A Song in the Dark

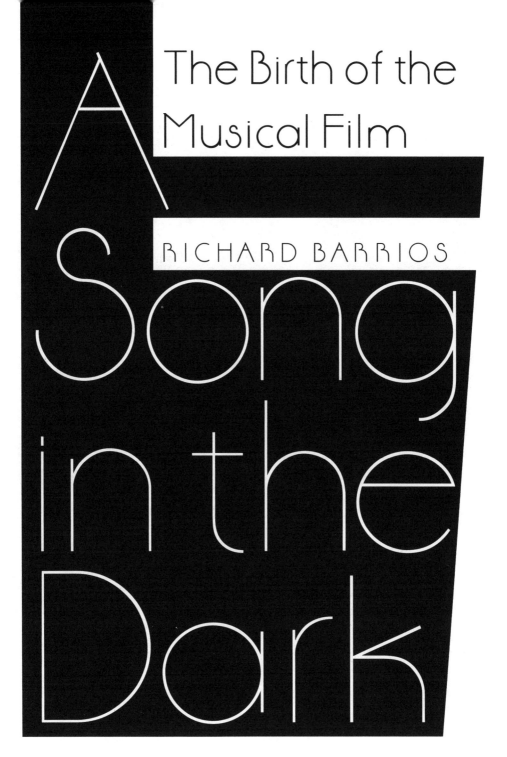

A Song in the Dark

The Birth of the Musical Film

RICHARD BARRIOS

New York   Oxford   Oxford University Press   1995

OXFORD UNIVERSITY PRESS

Oxford   New York
Athens   Auckland   Bangkok   Bombay
Calcutta   Cape Town   Dar es Salaam   Delhi
Florence   Hong Kong   Istanbul   Karachi
Kuala Lumpur   Madras   Madrid   Melbourne
Mexico City   Nairobi   Paris   Singapore
Taipei   Tokyo   Toronto

and associated companies in
Berlin   Ibadan

Published by Oxford University Press, Inc.,
200 Madison Avenue, New York, New York 10016

Oxford is a registered trademark of Oxford University Press

Library of Congress Cataloging-in-Publication Data
Barrios, Richard.
A song in the dark: the birth of the musical film/Richard Barrios.
p. cm.   Includes bibliographical references and index.
ISBN 0-19-508810-7.
ISBN 0-19-508811-5 (pbk)
1. Musical films—United States—History and criticism.
I. Title.   PN1995.9.M86B37   1995   791.43′6—dc20   94-27595

1   3   5   7   9   8   6   4   2

Printed in the United States of America
on acid-free paper

For Edna

who taught me

and for Jared

who also loves movies

Contents

Acknowledgments

While a book is being researched and written, one's level of isolation can occasionally become quite intimidating, reaching a point where it can momentarily seem as if one were truly alone in these tasks, that all this work is being carried out without reference to others. Fortunately, such negative feelings quickly vanish in the face of the greater truth, which is that without a large number of people and institutions who have aided, advised, and encouraged me this book could not possibly have come into existence.

First and last are the films themselves. My thanks to the following institutions who have maintained the films and in many cases preserved them and made them available for study: the UCLA Film and Television Archive, the British Film Institute, the Library of Congress, the Museum of Modern Art, and the George Eastman House. A special appreciation for the efforts of David Parker at the Library of Congress, along with my apology to him that this book ends before the advent of Eleanor Powell. Thanks as well to Jackie Morris and Elaine Burrows at the British Film Institute, and to Madeline Matz at the Library of Congress.

Without the work of film preservationists, a daunting number of these films would be lost forever. I am profoundly obliged to all those who work to retain and recover our film heritage, and to those institutions that fund this work. First and foremost, there is Robert Gitt, Preservation Officer of the UCLA Film and Television Archive. The sheer breadth of the work he has done (*Dixiana*, *Viennese Nights*, and *The Vagabond King*, among many others) is more than matched by his skill and attention to detail in working with fragile and fragmentary materials, and just as his love for the films shows through in his work, so have his generosity and good counsel informed much of my own effort. Keep up the search for "The Ga Ga Bird,"

Bob. Among the institutions who fund preservation efforts, The David and Lucile Packard Foundation has been notably generous in facilitating the survival of many of the films discussed in these pages. For any readers seeking new venues for tax-deductible contributions, consider film archives; they do need the money. And while other film companies often neglect or ignore the works of the past, the Turner Entertainment Co., primarily through the efforts of Richard P. May and George Feltsenstein, has made many of these films available to wider audiences than their creators could ever have dreamed. (Even *Golden Dawn* . . .)

In cases where the films themselves do not survive, there often remain paper trails detailing how they were made and what they meant to their audiences. Studio records and reports, ads and reviews, and miscellaneous documents all have formed a cornerstone of the research for *A Song in the Dark*. Little of this material survives unscathed; some studios seem to have worked hard to destroy any evidence of their films' production. Other ravages exist also, such as the fact that many of the files at the New York Public Library's Performing Arts Division seem to have been eviscerated or pilfered over the years. (Some mavens seem less interested in sharing information than in retaining a private stake on it.) Luckily, a great deal remains, much of it maintained by institutions and curators who understand the importance of the retaining and respect the integrity of film scholars. The Cinema-Television Library at the University of Southern California was extremely valuable for its materials related to films produced by MGM, Warner Bros., and First National. I gratefully acknowledge the unstinting help of Ned Comstock, whose diligence must surely qualify as one of his library's prime assets, and of Stewart Ng and Leith Adams. The Margaret Herrick Library of the Academy of Motion Picture Arts and Sciences is another estimable source, with a expansive selection of materials. It's regrettable that the Academy's Samuel Goldwyn Collection is at present (1994) not available to scholars, but there are innumerable compensations— for example, the comedy-horror show that makes up the Production Code Administration (Hays Office) files. Sam Gill of the Academy Library could not have been more accommodating and helpful, and his professionalism and courtesy, as well as that of the entire Library staff, is the sort that makes a researcher's job considerably more gratifying. I am also indebted to the other institutions whose resources I employed: the Bobst Library of New York University, for its fine microfilm collection; the New York Public Library for the Performing Arts at Lincoln Center; the Museum of Modern Art Film Library; the Library of Congress; the UCLA Library; and the British Film Institute Library. Also, to the Society for Cinephiles, The American Museum of the Moving Image (Astoria, Queens), The Museum of the Moving Image (London), and David Packard and the Stanford Theater. For those who are already familiar with some aspects of the early musical films, the name of Miles Kreuger will quite likely be familiar. His study and work in this field, and his enthusiasm for it, have made possible the work of all those who have followed, myself included.

Howard and Ron Mandelbaum and the Photofest staff made the search for some of the rarest of the photographs contained herein an experience both pleasurable and rewarding. I am likewise grateful to the following people who answered questions or supplied research materials: Jeffrey Carrier, Alex Gordon, Leonard Maltin, Sandra Gorney, Eric and Larry Chadbourne, Lawrence Greenberg, and Robert C. Stewart. A special word of thanks, also, to Anthony Slide, for his graciousness as well as his vast achievements in film scholarship.

It was a conscious choice to concentrate the research for this book on the films themselves and the written word, rather than the recollections of the relatively few surviving participants, whose memories have often been shared in other places. Nevertheless, I would like to thank those who (in private as well as public forums) answered questions and recalled their association with the earliest musicals: the late Ruby Keeler, the late Mervyn LeRoy, the late Myrna Loy, Billy Barty, Jackie Cooper, Dorothy Lee, Patsy Ruth Miller, Anita Page, Penny Singleton, Gloria Stuart, and Toby Wing.

Most readers with an interest in film history will know the preeminence in that field of William K. Everson. He is, simply, an international treasure, and all who love film are in his debt. His interest in the project, his guidance and support and friendship, were instrumental in making this book a reality. And to Karen Latham Everson equal thanks, not least for being a voice of sense and civility in an often peculiar world.

Romano Tozzi's knowledge of musical theater and film is, apparently, limitless. That alone would make him a prized resource, but coupled with this is a sense of courtesy and generosity as rare in this field as in any other, to which I can respond only with deep appreciation. On fronts both professional and personal, Marty Kearns has been enthusiastic, helpful, and unfailingly kind, as has Ken Richardson. David Lugowski is certainly the best audience any writer or raconteur could ask for, and his wide-ranging knowledge of film, keen perceptiveness of the film world and the universe at large, and profound sense of goodwill have colored and enhanced my work at innumerable points. Without Jerry Bryant I likely would never have decided to turn my interests in film into a career; he has, happily, long been one of the constants in my life. My abundant gratitude must go also to my parents, family, friends, and associates, for their support and for understanding how much writing this book meant to me; I would like, especially, to thank Vince Vitale and his computer skills, Yaacov Gershoni, Diane Allen and Francesca Rhys (and the wonderful support network at St. Paul and St. Andrew), Elisabeth Scott, Jeffrey Lipton, Mark Lechter and

Michael Opperman, and Eric Spilker. Without early support and advice from Jonathan Katz, this work might not have been started, let alone completed. A special word, also, in tribute to the late David Huntley. During much of the earlier stages of research and writing, under circumstances which were often quite trying, Rick DeCroix offered constant encouragement and innumerable welcome suggestions, for which many words of thanks could not be ample repayment.

Sheldon Meyer, Senior Vice President at Oxford University Press, believed in this project and supported it, and Joellyn Ausanka's copyediting was performed with skill and good sense. To an author with a first book, this kind of sponsorship is immensely gratifying.

Finally, there is Alan Boyd. Anyone first encountered at a screening of *Viennese Nights* might predictably play a large role in a work such as this—and the role has been played with the relish of a Noah Beery and the skill of a Rouben Mamoulian. With unfailing humor and grace he has given me assistance and advice, serving as a sounding board, confessor, and cheering section; one's life is blessed and one's work enriched by such friends. My gratitude to all who contributed to this work, as well as my affection, are on each page that follows.

New York City   R. B.
July 1994

A Song in the Dark

Introduction

For the past century, film has been bullying and beguiling its way into our lives and our cultures. It stimulates its audience's perceptions and responses and sometimes defines them, after which the audience uses those responses to endorse or reject each new film trend. The process can continue back and forth in endless permutation, and in the process film has sometimes attained and occasionally earned an elevated status. It has been, all in all, quite a progression—a throwaway diversion that came to define a large bloc of the collective sensibility.

Some of film's most extravagant stake on its audience's attention has come with its musicals. Despite the many distinguished specimens made abroad, musical film is a peculiarly American concept, alternately loved and derided. For many years musicals had—the past tense need apply—a remarkable propensity for fulfilling wishes and making fantasies seem reasonable. Innocence and cynicism, decorum and ebullience seem to meet at the point where some quintessential images are forged—Astaire and Rogers dancing cheek to cheek, Garland on the trolley, Kelly in the rain, Monroe and her diamonds. For all their putative triviality and the disrespect paid them by some elitists, musicals create unexpectedly powerful impressions. Their songs and stars resonate, they've been remembered and treasured and imitated, they constitute a singular legacy. And now they now seem an extinct species, a gleaming memento of an irretrievable and far less complicated past. The special area of escapism they once dominated has been displaced by television and, on the big screen, by action pictures that use comic strip violence to create brutal latter-day "production numbers." There have been other displacements too, including the most cynical of all, music videos. The musical was a comparative latecomer to film genres, and while earlier types of film have mutated and survived, it has not. While it still exists on stage and remains popular in retrospective presentation, the musical has little to do with film in any current or ongoing sense. We are, apparently, beyond the end of the rainbow, no matter how much we choose to bask in its glow.[1]

When the movie musical was born in the late 1920s, the American film industry dictated to the world, and the world was beginning to listen as well as watch. That time is the most chaotic era in the history of American entertainment, possibly its most dynamic and in some ways among its least understood. Starting in 1926 and continuing to 1930, the film industry—indeed, popular culture around the planet—was irretrievably altered, turned completely around in reaction to one word: *Sound*. In a stunningly brief period of time the established art of silent film became extinct, thrown over in favor of the virtually untested medium of talking pictures. No aspect of the entertainment business was free from the repercussions, and the ingrained traditions of film were radically affected. Timing, exposition, styles of acting and direction were all transformed, ultimately more than anyone could have conceived. With all this, however, there was only one completely new type of film, one not possible before the advent of sound. At once a logical and an extraordinary progression, the musical became the testing ground upon which sound film proved itself, an agent for the exhaustive trials and tests—technical and aesthetic alike—that turned sound from a freak gimmick to a standard-bearer. Nor was the musical a slow-developing sensation: it took off like a shot from day one and instantly became a quintessential form of popular diversion in America and around the world. Small wonder, considering what it brought to the new sound cinema: song and dance, visual and aural spectacle, lyrical intrigue, show-must-go-on heartbreak, and some unforgettable performers, all assembled in a package that rival media—live theater, vaudeville, radio—could not emulate. For nearly two years its popularity flared, then suddenly halted, a victim of changing times, evolving tastes, and oversaturation. Several years passed while it lay nearly dormant, save for a few who cared to keep the spirit alive. Then it returned stronger than ever to become one of the prime morale-rousers during the Great Depression.

The musical film's early history was its most vital and unpredictable time, a key phase completely unlike its later years; yet it has seldom received extensive scrutiny. In fact, by a breathtaking fluke, the most thorough tribute given it was on screen, not on paper. Had not Arthur Freed

1. The latter-day absence of musicals is demonstrated periodically by the ill-fated attempts to buck their cessation, a conspicuous example being in release as this is being written. *I'll Do Anything,* director James L. Brooks's attempt to bring back the integrated musical, fared so badly at previews that all the songs were deleted—an eerily precise equivalent of the musical massacres of late 1930, as recounted in Chapter Fourteen.

been MGM's preeminent producer of musicals, and prior to that one of its leading songwriters, *Singin' in the Rain* would likely have never been made. For it was Freed's song catalogue and recollections of the birth of the musical—especially the first true musical, *The Broadway Melody*—that led the creators of *Singin' in the Rain* to that fraught and funny time more than two decades earlier. And if writers Betty Comden and Adolph Green and directors Stanley Donen and Gene Kelly made a number of elisions and oversimplifications, *Singin' in the Rain* remains true to the spirit of its sources. How marvelous that life and art can close the circle so neatly on occasion—that the first, in some ways most important, musicals should be paid homage by possibly the greatest of them. Such an achievement cannot be duplicated in a book, even the first full study of the era. But the fact remains that however compelling is that catch-line "You ain't heard nothin' yet!," Al Jolson and *The Jazz Singer* are only the tip of a fascinating iceberg.

These films trafficked in dreams and escapism, yet the history behind their magic-making is rather more improbable than anything they themselves depicted. It's a mythically "American" saga, a true adventure, a boisterous and frequently ill-planned start to a major enterprise. Sex, power, reversals of fortune, nefarious dealings, and corporate skullduggery were all part of the game. And, always looking on in amazement, there was first the American public, and then the world. The musical's rocky origins, its successes and failures, occurred in full view of a vast, rapt, and sometimes exasperated mass audience. Entranced by the novelty, the public overlooked many things—technology plagued by glitches, carbon-copy storylines and songs, and performers who were (to put it graciously) sometimes less than ideal for the job at hand. For a brief, boom-town period of time none of that mattered, as darkened movie theaters were suddenly filled with words and music, ringing out over primitive amplifiers, enthralling huge crowds.

The birth of the talkies was a complex and colorful period, so drastic and frenzied that few accounts have accurately conveyed its character. Indeed, it's often considered desirable to leave the era virtually untouched and move on to the more tractable early 1930s. In the light of such discomfort the profound historical importance of the films, even the most essential and substantial works, tends to become lost. Foremost among the neglected works are the first musicals, and as with other aspects of the dawn of sound, they require certain efforts and perspectives not all observers are prepared to muster. Otherwise assiduous studies of film suddenly wax hostile when referring to these movies, invoking words such as "dinosaurs" and "savage incompetence" and the like, comments that can apply in individual cases, but inaccurate and unjust when administered to the entire output. So why are these films so elusive, why do they seem to defy the critic's and historian's grasp with such lubricity? Accessibility accounts for some of it. Many of them have not been seen by more than a few people in over sixty years. Some do not survive at all, others do so only fragmentarily, or in a way (black and white prints of the original color film) that renders them misrepresentative. A sizable quantity of the work that does survive is almost impossible to see, owing to rights problems and the underfunding that constantly puts a stranglehold on the restoration work performed by film archives. But many films are intact, and in most cases bring up the question of historical context vs. aesthetics. Begin having a conversation about film. Not current; old movies, Classic Hollywood. Say the term "early musicals." The usual reaction will be, "Yes, Busby Berkeley; Fred Astaire and Ginger Rogers." Reply, "No, before that. The *first* musicals. 1929. *The Broadway Melody* and *Sunny Side Up*." There are several possible reactions—stony, uncomprehending silence; confusion, since it's commonly thought Berkeley came first; and, at times, a peculiarly condescending strain of hostility. This is the reputation the earliest musical films have garnered, and it has resonated down the decades. More than most commercial filmmaking, musicals seem to favor their time and ethos with uncanny accuracy, and the first of them seem to evince too well the technical disarray and artistic indecision from which they arose.

It is no surprise, therefore, that these early efforts are considered the illiterate stepparents of the *On the Town*s and the *Gigi*s of later years. Anything manufactured amidst such circumstances would likely be so. And the gap is one that many seem to wish not to bridge. How, after all, can these crude, stodgy and often absurd specimens retain anything other than the most esoteric historical claim? Surely, mainstream cant goes, they were popular only due to their novelty, for they could never be seen as viable entertainment. The essence of this type of thinking, and it is discussed in some depth in Chapter Three, concerns the first true musical film, *The Broadway Melody*. The comparatively unimportant (at the time) distinction of an Academy Award as Best Production has ensured the film a historical asterisk, and writers have been apologizing for it ever since. But—and it is central to this book—for audiences in 1929 there was far more than novelty. They did not go to *The Broadway Melody* or to *Rio Rita* or *Gold Diggers of Broadway* or any other of the massive hits simply because they were new and different. They were also innovative, in technique and sometimes in content, and both audiences and many, often surprised, critics perceived them to be works of genuine quality. Novelty value was of course a factor, as in the first filmed operetta, *The Desert Song*, and in the first all-color talkie, *On With the Show!* Yet even these, and works of lesser importance and success, were perceived to have the substance to fulfill their hype-ridden promises. Because they are films of their time, with all the artistic naïveté and technical instability this connotes, they are often spoken of as if they were unsuccessful. Factual data, in the form of Warner Bros.' financial figures, offer a different story. *The Desert Song* grossed over eight times its negative cost, and *On With the Show!* nearly five times. Even accounting for distribution and other expenses, these yield profits impressive in 1929 and today. So perhaps some revisionism is needed in order to keep the facts straight, and to ensure that these films—and their audiences—are not seen in terms of events and films coming many years later.

Any attempt to chronicle this time accurately requires, of necessity, specific perspectives. Time, breadth of work, and intention come immediately to mind, yet perhaps the most vital perspective concerns those aspects that seek to examine film from theoretical points of view. Musicals, mostly the works of the later 1930s through the mid-1960s, have been comprehended from a variety of promontories, quite often cogently and provocatively, occasionally in such a way some may find dense to the point of obfuscation. (If a 1929 film seems a turgid thing to plow through, try certain analytical pieces.) The exuberance with which these films were made and the enthusiasm with which they were received are arguably among the most crucial parts of their historical, critical and sociological makeup. Dealing with them in an excessively clinical manner may seem to miss their point. Some assistance, in fact, may be needed to unlock the secrets of why they were loved and then rejected. The traditional critical/theoretical viewpoint of using early musicals as straw men—targets for scorn, as compared with more accomplished films of later years—does history a disservice. Context, in this case, is all, and the theoretical premise that reflects it most decisively is contained in Hans Robert Jauss's *Toward an Aesthetic of Reception*. In examining works of the past, Jauss sees "in the triangle of author, work, and public the last [as] no passive part . . . but rather itself an energy formative of history." The early musicals, in other words, were a channel between their creators and their audiences, which sometimes worked in mediative harmony and sometimes in discord. "A literary work," Jauss writes, "is not an object that stands by itself and that offers the same view to each reader in each period. It is not a monument that monologically reveals its timeless essence." And a film is the same way. Viewing an early musical, a film so much of its time, through pseudo-objective historical prejudices, i.e., in terms of the more polished work that followed, is to misread it. The farthest interpretation of this philosophy would be to view a film such as *On With the Show!* in sole terms of a 1929 mindset and background. Illuminating, yet perhaps not totally practical or even possible. That being stated, *A Song in the Dark* brings to bear on its subject from three simultaneous bases of operation:

1. *Background and production history.* Much of this information has been previously inaccessible or overlooked. It becomes particularly relevant in the case of a film such as *Glorifying the American Girl*, which becomes comprehensible only when the circumstances of its creation are addressed.

2. *Our changing perceptions of these films.* What audiences and critics saw in 1929–30 versus what we see today. Time and hindsight are unpredictable factors; many of the films are as enjoyable as today as they were when they were new, while others, some works of the biggest hits of the time, are now nearly unwatchable. Conversely, some works ignored then have become classics. The initial enthusiasm given *Puttin' on the Ritz*, for example, is startling; likewise some of the hostility that greeted *Follow Thru*.

3. *The singular and precarious relationship these films had with their audiences.* This is a factor of film history often not stressed enough, yet obviously a crucial factor in this case, in which affection turned to disdain (and later back again) virtually overnight.

The view from these vantage points is founded on a mix of research, analysis, criticism, and extrapolation. The research, from extant sources such as studio documents and reports in the trade press, uncovers hordes of facts previously not covered. Some qualify as trivia—Mae West as the potential star of *Applause*—and some as more straightforward history, such as the previously unmentioned credits for such figures as Fatty Arbuckle (comedy direction of *The Cuckoos*), Ernst Lubitsch (retakes on *The Vagabond King*), and Joan Crawford (MGM's *Wir Schalten um auf Hollywood!*). Capturing the tenor of the audience requires research of different types—box office receipts (where those survive), exhibitor reports, preview responses, even letters to movie magazines, whose readership was somewhat more perspicacious than might be guessed. The critics of the era were not always as observant and should be approached warily, although in the case of lost films their reports are sometimes among the few remaining sources. What reviews offer in terms of what can be observed in extant films today is highly variable, even apart from criticism's inherent subjectivity. The critical esteem in which musicals were held was sometimes remarkably high; it was not then as "low" a genre as some later reports intimate. The respect did vary wildly, however, engendering a confusion of critical reactions and thus, sometimes, an uncertain response from the public.

For the more obvious perspective of the time period covered, there is a brief overview of prehistory, followed by the main event in 1926, the beginning of the age of Vitaphone sound films, which eventually led to *The Jazz Singer* and everything that followed. When to wrap up the narrative offers more options. The release of *Love Me Tonight* (1932), the pinnacle of early-musical filmmaking, is one possibility, as is the advent of *42nd Street* in 1933, which helped bring back musicals after their near-moratorium. But musicals would have returned even without *42nd Street*, and the films of 1933 and early 1934 are essential to this study in their demonstration of how the old was giving way to the new. Several converging events in 1934 seem most clearly to form a line of demarcation where earlier musical ideas are finally put to rest. One was the corner turned on the Depression, after which optimism, if not actual better times, could inform an audience's grounding and color its preferences. The other, more critical factor concerns something that also influenced spectator tastes: the rise of the enforced Production Code in 1934, about which much more in Chapter Seventeen. The extent to which these forces propelled the musical to ever more standardized lines cannot be underestimated . . . and cannot be fathomed until the range of work from the earlier times is fully considered. For along with the crudity and the incompetence and unformed ideas there was also a sense of daring, a pioneer-spirit exhilaration that made film people willing to try almost anything once. The codes and overused procedures had not yet been formed, so anything went. Not surprisingly, the successes were often outnumbered by the failures in hindsight and at the time. Imitations of stage work went alongside odd attempts to render traditional silent-film forms in musical terms, and the results altered both forms. The musical stage became gradually informed by less stilted dramatic conventions and vocal styles, and film was forced to confront heightened notions of stylization and artifice. In any case, the scope of musicals on film was wider than it would ever be again.

One variable aspect of the time frame concerns finance. There are frequent citations in the text of film costs and grosses, as well as performers' salaries and admission prices. While some accounts strive for a rule of thumb to equate 1929 dollars with those of the current day, the circumstances have changed so vastly that there are simply no generalizations that can apply. John McCormack's $500,000 salary in late 1929 for *Song O' My Heart* is easily equivalent to the $15-plus million star fees given today. Yet to apply that "times thirty" stricture to admission prices would obviously not work, for audiences in the 1990s are not paying $15 and more for general admission tickets. Production figures are a similar case: the cost of *King of Jazz* in 1930 was around $1.5 million; a comparable figure today might be in the area of $75 million, or fifty times. But a more realistically priced big-studio product such as *The Broadway Melody* cost $379,000 and surely would run more than $19 million today. With grosses the circumstances are similar. Thus, since the financial dynamics of the big-studio-and-theatre-chain systems were vastly unlike anything in the present day, most of the financial figures mentioned here must be seen in relation to each other, with only a tenuous connection with the vastly different finances of today.

To keep the scope of the work within reasonable limits, the great majority of the films being discussed are American feature films, mostly by the major studios. In the earliest time, 1926–28, when they often mattered more than features, short subjects are given some attention. Otherwise, the musical shorts of the early sound era rate their own book. These are priceless pieces of history: opera singers, stars of Broadway and vaudeville, dancers, all viewed through the unblinking eye and objective ear of primitive photography and direct sound. The caliber of performers making their film debuts in these shorts is formidable: Burns and Allen, Judy Garland (as Baby Gumm), Humphrey Bogart, Ginger Rogers, Cary Grant, Bert Lahr, Joan Blondell, later Bob Hope and Sammy Davis, Jr. And there are precious recollections of legends, such as Bessie Smith in *St. Louis Blues* (1929), her only film. With foreign films the considerations are slightly different, though they too rate a full-length study. By the time of the first foreign musicals late in 1929, the American work had already established its predominance. Most of the first European efforts were closely modeled on the stateside originals and were generally considered so derivative that they were given minimal import. They came into their own in the darkest days of the American musical in 1931 and early 1932, with outstanding works from France, Germany, and Britain sufficiently influential to affect their American counterparts. Apart from these, the inclination remains chauvinistically pointed toward the Yankee progenitors.

How to watch and analyze these films is, if not a dilemma, clearly a major consideration, for their curious and complicated legacy is one many will feel is not worth recapturing. How stilted they can seem at first glance, how antiquated their conventions, desultory their craftsmanship, and inappropriate many of their performers. And yet with equal parts persistence, adventurousness, and imagination, they can begin to reveal themselves.[2] When this occurs, after one becomes accustomed to the retrograde technique and the archaic protocol, they evoke their time as thoroughly as the most candid newsreel and give an arresting look at how the movies dominated and mirrored American life at that crucial point when the roar of the Jazz Age was giving way to the moan of the Depression. The fantasies that these films attempted to fulfill are quaintly, often poignantly simpleminded, and their contrast with the imminent national temper stark and unnerving.

What brings back the magic for today's viewers? Sometimes it's a sudden jolt or an isolated moment: seeing Marilyn Miller cavort through "Wild Rose" in *Sally* and sensing the joy she gave to audiences; or feeling the history as Maurice Chevalier introduces "Louise" in the otherwise lachrymose *Innocents of Paris*; or seeing the filmmakers stretch, trying to amuse and outrage with a sequence such as "Turn on the Heat" in *Sunny Side Up*. Occasionally a jolt can come with the unwitting, often endearing candor

2. One somewhat distancing factor about these films that should be stated is the way in which, today, many of them seemed poorly framed, with off-center composition and, in 16mm, heads and feet lopped off. Most of this is due to the transferal to safety film of old Vitaphone prints. Since they had no soundtrack on the film they had full-frame pictures. When they were preserved, mostly in preparation for television, the different aspect ratios of the pictures were disregarded. A film such as *Show of Shows*, which has enough problems as it is, can thus be made even worse by being presented in such a literally disproportionate fashion.

present—hearing singers live-recorded, bad notes and all, or seeing numbers with the dancers' mistakes left in. In some films there never was any magic, as in *Glorifying the American Girl,* a peculiar botch then and now, and in others it takes a large audience to ease one into the spirit, as can happen with a film like *Just Imagine.* Patience is also a requirement, and it's a far cry from the immediate gratification most of today's viewers brandish as their prerogative. As something woefully undistinguished (or worse) is being run, one can sit waiting, *waiting* for something to perk things up. Suddenly, there's an unexpected felicity—a performance or song, an exchange of sharp dialogue, some surprising camerawork, a fleeting glimmer of improved film technique—and then comes a sense of why audiences were delighted.

Video is the film historian's mixed blessing, for it has made these films more accessible than ever, while at the same time occasionally compromising their effect. Who, after all, could ever have imagined that *Sally* or *Show of Shows* would be released on home video, and who would have had the temerity to envision that *Golden Dawn* would again be unleashed upon an unsuspecting public? And when one encounters the likes of *Tanned Legs* on video, a fast-forward button seems an immense beneficence. Yet seeing these films in such a way is at best only two-thirds of a loaf: video, which often enhances a film's archaic mien, ruthlessly diminishes the technical innovations and creative daring of these state-of-the-1929-art works. Nor, sometimes, do some of the niceties translate; it seems to be quite difficult to render two-color Technicolor onto video accurately, and thus the original effect is often misrepresented. The commercial video of *King of Jazz* is a different film from that made in 1930 and extant in a few surviving prints. Nevertheless, film preservation, which has occasionally benefited from the demands of the video market, has of late done well by these early musicals. More of them are in some kind of availability than at any time since their production, courtesy of film archives, charitable endowments, and sometimes even film companies, which more often shun contact with their earlier, potentially nonprofit-making product. The research and writing of this book, in fact, was greatly enhanced by the sudden resurfacing of major works not available earlier—UCLA's preservation prints of *The Vagabond King* and *Dixiana* are good examples, as is the British Film Institute's rediscovery of a fragment from *Gold Diggers of Broadway.*

Obviously, a variety of tools is required to address these films and to evoke their importance in their era and invoke their relevance to a time many years later. Gossip, for instance, was part of the time—*vide* the peculiar collaborative triangle of Gloria Swanson, Joe Kennedy, and Franz Lehar in Chapter Thirteen—and so were drama and humor. It's all accounted for here, and the occasional pointed or facetious observations within the text or in the footnotes attempt to access impressions otherwise nearly irretrievable. Should the giant musical chickens and insects of *The Great Gabbo*, presented therein with quite a straight face, be reported without intimating the unintentional laughs they educe? And the "dinosaur" allusion cited earlier is notably pertinent, too. Coming to terms with these films, taking into consideration how audiences received them, seeing and portraying them as other than the clunky and boring and trivial (somehow simultaneously) pieces they can seem to be, is rather like reassembling the skeletons of a particularly fabulous species. When the work has been done, the rewards are self-evident.

The early musicals, so seemingly remote and irrelevant, sometimes impact on our lives in surprising ways, implying entire lost worlds when the pieces come together. The hit songs (from "Puttin' on the Ritz" to "Am I Blue?" to "Tip Toe Through the Tulips With Me") are imperishable, and even some of the images remain fresh. Winnie Lightner bursting through the ennui and inertia of the revue *The Show of Shows*, or Buddy Rogers and Nancy Carroll playing out a light and seemingly improvised romantic scene in *Close Harmony*, or Maurice Chevalier elegantly yet unmistakably alluding to his frustrated sex drive in *The Love Parade*, or Louise Beavers bursting through racial stereotyping to swing out a jazzy ditty in *Safety in Numbers*—such moments may not always be timeless, but they are cherishable and worthy. Even lost films can offer strong impressions, such as Lawrence Tibbett roaring through *The Rogue Song* or Fannie Brice demonstrating her art in *My Man*.[3] So there is much to retrieve, a wealth of films and memories to respond to with amusement, rapture, indifference, and occasionally derision. And there is a time not quite beyond recall, when a group of people of wildly varying levels of competence undertook to determine just what a movie musical should be. Sometimes it was done boldly and well, sometimes adequately, occasionally hideously wrong. All in the name of pleasing spectators and making money, and even, at rare times, attempting to access a new type of expression, to reveal truths or dreams not otherwise manifested in conventional forms of communication. The era is gone, the studio system that produced it has vanished, the audience has undergone untold change, and the film musical is, essentially, no more. Yet in a small pocket of the American public's collective unconscious, the birth of the musical film remains an odd and stirring memory. It is to this memory, and to all those who contributed to it, that this book pays tribute.

---

3. At the time of her early film appearances, Brice was spelling her name with "ie" instead of the more familiar "y"; the spelling came and went through much of her career.

CHAPTER 1

Vitaphone Prologue

Popular history always seems to crave the convenience of significant events that can be labeled "THE FIRST." Unfortunately, there are not many major incidences that are worthy of the designation; history seldom permits such tidy corners. Since the drive persists, folklore has passed off *The Jazz Singer* as various Firsts in the history of film: The First Sound Film, The First Talking Picture, The First Movie Musical. It was none of these; it was not even Al Jolson's first film. With or without Jolson, sound film did not occur overnight. It evolved over many years in a number of places through varied technologies, and while some of its early history will never be completely fathomed the certainty is that music was always on the front line of its development. This is the background from which the musical film emerged, and its lineage is complex and checkered and frequently surprising.[1]

Two factors need be remembered in scanning the early history of sound. One is that silent films were, from their earliest days, never truly silent. The most insignificant movie theater featured a piano or an organ, and as the economic scale ascended so did musical assets. The pipe organs in many medium-sized houses featured instrumental stops in overwhelming variety, up to and including percussion, and the largest silent movie palaces featured full-time orchestras and sometimes singers and sound-effects people. From the mid-teens onward some major films, such as *The Birth of a*

---

1. The archaeology of sound film is too involved and engrossing to be considered on the basis of the minute précis it receives in this chapter. Harry M. Geduld's *The Birth of the Talkies* (Indiana University Press, 1977) is the chief source, and *Film Sound: Theory and Practice*, ed. Elisabeth Weis and John Belton (Columbia University Press, 1985) approaches the complexities of the issue from several perspectives. A definitive history may still be needed.

Nation, were given newly composed scores; less opulently and more often, studios listed suggested themes on detailed cue sheets. In any case, sound film, when it came to stay in the late 1920s, did not dislodge total outright silence. Another factor to bear in mind concerns the mechanical end. Two discrete technological constructs governed the sound revolution prior to 1930. The earlier kept the elements of sound and sight as separate entities. The visual was on a film strip, the audible on a phonograph disc (or, earlier, cylinder), and attempts would be made to synchronize the two into cohesion. The second process, more sophisticated and harder to engineer, involved the coexistence of visual and audible elements on one strip of film as picture and sound track. This made sound film into something of a genuine (not merely perceived) unity and would be the technology that endured.

In the Stone Age was the phonograph, developed by Thomas Edison and others from 1877 on, and immediately there began thoughts of coupling the sonic to the visual. *Scientific American* predicted early on that Edison's device could be linked with stereoscopic photography to provide a close simulation of nature. The stereopticon's claim as a reproducer of living images was promptly overturned by the invention of motion pictures, and again Edison was there. Shortly after the development of his Kinetoscope in 1889, he charged his assistant W. K. Laurie Dickson with the job of combining sight with sound. The result was the Kinetophonograph (or Kinetophone), a one-on-one peepshow which connected a Kinetoscope to a Gramophone. The spectator watched short films through an eyepiece while background music was piped in through stethoscope-like ear tubes. Sound was wedded to projected film at the Phono-Cinéma Théâtre, the sensation of the 1900 Paris Exposition. Cylinder recordings, a horn speaker, and a hand-cranked projector combined to give approximate synchronization to performances by such artists as Sarah Bernhardt, Coquelin, and baritone Victor Maurel, creator of Verdi's Iago and Falstaff. This contraption retained its popularity for a while after the exposition—three years before *The Great Train Robbery*—before falling victim to its many technical limitations. The main drawbacks, present in all such experiments until the mid-1920s, were insufficient amplification and faulty synchronization. The big horns over which the recordings were played were insufficiently audible, and there was the intractability of coordinating the film projector with the phonograph, both machines with peculiar concepts of speed and consistency. Anything less than perfect synchronization, even a hair's-breadth separation between picture and sound, could be magnified many times in just a few seconds. And was.

Others tested the waters over the next few years, most notably film pioneer Léon Gaumont, and Edison returned with a vengeance in 1913. His Cinephonograph, marketed under the old and still useful brand name Kinetophone, was the most viable try thus far, and attracted curiosity-seekers in the U.S. and England for about a year until a fire at the Edison labs forced the company to discontinue efforts to make pictures talk and sing. The Kinetophone occasionally achieved the desired synchronization between a projector and a cylinder player, and some of its films survive to give an idea of what constituted a 1913 talkie—and a 1913 movie musical. The best-known is *Nursery Favorites*, an eight-minute operetta that plays as "Jack in the Beanstalk" retold by Gilbert and Sullivan. The naïveté of the material is matched by the crudity of the technique—one static shot comprises the whole film—and by an abundance of innocently primitive charm. But underscore the word "primitive": the sound quality is barbaric, the voices reproduce as a drugged drone, and the synchronization of voices with lip movement is halting and often nonexistent. With recording done into one oversized acoustical horn, there is absolutely no sense of space or direction to the sound. The aural and the visual are and remain on autonomous planes, demolishing the attempted illusion. Considering that the prints seen today have been enhanced through modern technology, how it sounded in 1913 can only be imagined.[2] Even without the ruinous fire, the drawbacks to Edison's system would have ensured it only a short and insufficiently audible life. The last notable attempt at a film-disc linkup prior to Vitaphone was made in 1921 by one Orlando E. Kellum, whose work received an august boost when D. W. Griffith decided to add a song sequence to his film *Dream Street*. Griffith also appeared in a short talking prologue to praise Kellum and plug his own picture. The song, which featured Ralph Graves, was discarded shortly after the opening engagement at Town Hall in New York. Neither the synchronization nor audibility were adequate, while the sound quality proved exasperatingly scratchy. *Dream Street*, one of Griffith's weakest films, is left to history as the first major—if brief—use of recorded sound in a feature film.

Amid the disc experiments, work had also begun on sound-on-film systems. In the early 1900s Charles E. Fritts and Eugene Lauste devised the means to photographically record and reproduce sound, after which Lauste invented the string galvanometer, enabling the recording of sound directly onto motion picture film as an optical sound track. Though unable to develop adequate amplification, Lauste was the first to create a true sound-on-film process. Later, the Swiss-German triumvirate of Josef Engl, Joseph Massolle, and Hans Vogt devised the Tri-Ergon system, with a flywheel-sprocket assembly that could regulate speed and synchronize image and

2. One of the players appearing in Kinetophones, Viola Dana, later starred in silent films. Sixty-plus years after the fact, she recalled with amusement and amazement that when her sister Edna Flugrath played the Queen of the Fairies in *Nursery Favorites*, her girlish soprano reproduced as a booming bass. Another Kinetophone veteran, Harry Beaumont, made a more lasting contribution to sound films fifteen years later as director of *The Broadway Melody*.

sound track. Film mogul William Fox bought the rights to Tri-Ergon in 1925, and it became the basis of his Movietone sound-on-film system.

The most extensive work in sound-on-film was carried out by Lee De Forest, esteemed and somewhat controversial pioneer of radio and early sound film. It has been argued that his skill was less in invention and more in acquiring others' patents; in any event, he was in some way responsible for the innovation of the audion amplifier, which made public-address systems feasible and would eventually solve one of sound film's most persistent problems. After overseeing numerous experiments with microphone recording, De Forest marketed his Phonofilm process in 1923. It was the first time a film frame was successfully joined to a sound track on the edge of the film strip, to make sound films both synchronized and audible. All manner of performers made the trip to De Forest's Manhattan studio to appear in Phonofilm shorts—DeWolf Hopper, Fannie Ward, Chic Sale, Weber and Fields. There was a two-reel drama, *Love's Old Sweet Song* (with Una Merkel), plus several experimental sound cartoons on which De Forest collaborated with Max Fleischer, and the first sound newsreel, filmed in Washington in July 1924 and featuring President Coolidge. Not surprisingly, music played a preeminent role in the Phonofilm shorts, with contributions by Eddie Cantor, George Jessel, Molly Picon, vaudevillians Eva Puck and Sammy White, songwriter/performers Noble Sissle and Eubie Blake, and Abbie Mitchell ("The Colored Prima Donna"). And many more: opera and popular singers, vaudeville teams, dance troupes. There was even a botched attempt at adding a Phonofilm score to the silent epic *The Covered Wagon*.

Much of De Forest's work survives, and while his films make no great impact today they seem no less effective than the Vitaphone shorts produced three and four years later.[3] That they did not make a bigger splash had mostly to do with the antipathy of the film industry. Studio heads, who had seen sound-film devices come and go, remained unimpressed despite the inventors' pleas. Producers and spectators considered silent film an art and entertainment complete unto itself. Sound—specifically the sound demonstrated prior to 1923—added nothing, even detracted, and radio was not yet the great threat it would become a couple of years later. All this, plus his own predilection for nefarious deals, conspired to quash Lee De Forest. The industry viewed his films as both irrelevant and threatening, and he lacked the power base and entrepreneurial spunk to make a go of his concern independently. With insufficient marketing his films could not begin to compete with large-studio product. So adverse were these forces

---

3. The drawback to seeing many De Forest films today is technological. Shot at a speed significantly slower than the later standardized sound-film speed of twenty-four frames per second, they look absurdly speeded up when run on modern equipment. Some (Sissle and Blake, Cantor, Coolidge) have been preserved; others await proper restoration.

that his most ambitious project, excerpts from the intimate revue *Chauve Souris* shot in early Technicolor, was never screened publicly. Most ruinously, he was completely enmeshed from 1926 onward in a litigious snarl over the rights to and patents of his Phonofilm equipment. His chief adversary in this convoluted legal mess was William Fox, from whom much more will be heard shortly.

In 1924, while De Forest was hawking his sound-on-film device, disc-recording processes were being refined substantially. Bell Telephone Laboratories, working in conjunction with Western Electric, perfected a new method of electrical phonograph recording that replaced the old acoustical horn with a microphone, resulting in a clarity and fidelity previously lacking. To apply the device further Bell began experimenting with a sound-on-disc film system and soon came up with the first device to smoothly coordinate the projector with the phonograph. A fan belt attached to the motors of both machines could now ensure a consistent speed, and each phonograph disc could run as long as ten minutes, the same as one film reel.[4] Since feature films required two projectors running in alternation, there was a second pair of devices, with which the sound was fed to speakers via a double-rheostat system that switched from one unit to the other. When everything was functioning properly the setup could be used on longer films and, with the amplifier, was fully audible. Carrying far more clout than De Forest, Bell Labs began to peddle their system to the film industry through mediators. They quickly found a taker.

Legend has it that when the Warner brothers decided to invest in sound films, their company was facing bankruptcy and they were grasping at a do-or-die gamble. Nothing of the sort. The Warners began their association with the film industry in 1903, when their father, a Polish immigrant, bought a nickelodeon in New Castle, Pennsylvania. Two years later four of the twelve Warner children—Harry, Albert, Sam, and Jack—made an unsuccessful stab at film distribution. They tried again in 1912, dabbling in production until the success in 1917 of *My Four Years in Germany*. Through struggle and ingenuity they continued to progress until they formally incorporated in 1923 and opened a studio in Hollywood.[5] Their early successes included *The Gold Diggers*, *Beau Brummell*, and a series of vehicles for the studio's leading profit-earner, Rin-Tin-Tin.

At that time as well as later, the Warner ethos was characterized by what might be gently and euphemistically termed an ardent appreciation for

4. To achieve this duration, it was not possible to use the standard ten-inch disc played at 78 rpm. Instead, it was a whopper of a sixteen-inch disc, played at a speed of 33⅓ from the innermost grooves out to the edge and tracked by massive industrial-strength needles.

5. The official company title was Warner Bros. Pictures, Inc. The word "Brothers" was always abbreviated, and so for the sake of consistency the studio will be referred to hereafter as Warner Bros., or just Warners.

thrift. Over two generations of employees, the studio's attitude was to spend the least amount of dollars to get the maximum amount of work. In the six-day work weeks that were the norm in 20s and 30s Hollywood, the work conditions at Warners were the most spartan, stretching to fifteen-hour days and beyond. But along with the insistent cost-cutting and the often lowbrow outlook, the brothers fought and worked and borrowed to push their enterprise into the industry's higher echelons. At great cost they acquired the services of John Barrymore, then the country's most prestigious actor, and gambled on German director Ernst Lubitsch—both times resulting in prestige and profits. In 1925 the Warners began to consolidate their success with the purchase of the Brooklyn-based Vitagraph company, one of the first successful studios and possessor of a number of film-booking exchanges. They also started their own chain of movie theatres and, revealingly, expanded their holdings in an audible direction: KFWB, Los Angeles's third radio station, began broadcasting on March 3, 1925, its programs dotted with steady plugs for the studio's current offerings.

To serve as KFWB's sound engineer the Warners hired Major Benjamin Levinson, Western Electric's former West Coast director. Hearing of Bell Labs' improved film-disc system, Levinson quickly passed the news on to Sam Warner, the most technologically oriented brother and the most adventurous. Possessing his family's avid appreciation for music, Warner was immediately drawn to the description of a test film in which a pianist could be heard as well as seen. He went to New York to learn more, and after watching and listening to a film of a twelve-piece orchestra, he knew. This enthusiasm had little effect on his less visionary siblings until he began to discuss marketing and profits, along with attendant publicity, that could make Warner Bros. leap from ambitious second-rater to one of the majors. As originally discussed, the intentions for the device were *not to make pictures talk*. As Sam Warner argued and his brothers finally concurred, the system would bring orchestral accompaniment for silent films to even the smallest towns. Warner Bros. could be Santa Claus to exhibitors, furnishing the movies and providing the music. And, like the live vaudeville that played with silent features in most cities, there could also be filmed variety acts between the features. A democratic technology, this—bringing the finest available talent to audiences everywhere. Legend recounts that as an afterthought Warner also mentioned the possibility of talking pictures—to which his business-minded brother Harry shot back, "Who the hell wants to hear actors talk?"[6]

6. That remark appears in Jack Warner's 1964 memoir *My First Hundred Years in Hollywood*, and as with many such anecdotes doubtless got punched up in the retelling. Still, it neatly encapsulates the extraordinary blend of chutzpah and myopia that characterized Warner Bros.' entry into the sound film business.

Sam Warner did his convincing sufficiently well to lead his company, in June 1925, to sign an agreement with Western Electric to further investigate the technical and commercial possibilities of the film-disc system. Warners dubbed the process Vitaphone, in part after the Vitagraph studio they had just bought, and the brand name became synonymous with the technology. Work on test films continued in the East, with most shot in a simple static fashion to work out the remaining bugs. For bugs there were, in abundance: despite the good impression it made, Vitaphone was plagued by any number of headache-producing snags. Chief among these were the drastic sensitivities related to simultaneously making a disc recording and shooting a movie. The microphones were, too often, maddeningly capricious: they might not register the performance taking place two feet away, yet never failed to pick up every whir of the camera motor and sputter of the arc lamps. To counteract this, camera and cameraman were placed into small booths, soundproof, totally unventilated, and pure torture. Even if it were possible to shoot more than ten minutes of film at one time, the camera operator could not have endured two additional seconds in that stifling prison, and upon hearing the director call "Cut" would invariably bolt from the booth completely drenched. Between the immobility of the camera booth and the nailed-down microphone, performers' movements were restricted to an unprecedented degree, with the result that the early Vitaphone films are among the most motionless motion pictures ever made. Cameras could not pan or tilt more than a few inches, and the only variety to the single-take tedium came in Vitaphone's grander moments, when cameras set up in adjacent booths would be deployed to shoot simultaneous close-up, medium, and long shots which could later be intercut. Also housed in booths were the sound technicians, with hardships of their own. Since remixing was not yet possible, each successful take had to produce a flawless phonograph recording. Additionally, there had to be steady hands on the controls to obtain proper volume while ensuring that the equipment would not blow out (which it did, time and again). For performers and crew, there was the agony of the new, unendurably hot incandescent lights, made necessary by the demands of the microphone and the process's need for a "slower" film stock. Those miserable lights turned the first soundstages into a hell as much literal as figurative, and doubtless in that summer and early fall of 1925 there were times when it did not seem worth the effort. For Warners, the financial aspects were equally nightmarish—costs soon exceeded the million-dollar mark and kept climbing.

Vitaphone was pronounced worthy if not precisely bug-free early in 1926, and the Vitaphone Corporation was formally launched in April. The charter included a strategic proviso entitling Warners and Western Electric to license the system to other film companies. The plans for Vitaphone's premiere presentation made Warners' intention for the system unmistakable:

a silent feature film with a recorded orchestral score synchronized to it, preceded by a potpourri of short filmed musical acts. The logical choice for the feature was *Don Juan*, already in production under the direction of Alan Crosland. The company's most costly film, it promised spectacle, sex, and action—plus, in the person of John Barrymore, a touch of class. *Don Juan* was filmed like any other Hollywood silent, after which Vitaphone's East Coast technicians and Sam Warner took over. To enhance *Don Juan*'s pseudo-classicism with posh trimmings, Warner hired the New York Philharmonic and its music director, Henry Hadley, to record the newly commissioned William Axt-David Mendoza score and appear in a filmed overture. Any hope of doing it at the Vitagraph studio in Brooklyn was dashed when the sound people heard the subway rumble by under the building, and a search for something more soundproof led to the Manhattan Opera House on 34th Street. This time recording was impaired by blasts from a nearby construction site, which nearly popped Vitaphone's stylus out of the groove. With New York even noisier in 1926 than it is today, it was decided to yield to the unavoidable, stay on 34th Street, and do the recording late at night.

In spite of the costs, Sam Warner pushed continually to give the *Don Juan*/Vitaphone show a maximum quota of prestige and polish. For the remaining acts on the opening program he reached not to vaudeville or Broadway but to the concert hall and opera house. Aiming high and successfully, he enlisted the services of several of the most famous and accomplished artists in serious music. Then, in a final and infinitely shrewd touch, Warner underscored the import of the occasion by enlisting the services of Hollywood's unofficial commander-in-chief. Will H. Hays, former Postmaster General of the United States, had been appointed in 1922 to head a new organization set up by the film industry to regulate itself: the Motion Picture Producers and Distributors of America, Inc. (MPPDA), known in time simply as the Hays Office. Hays may have had the manner of a small-town alderman and the face of an enervated weasel, but he was nobody's fool. He reigned for years as the film industry's official spokesperson and apologist, his domain extending to the moral tone of Hollywood's citizenry as well as its product. A bland despot, he wielded his authority in such a way as to set the most hardened studio executives trembling. When Hays consented to lead off Vitaphone's proceedings with a filmed introduction, Warner's coup was complete. The investment as it stood had reached the $3 million mark before the public had a chance to find out what it was about.

On August 6, 1926, a rather ostentatious audience filed into the new flagship Warner Bros. Theatre on Broadway, having paid a steep $10 and more per seat. The exhaustive ballyhoo appeared to cynics as much noise about another abortive gimmick; the more impartial may have detected something different in the tone of the event, since the likes of Mischa Elman and Giovanni Martinelli were not normally associated with cheap stunts. Neither was Will Hays, and his presence indicated as much as anything that the occasion might be exceptional.[7] And so it was, to the extent that Vitaphone's opening night marks the true beginning of the sound era.

VITAPHONE PROGRAM
August 6, 1926

Address by Will H. Hays

Prelude to *Tannhäuser* (Wagner)
—New York Philharmonic, Henry Hadley cond.

"Humoresque" (Dvorak) and "Gavotte" (Gossec)
—Mischa Elman, violin, assisted by Josef Bonime, piano

"His Pastimes"
—Roy Smeck, Hawaiian guitar, ukulele, harmonica, banjo

"Caro nome" from *Rigoletto* (Verdi)
—Marion Talley, soprano;
   Vitaphone Symphony Orchestra/Heller

Theme and Variations from the Kreutzer Sonata (Beethoven)
—Efrem Zimbalist, violin; Harold Bauer, piano

"Vesti la giubba" from *I Pagliacci* (Leoncavallo)
—Giovanni Martinelli, tenor;
   Vitaphone Symphony Orchestra/Heller

"La Fiesta"
—Anna Case, soprano; The Cansinos, dancers;
   Metropolitan Opera Chorus;
   Vitaphone Symphony Orchestra/Heller

The first sounds the audience heard from the screen, in fact the only spoken words in the evening's program, were Will Hays's prosaic midwestern tones. His overwritten speech, delivered with a few ludicrous attempts at dramatic pauses and gestures, doled out praise, self-righteousness, and baloney in equal measure, plus a trace of prescience:

> My friends—No story ever written for the screen is as dramatic as the story of the screen itself. Tonight we write another chapter in that story.

---

7. Note that Hays's endorsement came when most of the industry shunned the suggestion of sound. Like other informed observers, he probably saw sound film—in whatever form it would take—as a tool to fight the encroachment of radio.

Far indeed have we advanced from that few seconds of shadow of a serpentine dancer thirty years ago when the motion picture was born to this public demonstration of the Vitaphone, synchronizing the reproduction of sound with the reproduction of action. . . . In the presentation of these pictures, music plays an invaluable part. The motion picture too is the most potent factor in the national appreciation of good music. That service will now be extended as the Vitaphone will carry symphony orchestrations *[sic]* to the town halls of the hamlets. It has been said the art of vocalists and instrumentalists is ephemeral, that he creates but for the moment. Now, neither the artist nor his art will ever wholly die. . . . To the Warner Brothers to whom is due credit for this, the beginning of a new era in music and motion pictures, I offer my felicitations and my sincerest appreciation. It is an occasion indeed with which the public and the motion picture industry are equally gratified. It is another great service, and service is the supreme commitment of life.

To a hall filled with industry insiders (including Hays), the initial impression was startling. What sounded like Hays's voice appeared to emanate from the screen and was clearly amplified throughout most of the large theater. Furthermore, the lip movements of the projected image seemed in close if not perfect synchronization with the words. The real test came with the musical performances, which the Philharmonic got off to a Wagnerian start. Again this was a right choice, offering culture and bombast in a familiar and accessible piece. As Hadley led the 107-piece orchestra through the prelude, several of Vitaphone's drawbacks became apparent to the more discerning spectators. One was visual, for the fluid camera work and rich monochrome tones of silents were obviously lacking. Though there were nods in the direction of photographic variety by panning over the different instrumental sections, it remained a static performance. Also, no matter how much improvement the Vitaphone sonics offered over previous sound films, they still left much to be desired. The sound was rather constricted and tinny, the brass especially lacking in resonance and sheen. This canned rendering could never truly replace the sound of a live orchestra. But novelty ruled the day, and most observers were entranced.

The largest part of the bill was given to solo performers, with mixed technical and artistic results. It was rather lopsided programming to have two virtuoso violinists on the bill, and opinions varied on just how well the string tone reproduced. Elman probably had the edge with the much-loved "Humoresque." Vaudeville guitarist Roy Smeck, billed without apology to Elman and Zimbalist as "The Wizard of the String," was judged a success with the lightest fare on the program.[8] Viewed today, the merits of these

8. In the copies of the Vitaphone program available today, Smeck's harmonica is not nearly as audible as his ukulele, and it's pretty safe to assume that this fault would have been compounded with the primitive 1926 sound systems.

segments are undercut by the unutterably pedestrian film technique: a single shot by a camera that never moves or changes its angle during a six- to nine-minute performance. Smeck's is the dreariest, one medium shot of him sitting there, playing one instrument after another.

For reasons good and otherwise, a major share of the attention accrued to the three singers. Since it was the most elaborate of all the acts, Anna Case's "La Fiesta" was put in the final spot, its Spanish flavor logically paving the way for *Don Juan*. As clearly as it foreshadowed the production numbers made possible by sound film, "La Fiesta" also showed that a staged musical number could not be statically photographed and put on the screen in toto. Impressive to audiences in 1926, it seems today an underdirected piece of commotion, with choral, dance, and solo performers—Case was a competent if not quite top-drawer singer—all lumped together for the camera's unyielding yet undiscerning eye.[9]

The decision to put Marion Talley on the program was more commercial than artistic. A few months earlier, her debut at the Metropolitan Opera had drawn nationwide attention: this eighteen-year-old "Kansas City Canary" was a press agent's dream, a Horatia Alger of classical music scaling heights normally set aside for more seasoned artists. Striking while the iron was hot, Warners filmed her in the role of her Met debut, Gilda in *Rigoletto*. Unfortunately, an artistic immaturity that was obvious enough onstage at the Met was magnified on film, and more than any other part of the program, the Talley segment drew heavy critical fire. The synchronization problems that occasionally arose in the other acts were rampant here, her voice constantly preceding her lip movement. Not that the voice was heard all that well, for her immature coloratura was judged meager in both tone and amplitude. To add to the misery, she made some rather strange faces during the aria's more difficult passages, prompting blunt comments on her well-fed and not terribly photogenic appearance. *Photoplay* was the rudest: "Her voice was far from attractive. As to her face, the producers made the mistake of allowing the camera to come too close. . . . Long-shots—and good, long ones—were just invented for that girl." Today, enhanced by vastly improved synchronization and sound, it's one of the more successful and cinematic of the shorts. There are modest attempts at dramatic staging and camera movement, and Talley's performance is at least passable. More training could have bought this comet a decent career. As it was, she couldn't live up to the hype, and her fame was short-lived.

In the greatest possible contrast to the timorous Talley, Giovanni Martinelli's *Pagliacci* solo was a sensation. If Martinelli lacked the golden instru-

---

9. The Cansino dance team seen in "La Fiesta" comprises Eduardo Cansino and his sister Alisa. It has been written that Eduardo's daughter Margarita, later known as Rita Hayworth, also appears in the number; she does not.

ment of his rival Beniamino Gigli, his musical and dramatic strengths were unquestioned. The leading dramatic tenor since the death of Caruso, he was a better actor than either Caruso or Gigli and had everything Marion Talley did not: experience, training, and a keen ability to seize upon the crucial point in opera where music and drama intersect. The laugh-clown-laugh aria was ideal material for his ringing tenor, his exceptional breath control enabling him to take the piece at a slow tempo in extremely long phrases, extracting the maximum amount of pathos through good musicianship and communicating it directly to the audience. The flat one shot/one camera format could not deter his stunning impact, and this single three-and-a-half-minute performance was crucial to the successful entry of sound film. In a very real way Martinelli was the first musical film star, demonstrating more than a year before *The Jazz Singer* the power resulting from the meeting of amplified voice and projected image.

Don Juan, following after the intermission, seemed anticlimactic in comparison. Barrymore's lovemaking and swordplay were enjoyable and the Axt-Mendoza score and scattered sound effects a fit accompaniment, yet it was evident that even Hadley and his forces were no match for a live theater orchestra. Nevertheless, most critics were enthusiastic the next day and some were ecstatic—at least in part because Warner flacks had taken care to package and cushion the event to hold unfavorable response to a minimum. The August 7 newspapers ran preplanted announcements of the evening's triumph, and several days later the trade and popular press were emblazoned with a carefully selected smattering of press quotes. A comment of "marvelous" from *The New York Times* was a big help (then as now), and the *New York Evening Journal* dubbed the device "the greatest sensation of the decade next to radio." Some observers did note the technical imperfections. In addition to the problematic Talley segment, many felt Vitaphone's mechanics to be obtrusive. Spectators were not generally accustomed to the peculiar properties of amplified sound, and both the constricted quality and the surface noise from the discs tended to mitigate against the desired illusion. *The New Yorker* complained that "the snap, or edge, of real acoustics" was lacking. Nor did *Don Juan* receive full endorsement, for some thought its florid melodrama past the pale, lacking the requisite Douglas Fairbanks panache. As many realized, the inadvertent truth was that *Don Juan*, whether transcendent or foul, was beside the point. The big excitement lay in Vitaphone's possibilities, and after August 6 New Yorkers had two main topics of conversation: Gertrude Ederle's successful swim across the English Channel and the new sound films at Warner's Theatre. The editors of *The New York Times* got into the act on August 8 with a piece entitled "Audible Pictures." It ran next to an editorial in praise of Ederle, and neither press agents nor Will Hays's speechwriter could have given Warners a bigger boost:

No single word . . . is quite adequate to suggest the amazing triumph which man has at last achieved in making pictures talk naturally, sing enthrallingly and play all manner of instruments as skillfully as if the living beings were present instead of their shadows. Those who first heard and saw the pierrot of "Pagliacci" in the person of the moving likeness of the living Martinelli fill a great hall with the vibrant sound which moved the audience as the presence of the singer could not have done more effectually, perhaps not as affectingly, were present as at the performance of a seeming miracle in which the tongue of the dumb image was made to sing. One can but regret that Caruso went away before this miracle had been accomplished.

The most obvious fact is that this invention in its various forms will enable the smaller communities to participate to a greater degree than even the radio permits in the cultural advantages that have been possible in the past only in places of large population. But the more stirring fact is that it will give immortality to the faces and voices of those whom the world wishes immortally to keep among the living. Any supreme skill of voice or hand that comes into the world hereafter in any generation may be kept for all generations, with a mimicry that needs only color to make it perfect. . . . In pictures such as these, the eloquent dead will hereafter still speak.

In the midst of all this razzle and twaddle, *Billboard* had the temerity to invoke the predecessor Warner publicists had tried to make everyone forget.

Whether the Vitaphone is any better in its voice reproduction and synchronization than the De Forest Phonofilm, is left open to dispute. The only conceivable difference between the two is that Vitaphone has been launched on a more elaborate scale, with Metropolitan Opera and concert stars singing before it instead of the vaudeville artistes De Forest has used thus far.

Not mentioned was the fact that Phonofilm was also more technically advanced than Vitaphone. Nevertheless the observation was apt: while not first with sound, or even best, Warners had promoted their device more astutely than De Forest ever could, and Sam Warner's intuition and skill enhanced the product with cultured trappings and polished packaging that made sound film seem special. It was inevitable that some spectators felt, as one critic noted, that "it may be only a relatively short time before a talking photoplay is produced," yet any intimation that silent film would be displaced was sheer anathema. Warners had already expressed its intentions in the Vitaphone/*Don Juan* program book, along with the lily-gilding assertion that "Vitaphone . . . will be a tremendous factor in promoting good will by and between the people of all nations." The care exercised in nearly every aspect of the presentation showed most conspicuously in a last-minute change made on the morning of the premiere. There had originally been one more musical act on the program, a dreary cobbling of balalaika melodies called "An Evening on the Don," which, after eliciting a humdrum response at the August 5 press screening, was removed from the lineup.[10] Showmanship was clearly the key, and as a result demand far exceeded supply for tickets at Warner's Theatre. The most expensive prices for the two-a-day showing were at the standard $2 high, though scalpers charged more. Seeing the long lines, Warners raised the price by another dollar—an unheard-of price for a film, almost equal to the highest theater tariffs—but it worked for two months. Vitaphone's New York run stretched to a significant eight months, and more cities followed in the fall: Chicago, Boston, Hollywood (briefly, at Grauman's Egyptian), and Atlantic City.

As a few exhibitors began to wire their theaters for sound, Warners realized that one of Vitaphone's ongoing difficulties would lie in convincing theater owners to cover the steep cost of installation. It averaged $23,000 for a pair of the projector-phonograph devices (for which the projectionist needed two assistants), a speaker-horn system, and a new screen, made of more reflective material to partly compensate for the less luminous new film stock which made synchronization possible. The system was troublesome as well, for the discs were not exactly low-maintenance. They were easily broken and prone to sticking and skipping. Plus, like any other phonograph records being tracked with extremely harsh needles, they were good for only a limited number of plays, after which they sounded awful.[11]

Sam Warner and publicist-organizer A. P. Waxman shrewdly stretched Vitaphone in a different direction for its next outing, on October 7 at another Broadway theater, the Colony. Both the feature and the short subjects were far more populist, i.e., less highbrow, in their aims. A forgettable war comedy called *The Better 'Ole*, starring Charlie Chaplin's brother Syd, was accompanied by an hour-long potpourri of artists from vaudeville and Broadway. This time when the Philharmonic opened the evening, Wagner gave way to "The Spirit of 1918." The rest of the program proceeded, as a critic put it, "almost precisely as the most extravagant booker would build a show for his vaudeville house." The one serious singer on

10. Although many reviews on August 7 mentioned the number, it had not made it to the premiere. After August 6, Warners continued to monitor its brainchild. During the fall of 1926, with the program running in several cities, it was decided that the Talley aria was not worth the brickbats, and it too was dropped. Later in the New York run, the Zimbalist/Bauer number was also pulled, likely due to technical inadequacy and excessive similarity to Elman's segment.

11. Each disc had to be replaced after ten plays (twenty for later discs). To remind the projectionist, the label of each record was imprinted with the appropriate number of boxes, one to be checked after each use.

the bill, concert baritone Reinald Werrenrath, sang not opera but "The Long, Long Trail." Everything else was indisputably pop: "jazzy songs and melodies" by The Four Aristocrats, Elsie Janis and chorus in a medley of her Great War morale-rousers, Eugene and Willie Howard in a comedy sketch. There was also a song and monologue by George Jessel—talk was creeping into the Vitaphone scheme, here and in the Howard sketch—and, most crucially, there was one other specialty artist: Al Jolson. His presence, and that of Jessel, give a hindsight jolt to the fact that *The Better 'Ole* opened one year less one day before *The Jazz Singer*.

What Martinelli had done for the first Vitaphone program, Jolson did for the second. He had been one of the highest-paid stars in show business for a decade, and Broadway, vaudeville, recordings, and radio all bore witness to his audience-enthralling self-aggrandizement. With a voice and manner that were naturals for Vitaphone, he donned his trademarked blackface to sing three of his biggest hits: "April Showers," "When the Red, Red Robin Comes Bob-Bob-Bobbin' Along," and "Rock-a-Bye Your Baby with a Dixie Melody," surefire songs in nearly any context. It was dynamite, and audiences were riveted. As in the first program, the most triumphant performance had not occurred in the headliner slot at the end of the bill, which had been given to Jessel. This less-than-astute showmanship was due to the fact that Jessel was under contract to Warners, and his first film *(Private Izzy Murphy)* was being readied for release. But while his work was warmly received, everyone knew who the real headliner had been. However much Jessel fancied himself Jolson's chief rival, there was no question who could sell a song better—or who came across on film more dynamically.[12]

Once again the Vitaphone program overshadowed the feature, and eager spectators paid reserved-seat prices to see and hear for themselves. In the critical community and in the industry, there was some apprehension along with the applause. The first program had caused everyone to comment benevolently on the system's ability to present first-rate classical music. Adding a popular slant for the second program was a different proposition, in fact the first demonstration that talking pictures could be a threat: in small towns featuring this caliber of entertainment, live vaudeville seemed infinitely dimmer. Once again, little mention was made of Vitaphone breaking into feature films, but other areas of show business were beginning to feel pressure and would continue to do so.

12. Seven decades after the fact, it's hard to imagine Jessel and Jolson as true rivals. Jolson has come down as the dynamic mammy singer, while Jessel's ultimate image for most people is that of a tiresome toastmaster telling limp jokes. In the 1920s, however, Jessel had also achieved success in vaudeville and—something Jolson never did—as a dramatic actor. He was perceived as being more versatile than Jolson, and in some ways he was; just not nearly as charismatic.

Although most of the industry felt it politic to ignore Vitaphone as conspicuously as possible, William Fox did not. One of the more adventurous of the pioneering motion picture pirates, he had already acquired the Tri-Ergon sound-on-film system. The *Don Juan* premiere, which he had attended, further consolidated some of his own ideas and schemes. Four days after the premiere of *The Better 'Ole*, it was announced that the Fox Film Corporation had bought a significant interest in the De Forest Phonofilm and that De Forest's films and sound equipment would be leased to the chain of Fox movie theaters. The announcement, as it turned out, was premature; relations between Fox and De Forest quickly deteriorated, and they ended up spending years suing each other. This was partly because Fox had already begun dealing with a colleague-turned-competitor of De Forest's, Theodore W. Case. Case and his assistant Earl I. Sponable had devised a sound-on-film system very similar to (and perhaps based on) Phonofilm, with even greater technical refinement. Fox was sold on the Case process not through any musical performances, but by a simple short of Sponable's pet canary in which every chirp came forth loud and clear.[13] Fox, who dubbed the system Movietone, cannily perceived that he should spend time realizing the system's potential instead of rushing to compete with Vitaphone. The sound-on-film process had certain major capabilities that its rival lacked. With no discs to worry about, filming could done with far less equipment and without Vitaphone's hyper-controlled studio environment. Shooting out-of-doors, which Warners' engineers shuddered to contemplate, posed no problem for Movietone, and the process allowed easier editing. The fact that it did not sound quite as good as Vitaphone was, for exhibitors, partly offset by a far simpler projection system. For months after the initial contracts were signed, Movietone's engineers concentrated on refining the process, including experiments with outdoor shooting and tests of big-name musical performers.[14]

Early in 1927, with Movietone's public debut still a few months away, Fox maneuvered the Vitaphone Corporation into an agreement by which each company could use the other's system when needed. This was a mutual boon: Fox needed Vitaphone's superior amplification equipment to

13. Many of Case's test films have survived, including the one of the canary. The most indelible is "Ma, He's Makin' Eyes at Me," as performed by a stringy vaudevillian, Gus Vysor, and his duck, the latter yakking out each interjected "Ma." If not to display the potential of sound film, this might at least inspire audiences to ponder the deeper meanings of life and art.

14. One of the biggest names to make a Movietone test was Harry Lauder, who ensured that the test would not be marketed without his permission by stopping in the middle of "Roamin' in the Gloamin' " to announce in a solemn brogue, "Thees is a taste." Nor were his suspicions unfounded: another performer used to try out Movietone was young hoofer Ruby Keeler, whose test was subsequently shown commercially—without, she later asserted, her knowledge or consent.

give Movietone extra finish, and Vitaphone could place its equipment and films in the large and lucrative Fox theater chain. Fox convinced Warners that they were both underdogs in the Hollywood community and needed to be allies as well as rivals. This was not idle paranoia. Five of the biggest studios—MGM, Paramount, First National, Universal, and C. B. De Mille's Producers' Distributing Corporation—had met in secret sessions to plot strategy regarding Vitaphone's encroachment into their territory. They agreed that the threat of sound should be officially ignored, totally abrogated, or at least forestalled as long as possible. If sound continued, they would all plunge in at the same time, and in so doing they would not resort to going hat-in-hand to Warner Bros., which was despised as a pushy upstart. Instead, they would use some system other than Vitaphone. In addition to Movietone, General Electric and RCA were nearing completion of work on their sound-on-film Photophone process, and following the birth of Vitaphone a number of schemers had started tinkering with their own questionable talking-picture devices. Sensing the heat, Warners mounted an intensive drive to bring Vitaphone to more theaters. Despite the expense, exhibitors in city after city signed on: Detroit, Cleveland, Baltimore, and more, always leading off with the *Don Juan*/Martinelli package. By mid-February, Vitaphone was boasting that over seventy cities, almost all of them in the Northeast and Midwest, had signed installation agreements. This certainly sounded good, in fact better than Vitaphone often did; reports indicated that the system's acoustics were less than superlative in most theaters outside New York.

A long four months went by between Vitaphone's second and third outings. The nature of the new program, coupled with the inordinate amount of time elapsed, indicated Warners' uncertainty about what direction to take. The feature was another Barrymore/Crosland special, *When a Man Loves*—*Manon Lescaut* under any other name—and its premiere on February 3, 1927, was preceded by a grab-bag of Vitaphone shorts split evenly between classical and popular music, with not enough for devotees of either art. Beniamino Gigli and Giuseppe de Luca performing Verdi on the one hand would not necessarily please those coming to hear vaudevillians Van and Schenck singing "She Knew Her Onions" on the other. Gigli and De Luca were joined by Marion Talley and mezzo Jeanne Gordon for the *Rigoletto* Quartet, with tenor Charles Hackett on hand for other *Rigoletto* arias. Fred Waring and his Pennsylvanians joined Van and Schenck on the pop end, and somewhere between the two poles Met soprano Mary Lewis went folksy with "Carry Me Back to Old Virginny." The praise was less glowing this time, even with technical improvements, and *Variety* complained about the "monotonous similarity of material," adding that "Warners may have been misled into believing that names mean more than entertainment." The Marion Talley jinx, incidentally, was still in effect; she could not win where Vitaphone was concerned. Assessing her contribution, *The New Yorker* stayed well this side of chivalry: "[She] is caused to utter sounds that could only be duplicated by the twittering of tightly-locked subway brakes." With the novelty beginning to fade, content and form were open to far greater scrutiny. Despite the star names and the production gloss of *When a Man Loves,* box-office response was tepid.

Warners next began to take a new tack, breaking down the Vitaphone package to put the shorts on the bill with ordinary silent films without recorded scores, in continuous regular-price showings instead of the two-a-day roadshows. New Vitaphone shorts suddenly began to flood the market, with more popular items like Jolson and Martinelli held over while the other acts changed. There was just enough variety in these new shorts to demonstrate the possibilities. Broadway entered the equation with the "Will You Remember?" duet from Sigmund Romberg's *Maytime,* well performed by baritone John Charles Thomas and operetta's Vivienne Segal. Other new Vitaphone stars included "Whispering Jack Smith," Broadway ballerina Maria Gambarelli, jazzy soubrette Sylvia Froos, monologist Joe Browning, and the great contralto Ernestine Schumann-Heink. There was even a Vitaphone mini-revue, a decidedly non-deluxe affair highlighted by a horse that danced the Black Bottom and waggled its tail at the camera. Put all together it spelled canned vaudeville, and in March of 1927 vaudeville began to complain. The Keith-Albee Circuit, one of the largest chains of vaudeville theaters, made an official declaration branding Vitaphone and other sound films "opposition," and threatened to add no-Vitaphone clauses to its artists' contracts. Warners shot back that it was not intimidated, that Vitaphone would continue to feature the biggest names.

More theaters were wiring for sound each week, yet the procession of acts, even with names like Gigli and Jolson, could not sustain indefinite interest in a limited medium with a constricted technology. William Fox knew this, and when the time came to unveil Movietone he scored a direct hit. He had earlier dabbled in Vitaphone-style musical shorts, but for Movietone's first official press screening on April 29 at the Roxy Theatre he offered something totally different from Warners, simple yet devastatingly effective: a sound newsreel. As with Vitaphone shorts, Lee De Forest had done it earlier, but perceptions had changed since 1924. The newsreel—a West Point military parade—was utterly innocuous and thoroughly successful, shot outdoors to flaunt Movietone's technical superiority. It also succeeded in another of Vitaphone's deficient areas, that of sound perspective. The military band was heard to grow louder as it drew nearer to the camera, and, especially when heard in the cavernous Roxy, the possibilities of sound film also seemed to expand. Movietone formally opened in New

York on May 25 as a prologue to the Fox feature *Seventh Heaven*.[15] Once again the newsreel stole the show, this time as adroitly as anything Warners ever dreamed of: a sound film, shot only five days earlier, of Lindbergh's takeoff for Paris. Lindbergh and his flight were already an international obsession, it was absolutely unprecedented for mass audiences to actually see *and* hear such a talked-about event, and crowds went wild. The other items on the bill, the icing on the cake, more directly threatened Vitaphone's supremacy: big-name musical performers Gertrude Lawrence, Ben Bernie and his orchestra, and Raquel Meller.

With Movietone an emergent threat, Warner Bros. was running scared. Clearly the status quo could not remain in the realm of snippets and canned vaudeville. The studio had already raised its ante in May by completing work on its first Hollywood soundstages, which would replace New York as the base of Vitaphone operations (Vitaphone work would resume in Brooklyn the following year). But by late spring of 1927 Vitaphone was in a slump, with dwindling grosses and an expanding public awareness of its many technical and aesthetic shortcomings. Several theaters terminated their contracts with Vitaphone, saving hundreds a week in royalty fees and personnel costs. The idea of using recorded scores for features was, from *Don Juan*'s first night, neither here nor there. The scores had inspired neither excessive favor nor, except among the theater musicians they displaced, aversion. To recoup its investment, Warners would need to expand Vitaphone into more attention-getting areas. This ultimate solution was conceived as early as autumn 1926, most likely by mastermind Sam Warner. It was, of course, *The Jazz Singer*.

The creation of *The Jazz Singer* has long since passed into folklore: George Jessel's unexpected replacement by Al Jolson; Jolson's inserting extemporaneous dialogue into two scenes and thus giving birth to "talkies"; and, inevitably, the motion picture industry miraculously undergoing an overnight revolution based on the response to this one film. When examined away from the glare of Jolsonesque bravado and Warner drum-beating, there is a different tale. In neither conception nor production was it quite the legendary go-for-broke gamble forged from chance and accident, nor was its initial reception as dazzling as legend reports. The myth of *The Jazz Singer* lies somewhere between a rock and a hard place: its importance cannot be underestimated, yet perspective and balance and leavening are needed to put it into the larger picture of the sound revolution. Its creation was marked by a singular fusion of catalysts—calculation, luck, and bun-

15. Since *Seventh Heaven*'s planned Movietone score was not yet ready, it was run as a silent film with organ accompaniment. When the score was added to the film some weeks later, it proved more attention-getting than any of the Vitaphone scores, chiefly because its love theme, "Diane," became a hit, helping establish the trend of popular theme songs.

gling, with a guest appearance by that show-biz staple, triumph in the face of tragedy.

In April 1917 an undergraduate student named Sampson (later Samson) Raphaelson saw Al Jolson perform in *Robinson Crusoe, Jr.* He immediately noted the similarity between the star's force-of-nature performing style and the Lower East Side cantors of Raphaelson's and Jolson's youth, and eventually used incidents from the life of the former Asa Yoelson as the basis for a short story. "The Day of Atonement," published in January 1922 in *Everybody's Magazine,* recounted the saga of Jack Robin (né Jakie Rabinowitz), who pursues a career in show business in defiance of the stern Orthodox father who assumed he would follow family tradition and become a cantor. Jolson, believing the story ideal for his screen debut, attempted through intermediaries to sell the idea to D. W. Griffith and other film producers, none of whom was interested.[16] Jolson then proposed a stage adaptation to Raphaelson. The author, not anxious to see his work reduced to the level of a standard Jolson extravaganza, had other ideas. Over the next two years he transformed "The Day of Atonement" into a drama he called *Prayboy,* which producer-director Al Lewis bought to launch the dramatic career of singer-comic George Jessel. As *The Jazz Singer,* it opened on Broadway on September 14, 1925, to mixed-to-negative reviews (the word "hokum" came up fairly often) and enthusiastic spectators, many of whom saw the play's sincerity as a pleasing antidote to the gross stereotypes of the current smash *Abie's Irish Rose.* In April 1926 George Jessel signed a three-year contract with Warner Bros., and the day before *The Jazz Singer* closed on Broadway on July 5, Warners paid $50,000 for the rights, agreeing to hold up the release of the film until the play completed its tour. The purchase was apparently made at the behest of Ernst Lubitsch, who—the mind reels that this master of cinematic urbanity considered such a thing—was eager to direct it.[17] Jessel's first film under his contract was a piece of

16. In mid-1923, Jolson did agree to star for Griffith in *Black and White* as a mystery writer who dons blackface to track down a murderer. After making a screen test, Jolson began rehearsals without a signed contract. On the first day of shooting he was a no-show, and two days later he sent Griffith a radiogram stating that doctor's orders compelled him to take an immediate ocean voyage. (In truth, he had hated his test and decided the whole thing was a colossal mistake.) Griffith, immensely and naturally frustrated, brought breach-of-[verbal]-contract charges against Jolson. By the time it got to court in September 1926, *Black and White* had been filmed by others as the massively unsuccessful *His Darker Self,* and Jolson had already entered films courtesy of Vitaphone. Griffith received a token award for damages.

17. Just as strangely, it was reported in 1927 that after Lubitsch moved to Paramount, his first project there was to be the film version of *Abie's Irish Rose.* Logic soon prevailed, and he was replaced by Victor Fleming. The director's connection with *The Jazz Singer* did continue, happily, in an ongoing association with Samson Raphaelson. The creator of Jakie Rabinowitz co-wrote some of Lubitsch's finest films, among them *The Smiling Lieutenant* and *Trouble in Paradise.*

dreck called *Private Izzy Murphy*, shot in Hollywood in summer 1926. Warners first contemplated shooting *The Jazz Singer* back-to-back with *Izzy*, then moved the shooting date forward to May 1927 to allow Jessel to complete his tour with the play. Any plan to use Lubitsch collapsed when he left Warners in August 1926, and later that month Jessel and Jolson both starred in Vitaphone shorts.

In the fall of 1926, Warners decided that *The Jazz Singer* would include Vitaphone sequences, and the December issue of *Photoplay* announced that it would feature several songs. Later reports named Alan Crosland as director and May McAvoy as costar opposite Jessel. By May, the planned time of shooting, there was trouble. *Variety* reported:

> Jessel has a contract for $2,000 a week to play in the screen version of "The Jazz Singer." While the production was being discussed Jessel pointed out that since he would be expected to make two or three records for Vitaphone to accompany the picture, this matter should be taken care of in some form of additional compensation. He reasoned this would be only just, considering that Vitaphone was an entirely separate proposition from Warner Brothers. . . .
>
> Warner Brothers cut communications with Jessel, and it is understood overture[s] have been made to Al Jolson to take the lead. If Jolson signs he will not be able to go to Hollywood before next February. . . .
>
> Jessel claims that he will get two more years of service out of "The Jazz Singer" as a spoken drama and does not wish to appear on the Vitaphone as opposition to himself.

By May 26 Jessel was out and Jolson was in, and that day he signed a contract with Warners stating that *The Jazz Singer* would include his performance of six Vitaphoned songs. "Kol Nidre," "My Mammy," "When I Lost You," "Yes Sir, That's My Baby," "Mighty Lak a Rose," and " 'N Everything" were the songs first mentioned. Jolson was to be paid far more than Jessel: $75,000 for eight weeks of work starting on July 11, 1927, and $9,375 per week for anything beyond eight weeks.[18] Following preliminary tests of Jolson, filming began without him in June. The New York location sequences were shot first, then work continued in Hollywood. Jolson joined the company in mid-July and filmed his silent scenes in about one month. It had already been decided that incidental dialogue would be employed along with the songs, and the Vitaphone sequences were filmed in the latter part of August without excessive difficulty. "My Mammy," for exam-

18. Rumors have persisted about financial arrangements between Jolson and Warners that were not written into his contract. The best known allows that Jolson was paid partly in Warner stock, which seems reasonably possible. Less probable is Jolson's later claim that he himself was required to invest money in the production.

ple, was pulled off in three takes on the afternoon of August 18. Filming wrapped early in September, with the final negative cost coming in at a sizable $422,000, and the buildup quickly started. The opening was set for October 6 at the Warner Bros. Theater in New York, and one day before the premiere Sam Warner died in Los Angeles of a brain abscess precipitated by an acute sinus infection. He was an appallingly young forty-one, the illness had been brief, and the studio was plunged into a state of shock. His brothers, in New York for the premiere, returned to California immediately. At his funeral they played Jolson's Vitaphone recording of "Kol Nidre," a poignantly crass touch.

It is absolutely no secret that *The Jazz Singer* is, to all intents and purposes, a lousy movie. Many knew it in 1927, and anyone who sees it today expecting a masterpiece will be rudely awakened. Incredibly corny and hokey, it's also repellently manipulative. As silent filmmaking—at least 75 percent of it is silent—it is miserably regressive, with title cards that would have been considered dated in 1907, let alone 1927. (Examples: "God made her a woman and Love made her a mother"; "That I should live to see my baby again!"; and the inevitable "A jazz singer—singing to his God.") And the staging and general dramatic tone frequently match the titles in subtlety. But in many ways it doesn't matter, for despite all the tripe this first feature film to include both talk and song always discloses its historical resonance. Some of the history, for better or worse, was quite inadvertent. Lubitsch, for example, might have directed it as a 1926 silent with Jessel, shot immediately after *Izzy Murphy*. And, inevitably, it must be wondered how on earth would it have turned out with Jessel in the lead. Today that prospect may seem as inconceivable as it is disheartening, and it did come close to happening. The reasons for Jessel's replacement have always been somewhat unclear, and further clouded by the predictably divergent stories told after the fact by Jolson and Jessel themselves. The truth is fairly simple. Jessel had been signed as a *silent-film* performer. The decision was made some months later to give Vitaphone a boost by putting singing sequences into the silent film of *The Jazz Singer*. Jessel decided that the circumstances and prestige warranted a higher salary and probably assumed that if he waited until just before filming to make his demands Warners would be forced to capitulate. As the haggling dragged on Jolson was waiting in the wings, probably at the behest of Sam Warner. It's hard not to assume that Warners was delighted with this turn of events.[19] Jolson was the obvious choice: *the only choice*. His success with Vitaphone had already been demonstrated, he was a bigger name and far better singer than

19. The more suspicious might come up with a conspiracy theory. Was it simple avarice that made Jessel relinquish his prior claim on *The Jazz Singer*, or did Warners surreptitiously stage-manage his discontent to get him out and Jolson in? Maybe it did happen as advertised, but remember, this is Hollywood we're talking about.

Jessel, and his appearance in the film would basically constitute autobiography. His face dominated the ads in an unforgettable white-on-black logo and, far more than Vitaphone, he was the chief selling point.

The most detectable asset of *The Jazz Singer* is the conviction put into it—Warners' and Alan Crosland's belief in the project and Jolson's belief in his powers as a musical entertainer. Whether the material was worthy of belief is another issue; what matters is that this story carried a force that more conventional screen fare lacked. Jewish themes were not uncommon in 1920s cinema, not only trivia of the *Private Izzy Murphy/Kosher Kitty Kelly* variety but sensitively considered dramas such as *Humoresque* (1920) and *His People* (1926). Raphaelson's play, with its ongoing conflict of tradition vs. assimilation, offered intensity and substance as well as schmaltz, and if the film adaptation was epically unsubtle and trite, it did pack some power. So did Crosland's strong visual sense. While he couldn't keep the actors from chewing the scenery to atoms, he often made it and them look good. The early shots of the Lower East Side have a documentary vigor, and the backstage vignettes and theater scenes (staged by Ernest Belcher) seem vivid and authentic, up to and including a few shots of young Myrna Loy as a nosy chorus girl. And however incompetent Jolson's pantomime, it's hard to forget the sight of the luminous smile breaking through his blackface while Louis Silvers's orchestra score gives out with a few bars of "My Mammy."

Jolson. Not only this film, the entire sound-film revolution is inconceivable without him. He *was The Jazz Singer.* Not the character of Jakie Rabinowitz, for Jolson's sense of self was too great and his dramatic ability too slight to portray a character other than himself. No, he is the film, and not even the good actors in the cast—May McAvoy, Warner Oland, Eugenie Besserer, William Demarest in a bit—matter greatly. Whenever they attempt to perform in a coherent drama, on comes the Jolson juggernaut, on full throttle the moment he opens his mouth. The man was, truly, spectacular, and his six songs and few words of patter clearly illuminate character and situation in ways that film had not done before and shorts subjects could not do. Jakie's near-Oedipal fixation finds its ultimate expression in "Mother of Mine, I Still Have You" and the indelible "My Mammy," as well as "Dirty Hands, Dirty Face." The exuberant "Toot, Toot Tootsie" and "Blue Skies" both illustrate the performer's energy that finds its most compatible outlet in "jazz" (i.e., pop) singing, where even whistling and scat syllables could be made vivid and immediate. "Kol Nidre" gives resolution to the central conflict as Jakie makes peace with his faith and his father. If the dramatic connections between song and plot are as rudimentary as they are hokey, at least the effort has been made, as it would be in most of the best early musicals, to integrate song and plot.

Jolson in *The Jazz Singer: (above)* In atypical repose, he sings "Kol Nidre" on the Day of Atonement. *(below)* With May McAvoy, silent but more in character. Both: *Photofest*.

Whatever breakthrough *The Jazz Singer* comprises is due to its sound sequences being placed, for the first time, at the service of the characters and plot of a feature film. In this context, sound seemed to add a new dimension, one underscored by Jolson's overpowering style. The final scene, his rendition of "My Mammy," wraps up the whole corny business with an intensity that silent drama could never duplicate. No title card could have conveyed the power of those hysterical cries just prior to the final sung lines—"Mammy, I'm comin'! . . . Oh, God, I hope I'm not late!" That is the significance of *The Jazz Singer*. The hoary legend that it instantaneously made silent film an outmoded curiosity is rubbish. Most observers in 1927 did not foresee the birth of a new kind of film. Instead, they saw that for all its potential *The Jazz Singer* was essentially several Vitaphone short subjects patched into a silent melodrama. The sound and silent sequences were considered segregated entities, not parts of a cohesive whole. Even some of the print ads reflected this, listing Vitaphone as a supporting *player*, after May McAvoy.[20] Only later was it recognized the extent to which *The Jazz Singer* expanded upon the potential, previously intimated by Vitaphone and Movietone, for new forms of entertainment; this ultimately bore fruit as talking pictures and musical films.

Numerous legends have arisen about the "Blue Skies" sequence; allegedly, the manic Jolson suddenly began to ad-lib dialogue, forcing the terrified Besserer along with him in what had been intended only as a song number. Again, this is not quite as advertised. It had already been stated that some dialogue would be used, so it's safe to infer that the final result was more calculated than accidental. It was also a retake of a previous number. On August 16 and 17 Jolson and Besserer shot the scene using "It All Depends On You," then reshot it with "Blue Skies" two weeks later.[21] Most likely, Jolson's spiel was partly written and partly improvised. Adlibs were never a problem for him in any case: "Mama, darlin', if I'm a success in this show, well, we're gonna move from here. Oh yes, we're gonna move up in the Bronx," and on and on. His other dialogue scene is briefer, but that "You ain't heard nothin' yet" line, just before his barreling into "Toot, Toot Tootsie," became an emblem of the sound revolution. No, Jolson did not make it up on the spot; probably he was told to say a line or two between songs, and the "nothin' yet" line was a phrase he had used many

20. There's far more song than talk in *The Jazz Singer*, though the other audible performers were virtually ignored. These included Bobby Gordon, who plays Jolson as a boy and sings "My Gal Sal" and "Waitin' for the Robert E. Lee"; Cantor Josef Rosenblatt, who plays himself in a concert sequence; tenor Joseph Diskay, dubbing for Warner Oland; and Eugenie Besserer, who as Jakie's mother mumbles occasional comments during his song and patter to "Blue Skies."

21. Bert Fiske filled in off-camera for Jolson's piano playing of "Blue Skies." "It All Depends on You" was put on hold until the following year, when Jolson sang it in *The Singing Fool*.

times on stage. His delivery of dialogue is, like his songs, as watchable as it is overbearing, infinitely more accomplished than the uncured ham of his silent scenes.

More than the opening night of *Don Juan*, the *Jazz Singer* premiere has traditionally marked the beginning of the sound era. At the time, it was not judged that outstanding an occasion. No ads heralded the event as with *Don Juan*, and tickets were half the price of that first night.[22] The program opened with the standard Vitaphone olios, all in a popular key—and with a comic banjoist, a twin-piano duo, and a close-harmony quartet, nothing to compete with Jolson. More interesting was Vitaphone's initial "dramatic" effort, *When the Wife's Away*, a ten-minute sketch with William Demarest. This time the feature dominated the night. More correctly, one person dominated. The huge ovation at the end of the evening was only for Jolson, not for any perceived cinematic breakthrough:

> Mr. Jolson's persuasive vocal efforts were received with rousing applause. In fact, not since the first presentation of Vitaphone features, more than a year ago at the same playhouse, has anything like the ovation been heard. . . . In the expression of song the Vitaphone vitalizes the production enormously. The dialogue is not so effective.
>
> Mordaunt Hall, *The New York Times*

> Probably nothing ever put on in a Broadway motion picture theatre evoked such hearty and prolonged applause as was shown time after time during the picture.
>
> But . . . it was for Al Jolson and his songs. The picture itself didn't cause a ripple.
>
> "The Jazz Singer," primarily, is scarcely a motion picture. It should more properly be labeled an enlarged Vitaphone record of Al Jolson in half a dozen songs. . . . .
>
> Samson Raphaelson's sad little story . . . is used by Warner Brothers simply as a background for putting over Al Jolson and his songs with the Vitaphone. It would be sad to think of what would happen to the picture without the Vitaphone and Jolson's songs.
>
> John S. Spargo, *Exhibitors Herald*

> Undoubtedly the best thing Vitaphone has ever put on the screen. The combination of the religious heart interest story and Jolson's singing . . . carries abundant power and appeal . . . .
>
> But "The Jazz Singer" minus Vitaphone is something else again.
>
> Sid [Silverman], *Variety*

22. Some tickets, in fact, were still available on the morning of October 6, even with the announcement that Jolson would attend. Warners publicists seem to have been asleep at the switch on this one, and after opening night as well. Again in contrast to *Don Juan*, there were no big ads or review quotes—or talk of overnight sensation—in the daily or trade papers.

The most hostile review was based more on politics than aesthetics. *Photoplay*'s powerful editor James R. Quirk sided with the Hollywood establishment ignoring sound films. His review of *The Jazz Singer* was relegated to the rear pages of the December issue where, stuffed in amid reviews for routine and low-budget films, it read in its entirety:

> Al Jolson with Vitaphone noises. Jolson is no movie actor. Without his Broadway reputation, he wouldn't rate as a minor player. The only interest in the picture is his six songs. The story is a fairly good tear-jerker about a Jewish boy who prefers jazz to the songs of his race. In the end, he returns to the fold and sings *Kol Nidre* on the Day of Atonement. It's the best scene in the film.

Samson Raphaelson, who attended the premiere, seethed as Jolson took his bows:

> I had a simple, corny, well-felt little melodrama, and they made an ill-felt, silly, maudlin, badly timed thing of it. There was absolutely no talent in the production at all. . . . Jolson [is] a lousy actor. He's a non-actor. . . . It was embarrassing. A dreadful picture. I've seen very few worse. . . .
>
> My characters were real, they were out of my childhood. There were no characters in the movie. Just a line here and a line there, . . . then Jolson would sing a song, and the songs were ill-chosen.

The New York public reacted far differently, more positively than the most generous critics had predicted. The lines at Warner's Theatre grew longer than those for *Don Juan* or any other sound program. Week after week, *Variety* attempted to ascribe the hefty grosses to such factors as New York's support for one of its own and the appeal to Jewish audiences. It was a smash locally, but the precise nature of the phenomenon was not evident for four months. By late December it had also opened in Philadelphia and Chicago, and over the following weeks in several dozen more cities. By early February Warners was boasting that *The Jazz Singer* was playing to one million people per week, and in cities where a film normally ran for one week was holding over for eight weeks and more.

Warner Bros.' reaction to the sensation was extremely peculiar. Just when *The Jazz Singer* was making its deepest impression, its producers were idle. The studio shut down all production for the entire month of December and part of January, and there were momentary rumors that Warners was closing for good. Denying this, Jack Warner promised twelve Vitaphone "speaking pictures" for 1928—and then, for many weeks, there was silence. Without Sam Warner as a guiding force, Vitaphone seemed to lose the finer part of its bearings. He had been responsible for nearly everything that remotely suggested planning or vision for Vitaphone, up to and including "Warner Bros.' Supreme Triumph, Al Jolson in *The Jazz Singer*."[23] More than anyone, Warner would have understood the implications of *The Jazz Singer* and the reasons for its success. While the Vitaphone show would continue without him, it would lack his imprint, his taste, and his savvy.

There's no question that *The Jazz Singer* was essential to the development of sound film—but this was due to star power, not the film itself. Inserting Vitaphone songs into a feature probably should not have caused all that much fuss, and with George Jessel's whiny voice and mousy demeanor it wouldn't have. But Jolson blew through that film like a hurricane, and after a few months of down-time nothing would be the same. Audiences lining up to see *The Jazz Singer* in the early months of 1928 could not realize the immense changes they would soon experience.

23. In that slogan, as in much of the advertising apart from print ads, there was no mention of Jolson's singing or of Vitaphone, because like many early talkies to follow, *The Jazz Singer* was also available as a silent film for the many theaters not yet wired for sound. It was cheaper to use only one style of posters, lobby cards, etc., for both silent and sound versions, and for the most part sound was mentioned only in newspapers and periodical ad sheets. That *The Jazz Singer* had little allure as a silent film did not stop Warners, or anyone else, either: silent versions of sound films, produced by all the major studios, were notoriously deadly. The situation had its absurd aspects. In 1928, when Warners' publicists were rooting around for something wonderful to say about the silent version of Jolson's *The Singing Fool*, the best they could do was a timid paraphrase of a Jolson catchphrase: "You ain't seen nothin' yet!"

CHAPTER 2

1928: Breaking the Sound Barrier

1928 is the great lost year. Its events have been forgotten, its films consigned to oblivion. But make no mistake—it was the year of revolution, of change, of opportunism and jumping on the bandwagon regardless of the consequences. It was the year in which a number of outstanding silent films were produced and suddenly were held to be wholly irrelevant. It was the year of the big gamble, a time when careers started and careers died. 1928 was when sound came to stay.

If it seems a paradox that most of the important and influential films of this momentous and terrible year are unknown, it is because the technology of sound film preceded the art by a good distance. The studios came to grips with sound and made the musical film possible, in a mechanics-mastering baptism by fire. These first talking features, often using music and songs, were not musicals, not just yet. Nor did they possess any genuine quality, such aesthetic merit as occurred being almost always inadvertent. Unintended monuments to the crassness of the American film industry, they were made quickly and poorly and rushed out to beat rivals to the punch. So curious were audiences that initially even the worst of them—and their worst was considerable—earned big profits. Novelty was the drawing card; creativity took a vacation.[1]

So the first year of sound film was not the time to reflect on artistry.

---

1. It's an axiom of film history that novelty spells success for any technical breakthrough, regardless of deficiencies. Sound films are the supreme example, and it would be equally true with wide-screen and 3-D in the 1950s. But it isn't always true. The early features in "perfected" three–strip Technicolor drew an extremely uneven response, despite the publicity, and some were out-and-out flops. So was *Scent of Mystery*, in 1960; what ever happened to Smell-o-Vision?

The world could see Hollywood at its most vulnerable and sometimes most ludicrous, groping to produce offspring that were, often as not, both trials and errors. Painfully adjusting their viewing habits, audiences often felt assaulted, yet came in huge numbers, fascinated witnesses to the newest wrinkle in American ingenuity. Today even the most disagreeable aspects of the 1928 sound films retain peculiar appeal. The sheer desperation of these pioneers, flying blind in a struggle to harness the intransigent new process, is quite palpable. Many decades after the fact, we are amused by the participants' ineptitude, admiring of their dauntlessness, and frequently dumbfounded that anything this miserable could ever be merchandised as a piece of entertainment. Given their transitional and artistically negligible nature, it's easy to see why history has given short shrift to the earliest talkies and why the events surrounding the changeover to sound have been forgotten or ferociously oversimplified. This, alas, is coupled with the studios' indefensible (if understandable) negligence in preserving these museum pieces, which played a far greater role than has generally been credited in bringing forth the new medium of sound and the first musical features. They were made for the moment, and they stayed that way; call them the iceberg under that tip known as *The Jazz Singer*.

It was in the spring of 1928 that the film industry initiated its main drive toward sound. On May 15, the biggest single deal to clinch the changeover came when MGM, Paramount, and United Artists signed contracts with Electrical Research Products, Inc. ERPI was Western Electric's marketing subsidiary, and the deal called for the purchase and installation of sound equipment in both the studios and their chains of theaters. This unequivocal move was in direct response to *The Jazz Singer* and to its two follow-ups, the second and third features with dialogue. Al Jolson was in neither of them, so their huge success was attributable to sound, not star power. Both were produced by Warner Bros., and they're as little known today as *The Jazz Singer* is famous. Neither *Tenderloin* nor *Glorious Betsy* had started out to be a talkie, for despite announcements to the contrary, Warners had been caught unaware. Forced to improvise, it hastily decided to tack on some dialogue scenes to *Tenderloin*. More than *The Jazz Singer*, this marked the beginning of one of film's stranger eras: the age of the part-talkie, when films intended to be silent had scenes or bits of dialogue added as an afterthought. These synchronized moments came and went, tenuously interspersed among traditional silent scenes with musical accompaniment without regard to logical pattern. If a seven-reel feature had only one minute of dialogue added to it—and some did have that little—it could be advertised as a talking picture and consequently would make money. "Goat-glands," they were nicknamed, after the strange and spurious attempts at medical rejuvenation. Again and again they proved that sound and silent film were different media that wouldn't mix well, especially with dialogue as unsatisfactory as it was superfluous.

Given a hoopla opening at Warner's Theatre in New York on March 14, *Tenderloin* starred Warners' leading lady of the moment, Dolores Costello, a lustrous Botticelli beauty and an indifferent actress. Her presence in *Tenderloin* was marketed as a dividend to sound's inherent curiosity value, giving audiences their first chance to hear the voices of established, hitherto silent, players. Tearing down this wall of mystery was in some ways an astute way to proceed with talking film, adding both name recognition and the element of surprise. To Warners' dismay, the ploy was very much a double-edged sword, for not all the surprises turned out to be pleasant. *Tenderloin* proved that right off the bat. "You will see and you WILL hear Dolores Costello in *Tenderloin*!" ads chimed, and audiences did so in numbers undreamed-of by critics forecasting a modest response for an ordinary underworld melodrama that happened to have less than fifteen minutes of bad dialogue tacked on. Marketed as the first talking drama, it did astounding business through the spring and summer of 1928.

While *Tenderloin*'s trump card, talk, was embraced by audiences, its other purported asset, its star, was a bust. At that time and for long after, Warner Bros. was unwilling or unable to recognize what soon became a byword: Vitaphone was a sexist technology, recording and reproducing men's voices more accurately than women's from Marion Talley on. Conrad Nagel and Georgie (later George E.) Stone were the vocal winners in the *Tenderloin* cast, Nagel's phonogenic voice in such demand over the next two years that his career was nearly killed by the overexposure. Dolores Costello's voice, in life relatively warm and attractive, did not come through adequately on the Vitaphone discs. Exacerbated by intense self-consciousness and poorly written dialogue, her feeble delivery was up there on the screen for everyone to hear and see. She was not helped by Michael Curtiz's inadequate direction, horrendous tension on the set, and by another mechanical failing, a tendency toward sibilance. The lisp, though Costello got the rap for it, was Vitaphone's, usually caused by a deadly combination of primitive amplifiers and worn discs. In this case it rendered one of her lines as "Merthy, merthy, have you no thithter of your own?" To make matters worse, she was completely stymied by the notion that visual and vocal acting could be correllated into a seamless whole.

Therein lies one of the major lessons of early talkies: while Dolores Costello's lack of a good voice and dramatic training would be cited as her downfall, the truth was, as so often, far more complicated. The greater difficulty lay in her inability to properly combine speech with gesture for the camera. As it was with her so would it be repeated with a number of silent stars, most legendarily John Gilbert, due not so much to bad voices as inadequately coordinated performances of poorly written dialogue, aggravated by changing audience tastes.

Costello's audible failure, Vitaphone's defects, and *Tenderloin*'s rotten dialogue made for a lethal mix, and when the opening night audience of hardened Broadwayites fell over itself laughing at the "thithter" line and the tinny sound, Warners deleted two of the four talking sequences. Had the studio approached the enterprise with a bit more care and—too-rare commodity—time, it might have fared better. In many ways, Warners did not yet know what it took to make talkies and would not for a long time. One critic's comment on *Tenderloin* applied to most immediate successors: "The players sound more like children speaking pieces than persons carrying on a conversation."

Glorious Betsy opened in New York and Hollywood a month later—the first talkie to premiere in the film capital. All the Vitaphone openings had been in New York, and *The Jazz Singer* had run in downtown Los Angeles, away from the more rarefied precincts of Tinseltown. Curiosity atop hype draws crowds, and as Conrad Nagel remembered many years later, "My God, all of Hollywood was there to see it." No—to hear it. *Betsy* intimated the possibility of a new resonant future as never before, and the impact of its premiere was such that the studios made the final decision to push toward sound. It boasted the same stars as *Tenderloin*—Costello again trying hard—and was otherwise classier than its lurid predecessor, somewhat better recorded and with more palatable subject matter (Jerome Bonaparte's romance with Maryland belle Betsy Patterson) and effective musical sequences. *Tenderloin* had used song as well, a comic rendition of "Sweet Adeline" in the last scene that was likely its best-received moment. In *Betsy* Warners went this two better with a choral rendition of "Nellie Gray" and a rousing "La Marseillaise" by Metropolitan Opera baritone Andre de Segurola.[2] Certainly song fared better than dialogue which, as in most early talkies, never failed to draw scornful critical comment. Low-grade dialogue badly recited was as much a part of the era as stiff photography and jangly sound reproduction. The problems stemmed from Hollywood scenarists' lack of experience, the completely gratuitous nature of most talking scenes, and the ponderous monotone delivery insisted upon by the sound technicians. These petty eminences, implacable in their belief that the sonic preceded all else, revelled in their newfound leverage, demanding and receiving an anesthetized drawn-out speech that gave e-ve-ry syl-la-ble maximum impact without resorting to emphases that might blow out tubes and ruin equipment. Adding insult to injury, the immobile microphone forced the mountain to go to Mahomet: actors were compelled to position themselves

---

2. A better known opera star in *Glorious Betsy* was veteran baritone Pasquale Amato, seen but not heard as Napoleon.

within pickup range before each line. Mikes were concealed in vases, telephones, any object an actor could address without looking completely balmy. And always those same monotones! Just the same, in the boom town of mid-1928, most audiences were entranced.

Early June saw the release of Vitaphone's next part-talkie, the first not to use singing. Lloyd Bacon's *The Lion and the Mouse*, adapted from a 1905 Broadway hit that hadn't aged well, was a further primer course in sound dos and don'ts, with a whopping twenty-nine minutes of talk. Despite massive audience turnout, critics again rejected the dialogue and the silent-film actors who tried to speak it. Dolores Costello being busy elsewhere, the chief female offender this time was May McAvoy, a talented silent actress who'd earlier escaped the talkie bug in *The Jazz Singer*. Here, in unfortunate juxtaposition with the vocal skill of Lionel Barrymore, she was clearly and audibly in trouble. Once again name-recognition had substituted for quality. In marketing terms it succeeded for a while, but this type of short-sightedness and miscalculation would be evident again and again over the next few years and would help to kill Warners' preeminence in talkies. The object was to extend a minimum of effort to make the greatest possible splash, with little in the way of test-market previews to make sure that it would work with an audience. This type of thinking did not show the care and showmanship that had characterized the studio's plunge into sound; instead, it recalled the company's poverty-stricken origins. Had Sam Warner lived to oversee the transition, things might have proceeded more intelligently. No such luck—the studio, anxious to keep raking in those huge grosses, would continue to misjudge the tastes of its audiences and misinterpret the demands of the new medium.

By the time of *The Lion and the Mouse*, the major film companies had begun to buy and install sound equipment in their studios and in their theaters. It seems preposterous that such a major decision and investment were made on the basis of three features and some short subjects. The speed with which silent films were replaced and overthrown by sound films, while not quite as great as legend recalls, was plenty rapid enough; what strains credulity is the *vehemence* propelling it. The industry had not deigned to consider sound for years—and here it was, going overboard in the opposite direction. Never before or since in the history of popular culture has so much changed so fast. Even the rise of television in the late 1940s was a more gradual process. By mid-1928 hysteria was definitely in the air, though the panic was tempered by braggadocio and even nonchalance, plus the drive to compete with the audible entertainment available at home. The telephone had introduced people to the sound of the mechanically reproduced voice, after which the phonograph and the radio channeled the process into professional entertainment. For film, operating in the realm of the visible, it was deemed necessary to add the vocal just to keep up.[3] The chief mystery, at least in hindsight, is how so much could be gambled with such scant evidence. However inevitable it seems in retrospect, there was ample room for doubt at the time. Yes, the four part-talking features released by June 1928 had been huge moneymakers—*The Jazz Singer* over $2 million, the others about a million each—and more theaters were wiring for sound every week. The studios, confident they could overcome the problems over the long haul, overlooked damning evidence: the utter inadequacy of the films made so far. Regardless of novelty, initial enthusiasm, Jolson, or "La Marseillaise," they just weren't good.

But money talked. It talked more than these films and even louder than Jolson sang, and at a time when producers were becoming aware that silent films were sources of art as well as commerce. *The Crowd, Docks of New York, Sunrise,* and *The Wedding March* were among the concurrent silent films being produced, pictorially sumptuous and with a new maturity in technique, acting, subject matter, presentation. If the artistry was often self-conscious, it was nevertheless an enormous achievement for an industry that had risen from paltry beginnings less than thirty years before. In 1928 these films seemed almost elegiac, for it seemed that art would die with the birth of sound film. The contrast between *Sunrise* and the earliest talkies is daunting on every conceivable level, and looking at the sound revolution many decades later, we have the right to doubt that those responsible for its rapidity realized the full ramifications of their actions. That silents were thrown over so quickly and not allowed to coexist with talkies for more than a brief time is a graphic demonstration of one of the truisms in the American business ethic: the conflict between artistry and commerce has only one possible victor.

Still, there was a joker in the deck. Proof would be forthcoming, later in 1928 and into 1929, that audiences did want silent films as well as talkies. Polls taken in such cities as Los Angeles and Syracuse showed that while the public did like talkies, almost no one wished silents to go away entirely. Part-talkies fared the worst; few were at all partial to them. Hollywood's all-or-nothing rush to talkies may have been hastier than most audiences were willing to absorb. And even the viewers craving them had an ambiguous relationship with the first talkies. (That word, incidentally, only came into common use a bit later; in 1928 the preferred term was "talkers.") There was bad recording and inadequate amplification to contend with, and not even one's eyesight was immune to the upheaval. No camera lens, however fine, could give sharpness and detail to images photographed through the window of a soundproof booth, and the problem was compounded by harsh incandescent lighting that made surfaces flat and drab,

3. As clear as the links seem today between the popularity of radio and the advent of talkies, the connection was little remarked-upon by observers at the time, even with such performers as Al Jolson achieving success in both media.

complexions sallow, textures indistinguishable. The editing, mostly a matter of cutting between three cameras setups, seemed rudimentary at best. Arid long takes were the rule, camera movement was almost completely eliminated. A lot of these films looked as bad as they sounded.

And few films could have looked or sounded worse than the next major event in sound films: that most egregious of cinematic milestones, the first 100 percent All-Talkie. Mathematical improbability is the least of the problems with *Lights of New York*, which premiered in New York on July 8, 1928, and today inspires marvel that talking films could overcome such a horrendous sendoff. Small-town barbers victimized by gangsters in a wicked big city . . . who was responsible for this? Warners, naturally, who may have intended this film only as an experiment, expending a Poverty Row budget (studio records give it as a chintzy $23,000) and using a novice director, Bryan Foy, with no feature experience. Whatever the circumstances, it's a graphic demonstration of the money-grubbing mind-set of the period that Warners would deem this sorry thing worthy of release as the first all-talking feature. Tellingly, it wasn't launched with one of the $2 reserved-seat engagements given the previous sound features in their first runs. Instead, it opened at the lesser Mark Strand Theatre on a lower-price—and appropriately named—"grind" run.

Lights of New York's gross of well over a million dollars is devastating proof of the public's voracious appetite for sound in mid-1928. Interest was so great that some audiences burst into applause at the conclusion, although perhaps they were just grateful that the ordeal was over. Some critics also tried to be charitable, although *Variety* was frank in discussing the film's inadequacy as well as its implications and, grudgingly, the Warners' guts.

> Hokumed junk. . . . As a picture this is an open-face story with roll-your-own dialogue. . . . In a year from now everyone concerned . . . will run for the river before looking at it again.
>
> This 100 per cent talkie is 100 per cent crude . . . but still this talker will have pulling power, and the Warners should get credit for nerve even if they didn't do it with a polish.

Lights of New York is cheap in every sense of the word, and most likely no other major studio would have allowed such a bad piece of work to carry the prestigious burden of being the first all-talking feature. It's less *actively* bad than it is a catalogue of missed opportunities, and whatever else his many directorial failings Foy could see that Vitaphone worked best when music and song were involved.[4] What little merit *Lights* contains comes from its musical elements, including a score that provides some relief from

---

4. As one of Eddie Foy's seven vaudeville-trained children, he certainly had the proper musical background.

the vocal monotony and clearly points the way for film scoring, and night-club sequences given vitality by their use of song and dance. The Pirate Girls' routine to "National Emblem" is neither graceful nor adept, as choreographed by Larry Ceballos, but at least it's there, with their taps relatively well recorded. So is the Jolsonesque rendition of "Dawning" by Harry Downing. But all of this must yield to the script's monumental inadequacy; several of the inept and inane turns of phrase contained therein have reached mythic status. "Take . . . him . . . for . . . a . . . ride" is the classic, as funny for Wheeler Oakman's lumbering delivery as for the cliché it became. The broken mistress (Gladys Brockwell) also speaks memorably, in an angrily off-center riposte to her former protector: "You think you can take any chicken you want and throw *me* back in the deck!"[5]

At the same time that *Lights of New York* was making its timid plunge into the realm of all-talking features, the sound shorts continued apace, nearly always better than the full-length efforts. Fox's Movietone, with its ability to shoot live sound out of doors, was far more flexible than Vitaphone, and its newsreels offered a welcome respite from Warner-induced claustrophobia. Unexpectedly, Fox trumped Warners by producing a one-reel visit with George Bernard Shaw that was, except for Jolson and Martinelli, the most rapturously received sound film thus far. "That white whiskered lad is some bimbo," *Variety* complimented, and audiences agreed. Quite a contrast to Warners' concurrent offerings—poor May McAvoy fighting a losing battle against *The Lion and the Mouse*, and the terminally dim *Lights of New York*.

Nine months after the premiere of *The Jazz Singer*, Hollywood's initial wait-and-see attitude was giving way to a mad scramble. Four major studios released synchronized films immediately after *Lights*, including MGM's lushly photographed *White Shadows in the South Seas*. The only one of the quartet to contain dialogue was *The Perfect Crime*, an odd shambles produced by Joseph Kennedy's Film Booking Office. FBO was on the verge of being acquired by RCA, who intended to buy into the talkie market with its sound-on-film Photophone system.[6] One week later came *The Terror*, Warners' second try at an all-talkie and a marked improvement on its tacky predecessor, even if May McAvoy did have trouble making herself heard above Louis Silvers's elaborate wraparound musical score. At least, most

5. Brockwell's aptitude for sound film, revealed in this and other early talkies, was cut short with her death in an auto accident in 1929. Fan magazines offered a sweetly macabre sidelight to the dawn of sound by reporting that her mother was sighted at every Los Angeles showing of her last, posthumously released film, *The Drake Case*. Talkies had permitted her to grasp the memories a bit longer.

6. More technically refined than either Vitaphone or Movietone, Photophone employed a variable area soundtrack (as opposed to Movietone's variable density track), which offered a wider range and greater clarity. It's still in use today.

reviewers felt, it gave audiences more than merely talk for its own sake.[7]
The Terror was the second dialogue film to play London, several weeks after
The Jazz Singer opened to a smashing response. A Hollywood thriller that
faked a London setting and characters was a sitting duck for British critics,
who reacted to the whole affair less with terror than with horror, although
the English public remained abundantly interested.

Other studios now started their dialogue films—Fox's *The Air Circus*, William Wellman's *Beggars of Life* (Paramount), and Paul Fejos's *Lonesome* (Universal). The latter pair, probably the finest talking pictures of the year,
were artistic successes despite their dialogue, and, like Warners' next two
part-talkies (*State Street Sadie* and *Women They Talk About*), did less business
than their predecessors. The public was sending the message that it would
not be pleased indefinitely with this type of work. A shot in the arm was
needed—and Al Jolson gave it.

It's not likely that many people attending the Winter Garden in New
York on September 19, 1928, soon forgot the experience. The theater, Al
Jolson's home base for his Broadway shows, had recently been converted
into a Vitaphone house. Jolson was in the audience and on the screen, and
afterward he was onstage to take bow after bow. Most spectators could not
stop crying, Jolson included. *The Singing Fool* made him the biggest star in
the world.

Since it's rarely seen today, *The Singing Fool* is frequently confused with
The Jazz Singer, although besides Jolson and a pervasively maudlin air the
two have little in common. In the earlier film Jolson was inordinately
attached to his mother and sang "Mammy"; here the fixation was on his
young son, and "Sonny Boy" became an enormous hit. So did the film,
which amassed a stunning world-wide gross of $5.9 million.[8] The timing
was perfect. A number of theaters in medium-sized American towns had
just been wired for sound, and for many of them *The Singing Fool* was the
premiere sound attraction, most likely the first talkie that many people
saw. Its Winter Garden run continued well into 1929, by which time its
technical aspects were pitifully outdated by those of other talkies. It even
went over in towns without wired theaters, where some exhibitors simply
played Jolson's commercial recordings at the appropriate moment on jerry-
rigged phonograph hookups. No question about it, Mr. Show Biz had
done it again, with an aura of excitement largely absent from recent sound
films.

---

7. How much more we don't exactly know, since it has long been considered a lost film.
The soundtrack discs, at least, were recently rediscovered . . . and no, McAvoy doesn't lisp.

8. Some sources give it as the highest gross of *any* film in its initial release prior to *Gone
With the Wind*. This is probably overstating it—MGM's records show that *Ben-Hur* and *The Big
Parade* grossed more, and no one knows just how much *The Birth of a Nation* brought in. Still,
by the standards of the time it's an amazing amount.

As a vehicle, *The Singing Fool* left *The Jazz Singer* far behind. By the time he made this film in summer 1928 Jolson was a major, upper-echelon movie star. He and Warners and the public all knew it, and except for a few minutes of unaffected charm by little Davey Lee, Jolson took over the whole show. That was quite enough for audiences in 1928 and for many critics, who showed a startling willingness to overlook the film's many faults in the face of Jolson's dynamism and his rendition of seven songs. Even the ordinarily skeptical trade press was sold on it, or at least on its star. *Billboard* gushed:

> Great entertainment and the strongest argument in the world that talking pictures are the real thing. . . . Jolson wasn't much of an actor in *The Jazz Singer*, but in *The Singing Fool* he does highly impressive work. He looks better in celluloid now than before, sings his songs better, has lost his consciousness of the camera . . . and actually stamps himself as a great actor.

Is this the same *Singing Fool* we see today, this banal, awkwardly part-talking sob story alongside which *The Jazz Singer* looks like Ibsen? Constant reminders of its historical importance and phenomenal success are necessary just to sit through it. (For those who dislike Jolson, forget it.) The disparity between this perception and what its initial audiences saw is nearly unbridgeable—proof that even the most potent star power can go flat.

It's illuminating to see just why and how *The Singing Fool* doesn't hold up as well as its predecessor. No matter how inaccurate those "First Talking Picture" claims, *The Jazz Singer* has retained its historical resonance—along with that iconic image of Jolson on one knee singing "Mammy." It also made some attempt to deal with the subjects of cultural assimilation and parental responsibility, plus there was Alan Crosland's visual skill. *The Singing Fool* lacks such niceties to deflect from its camera-hogging star, who is kept center screen for a prolonged 105 minutes. Lloyd Bacon's direction has no breadth, and his original story is even more rudimentary than *The Jazz Singer's*.[9] Songwriter *cum* nightclub waiter Al Stone becomes a singing star overnight and marries a gold digger; his career goes down the tubes after she ditches him, and just as he's making a swell comeback his beloved "Sonny Boy" dies, after which he goes out and sings his heart out while the faithful cigarette girl who has always loved him watches tearfully.

The millions of spectators who went to see *The Singing Fool* in the fall and winter of 1928–29 made little note of its trite dialogue and manipula-

---

9. The original story is credited onscreen to the pseudonymous Leslie Burrows, listed in press materials as Barrows. The initials gave it away, as they did the next year with another soggy Burrows/Barrows/Bacon musical, *Honky Tonk*.

Shooting early sound: Al Jolson, Davy Lee, and Vitaphone equipment in the bedtime story scene from *The Singing Fool*. *Photofest*.

tive storyline. They didn't care that much of the film centered on a custody battle between Al and the two-timing Molly that was both soggy and distasteful. What mattered was Jolson, and surely his manic rendition of "I'm Sitting on Top of the World" carries as much presence and conviction as any musical number in film history. Unfortunately, his high-pressure cockiness, an essential ingredient of his star image, makes a mockery of the fact that he's attempting to play a character. Al Stone's struggle for happiness is grotesquely transformed into Al Jolson's interminable grabbing of the spotlight. Charismatic as he is, his presence becomes oppressive fairly early on, and his promise to sing a thousand songs feels like a threat. This movie's sole justification, as a showcase for Jolson's performing ability, becomes its own downfall. And his drawn-out "dramatic" scenes point out the vast gulf separating Jolson's conception of his acting ability from its actual paltry nature. The "Sonny Boy" song was what most people remembered, and it is indeed a significant moment in the history of the film musical. But it does not wear at all well, with its drippy sentimentality and droopy melodic line. Matters are not helped by the tearful reprises we get during and after Sonny Boy's death; the final one, in blackface, attains a level of bathos that defies rational description.[10] Jolson is in optimum voice, but the self-confidence that had inflated since *The Jazz Singer* makes his performance desperately overbearing. Magnetic as he is, he's done a great disservice by the film's utter lack of proportion. As Sonny Boy, three-year-old Davey Lee (billed as David) demonstrates more affinity for sound-film acting, especially in one lengthy bedtime story scene that even the more exacting critics praised. The ever-unhelpful Vitaphone mitigates notably against both Josephine Dunn and Betty Bronson; the former (as the wife) speaks in nasal singsong, and Bronson, a charmer in silents, is practically inaudible.

The Singing Fool is a true hybrid, a curious mix of the assurances and doubts of an era when sound (and later, color) came and went with extreme unpredictability. It's a source of wonder that Warner Bros., with two all-talkies already completed, didn't extend itself to make this a third, truly special, effort. The value in publicity and prestige for the new medium would have been immense. Unable to give Jolson a sturdier vehicle for his talents—and perhaps he didn't want that—the studio could have at least gone all the way on the technical end. Then again, Warners' cheapskate showmanship didn't *need* to go any further for *The Singing Fool* to pull in the maximum number of bucks. So its now-silent/now-talking format lurches all the way through without discernible logic:

13½ minutes silent
  (musical score)

         45 minutes sound
          (with many silent transitional passages and some intertitles)

3 minutes silent

         5½ minutes sound

9 minutes silent

         4 minutes sound

1½ minutes silent

         9 minutes sound

3 minutes silent

         12 minutes sound[11]

10. Allegedly, tunesmiths DeSylva, Brown and Henderson originally intended the song as a joke, but Jolson took it seriously and, as was his custom, demanded and received co-credit. They shared in extremely gratifying royalties—record sales topping a million and sheet music sales far higher. Then, in 1941, the Andrews Sisters made it a hit all over again.

11. Existing prints contain less sound than this chart indicates. Jolson's rendition of "The Spaniard Who Blighted My Life" (in Reel 3, just before "There's A Rainbow 'Round My Shoulder") has been deleted. In March of 1929 Billy Merson, who wrote the song, sued to have it removed from all prints except those exhibited in the U.S. and Canada. In 1929 he was still making a healthy living performing the number in British music halls and didn't need the competition, though Jolson had sung it for years. The only prints of the film to survive are of the overseas version, with the song omitted; the soundtrack disc for the song also survives. Ironically, the stills most often used to depict *The Singing Fool* are of this number, with a wild-eyed Jolson wrapped in a Spanish shawl, castanets a-clatter.

In addition to the many silent shots and unnecessary titles, the sound sequences are riddled with a curious barrage of incidental noises that never seem to register. Doors slam in silence, footsteps and tap dancing make no impression, and, most distractingly, Jolson's nightclub performances are sometimes greeted by huge mute ovations. If they did exist, these noises might not be heard over Louis Silvers's nearly constant background music, wildly far from what is now understood as sound-film underscoring. Its pervasiveness was presumably intended to ease 1928 spectators from silent to talking sequences, and relief comes only in the New Year's Eve scene when party noises are able to drown it out. Silvers's worst inspiration comes near the end, when the heartbroken Al dons blackface to the strains of "Vesti la giubba," which worked far better when Martinelli sang it. The sound throughout the film has a dead, detached quality that's most disconcerting. Critics in 1928, quick to comment upon such technical drawbacks in other films, became rather lenient about their presence here—a tribute solely to Jolson's energy, personality, and star power. While there is no gainsaying the success and influence of *The Singing Fool*, it's a milestone of the most disposable sort, seldom revived and never revered.

September 1928 was a good month for overbearing parents. An archetypal stage mother formed the basis for Edna Ferber's novel *Mother Knows Best*, adapted by Fox for its second part-talkie. Ferber's characters had real-life counterparts in musical showperson Elsie Janis and her omnipresent mama, and as filmed her story played as *The Jazz Singer* turned inside-out, with good backstage vignettes and dialogue that clearly improved on previous movie talk. Though no Elsie Janis, Madge Bellamy was sufficiently game to offer impressions of Harry Lauder, Anna Held, and . . . Al Jolson. In blackface. Audiences really perked up when they heard Louise Dresser (as Ma) give Bellamy a dressing-room pep talk: "Dear, don't forget to get down on your knees for 'Mammy.' " No one was about to forget *The Jazz Singer*, not at this point.

By the mid-fall, as the initial fascination dimmed, spectators were increasingly less inclined to forgive the technical inadequacies in the ways sound films were made and exhibited. This last aspect was memorably recalled in *Singin' in the Rain* when disc and film lose their synch and the heroine and villain begin to speak with each other's voices; and something similar did occur during a Chicago screening of Warners' *Noah's Ark* in 1929, naturally involving the hapless Dolores Costello. The breakdowns were usually less funny, and first-hand reports testify to the grisliness of the experience, even during opening engagements. Case in point: Paramount's third all-talkie, *The Wolf of Wall Street*, in January 1929, as reported by *New York Times* critic Mordaunt Hall:

> On Saturday, when this film was screened for its second running [at the Rialto Theatre], the characters lost their voices, or, at least, the audible

device refused to function. It was rather nice to hear their muffled tone, but quite a number of spectators decided that they wanted to have their money's worth of sound. So they clapped their hands impatiently. Still there was a hush about the proceeding. Then there was further clapping, which must not be construed as applause. . . . [12]

This same mediocre film was used in a public relations attempt to promote talkies to audiences heretofore unable to experience film. In Des Moines, a special screening of *The Wolf of Wall Street* was given for an entirely sightless audience, which was able to follow the plot entirely through the dialogue and apparently enjoyed the experience. This was well and good—but many talkies were far less assiduous in generating such good will.

The third all-talking film arrived early in October, not from Warners or Fox. The enterprising underdog Universal got the jump with a shoddy opus titled *The Melody of Love*, a flimsy mélange of Tin Pan Alley and Great War motifs, complete with a great deal of stock combat footage and several songs. Directed by A. B. Heath, who normally worked only in short subjects, it starred Mildred Harris (an ex-Mrs. Charlie Chaplin) and Walter Pidgeon, who sang nearly as well as he talked. Far more interesting than the film was how it was made. In the late summer of 1928, before Universal bought its own sound equipment, studio head Carl Laemmle borrowed one of Fox's Movietone sound trucks, ostensibly to make sound tests for its production of *Show Boat*. Fox executives, apparently distracted by the hysteria of the era, seem to have made no contractual stipulation for the use of their machines. So Universal went to town. In a ploy that makes Warners' rush to sound seem demure, talking sequences were turned out speedily for several films, and then in about nine days, for an insignificant $30,000, Heath shot *The Melody of Love*. Fox finally reclaimed its equipment, after which "Carl Laemmle's 100% Talking Sensation" was given a gala premiere in, truthfully, Kenosha, Wisconsin. Though *The Melody of Love* no longer seems to exist, its quality can perhaps be gauged from a comment in the *New York Daily Mirror*—"It is [as if] a gang of children [had] gone out in the backyard and said 'Let's make a talker.' " Even Universal, no stranger to mediocre filmmaking, had trouble finding first-run engagements for it, as when a Philadelphia screening for prospective exhib-

12. This type of hazard extended quite democratically to the industry's most powerful presences. *Coquette* was Mary Pickford's talking debut, and the New York premiere on April 5, 1929, was a major event, for Pickford's embrace of the new medium gave it added credence. Trouble started almost immediately: the blaring rendition of "Old Folks at Home" under the credits proved too much for the Rivoli Theatre's amplifiers, the system blew its fuses, and the mortified V.I.P. audience sat for several minutes watching a mute talkie. Finally the projectionists brought up the lights, fiddled with the equipment, and rewound the film. Though this time it ran in its entirety, the damage had been extensive and the volume severely reduced. The dialogue was nearly inaudible, and nobody had a good time.

itors was greeted with outright hostility. Only the *third* all-talkie, in the midst of total industry upheaval, and with a minor claim as the first musical, and all it could rate from *Variety* was "Most of the talking sequences are brutal. . . . It's nothing to get unduly excited over." Today, we can only wonder just how bad.

The regressive nature of this kind of claptrap was underscored by several late major silent films, such as Ernst Lubitsch's *The Patriot* (Paramount) and Harry Beaumont's *Our Dancing Daughters* (MGM). The latter was less an artistic achievement than a sensation, and in addition to encapsulating an era it made stars of its heroine, Joan Crawford, and its villain, Anita Page. Both of these silent films were sold as "Sound," with synchronized score and effects, but nobody was fooled. In any case, even lesser silents looked superb alongside the next two Warner all-talkies, *The Home-Towners* and *On Trial*, claustrophobically filmed plays that caused a critic to gripe, "Sooner or later, Warners must go outside." Talk *qua* talk would not do the job any longer, and even veteran actors suffered defeat under Vitaphone's caprices. Pauline Frederick, whose prestige and experience spanned stage and film, was top-billed in *On Trial* and received terrible reviews; Vitaphone had rendered her throaty tones totally unintelligible.

Short subjects returned to the fore in November with John Ford's three-reel *Napoleon's Barber* (Fox) and particularly Walt Disney's *Steamboat Willie*, which legend avers is the first sound cartoon. Wrong; it was the first *successful* sound cartoon. Lee De Forest had been there first, and there had also been the synchronized *Dinner Time*, released in August 1928 by the Van Beuren cartoon studio as part of its "Aesop's Fables" series. But *Steamboat Willie* made the impact. Disney and company had used a metronome while recording Mickey Mouse's rendition of "Turkey in the Straw," helping the rhythm and music to flow with the visuals instead of against them. For the first time, a sound film was an integrated work, and both cartoon features and musical films have their roots here.

The last two months of 1928 and January 1929 were about the worst of the era. With studios busily hiring new personnel, installing equipment, and testing voices, they temporarily forgot their audiences. Grosses dropped detectably at year's end, and some heavily publicized efforts did disappointing business as people started to wonder why talkies didn't look and sound and move better. Even Warners announced that it would make no more all-talking films, stating that a ratio of 75 percent talk to 25 percent silence, as in *Singing Fool*, was preferable. If Jack Warner genuinely believed that *Singing Fool* succeeded because it was one-fourth silent, instead of because Al Jolson was the world's most popular entertainer, the pressure (Warners was in the process of acquiring First National Pictures, which eventually led to a move to new quarters in Burbank) was obviously affecting his thinking. The release of several major Warner all-talkies, including a full-blown operetta, was held back for many weeks, well into 1929. This moratorium gave other studios a clearer track, and Paramount opened its first all-talking picture, *Interference*, in November, then reshot a few scenes prior to general release. *Interference* attempted to outdo the Vitaphone films with its name cast—Clive Brook, Evelyn Brent, William Powell, Doris Kenyon—and general air of class, though many found it less elevated than stilted.[13] Concurrently, MGM made a reticent and belated talkie debut with a few shorts and a feature, *Alias Jimmy Valentine*. That *Jimmy* talked only in its last two reels did not prevent the studio's crack publicity corps from promoting the dickens out of it and reaping big grosses.[14] The one indisputably good talkie at the time was *In Old Arizona*, Fox's first all-talkie, which survives as the most fluent of very early sound films. They gave this Cisco Kid yarn the works: an effective theme song ("My Tonia" by DeSylva, Brown, and Henderson), spectacular locations with live sound, an intriguing O. Henry trick ending, and an eloquent performance by Warner Baxter. Here again sound was used to point the way for musicals, and audiences were as delighted as Fox's accountants.

Amid further Vitaphoned trivia, Warners premiered two important films, one of them musical. Its biggest film to date, Michael Curtiz's *Noah's Ark* opened in November and represented an enormous outlay for the studio—over $1 million as well as at least one drowning. As a talkie, it was something of a flub. Even more than in other hybrids, the talkie portion of *Noah's Ark* (directed by Curtiz and Roy Del Ruth) was stilted and poorly photographed, weakly spoken by Dolores Costello, and unable to compete with the scenes of spectacle cramming its silent portions. Not even Warners could let this mess stay as it was, and so the New York opening was held up for four months while the studio hacked out about thirty minutes, including all of Noah's dialogue. By the time it went into general release in mid-1929, *Noah's Ark* was an outmoded artifact.[15]

The studio's last talkie of 1928 was a clearcut imitation of the Jolson pictures, with an equally magnetic star.

HEAR HER RUN THE SCALE OF HUMAN EMOTION VIA VITAPHONE

Irresistible . . . FANNIE BRICE in *My Man*

13. It was marketed as the most prestigious talkie event to date, with theater producer Daniel Frohman appearing in a filmed prologue to proclaim how superior it all was. Well, sure, in comparison to *Lights of New York* or *Melody of Love*.

14. The talkie revolution occasionally made for strange bedfellows. So behind the times was MGM just then that it had not yet installed its Movietone equipment, so *Jimmy Valentine*'s talking scenes had to be shot off-hours at Paramount's new sound stage.

15. UCLA's exemplary restoration of *Noah's Ark* is of the general-release (cut) version, with about 12 percent dialogue and a phenomenon common to major early talkies, an overture and exit music. Both plug the theme song, a rather bad Billy Rose effort called "Heart O' Mine," sung in part by an excruciatingly shrill and blessedly anonymous soprano.

It sounds irresistible, Barbra Streisand notwithstanding, but Archie Mayo's film gave Brice a raw deal. Like *The Singing Fool* it alternated in a gauche fashion between sound and silence, forcing the star's songs and comedy routines to confront a trite ugly-duckling plot. Fannie Brand, who works in a costume shop, makes good in show business and gets her man (Guinn Williams) despite adversity in general and a beautiful bitchy sister in particular. The whole Brice oeuvre was on display, which makes the loss of this film all the more frustrating: "I'm an Indian" and "Second-Hand Rose" and "Mrs. Cohen at the Beach," the inevitable title song, and a new winner, "I'd Rather Be Blue"—all are quintessential Brice. Nevertheless, *My Man* was a disappointment. The reviews were mixed and the box office take, while equal to that of earlier all-talkies, was far below that of the Jolson pictures. The problem was Brice. However luminous and loved on Broadway, she lacked Jolson's national drawing power and, years away from her Baby Snooks household name phase, was unknown in many parts of the country. This became obvious when the low returns started coming in from smaller towns. Brice, with her individual look and sound and manner, was too special, too subtle an artist for this type of mass appeal. Moreover, her trademarked urban ethnicity didn't carry over as well as Jolson's, and her sublime musical performances and comedy sketches did not belong in such a story.

Over and over again in the next two years, the same thing happened: studios desperately grabbed for the résumés that listed established names with good voices and stage experience, thinking "Jolson did it, so others should too. Isn't that how talkies were born?" The hoofers and vaudevillians and Broadway and operetta stars went West to seize talkie fame—the Harry Richmans, Belle Bakers, Ted Lewises, Irene Bordonis. And then they wondered why it seldom worked out. Because it couldn't: the media and audiences were different, and idiosyncratic performing styles that played well across Manhattan footlights wouldn't necessarily go over well in Topeka in big unflattering close-ups. There were instructive lessons to be learned from *My Man*, if only the studios had been willing to pay attention. They weren't, and later on there would be the devil to pay.

In spite of the December slump, it had been, conservatively speaking, an astonishing year. For its first issue of 1929, *Variety* ran it on a front-page banner headline:

PICTURES' MOST SENSATIONAL YEAR

Sound didn't do any more to the industry than turn it upside down, shake the entire bag of tricks from its pocket and advance the Warner Brothers from last place to head of the league.

The report went on to qualify this by noting that the "anything goes" period had ended and that merit was again a leading consideration. Talk—or song—per se was no longer enough, and spectators were clearly starting to search for the rare talkies in which the aesthetic was up to the demands of the process. January of 1929 was a time of retrenchment, with little new or intriguing and nothing musical. Like the weeks prior to *The Singing Fool*, it was a slump time; another breakthrough was needed, another bench mark to indicate that sound was worth all the money and headaches.

At the beginning of February, the milestone arrived.

CHAPTER 3

The Broadway Melody

Early in 1990, *The Broadway Melody* was shown in Los Angeles as part of a "birth of the talkies" film retrospective. One major daily paper led off its notice with a slam—"The novelty of sound made it a huge hit, but this may be the worst film ever to win a best picture Oscar"—and proceeded downhill. This was by no means a conscientious statement, yet it was superficially accurate. For all its enormous success and its Academy Award as Best Production, *The Broadway Melody* appears infinitely primitive after all this time. No surprises there. Some things, however, went unmentioned, as they typically do when uncomprehending reviewers try for pre-emptive putdowns.

Most conspicuously, *The Broadway Melody* is the first true musical film. It is also: The work that established movie musicals as potent and viable entertainment. The film giving stature to sound film at a crucial time. The instigator of a host of technical advances that greatly enhanced the production of talking pictures. A phenomenal worldwide success with audiences and critics. The first all-talking film produced by the industry's biggest company. The model for a multitude of successors and imitators. A showcase for a central performance establishing a high standard for sound-film acting. And on and on. The Academy Award is beside the point, as it often is, and so is the fact that *The Broadway Melody* now seems irreparably dated. Its value resides in loftier places.

All those firsts are valid, unlike many claims made for *The Jazz Singer*. Yet the greater significance of *The Broadway Melody* is not what it did first, but what it did *right*. Musicals were, after all, predestined front-runners in the infant talkie, the one genre not possible in silent film. People were eager to see them, and the Jolson and Brice pictures and *The Melody of Love*

59

had already led the way. Getting there first was not the issue, for by the time of *Broadway Melody* Warners had already filmed a very literal transcription of the operetta *The Desert Song*, though it would hold up its release for many months. In contrast to such fumbling, *The Broadway Melody* was a product of MGM, and corporate style made all the difference. The world's largest film factory approached sound with more skill and sense than most of its rivals and was repaid for its effort, as was posterity: everything that would go into making a film musical can be found in *The Broadway Melody* in one form or another. For understanding audiences, this quaint and clanky museum piece retains just enough luster to show not only why so many went to see it but also why they *loved* it. But the history is what matters the most. The evolution and creation and reception of this one film were instrumental in establishing the talking picture as something more than a garish fad or a conduit for overblown solo acts like Al Jolson.

The standard historical account of the making of *The Broadway Melody* is not unfamiliar. Director and screenwriter Edmund Goulding wrote "Whoopee," an original story about a small-time sister act that crashes Broadway. Its unmistakable potential for both talk and musical numbers was observed by studio production head Irving Thalberg, who then engaged actor-writer James Gleason to jazz up the script with hard-edged New York argot similar to that in his play *Is Zat So?* Nacio Herb Brown and Arthur Freed were commissioned to write a score, and Thalberg liked the work-in-progress so much he decided to go from part- to all-talking. Technical innovation entered when Thalberg decided to retake the Technicolor "Wedding of the Painted Doll" sequence, and sound technician Douglas Shearer suggested that they could reuse the recording made the first time, thus giving birth to playback recording. Rushed into release before other studios' competition, *The Broadway Melody* scored a big hit and a crowd of imitators, later winning an Academy Award due to its novelty value and to heavy MGM lobbying.

There are a few errors in this recounting, and most importantly, the omission of all the factors that made *The Broadway Melody* special and made other good talking pictures a more attractive prospect. "You Were Meant for Me," one of the hits songs in the Brown/Freed score, is an appropriate motto for this film and its audience. Its creators, in remembering to keep the audience in mind, packaged it far more meticulously than earlier sound films. Every major aspect of *The Broadway Melody* reflected this extra care—part MGM professionalism, part instinct, and dashes of luck and happy accident.

One of the accidents came with its status as MGM's first all-talkie. That was originally to have been *The Trial of Mary Dugan*, a theatrical adaptation starring Thalberg's wife, Norma Shearer. *Dugan* was announced in July

1928, several weeks before Thalberg met to discuss a new part-talking musical with Edmund Goulding, director Harry Beaumont, and scenarist Sarah Y. Mason. With the title "Whoopee" already taken by Florenz Ziegfeld and Eddie Cantor, the script was called *The Sister Act* for a brief time, then *The Broadway Melody*.[1] Goulding based his characters on vaudeville's Duncan Sisters, and like them there are two Mahoney sisters, one short and feisty (Hank), the other willowy and docile (Queenie). Unlike the Duncans, who were top-rung headliners, the Mahoneys are a smalltime act who land in New York after years of touring the boondocks. Script conferences turned the story into a triangle with the addition of Hank's fiancé, songwriter-hoofer Eddie Kerns, who has landed a spot in Francis Zanfield's new revue *The Broadway Melody*. After a harrowing audition the Mahoneys also join the show, and when it opens, Queenie enters the fast lane with a stage-door playboy. As Hank grows disenchanted with the realities of big-time Broadway, Eddie starts to fall in love with Queenie; realizing this, Hank decides to quit the show. She sends Eddie off to rescue Queenie from the playboy, and when Eddie and Queenie return from their honeymoon they find Hank starting over with a new partner, a brassy chorine with whom she'd previously clashed.

There was little even remotely original about this story, which neatly dovetailed the two most frequent strands of backstage plots, putting on the show in the first half and love and anguish behind the footlights in the second. The Jolson and Brice pictures, *Melody of Love, Mother Knows Best*, and even *Lights of New York* had all hit upon some of the same motifs, yet Goulding and company buffered the clichés with a degree of care and fresh detail: Eddie Kerns on Tin Pan Alley, rubbing up affably against the competition; the Mahoneys' audition, which falls apart when Hank's adversary sabotages the piano; Queenie landing a feature showgirl spot after her predecessor collapses from exhaustion; the high-strung tenor who gripes about everything until a fed-up stagehand attempts to conk him with a spotlight; the costume designer locking horns with a wardrobe woman far larger and tougher than he. Not even Ziegfeld/Zanfield or the society swells bring in any glamour. Putting on a show is tough work, and personal feelings don't matter, as Hank learns the hard way when she's cut out of one number. As a pivot for the action, the character of Hank is far from the Jolson style of star takeover. This was a new type of heroine for the new medium, and only dialogue could give such impact to her slangy veneer and the susceptible nature it camouflages. Hank, who collides head-on with New York's

---

1. While a brash backstage story called "Whoopee" seems atypical of the polished British director of *Grand Hotel, Dark Victory*, and *The Razor's Edge*, Goulding did have previous experience in such areas with the 1925 hit *Sally, Irene, and Mary*. Inordinately interested in the emergent talkies, he wrote an in-depth article on them for *Variety* in June 1928.

showgirl-devouring maw—"Broad's Way," she calls it—and fires insults at anyone who crosses her, is blindly devoted to Eddie and maniacally protective of her sister. As the script developed and Hank took center stage, it was clear that the climax came not with Eddie winning Queenie but with Hank's sacrifice of her career and happiness.

Harry Beaumont, recently transferred over from Warner Bros., was chosen to direct on the basis of his first MGM feature, *Our Dancing Daughters*, then awaiting release. *Daughters'* fusion of jazzy verve and romantic melodrama showed a deft hand, and studio records point out that he was present at all the script conferences. Auteurists take note: while many contract directors were simply chattel or hired guns assigned to available properties, this forgotten figure had major impact on the project from its inception—far more than Goulding, who left for another studio during the early stages of production. Thalberg assigned staff writer Norman Houston to flesh out Mason's scenario and, deciding to go from part- to all-talking, brought in James Gleason to provide greater urban wallop. Although Gleason's contribution is traditionally given as a major factor in the film's success, the scripts and notes indicate that little of his work was used. Most of the dialogue in the completed picture was the work of Houston and Beaumont.

Thalberg and his production supervisor (and brother-in-law) Lawrence Weingarten were charting untested waters, and it was an experimental job all the way. Music would naturally play a crucial role, and since musical programs in previous films had mainly been a matter of Jolson and Brice hauling in their own material, this would be something new. Songs could be written for or molded to specific plot requirements, and as with theme tunes in late silents, a new song hit could attract that much more attention to the film.[2] Thalberg and his staff began to audition songs from a number of writers, including the Los Angeles-based team of Arthur Freed and Nacio Herb Brown. Singly and in tandem, the duo had been around for some years, achieving modest success jointly (the *Music Box Revue* in Hollywood) and individually (Brown's instrumental "Doll Dance," Freed's lyrics for "I Cried For You"). Billy Rose, one of show business's archetypal hustlers, was also competing for the assignment and went to the trouble of hiring an orchestra to play his songs for the MGM brass. But Thalberg went with the lesser-known Brown and Freed, whose seven songs for the new musical talkie were a mixture of new pieces and older unused material from their trunk. Three were particularly strong—the title number, "You Were Meant for Me," and "The Wedding of the Painted Doll" offered all the needed variety, from uncluttered sentiment to syncopated flash to ur-

2. And if published under MGM auspices would add to the company till. In September 1928 MGM became the first studio to bid for those profits by buying 51 percent interest in the Robbins Music Corporation, a major Tin Pan Alley concern.

ban brio.[3] "The Broadway Melody" received the most intensive spotting in the final cut, played under the credits and sung three times before any other song is performed. Fortunately it was good enough to hold up under the plugging, with defiantly upbeat lyrics that tie in specifically and affectingly with the character of Hank.

Going to the source, Thalberg tried to sign the Duncan Sisters. Earlier they had crashed Hollywood to make an execrable silent version of their stage hit *Topsy and Eva;* they now were booked up and could not make the time. As it emerged, the casting of the leads covered three crucial bases: rising young comer, musical comedy pro, seasoned film veteran. After her excellent showing in *Our Dancing Daughters*, eighteen year-old contractee Anita Page was considered a safe bet for stardom and was given the role of Queenie. Though she had no musical training or experience with dialogue, the main criterion was visual, a bill she could fill with no problem. Eddie, who carried the musical burden, was the hardest role to cast; after numerous tests the final choice was Charles King, making his film debut after two decades on the musical stage in such hits as *Present Arms* and *Hit the Deck*. For Hank: Bessie Love, wisely. Starting in 1915 with a small role in *Intolerance*, she quickly rose to the status of leading player, never irreplaceable star.[4] Perhaps her appeal was too offbeat for the Twenties. She was pretty, not beautiful; glamour seemed alien to her, and she was too homey for jazz-baby roles. By 1928, as she neared thirty, she was finding less work, and like many film players approaching has-been status, tried a personal appearance tour in vaudeville. When the call came from MGM she refused to make a test. "I had done enough films for them to know my work," she later recalled, "and if they wanted to hear me, they could see me in the variety show." Or in a two-reel Vitaphone comedy called *The Swellhead*, which proved she had no problems with microphones. Swallowing her pride, she finally agreed to test and impressed everyone.

---

3. The others were "Love Boat," "Harmony Babies From Melody Lane," "The Boy Friend," and "Lovely Lady," the last of which didn't make it in and was never used again by the team, normally inveterate recylers. Another song in *The Broadway Melody*, "Truthful Parson Brown," was the work of Willard Robinson.

The engagement of Arthur Freed carried far more weight for the history of the musical film than anyone could have imagined. While his partner remained a composer Freed gradually moved into production and by 1939 was a full-fledged MGM producer. Over the next two decades his name was on many of the greatest musical films ever made—*Meet Me in St. Louis* and *The Band Wagon* for starters, as well as *Singin' in the Rain*, which used three Brown/Freed songs from *The Broadway Melody*. When he spoke near the end of his life of his entry into film, his memories were quite inconsistent, as with one assertion that he and Brown had written all the songs especially for the film, which is likely wrong. One of Freed's memories that does seem valid concerns the experimental nature of the film, everything being tried for the first time and no major stars cast in case the whole thing didn't turn out well.

4. She had had several attention-getting roles, most notably as a junkie in *Human Wreckage* (1923), and at least one smash success with *The Lost World* (1925)—in which she played second fiddle to a pack of animated dinosaurs.

Production started in mid-October 1928 under the most trying makeshift conditions, everything from scratch and everyone at sea. Costumer David Cox, for example, was appalled to find out just how loudly a pair of silk bloomers could rustle when it passed too near a microphone. The twenty-six day shooting schedule was a nightmare of barely organized chaos, and the pressure never let up. The object was to do it fast as well as good, for everyone knew that other lots had musicals in the works: Warners had *The Desert Song,* Fox was working on *Movietone Follies,* and Paramount was putting sound into the silent backstage drama *The Shopworn Angel.* Many years later Bessie Love remembered:

> At the time we had no unions, and we were worked all hours. They were really terrible; to get the film out before anybody else could beat them to it, we worked day and night. The film had a four-week shooting schedule, and we would have to be on the set ready and made-up to shoot at 9 A.M. and we wouldn't finish until about 9 or 10 at night.

It was particularly hard on the inexperienced Anita Page, and in the middle of one emotional scene she flew into a hysterical fit and had to be sent home.[5]

For Harry Beaumont, who was probably averaging four hours of sleep per night, camera mobility was a leading concern. His intention, to inject some of the flowing visual quality of silents, was a tall order when it involved lugging around camera booths that each weighed about a ton. To impart some vitality, Beaumont and cinematographer John Arnold devised what they dubbed a "coffin on wheels," a camera booth compact enough to be moved around, used most successfully in a scene of Anita Page and Kenneth Thomson (as playboy Warriner) dancing while carrying on a conversation.[6] Arnold shot most scenes with four cameras running simultaneously from different angles, and when editor Sam Zimbalist pieced it together the result moved more smoothly than the earlier static talkies. Beaumont later praised the comparative pliability of the sound-on-film process.

Thalberg's other brother-in-law, Douglas Shearer, had recently assumed the mantle of studio sound engineer, due not to nepotism but because no one else wanted the job and he happened to have an inquisitive mechanical bent. A musical was an ideal focus for his experiments, and he poked and manipulated equipment, constantly moving the mikes all through filming

5. Dialogue changes sent to Page on November 1, just prior to this incident, survive in the MGM files and bear an obviously futile message from production associate Jack Cummings: "Anita Baby—Read these and don't worry."

6. However ordinary this seems, for viewers in 1929 it was a revelation. Not only the booth but the microphone needed to move, so a stagehand in stocking feet followed the actors with a mike just out of camera range. During one take the stagehand stepped on an exposed carpet tack, and since a bloodcurdling yell could not be written in, the scene had to be reshot.

to get the best possible pickup. One of the breakthroughs was sound editing, joining pieces of soundtrack in the same way a film editor pieces together different shots. Eventually a highly cultivated craft, here it was a humble corner-cutter. In one scene, an actor spoke the word "things" without sounding the final "s," a gaffe which for Vitaphone would have warranted a retake. With Movietone, Shearer and Zimbalist found they could cut in an "s" at the appropriate moment.[7] Shearer's best-known accomplishment came with "The Wedding of the Painted Doll," filmed while Thalberg was in New York. When he returned to Culver City and ran the sequence, he complained that it was not a movie at all, only a stage performance—nothing cinematic about it. He demanded it be reshot to include different angles, an edict well in line with the studio procedure that gave MGM the sobriquet "Retake Valley." The retake was going to be expensive, what with Technicolor film requiring extra illumination, and the need to rehire the dancers and orchestra and tenor James Burroughs. Then it occurred to Shearer that musicians weren't needed. There was nothing wrong with the recording they had made the first time, and since Burroughs sang from offscreen, the dancers could go through their routine and the new film would be combined with the old soundtrack in the lab. In the face of skepticism Shearer went ahead and created the process of prerecording and playback. What seems like an obvious tactic was in fact a huge advance that saved time and money, helped to liberate musical films from technical paralysis, and ultimately defined a leading difference between musicals on film and on stage.[8]

Shooting proper concluded in November, after which the ethos of Retake Valley asserted itself. Except for a few passages by Gleason, most of the new material was written by Beaumont, including Queenie's drunk scene and Hank's shouting match with Eddie ("You're yella!"). Ending the film with Eddie and Queenie's embrace now seemed inappropriate, since Hank was clearly the protagonist. Beaumont added one more scene, the last to be written and shot: Hank en route to the train station, down but not out, vowing to return to Broadway before too long. By the time all the work was finished in January, the cost had reached $379,000, higher than planned but still only the upper end of average for an MGM "A" feature, and $8,000 less than *The Singing Fool*.

A few months earlier, MGM had looked like the tortoise in the race to sound and except for United Artists was the last major studio to begin work

7. It happens during the birthday party Hank throws for Queenie. An actor tells a Scotsman joke with the punchline "The best things in life are free," and the added "s" in "things" is clearly audible. Like Arthur Freed, Sam Zimbalist moved up the MGM ladder to become a producer, eventually specializing in spectacular remakes: *Quo Vadis*, *Ben Hur*, etc.

8. The other numbers in the film were all shot with live sound, as with the Vitaphone films. If the orchestra was not onscreen, it was right out of camera range, playing into microphones.

on talkies. Now this reticence would prove one of the wisest judgments of the era. So would Louis B. Mayer and Thalberg's decision to shoot *The Broadway Melody* under wraps in the event that the trial and error produced a disaster.[9] *The Trial of Mary Dugan*, also in production, seems to have been retained as backup which could go out as MGM's first all-talkie if the musical experiment didn't pan out. Only when the studio saw the high-grade finished product did the promotion heat up, including, from the publicity department, a legendary slogan:

ALL TALKING

ALL SINGING

ALL DANCING

For the premiere on Friday, February 1, 1929, at Grauman's Chinese Theater, MGM recruited its highest paid actor, John Gilbert, to host the proceedings and introduce the opulent stage prologue. For the New York opening at the Astor Theatre one week later, there was ballyhoo unprecedented in sound films except for the first Vitaphone show and possibly *The Singing Fool*. For the week prior to February 8 the ads in the New York dailies sold the film as everything under the sun, each day a new ad hustling a different facet: Musical (A music staff of "You Were Meant for Me"); Woman's Picture: ("Her little sister had won out in the game of love!"); Sex Drama (Warriner and Queenie, captioned "I'll buy you a Rolls Royce!"); Spectacle and Media Event ("All Pictures Fade into Insignificance Beside *The Broadway Melody*"). Advertising was only one phase of the onslaught. Harry Beaumont, accorded an unusually high profile, praised sound film and the emerging musical in one interview after another. His words were given added import when he discussed the ins and outs of sound filming, and specifically what it took to turn out a good talkie. It was one of the first times an insider had given the public a frank assessment of talking films and their capabilities, and the effect was to heighten audience interest in this film and the medium as a whole. Sound is indeed here to stay, he affirmed, and it's steadily getting better. Not since *Don Juan* had the technology been promoted so astutely, and the diligence extended beyond the standard venues to the auditory end. As it was, *Melody* was the best-recorded sound film to that time; then, MGM technicians spent days

9. Even more than the high-pressure promotion given film projects today, studio publicists in the late 1920s were always willing to pitch film plans that never came to pass, as later chapters in this book attest. MGM's restraint with *The Broadway Melody* was refreshing as well as sensible and kept the studio from looking foolish if the film didn't come off. That this was a good policy can be seen by another musical in production shortly after *Broadway Melody*, *The Five O'Clock Girl* starring Marion Davies. See Chapter Nine to discover why this much-publicized film never saw the light of day; just let it be noted here that the economic security of the old-time studio system was such that *Heaven's Gate*-style disasters were usually averted, at least before they reached the public.

One major factor in the smash of *The Broadway Melody* was its deft combination of on-stage hoopla and backstage conflict. The former may be seen on the front cover of this book. A prime example of the latter is this dressing room scene. Bessie Love, Charles King, and Anita Page have it out just prior to Love's climactic breakdown.

performing acoustical tests at Grauman's and the Astor to ensure that the reproduction surpassed anything heard so far, with Beaumont helping to calibrate the Astor's synchronization and volume levels. Little work of this type had been done before, and never to this meticulous extent; quite a contrast to *Tenderloin* or *Melody of Love* or, for that matter, *Interference*, withdrawn after its premiere for retakes.[10]

As had become common with big-time talkies (whether they warranted it or not), the opening engagements and the subsequent runs in major cities were road show bookings, two- or three-a-day showings with reserved seats at a $2 top. With all the hype and novelty, *The Broadway Melody* would have made money even if it had been a lemon. But it wasn't: the crowds at Grauman's and the Astor cheered loud and long, and then the reviews came in. "The best talkie (also singie) yet . . . points the way to an even greater future than it actually fulfills. . . . But as an achievement at this

10. The attention to reproduction extended to other first-run engagements with MGM's decision to transfer the Movietone tracks to discs. The explanation was that the discs offered superior sound in theaters, which was probably accurate. Also a likely factor: more theaters at that time were wired for Vitaphone than Movietone, and thus films in that format would get wider circulation.

time it is a wonder" *(Los Angeles Times)*. "The best talkie ever made . . . the most human, the most intriguing, the most genuinely satisfactory picture to come out of Hollywood in a year. . . . Though in the past year most skeptical of talking pictures, I must unconditionally surrender to *The Broadway Melody*" *(Los Angeles Evening Herald)*. "[Four stars] What a picture! . . . Direction, dialogue, songs, all done by experts. . . . And acting that is superb" *(New York Daily News)*. "Knockout entertainment. . . . Not since 'The Big Parade' has a movie been accorded such a tremendous reception" *(New York American)*. And so on through the trade and regional press. The reviews were sufficient to lead MGM to take the rare (for 1929) step of placing review snippets in newspaper ads, under a banner that gloated "AS EXPECTED."

Also expected were a few conspicuous absentees. The dissent was led by New York critics such as those in *Time* and *The New Yorker*, for whom *The Broadway Melody* seemed moth-eaten and bathetic alongside the polished Broadway norm. For Mordaunt Hall of *The New York Times*, who had earlier evinced a low tolerance for talkies, the notion of attractive young women spitting out wisecracks was cause for prodigious distress. Hall liked the songs and the color sequence and praised Bessie Love, but in his review and a follow-up piece sputtered endlessly about the uncouth discrepancy between "Fair faces and wild slang." Aural incongruity would indeed be an issue in talking film, yet the greater pertinence in this instance was that Hall was perhaps the least perspicacious critic of the time, his quaint dismay over the dialogue being of no consequence to anyone other than himself.

More perceptive observers, including those with valid criticisms, used the film as a spyglass to a future of music and sound. Some of the most persuasive words came from an utterly unexpected source—René Clair, already established as French cinema's most imaginative talent. Initially resistant to talkies, he saw *The Broadway Melody* in London in May 1929 and in a letter home (later published as "The Art of Sound") had high praise:

> For anyone who has some knowledge of the complicated technique of sound recording, this film is a marvel. Harry Beaumont . . . and his collaborators . . . seem to delight in playing with all the difficulties of visual and sound recording. . . . This film['s] makers have worked with the precision of engineers, and their achievement is a lesson to those who still imagine that the creation of a film can take place under conditions of chaos known as inspiration. . . .
>
> The immobility of planes, that curse of talking films, has gone. The camera is as mobile, the angles as varied as in a good silent film.

Clair detailed Beaumont's resourceful deployment of sound and image to attain dramatic harmony, singling out a few scenes in which sound was portrayed allusively, heard off-screen and reacted to. Whatever Clair's reservations about the overall nature of talkies, *The Broadway Melody* seemed to act as a catalyst for a decided change of heart regarding the potential of sound film. Is it too great a stretch to theorize that *The Broadway Melody* had some influence on *Sous les Toits de Paris*, *Le Million*, and *A Nous la Liberté*? Probably not, for this is the film of which Clair wrote, "The talking film has for the first time found an appropriate form: it is neither theatre nor cinema, but something altogether new."

The financial figures naturally reflected the enthusiasm—$2,808,000 in the U.S. and $1,558,000 overseas, second only to *The Singing Fool* among films of the period; angry exhibitors complained that MGM's distribution arm, Loew's Inc., had raised its rental fees to realize a higher profit margin than usual. The high domestic figures were less unexpected than the strong foreign reaction to this quintessentially American product. A success in London, where the Jolson films had scored well, could be predicted, but records were also set in such places as Rio de Janeiro, Amsterdam, and Marseilles. The language barrier was little problem, for one of the lesser-known distinctions of *The Broadway Melody* is that it was the first sound film that successfully employed superimposed subtitles— about thirty translated titles laid over the action to explain plot points and key lines.[11]

The Broadway Melody's prime achievement, in any language, was its role in restoring public faith in filmgoing. It made it safe for audiences to attend the talkies, for as with silents, they could again go to the movies fully counting on a completely enjoyable evening and not be thwarted by technical or creative incompetence. Films as good as this could make talkies work. Much of this, of course, came with that MGM pride-in-product attitude and quality control. The much-vaunted novelty value, too, is a more complicated issue. However easy it is to assume that the first movie musical scored its bull's-eye with songs and dances, many of its most decisive accomplishments were not necessarily musical, even with the huge success of the three lead songs. As those variegated newspaper ads intended, there was a wealth of reasons drawing the crowds and the high grosses, and the most conspicuous of these was a new level of assurance in talking-film technique. What can only now seem plodding and crude was seen then as smooth, dynamic, rapid—a near-epic parable of winners and losers. In comparison to the stiff, lumbering, frequently inane tread of most early talkies, *The Broadway Melody* was a blast of fresh air, and viewed alongside its con-

11. Few early sound films received this treatment. Before foreign-language dubbing became the norm, the studios sometimes dealt with the problem in a more costly and troublesome fashion: they shot foreign versions of their films concurrently with those made in English, often with the same stars. Asking Claudette Colbert and Maurice Chevalier to act in French was easy; getting Laurel and Hardy to speak Spanish necessitated quick and erratic phonetic cramming.

temporaries—*Noah's Ark, Interference, In Old Arizona, The Singing Fool*—its superiority is unequivocal.

The first frames after the credits give testament to the progress, as a bouncy arrangement of "Give My Regards to Broadway" accompanying a dizzying montage of aerial views of Manhattan immediately establishes the city as a frantically magic mecca for small-timers like the Mahoneys.[12] Right after this opening flourish, the Tin Pan Alley sequence starts with a bravura visual and aural collage of singers, instruments, and bits of melody that seems to push early sound film as far as it can go. As Eddie shows off his song to jealous competitors and the Mahoneys arrive at a seedy midtown hotel, the writing and direction and acting have an energy and authenticity new to talkies. To maintain freshness and zip throughout the entire 101 minutes, a concerted effort is made to revitalize the clichés and avoid becoming a stolid talkfest. The grungy rigors of putting on a Broadway revue, the hard-bitten showgirls and slimy stage-door Johnnies, the conflicts and the exhaustion—all are presented with more dexterity and conviction, and more movement, than any previous sound picture. As René Clair had noticed, the action and sense of space move into planes deeper than a one-dimensional playing area, and the mobile camera gives such a lift to the scene of Anita Page and Kenneth Thomson dancing and talking that it was probably worth the distress of that wounded stagehand.

The attempts at cinematic propulsion don't disguise the fact that *The Broadway Melody* comes to a halt whenever a musical number draws near. Even in 1929 the song sequences were notable more for implication than achievement. "The possibilities," *Variety* observed, "are what jolt the imagination." If putting together production numbers for film was not totally unprecedented, it was still pretty much virgin territory for Beaumont and dance director Sammy Lee.[13] Their efforts raised one of the perennial dilemmas in backstage films: in (re-)creating numbers that ostensibly occur on a stage, how much cinematic license should be taken? Is so-called realism a leading concern, or do imagination and spectacle come to the fore? The primary methodology over the next two years was to keep it simple, act like it's in the theater. It was easier that way, more traditional, competing with Broadway on its own turf. But Thalberg was onto something when he scrapped the first "Painted Doll" number. Literal transcriptions of stage

12. As first released, the Manhattan montage was somewhat longer than it is now in most existing prints, including the copy on home video (which also puts ill-fitting updated music under the MGM logo). "Give My Regards" originally segued into Victor Herbert's "Little Old New York," set to a sharp succession of urban images (neon marquees, traffic cops with synchronized whistles, Times Square, etc.). The transition to the first scene is thus more jarring than intended.

13. The biggest "musical numbers" in any film prior to this were in fact for a silent MGM backstage drama. *Pretty Ladies* (1925) featured spectacular *Follies* numbers devised by director Monta Bell, some in two-color Technicolor.

numbers were hopelessly dull. Shooting straight through the proscenium was too easy and made for boring theater, not stimulating film. Unfortunately, Thalberg's good intentions were insufficient. The technique in November 1928 was too cumbersome, the sense of a musical-film aesthetic too nascent, to give much cinematic life to the numbers, and the attempts at editing and multiple camera angles are too sparse to add anything. These are basically stage tableaux shot head-on from chained-down cameras, much the same as the larger Vitaphone pieces.

"Love Boat," upon which Anita Page serves as an underdressed living masthead, is the stiffest. Literally the only movement in the entire number is when Page raises her arm, perchance to salute a ship that passes in the night. The problem is compounded by the worst recording in the film. With tenor Burroughs, a male chorus, and the orchestra clearly too much for the microphone, words and music become unreconstituted mush. The only cinema in the sequence lies in the emotional underpinnings of the reaction shots: Queenie's dazed excitement, Hank's sad resignation, Eddie and Warriner offering variations on sexual attraction. "The Boy Friend" is a little more kinetic, as Love and Page lead a line of chorines in one (before the curtain), yet the makeshift becomes obvious when the dance starts up and Page saunters off. While Bessie and friends cavort jazzily, Anita stands on the side, swaying and twirling her plumes sort of in time to the music. Such inadequacies also show up in the impromptu version of the title song in their hotel room, when Love does all the work, and especially in an excerpt from the Mahoneys' vaudeville act. "Harmony Babies from Melody Lane" recalls every wretched variety routine from the Cherry Sisters on, and as shown here, Hank and Queenie could barely cut it on the bottom of the bill in Hay Springs, Nebraska, let alone on Broadway. Love was a beguilingly fidgety dancer and could sing a little, but Page could go no further than looking nice and carrying a tune. This does work to the script's advantage when it becomes clear that Queenie's looks are responsible for getting Zanfield to hire the act. Hank is the born trouper, but a half-naked blonde captures more eyes on "Broad's Way."

The most effective musical sequences are the least pretentious: King's first rendition of the title song, backed by a Tin Pan Alley combo (Nacio Herb Brown on piano); "Truthful Parson Brown," given a relaxed workout by the Biltmore Quartet in a party scene; and especially "You Were Meant for Me," which takes song out of presentational mode and puts it at the service of the plot. Eddie sings it to Queenie in her apartment, he earnestly assured, she troubled and interested, a quiet unpretentious little scene. "I wrote it for you, Queenie . . . I wrote it *about* you!" King gives the simple ballad the right kind of soft sell, and the closeness of the camera adds an intimacy Broadway could never duplicate. Here's where movie musicals would mine some prime ore.

The title song (in its second reprise) and "The Wedding of the Painted Doll" are the most expansive items on the bill, each with a cornucopian array of gauche puppetlike dancers, bovine chorines, and stagebound presentation. Beaumont and Sammy Lee lacked the time and know-how to move much past the rudimentaries with these and, as *Variety* discerned, only hick audiences were fooled into thinking them the equal of Broadway's finest. "The Broadway Melody" at least has stylish high-contrast Art Deco design and some bizarre two-tone wigs. And for all its staginess it does briefly turn into a film instead of a canned routine. When soloist Joyce Murray begins a tap dance on pointe, the movie audience is given a perspective not possible in the theater: interspersed with the medium and long shots are three close-ups of the tapping feet. Although ballet-tap was common in twenties show dancing, no audience had been this close to it, hearing the taps register clearly and seeing the feet from a few inches away. That it looks excruciatingly painful is further testimony to film's ability to alter the most familiar theatrical rites.

"The Wedding of the Painted Doll" is the first true large-scale production number on film, and its significance is vastly out of proportion to its three and a half minutes on the screen. By combining recorded sound with photographed color, it represented an attempt by its creators to provide the ultimate simulation of the real thing, i.e., "live theater," but the intention became somewhat derailed by the nature of the color itself. This is not the Technicolor of later years that put rainbow hues in the Land of Oz and made Betty Grable golden. Long before achieving full-spectrum color photography, the Technicolor Company's founder, Herbert T. Kalmus, had already devised a more limited compromise process known today as two-color Technicolor. Used in Hollywood films for six years prior to *The Broadway Melody*, this color was anything but lifelike. Indeed, it was unable to reproduce much of the visible spectrum, being primarily based on hues of green and red. Anything else was a gamble. For starters, no blue, ever. Skies came out a metallic sea green, and any designer using blue in sets or costumes found out that it photographed as something altogether different and usually somewhat muddy. Yellow was approximated as brassy beige, and purple was out of the question. Colors that did reproduce were generally compromised. Reds commonly had a harsh brick-like tinge, greens could lean toward gray or brown, and the process was prone to graininess and inconsistency, tending to blur in long shots. This sounds immoderately limited, and so it was. Nevertheless, it had many good points when properly applied. Flesh tones could be rendered accurately, enabling special showcasing for star performers; pinks and turquoises worked well; and browns, tans, and golds were particularly warm and rich. Technicolor's lab mandated painstaking quality control over printing, more akin to dye-transfer lithography than modern color photography, and the results could be quite attractive and sometimes better. A well-conceived design augmented by careful lighting, photography, and printing could produce a fairly stunning unreality far more appealing than common naturalism.

A few silent films had been filmed entirely in Technicolor, most notably *Toll of the Sea* (1922) and *The Black Pirate* (1926). Most often, the inherent artifice and expense plus complaints of eyestrain made it sufficient to use color for only a few minutes at a time. Technicolor gave splashy dressup to key moments in a number of black-and-white films: the Exodus in *The Ten Commandments* (1923), Gloria Swanson's dreams of glory in *Stage Struck* (1925), a fashion show in *Irene* (1926), and so on. As the use of color increased, Kalmus worked steadily to make it less whimsical and more workable. Traditionally called "2-strip," it literally consisted of two strips of film cemented together, each carrying a separate color record, and so obtrusively thick that it tended to scratch and buckle when run through projectors. By 1929 Kalmus amended this by fabricating a single double-emulsion strip upon which both color records were printed. It make projection easier, cut down on the grain, and yielded more vibrant colors. With this development waiting in the wings, it was preordained that color would pop up in early movie musicals. In much the same way as in silent films, "The Wedding of the Painted Doll" used Technicolor to add pizazz to a short spectacular scene, in this case a fantasy so self-contained that none of the principal players appear in it. With Freed's lyrics as their cue, the color's eccentricities became desirable and even mandatory, as did the heavy makeup deemed necessary for the process.[14] Today, unfortunately, it survives only in black and white, leaving the imagination to divine which dancers wore pink and which wore green. Shearer's employment of playback recording, as seen here, is hardly impressive, for this is still clearly a silent film, with frenetic dancers lurching about at wildly varying levels of skill and coordination. The one trait they share is total silence, with no taps or footfalls, and the deadened quality is in some ways more alienating than the various failings of the other numbers. At the time such things mattered little, for this eye-catching diversion pleased almost everyone except the British journal *Close-Up* ("The Only Magazine Devoted to Films as an Art"), which not surprisingly decried *Broadway Melody* as a raucous and basically irredeemable piece of bad news and reserved special venom for the color sequence: "The faces of the players remind you of the colour of milk chocolate and their limbs have the appearance of that delightful old gentleman who exhibits part of his nudity in a case in the British Museum."

14. Maybe it looked acceptable in original nitrate prints, but the makeup in some early color films is pretty extreme. In the Resurrection scene of DeMille's *King of Kings* (1927), H. B. Warner (Jesus) is not heavily done up and looks fine; Jacqueline Logan's Mary Magdalene has chalky skin with carmine lips and cheeks—a garish expressionistic mask.

Such an objection was relatively uncommon. Most observers were willing to meet *The Broadway Melody* on its own level, away from undue claims of Art. And in Bessie Love nearly everyone found one achievement above criticism—a performance establishing an early high standard for acting in sound films. What a contrast to all the Dolores Costellos and May McAvoys! Finally, definitively, a woman's vocal and dramatic efforts registered as well or better than a man's, and the tremendous impact of Love's performance revived her career. In the midst of the hackneyed plot mechanics and dated slang so abhorred by Mordaunt Hall, there she is: the one element of the film holding up without reliance on historical context, validating everything around her with a combination of solid technique and emotional directness. With a low and pleasant voice (except when Hank is crossed and becomes shrill) she delivers the show-biz lingo in wholly authoritative fashion, and combines it with the physical coordination of the finest silent acting. The result is an intensely credible character who's always acting or reacting, as often as not running scared, unwilling to face facts about either love or show business. The performance builds in intensity as the conflicts add up, until the cathartic dressing room scene when Hank realizes the truth and goads Eddie into saving Queenie from Warriner. Alone, she starts to put cold cream on her face and breaks down, careening between tears and uncontrolled laughter as everything comes off—makeup, illusions, ideals. The scene is a star turn, almost an aria, and Love holds nothing back. Finally containing herself enough to get through a phone call, she asks her agent to set her up with a new partner, and after she hangs up Beaumont fades out, one last sob heard after the screen has dimmed to black.[15] There were many reports of teary spectators bursting into applause at that same moment, aware as never before of the kind of quality sound films could achieve. Though the narrative focus then shifts back to Eddie and Queenie to give their love story a happy (not totally convincing) resolution, Beaumont made the right decision to end not with a clinch but with that last-minute scene of Hank the loser, on her way to rebuild her career and her life, still making cracks. Her face and mien are changed, and it's clear that some of the old spark is gone, perhaps for good. Love's skill is such that the crude manipulation of *The Singing Fool* seems a century earlier instead of just a few months, and as one of the big winners of the early sound era, she received fine reviews, general career-rebirth acclaim, a new MGM contract that quadrupled her salary, and an Academy Award nomination.[16]

15. René Clair singled out this final moment to praise its adroit manipulation of sound and image. He added that "Bessie Love talking manages to surpass the silent Bessie Love whom we loved so well in the past."

16. The winner was Mary Pickford, ostensibly for *Coquette*, more realistically for being a star longer than anyone could remember. The other nominees—Ruth Chatterton *(Madame X)*, Betty Compson *(The Barker)*, and Jeanne Eagels (posthumous nomination for *The Letter*)—

Charles King and Anita Page, billed above Love in the credits, collected favorable notices—but there was never any doubt about who carried the film. King, with his ingratiatingly overbearing hoofer's personality, doesn't act so much as dispense a catalogue of shtick. The intimacies of romantic film acting are clearly beyond him, hearty bluster not sufficing when smaller emotions are required. The performance does work when, in winning Queenie back, Eddie is beaten in both person and pride—a scene that surprisingly rejects a macho ethos. More than King, Anita Page occasionally comes in for censure from modern observers. The character as written is one-dimensional—sweet and lovely and dumb—and as distasteful as it is dated; Page, who later gave some skillful performances, lacked the training at this point to overcome the role's inherent limitations. Her movements are less coordinated than those of the more compact Love, her posture is slouchy, and that accent, straight from Flushing, Queens ("Haaaank, I'm noivous!") gives the lie to Queenie's midwestern background. With all this, she is intensely likable—sincere, well-meaning, endearing in much the same fashion as Ruby Keeler several years later—and, of course, quite beautiful.[17] Of the other performers, Jed Prouty is most prominent as the interminably stuttering agent. His routine (grope for the right word and come out with something entirely different) came off as a novelty, and so he became the first of many unfunny comic-relief figures plaguing early musicals. More effective are Kenneth Thomson as Warriner, Mary Doran as the nasty showgirl (Hank calls her a bimbo), and Drew Demarest as the sissy couturier, the talkies' first gay stereotype.[18]

The key films, the groundbreakers, the seminal works, the *Citizen Kane*s and *Potemkin*s and *Intolerance*s, remain basically timeless. When the details fray with age, the inherent unshakable permanence remains. In some ways *The Broadway Melody* is equally influential, but it was made by craftsmen rather than artists and lacks the transcendence of the most significant work. Moreover, its many innovations were of a kind to ensure that it would

were all high-grade, Eagels in particular. For 1929–30 the awards were in seven categories only, and *Broadway Melody* copped nominations in three: Picture, Actress, Director. While the Best Picture citation was partly prompted by MGM "encouragement," it did serve to confirm *Melody*'s success and repercussions.

17. Unlike Bessie Love, who continued to work into the 1980s, Page and King's film careers were notably short-lived. After the first musical boom King returned to the stage, with only fleeting film work afterward, and died in harness in 1944 during a USO tour. For Anita Page, who retired from film in her mid-twenties, *The Broadway Melody* had personal as well as professional consequences—a brief marriage to Nacio Herb Brown.

18. Co-writer James Gleason also turns up in a bit in the first scene. Thomson's role as smarmy Jock Warriner became an industry in-joke when the crude recording in some scenes made the name come out as "Jack Warner." Obvious as Demarest is, Norman Houston's original draft was even more extreme. When the designer starts fussing about his hats, the Mary Doran character was to have remarked to her colleagues, "Don't mind him! She's just one of us!"

outdate itself. More than most works of vast consequence it was a film inextricably of its time, to be relegated to the status of an antique when that time was past. Other than the perennial songs, about all that was left was the Academy Award and an advertising slogan that passed into folklore as a symbol of the talkie revolution. Some fond memories too, for it remained for many viewers the one backstage musical they had really loved, and not just because it was the first. Certainly MGM didn't forget. In 1935, well into the second wave of musical cinema, the studio produced an expensive and tune-filled backstage film with a familiar title: *Broadway Melody of 1936*, followed by further unrelated installments in 1938 and 1940. Also in 1940, MGM released *Two Girls on Broadway*, an unpretentious B-film that turned out to be a remake of its first all-talkie. With the Mahoney sisters now named Pat (Queenie) and Molly (Hank), the plot was updated and smoothed out, once again with a scene of tearful self-sacrifice that climaxed with a phone call. None of the original songs was used, and this time Brown and Freed's contribution to the score delivered no hits. The most interesting feature of *Two Girls* was its cast, which exactly matched its predecessor in the choice of a star trio: glamorous up-and-comer (Lana Turner), experienced hoofer (George Murphy), and feistily seasoned film veteran (Joan Blondell).[19] It came and went pleasantly without making much splash, its connection with its illustrious predecessor little stressed except by some critics, who noted that spectators might feel they had seen it all somewhere before.

There's no question that much of the impact of *The Broadway Melody* was due to its status as first of the breed, yet that alone does not account for the worldwide enthusiasm. It was seen as a watershed, the first talkie yardstick, proof of sound film's positive effects. You Were Meant for Me, indeed. Nor could the studios stop thinking about it; Lord knows it was imitated and stolen from incessantly. What couldn't be copied or faked were the adventurousness and finesse that Harry Beaumont and Bessie Love and Douglas Shearer and all the others put into it. They had done their pioneer job well, with a degree of spirit and integrity few of their many successors would match. Talkies could hardly have asked for a more relevant boost. This is what matters, not the plot and absurd dances and archaic technique that show today. This is where it began, and its greatest importance lies in everything that follows.

19. The Thomson and Prouty roles were taken by Kent Taylor and a non-stammering Wallace Ford. This was the second remake, in a way. In 1930 MGM released a nightmarish series of anthropomorphic live-action comedies in which trained dogs were forced to stand up on hind legs, wear costumes, move their mouths to dubbed dialogue, and other indignities. One of the earliest of these "Dogvilles" was *The Dogway Melody*, complete with "You Were Meant for Me," a parody of "The Love Boat," and bits cribbed from *The Jazz Singer* and MGM's *Hollywood Revue*. It's enough to turn the most apathetic cinephile into an animal rights activist.

CHAPTER 4

On With the Show

Many years after the fact, actor William Haines described the coming of sound as it affected his studio, MGM. "It was the night of the *Titanic* all over again," he said, "with women grabbing the wrong children and Louis B. [Mayer] singing 'Nearer My God to Thee.' " This was the film industry, mid-to-late 1928. With crisis mentality to the fore, careers and reputations and value systems were suddenly upended, even tossed aside. Along with the race to sound, there were steady rumblings in studio board rooms. A sort of revolutionary zeal (i.e., greed) led moguls and speculators to outdo each other in conceiving grandiose mergers and buy-out schemes. Some of these did come to pass, as with Warner Bros.' takeover of First National, while others remained noisy rumors. Either way, this behind-the-scenes hustle contributed to the tone of the era, everything freewheeling and up for grabs. Haines's description was apt: it was a whole armada of *Titanic*s, with the *Lusitania* and *Mary Celeste* tossed in for good measure.

Amid the chaos, the musical film was undergoing a torturous infancy. The early days were wide open, and the first films, released in the first half of 1929 in the wake of *The Broadway Melody*, are an incredibly mixed bag, in some ways the most straightforward, even guileless films ever made. Not the material, of course, which is mostly secondhand and tattered. It's the craft and technique, the drive for an aesthetic, that are upfront here, desperately trying to assert themselves and find their way around the daunting hurdles. In this most frivolous of genres these are the no-frills efforts, every ingredient open to inspection and consent. "What on earth is a musical film?" these films seem to ask the audience. "Do you approve? We're doing the best we can. Tell us we're doing it right."

With the time factor serving as a pressurizing agent, filmmakers were seldom granted the latitude to think through the fundamental issues they were compelled to address. Stopgap was the order of the day, and no one had rounded notions of what might constitute a musical, or indeed any kind of talkie. Some leaned heavily on the stage as a prototype. The trained voices, the properties with pre-sold titles, the sheer ease of doing it that way ensured that many early talkies were intemperately stage-oriented. Musicals, where notions of artifice and reality were in constant collision, added more pieces to the puzzle, raising desperate questions that did not receive binding answers. Given the intimacy of film, how should the musical's calculatedly unreal and stylized world be depicted? Can music and song and dance factor into naturalistic presentation or should it only be used as part of an onstage performance context? A statistical consideration: most stage musicals have a dozen or more songs—is there any set number that a film should have? No one was sure at first, and everyone had different ideas. The flaws in the resulting films were obvious to audiences, yet spectators, invigorated by the newness, were more patient than the circumstances warranted and paid less heed to the technical blunders and artistic deficiencies than the critics. The people went, they watched and listened, and most of the time they enjoyed. And they knew that these early efforts would do until better things came along.

Plans were already under way for several musicals in the summer of 1928, and in a sane time and place Warner Bros. would have been there first. Logic not being the reigning factor, it was the talkie latecomer, MGM, who ended up with the first musical. The one irony about William Haines's remark was that the chaos at Metro was nothing as to that at other studios. However difficult it had been to produce, *The Broadway Melody* charted a critically simple progression: conceived, written, assembled, cast, shot and reshot, edited, marketed, premiered. Just like any other big-studio picture at any time—except late 1928. To look at the other musicals in production at the same time is to gauge the breadth of MGM's success. Those responsible for *The Broadway Melody* were aware that a straight line was the shortest distance between two points. That many of their rivals did not was proved by the films they created.

Surely Warner Bros. had the right idea for its first all-talking all-musical effort, ambitious yet sensible. Instead of extending the Jolson concept to make a low-rent backstager with songs and dances and schmaltz, the studio's plans were far more ostentatious. In the spring of 1928 Warners bought the screen rights to the 1926 Broadway hit *The Desert Song*. All of operetta's ingredients were here clustered in intense array: Sigmund Romberg's sumptuous music, florid lyrics by Otto Harbach and Oscar Hammerstein II, exotic settings and colorful costumes, larger-than-life lovers, picturesque and stereotypical supporting characters, and, true to the medium, a plot approaching parody. It encompassed the French Foreign Legion on

Two alone: Red Shadow (John Boles) encounters Margot (Carlotta King) in *The Desert Song*. Photofest.

a Moroccan outpost, the Riffs' struggle for freedom, a hero with a dual identity, and a woman threatened with numerous affronts probably worse than death. Operetta had no mandate toward believability, and with this score no one cared. There was an unusual quota of hits for this type of show—"One Alone," "The Riff Song," "French Military Marching Song"—along with a title song that summoned rapturous intrigue and moonlit sands ("Blue heaven and you and I . . ."). It was quite a package. The two leads of *The Desert Song* are more excessive and appealing than most operetta archetypes. Pierre Birabeau, a general's son, feigns the person of a prissy wimp to conceal his alter ego, the dashing insurgent Red Shadow. Margot Bonvalet pursues romance and adventure with an ardor and spunk beyond her genteel upbringing, yet is too naïve to see Pierre's disguise. There's also the exotic menace of the half-caste Azuri, as well as Ali ben Ali and other such condescension. It plays as the plot of a particularly lunatic piece of silent-movie escapism, and indeed operettas had proved viable on the silent screen (e.g., *The Merry Widow* and *The Student Prince*). With Vitaphoned songs and Valentinoesque sand dunes it was, Warners judged, an obvious choice.

The Desert Song was originally intended as a singing part-talkie, a more illustrious companion to *Tenderloin* and *State Street Sadie*. After *Lights of New York* it was changed to an all-talkie. The screenplay by Harvey Gates, who had worked on *The Terror* and other Warner talkies, kept the two-act stage structure totally intact, cut some songs (most conspicuously "Romance" and "It"), and left in most of the purplest stage dialogue. There was also room for exterior shots of horses and writers and desert sands, to be shot silent to accommodate Vitaphone's temperament. By mid-September 1928 director Roy Del Ruth (another *Terror* veteran) was testing for the leads. A comely face and figure and an outstanding singing voice are the most obvious prerequisites for operetta. Less prominent, if just as pressing, is the ability to balance romantic sincerity with a sense of the absurd—and neither poise nor dash was exactly a strong suit in Vitaphone's actors so far. John Boles, a former musical player who had come into silent films in 1924, filled the role of Pierre with unexpected ease. For Margot, who ideally would combine Dolores Costello looks with the voice of Melba, Jack Warner cast Carlotta King nearly sight unseen, after hearing her on the radio. If she looked halfway good, he decided, she would be Margot; she did, and she was. The remaining cast was drawn from such Vitaphone veterans as Johnny Arthur, Louise Fazenda, John Miljan, and, already in her fifth talking picture, Myrna Loy, then coming into her infamous all-purpose ethnic vamp phase.[1] Despite the obstacles, the six-week shoot of *The Desert Song* (October–November 1928) proceeded rather smoothly, King and Boles singing loudly as Louis Silvers conducted the one-hundred-plus-piece Vitaphone orchestra off camera. By early December everything was done. It was a creditable job, brought in by Del Ruth at the reasonable sum of $354,000. Warners had the jump on its competitors, and the first film operetta could make a smashing way to launch 1929.

Warners blew it. *The Desert Song* sat on the shelf for five months, during which time every other major studio released at least one musical. The delay was due partly to legalities and mostly to corporate incompetence. The legal obstacles were prompted by Mrs. Louis O. Macloon, a theatrical entrepreneur who already owned the stage rights to *Desert Song* for the western sectors of the U.S. and Canada. Learning that Warners was filming it, she sued to prohibit the exhibition of the film in her territory. The courts decided that film rights, whether for silents or talkies, had nothing to do with theatrical performances—a ruling that did nothing to alleviate the burgeoning animosity between the musical stage and its new rival. Macloon appealed the decision and lost, and by the time the matter was resolved it was mid-February of 1929. Blocks-long lines for *The Broadway Melody* were forming in New York and Hollywood, and Warners could have competed.

---

1. As is well known, Loy played dozens of these hot-blooded oversexed roles—Asians, Gypsies, and whatnot—before finding her bearings as screen's model *bonne vivante*. Compelled to make a test for Azuri, she came up with suitably outlandish makeup and an incredible all-purpose "native" accent. Even Warners' skeptical production supervisor, Darryl Zanuck, was convinced, and Loy went on to more of the same for several years.

Its decision to wait two more months was due to the cockeyed and backward-looking schedule by which its films were made and released. In the Warners release program, a year's worth of studio product was predetermined, promised to exhibitors before the beginning of the season, and rushed through assembly-line production—so many Dolores Costellos, so many Rin Tin Tins, etc., and a few higher-priced road show "specials" like *The Singing Fool* and *Noah's Ark*. From Warners' point of view, this type of stockpiling was advantageous; late in the year, having completed its product for the season, the studio was able to shut down its plant for as long as two months, laying off nearly all its employees. Other studios also had a release program but, seeing the extraordinary events of the time, were able to sidestep it to rush their sound films out to an eager public. Not Warners. The company adhered to its program so rigidly that it often botched the timing on its early talkies by keeping them on the shelf until their allotted time arrived. With more polished work arriving on a weekly basis, films like *The Redeeming Sin* (Dolores Costello again) and *Conquest* began to date all too quickly.[2] It had been predetermined in the fall of 1928 that *The Desert Song* had a particular slot in the Warner schedule, and there it remained, waiting for its audience while the parade passed by.

Miscalculated timing also played havoc with Universal's *Show Boat*, for neither sound film nor a smash-hit Broadway musical had factored into the original plan. Universal was and is the oldest of all major studios, and under the watchful lower-brow eye of "Uncle" Carl Laemmle it maintained an even, uninspired keel through most of the 1920s.[3] That con job *Melody of Love* was an extreme example of the house style—quickly and cheaply made, utterly unmemorable. Occasionally during the 1920s Uncle Carl tried for more by raising the sights and budgets of a few pictures, with varied and sometimes impressive results *(Foolish Wives, The Cat and the Canary, The Phantom of the Opera)*. His most costly venture, a 1927 adaptation of *Uncle Tom's Cabin*, was less effective, especially after his attempts to interest D. W. Griffith in the project—*The Rebirth of a Nation*, as it were—met with no success. The job passed to the far less significant hands of Harry Pollard, a hack who had directed some of Universal's lighter fare, and before Pollard started work, Laemmle had already prepared a follow-up.

Edna Ferber's novel *Show Boat* had been published in August 1926 to fine notices and immense public favor. Its tale of impermanence and en-

---

2. Both of these were shot in the late summer and early fall of 1928 and were held back for at least six months. When they finally did go into release, audience interest had diminished somewhat and the reviews were horrendous. *Variety*'s irked summation of *Conquest* was "There can be no permanent place or toleration of such cinematic blah."

3. Laemmle's legendary nepotism was thusly limned by Ogden Nash: "Uncle Carl Laemmle/Has a very large faemmle."

durance on the Mississippi, with vibrant characters and magnificent natural backdrops, was a sure thing for film, and Laemmle bought the rights for $65,000, tagging it as another Southern-set spectacle for Pollard. Days after Ferber sold the rights, she signed a more momentous contract with Broadway's master showman Florenz Ziegfeld. The result was the Jerome Kern/Oscar Hammerstein II musical drama *Show Boat*, the outstanding musical of the decade and possibly the most significant and beloved show of all time. Even as Laemmle and Pollard were preparing their silent *Show Boat*, the musical had become Broadway's biggest hit. Uncle Carl calculated that by the time *Show Boat* was released, talking and singing pictures might be a going proposition, and the idea of a silent *Show Boat*, without "Ol' Man River" or "Can't Help Lovin' Dat Man," seemed terrifically unprepossessing. His options were to leave *Show Boat* as a silent, with a synchronized score and effects, or to postpone shooting until it could be made at least part-talkie, for which he could buy the musical rights from Ziegfeld. Or he could pretend to disregard the show and put in other songs.

The final plan involved all of these. *Show Boat* began filming as a silent in mid-July 1928, cast with non-singers—Laura La Plante, Joseph Schildkraut, Otis Harlan, Emily Fitzroy, Alma Rubens—and with a proviso that sound sequences might be added later. Around this same time Laemmle contacted Ziegfeld, who was either uninterested in selling the rights or asked too much money. Laemmle floated a trial balloon that Irving Berlin would write a theme song and possibly a special score for *Show Boat*, and when that fell through he turned to the enduringly shifty Billy Rose, who captured Laemmle's interest by offering a package of himself to write the lyrics for new *Show Boat* songs and Al Jolson to write the music. Jack Warner quickly said no to any possibilities regarding his most valuable player, and as Laemmle continued his search, *Show Boat* was put back into production. A number of dialogue scenes were added, as well as a few new songs and spirituals, some performed onscreen and others as synchronized accompaniment. When it was completed, a premiere was announced for sometime around New Year's, then Uncle Carl took a long look at it and knew that it would not play. The stage songs were by then an integral part of *Show Boat* and nothing less would be acceptable to the public. With renewed ardor Laemmle returned to Ziegfeld, and they signed a deal on January 17, 1929, probably (the amount has been variously stated) for $100,000 plus a share of the profits. Again *Show Boat* went back before the cameras, and its premiere was postponed indefinitely.

While the *Show Boat* business trudged on, other studios were also trying. United Artists tried for and missed first place in the fall of 1928, when producer Joseph Schenck signed Broadway's Harry Richman to star in an Irving Berlin musical, *Say It With Music*. Casting and other delays forced the project back many months, until it surfaced in 1930 as *Puttin' on the*

Ritz. After MGM, Paramount (otherwise known as the Famous-Lasky Corporation) was the industry's most efficiently run factory, with a massive contract roster. During most of the 1920s it operated on two fronts: a Hollywood lot and an East Coast studio in the Astoria section of Queens, across the 59th Street Bridge from Manhattan. Although it lacked a large back lot and some of the extended facilities of Hollywood studios, Astoria was ideal for films using New York locations, several major stars (including Valentino and Gloria Swanson) finding it particularly congenial to work a continent away from the interfering front office. The cost of running two large plants finally led Paramount to suspend its Eastern operation early in 1927, a decision to be rued in very short order. As sound began its approach, an easy access to audible stage talent seemed most desirable ("Broadway stars on film!"), and Astoria was reopened in the summer of 1928. Paramount began work on its first musical shorts with such New York performers as Eddie Cantor, Ruth Etting, and Borrah Minevitch and his all-harmonica orchestra, meanwhile contemplating several major projects. *Glorifying the American Girl* was chief among them. In 1926 Paramount paid Florenz Ziegfeld for the use of his name in an elaborate silent drama to bear his production slogan as its title and set to star Ruth Taylor and Ziegfeld graduate Louise Brooks. It was postponed after Paramount failed to develop a script to match the spectacular concept, reactivated with the arrival of sound, and shelved again when it was clear there was still nothing in the way of an adequate script. Next choice was *Burlesque,* from the hit play by George Manker Watters and Arthur Hopkins. This tale of a seedy alcoholic hoofer and his doormat partner had made Broadway stars out of Hal Skelly and young Barbara Stanwyck, and for all its corn carried gritty potency and ample musical possibilities. *Burlesque* was announced as Paramount's first all-talkie, to be directed by Victor Fleming in New York or on the coast with contractee Nancy Carroll costarring. The Skelly role was a stumper, and after Lee Tracy, Jack Oakie, and even Eddie Cantor were considered and rejected, *Burlesque* was postponed.

With its larger strategies continually delayed, Paramount proceeded with a far smaller Astoria musical. Along with its short subjects, the studio tried to dash off a musical feature, just to see if it could be done. Novelist Katherine Brush slung together a few story fragments with a cabaret background and specialties and appearances by dancers Ann Pennington, Bobbe Arnst, Pat Rooney Senior and Junior, and Tamara Geva; writer and monologist Donald Ogden Stewart; and also Fannie Brice, just returned from *My Man.* The ineffective result, generically entitled *Night Club,* was directed by tyro émigré Robert Florey, making an early stab at some of the visual resource for which he would later be commended. The embryonic circumstances gave him little chance for good work, and much of the footage turned out unusable. By the time *Night Club* was assembled into a quasi-coherent whole, it came to barely four reels: not enough for a feature, too much for a short subject, not quite a total loss, yet obviously not state-of-the-art talkie-making. After some months on the shelf it was released as the longest component of an all short-subject program, and the studio wisely limited its early bookings to cities well out of critical harm's way. If a film plays Minneapolis in early March 1929 and does not arrive in New York until late August, something's wrong. Critics were quick to recognize *Night Club* as the trial run it was, and like *Melody of Love* it was quickly passed over.[4]

Considering that it was Warners' earliest rival, Fox was unduly slow in formulating a musical response. With most of the studio forces marshalled to produce *In Old Arizona*, plans for a musical revue were laid aside until October 1928. *The Movietone Follies*, intended to showcase the talent on the Fox lot, was not a bad idea, except for the fact that neither director Marcel Silver nor anyone else knew how a filmed revue should work or how to make use of the limited musical talents of such players as Lois Moran, David Rollins, and Sue Carol. Gertrude Lawrence, who was also approached, wanted too much money. Filming was done under such secrecy that even the company's East Coast executives were kept in the dark, and it continued on and on into 1929.

With the bumbling and bungling fueling these films it's easier to comprehend how the professionalism behind *The Broadway Melody* propelled it to first place without undue fuss. Its first successor was something of an anomaly, made quickly and inexpensively to beat a better-known film to the screen, and in many ways not a conventional musical at all. With the delays on *Movietone Follies*, *Hearts in Dixie* became Fox's first musical by default. Earlier in 1928 MGM's King Vidor had announced plans to direct a drama with an all-black cast. It was a scheme no studio would have touched as a silent, but sound film, and the prospect of using the music ranging from spirituals to jazz, made the project extremely appealing. Vidor's film, *Hallelujah!*, would be many months in production and editing; seeing a window open, William Fox and production head Winfield Sheehan put into speedy work a similar drama with music. From first thoughts to premiere, *Hearts in Dixie* was one of the fastest jobs of the time. The cast was headed by Clarence Muse (replacing Charles Gilpin after shooting began) and Stepin Fetchit, né Lincoln Theodore Perry, who had recently completed roles in *Show Boat* and in Fox's *The Ghost Talks*. The musical performances were supplied by the Billbrew Choir, who had also participated in *Show Boat*. Unlike *Hallelujah!*, this was an in-California-only affair, the Fox ranch standing in for Kentucky. Rehearsals began at the end of November under

4. While *Night Club* per se is apparently lost, parts of it survive as a two-reel version called *Broadway Nights*, released in the early 1930s. No plot scenes remain—no great loss—and what's left is a succession of specialty numbers. Bobbe Arnst shimmies, the Rooneys do some eccentric tap, and, memorably, Brice performs "I'm Sasha, the Passion of the Pasha."

director and co-scenarist Paul Sloane, shooting was completed by mid-January, and Fox rushed it into theaters by the last week of February, while *Hallelujah!* was still being filmed.

Hearts in Dixie is seldom mentioned today, save by those who know only of its cloying title and of the notorious presence of Stepin Fetchit. Assumed to be a blatantly nostalgic tribute to pre-Civil War slavery, it's actually set after the war, among free people, and the unavoidable comparisons with *Hallelujah!* are not entirely invidious. Despite its flaws, Vidor's film is an authentic folk epic, an outsider's sincere attempt to distill the essence of a people and a culture. *Hearts in Dixie*, aiming less high, lacks a certain degree of pretentiousness. It's less a conventional narrative than a series of mood-piece incidents centering on the theme of family solidarity in the face of change—a humble predecessor, perhaps, to *Meet Me in St. Louis*. The central character is the patriarch Nappus (Muse), and the music sets off several major episodes: Nappus's oldest daughter dies because he relies on superstition and waits too long to seek medical help; his lazy son-in-law (Fetchit) remarries a woman who puts fear and a little pep into him; over everyone's objections, Nappus sells everything he owns to send his young son north to be educated.

Charges of condescension and racial insensitivity can't be ignored. Yet, Stepin Fetchit aside, *Hearts in Dixie* attempts to offer a positive portrait. Yes, it's impossible not to squirm in discomfort at the tendency to show the characters as charmingly quaint and simple. But this is 1929, the year of such horrors as Paramount's *Why Bring That Up?*, with a blackface duo billed as "The Two Black Crows," and next to such atrocity the basic good intentions of *Hearts in Dixie* are most apparent. Stepin Fetchit shuffles out of range long enough to put most of the focus on the intelligent and infinitely dignified Clarence Muse, and with him, as with most of the other actors, there's none of the painful self- and mike-consciousness rampant in early talkies. *Hearts in Dixie* is perhaps the most *physical* film of its day, with speech and gesture giving gradual and natural way to song and dance, and the lack of conventional musical structure is superseded by a far more compelling conviction that music can carry greater meaning for its people than speech. King Vidor's similar efforts in *Hallelujah!* were somewhat compromised by the slickness of the Irving Berlin songs foisted upon him. In *Hearts in Dixie* the musical program is traditional and homespun—spirituals, "Lil' Liza Jane" and the like—and performed with an exuberance nonexistent in musical comedies and operettas of the time. Even Fetchit's character, unfortunately and aptly named Gummy, comes alive when he dances. Sloane also used the superior Movietone process to advantage in many outdoor scenes, in an attempt at sound montage as wagonloads of people sing their way to a party, and to create an eerie mood for the scene of Nappus's ailing daughter being attended by the Hoodoo Woman. With a screech owl as her noisy familiar, the Hoodoo Woman (A. C. H. Billbrew) moans, prays, and carries on in an *agitato* style unlike anything in the early sound era. The final scene of Nappus's farewell to his son is made especially poignant by Sloane's eloquent juxtaposition of image and sound.

Without Stepin Fetchit, it's easier to see all the good, if patronizing, intentions and achievements of Sloane and his cast. But Fetchit is too conspicuous a presence to be ignored and is so against the grain of the other actors that he seems incapable of interacting with them, content instead to loll in his own incarnation of the ultimate stereotype. Renewed interest in Fetchit since his death has prompted a revisionist view that his self-created role was subversive, not subservient, that he was actually mocking a oppressive white culture by expanding on its prejudices in the most garish fashion imaginable. Possibly so, probably not. A clever and shrewd comedian, he knew what made the majority of spectators happy and received the lion's share of the good notices for *Hearts in Dixie*. He parlayed his success into a long-term contract with Fox—the first black performer to sign a deal with a major studio—and in his own way was a pioneer and innovator, so although it's impossible to watch him without cringing, he should not, for better and worse, be ignored.

Racial concerns of a different sort prompted Fox to open *Hearts in Dixie* with an absurd prologue better suited to an ethnographic documentary. A solemn white emcee informs the audience that it will now behold "the joys and sorrows of other people. . . . Our skins vary in color . . . but we both laugh when we're happy." Even in 1929 this kind of garbage was treated derisively, *Variety* noting that "Balconies are liable to razz it." Some exhibitors did express fear about spectator reaction to the racial content; though, billed as "The William Fox All Talking, Singing and Dancing Novelty," *Hearts in Dixie* ultimately drew sizable crowds and positive reviews around the country.

The next musical to reach the screen, *Syncopation*, was more significant in its background than its achievement. In 1927 Joseph P. Kennedy, then in the would-be movie mogul phase of his colorful career, assumed control of FBO, a moderately successful independent film company. In October 1928 he joined with David Sarnoff of RCA to contrive a large merger in which FBO was joined with the Keith-Albee-Orpheum chain of vaudeville theaters (in which Kennedy also held major interest) to form a major subsidiary of RCA. The new company was dubbed the Radio-Keith-Orpheum Corporation, Radio for short and presently RKO-Radio, and it would produce sound films using RCA's Photophone process. A major studio, with its own technology and chain of theaters, had been created almost overnight. Kennedy then bowed out with an ample profit, and the new studio began to seek its bearings. FBO, which normally specialized in lower-case genre items, had resolved prior to the merger to take the plunge with a musical comedy. After the deal this production, *Syncopation*, would be the first to bear Radio's new trademark. Designed as a vehicle for Fred Waring and his Pennsylvanians, the country's most popular musical group after Paul Whiteman's band, *Syncopation* was shot in New York in late December and early January 1928–29, not at Astoria but at the smaller FBO/Pathé studio in Harlem. It was only the third sound feature filmed in the East (after Paramount's *The Letter* and *Hole in the Wall*, and not counting the abortive *Night Club*), which enabled FBO's Hollywood facility to undergo a technical overhaul. Director Bert Glennon, formerly and afterward an expert cameraman, brought it in quickly and cheaply, and the new company's publicity department did the rest. "THE BIRTH OF A TITAN," read exultant ads for Radio Pictures, which were "Dedicated to the advancement of electrical entertainment." The company's first great picture of the 1929–30 season, the ads asserted, would be another musical, *Rio Rita*. In the meantime there was *Syncopation*, opening in late March.

Had it been released a couple of months later, or without intensive ballyhoo, *Syncopation* would have come and gone without a peep. The production values were dowdy, the songs undistinguished, and Gene Markey's story was ordinary and derivative. Based on Markey's novel *Stepping High*, it told of a husband/wife dance team (Barbara Bennett and Bobby Watson) who succeed in a nightclub revue, break up, and later reunite. The weak casting was no help. Bennett lacked the appeal of her sisters Constance and Joan, and Watson was no one's idea of an audience-pleasing romantic lead.[5] Waring and the Pennsylvanians, for all their star billing, were merely incidental participants, playing a few numbers in nightclub scenes. A bigger impression was made by tenor Morton Downey, as a wisecracking song plugger, with good comic lines and warm vocalizing. Opposite him was Dorothy Lee, a teenager from California who had to go to New York to break into movies. Radio was so pleased with her that she was signed for *Rio Rita*, ultimately to a long-term contract. Also in the cast were stage actors Osgood Perkins, Verree Teasdale, and McKenzie Ward, the latter playing what *Variety* termed "a nance interior decorator."

The attention and profits attracted by this film become comprehensible only when the RKO publicity team and corporate identity are taken into consideration. Between its high-powered parent RCA and the ready-made conduit of the theater chain, *Syncopation* was built to win. Waring and Downey plugged the songs on the radio incessantly, and the release plan was

5. Before the film opened, Bennett married another performer in *Syncopation*, Morton Downey; the union produced Morton Jr., the infamously confrontational talk show host. Watson's main film success was in the 1940s, when the appropriate haircut and mustache made him a dead ringer for Hitler, thus much in demand for a number of wartime efforts. His own tribute to the coming of sound came with his role in *Singin' in the Rain* as the voice coach whose studio is demolished by Gene Kelly and Donald O'Connor.

timed to coincide in most places with *Broadway Melody*, for which it served as a lively if far inferior competitor. RKO went so far as to set up traveling *Syncopation* units à la vaudeville, lugging in prints and portable sound equipment to play in unwired houses in smaller towns. If that weren't enough, multimedia events were concocted in which the entire film was broadcast over the radio in selected cities, apparently a first for a talking feature. Such stunts made the country *Syncopation*-conscious, and this minor and forgotten film did much to abet the public's emerging awareness of musicals.

Paramount finally got through a musical production just after *Syncopation*. It was typical of the era that the studio's first effort was not one of its heavily publicized projects but a small film produced quietly on the West Coast. Again based on a Gene Markey story, this time in collaboration with Elsie Janis, it had a grabber of a title: *Close Harmony*. Janis injected some of her own experiences into this tale, more anecdote than story, of a savvy vaudevillian who helps and eventually falls in love with a struggling bandleader. Its saving graces were a total lack of pretension, some believable conflict (vaudevillian is suspected of sleeping around to advance herself), and the bull's-eye casting of Buddy Rogers and Nancy Carroll, who became key players in the new musical boom.

Nancy Carroll was a talented performer and an interestingly complicated person. A two-fisted redhead from a tough New York neighborhood, she had gone on the stage in her teens to middling results, then moved to California. Her Irish-sweetheart beauty attracted numerous screen tests, and after signing with Paramount she rose to quick prominence in the title role of *Abie's Irish Rose*. By late 1928 she was the studio's major comer and a clear threat to Clara Bow. Her sound debut had been in a song sequence added to *Abie* for its general release, and she consolidated that success by starring with Gary Cooper in another part-talkie, *The Shopworn Angel*, where she scored with a tough-tender rendition of "Precious Little Thing Called Love." With musicals coming in Carroll was a natural, her acting ability and charm more than compensating for limitations in song and dance. That she was driven and temperamental was not evident onscreen; for 1929 audiences she was aces, a sexy valentine for the waning days of the Jazz Age. Charles "Buddy" Rogers was even bigger at Paramount than Carroll, his fame coming with a lead in the hit *Wings* and as Mary Pickford's leading man (later, real-life husband) in *My Best Girl*. His nickname, "America's Boyfriend," was apt: unthreateningly cute and dimpled, the beau every mother wanted for her daughter, with a slight sweet singing voice and a way with a trombone. While it was a persona perilously close to male ingenue, Rogers's guileless sincerity was authentic and his oh-gosh appeal considerable. His teaming with Carroll made for potent chemistry; they looked smashing together, and the role-reversal aspects were tantalizing. She was the experienced one, he the innocent who learns about life and love.

Since the Carroll-Rogers dynamic was central to *Close Harmony*, it's curious that it had originally been cast with Ruth Taylor (Lorelei in Paramount's silent *Gentlemen Prefer Blondes*), who Carroll replaced just a few days before shooting began in early January. Richard Whiting and Leo Robin, gifted workhorses of Paramount's new music department, supplied four affably unpretentious songs, and the cast was rounded out by Jack Oakie and Skeets Gallagher as a vaudeville duo and dialect comic Harry Green as an apoplectic producer, with a young unknown Jean Harlow momentarily visible as a chorine. The studio often used a dual director system for its sound films, and on *Close Harmony* credit was shared by stage director John Cromwell, who staged the action and coached the dialogue, and Hollywood veteran Edward Sutherland, who attended to camera angles and other cinematic aspects. The pairing worked smoothly enough to bring in *Close Harmony* in a few weeks, and it was ready for release by the end of March.

Even today, as a piece of early-talkie hooey *Close Harmony* retains its appeal and off-the-cuff modesty. Unlike the more ambitious *Broadway Melody*, it's simply a sweet seventy-minute story about a boy and a girl and a band, everything done on a small scale. Rogers has a couple of songs with his band, Gallagher and Oakie do a comic novelty, Carroll prances with a few chorus girls. Cromwell and Sutherland keep it moving without undue lag, occasionally with some fluid camerawork, and save their biggest coup for the climax. After a dressing-room fight with Carroll, Rogers is stalked by a violent tracking shot as he tears onstage. As his band strikes up "Twelfth Street Rag" he pushes them harder and harder, finally shoving the band members aside one by one to play hot riffs on their instruments—cornet, trombone, piano, drums—and he sings, too. It's clearly calculated to bowl over the audience, and it works. Rogers and his character are both up there knocking themselves out, in undubbed live sound, and it's a whale of a moment. It resolves all the plot conflicts and incidentally ratifies Rogers's star status.

With its New York premiere delayed in favor of regional openings, *Close Harmony* was released, like *Syncopation*, in a pattern designed to parallel the general release of *The Broadway Melody* and to pilfer that film's business wherever possible. As the first musical film to open in a number of small towns, *Close Harmony* drew consistently large crowds and, more than *Syncopation*, good reviews. Carroll was already becoming a critic's pet, and Rogers's versatility wore down resistance to his pretty-boy aura. The radio broadcasts and promotional whatnot were not needed here. With sufficient substance to deliver on the promise of its stars and title, *Close Harmony* was a model commercial product for the spring of 1929.

Show Boat, in the meantime, had not yet docked. After Ziegfeld and Laemmle finalized their agreement, work started on transforming *Show Boat* into a quasi-musical movie. There was no thought of a wholesale reconversion to integrate large sections of the Kern-Hammerstein score. Instead, the centerpiece of the musicalization was that bane of the goat-gland era, a talking prologue, filmed on the Fox Movietone soundstage in New York. Ziegfeld introduced three members of the original Broadway cast (with chorus) in five songs: "C'mon Folks" and "Hey Feller" by Tess Gardella (billed, as always, as "Aunt Jemima"), "Ol' Man River" by Jules Bledsoe, and, memorably, Helen Morgan in "Bill" and "Can't Help Lovin' Dat Man." Back in California, A. B. Heath and Harry Pollard patched a couple of the stage songs into the film where they could, giving Laura La Plante dubbed renditions of "Ol' Man River" and "Can't Help Lovin' Dat Man" and using some of the music for the synchronized score. It was, in all, a big fish-nor-fowl paste-up, with a magic title that Laemmle proceeded to exploit with far more flair than anything he had put on the screen. Weeks earlier, he had served New York a clever hors d'oeuvre by importing a genuine showboat troupe, Norman F. Thom and the "Princess" Showboat Company, to perform barnstorming melodramas (one of them, *The Parson's Bride,* excerpted in *Show Boat*) on Broadway. Audiences cackled happily at Thom and his fellow incompetents for several weeks before the main event, which was something of an anticlimax.

Given all that had transpired no one should have been shocked that *Show Boat*'s premiere was an unconditional disaster. It had been set for Miami on March 15, 1929, with a follow-up opening at Palm Beach the next evening—Florida the choice because it was the end of the winter season and a large number of film moguls were there to mix with the socialites. Unfortunately, Miami's Capitol Theatre had been plagued by union strife for months, and it came to a head on premiere night. While fifteen hundred glittering attendees sat fuming, it was discovered that agitators had sabotaged the projectors. There was no movie, and following some impromptu entertainment by attendees Helen Morgan and W. C. Fields, the audience demanded a refund. The premiere defaulted to Palm Beach, and other regional galas preceded the New York opening on April 17. The critical consensus was that it was long (over two hours plus prologue and intermission), prettily photographed, had some effective moments, and in general was exceptionally tiresome. The dialogue scenes and Pollard's aversion to dynamic editing both drew harsh comment, and for New Yorkers, who had loved the stage show, it was particularly dreary. Nevertheless, the final box office returns for *Show Boat* were good, especially in smaller towns, where its title was magic and it could not be compared with its illustrious predecessor.

Show Boat survives in fragmentary form, in an unfortunate inverse of many Vitaphone films as a picture (in the shortened general-release version) without a sound track. The first half of the prologue has also resurfaced, fortunately with sound and picture. Despite the missing pieces, it's easy to see what a patchwork this *Show Boat* was. At the center of it is Harry Pollard's notion of pacing, which began and ended with a resolve to keep scenes going as long as possible. Most of the actors seem miscast, and with the dialogue gone it seems still more funereal. It's good to look at, more authentically so than the glossy 1951 version, yet this particular Ol' Man River rolls along without ever getting anywhere. The prologue is also not quite right. While it's good to have "creator" films of Gardella (she did not otherwise record "Hey, Feller!"), this tab-show preamble could only detract from the feature. After hearing Helen Morgan's Julie sing "Bill" with devastating poignancy, how could audiences be held by Alma Rubens's pantomime in the same role? The missed opportunities are self-evident, and perhaps if Laemmle had continued to spend money and time he would have had a major work. That he didn't, and let it be released as the hybrid it was, was typical of that studio, and generally of that era.

Meanwhile, back in the desert, April was drifting in, and Warner Bros. looked at its release schedule to find that it also had a Broadway adaptation ready to open. Nearly six months late, *The Desert Song* opened in Hollywood on April 8 and in New York on May 1, and even with the interminable delay Warners lucked out by the juxtaposition to *Show Boat*. Next to a this-and-that semi-version of a stage hit, here was a literal transcription of Broadway's most popular operetta with most of its score intact. Eager to discover how movies would represent operetta's rarefied exoticism, audiences formed long queues, finding few surprises other than a couple of genuine desert vistas in Technicolor plus the pleasant revelation that John Boles had a fine voice. The delayed release was particularly evident to critics, who quickly commented on how far cinema technique had come in the intervening months. The recording was already dated, and it was obvious that unreconstituted operetta could seem more than a mite ludicrous as viewed in tonsil-baring closeups. Mordaunt Hall of the *Times*, stuffy as ever, was at least precise:

> It is an interesting experiment but one wherein the story, even allowing for the peculiar license needed for such offerings, lays itself open to chuckles rather than sympathy or concern. . . .
>
> The characters . . . seem to seize upon song at inopportune moments, which fact might be very well on the stage but it is a weakness in a

picture, for it causes sudden fluctuation of moods, of the persons involved, and are conducive to merriment.

Less kind others noted that by and large this was only a movie in the sense that it had been printed on celluloid and was run through a projector. Yet the public, much of which had not seen a great deal of operetta, came in droves in America and abroad. The worldwide gross of *The Desert Song* tallied at just over $3 million, more than any Warner film to date save *The Singing Fool*. With such an enticing return on its investment, the studio immediately began to search for more operettas.

Warners got still more return on *The Desert Song* with remakes in 1943 and 1953.[6] The original, considered very much of an antique, was kept out of circulation for many years and finally presumed lost. Around 1970 a black and white copy was found in Jack Warner's personal vault, and, as it turned out, the critics and the public had both been right. Cinematically, *The Desert Song* is primitive nearly beyond contemplation. Roy Del Ruth did little more than re-create the play on the soundstage, aiming the camera at whoever happens to be talking or singing at the time. The photography is drab, the editing as four-square obvious as can be, and the divisions of acts and scenes rigidly observed. But the material is so floridly excessive that the crude technique is less a hindrance than a queerly apt complement, and the cast believes in every inane turn of the plot. The paralysis-infected actors of *Lights of New York* have been supplanted by a voracious pack of hams who clearly realize they're in a farfetched melodrama and make doubly sure the mike and camera don't miss a thing. John Boles, before he behaved so drearily in early-thirties soap operas such as *Back Street*, was a competent musical actor, and with his baritonal tenor and unshakably loony conviction he's completely credible as both the old-maidish milquetoast and the dashing Red Shadow. Opposite him, the Margot of Carlotta King is problematic and pallid, vocally adept but without the sense of abandon the character needs. She's especially dull alongside Myrna Loy, outrageously campy and invincibly magnetic as the ultimate half-caste vamp.[7] King, in comparison, is cardboard, standing there and flatly reciting lines. As some noted, the camerawork does nothing to enhance her not-unattractive looks, and she generally wakes up only when called on to ladle out her ample soprano. Suddenly, three-quarters of the way through, she

6. Neither remake used as much of the score as the 1929 version, and both had fascinatingly topical alterations factored in. The plot was massively overhauled in 1943 to make the Red Shadow lead the Riffs against the Nazis; lyrical patriotism sold very well during World War II. The patriotism had a more sour tinge in 1953. The plot was back to its original outline, but the Red Shadow was now called El Kodar. In the age of McCarthy, a hero could not be called a Red anything.

7. Her belligerent cries of "Vherre ees Piehrrre?" in the last reel are especially choice. In her memoirs Loy recalled how the role's impact became clear later on when people would approach her, squint biliously, and go into Azuri imitations.

is excitingly transformed when Margot grasps the Shadow's sword and gives vent, via the "Sabre Song," to her conflicted feelings about the two men in her life. It's Romberg and Freud in almost equal measure, and given a chance with a showcase aria King finally comprehends that song and drama can link. She slams through Romberg's roulades with force and comprehension, capping the performance with a potent high C that, coming over Vitaphone equipment, was a real stunner. Johnny Arthur, as the spineless society reporter Benny, is equally overwhelming. Benny is intended to make Pierre seem less effete by contrast—and oh, how Arthur succeeds, flaming brightly across the screen from Scene One onward, leering at passing soldiers and admonishing a Riff, pot to kettle, to not be "so effeminate." When the flirty Susan (Louise Fazenda) convinces him she's his ideal partner, there is removed the last shred of doubt that this show is, after all, a fantasy.

The Desert Song, then, is nothing like a masterpiece, though it does contain musical virtues lacking in some of its contemporaries. Its main importance is its indication of new directions such as the departure from the dominant backstage milieu. By April 1929 this seemed particularly welcome, for one specific precinct of the backstager had of late been attracting undue attention. The figures had been coming in on *The Singing Fool,* and, as expected, an array of Jolsonesque stories and performers began to turn up: Eddie Dowling, Morton Downey, that first-pick Jazz Singer George Jessel, even Maurice Chevalier. It was the most derivative trend of the age, the most limited, maybe the silliest, and likely the most outlandish; it will be covered separately in Chapter Six.

After the false start of *Night Club,* Paramount's East Coast plant had concentrated on dramas and short subjects. With *Glorifying the American Girl* put on hold, the studio began work on *The Cocoanuts* at the beginning of February. The 1925 musical comedy had attempted to spoof the Florida real estate furor, yet all such efforts were subsumed by the Marx Brothers, who made it an anarchic smash at the expense of the composer, Irving Berlin, and the writer, George S. Kaufman.[8] With verbal pandemonium and instrumental solos, the Marxes were ready candidates for talkies, and Paramount figured that *The Cocoanuts* would fit well as their group debut (Harpo had already appeared for the studio in a silent). Its being the first Broadway musical comedy adapted to the screen was not the primary factor, and became less so as time went by. The brothers had opened in *Animal Crackers* the previous October, and during the four-week shoot of *Cocoanuts* they and Margaret Dumont did double duty, at Astoria by day

8. Somewhat disappointingly for Berlin, his first "book" (plot) show produced no hits. This might have been otherwise had not Kaufman insisted on cutting one Berlin ballad prior to opening night. Its sentimentality, opined Kaufman, was incongruous with the satiric thrust of his script. The song was titled "Always."

and at the 44th Street Theatre at night. On Wednesdays, matinee day, shooting focused on the remaining players, all drawn from Broadway. Romantic leads Mary Eaton and Oscar Shaw had recently starred in *The Five O'Clock Girl*, and the glamorous villainess was Kay Francis, in her second film. The two-tier director arrangement enlisted Joseph Santley from the stage, with Robert Florey attending to the cinema end, and there were the usual microphone-induced nightmares. When a map clattered when Groucho handled it, Florey soaked it in water—and as such it can be seen on screen, noiseless and droopy. As filmed, it was a true musical comedy, with much of the stage score used, plus interpolations. By release time over forty minutes had been cut, mostly music, and retakes shifted the emphasis further away from Eaton and Shaw and the Gamby-Hale dancers onto the Marxes. More properly, onto three Marxes; Zeppo, as usual, was an adjunct. *Cocoanuts* opened at the end of May and was an immediate hit with audiences and critics. About all that anyone said about the musical aspects or the plot was that they intruded stodgily upon the comedy.

Because of Groucho and family, *The Cocoanuts* is probably the most frequently shown 1929 musical and thus generally assumed to be a typical specimen. That's not the case any more than *A Night at the Opera* is a standard musical from 1935. The Marxes were a self-contained law and, as Irving Berlin discovered, juxtaposing them with more decorous and lyrical matters provides off-kilter results. Groucho's Mr. Hammer (Schlemmer in the play) does not willingly suffer these musical fools any more than he respects Margaret Dumont's dignity, and so comedy takes the usual Marxist precedence over romance and music. Despite the terminal staginess, some of the team's best bits are here: the "Viaduct" routine, Groucho as auctioneer, Harpo in eternal satyric pursuit, and some well-timed hide-and-seek in and out of Kay Francis's hotel room. It's no pity that this occupies far more footage than the songs, although the excision of a song by Groucho ("A Little Bungalow") is cause for regret. But the visually oriented Florey did his best in the musical sequences with the ultra-limited means at his disposal. Considering the mobility problems, confining painted scenery, and routine dancing, he managed a few vivid touches—a dance scene run in negative as background for the opening credits, Mary Eaton and the dancers in the "Monkey Doodle Doo" number (a less-typical Berlin work) captured in both crane and low-angle shots. Later, a ballet troupe is introduced in overhead floral patterns long before the advent of Busby Berkeley. Other than the visuals and Frank Tours's punchy musical arrangements, the program is pretty barren, and except for "Monkey Doodle Doo" only a few shards remain from the original score. "When My Dreams Come True," a new Berlin number intended as the hit of the show, is a dreary and insipid thing, so far out of the league of the classic Berlin ballads (cf. the banished "Always") that not even Harpo's solos, including one on clarinet, make it inspiring. As for the singing lovers, Eaton is pretty and cool, while the stolid Oscar Shaw is apparently the oldest juvenile in the history of musical comedy and photographs like a slug.

Received more as comedy than musical, *The Cocoanuts* remained apart from several concurrent large-scale entries: another Universal blockbuster, *Broadway*; Fox's long-delayed *Movietone Follies of 1929*; and Warners' all-Technicolor *On With the Show*. All these opened within a few days of each other. The momentum was escalating.

Broadway was another result of Carl Laemmle's quest for class and coin. The smash 1927 melodrama by Philip Dunning and George Abbott seemed to condense all the dark brash myths about Prohibition into one parcel confined entirely to the backstage area of a seedy nightclub. The ambitious hoofer, sweet chorine, ruthless lech of a gangster, smart police detective, and vengeful moll all spout dialogue couched in the most colorful and evocative slang possible this side of decency. Laemmle outbid his competitors with an astronomical $225,000 for the rights and assigned his newest producer, Carl Laemmle Jr., to oversee another spectacular silent drama. As with *Show Boat*, these plans soon required speedy revision, the time factor in this case permitting *Broadway* to be shot in both all-talking and silent versions. For the former, as might be expected, the urge was not resisted to move out onto the nightclub stage and add a healthy dose of song and dance. Laemmle, who had to pay an extra $25,000 for dialogue rights, carried over most of the stage sides verbatim and quickly cast studio regular Glenn Tryon as the hoofer. Betty Bronson was originally mentioned for the part of the chorine, then, near the last minute, the role was filled by Merna Kennedy, who had fared adequately opposite Chaplin in *The Circus* and declined a rematch with him in *City Lights*. The choice for director was notably provocative. Dr. Paul Fejos (as he was often billed) was a remarkable character, surely one of the few people in history to juggle the careers of film director and bacteriologist. After directing a few films in his native Hungary, Fejos came to America in the mid-twenties and practiced his other trade for a time. When he began to dabble in film again his work came to Laemmle's attention, and he was signed to a contract. His direction of the part-talkie *Lonesome* was highly praised, and as a reward he was assigned *Broadway*.

Fejos immediately proceeded to put an indelible imprint on this combination backstage musical and gangster melodrama. The keynote of his concept, he reckoned, was tempo, which had given the play its glittery vitality. This obviously could be a major problem for a film shot in late 1928–early 1929, yet Fejos was not deterred from pushing on ambitiously. His vision transformed the Paradise Club from a seedy dive to a staggeringly grandiose Art Deco monument, and the nightclub set, designed by Charles Hall, was far larger than anything in talkies thus far. The tempo entered in with the true star of the production—a fantastic camera crane, devised by Fejos and camera wizard Hal Mohr, the likes of which no one had ever seen. Based partly on the same principles as fire-truck ladders, it offered unprecedented flexibility and speed and enabled Mohr's camera to prowl the huge set at will, swooping up and down to catch actors or architectural detail. Fejos' calibrations were so precise that the crane could change direction in midair, stop on a dime, and in general do everything short of serving tea to the cast. The price tag for this technological wonder was about $50,000, which must have made Uncle Carl choke.[9]

Broadway was kept in reserve until after *Show Boat* was well into release. Then in May 1929 it was sent out amid reams of publicity centering on its celebrated source, musical sequences, and million-dollar cost. The reviews, while better than those for *Show Boat*, were hardly in the rave category. It was the same complaint, over and over. The play had been imitated and stolen from so much (*Lights of New York*, on up) that after as little as two years it seemed stale. Also, and more to the point, Fejos's powerful visuals, and that crane, became its true centerpiece. The cast, the music and dance, the play itself, became secondary to those spellbinding images. Making the nightclub so huge seemed too Hollywood a thing to do. It was no one's idea of Dunning and Abbott's shabby Paradise Club, and the *Billboard* critic compared Fejos's nightclub to the Cathedral of St. John the Divine. The actors also suffered in comparison with their predecessors, especially Glenn Tryon, an agreeable light comedian who lacked the tangy incisiveness Lee Tracy brought to the part onstage. Merna Kennedy fared poorer still, and what kudos there were went to Evelyn Brent as the moll and Thomas E. Jackson, repeating his stage role as the detective. It was correctly predicted that the title and the surefire melodrama would carry the day for most spectators, as indeed they did, along with the highly touted musical sequences; *Broadway* ultimately attracted enough viewers to make back its great cost.

Broadway is a fascinating film and a schizophrenic one. On the one hand there's a play, with museum-quality twenties underworld dialogue and a formula revenge plot. All hands, except Merna Kennedy's eternally simpering "good girl," seem ponderously compelled to turn every exchange into a slangfest.[10] This is all juxtaposed, most jarringly, with a dynamically bizarre and totally unrelated visual meditation by Paul Fejos, a piece of film

9. Some reports listed a higher cost; in any case it's equivalent to well over a million today, and Universal redeemed its investment in publicity. Photos were issued of the crane, proudly emblazoned with logos for the studio and *Broadway*.

10. "Cut 'em deep and let 'em bleed!" is probably the most arresting moment of dialogue. (Translated, it's Tryon's exhortation to the chorus to go out and give it all they've got.) Another good one is a fellow chorine's take on Kennedy: "If I ever seen a professional virgin, she's it!"

Lining up a shot for *Broadway*, with the two real stars of the production well in evidence: the celebrated 28-ton camera crane, and a portion of Charles Hall's Paradise Club set. Atop the crane are its designers, director Paul Fejos and cinematographer Hal Mohr, and their assistants. *Photofest.*

that might be titled *New York Nocturne*. It certainly is not *Broadway*, the play that it parallels and eventually inundates. Fejos opens his fantasia on a meticulously detailed model of Times Square, which is set upon by a half-naked leering giant who finally rouses the city into debauched life. A startling and stimulating metaphor for Prohibition-age iniquity, it bears minimal relation to the characters who come on presently. The technique is quiet for a couple of reels, then when the club comes alive so does the camera crane. As Glenn Tryon and the chorus come out and begin to sing "Hittin' the Ceiling," the crane takes its cue from the song and blasts off. It occurs time and again: whenever a musical number starts, Fejos will inevitably cut away from the performers and play with the camera. One can only admire the capabilities of the crane as it sweeps and swirls about that incredible set, yet the virtuosity is ultimately empty. Like the opening sequence, it has no real connection to the plot and characters, and the necessity to shoot the crane shots silent and add the sound later gives them a disembodied quality which contrasts weirdly with the backstage scenes, which are shot with a chained-down camera and droning voices.

Visual virtuosity is on one end of *Broadway*, audible histrionics are on the other, and in between is a limbo dumping ground for the musical numbers. The songs are presented apologetically and staged perfunctorily, and the performers are nil. The voice dubbing for Tryon and Kennedy is so poor that Fejos's constant cutaways to his crane are a relief. Musical aspects come to the fore only after the plot is resolved, but the finale, a Technicolor production number, is now missing and presumed lost.[11] So *Broadway*, as it survives, is less a musical than ever. Its greater importance, then as now, is as a one-of-a-kind transitional piece, an uncommonly baroque hybrid.

Opening concurrently with *Broadway* was the long-delayed and far less florid *Fox Movietone Follies of 1929*. Contrary to its title and historical report, the *Follies* was not the first of the all-star revue films, for it was neither star-laden nor quite a revue.[12] Once again the background seems to offer greater interest than what was put on the screen—"seems" being the operative word, for this is another lost film for which surviving reports must suffice. Like *Night Club* and *Glorifying the American Girl*, it had started out, back in October 1928, as another candidate for "The Screen's First Musical Comedy," shot in great secrecy and at interminable length. Jackie Cooper, who made his feature film debut in a bit in one of the musical numbers, has recalled the great tension on the set, much of it likely due to the uncertainty of intention. When completed late in the winter, it seemed to have no cause to exist, being a plotless procession of unrelated sequences with little style and less consistency. Back to square one, as Fox writers quickly devised a plot to stuff around and between the songs, and director David Butler shot it in March. It was, no surprise, another backstage story, "appropriated" from George S. Kaufman's play *The Butter & Egg Man*, about a young Virginian (John Breeden) who sells his plantation to buy a failing revue featuring his sweetheart (Lola Lane). While a vamp (Sharon Lynn) and some creditors run interference, the show is turned into a hit with an assist from a rather meager array of Fox talent. To make room for so masterfully contrived a story, many of Marcel Silver's revue scenes were excised, and among the performers left in the cold were Robert Benchley, Lois Moran, and Dorothy Jordan.[13] By early May, when it was all pasted

11. The number centered around a title song performed by Tryon and the chorus. It's tempting to speculate how color might have combined with the moving camera and that set, which allegedly required a two hundred-electrician crew for the finale. A few frames of test film exist to show, impressively, how Fejos's grandiose nightclub looked in color.

12. According to its self-promoting title, the star billing goes to the studio and the technical process. The copyrighted title was still more upfront—*William Fox Movietone Follies of 1929*. Most of the advertising dropped Fox's first name.

13. Waste not, want not: months later, Fox exhumed the Moran and Jordan numbers and spliced them into a paltry college musical titled *Words and Music*, notable only because the second lead was played by Duke Morrison—a very young John Wayne.

together, the cost had reportedly ascended to the lofty region of $750,000, and with such an investment Fox hyped it ferociously. Despite this and its showcase presentation at the Roxy Theatre, critics and exhibitors felt let down. Two ingredients had been slighted—substance and showmanship. The numbers were not good enough to stand on their own, and the story was too thin to carry them. It lacked the drama and score of *Broadway Melody*, the spectacle of *Broadway*, the charm of *Close Harmony*. Except for Sue Carol's success with a dance-craze song titled "The Breakaway" and Stepin Fetchit's comedy and dance stint, everything seemed flat. Using trick photography on an energetic group of black singer-dancers performing "Walking With Susie" seemed so-what, and "Pearl of Old Japan," a faux-undersea ballet in Multicolor, was insufficiently dazzling. Notwithstanding the letdown, and aided by the popularity of "Breakaway," the *Follies* made money, especially in the smaller towns where its novelty was still pronounced. Yet it was clear that such an uninspired outing did the new medium little good.

Another mistimed aspect of the *Follies* concerned William Fox's ongoing fascination with film technology. Searching for a new front after launching Movietone, he turned up something literally bigger than sound. Engineer A. E. Sponable, who had worked with Theodore Case on Movietone, created a film strip seventy millimeters in width, yielding an image twice as wide as usual. Christened "Grandeur," this was the direct parent of the widescreen processes of the 1950s, Cinemascope and the rest. Its outsized proportions and startling shape were excitingly innovative, plus it sounded better than other talkies due to its soundtrack also being twice as wide, imparting far greater clarity and fidelity. Grandeur's maiden voyage was the *Movietone Follies*, which had been shot both in normal ratio and on the new wide film. Technical complications held up the unveiling of the Grandeur *Follies* until September 1929, when it was rerun in New York. While few were amused to return to a movie that had not been great the first time, a fair amount of the curious did turn out for The New Improved *Follies* In Grandeur. But Fox's timing had been terrible. Theater owners, just finishing with the expense and trouble of installing sound, would be required to put in new projectors, speakers, and screens, and not even large theaters cared to consider it yet. Grandeur bade its time for a few more months.

For showmanship of more viable stripe, a return to Warner Bros. is required. As 1929 began, the studio returned from its hiatus renewed and with music on its mind. The first films put into production in the new year were the Sophie Tucker vehicle *Honky Tonk* (covered in Chapter Six) and an easygoing comedy with songs based on the old stage musical *The Time, the Place, and the Girl*. More ambitious plans were in the offing a few weeks later with Warners' answer to *The Broadway Melody: Shoestring*, from an unproduced play by Humphrey Pearson in which an underfinanced show trying out on the road reaches make-or-break status on opening night in Newark. The performance goes on as the producer fights off creditors and stalls an unpaid cast, and there is a box office theft, a no-pay/no-play star, a gaggle of bickering costars, and a hat-check girl who goes on successfully in place of the balky diva. This was as much backstage as a plot could attain, and with Vitaphone's profits rolling in Warners had begun to raise film budgets above its own shoestring. At just under half a million this was the company's biggest project since *Noah's Ark*, its largest splurge and biggest gamble being the decision to use Technicolor throughout, which reportedly accounted for nearly half the total cost. The response to "The Wedding of the Painted Doll" having been forecast even before *Broadway Melody* opened, Warners signed contracts with the Technicolor Company for first access to the improved single-strip process. While there were still no blue tints, the spectrum was somewhat wider, the hues stronger, and the images sharper and better-focused. With a working title of *Broadway or Bust*, it went into production in February under Alan Crosland, directing his first Warner effort since *Glorious Betsy*. Grant Clark and Harry Akst were enlisted to create the songs for the show-within-a-show, *The Phantom Sweetheart*, and the cast was marshalled from notably nonmusical talent—Betty Compson, Sally O' Neil, Arthur Lake, William Bakewell, Louise Fazenda, Sam Hardy—with two major supplements. Joe E. Brown, an ex-acrobat and vaudevillian who had starred on Broadway, entered movies in 1928. His trademark was a mouth wide enough to span several counties; there was also a vast repertoire of whines and grimaces, a vital affinity for slapstick, and a way with rubber-legged dancing. A sure bet for sound comedy, he would soon become Warners' preeminent clown. Ethel Waters's mark on show business had come in black vaudeville, recordings, and nightclub revues. For this, her film debut, she was hired only as a specialty, playing herself and singing two songs. It was enough.

By the time shooting ended in April the title had been changed to *On With the Show!*[14] For once Warners timed it right, speeding up postproduction for a New York opening just four weeks after *The Desert Song*. The ads left no doubt as to the prime selling point: "Now COLOR Takes the Screen!" This, it was alleged, was the closest possible equivalent to a live theatrical experience—"real life," whatever that is, could not be simulated any closer. In the event, the color was received with qualified rapture, more than the film as a whole, and it gave Mordaunt Hall a new angle from which to revile his bête noire, uncouth backstage dialogue: "One imagines the lovely hues writhing in agony upon being called on to decorate such a story." If the public listened, or if it had started to notice that four out of

14. The exclamation point came and went. It appears in the credits on the main title, although most of the advertising leaves it out. Somehow, given the tenor of the time, it seems warranted.

five talkies seemed to be backstage musicals, the diversions of *On With the Show!* were sufficient to overcome the objections. In some towns the take exceeded that of *The Broadway Melody*, and a final worldwide tally of $2.4 million seemed to indicate, powerfully, that audiences wanted more musicals and more color.

On With the Show! has passed into legend for right and wrong reasons, the former being that it was the first all-color all-talkie and Ethel Waters introduced the hit song "Am I Blue?" A later Warner backstage musical is the axis for the misconceptions, for it has been alleged by some apparently not knowing either film that *On With the Show!* was remade as *42nd Street.* Wrong, for all they share is the plot device of a sweetly talented unknown replacing a less worthy star. The *Movietone Follies* had already engaged the same gambit, and so, in a way, did *On With the Show!* itself, in an earlier scene of the producer (Sam Hardy) ineptly going on after an actor has suddenly fainted. *42nd Street,* with its nifty musical numbers and Depression-era verve, makes *On With the Show!* resemble a relic from the Bronze Age. It has consequently acquired the aura of a turkey, which it is not. Primitive and often unpolished, it does contain a share of clever ideas and worthy features. The primary one, and it can no longer be savored, is the color. The dim black and white prints that survive offer only anemic echoes of what audiences saw, for apparently the color design was both tasteful and vibrant.[15] There do remain a number of strikingly composed shots, and Crosland, with his strong visual bent, moves the camera as much as he can to give the backstage scenes a sense of hectic bustle, crosscutting them cleverly with the song numbers to show the mechanics bolstering the onstage festivities.

The loss of color throws a less forgiving light on the script. With Pearson's material as an adequate foundation, scenarist Robert Lord devised a valid structure in which the frivolous show onstage could be followed as the various behind-the-scene crises enfold. Unfortunately, the dialogue, not the musical numbers, supplies the most hapless contrast to *42nd Street.* These heavily expository, supposedly breezy one-liners are rancid to the point that the adept Brown and Fazenda are completely thwarted, and *Photoplay* could report accurately that "The conversation consists of snappy comebacks, 1910 variety." Bad as it is, the dialogue becomes even duller when spoken by Sally O'Neil, cast as the hopeful young Kitty on the basis of her fame in silent pictures and pert Irish looks. It's an appalling performance, one of the very worst of the era. The only compensation is her pleasant appearance, and indeed Crosland's camera is fond of ogling her

---

15. By all accounts, the color was far more vivid and clear than anything yet seen. When a taxicab drove across the screen in the first scene, the premiere audience burst into applause at seeing yellow rendered accurately. Less well received was the excessive quantity of henna used on Louise Fazenda's hair; her scarlet frizz tended to dominate all her scenes.

Yes, it's Ethel Waters, singing "Am I Blue?" in *On With the Show!* with the Harmony Emperors Quartet. The costume is by Earl Luick; the sizzle is by Waters. *Photofest.*

round little bottom, nicely encased in usherette trousers. The acrid Bayonne accent, the misinflected line readings, the metallic Vitaphone recording—it's akin to being bludgeoned by a cast-iron Kewpie doll. Between the script and the uneven cast, there is no central axis other than the show itself. Arthur Lake whines fulsomely as *Sweetheart*'s juvenile lead, and William Bakewell (as Kitty's boyfriend) and Sam Hardy are defeated by their lines. Betty Compson fares better as the aging beauty Nita, stylishly exuding attitude and crackle until deciding, with rueful grace, to retire. Compson gives the script more than it warrants when Nita muses about the ironies of a business that washes you up by the time you're thirty.

With the problems in script and cast of *On With the Show!*, much of the merit passes onto the music, presented entirely in the onstage context of *The Phantom Sweetheart*. Unlike the revues that form the backdrop for most backstage films, it's a conventional book show, some nonsense about a young Southerner who returns to his plantation to be married and is lured from his fiancée by a mysterious veiled beauty. For all its silliness it's oddly charming, an example of pop twenties musical comedy genuine enough to pass for the real thing instead of a movieland pastiche. The kickline choruses, dance specialties, comedy relief, ballads and ensemble numbers are all here in pristine form. Crosland and dance director Larry Ceballos present them as filmed theater, yet with spirit and verve and a sense of fun. Aside from the smashing "Am I Blue?," Akst and Clarke's score suits the occasion acceptably, with big choral pieces (including the sublimely idiotic "Lift the Juleps to Your Two Lips"), an attractive ballad ("Let Me Have My Dreams"), and a Ziegfeldian dream sequence called "In the Land of Let's Pretend," complete with a showgirl parade down a staircase.[16] The dances seem equally authentic, with a comic-drunk solo for Brown, a fox-hunt ballet with hobby horses, and a couple of terrific appearances by the mixed-double black tap group, the Four Covans. Best of all, there's a treasurable contribution by one of the greatest American singers. Ethel Waters has only the briefest opportunity to interact with the white performers on or off stage, and given a greater chance she would have stolen the film even more than she does with her two songs. With a persona far removed from her later incarnation of revival-meeting earth-grandmother, she's slim and cheeky, the same Waters who earned early fame as "Sweet Mama Stringbean." For "Am I Blue?" she's done up as a peculiarly chic cotton-picker, belting torchy and hot. After an absence of over an hour, she returns in high style for "Birmingham Bertha." Cotton field and headrag have been swapped for an urban street and flapper feathers as Waters invades Chicago to reclaim her man. Snarling and purring, mugging her way through Clarke's lyrics, she projects more musical authority than anyone since Jolson. The briefness of her appearance is as regrettable as the fact that her film work was so sparse. In general, *On With the Show!* is an engaging and significant antique; Ethel Waters's participation ensures that for just a moment it becomes the celebration of one person's art.

On With the Show! is the Janus of the earliest musicals, with its writing and other incompetencies looking back to the earlier days of Vitaphone and Jolson, its absorption in backstage life remembering that of *The Broadway Melody*. At the same time, its own influence echoed over the years to *42nd Street* and beyond. With some success and some technical assurance, it attempted to render musical comedy in motion picture terms, a documentary context that discloses just how that *Phantom Sweetheart* is made to happen. The use of Technicolor was also progressive in its confident expansion on

16. Betty Compson performs the latter two in an attractive dubbed soprano which has been credited, possibly erroneously, to Josephine Houston. Houston appears in the film as Arthur Lake's sweetheart—a part originally slated for Carlotta King—and while she possibly did double duty, it doesn't sound like the same voice. Sally O'Neil also has a dubbed go at "Let Me Have My Dreams," seemingly with the same voice that Compson used. The contrast is amusing—the ghost singer's smooth tone and cultured diction is pitted against O'Neil's speaking voice, which seems made of molten tin. Don't, by the way, attempt to take dictation from the vocal choruses, as recorded in performance by a line of mikes in the orchestra pit. The mikes don't favor multiple voices at all, so only about one word in twelve is comprehensible.

earlier works, the makers' strengths and failures are all available for viewer inspection. Though neither it nor the other films in this chapter touched all the bases in as persuasive a fashion as *The Broadway Melody*, their newness ensured their popularity and influence. As a result, the tropes became increasingly standardized. *On With the Show!*, for example, should have been the culmination of backstage movies, not the gateway to more. Its good ideas and technique, not subject matter, are what the imitators would have been wisest to emulate. And some of them did. Over the next months, as the technique continued to develop, the smart ones expanded on content as well. There was an entire musical world waiting to be revealed and an eager public awaiting Hollywood's next steps. These first films had indicated the possibilities as well as the pitfalls, and in the summer of 1929 Hollywood geared up to deliver even more.

CHAPTER 5

Finding a Voice

Open season had officially started, with no rules. The frenzy and clamor made it immensely convenient for most of the studios to plow ahead without looking. So many factors to heed, so little time, so many shortcuts and, as ought to be expected, such frightfully mixed results. Often as not, the final product made it clear that the new and unfamiliar demands led films to be conceived in panic and manufactured in ignorance. In the beginning, about all they had was enthusiasm and microphones, backed up by a modicum of intuition and an avid yen for profits. Every other component, personnel and matériel alike, had to be built or bought or hauled in or finessed or fudged. A human avalanche, an epic influx of new people invaded the film industry, mostly from the stage—from Broadway and vaudeville and burlesque and stock companies and puppet shows and Lord knows where else. But the talent turnover was not entirely an outsider job, for a surprising amount came from within the industry. Some veterans revealed unanticipated lyrical gifts before and behind the cameras.

The production of musical films has always encompassed a sizable number of technical and aesthetic components. This was never more valid than with early musicals, in whose aspects audacity and insecurity, panache and ineptitude, resourcefulness and mediocrity were all incorporated. To synthesize all the elements, locate the ground where film and stage needed to meet, was an ongoing challenge met with many solutions. The variables included the property at hand, the creativity of those involved, the available resources. Some of the films were in fact assembled of fairly sturdy stuff. In slow steps, not always aware of what they were doing, the filmmakers inched toward a viable balance, and examining the elements helps make the films more accessible.

I

SOUNDS: MUSIC, LYRICS, TECHNOLOGY

Theme Songs

Music was always first. Long before sound came, song and film had been linked to form a prosperous side industry nicely tailored to a mutually beneficial end: the song channeled attention to the film, which could then plug the song. The phenomenon originated in the mid-teens with a less clearcut intent. The emerging star system prompted songwriters and publishers to market their wares by dedicating them to an established player to whom a song might or might not have any connection. Charlie Chaplin, Fatty Arbuckle, Theda Bara, and Mary Pickford were among the many faces on sheet music covers. As the songs sold, producers slowly began to notice how the music connection gave the star an attractive new facet and how a music store could be a salutary place in which to plug an upcoming movie. The tie-ins became more specific as producers commissioned theme songs bearing the title of a film, ideally to be played as the film was run, and afterward on sale in the lobby. One early title song—for Mabel Normand's *Mickey* (1918)—was a genuine hit. Otherwise the field was rather haphazard and disorganized.[1]

The galvanizer for movie theme songs arrived in the mid-1920s in the alluring person of Dolores Del Rio. "Charmaine" and "Ramona" were the characters she played in *What Price Glory* (1926) and *Ramona* (1928), and both became titles of song hits. *Glory*, with its raunchy Broadway reputation and surefire ingredients, would have been a smash whether or not it had a theme song, so the graceful waltz "Charmaine" rode to popularity on a preset wave of enthusiasm. *Ramona* was another story. In its completed form it was judged less monumental than superfluous; its sentimental story was already over-familiar through a novel, a play, two previous films, and scads of knockoffs. A hit theme song might generate particularly welcome attention, so Mabel Wayne and L. Wolf Gilbert created another Del Rio-inspired waltz. The result was even catchier than "Charmaine," with a sweet melody that seemed to cascade like the waterfall mentioned in the lyrics. As with its predecessors the theme was employed liberally in the scores issued to exhibitors, so a certain success was inevitable. But then, in the most cunning of tactics, United Artists put Del Rio herself to work. She sang "Ramona" on a coast-to-coast broadcast six weeks before the pre-

---

1. In addition to such predictable entries as "Daddy Long-Legs" (from Mary Pickford's 1918 success), there were real curiosities. When the Babylonian segment of D. W. Griffith's money-losing *Intolerance* was reissued in an expanded retitled form, some genius thought that a hit song would fuel its chances. The result was the deathless "(I'll Be With You At) *The Fall of Babylon.*"

miere, then recorded it in her heavily inflected English and fetchingly erratic soprano. Next she made personal appearances at the film's major openings, singing the title song at every one of them. Days after *Ramona* began to run in theaters, one would have had to live on Neptune not to know that song. It was the waltz of choice at cotillions and proms, on the radio, and on cover recordings by countless dance bands. By general acknowledgment, it made a surefire hit out of a so-so movie. This success, plus the concurrent rise of synchronized scores, ensured that other hits would soon emerge. Fox, which had already scored with "Charmaine" and *Seventh Heaven*'s "Diane," continued with "Little Mother" *(Four Sons)* and "Angela Mia" *(Street Angel),* and First National followed suit with "(Jeannine, I Dream of) *Lilac Time*." Less successful but longer lasting was Irving Berlin's "Marie," from Sam Goldwyn's *The Awakening.*[2]

Dolores Del Rio's compatriot Ramon Novarro was the next silent star to win with a theme song. Late in 1928 MGM produced *The Pagan,* a South Sea romance in which script played second fiddle to scenery, including unbridled displays of Novarro in a sarong. When his tenor was found to be as comely as his torso, Metro powers commissioned Brown and Freed (just finished with *Broadway Melody*) to run up a little item called "The Pagan Love Song." One more waltz, simple tune and lyrics, nothing much. Novarro sang it on the soundtrack of the otherwise silent film, and it was enough to make the song a smash, with sheet music sales in excess of 1.5 million and $100,000 in royalties to Brown and Freed. Had Novarro made a record of it (he did do so years later), sales might have been greater still. Even as movie musicals were entering the scene, then, it had been discovered that song hits could emerge from movie houses as well as music halls.

Songwriters and Music Publishers

The Singing Fool was proof definitive that onscreen performances could be the best possible promotion for a song. With combined record and sheet sales of well over three million copies, "Sonny Boy" whetted the studios' appetites for profits and heralded everything that followed. While its huge success contributed vastly to the popularity of *The Singing Fool,* Warner Bros. saw none of the song's profits. Those went to composer-publishers

---

2. Before the silent-film theme craze wound down in early 1929, it reached a memorable nadir. Just as "Ramona" was cited as the song that solidified the trend, the era's best-known embarrassment arrived with the release of Norma Talmadge's *The Woman Disputed.* Somehow "Woman Disputed, I Love You" added little to the appeal of the enterprise.

Talkies were seldom better in their thematic choices. In 1929 Warner Bros. went so far as to announce that all its productions would feature theme songs. The edict was blessedly short-lived, though it did produce the less-than-gem-like "Ship of My Dreams," from *Isle of Lost Ships.* And veteran Gus Edwards, who knew better, came up with something for MGM's *The Trial of Mary Dugan,* albeit not used in the film. "Poor Little Mary Dugan" topped few charts.

DeSylva, Brown, and Henderson, who parlayed that success into a gainful deal with Fox Films. Warners rectified the issue by buying into Witmarks, Inc., one of the most established of music publishers. MGM had already made its deal with the Robbins Company, and other studios followed when William Fox formed Red Star Music and Paramount allied with publisher T. B. Harms to form the Famous Music Company. These labyrinthine and lucrative deals were responsible for pushing more songs into more films and form the key to one ongoing peculiarity: when even established stage hits were transferred to the screen, new songs often replaced superior (and audience-identifiable) tunes from the original score. *Paris*, *Sally*, and *No, No, Nanette* were just three cases where nearly all the stage songs were cut in favor of inferior new pieces by studio composers. The official excuse for this irritating predilection was that audiences would be overfamiliar with the stage songs by the time of the film's release. While this is partly true—the concept of a song's being a standard was less binding then—the more dominant reason was that the most resolutely mediocre new song would bring more profit to a studio-owned outfit than a preexisting one over which the studio had no dominion. The studio-publisher agreements guaranteed these songs an unusually long shelf life, for unlike many pop hits they did not vanish after the films' release and the first flush of popularity. Studios, owning the songs in perpetuity, gave them residual use in subsequent productions as scoring in dramatic films and occasional onscreen reprises. Such constant play was a major aid in molding a pop song into a standard. MGM was an early trailblazer, as with its drama *The Divorcée*, released in April of 1930. Its first scene, depicting typically Metro socialites at play, was accompanied by a medley of MGM-owned hits: "Singin' in the Rain" *(The Hollywood Revue of 1929)*, "Pagan Love Song," and "Just You, Just Me" *(Marianne)*.[3]

By the middle of 1929 songwriters had replaced the sound men as the most conspicuous new presence at the studios. Few of the best or busiest tunesmiths were able to resist the call and the money, and the result was an immense quantity of songs emanating from Hollywood in the first two years of talkies. So prominent were the songwriters and publishing arrangements that the September 1929 issue of *Photoplay* covered them in a long, fairly frank article titled "Westward the Course of Tin-Pan Alley," which detailed the exodus as well as the deals and profits made by the studios. (The magazine also instituted a monthly column reviewing the latest movie songs and records.) Most songwriters shipping out to Hollywood were brash New Yorkers utterly bemused by California, moguls, and talkie hysteria. It

---

3. This practice continues today, some film scores having been gold mines. One of Rodgers and Hart's finest scores graced Paramount's *Love Me Tonight* (1932), and "Lover," "Mimi," and—especially—"Isn't It Romantic?" have been heard in Paramount films (and, later, television programs) ever since.

was a situation best suited to tyros and second-stringers, though some, like DeSylva, Brown and Henderson, had numerous Broadway successes on their résumés. The biggest names—Jerome Kern, Oscar Hammerstein II, Irving Berlin, Sigmund Romberg, George and Ira Gershwin, Richard Rodgers and Lorenz Hart—all dabbled at some point, often with less success than their inferiors. Occasionally, their film work made it too clear that the art was not what had attracted them.

Inveterate self-promoters, the songwriters figured in a curious subgenre of musical shorts in which they celebrated themselves and advertised their studios' melodic bounty. MGM's *The Songwriters' Revue* (1929), hosted by an edgily sardonic Jack Benny, featured all the composers and lyricists then under contract and demonstrated that songwriters such as Brown and Freed performed their wares with a great deal more enthusiasm than skill. Paramount's *Makers of Melody* (1929), in which Rodgers and Hart purported to reenact the stories behind the composition of three of their hits, was one for the books. The mini-scenarios were absurd, the songs given indifferent performances; and there in the center were Rodgers and Hart, abashed and numbingly self-conscious.

Apart from the dubious notion of turning tunesmiths into movie idols, sales figures for both records and sheet music demonstrated that America did want to sing the songs after seeing the movies in which they appeared. In September 1928, in the same week that MGM bought 51 percent interest in Robbins Music, *Variety* reported that the top-selling songs in the country were mainly film themes—"Jeannine, I Dream of Lilac Time," "Angela Mia," and "Ramona." The covers of the song sheets gave an additional boost to film promotion. A portrait of the pertinent star might grace the cover (Mary Pickford in *Coquette*, Lon Chaney in *Laugh, Clown Laugh*), or it might be a reconfiguration of its film's advertising art. Some were quite attractive, often in full color, and made appealing take-home mementos for music-minded moviegoers.

Recordings and radio were other ancillary tools in marketing the songs and the films, the trend toward more direct film/audio tie-ins being cinched when Jolson's Brunswick recording of "Sonny Boy" sold over a million copies. With 1929 and proliferating movie musicals, film-related records and radio appearances multiplied. Nearly every singing star who appeared in a film cut records of its songs and went on the radio to plug both products: Fannie Brice, Charles King, Sophie Tucker, Ethel Waters, Nick Lucas, Rudy Vallee, and so on. There were also the expected cover recordings, many dozens of them, by major radio and dance orchestras: Paul Whiteman, Fred Waring, Abe Lyman, Ben Bernie. Adding to the stacks, Hollywood furnished true curios in the form of singing movie stars. A precedent for this had been set in 1923, when Rudolph Valentino went into the recording studio and proved conclusively that his strengths lay in non-vocal areas. As talkies beckoned, more film stars came forth on radio and records. Dolores Del Rio was the first, followed by her compatriot Lupe Velez and, ultimately, a host of unanticipated others (see Discography in Appendix I). If art was not always served, the publicity value was considerable, and some of the records sold surprisingly well.[4]

Songs in Early Musicals

Hollywood always seems to have had unspoken and irrefutable precepts regarding the relative merits of quality versus those of quantity. While the one might be desirable, the other is mandatory, and the songs of early sound cinema could well be Exhibit A. The sudden demand for musicals was matched by profuse supply, of which, inevitably, only a small portion was on a par with the best turned out by Broadway at the same time. Amid the classics and gems, the gap between the volume and the substance of this work was glaring. The reasons began with the perceived audience for the films and their songs. It was the least-common-denominator phenomenon: the film spectator was deemed on a lower plane than the more sophisticated Broadway equivalent, and songs had to be tailored accordingly. Simpler and more accessible models of current pop tunes were held as the prototype for film use. In this formula, lyrics were kept plain and often repetitive, rhyme schemes obvious, melody and harmony nonadventurous. The artless "You Were Meant for Me," which works fine in the intimate and modest context given it in *The Broadway Melody*, would likely have made far less impact on Broadway. In this case the song was sufficiently worthy; more often, in aiming for a wide audience, the songwriters set their sights too low. With dance-craze numbers all the rage in 1929, "Breakaway," written by Sidney Mitchell, Archie Gottler, and Con Conrad for *Fox Movietone Follies*, became a hit. Unlike the songs for *Broadway Melody*, however, its popularity was fleeting. "Breakaway" was too musically uncomplicated for its own sake, its anemic melody and so-what rhythms never stimulating enough to evoke the dance it professes to celebrate.

One major deterrent to quality composition was the rigidity by which the studio system was set up. Seldom was there much collaboration; a composer was merely one of many cogs on the assembly line, required to shoehorn the songs into die-cast slots, and the situation was not necessarily conducive to greater contact with one's muse. The *Photoplay* article hinted at the battle between inspiration and remuneration:

4. Hal Roach was one of the first producers to observe the possibilities. In April 1929, when he signed Thelma Todd to costar in two-reel comedies, he inserted a clause in her contract by which she was permitted to cut records for Victor. The clause was never exercised, however, and Todd never made a record.

Never before were things as easy for a composer or lyricist as the present. That goes, financially, artistically and comfortably. Named in the order of importance to the songwriter.

During the so-called "good old days," the song-writer sweat agonies before an idea came for a song [and] after writing it, the trouble of getting the song marketed began. . . .

Prior to the Hollywood era of song-exploitation, song writers were paid strictly on a royalty basis. Every dollar . . . was charged against the financial earnings of their songs. . . . The new arrangement has made Hollywood brighter than any blue heaven for the composer and lyricist. He is paid a salary plus drawing account against royalties. . . . *Whether his songs have earned a single penny or not—he does not owe the publisher or producer a cent.*

The system worked well for a time, as hit parade lists were dominated, weighed down, by movie songs. Some weeks in November 1929, some 90 percent of the nation's most popular songs were film-related. In their crassest manifestation, the studios became ditty factories where style and substance were tertiary considerations. That there were hundreds of songs in 1929 alone was not exactly a deterrent to uninspired and slipshod work. In *Tanned Legs* (Radio 1929), Sidney Clare's lyrics were so carelessly coordinated with Oscar Levant's tunes that the song "You're Responsible," accented both the second and third syllables of "responsible" to produce an unintended and infelicitous "ReSPON-SIByl."

The level of melodic composition was generally adequate; lyrics were another matter. Cheap gimmicks, nonsense syllables, and repeated words appeared with regularity, resulting in such pieces of work as "Shoo Shoo Boogie Boo" from *Why Bring That Up?* (Paramount 1929) and "Jig Jig Jigaloo" from *Broadway Babies* (FN 1929).[5] The sheer inanity of lyrics reached a pinnacle with "Li-Po-Li" from *Show of Shows* (WB 1929), which pitted Ed Ward's bouncy melody against Al Bryan's racist and asinine words. Uptempo songs often tended to fare better than ballads. In the score for *The Great Gabbo* (Cruze/Sono Art, 1929), "Every Now and Then" (Donald McNamee and King Zany) matches a breezily syncopated tune to simple serviceable lyrics. But an attempt at a grand romantic statement, "(Caught in) The Web of Love" (Lynn Cowan and Paul Titsworth) is simply disastrous, rhythmically dreary and textually atrocious.[6] The biggest names could also founder, as with Irving Berlin's simpleminded "When My Dreams Come True" *(The Cocoanuts)* and operetta master Rudolf Friml's

5. The latter also exemplifies the lack of originality then current: its words and music are blatantly lifted from a far superior Broadway original, Dorothy Fields/Jimmy McHugh's "Diga Diga Do" from *Blackbirds of 1928*.

6. And it gets the staging it deserves, too. See Chapter Eight.

score for *The Lottery Bride* (UA 1930), an utter failure. The songs in *Rose-Marie* and *The Vagabond King* found no distinguished successor here, not with the turgid likes of "My Northern Lights" and "You're an Angel." The Gershwins' score for *Delicious* (Fox 1931) moved one critic as follows:

> The principal [song is] such an unutterably banal ditty that I must print its opening line:
> "You're so delicious (pronounced delic-i-ous).
> "And so capricious (pronounced capric-i-ous)."
> Well, it's probably malic-i-ous of me to print these lyrics out, but they are really so stupid that I am certain that they will be popular.[7]

One of the less conventional songwriting talents of the time was Dorothy Parker, who was somewhat fazed to find herself assigned to furnish lyrics for Cecil B. DeMille's first all-talkie, *Dynamite* (MGM 1929). A more inappropriate collision of talents and personalities cannot be imagined, and it was not observed that Parker took to her job with undue gravity. Her first suggestions for a theme song were stoically rejected by DeMille—"Dynamite, I Love You" and "Dynamite, Blow My Sweetie Back to Me." Finally she subdued the bile long enough to produce a more tractable lyric called "How Am I to Know?," set to a slightly meandering tune by Jack King and sung in the film by a then unknown Russ Columbo. It became something of a hit and eventually a standard, although *Photoplay* had commented that "Though all the orchestras" who recorded it "do their darndest they cannot make a silk purse out of a whateveritis."

Other songwriters fared more advantageously, occasionally equaling or exceeding Broadway's norm. Brown and Freed had numerous hits after *Broadway Melody*, notably "Singin' in the Rain" from MGM's *Hollywood Revue*. DeSylva, Brown, and Henderson matched their biggest stage hits with their score and script for Fox's 1929 smash *Sunny Side Up*, though faring less well the following year with the science-fiction extravaganza *Just Imagine*. Irving Berlin gave *Puttin' on the Ritz* an evergreen title song and contributed good numbers to *Hallelujah!* and *Mammy*. Others turning out solid work included Richard Whiting, who collaborated on "Louise" *(Innocents of Paris)* and the score of *Monte Carlo,* among others; Victor Schertzinger and the prolific Clifford Grey *(The Love Parade)*; Grant Clark and Harry Akst ("Am I Blue?" and "Birmingham Bertha" from *On With the Show!*); Raymond Klages and Jesse Greer, teaming up on "Low Down Rhythm" and "Just You, Just Me" (originally for *Hollywood Revue*, the second moved to *Marianne*); and Bert Kalmar and Harry Ruby, who in 1930

7. So said John S. Cohen Jr. in *The New York Sun*. Quite possibly Ira Gershwin was mocking other film songs (and unmusical movie industry executives), though the joke isn't so apparent in context. The wit of "Blah, Blah, Blah," from the same score, is more self-evident, despite its performance by the alleged comedian El Brendel.

Star treatment was occasionally extended to composers as well as actors. In 1931, after most of his peers had fled Hollywood, Nacio Herb Brown remained. He composed "Paradise" for Pola Negri to sing in *A Woman Commands*, thus prompting this dramatic study of diligent composer and rapt star.

did well with *The Cuckoos* and gave the abysmal *Check and Double Check* its only touch of class with the standard "Three Little Words."

Few of the best film songs seemed to share any magic formula. As with so much popular music, most were fortunate combinations of music and words rather than truly arresting or adventurous pieces. Occasionally there were boons. It's easy today, for example, to scoff at the ricky-tick "Tip Toe Thru the Tulips with Me," the hit from *Gold Diggers of Broadway;* its cloyingly naïve words and simple stepwise tune invite little musical investigation.[8] It is all the more surprising, then, when melodist Joe Burke launches the break (central section) with a startling device: "Knee-deep in flowers we'll stray" is set with a bracing downward leap that gives the words credence and illustration. The musical interval of the descent from "knee" to "deep," a minor seventh, is a greater distance than common for this type of song, unexpected and harmonically somewhat daring. The next line's "We'll keep the showers away" also leaps downward, this time a full octave, and as it resolves the harmonic tension and sets up the return to the main theme, Burke's musicianship gives punch to an otherwise ordinary piece. A more deliberately silly song, "Singin' in the Bathtub," was written by Herb Magidson, Ned Washington, and Michael Cleary for Warners' *The Show of Shows* as a deliberate parody of "Singin' in the Rain." Wacky as it is, this ode to crooning and cleanliness was crafted with some skill, its alternating major-minor harmonies and clever lyrics receiving extra point through Winnie Lightner's clarion tone and crisp diction. Best of all is the "recitative" between the first and second choruses, exhorting the "knights of the bath" to "wash all your sins away." The genuine good humor of both words and music make the song a definite standout amid dreary surroundings.[9]

Conductors and Arrangers

The music departments at each major studio were, in the first years, used primarily for musicals and less so for main-title and incidental music in dramatic films. This proved a boon to a minor segment of the music community: musicians based in Los Angeles, who before 1929 often found only sporadic jobs in dance or theater orchestras. Both arrangements and playing in the first musicals sound starchy and crude to modern ears, and as with recording it was an area that warranted much refinement. Dance numbers were especially hazardous, the orchestra often sawing away at the same old song over and over with little variation. It all gradually improved as the studio orchestras, conductors, and arrangers worked to raise their expertise to increasingly stylish levels. MGM's house forces progressed in a few months from the play-by-numbers technique of *The Broadway Melody* to a more assertive style in *Hollywood Revue.* Among the early arranger/conductors were MGM's Arthur Lange, the gifted Victor Baravalle at Radio, Howard Jackson at Fox, Louis Silvers at Warners, and Leo Forbstein, whose

8. For modern listeners this is compounded by its use in the late 1960s by the outré ukulele-strumming Tiny Tim.

9. Warner Bros. clearly knew the value of the song. It was soon used as the theme of their first Looney Tune, *Sinkin' [sic] in the Bathtub,* and for the next forty years, any Warner cartoon with a bathtub would likely use it as underscoring.

work at First National (later at Warners) helped define the blaring studio sound associated with Warners' urban dramas and musicals of the mid-1930s. House styles progressively emerged at each studio, and even in the mostly stodgy song-and-dance arrangements of 1929 there was the occasional felicity—a honky-tonk piano for "Singin' in the Bathtub," an elegant obbligato for solo violin that gives *Gabbo*'s "Web of Love" more beauty than it warrants, the jumpy Broadway-pit-band playing in *The Cocoanuts*. MGM's scoring was the least interesting of the studios, bloated and plodding, and early Warners scores also tended toward the ponderous. At Radio/RKO, Baravalle (and later Max Steiner) energized the brasses and saxophones of the house forces, and at Paramount, where music was given more prominence than elsewhere, department head Nathaniel Finston developed the first truly individual studio sound. Finston's pianists and percussion players were of especially high quality, the muted trumpets and clarinet glissandi were immediately recognizable trademarks, and the happy results can be heard in a wide variety of films—*Paramount on Parade* (1930) to *June Moon* (1931) to *This is the Night* (1932). Some famous pop orchestras also turned up: the bands of Paul Whiteman *(King of Jazz)* and George Olsen *(Whoopee!*, among others) offered a distinctive sound and virtuosity seldom exceeded since then.

Sound Recording

In 1929 and 1930, musicals were always at the vanguard of sound technology of necessity, for by their nature they constantly posed the most complex problems. After the first flush of sound technicians' power in late 1928, their high-profile jobs receded into a more reasonable standing, which enabled Douglas Shearer and his peers to push for more crispness and resonance, with minimum extraneous noise. The earliest days of hide-the-mike-in-the-vase were over in due course, as several sound technicians worked with imaginative directors to determine that microphones could in fact move, could follow the actors and be at their service instead of vice versa.[10] Another challenge lay in maintaining proper levels of volume and balance, the ruinous microphonic overloading in *Broadway Melody*'s "Love Boat" number being a case in point. Conversely, the amount of sound produced on the set was sometimes too little, for it was all too easy to leave the pickup range. It was a frequent complaint that several actors might carry on a conversation at inexplicably differing levels of audibility. Production numbers shot with live on-set recording were especially prone to diffi-

10. Dorothy Arzner, the only leading woman director in Hollywood in 1929 (and for many years after), is often credited with devising a mike boom to follow the movements of the perpetually mobile Clara Bow in *The Wild Party*. Other directors also took credit for it and no doubt many hands contributed.

culties in balance. Instruments could drown out singers, choruses could overwhelm soloists, and those moving around the stage during lively numbers were not always heard clearly. The microphones were quite exasperating: as temperamental as they were in picking up sounds, they themselves often made unwanted noise, being condenser (electrostatic) mikes prone to sputtering when the humidity level rose.

After its introduction in "The Wedding of the Painted Doll," prerecording gradually became the norm. The loss in spontaneity was offset by advantages numerous and obvious: it eliminated the need to keep a full orchestra on the set; staging rehearsals were more manageable; camera setups and editing were far easier; retakes were more feasible. As with other technical advances, some refinement was in order. Moments of transition, in which songs and underscoring would be cued up and faded in, could be abrupt and jarring. Blending live sound with prerecorded music and song required subtlety and technical skill, and editors and sound people, burdened with rudimentary and unruly equipment, were not always up to the job. Introducing songs into the essentially naturalistic medium of film raised tricky aesthetic questions which primitive sound mixing could not answer. Songs popping up from nowhere, accompaniments suddenly blaring forth—such did not alleviate the inherent absurdity. Lower-budget efforts were notable prey to these complications. In the musical western *Under Montana Skies* (Tiffany 1930) the songs begin and end without preparation, completely unrelated to the dialogue scenes or their ambient sound. When Dorothy Gulliver finishes singing "Underneath the Blue Montana Skies," the prerecorded orchestral coda suddenly cuts off, with a nearly palpable *bump*, in mid-note, forcing the spectator to put technical considerations ahead of all else.

The most intense problems with sound occurred in connection with Vitaphone. However better it may have sounded in theaters, disc recording was never less than a pain, both at the studio and for exhibitors. Since Vitaphone made prerecording difficult and sometimes impossible, Warner and First National films shot their musical sequences with live sound long after other studios stopped. Even plain dramatic films often had underscoring done *in situ*, an orchestra grinding away just beyond camera range. In theory this added spontaneity and life to the performances, but two of Warners' biggest musicals of 1929 furnish good examples of the potential pitfalls. In *Gold Diggers of Broadway*, as Nancy Welford sings "The Song of the Gold Diggers," a line of tuxedoed chorus boys punctuate her singing by tapping their canes on the stage floor. Since it was all being recorded by a row of microphones placed just below the front of the stage, Welford's vocal efforts are briefly overwhelmed by the racket of cane upon wood. Ethel Waters's wonderful rendition of "Am I Blue?" in *On With the Show!* is hampered by the overloaded mikes, especially in the second chorus. The combined forces of Waters, the orchestra, and the Harmony Emperors Quartet are just too much for the system, and Waters's high notes are all but drowned out by an aggregation of white noise and sonic slush.

Many of the later Vitaphone films did resort to more complex sound elements, such as overscoring and prerecording, and also to a primitive type of sound mixing, with the result being that these discs—Vitaphone's most technically sophisticated—have a duller and more constricted sound than the system's early direct-to-disc recordings. Although more mobile than it had been in 1926, the system was in 1930 still hobbled in many ways. Exhibitors had the worst of it—discs forever requiring replacement, surface noise and scratches an ever-present danger, synchronization problems never being totally avoided. As sound-on-film reached higher grades of sophistication and efficiency, the disc system seemed increasingly antiquated, and by the spring of 1930 the handwriting was on Vitaphone's wall. A planned switchover to sound-on-film technology put Warner Bros. in something of a bind, however. The change was obviously necessary, but with millions already spent on Vitaphone at the studio and in the theaters, Warners was hard-put to justify the complete junking of its signature technology. Ultimately, the plan was executed as quietly as possible, Warners discreetly leaking to the trade press that it would slowly move to a sound-on-film system. On May 26, 1930, it was announced at the annual Warners–First National sales convention in Atlantic City that Warner films would be available with sound-on-film as well as sound-on-disc, and the following January Warners and First National began shooting with Western Electric sound-on-film. Not surprisingly, many theater owners were none too pleased. It had not been long since that they had spent thousands on Vitaphone installation, and as the Depression took hold they were in no hurry to subsidize another changeover. To alleviate the situation, many films were made available to theatres in the disc format until mid-decade. Despite its being dead as a production tool from 1931 on, the name "Vitaphone" did continue as a trademark for years afterward, as did Movietone, used as the trademark for Fox's newsreels.

The unquestioned supremacy of sound-on-film brought steady improvements, though quality tended to vary from one studio to another. What they all shared by 1930 was the desire to make sound as unobtrusive as possible. Film sound, with its attendant mechanical eccentricities, no longer needed to call undue attention to itself, and certain subtleties of recording had to be effected. Extraneous noise was an ongoing problem in all sound formats. Silence was supposed to be just that, and a whoosh or hiss or thump on the sound track in ostensibly silent moments was not an enhancement. By 1931 several noise suppression devices had been developed to silence much of the hissing and give increased fidelity to film sound in general.[11] Another trouble area was the proper coordination of spatial and sonic perspective, for microphone placement and prerecording could make characters far away from the camera sound every bit as loud as those two feet away from it. *Montana Moon* (MGM, 1930) was a conspicuous example, Joan Crawford singing on horseback zillions of feet away from the camera sounding just as loud as the cowboy chorus warbling up in the foreground. More and more, audiences began to notice such things (critics had long taken potshots), and technicians became more attentive to the need to make volume levels closer simulations of actual sound perspective. Except for the deliberately artificial world of the musical, talking pictures entered a period of sonic austerity after mid-1929 and underscoring became nearly extant for several years. Part of it was the drive for naturalism and much of it the technical difficulty of proper sound mixing. Supposedly "realistic" sound (i.e., no background music) became the rule even in some musical comedies, to the point that actors would occasionally be shown turning on radios to give underscoring a putative alibi.

II
IMAGES: PHOTOGRAPHY, EDITING, COLOR

Moving the Camera

More often than not, any discussion of 1929 films fast turns to the issue of camera mobility—specifically, the lack thereof and how the camera booths and the intransigent mike put an unconquerable stranglehold on film. This was true only up to a point, for starting in the late summer there was often the capacity for more mobility. It was the filmmakers who were at fault, so afraid of the new process that they forgot that "move" was the root word of "movies." This fear continued into 1930, for the first covey of sound men had ensured that their reign of terror would hold fast long after their real power diminished.

Those who tried for more movement were often resisted, put down, disobeyed. One of the mavericks was stage director Rouben Mamoulian, who shot his first film, *Applause*, at Paramount's East Coast studio in the summer of 1929. Full of ideas, full of himself, Mamoulian was not about to have this

11. Many early talkies sound better today than ever before, and not only due to improved reproduction. In the 1950s, when most of them were preserved and transferred for 16mm play on television, the work was often rushed and sloppy, which made the original tracks, not great to begin with, sound positively dreadful. The "restored" prints and tape transfers made since the mid-1980s are far better. Intelligent engineering, as well as the bells and whistles of modern technology—equalizing and Dolbyizing and digital remastering—can make the absolute most out of what's there.

seamy backstage yarn degenerate into a series of static confrontations in dreary two-shots. He wanted it to move, be exciting and daring, give the visuals as much force as the sound and then some. When he started giving his ideas to the crew there was amused incredulity. "No, no," they said, "you can't do that, and we aren't even going to try." For a while, stalemate—then Mamoulian decided it was his show and would live up to his vision. "We *are* going to do this and this, and also this," he told the crew, handing them scenes with complicated setups and elaborate movements. "When I want that camera to move you'll move it, and make the mike follow along." And, grumblingly, they did. Mamoulian's work on *Applause* was inspiring proof that talk-ies could indeed be a place for visual adventurousness, and that microphones were less the obstacle than the intractable people who controlled them and the spineless toadies who feared them.

Mamoulian's efforts were a shining and singular exception to a relatively dreary rule. Visual mobility was far less evident in 1929 Hollywood than voice coaches or dance instructors. Most scripts lacked even the punchy dialogue of *The Broadway Melody*, and the results could deteriorate into dire aural and visual monotony, often on a large scale. Harry Beaumont's coffin on wheels was, alas, not always emulated by his successors. While musicals were generally a little more mobile than most dramas, much was still missing, especially when mediocrities were in charge. In *Fox Movietone Follies of 1929*, Marcel Silver's attempts at special effects in the production numbers weren't enough, as *Variety* made clear: "Photography seems dead, but here it must be remembered that a cameraman these days is pretty thoroughly handcuffed." Exceptions turned up now and again, such as visual stylist Robert Florey, who was somehow able to put a few eye-catching touches into *The Cocoanuts*, and Paul Fejos with The Camera Crane that Conquered *Broadway*, and King Vidor's moody silent-shot backwater visuals in *Hallelujah!* As the year progressed, it was discovered that the camera could be taken out of its booth, made soundproof, and given far greater freedom. The first portable camera setups were called "blimps," for with all the padding to ensure silence, that's what they resembled. Several directors took credit for the innovation, most conspicuously Cecil B. DeMille, who claimed that when the camera just had to move for a scene in *Dynamite,* he liberated it. As with movable microphones, it was most likely a matter of several people coming up with similar ideas around the same time and implementing them in slightly differing ways. By the late summer the camera was free enough to enable director David Butler to come up with an uncommonly strong opening for *Sunny Side Up*, released in October: a traveling camera roves around the outside of a tenement building, peeking through some of the windows to pick up a variety of sights and sounds, a clear harbinger of a similar scene twenty-five years later in Hitchcock's *Rear Window*. Even Vitaphone films began to loosen up a bit, to the point of venturing outdoors with newly portable recording equipment for such films as First National's *Smiling Irish Eyes* and Warner's Technicolor operetta *Song of the West*.

Pictorial Quality

While the stagnancy of the camera was the most onerous attribute of early-talkie photography, other infelicities also persisted. The flat visual look of the early Vitaphone shorts and features, that one-dimensional grayish dreariness, was slow in dying. All too often the pearly sheen of the silent days turned into all-purpose pallor on the restrictive new soundstages, and large-scale musicals, dependent upon sparkling visuals, were especially hampered. The photographic restrictions could make production numbers resemble overcrowded, underdirected, and ineptly designed harbingers of bad early television. *Show of Shows* is one of the most calamitous of early talkies for these reasons: even taking into consideration that current prints are black-and-white shadows of the original Technicolor, its incessant and interchangeable dance numbers resembling incompetent halftime shows are stiffly photographed from distances of near-Goodyear Blimp proportions.

Another visual problem brought up a more delicate issue. It was frequently conceded that talking-picture visuals were less than photogenically gracious to many players, musical performers being prime victims. Unlike the stage, where projection of voice and personality mattered far more than looks, it was soon apparent in film that sight and sound would carry pretty equal weight in musicals. In a less photographically restricted era such imported players would often be able to pull it off before the camera; what Fred Astaire lacked in looks he compensated for in camera-wise magnetism. In 1929, when stage folk needed all the help they could get, little was forthcoming. Talkies' blunt visual approach only amplified facial irregularities or advancing years, and women were especially ill served.[12] The fortyish Maurice Chevalier did luck out, for careful photography and natural ebullience made him seem years younger. Unfortunately, the glamour attained onstage by a Marilyn Miller, a Gertrude Lawrence, an Irene Bordoni tended to erode when the camera drew close. Worse, the unyielding lens tended to expose, even magnify the artifice and effort through which these stars realized their charisma.

---

12. Stage performers weren't the only ones dealt with so unbecomingly. No one had difficulty finding fault with *Lights of New York* or with the performance of Helene Costello (Dolores's sister) therein, yet so dire was the situation that even her one unquestioned asset, her looks, suffered in the primeval circumstances. *Variety*, gracious as always, commented: "Helene Costello . . . failed to convince vocally [and] also photographed blah, giving her a horse collar on both ends of the racket." At least Marion Talley could sing.

The situation improved only slowly, as the industry's most distinguished cinematographers strained to take one step forward after the seventeen-step regression. Much of the recovery was conducted in musicals, most prolifically by the brilliant Lee Garmes. Between mid-1929 and mid-1930 he all but cornered the market by shooting *Say It With Songs, Spring Is Here, Kiss Me Again, Song of the Flame, Bright Lights*, part of *Whoopee!*, and the semimusicals *Lilies of the Field* and *Morocco*. Other shining contributions were made by Victor Milner *(The Love Parade, Monte Carlo)*, Gregg Toland *(Palmy Days* and portions of *Whoopee!)*, and Ernest Palmer *(Just Imagine* and part of *Sunny Side Up)*. Their work was aided by the return in 1930 of arc lights in a new incarnation. The lights' former propensities for sputtering and humming greatly curbed, they provided more dynamic illumination that gave back some of the old visual zip. Around the same time, new film stocks and photographic techniques made the monochrome spectrum wider and nearly as pleasing as in silents.

Editing

At this stage in its development, film editing tended to be more a craft than an art and suffered notably during the early sound days. The finest editing in the late silent era provided a seamless succession of images, seldom calling attention to itself through flashy techniques, allowing for unimpeded visual flow. Dynamic principles of montage, as pioneered by Eisenstein in *Potemkin*, also influenced American cinema. All this died for a spell after sound arrived. Multiple-camera setups and interminably long takes plunged editing into its most aboriginal form, and the rigidity of the early Vitaphone shorts carried over with only slight progress into features. Two-shots of actors talking were particularly prone to the stasis, and even *The Broadway Melody* had scenes dragged out to the point of inertia. Again, as with cameramen, editors gradually regained a toehold. Camera booths became a thing of the past and in 1930 the sound Moviola was introduced, enabling the cutting of both sound and picture elements. With the editor's job becoming easier, it also became more creative. Cross-cutting and other such techniques came back into fashion, with underworld films as their most conspicuous forum, yet the visual languor was slow in dying off. The coming of sound had siphoned off a great deal of confidence, and only haltingly was film pace returned to its former snap and flow.

Besides the slow cadence it entailed, early-talkie editing had an occasional and singularly annoying propensity. In some 1929 and 1930 talkies the editor's splice can be heard as a slight thump when the shot changes. Once again it was a bug that didn't always get worked out, due either to technical inadequacy or sheer sloppiness. The solution lay in blooping, which had been devised by Theodore Case as early as 1926. Case had observed that when a Movietone negative was edited and printed, the photoelectric cell gave distinct audibility to edit points. As a remedy he covered the splice on the negative with a glob of heavy black ink, rendering the splice silent. Unfortunately, not all editors and sound people availed themselves of "Movietone Ink" (as it was marketed), and some films were released with unblooped scenes which provide a steady distraction when seen today.

Color

One of the most conspicuous visual aspects of the early musicals had nothing to do with inert camerawork or recalcitrant editing—and everything to do with the box office. Technicolor, two-color incarnation, soon became one of musicals' most prominent attributes as Herbert Kalmus, promoting his process with great enthusiasm, found avid takers at the studios. From mid-1929 to the end of 1930 well over fifty features, nearly all musicals, employed color photography entirely or in part. Once again "The Wedding of the Painted Doll" led the way, followed by *The Desert Song* and *Broadway*. Then came *On With the Show!*, whose publicity left no doubt as to its major selling point. "Colors that make the rainbow turn pale!" boomed ads. Other publicity expanded on the theme with about the same degree of restraint, putting the film on a level with a trip to the Louvre:

> Now COLOR Takes the Screen!
>
> Now Warner Bros. pioneer again with another radical development in motion picture reproduction—COLOR! Full colors—natural colors—real colors, reproduced direct from life! Color breaks the last barrier between you and Broadway at its best. Now the Screen can give you *everything* the Stage can offer—and more . . .
>
> "ON WITH THE SHOW" would be superb picture entertainment, even in black and white . . . But the added thrill of Technicolor makes it an artistic event of commanding importance in entertainment history.

The combination of color and music was sufficiently potent to give *On With the Show!* a huge gross, and *Gold Diggers of Broadway*, a few months later, even more. The industry could only take notice, despite the money and trouble that were an integral part of Technicolor work. Film stock, adding $50,000 or more to the negative cost, was about 1000 percent the expense of doing it in black and white, and the numbers rose greatly when hundreds of prints were made up. Somehow it seemed worth it—1929 audiences clearly liked color with their sound and their music. For more economy-minded producers there was the viable option of color sequences. The advertising value alone ("Revue scenes in COLOR!") justified the ex-

The rigors of shooting in early Technicolor, as shown in an on-set shot of the "Dancing the Devil Away" number for *The Cuckoos* (Radio 1930). Technicolor necessitated a great deal more light than usual—in this case, according to publicity, "300 huge lights, totaling 13000 amperes of electricity." Whatever it was, the body paint couldn't have been much fun. Note also the production people gathered on the far right. Barely visible above the lone spotlight is, most likely, dance director Pearl Eaton.

pense, although some of these served neither art nor showmanship. In a few cases they needn't have bothered, as in a three-minute scene of pseudo-Bretonese dancers cavorting in the gardens of Versailles in MGM's Napoleonic operetta *Devil May Care* (1929), which adds nothing to audience enjoyment or comprehension. Likewise a brief chorus routine in *Pointed Heels* (Paramount 1929), which contributes only an irrelevant flash.

The heyday of two-color Technicolor seemed like a second birth of Vitaphone, Warners again clinching a deal that gave it the jump on the competition. Radio (RKO) quickly signed its own agreement with Technicolor, while MGM and Paramount made more conservative smaller commitments. By fall 1929 the overwhelming demand far outstripped the supply: with only a dozen cameras in existence, studios had to cut back on their color plans. Before Kalmus could manufacture more cameras, the shortage was so acute that scheduling had to be put on a round-the-clock basis. RKO, forced to shoot *Rio Rita*'s color scenes in the wee hours, bicycled the cameras to the set after other companies were done with them. All the undelightful inconveniences—scheduling problems, expense, major design and lighting difficulties—simply had to be tolerated, for color was king just then. The response to the use of the process in such films as *Sally* (FN 1929), *The Vagabond King* (Paramount 1930) and *The Rogue Song* (MGM 1930) seemed to consolidate the success of the enterprise. In early 1930, James R. Quirk, *Photoplay*'s influential and opinionated editor, peered into a cloudy crystal ball: "Six months ago Technicolor pictures were just starting. In twelve months more the untinted shadows will be obsolete." Herbert Kalmus, elated with these developments, began a high-pressure advertising campaign in the national press. *The Saturday Evening Post* was emblazoned with full-color stills from some of the Technicolor productions, along with the legend "TECHNICOLOR is *NATURAL* Color."[13]

The success of Technicolor in 1929 sent a number of technicians in the U.S. and Europe into the laboratory to produce rival processes, most of them pretty awful. Little impact was made by such systems as Photocolor, Raycol, Harmonicolor, and, no kidding, something called Coloratura, used in a few Pathé newsreels. Even Mack Sennett got into the act by employing Sennett Color ("Nature's Reflection") in some comedy shorts. For a time William Fox was enamored of Multicolor, a two-color system descended from the British Prizmacolor system of the 1910s and 1920s. First used by Fox for one sequence in the *Movietone Follies*, Multicolor was at its best about as pleasing as two-color Technicolor. It too could not capture anything like a full spectrum, for once again there were no yellows, purples, or pure primary colors. Unlike Technicolor's brick reds and mossy greens, Multicolor was based on shades of red-orange and blue, which gave it a softer and cooler look than its rival. Flesh tones reproduced nicely, grain was not excessive, and if Kalmus & Co. had not had a near monopoly on studio business, it would doubtless have been used more.[14] After the *Movietone Follies*, Fox put Multicolor sequences into *Married in Hollywood* and *Sunny Side Up* (the "Turn on the Heat" number), and the process also turned up in *The Great Gabbo* and Pathé's *Red Hot Rhythm*. After Fox gave up on Multicolor, he announced plans in 1930 for Fox Color, which for sundry reasons was soon discarded.

Technicolor, meanwhile, was thriving, too much so for its own good. Seeing the orders pouring in, Kalmus expanded the operation by build-

13. It was of course nothing of the sort, at least in the sense of reproducing nature accurately. And these ads were deceptive enough to doctor photos from such films as *Sally* and *The Vagabond King* with blues and yellows, colors Technicolor was incapable of reproducing. The ads for *On With the Show!* also lied when bragging of "A new all-color process that brings out every shade in its true value." To add irony to deceit, it will be recalled that this is the film that introduced "Am I Blue?"

14. Actually, it was. The direct descendant of Multicolor was Cinecolor, which for years was a commonly used, far cheaper alternative to three-strip Technicolor. Most often seen in low-budget Westerns, it lasted from the late 1930s into the 1950s.

ing more cameras and enlarging his facilities. These seemingly sensible moves ultimately robbed the process of its chief asset, tightly managed quality control. A lack of careful supervision coupled with an immense upturn in volume yielded increasingly shoddy results. Actors could look like they were infected with terminal sunburn or jaundice, tints veered between the garish and the sickly, there were countless complaints of blurred out-of-register images, and the grain problem worsened. Print quality apparently varied wildly, as did spectator reaction. The color sequences in First National's *No, No, Nanette* (1930), judged by *Photoplay* "the finest to date," received a rigorous drubbing in the trade journal *Harrison's Reports:*

> The Technicolor work is the poorest yet seen. The emulsion grain is so noticeable that it makes the picture appear that the heavens were raining sand. The long shots are one big blur. The color in the medium shots is mostly washed out. The faces of the players are expressionless. In some scenes they look like death masks. . . . Unless better work is done, color had better be left out of talking pictures.

After several months of such experiences audiences began to be hostile, and so did studios. But in mid-1929 all the objections, the raining sand and greenish skies and nightmare blurs, seemed far away. At that point, with shooting starting on a number of major productions, Technicolor was blazing brightly. For just a few giddy months it seemed that the world of musical films would ever be made of shades of salmon and turquoise.

III
THE PERSONNEL: DIRECTORS, WRITERS, PERFORMERS

The dawn of nearly every decade seems to herald enormous changes in the American film industry. A new group of players comes in, there are new ways of doing business, sometimes different directors, other types of stories and styles. The 1910s, the era of Griffith, saw the dawn of the feature film and California-based production. The 1920s brought new icons, like Valentino, and a more aligned studio system. With the 1940s there was film noir, Orson Welles, and a new generation of players, and in the 1950s came television and innumerable corporate and social shifts. And so on to the 1990s. If sound had not come, the late 1920s would have had its turnover, its new names and structures and trends. Such changes could not, however, approach those wrought by the advent of sound. A flood of people from the stage, a demotion of the Old Guard, an incredible herd of opportunists—all were part of the new era of sound, with musicals as the central point at which these forces met.

At the beginning of its existence, the film musical had perhaps more prestige than ever again, or at least until the bloated Broadway adaptations of
the 1950s and 1960s. This was due partly to newness and mostly to the
caliber of people involved before and behind the camera. Although directors in the movie-factory heyday were frequently considered little more
than well-appointed traffic cops, the best of them left considerable imprint
even after the immense modification to their craft dictated by sound. The
majority of silent directors had a relatively easy time making the transition,
and many stayed on and flourished.[15] Some plunged in without preparation, while others, especially at MGM and Fox, were given the chance to
first try out their skills on talking short subjects. Either way, musicals were
an early destination, for some of the most distinguished silent directors
chose or were assigned musical or related subjects for their entry into the
new era.

Ernst Lubitsch, Hollywood's preeminent émigré, moved to the head of
the line his first time out; no one could have asked for a bigger sensation
than *The Love Parade*. Other top-rank silent directors checking in musically
were King Vidor *(Hallelujah!)*, Josef von Sternberg *(The Blue Angel, Morocco)*,
Raoul Walsh *(The Cock Eyed World, Hot for Paris)*; and, less happily, James
Cruze *(The Great Gabbo)* and the fast-fading Marshall Neilan *(The Vagabond
Lover, Tanned Legs, Sweethearts on Parade)*. After his *Broadway Melody*
involvement, Edmund Goulding moved on to *The Trespasser* (1929), one of
many nonmusicals in which song furnished major support. Goulding's role
in its success was hardly supporting: in a nonauteur time he was producer,
director, screenwriter, and co-songwriter. Frank Borzage followed a run of
hit love stories with the equally sentimental John McCormack vehicle *Song
O' My Heart* (1930). Other impressive imports included Paul Fejos with
Broadway and Ludwig Berger, bringing a Viennese operetta background to
The Vagabond King. More domestically, and far out in left field, there was
Cecil B. DeMille, fresh from his encounter with Dorothy Parker. His trademark ostentation well in evidence, he tested lyric waters with *Madam Satan*
(1930) and nearly drowned in the attempt.

In the anything-goes time of 1929, neither genres nor directors were as
standardized or specialized as they would be later. Other than the most
important figures, who might have their pick of properties, the studios were

15. There were also major silent directors whose careers ebbed with sound. D. W. Griffith,
already in decline, went into unhappy semiretirement after two talkies. The vastly respected
Herbert Brenon, who was averse to the idea of talkies in the first place, undertook them only
with great reluctance and soon left Hollywood. Others whose careers suffered or changed
included Fred Niblo, Rex Ingram, who moved abroad, Joseph Henabery, who switched over
to short subjects, and Mal St. Clair, who plummeted from elegant comedies in the mid-1920s
to routine drivel by the early 1930s.

not averse to putting any contract director on a musical whether or not there was any affinity for the job. Sidney Franklin, a specialist in costume dramas and literary adaptations, was assigned to MGM's first operetta, *Devil May Care* (1929) and to the Jenny Lind bio *A Lady's Morals* (1930), in which the lack of a lyrical touch revealed his unsuitability. For a brief time in 1929 Lionel Barrymore became a favored MGM director after the huge success of *Madame X;* as a reward he was given *The Rogue Song,* and a lack of directorial affinity was again evident. At Warners and its associate First National there was little room or time or money for specialization. Every director was expected to handle every type of story with unvarying expertise, and since music was high on the agenda in 1929–30 all the regular hands—Michael Curtiz, Roy Del Ruth, Lloyd Bacon, Archie Mayo, Mervyn LeRoy, Ray Enright—turned out several musicals apiece, rarely with any personal stamp. *The Jazz Singer* behind him, Alan Crosland was Warners' closest approximation of a specialist. His five musicals were of widely varying quality and occasional distinction, culminating with the superior *Viennese Nights* (1930). Experts in silent comedy were judged particularly suited to song and dance, and at First National, comedy aces William A. Seiter and Clarence Badger stayed busy with the lighter musical fare, as did Frank Tuttle and Edward Sutherland at Paramount and Charles Reisner at MGM. Radio, most compact of the major companies, gave the undistinguished writer-director Luther Reed a brief time in the sun with its three biggest productions: *Rio Rita* (1929), *Hit the Deck* (1930), and *Dixiana* (1930). And David Butler, who had switched from acting to directorial chores in 1927, was entrusted with most of Fox's top musicals, including *Sunny Side Up* and *Just Imagine.*

With theater the reference point for most early talkie work, stage directors came to film in what might be called tempered droves. Many of them ended up as codirectors (sometimes billed as "Dialogue Directors"), working with the actors while a film-trained director tended to the cinematic side. Paramount was especially disposed to this tandem system, as with John Cromwell and Edward Sutherland on *Close Harmony* and *The Dance of Life.* Later, George Cukor had an ill-starred association with Ernst Lubitsch on *One Hour With You* (see Chapter Fifteen). Other Paramount duos included directors of *The Cocoanuts* (Joseph Santley and Robert Florey) and *Follow Thru* (Lawrence Schwab and Lloyd Corrigan). MGM's *Good News* carried the credit "Stage direction: Edgar J. MacGregor; Screen direction: Nick Grindé." Interestingly, few stage directors who received solo film credit worked on musicals. Two major maverick exceptions attained artistic—not financial—success. Rouben Mamoulian, with an opera and Broadway background, opened new cinematic doors with *Applause* and, three years later, *Love Me Tonight.* And Broadway's master of revue, John Murray Anderson, was imported to work his brand of magic on film. Anderson's perfectionist ways were anathema to his economy-minded studio, Universal, although *King of Jazz* (1930) boasted high quality as well as a high price tag.

Writers

The production of early talkies seldom allowed for a personal touch, and writers were often in a less desirable position than directors. Few productions were not written by committee, and as the early Vitaphone features made painfully obvious, movie dialogue was a tricky business. As written by silent-film writers it tended to sound like recited titles, and stage dialogue could not be transcribed onto film intact. Comedy material set its own trap with spotting gags and holding for laughs; without a live audience to try it out, who could tell how audiences would react and how comic timing should be calibrated? Musicals, in which the script was seldom the strongest feature, had such peculiar hazards as the need to plausibly integrate songs into dramatic action. In fact, one justification for all the backstage films made in 1929 and 1930 was that they could skirt the issue entirely. It was far easier to cut to a revue or nightclub number than attempt an organic merger of song and dramatic action. Broadway, with its deliberately artificial musical aesthetic, could pull this off; motion pictures, more immediate and intimate, often could not, and early musicals were thus littered with song cues dropped in like bags of molten lead.

Once again, brash Easterners came to mix in with movieland veterans. In many productions the scenario (plot outline) and continuity (scene structure) were assigned to experienced movie people, and the newcomers wrote the dialogue. Like songwriters, few New York playwrights resisted the temptation to spend time in the sun, though many returned home shaken by the experience. This is not to imply that their talent was much exerted. The results of both camps, veterans and upstarts, too often emerged as stale and robotic, with devices and formulas used in less than infinite permutation. The prototypes—*The Jazz Singer, The Singing Fool, The Broadway Melody, Broadway, Burlesque [The Dance of Life]*—were stolen from over and over, nearly to the point of copyright infringement. Hoofersongwriters, vampy chorines, faithful sweethearts, feisty or malaprop-prone comedy relief—these stereotypes acquired little freshness when used with carbon-copy regularity.

While a notable name will occasionally surface on the writing credits for these films, the work does not always enhance the writer's reputation, partly because a fair rule of thumb is that for every writer credited, there are six or more who worked on the script. Ben Hecht, who provided the original story for *The Great Gabbo*, saw a provocative concept become irreparably botched in its final form. Herman J. Mankiewicz, a brilliantly erratic figure with such later credits as *Citizen Kane*, fared unevenly in adapting *The Vagabond King* and poorly with *Honey* (1930). After shocking Broadway with *Rain* and *The Shanghai Gesture*, John Colton embellished the story and dialogue of *The Rogue Song* with a few, not enough, trademarked lurid touches. Oscar Hammerstein II, having seen some of his work mangled upon transfer to the screen, did a superior job of putting old wine in new bottles for *Viennese Nights*. Some others succeeded, every so often, in giving musical scripts moments of distinction. Led by the Lubitsch operettas (mostly written by Ernest Vajda), Paramount musicals were often witty, even those as flimsy as *Let's Go Native* (1930, written by George Marion Jr. and Percy Heath), which had among its quota of mischief some intentionally clunky song cues that delightfully sent up the whole gambit.

Dance Directors

The inherent artificiality of musicals, as magnified by the eye of the camera, was never more apparent than in dance. A performer bursting into song in any but a rigid onstage-in-performance context could easily seem quaint or odd or silly; to follow it with a dance and bring on the chorus, as Broadway did, looked absolutely impossible. Integration into dramatic continuity was but one aspect of a greater difficulty, for nowhere did there exist a frame of reference for putting dance to film. It was apparent early on that the film frame functioned far differently than the proscenium as a vessel for action. Nonetheless, a 1929 movie dance director—the term "choreographer" was not yet in use—would simply come in and stage a routine, which the director would shoot straight through from several angles simultaneously, and the editor pieced together whatever came out. There was little thought of teamwork, let alone effecting a cohesive union of cinema and music and movement, and the results lay there. In these pre-Jerome Robbins/Agnes deMille/Gene Kelly times, dance direction on stage and film was neither an integrated nor highly developed art. The prime goal was to keep performers in something approaching unison, to which cinema could add only the occasional formation that the camera *might* find interesting. The studios hurriedly enlisted the services of some of the biggest (or at least busiest) names in theater to stage the early musicals numbers. The most prolific of them were Larry Ceballos and Jack Haskell (Warners and First National), Sammy Lee and ballerina Albertina Rasch (MGM), Seymour Felix (Fox), Dave Bennett (Paramount), and Pearl Eaton (RKO). Competent stage veterans, they generally lacked the creativity or instinct to rise above their restrictive and repetitive assembly line circumstances.

The dancing in *The Broadway Melody*, unrefined as it was, set the tone for most early film choreography: warmed over proscenium-bound routines, often shot nearly off the cuff with little cinema. Even so, Irving Thalberg's order to reshoot "The Wedding of the Painted Doll" is an early example of an intuitive attempt to try for something more. There was also Robert Florey, garnishing the routines in *The Cocoanuts* with overhead angles and other dynamic traces. Unfortunately, time and expediency and the proscenium mentality were all too powerful. Most often, it was set in stone—the singer sang, then the chorus came on and did the routine. If the soloist could dance, O.K. If not, he or she could hurriedly get out of the way. Over and over, ever longer lines of chorus girls kicked higher and higher as beplumed Follies girls paraded in the background, and the camera sat there. In *Glorifying the American Girl* (1929), Florenz Ziegfeld attempted to put his trademarked spectacles on film in toto, with predictably misconceived results. A *tableau vivant* of "The Lorelei" might have been impressive onstage; on the screen in Technicolor, with its performers frozen into position, it resembles nothing remotely cinematic. The only movement is provided by the camera, as cinematographer George Folsey pans across the performers in a jerky U-shaped formation, then cuts to an immobile long shot.[16]

Occasional respite came in the form of an accomplished dancer—Marilyn Miller, Lupino Lane, Ann Pennington—or a good song coupled with a lively concept, such as "Singin' in the Rain" from *Hollywood Revue*. Sometimes, as with *Sunny Side Up*'s "Turn on the Heat," a number could get by on sheer outrageousness. As Fred Astaire would certify some years later, intimate dances could work better on film than the mammoth productions. Smaller scale usually meant a more flexible camera and a more feasible projection of personality. In *Sally*, Marilyn Miller and Joe E. Brown's knockabout comic dance is far more beguiling than her later ballet with chorus. Instead of placing Miller statically within the frame, Ceballos and director John Francis Dillon permit her free movement and a sense of space in the smaller numbers, the camera following her (and Brown) along. In the formalized confines of a stage ballet she seems less fresh, for the stolid surroundings and regimented chorus work inhibit her.

Big-name soloists like Miller were far less prevalent than chorus numbers. Those, taken as a whole, are a pretty uninspiring lot, ponderous and pedantic and elementary. They were necessarily so, in order to accommodate the embryonic dance skills of their participants. Some of the most uncoordinated ensemble work ever beheld by a mass audience can be found in 1929 chorus routines; one might well wonder how some of these less-than-terpsichorean hoofers landed their spots and why so many onerous bloopers were allowed to remain. The first of several reasons is that movie spectators had not yet been conditioned to expect perfection in dance. Live

---

16. *Glorifying the American Girl* does have the most interesting choreographic credit of any film of the time: Ted Shawn, one of the century's early innovators. Nevertheless (like "The Lorelei"), the dances are nothing to write home about.

stage routines traditionally fell prey to problems with ensemble and precision, and film audiences did not necessarily expect anything different. Also, naturally, there are the two Hollywood mainstays: time and money. With over a dozen musicals in production at any given time in late 1929, low-priced available talent was in unprecedented demand. For once, all those starlets (of both genders) eternally flocking to Movieland could grab a spot. Some of them did have dance or chorus experience; many who didn't lied on their application forms, as the films make clear. A good appearance and a dollop of enthusiasm counted more than skill, and of course there were additional considerations related to the casting-couch school of musical training. In any case, so long as the number didn't go completely to pieces the dancers' mistakes might stay in the final cut. Lower-budget productions, lacking the wherewithal to reshoot, were obviously most susceptible, but some big-scale efforts had problems as well. Thus, eternity is left to contemplate the sight of tuxedoed gentlemen in *Gold Diggers of Broadway* and *The Great Gabbo* scrambling to retrieve the canes they've dropped, and one young lady in *Puttin' on the Ritz* who can't seem to stay in line or do any of the same steps as her fellow chorines.[17] In New York studios, bona fide Broadway people sunlighted (as it were) in features and shorts while hoofing in theaters at night. It's worth noting that despite their ostensible experience, these dancers, as seen in *The Cocoanuts* and *Glorifying the American Girl,* seem no more polished than their California counterparts.

As 1930 progressed trappings and overpopulation began to give way to energy and ideas. One big change came in mid-1930 when Busby Berkeley arrived to stage the dances for *Whoopee!* The former William Berkeley Enos was born (in Los Angeles) into a theatrical family, and after military service and an acting stint turned his attention to stage directing. When there arose jobs for dance staging he took them, even though he never considered himself merely a choreographer and was in fact not particularly adept at laying out steps. He made a name for himself first as a dance supervisor and later as overall director in more than twenty Broadway shows, among them *A Connecticut Yankee, Present Arms,* and *Golden Dawn.* After accepting Sam Goldwyn's offer of $1,000 a week, he immediately made his presence felt on the set of *Whoopee!* The nominal director, low-profile anonymity Thornton Freeland, had nothing to do with the dance numbers. Berkeley took over, making it clear from day one that he would approach the sequences less as precision drills than as routines conceived through and in terms of the camera's eye. His work on *Whoopee!* first put into play the techniques that rapidly became his calling cards: the overhead shots, the geometrical arrangements, the successive close-ups of chorus girls, the

17. That the latter two numbers were the work of dance director Maurice Kusell perhaps indicates something or other.

"waves" and other formations. Unlike his later extravaganzas at Warner Bros., Berkeley's early film work is as much stage as cinema, with many of his chorus groupings being fairly routine. Yet the intent and imagination are always there to show how far the musical had come in less than two years. Nor was Berkeley's the only imaginative mind at work in 1930. "The Varsity Drag," staged by Sammy Lee for *Good News* (MGM), and Dave Bennett's "I Want to Be Bad" in *Follow Thru* (Paramount) both indicate how much the numbers had improved: they were becoming more inventive, snappier, more fun. Filmed dance was beginning to find its own syntax.

Performers

Broadway pros, film veterans, vaudevillians, opera stars—on every fathomable level, onscreen talent provided 1929 audiences with a Pandora's box of musical offerings, a bounty of mixed blessings. In the court of misconceptions still surrounding sound's introduction, the realm of the performer is Exhibit A. Yes, there was a massive influx of new onscreen talent coming in from Broadway and points west. But for every Al Jolson there was a Bessie Love. These two can be said, in fact, to form the era's prototypes: the seasoned stage pro who seemed overscaled on film versus the camera-savvy movie actor with middling musical gifts. Certainly the stage performers were there in abundance, the Maurice Chevaliers and Helen Kanes and Lawrence Tibbetts. Less expectedly, so were the film people. Whether or not they had the ability, whether or not they had the desire, few movie actors, from Ramon Novarro to Myrna Loy to Buster Keaton, escaped contact with musical performing. Either way there were always surprises, for it was impossible to predict who would succeed in musicals and who wouldn't.

STAGE PEOPLE

Theater veterans are closely associated with the first era of movie musicals, and they surely made a great deal of noise. They were also held responsible for much of the audience disillusionment when it set in around the summer of 1930. Fannie Brice in *My Man* had been the first to prove that undeniable talent plus Broadway fame might not equal film stardom. Movie-star charisma could be more tenable than stage experience, and when the early novelty wore off the public tended to opt for known quantities. Packaging was as important as talent, and style could triumph over substance.[18] The

---

18. This concept would find its ultimate expression in the 1980s with music video, in which performers' abilities could matter far less than a high concept, and projection of effect took precedence over exigencies of voice or even music.

studios were continually scouring Broadway and vaudeville and touring companies for talent, which was then hurriedly signed to short-term contracts. The influx of stage people was so sudden and extreme that in June 1929 Actors' Equity mounted an effort to set up shop in the film colony. Not unexpectedly, studio plutocrats quashed this attempt, and unionization would have to wait for the formation of the Screen Actors Guild in 1935.

When the stage players arrived in Hollywood, their mettle would sometimes be tested first in short subjects; more often they were immediately starred in features. It was all hurry hurry hurry, and some of the people who might have done well after time and care and preparation were instead pushed out into the spotlight in what amounted to public screen tests. A few did succeed in this fashion. Jeanette MacDonald, for example, had the great good fortune to make her film debut in *The Love Parade* under the meticulous tutelage of Ernst Lubitsch. Similarly, Bert Wheeler and Robert Woolsey, joined together as a comic team for Broadway's *Rio Rita*, were given fitting showcasing when they made their cinematic debut repeating their stage roles.

Some performers worked out; many tried it once and failed. Unquestionably, the premiere musical comedy diva of late-1920s Broadway was Gertrude Lawrence. Here was true star magnetism: an erratic vocal instrument and a lack of conventional beauty combining to produce an overwhelming swell of appeal and glamour captivating audiences for thirty years. Her Movietone short had been judged successful back in 1927, so she seemed to be a natural for movies. However, *The Battle of Paris* (1929) was a flop of nearly heroic proportions in which nothing worked, not a self-indulgent and poorly photographed Lawrence nor Cole Porter's so-so songs nor, least of all, Gene Markey's heinous script. Charisma obviously did not always transfer onto film as it had with Jolson and would again with Chevalier and Tibbett and a few more. Others with less confident native ability could not understand the camera's ruthless habit of ferreting out any trace of insecurity or self-consciousness and magnifying it manyfold. Conviction, even talent, weren't enough. Harry Richman furnishes a case in point. However much he may have fancied himself Jolson's equal, however well he sang, it didn't play when it came time to put it up on the screen in the dramatic scenes of *Puttin' on the Ritz*. Notwithstanding a script that would have let Olivier down, Richman failed glaringly, unable to project even his own patented personality. Likewise Ted Lewis in *Is Everybody Happy?*, dumped into a story that made *The Singing Fool* seem like *King Lear*. Who could succeed against those odds?

With the more generic leading men from Broadway, the failure rate was also pronounced if less flagrant. Charles King led the way, and others soon followed. J. Harold Murray had scored on Broadway as the romantic lead in *Rio Rita*, and he had looks, acting ability and a voice that would all

Musical People: Buddy Rogers and Nancy Carroll in *Follow Thru*.

Ramon Novarro and Dorothy Jordan in *Devil May Care*.

transfer well to movies. Somehow, it just didn't work: the bravado seemed overblown, the heroism more than a mite hammy. Likewise Dennis King, a classically trained actor who became a matinee idol in Broadway operettas, climaxing with a smashing success as François Villon in *The Vagabond King*. Paramount paid him a great deal to do the film version, after which, noticeably, there was no follow-up. Audiences felt he was not so much acting as declaiming, with gestures to match. Magnetic it was, but after being subjected to two hours of such performing, especially in close-up, viewers felt exhausted. Such stage juveniles as Allen Kearns, Jack Whiting, Joseph Wagstaff, and the superannuated Oscar Shaw fared no better, managing to come off as simultaneously overripe and callow. One of the more conspicuous Broadwayites on the scene was second-rung operetta star Alexander Gray, whose fine baritone won him a series of major roles at Warners/First National. The voice projected far more than the personality, and when movie operettas died in late 1930 so did Gray's film career. Of all Broadway stars, in fact, the most lasting contributions came from musical comedians. Eddie Cantor was given a can't-lose star buildup by Samuel Goldwyn, Joe E. Brown fast became Warner Bros.' biggest comedy draw, and the Marx Bros. let nothing so incidental as film performing hinder their lunatic rampage.

Rouben Mamoulian, directing Joan Peers in *Applause*.

Alice White, in costume for "Jig Jig Jigaloo" in *Broadway Babies*. *Photofest*.

On the surface, Broadway's female headliners might have seemed to offer more possibilities. Marilyn Miller's success in *Sally* was encouraging and though audiences rejected *Applause*, Helen Morgan's personal reviews were glowing. Jeanette MacDonald, her spirit not deterred by a string of Broadway flops, bloomed on film as she never had on the stage, and as few of her rivals did. Onward they came: operetta's Vivienne Segal and Ethelind Terry, the piquant Irene Bordoni, *Show Boat*'s Norma Terris, Ziegfeld star Mary Eaton, stylish chanteuse Marion Harris. None worked out. Improper showcasing, weak stories, and unflattering photography all proved as much of a hindrance as they had with Gertrude Lawrence and Fannie Brice. Bordoni was a little long in the tooth to play the ooh-la-la coquette on film; Terry made no impression; Eaton came off as a blank clone of Marilyn Miller; Terris was gelid and unphotogenic; Harris was wasted. Vivienne Segal, given more chances to succeed, also suffered more. She had not had the opportunity to go to Warners to re-create her stage role of Margot in *The Desert Song*, and when she did make it out she was handed the tedious *Song of the West*, the feeble *Bride of the Regiment*, and the horrendous *Golden Dawn* (all 1930). In none of these did she have direction and photography to facilitate her projection of the lyric sensuality so attractive on Broadway, and by the time she appeared in a genuinely good movie musical, *Viennese*

Nights, neither the studio nor the public cared. A lesser stage name, Bernice Claire, fared better for a time, but like her perennial costar Alexander Gray was gone by the end of 1930. Irene Dunne was the exact opposite. Her debut in *Leathernecking* (1930) went almost unnoticed, yet somehow RKO/Radio saw beyond the singing ingenue; she was soon established as one of the decade's most popular and versatile players. It took longer for Ginger Rogers, also from Broadway. Following her feature film debut in early 1930, she thrashed about for several years before finding her niche.

Little by little, audience backlash built up against many stage performers. The influx of new talent had been too sudden and extensive, and the fan magazines began to accurately reflect spectators' disinclination to give up all their old favorites. MGM's *Lord Byron of Broadway* (1930), a fairly pungent backstage story, had an almost entirely stage-based cast—Charles Kaley, Ethelind Terry, Marion Shilling—with a recognition factor of nil. *The New Movie,* one of the more intelligent fan rags, nailed it unhesitatingly:

> The producers assembled a cast recruited from the stage and the result is a film almost utterly lacking personality. The one good bit is turned in by the screen actress, Gwen Lee. The story had real possibilities [and] might easily have developed into an excellent single—but didn't. The producers never will cease experimenting with stage players when they have plenty of Hollywood talents handy.

After Broadway, vaudeville and variety were the biggest suppliers of music-oriented players. Talkies, particularly in their musical wing, had already began to cut into vaudeville's business and would continue to do so. Vitaphone took an early lead in uncovering available and willing participants, most of whom proved better suited to shorts than to features. Vaudevillians attentive enough to detect the approach of the death rattle flocked to the soundstages in droves. One early comer was performer/producer/songwriter Gus Edwards, a legendary figure on the circuits and best known for cowriting "School Days" and other corny standards. Eyeing the future, MGM hired Edwards in the summer of 1928 to oversee their musical program and make occasional film appearances.

Only gradually did the realization sink in that few of these people could act, especially in that dreary procession of mammy stories tossed out to vaudeville stars of both sexes. Comedy-song team Van and Schenck fared no better with *They Learned About Women* (MGM 1930), in which brash numbers collided with a script fraught with phony pathos. Warner Bros. had at least the germ of the right idea with veteran compère Frank Fay, who was showcased as the host of the revue *The Show of Shows;* indeed, some critics and spectators liked his work, as unwatchable as it seems today. Attempted follow-ups clearly revealed that he belonged onstage, not in movies. Some of the more successful vaudevillians were those not shouldered with the burden of carrying films, but used to advantage in showy subsidiary roles. Marjorie White and Tom Patricola at Fox, Lillian Roth and Skeets Gallagher at Paramount, Cliff Edwards and Benny Rubin at MGM all honed their shtick in variety and in legit. Their sassy wisecracks and screwball songs and abundant energy were diverting, at least until they wore out their welcome by playing the same role again and again.[19] With radio aiding talkies in speeding vaudeville to its death, it was inevitable that radio personalities would turn up, typically with woeful results. In short subjects and cameos, perhaps; not in leads. Rudy Vallee's immense airwave popularity did not translate to movie fame when he starred in *The Vagabond Lover*. Likewise Morton Downey, who made little dent despite considerable promotion.

Whether through xenophobia or simple quirky fate, few big-name foreign imports did anywhere near as well as Chevalier. Despite the success of *Paris*, Irene Bordoni did not fare too well, her leading man Jack Buchanan little better. Then there was the delectable Evelyn Laye, a West End star who had beguiled Broadway in Noël Coward's *Bitter Sweet*. Lamentably, all her beauty and charm and talent went for little by the time of her film advent late in 1930 in Goldwyn's disastrous *One Heavenly Night*.

Vitaphone had staked much of its early claim with opera stars, and a few divas and divos made features. Lawrence Tibbett was the exemplar here, an absolute sensation in *The Rogue Song*. He could act, he was relaxed before the camera, and he could pull off a bravura grand manner without seeming ridiculous. Also, the fact that he was comfortably American cut through audiences' fear of opera as the habitat of elitist foreigners. All that, and he had a baritone voice to kill for. It was a package that others, even the Martinellis and Giglis, could not hope to emulate. Radio did make an attempt with a rival American baritone, Everett Marshall, in *Dixiana* (1930). While no one had reason to complain about Marshall's voice, his appearance and acting were far less impressive and compounded the film's failure. Fox engaged José Mojica, a good-looking Mexican tenor whose U.S. fame was made in Chicago instead of the Met. Visions of a singing successor to Valentino were dashed instantaneously by Mojica's *One Mad Kiss* (1930), a dire event. Fox did better by John McCormack, who was less of the opera stage than the concert hall and whose repertoire gave him a distinct edge. That he was neither youthful nor comely mattered little when that quintessential Irish tenor ladled out all the standards in *Song O' My Heart*. Perhaps seeing the example of Marion Talley, opera's more prominent women stayed away from the movies. The main exception was

19. Also from vaudeville, in an arresting musical appearance: Julian Eltinge. The best known female impersonator in the business sang several numbers in his only talkie, a quickie called *Maid to Order* (Jesse Weil Pictures, 1930).

Grace Moore, whose early work was hardly memorable; her film fame would not arrive for some years. Warner Bros., claiming high hopes for Metropolitan Opera mezzo-soprano Alice Gentle, squandered her talents with frightening ease. Costarring as a jealous Bolshevik in *Song of the Flame* would have been enough for many self-respecting professionals; it was thus no small achievement that Gentle had already outdone this with her previous appearance as the vengeful Mooda in *Golden Dawn*. She came close to making a complete fool of herself, and suddenly Verdi and the Met seemed very far away.

SCREEN VETERANS

If the newcomers to Hollywood tallied a mixed score, homegrown product fared better, on the whole, than might be presumed. After a few months it was apparent that the movie musical was going to find its own way and its own personalities. A trained voice (*vide* Carlotta King) and stage seasoning often counted for less than a face the camera could dote on or the ability to project gleaming self-confidence onto the screen. Accordingly, Hollywood's younger and older guard both took the plunge. For some it was a snap, for others (and for their audiences) an ordeal. It was the Dolores Costello-May McAvoy gambit again, name-recognition and movie star savvy outweighing good sense. This time, it often worked—as a once-only stunt or, in a few cases, a genuine career rebuilder.

Young contract performers bore the greatest work load at studios and so added the greatest amount of song and dance to their repertoire. Most of them were fresh faces without preset images and thus could move to musicals without jolting public expectations. Anita Page's casting in *The Broadway Melody* proved to be sound commerce if not great art, so others followed. First National's blonde bonfire, Alice White, found a ready niche in backstage tales; newcomer Joan Bennett was enlisted several times; and Robert Montgomery was put, sometimes uneasily, into a few musical roles at MGM. At Paramount there was Nancy Carroll, and however unwillingly she took to the genre, she certainly made an impression. Another audience sweetheart who had less pizzazz than Carroll but far more clout was Janet Gaynor, who had rapidly ascended to the position of preeminent actress at Fox and moved with unexpected éclat into her studio's biggest musical hit, *Sunny Side Up*. Her winsome untrained way with song and dance added new dimensions to the waif appeal cultivated in her silent romances and helped to solidify her position as one of the biggest draws in the business. Carroll and Gaynor each had a regular leading man whose approach to musicals echoed theirs, though, unlike Buddy Rogers, Charles Farrell always remained overshadowed by perennial costar Gaynor. In silents, along with drop-dead looks, he projected a uniquely innocent virility. Talkies erased much of that, alas, by exposing a nasal voice given to simpering line read-

(*above*) Winnie Lightner in *Hold Everything*. (*below*) Dance director Sammy Lee coaching Joan Crawford on the set of *The Hollywood Revue of 1929*.

ings and insipid song renditions. As a solo act in talkie drama he floundered, but in musicals, where Gaynor bore the main load, he made do with appearance and amiability and accumulated spectator goodwill.

The Rogers-Carroll and Gaynor-Farrell duos typified the conventional approach taken to musicals by Hollywood's younger generation. The trump card of older and more established players was the element of surprise. The prototype here was Ramon Novarro and his success with "Pagan Love Song." When it came time for his full-fledged talkie debut, MGM led off from the vocal division with the unstinting *Devil May Care*. A similarly unexpected singing success came courtesy of Bebe Daniels, who had been around for years as a middling-to-popular star. Fledgling Radio, searching for its Rio Rita, found Daniels unexpectedly up to the task, and her lush soprano and fervent romantic conviction carried the film to an immense success. One of the biggest of silent stars made a similar move to equal effect. By the middle of 1929 Gloria Swanson had been the quintessence of movie queen for nearly a decade, and the legend was starting to need some refurbishing. With a surefire soap opera as her talkie entree, she exceeded all anticipation, for *The Trespasser* was the most spectacular sound debut of any silent favorite except the white-hot Garbo. Swanson's incisive way with dialogue would have been boon enough, but the real ear-opener came with her ardent singing of "Love (Your Spell Is Everywhere)." Audiences heard, gasped, and applauded wildly, and Swanson was back on top. Other silent favorites manifested varying degrees of competence in singing and dancing roles. Colleen Moore, Billie Dove, Carmel Myers, Joan Crawford, and Dorothy Mackaill were among those who won somewhat bemused praise for their contributions. With Clara Bow, Corinne Griffith, and Marion Davies the enthusiasm was a bit more muted, and by 1930 it was clear that not everyone could pull it off. Leading men took the plunge as well, less conspicuously yet with some enthusiasm. The paragon of silent-screen villainy, Noah Beery, raised many eyebrows by channeling his arch-depravity into basso profundo in two operettas at Warners/First National. (After the mind-boggling *Golden Dawn*, there were few requests for Beery's musical services again.) More conventional silent leading men also became crooners: Lloyd Hughes, James Hall, Reginald Denny, and Ben Lyon all proved to have reasonably engaging voices, and second-string heart-throb Lawrence Gray took to song in a big way, despite an only passable tenor. Even Western star Ken Maynard came aboard, as the screen's first singing cowboy.

Voice Dubbing

For the film favorites who *had* to sing despite an ear-shattering lack of aptitude, there were voice doubles, commonly known later on as dubbers.

The situation depicted in *Singin' in the Rain* was not totally fabricated, for some tin-voiced idols did enjoy the services of offscreen vocalists. In the days before prerecording, dubbers were actually on the set, singing into the mike while the star mouthed the lyrics, as when Joseph Diskay gave voice to Warner Oland's mimed chanting in *The Jazz Singer*. The coordination was sometimes a bit off, and as the practice continued numerous observers smelled and heard a rat. *Photoplay* blew the whistle in its July 1929 issue in an article entitled "The Truth About Voice Doubling," which led off with the admonishment, "When you hear your favorite star sing in the talkies, don't be too sure about it." The highest-profile culprit cited was Richard Barthelmess, who had made a hit (part-) talkie debut in *Weary River* (1929) as an ex-con who turns tunesmith. The article confirmed what had been widely assumed—that he had not done his own singing—and added that First National had contracted the dubber, Johnny Murray, to sing for Barthelmess in future films as well. Also tagged as feigned vocalists were Laura La Plante *(Show Boat)*, Corinne Griffith *(The Divine Lady)*, and Barry Norton *(Mother Knows Best)*.[20] Later, there would be Betty Compson and Sally O'Neil in several films each and Mae Murray in *Peacock Alley* (1930). Audience impatience with this flummery was such that when MGM produced the all-star *Hollywood Revue*, studio publicist Pete Smith let it be known that Joan Crawford, Marion Davies, and other cast members would sign affidavits vouching for the authenticity of their singing voices. When MGM cast Greta Garbo as a 19th-century Italian prima donna in her second talkie, *Romance* (1930), she refused to be seen singing with a dubbed voice. Director Clarence Brown resorted to some fancy footwork: either she was heard singing from offscreen only or, when required to appear in an excerpt from Flowtow's *Martha*, was replaced by a stand-in shot from far, far away.[21] The vocal doubling was less convincing, for Diana Gaylen's fragile coloratura took to Garbo's Nordic contralto about as well as a duck to asphalt. Indeed, after the run of voice doubling in 1929 the practice was not used that much during the first musical wave. Nothing, certainly, to compare with the wholesale dubbing Hollywood took to later, such as the many voice replacements in adapted Broadway shows. Singers or not, players in early

20. Griffith sang for herself in later pictures. Eva Olivotti sang for La Plante and Sherry Hall supplied the voice for Norton, who did his own piano playing. La Plante was also dubbed in *Captain of the Guard* (1930). More extreme instances were Louise Brooks and Paul Lukas, whose speaking voices were dubbed by Margaret Livingston and Lawford Davidson. Lukas's Hungarian accent was too heavy, and Brooks, who did have a good voice, left Paramount before *The Canary Murder Case* was made over as a talkie. A later instance of a completely dubbed actor was another heavily accented performer, Anny Ondra, in Alfred Hitchcock's *Blackmail* (1929), voice furnished by Joan Barry.

21. Garbo also made use of a double the following year for her Javanese cooch routine in *Mata Hari*. She appeared in the close-ups only, while dancer Dorothy Wagner swung her hips in the longer shots.

talkies were most often forced to sink or swim on their own merits, such as they were. If it was sometimes a foolhardy thing to do, it did give the performances a certain unpolished appeal and integrity absent from the smooth-grained perfection in later Hollywood musicals.

That type of conviction, that confidence in the face of daunting obstacles, was surely as much a component of these films as Vitaphone discs and silly song cues. So was paradox, the trait most readily apparent when assessing the aspects of these movies. There were so many contradictory forces at work: second-rank songwriters achieving the greatest success, tone-deaf executives making decisions regarding placement and replacement of songs, technical successes achieved by those (like Douglas Shearer) with little training or preparation, financial failure setting in once aesthetic progress was made. And more: Technicolor, with its strange predispositions and bumpy rise-and-fall, the intractable ways through which some performers succeeded and others did not, the uneasy alliance of the new people and the old. It all proved an unavoidable and often forgotten maxim in the motion picture business: there are no magic formulas, no failsafe sure things, no one-way-only methods. It was the most haphazard epoch in the history of the industry, a time when chance and accident and reversal of fortune were all commonplace. This early on, without years of trial and experience, there never was any precise way to calculate what would work in a movie musical and what would not. Nothing else could account for Gertrude Lawrence's musical failure in the face of Bebe Daniels's success, or for those green skies shining brightly over Technicolor production numbers, or for so many other peculiarities. In this most superficially formula-bound of film genres, there were no formulas at this time. Tendencies, imitations, yes—but if the theme remained basically the same, its variations were without number.

CHAPTER 6

Dueling Mammies

The blare and brass of the Jazz Age was accompanied by a more mawkish side that abounded in books, plays, songs, and films.[1] The Victorian age's quaintly noxious brand of sentimentality was supplanted by a more aggressive hokum incarnated most audaciously in depictions of parent-child relationships. Plays and films such as *Over the Hill to the Poorhouse, Abie's Irish Rose, Madame X,* and *Humoresque* were among the many works cashing in their sentimental chips with an appeal weighted heavily toward familial guilt. Tracts could be, have been, written about the pathological underpinnings in these tales of motherly sacrifice and father-son conflict; no doubt about it, family relationships have been used to produce some dire popular culture. The twenties provided major examples, which Freud might have surveyed by starting with Oedipus and concluding with Fannie Hurst, and the coming of sound attained for this peculiar strain its deranged apotheosis.

Al Jolson, before entering movies, had not been aligned with such things. His Broadway shows were raucous, slimly plotted vaudevilles, and the main sentimental component in his image lay in an occasional syrupy ballad or paean to ersatz optimism: "April Showers," "Back in Your Own Back Yard," and the ubiquitous "My Mammy." He slid into the morass only when he went to Warner Bros. to become the center of the gluttonous clutch at the heartstrings that is *The Jazz Singer.* As Samson Raphaelson

---

1. In the film *Singin' in the Rain,* the Gene Kelly character overhauls a bad early talkie, *The Dueling Cavalier,* by turning it into a musical. He asks his sidekick, Donald O'Connor, to suggest a title; O'Connor, cognizant of the Jolsonmania rampant in 1929, comes up with *The Dueling Mammy.* (His second suggestion, *The Dancing Cavalier,* gets the nod.) Somehow, that silly mammy title seems to evoke the whole rash of Jolson clones taking over early talkies.

complained, the film was a sentimental distortion of the play, and much of this coarsening had been achieved by adding song to an already soggy mix. The mother love angle was underscored, the song "My Mammy" was brought in for a specific tie-in, and through Jolson's powerful vocalizing the old formulas were given a potent jump-start. Then, the epochal success of *The Singing Fool* seemed to back up the belief that the new soggier Jolson was infallible. Film moguls, themselves weird self-styled paternal figures, observed the tears and grosses, so it followed that the copycat Jazz-Singing Fools erupted in full force early in 1929.

These counterfeit Jolson vehicles, these "mammy pictures," were an early leading trend of the talkies for several logical reasons. First and last, there was the bottom line. While no producer had the right to expect *Singing Fool*-type millions, the profit margin could be substantial. Crass in intent and bereft of ingenuity, a mammy story could be shot on the cheap with a lowly backstage plot that did not require such trappings as production numbers, Grade-A supporting artists, or Technicolor; the only major item in the budget was usually the star salary. Ease in casting was another prominent factor, for it seemed that any high-powered vaudeville or Broadway headliner could be called on to sing a song, shed a tear, and do his or her monomaniacal best to elicit audience sympathy.

The plots of mammy films dealt, with only minor variation, with the struggle of one man or woman to overcome professional obstacles and family-related strife and find happiness as a singing superstar. In this basic recipe there was ample room for adversity and discord, show-must-go-on gallantry, self-sacrifice, and lots of songs. Along with frequent autobiographical overtones, a dash of ethnicity, usually Jewish or Irish, added some spice. Also often included were such exotica as childhood disease, imprisonment, custody cases, parental ultimata, and scene-stealing kids and animals. There was often an equivalent of the theater's "eleven o'clock song," a climactic heartwrencher modeled in spirit if not tune and text on "Sonny Boy." Style, flair, and taste were conspicuous only by their absence. If films such as *On With the Show!* and *Hearts in Dixie* at least attempted to extend the boundaries, mammy pictures were the lazy converse, forever looking back at *The Jazz Singer* and *The Singing Fool* and their huge profits. Such imagination as they contained was confined to the leap of faith that their stars' musical know-how could carry them through dramatic scenes. No wonder they were mostly one-shot affairs: these performers were not right for such stories, many of them not at all suited to film or indeed any kind of acting, and anything beyond a once-over might deplete their repertoire. As early as December 1928, with *My Man*, *Variety*'s Sime Silverman had perceived the cinematic limitation of Fannie Brice:

Having used up all the dynamite, it's going to be tough to parallel this concentration of material in another Brice picture. This one unfolds everything she can do and has done. If it has taken her all of these years to gather the material she has, how long will it take Fannie to get as much and as good stuff again?

As a whole, these films are as contemptible as they are ridiculous, and many in 1929 were aware that the concept of the lowest common denominator was here being taken to an extreme. Yet, for a time, even small film companies desired to join the mammy parade.

In typically self-cannibalizing fashion, Warner Bros. was the first to bring on the imitators; *My Man* was actually in production at the same time as *The Singing Fool* in the summer of 1928 (though released four months later), and very shortly the studio contracted Ted Lewis and Sophie Tucker for similar fare. One performer Warner did not enlist was George Jessel, who had departed the studio after the *Jazz Singer* contretemps.[2] In the face of Jolson's triumph, the best Hollywood contract Jessel could wangle was with Tiffany-Stahl Productions. For a small outfit churning out low-budget product, Tiffany occasionally aspired to big (and, with apologies, gem-like) things, much as Warners had a few years earlier. However, Tiffany's guiding spirits lacked the Warners' ambition and daring, also their chain of theaters. As with many small studios, Tiffany films were sold on an independent basis and did not always play the larger theaters or larger towns. When accomplished director John M. Stahl allied himself with the outfit in 1927, the company began going after more substantial properties and bigger names such as Jessel. He starred in two silent features shot back-to-back in the spring of 1928. One was *George Washington Cohen*, the other a blatant rip-off of *The Jazz Singer* at first called *The Schlemiel* and later renamed *The Ghetto*. Either way there was no doubt as to the slant of the material, with Jessel as a mother-fixated jeweler's son from the Bronx who longs to make good in show biz, eventually does, and woos a socialite. Its only interest lay in the lead character being named Georgie Jessel, although for all its similarity to Jessel's own life it could have been Paul Bunyan. Possibly with an eye toward the future, Tiffany shelved *The Ghetto* following its completion, then months later, around the time *The Singing Fool* opened, announced that it would be remade to include songs and talking sequences.

Graced with the more upbeat title of *Lucky Boy*, the film went back into production at the end of November as another of those early-talkie paste-ups, which *Photoplay* aptly termed "patched and vulcanized." By that point

2. While there was no lawsuit following Jessel's departure from Warners, there was rancor, apparently on both sides. In November 1928 Warners advised its Canadian office that it was not to spend any time promoting Jessel's Warner films.

it was commonplace for a silent film to have talking scenes tacked on, and sometimes, as with *Abie's Irish Rose*, a film already released might be withdrawn to have sound added. The makeover of the Jessel picture, for which he was credited with both dialogue and titles, was particularly interesting. Although the silent version had been filmed in California, it was decided to shoot the sound sequences (with a different director) in New York, in a makeshift studio on the eleventh floor of the RCA Building on Fifth Avenue. In hastily constructed mock-up sets, Jessel and a few other performers (including Glenda Farrell and perennial Marx Bros. nemesis Sig Rumann) remade about 40 percent of *Lucky Boy* as a talkie. Jessel's jokes and songs naturally dominated the sound footage, especially one of the five tunes, "My Mother's Eyes." It became permanently identified with him, not surprising considering he performed it in the film on four separate occasions. Silly and stopgap it may have been, yet the work on this bicoastal talkie was done with a certain measure of skill and effectiveness and with relatively superior sound recording that flattered Jessel's voice and partly obscured his singing's marked inferiority to Jolson's. Tiffany, which had already put brief sound sequences into a few other silents, quickly saw *Lucky Boy*'s potential, arranged for press screenings, and used the positive advance reviews to sell it to scores of independent exhibitors. In a Jolson-crazy atmosphere Tiffany hawked Jessel and "My Mother's Eyes" as a next-best substitute. His recording of the song also helped matters, and when it went into nationwide release in February of 1929, *Lucky Boy* quickly made a mint, particularly in the small towns where Tiffany films were prone to run most frequently. Jessel, who later asserted that the whole dumb affair was unworthy of him, was probably galled by the enforced comparison to Jolson, likewise the knowledge that he would never draw mass love as his rival did. Nevertheless, the timing was sufficient to make his film a success.

The next pretender to the mammy throne was a far different character. Eddie Dowling styled himself as a Broadway jack-of-all-trades—actor, singer/dancer, songwriter, scriptwriter, producer, impresario—as well as a self-proclaimed arbiter of wholesome "all-American" (i.e., Gentile) entertainment, such as the Broadway shows *Honeymoon Lane* and *Sally, Irene and Mary*. While lacking Jolson's force-of-nature personality and Jessel's nervy crust, he was as much an egotist as any of his fellows. With talkies on the way he signed aboard with a new company, Sono Art Productions, set up expressly to produce low-budget sound films. Dowling was enlisted to co-write and star in the company's initial offering, into which would be injected as much potential audience appeal as possible—translated, at this moment in time, as "keep it as close to Jolson as you can." The result was *The Rainbow Man*, with Dowling as Rainbow Ryan, headliner of an itinerant minstrel show, who adopts an orphan (Frankie Darro) and falls in love with the child's aunt (Marion Nixon). The standard ingredients were in place: stern grandfather, child-custody brouhaha, four songs (two cowritten by Dowling) and a carload of heart-tugging schmaltz. While there was nothing remotely distinguished about it, Dowling's reputation gave the project some luster and, as only the third musical all-talkie to play in New York, *Rainbow Man* was given a major-league premiere on April 16, 1929.[3] Public enthusiasm fast made it obvious that *Rainbow Man* would retrieve many times its modest cost, and even some critics felt that the corn had been presented palatably enough. *The New York Post*'s backhanded compliment was typical: "Seldom has the screen seen and heard a more successful blending of the wet-eyed sentimentalities and relentlessly cheerful platitudes which make a smashing boxoffice success." Quite so, as Dowling and Sono quickly signed a lucrative deal with Paramount, who distributed the picture in exchange for a share of the profits.[4]

Unlike most mammy stories, the appeal and success of *Rainbow Man* were based on the whole package; it was clearly, if unintentionally, not a one-man show in the Jolson manner, and modern observers may find both star and film reticent nearly to the point of nonexistence. Dowling was a curiously contradictory performer, an uneasy mix of brash confidence and insistent heart-on-sleeve sensitivity. He had neither a distinctive voice nor a forceful style, and unlike the flattering publicity portraits issued by his handlers, he had a very whimsical look on film, with an overbite and jug ears that give him the appearance of an elongated elf. He stacked the odds against himself rather intensively here by pitting his talents next to those of the engagingly precocious Darro and the fresh and attractive Nixon, plus a dog and a trained monkey! At one time or another they all steal the picture from its star, who forever keeps trying to steal it back, and the ongoing struggle provides inadvertent diversion over a drawn-out ninety-five minutes. Even so, and despite its contrivances and drab songs, *Rainbow Man* is so humble that somehow it's fairly endearing. The small-town setting is refreshing after the synthetic urban bustle of other early musicals, and the minstrel sequences give a quaintly authentic sense of an era in entertainment drawing to a close.[5] Dowling does manage to get the last word in a monstrous and unintentionally hilarious final scene, in which

3. To perform onstage at the premiere Dowling conscripted the services of one of his protégées, a large and large-voiced young singer named Kate Smith. She had earlier made her Broadway debut in Dowling's *Honeymoon Lane*.

4. Aside from its financial success, *Rainbow Man* achieved an interesting distinction in September 1929 when an exhibitor and sound engineers toured the Far East with a print. How audiences reacted is not known, yet it's emblematic of the era's topsy-turvy nature that this meek little film was the first talkie to play in some of the farthest corners of the world.

5. Dowling, who never wears blackface, loses points with an Irish-dialect story, in jaw-dropping bad taste, about his mother's train trip to New York and her encounter with a black porter—a sorry relic of "respectable" twenties entertainment.

Marion Nixon, Eddie Dowling, and minstrels (Sam Hardy, center), simulating happiness as *The Rainbow Man* grinds to its conclusion.

Rainbow's estranged sweetheart is tricked into attending the minstrel show, he woos her back by crooning "their song" (the dull "Sleepy Valley") and then proposes to the mortified girl before the entire audience. "Mary," he wails, "I'm not trying to embarrass you!" Really? Yet, outrageous as that last scene is, *The Rainbow Man* generally steers clear of the obnoxious over-kill of *The Singing Fool*.

If Eddie Dowling was too low-key to wrest the mammy spotlight from Jolson, the next entrant had no difficulty. It was strange that Paramount was eager to buy into *Rainbow Man,* considering that the studio had its own clone ready to roll two weeks later. With the premiere of *Innocents of Paris* everyone knew that talkies had a major new player, and Maurice Chevalier succeeded Jolson as the supreme musical film star of the age. Paramount was Hollywood's most continental company, with numerous European actors and directors on the payroll, and Chevalier was a logical addition to the roster. Up from the ranks of French music halls to, eventually, Folies-Bergères stardom, he had honed his effortless cafe style and manic-suave charm. An easy bet for talkies, he arrived in New York in October 1928 and shot a French-language musical short at Astoria. Directed by fellow expatriate Robert Florey, *Bonjour New York!* was intended for foreign distri-bution and as a screen test for Chevalier. He promptly went on to Califor-nia, where Paramount, surveying recent successes, felt it prudent to adhere to the status quo, even with such an unJolsonesque artist as Chevalier. Perhaps scenarist C. E. Andrews had peeked over Eddie Dowling's shoulder; *Innocents of Paris,* apart from Chevalier, might better have been called *L'homme de Rainbow.* The mimeograph mentality was beginning to accrue. Chevalier was cast as Maurice, an Apache junkman who stumbles across an orphan boy drowning in the Seine, fishes him out, and meets the kid's pretty aunt and stern grandfather. While the conflicts mount, Maurice wins an amateur singing contest and becomes a star. This script was so junky that Harry D'Arrast, the scheduled director, quit Paramount in frustration. His replacement, Richard Wallace, lacked D'Arrast's Gallic sophistication, which was perhaps just as well, and despite the primeval technical conditions and doleful scenario shepherded film and star through a smooth shoot in late 1928 and early 1929. The result was perceived as a double triumph for Chevalier—a victory at the box office and over his script. The premiere, on April 26, had made that immediately apparent, as reported in the *Exhibitors Herald-World:*

> It is rather a pity that he had to be introduced to American audiences in *Innocents of Paris.* . . . The reaction of the audience [at the Criterion Theatre] was unmistakable. Though they thought Chevalier magnificent . . . they found [the] story . . . so artificial and synthetic that it might have detracted considerably from his performance. . . .
>
> It is not particularly pleasant not to be able to go into a rave over Chevalier's first picture for Paramount. He is too great an artist, however, not to deserve the most minute and most critical inspection. Chevalier deserves the best, even of criticism.

Mass audiences, less exacting than an opening-night New York crowd, made *Innocents of Paris* one of the year's biggest successes. In quick time, as with Jolson, the impressionists were out in force. One did not have to go far to see a Chevalier parodist at work: the straw hat, the distended lower lip, the boulevardier/bedroom accent, the insinuating grunt-and-croon rendition of the hit song "Louise." But while the mannerisms were imitable, the persona was not. Even when dumped into a faux-Jolson vehicle which he despised, Chevalier was obviously an original, as well as a gift to the infant musical.

Needless to say, there was and is only one reason to see *Innocents of Paris.* One would never tend to associate pity with the indomitable Chevalier, yet it is hard not to feel sorry for him here: a major international star in a triumphant American debut, swamped by a story cobbled out of garbage. Wallace is unable to muster more than a dollop of Parisian flavor, and except for Chevalier and the overdone peasant attire of his parents it could all be set in Sioux Falls. Chevalier is also saddled with an uninflected Louise, Sylvia Beecher, of whom little was heard afterward. Reciting her lines in glassy tones, she is in charm and ability Chevalier's complete opposite;

she's certainly too dull to warrant his marvelous rendition of that song, though as shot by Wallace it's a classic scene, up to the birds in the trees that do twitter her name. Chevalier, surprisingly, radiates boyish modesty—a far cry from the familiar roguish-seducer persona. At the amateur show, performing "Nous avons les ananas"—a quirky, perky answer to "Yes, We Have No Bananas"—he gesticulates and uses a barrage of different voices and faces, like nothing seen in sound film so far. Later on, when he opens in vaudeville billed as "The Mysterious Prince," the straw hat comes out and the more familiar persona emerges. As Chevalier sings "Pardon Me, It's a Habit of Mine," Wallace cuts to a montage of adoring women, who finally come up and kiss the star. (It's the only intimation of sex in any mammy picture.) The Chevalier myth is officially codified and, fortunately, "Sonny Boy" seems very far away.

It was not far enough away for the Jolson cycle to be at an end, however. Morton Downey had made an agreeable debut in *Syncopation*, and shortly afterward was signed by the Pathé Film Exchange to headline its first venture into musical talkies, an excruciating item bearing the deadly and appropriate title *Mother's Boy*. It was *The Jazz Singer* with an Irish brogue—stern father, family conflict, beckoning showbiz fame. This one outdid all its predecessors by having Tommy O'Day leave his Broadway show just as the opening night curtain is rising to rush to his mother's sickbed, where he serenades her back to health with no less a theme song than "I'll Always Be Mother's Boy." Tommy's press agent makes sure this good deed receives front-page coverage, and in no time there's a new star on Broadway and a happy (and rich) old lady. This wretched pot of kitsch was shot in February 1929, in the same Harlem studio that had recently turned out *Syncopation*, by director Bradley Barker. (He usually handled only short subjects, and after his work here returned to them.) Pathé, who apparently had no more shame than scriptwriter Gene Markey, planned the film's release to coincide with Mother's Day and, insultingly, premiered it as a reserved-seat Broadway attraction. Opening night audiences reacted with ill-disguised hostility, and admirers of Downey's shamrock-croon tenor found little solace in the face of the miserable script, chintzy production values, and poor recording. Pathé had not even taken care to offer the critics seats with good sightlines and proper acoustics, and most of the reviews were horrendous. Just the same, *Mother's Boy* ended up in the profit column once it reached the smaller towns. Downey ("Broadway's Golden-Voiced Tenor") plugged the songs on radio and on records, and provincial audiences flocked to see what Pathé advertised as "A Story of Romance and Sentiment Tunefully Told."[6]

6. *Mother's Boy* does survive, although understandably it does not turn up often. It's difficult to pick out its worst feature from the array of choices: the heavyhanded stereotypes, the dumpy Downey's piercing high notes, the by-the-numbers drip of the screenplay, Barker's

Warner Bros., which missed Mother's Day, followed soon enough. Fannie Brice having done *My Man*, Sophie Tucker strutted in to do, essentially, *My Daughter*, otherwise known as *Honky Tonk*. By September 1928, when she signed for her film debut, she had been an institution for nearly two decades and, unlike Brice and Jolson, earned her fame away from Broadway, in vaudeville and music halls and on records, steadily modifying her material for a larger audience. "My Yiddishe Mama" became less germane to her image than "Some of These Days" and a slew of hot ballads belted out in her robust alto. Her billing, "The Last of the Red Hot Mommas," was anything but motherly. If she was fat, her double-entendre lyrics averred, it only meant there was more of her to go around. The enticing title *Honky Tonk* might have been the cue for a gamy, funny script showcasing her spicy songs and raucous allure. But not at Warner Bros. In pitifully unimaginative fashion, Tucker was shoved into that same dreary mold. Naturally she was cast as someone named Sophie, who sings hot ditties in a lowdown dive only because (surprise) she's putting her daughter (Lila Lee) through school. True to the genre, the girl is a bit of a snob, and upon discovering the source of the money, she denounces Mama; it's left to her society fiancé (George Duryea) to effect a reconciliation. Whatever did this kind of story have to do with Sophie Tucker—a lusty, vital performer who had little truck with melodramatics and less with self-denial? Not much, for scores of performers could have been substituted with little alteration.[7] The only compensation was a cabaret setting that gave ample latitude to Tucker's racy ballads; otherwise, the writing veered just short enough of tragedy to keep her from making a fool of herself, she was photographed with some care, and Lila Lee helped her carry the confrontational moments. All that remains of *Honky Tonk* are soundtrack discs, which deliver as expected: weak and perfunctory drama leavened by Sophie in optimum voice. She slings out a sassy "He's a Good Man to Have Around," a zesty "I'm Feathering a Nest (for a Little Bluebird)," and the inevitable "Some of These Days" and "I'm the Last of the Red Hot Mommas." Musically she falters only when called on to elicit pity with a torchy "I'm Doing What I'm Doing for Love." Heartbreak was never this woman's métier.

Honky Tonk opened in the summer to predictable reviews—respectful of

---

helpless direction, and cheap sets that give the production a bomb-shelter-type sparkle. Pride of place, however, may go to Beryl Mercer's cloying performance as Mother O'Day. Mercer's best-known role, as Jimmy Cagney's imbecile ma in *The Public Enemy*, was also her most typical, and in *Mother's Boy* she goes beyond even the usual excesses to provide possibly her most indelible demonstration of the fine art of the whine.

7. Some weeks earlier, Fox had released the similar part-talkie *Not Quite Decent*. Louise Dresser played a cafe singer with an illegitimate daughter and performed the theme song, "Empty Arms," in blackface—a trick Warners somehow missed.

the star, contemptuous of the plot. To audiences, too, the similarity of plots was growing apparent, and despite the Tucker name grosses were well below expectations. Though the economical production ensured that it turned a profit, Warners could not have failed to notice that Sophie's film brought in only half the return of *My Man*. She did not return for a follow-up and commented definitively on the whole affair the following year when she recorded "Hollywood Will Never Be the Same." In addition to various conquests among the ranks of leading men and cowboys, she boasts that "At first my director said he'd like to test me, and I let him know/That I've been tested by experts and okayed, long ago!"

Another studio, Universal, got on the Jolson bandwagon with what seemed at first a tinge of originality. In July 1928 it had announced *The Minstrel Show*, a tribute to that era in American entertainment to star Eddie Leonard, one of the last barnstorming minstrel men and also a major name in vaudeville. Harry Pollard was slated to direct the film as the second installment of a trilogy chronicling America's regional entertainment. *Show Boat* was the first, followed by the Leonard opus and concluding with *The Barnstormers*. These lofty plans deteriorated about the time Universal put the magic name Jolson on its payroll. Not Al—his brother Harry, who was mentioned for the star spot intended for Leonard. After weeks of uncertainty both *Minstrel Show* and *Barnstormers* were scrapped, and Jolson left. For Leonard, Universal underwent a burst of creative energy and decided to star him in another mammy knockoff. Directed by hack Robert Hill, it was filmed as *Harmony Lane;* by the time it opened in July 1929 it had been imaginatively retitled *Melody Lane*. Under any name it was a fiasco, the first mammy picture to engender outright hostility from audiences as well as critics. Leonard, in his late fifties, was called upon to play a youthful minstrel star with a baby daughter and a pretty wife (Josephine Dunn, repeating her *Singing Fool* role). Again there was marital strife, a custody battle, the slide from stardom, the daughter suffering injury, and show-must-go-on heartbreak. And this time nobody cared. Leonard was a total washout, so completely lost before the camera that he made not so much as a dent when performing his theme song "Roly Boly Eyes." The script's slavish lack of imagination inspired critics to offer little essays on the dangers of inordinate imitation:

> Here we go again. Al did it in "The Singing Fool," so why can't I? Eddie Leonard runs true to movie Freud and tries to cash in by redoubling another's bid. If Al cleaned up on a mere shower of tears, what price deluge? . . . As the lady behind my left shoulder remarked with considerable conciseness and precision—UNHOT.

The symbolic end of the mammy era came just a few weeks later, when the master returned to show just how little the matrices had varied. August

6, 1929, marked the third anniversary of Vitaphone's debut, which Warner Bros. decided to commemorate with a gala New York premiere. Warners could have vividly demonstrated the inconceivable changes in the intervening three years by flaunting one of its sharp new products, such as the Technicolor *Gold Diggers of Broadway*. Instead, sedentary and prosaic, it marked the epoch with a film that rather pathetically looked backward to prior glories. The film was Al Jolson in *Say It With Songs*, with Davey Lee. In other words, the fool sings again.

By early 1929 *The Singing Fool* was an industry legend, and Jolson was under some pressure to top himself. While his ego was not of the sort to reflect on the need to exceed past glories—he saw everything he did as the best—he knew that the world was waiting and that his next move better be sensational. While he was still shooting *The Singing Fool*, Warners announced his next film as *Mammy*, later mentioning that the new Mrs. Jolson, Ruby Keeler, might be costarring. When his third film finally went into production in March 1929, Mammy and Keeler had taken a back seat to Davey Lee, who had just scored a hit in the predictably titled *Sonny Boy*.[8] A rematch with Jolson was inevitable, so Warners pulled out Formula 1–A, titled it *Little Pal*, and to cinch the *Singing Fool* tie-in recruited director Lloyd Bacon (fresh from *Honky Tonk*). Imitation begat imitation: Marion Nixon had shown such appeal in *Rainbow Man* that she was engaged to provide distaff twinkle, and the Dowling film also necessitated a title change. It had featured a song called "Little Pal," so Jolson's film, which used another song with the same title, was renamed *Say It With Songs*. In addition to nailing the movies' current obsession with melody, it could have been, in its elucidation of Jolson's philosophy, the title of any performance he ever gave.

The Happy-Third-Birthday-Vitaphone/*Say It With Songs* gala on August 6 was the usual tinselly affair, Jolson playing to the gallery and exuding bogus magnanimity about how great it was to be making these swell talkies for the fine Warner people. But many in the know were aware of the rumblings beneath the good cheer. Jolson, whose sense of humor tended to evaporate when the subject of money arose, had been pushing Warners for a larger slice of the pie. When his suggestion of a profit-sharing deal was vetoed, he threatened to shop for a berth on another lot. Finally they agreed on two more films at a higher salary—yet insiders knew that the smiles at the premiere were forced and unfelt. This was entirely appropriate, too, for while *Say It With Songs* was a surefire hit, it was even more clearly a cynical rehash of the star's prior successes. The critics attacked Jolson's poor choice of material, and Darryl Zanuck, credited with the story, drew heavy fire.

8. Frequently and erroneously referred to as a Jolson film, *Sonny Boy* costarred Edward Everett Horton and Betty Bronson, with Jolson in an unbilled cameo; it was a farce originally titled *She Knew Men*, and Davey Lee sang the title song.

(One critic sneered that "Zanuck probably couldn't have written a weaker story but to date he has never tried.") The script merely slapped together the more lachrymose parts of Jolson's previous stories, added a couple of bits from other mammy pictures, and basted it with an extra gloss of melo-drama. This time Jolson was Joe Lane, a radio singer with gambling fever, a loving wife, and a son, Little Pal. When Joe's boss (Kenneth Thomson, replaying his oily seducer from *Broadway Melody*) makes a play for the wife, Joe deals him a fatal punch. Convicted on manslaughter charges, he goes to jail where, incredibly, things go downhill for everyone in the movie and in the audience. Joe nobly renounces his wife so she won't be shackled to an ex-con, Little Pal is run over by a truck, there's an emergency opera-tion, and on and on until a happy ending. Bad as the story was, its details were more outrageous: Jolson arrested during his radio show, over a live mike; Little Pal unwittingly implicating his father at the hearing; Jolson singing drippy cheer-up songs to the other prisoners in his cell block; the boy finding miraculous cure at the mere sound of Daddy's voice. To add to it, the production values were cheesy and the score lacked the catchy Jolson songs. Touted as a worthy successor to "Sonny Boy," "Little Pal" vanished on sight, and the only new song up to Jolson standards was the boisterous "I'm in Seventh Heaven," despite the censorship that diluted its "hell" into a meeker "heck." [9]

With a worldwide gross of $2.25 million, *Say It With Songs* was a hit, as anticipated. But it was a hollow victory; something was terribly wrong. For the first time Jolson's public did not leave the theater in a state of tearful ecstasy, and even setting aside the critics it was common knowledge that word of mouth on the picture was awful. There he was, The World's Great-est Entertainer, sobbing over Davey Lee once again—and suddenly seem-ing ridiculous. Not only was the previous excitement absent, but Jolson, Zanuck, and Warners had underestimated their audience and possibly cheapened it. With the same formula regurgitated once too often, the buildup of sludge and corn was becoming excessive even for committed Jolsonites. Significantly, Jolson's next Warner films, *Mammy* and *Big Boy* (both 1930), avoided parental heartbreak. Mammy films were obviously wearing out their welcome, and a few observers began to comment that there was a clear danger regarding excess quantities of *any* kind of musical. Had anyone cared to notice, the reaction to *Say It With Songs*, which had

9. Current prints of *Say It With Songs* are missing two Jolson numbers, the standard "Back in Your Own Back Yard" and "I'm Crazy for You," which he sang in the radio studio in the first reel. Due to rights-clearance problems, they were deleted prior to the first TV runs in the 1950s; their absence puts Jolson's first song nearly a half hour in, making things seem even more dismal. This is, by the way, the rare Jolson film in which he never appears in blackface.

little to do with its high gross, was a clear harbinger that the American public would not stand to have its tastes miscalculated.

Warners had something worse in store a few weeks later. Ted Lewis was one of the few big vaudevillians to push the pop pathos full strength, going so far as to bill himself "The High-Hatted Tragedian of Jazz." However, his basic appeal lay less in ballads than in other aspects of his profession. A first-rate clarinetist, he led a "jazz" band, in this case a pop type of Dixieland, and propelled his group to stardom in vaudeville, on records, and in Broadway revues. His raspy voice could talk through a song more convincingly than many skilled vocalists, and his trademarks were indelible: a top hat, a jauntily invincible manner, his theme "When My Baby Smiles at Me," and cries of "Yes, sir!" that punctuated nearly everything he did. Most of all, he had that catchphrase. "Is everybody happy?" was a showboating, applause-inducing gambit that never failed to draw cheers; inevitably, it became the title of his screen debut. Warners had the title in place long before a story was put together, and as was so often the case, that story turned out to be a major problem.

Warners first signed Lewis in July 1928, but difficulties related to both him and the script postponed the project for nearly ten months. When shooting did finally begin, director Archie Mayo found himself with a star totally at sea in all except his songs, and the filming went over schedule and budget as Lewis struggled to cope with the demands of dramatic acting. Not that the Joseph Jackson/James A. Starr screenplay could be termed drama: this was the balmiest, most dire scenario in all the mammy canon, with new and singularly ridiculous details sufficiently outrageous to warrant recounting:

> After retiring from the podium, Victor Molnar (Lawrence Grant), one of Budapest's leading conductors, emigrates to the United States with his wife (Julia Swayne Gordon), his young son Ted (Lewis), and his prized violin, a gift from Emperor Franz Joseph. In New York, Ted locates his former sweetheart Lena (Ann Pennington), now appearing in the Ziegfeld *Follies*. Success has gone to her head and she rejects Ted, who then fails in his attempt to get a job playing in a symphony orchestra. With the Molnars facing eviction for overdue rent, Ted secretly pawns the prized violin. One day, while practicing his clarinet in the park, he meets Gail (Alice Day), who works for a booking agent, and soon has a job fronting a jazz band in a Hungarian cafe. His parents go to the symphony, find that he is not in the orchestra and, badly shaken, decide to go to a Hungarian restaurant—the one where Ted is playing. Enraged, Papa Molnar tells Ted that he never wants to see him again. Though he and Gail become temporarily estranged, Ted (now calling himself Ted Todd) soon leads his jazz band to national prominence. Molnar, heartbroken

over losing both Ted and the violin, leaves home. After scoring a hit at a Carnegie Hall benefit, Ted discovers his father backstage, working as a janitor. On Christmas Day everyone, including the contrite Lena, is reconciled in Ted's posh new apartment, and Ted's band plays for the happy guests.

About all that was missing was a dying baby. It was a pity that the script was the woeful piece it was, for there was a kernel of an imaginative idea: the experiences of immigration and assimilation portrayed through music. This transition from classical Old World formality to boisterous New World jazziness might have been turned into stirring music drama in the right hands. Perhaps at another studio, where higher-profile directors were given leeway with musical subjects, it might have been possible. This, however, was Warners, churning them out to fill its release program for the season. There was no need for creativity.

As with many Warner films of the period, *Is Everybody Happy?* has long been considered lost. Two fragments have resurfaced, however, to give visual as well as aural testimony to the pros and cons of putting a performer like Ted Lewis in such a property. Fortunately for Lewis's reputation, both extant sequences are songs, thus sparing future curiosity-seekers the opportunity to assess his histrionic gifts. The songs bracket Ted's confrontation with his parents in the cafe. "New Orleans" is typically raffish Lewis, pushing his band through lively Dixieland paces reminiscent of King Oliver's early recordings. Lewis and his clarinet are the main interest here, with some virtuoso blowing as well as acrobatics, Lewis twirling the clarinet like a baton. After his parents storm out, he essays "I'm the Medicine Man for the Blues," which became a standard item in his repertoire. "With my melodic strains I amuse," he rasps, struggling to telegraph to the audience that his heart is breaking. This is the other Ted Lewis, the less engaging one not averse to shoveling maudlin slop, and with material far below his best blue song, "Me and My Shadow."

Is Everybody Happy? went into release in October, and in venerable Warner fashion the timing was notably off. It played some areas about the same time as *Say It With Songs*, and in comparison with even third-rank Jolson, Lewis suffered badly. It didn't help that his film's title virtually encouraged a negative reply, one duly submitted by many critics.[10] Those who restrained themselves sufficiently not to give the inevitable "No!" responded rancorously—the reviews were as bad as those of *Melody Lane*. Much of the public stayed away, too, except in small towns. While *Is Everybody Happy?* did not lose money, its profit margin was well below the Warner average

10. As it would be again some fourteen years later, when Lewis starred in a second, unrelated film bearing the same title, this time a low-budget item produced by Columbia Pictures.

for that boom year. All things considered, it was utterly absurd to keep retreading these Jolson stories, and with this one the point seems to have finally hit home. Warners attempted no more musical sob stories.

A few other studios did have similar efforts pending, and among them was George Jessel, trying there again. He signed with Fox, a company which normally avoided Jolsonesque headliners, and was cast in a role for which he would seem cosmically unsuited—an Italian immigrant named Luigi. *Love, Live and Laugh*, based on a play called *The Hurdy Gurdy Man*, was not really a mammy story, yet it had many of the usual components. After falling in love with Margharita (Lila Lee), Luigi returns to Italy to attend his dying father and, caught up in the Great War, is blinded and sent to prison camp. Landing in New York after the Armistice, he discovers that Margharita, thinking him dead, has married. (Timing was everything in these stories.) Not just any other . . . but the only doctor in creation who can restore Luigi's sight. Operation over, Luigi and Margharita consider running away, but self-sacrifice intrudes and Luigi goes off alone, concertina in hand.

In reality it was not as bad as it sounds. The intelligent William K. Howard was a vast improvement over the usual run-of-the-mammy directors of such films, and while a Jessel piece seems far out of his sphere, Howard did his best to keep things in balance. This didn't go over too well with Jessel. The songs were kept to a minimal three, and though Jessel received co-credit for the script, several of the other roles were built up. Considering the star's difficulties with his Italian accent, this was all to the good. *Love, Live and Laugh* opened in November of 1929, and once critics got over the shock of seeing Jessel switch from ghetto boy to *paisan*, they commended the drama and cheered the direction. Not so the public. Jessel was so closely associated with *Jazz Singer*-type doings that this was seen as too great a stretch dramatically and ethnically. Shortly after *Love, Live and Laugh* played a disappointing engagement at the Roxy in New York, Jessel and Fox parted company. He returned to the stage and never again starred in features.[11]

A more conventional essay in parenthood and showbiz heartbreak opening a few days after the Jessel picture turned out surprisingly well. Nearly forgotten today, Belle Baker was in the 1920s a major name in vaudeville and on Broadway and records. Like Fannie Brice, her Anglicized name (formerly Bella Becker) did not preclude contact with her roots: one of her trademarks was the impassioned "Eli, Eli." Baker's plush and poignant contralto was one of the best instruments in the business, with inflections

11. He had already filmed his bit in Fox's all-star revue *Happy Days* and in later years would make cameo and guest-star appearances in films ranging from *Stage Door Canteen* to *Valley of the Dolls*. Most of his later association with the industry was as a producer and, interestingly, nearly all of his films were released by Fox.

and phrasing that transformed simple ballads into moving statements of love and loss. She also knew how to swing out on uptempo numbers and had introduced Irving Berlin's "Blue Skies" ten months before Jolson performed it in *The Jazz Singer*. Despite a matronly appearance, she was an intuitive dramatic performer, as good a bet as anyone to star in a tailor-made film, and in June 1929 she signed with producer Edward Small for a vehicle to be released by Columbia Pictures, just beginning to emerge from the abyss of Poverty Row. Under the hard-driving and legendary Harry Cohn, and with a nascent directorial talent in Frank Capra, Columbia's product was rapidly improving if still economical, its casts mostly made up of has-beens, yet-to-bes, and never-weres. Acquiring Baker's services was a coup, albeit not quite up to Columbia's claim that it was "An event as important as the coming of sound." The newly slimmed-down Baker was placed in a variant on mammy themes titled *Cradle of Jazz*, which scanned as *Syncopation* laced with *Honky Tonk*, with Baker in a vaudeville act with her husband (Ralph Graves) and son (David Durand, who had attempted to steal *Innocents of Paris* from Chevalier). When mom retires from the act to raise the boy properly, husband tumbles into the arms of a siren (Eunice Quedens). Son in tow, Belle walks out and scores a hit as a solo; it's left to the boy to reunite his parents. As usual there was generous opportunity for Baker to play to strength with new songs ranging from torch ("I'll Still Go On Wanting You") to bounce ("I'm Walking With the Moonbeams [Talking to the Stars]"). During shooting, *Cradle of Jazz* gave way to the less flavorful *The Song of Love*, and it was under that title that Baker's film was given a splashy premiere (by Columbia standards) in New York late in November.

At this point the mammy cycle had run its course, and while the corny likes of *The Song of Love* would not change this, it was still a pleasant surprise for audiences and critics to discover that Baker on film lived up to the ballyhoo. Her sincerity and professionalism transcended the mushy script, and unlike most of her fellows, she was neither intimidated nor diminished by the camera. On the contrary, close-ups gave her songs added eloquence. It was the first time since Maurice Chevalier that a star of one of these films seemed genuinely suited to film, and within its modest boundaries *Song of Love* was a considerable success, at least in communities where Baker was known. Audiences could tell the difference between her skill and the more perfunctory work of Sophie Tucker and others. Yet the mold for vaudevillians on film had already been struck and, true to form, Baker starred in no more films. Perhaps in this case it was wise to go one for one and quit while ahead.[12]

12. Aside from attesting to Baker's skill, *The Song of Love* is notable for the presence of Eunice Quedens (kwuh DENZ) as the temptress Maizie. Ms. Quedens is a very young Eve Arden, making her film debut (and singing and dancing) under her real name.

Would that Eddie Dowling had taken the same advice. In an era not noted for underkill, his self-promoting tenacity was impressive. In due time he topped *Rainbow Man* with more music, plot(s), melodrama, and slush, bearing the unnervingly mistaken title *Blaze O' Glory*. This was an absurd thing, an overwrought mélange of scraps and shreds from other talkies, and one critic pegged its dramatic terrain pretty accurately:

> Here is a production that at least is generous. Ever since the movies learned to talk there have been four surefire themes. The court room, back stage, the war and the little pal. *Blaze O' Glory* gives you all four of them neatly wrapped up. . . .

Dowling cast himself as Broadway star Eddie Williams who, on trial for murder, tells his story through a complicated web of flashbacks. During the war Eddie (a) was gassed, and (b) saved the life of Hummel, an enemy soldier. Unemployed after returning home, the depressed Eddie finds his wife Helen (Betty Compson) in the arms of another. He shoots the man— Hummel. All ends well (except for Hummel) when one more flashback reveals that Hummel, believing Helen single, genuinely loved her. This somehow leads the jury to find Eddie not guilty, and he and Helen go off, presumably in idyllic relief. Tucked in with all the flashbacks (which confused and finally exasperated many) were such typical Dowling songs as "Doughboy's Lullaby" and "Wrapped in a Red, Red Rose." For extra Sonny Boy appeal, Frankie Darro played a feisty variant of his *Rainbow Man* role, and Henry B. Walthall added sonorous authority as the defense attorney.

By the end of 1929, when *Blaze O' Glory* premiered in New York, talkies had progressed beyond this type of slapdash uncategorizable melodrama, and the reception was such that a few days after the premiere Sono Art recut it to remove some of Dowling's melodramatic and musical excesses. The press, invited back for another look, did not observe the surgery to have been terribly productive. To sell it to wary exhibitors, Sono blazoned expansive ads with laudatory comments. Reviews being what they were, these were from priests, rabbis, ministers, American Legion commanders, and the secretary of the Bronx chapter of Gold Star Mothers, all of them sent complimentary tickets. This type of flag-waving promotion, coupled with Dowling's pronouncements about the vile "barroom humor" abounding in films, was an ill-disguised effort to brand *Blaze O' Glory* a heartfelt public service instead of a crass hunk of commerce. All was in vain, as *Blaze* soon found itself rapidly and ignominiously extinguished on the grind circuit in small towns.

By early 1930 the mammy film was officially dead, a victim of its own narrow intentions. Other singing stars coming into the movies, such as Rudy Vallee and Harry Richman, were spotlighted in less morose fare, and while vestiges of the old formula did pop up with the likes of John McCormack, there was never again anything on the order of *Mother's Boy*. Occasionally, too, there would be the ill-advised descendant down the decades—Danny Thomas, Jerry Lewis (on television), and Neil Diamond in remakes of *The Jazz Singer*, Johnny Ray in *There's No Business Like Show Business*. But after the mammy singers and stories were gone they left behind a booby trap that few seemed to notice. In the summer of 1929, when the studios announced their plans for the upcoming season, few mammy films appeared on the list; there was, however, plenty of everything else—backstage tales, operettas, revues, Broadway adaptations, and so forth. In the months that followed, production of musicals would reach dangerously large proportions. A glut of mammy films had already killed audience interest in one type of musical and, though few moviemakers cared to address it, there loomed the strong possibility that quite shortly history would repeat itself.

CHAPTER 7

Hollywood
Revued

Up to the summer of 1929, the musical film owed as large a debt to Holly-wood as to Broadway, if not in presentation or inspiration then in material and general texture. *The Desert Song* and *The Cocoanuts* and the hybrids *Show Boat* and *Broadway* aside, the first run of musicals attempted to interpret the genre from a standpoint of cinema. While production numbers re-mained static stage presentations, the stories were conceived in filmic terms, sometimes—even in the mammy stories—with looseness and en-ergy. This contrasted significantly with talking dramas: *Interference, The Let-ter, On Trial, The Trial of Mary Dugan, Madame X, Coquette* were all theatrical successes before being adapted, barely, to the screen. The musicals based on stage shows followed in due time, but before their advent there began a distinctive phenomenon very related to the proscenium consciousness: all major studios planned, and most released, all-star musical revues. While not genuine stage transfers, their hearts and souls were far more of the theater than the soundstage, and they form one of the most peculiar, some-times risible, trends of the age.

It seemed at the time to make a great deal of sense. The stage was the standard-bearer, and revues were the apogee of Broadway magic. During the 1920s they had reached unprecedented popularity, with a decline just beginning as talkies came in. After 1927 Ziegfeld would produce only one more edition of the *Follies*, in 1931, though other annual revues continued to succeed, albeit in diminishing capacity: the *Scandals*, the *Vanities*, *The Little Shows*. In the Depression revue glitz seemed increasingly expendable, with occasional exceptions such as Irving Berlin's *As Thousands Cheer* (1933), probably the greatest of them all. Hollywood, unable to detect that the form had peaked, saw the flesh and spectacle of the revues, the grab bag of jokes and sketches, the songs and blackouts. They saw the money these shows raked in and the fact that they required little pretext or plot to tie things together. The movie musical, still finding its direction, was viewed as a competitor to the stage: an *extension*, not an alternative, and at first lacking Broadway's slickness and skill. So, to show audiences and stage producers just what they could do, the studios gathered their forces—contract players, songwriters, and technical personnel, the newly hired people as well as the established ones—to produce all-star house parties where everyone got up and did something. A crucial error was being made here. More than any other type of stage presentation, revues were inherently theatrical, incapable of cogent translation onto celluloid. The spectacle endemic to revues seemed stiff and foreign on the screen, and cinema's dashing intimacy was inappropriate to the revue. Consequently, the contrast—tension, really—between the two showed up on the screen more glaringly here than in any other films of the time.

The revues were, to put it gently, mixed bags. Most had at least some adequate moments, and all had parts unwatchable then, let alone now. Yet for such museum pieces they can't simply be labeled collections of ineffectual turns by stars trying desperately to fake musical talent. What has not been mentioned to any extent was how different they were from each other. Each studio, as it ended the silent era and plunged into sound, had cultivated its own procedures and standards, its individual concepts of talking pictures and audiences. No one could ever mistake a Fox film for one by MGM, and the directors and players at Paramount were completely unlike those at Warner Bros. This all carries forward in these revues, money-making show-windows for studio wares generating "See what we can give you now!" goodwill during the first calm after the revolution. However ludicrous, each is a vivid signpost to its studio's approach to sound in general and musicals in particular: state of the Hollywood pop art, ca. autumn 1929.

It's generally assumed that the first was the most famous of them, MGM's *Hollywood Revue of 1929*—another genius stroke by Irving Thalberg to keep up the lead forged with *The Broadway Melody*. Actually there had been predecessors of sorts. Back in 1925 Lee De Forest produced the unreleased Technicolor *Chauve Souris*, which he proclaimed as an improvement over the *Follies*. More to the point, there was the false start of the *Fox Movietone Follies of 1929*, which ended up far less a revue than originally intended, not so much an entrée to the form as an indicator of its potential. It also implied the stepchild concept of using a plot as a lame excuse for unrelated revue scenes, as was later done with such films as *The Great Gabbo* and *Paris*.

The *Movietone Follies'* lack of commitment to its genre, its prissy defusion of stimulating ideas, is typical of its studio, which rarely put the goods together in a showmanlike way. Only in a precious exception like *Sunny Side Up*, produced some months after the *Follies*, did Fox rise to the challenge. Mostly, the studio's approach to sound and musicals in the early years was as set forth in its *Follies*: bland and banal, lacking star- and staying-power, with such good ideas as occurred often bungled, and an interminable reliance on formula. The performers most frequently encountered in the Fox musicals—Janet Gaynor, Charles Farrell, El Brendel, Marjorie White, Sue Carol, Frank Richardson, Sharon Lynn—each fit into an unalterable niche. Only Gaynor's spunky charm and some moments of vitality from White and others broke through the ennui, and script and music interrelated in only the most tenuous and perfunctory fashion. It would always remain so with the Fox musicals, even down the years to Shirley Temple, Alice Faye, Sonja Henie, Betty Grable, Carmen Miranda, Dan Dailey. Through internal upheavals and management changes, Fox musicals somehow stayed pretty consistent: skillful technique, competent song and dance, personable performers cubbyholed into stereotyped slots, content rarely above standard, and imagination that surfaced once in a blue moon.

The ads for *Movietone Follies* promised "Broadway's Dazzle Brought to You in the Screen's First Follies." First it may have been, but Metro-Goldwyn-Mayer formalized the revue with a lineup few could equal. *The Hollywood Revue of 1929* opened on June 20 at Grauman's Chinese amid a blatant amount of to-do. MGM, never averse to lily-gilding, turned the Hollywood and New York premieres into circuses: Grauman's and the Capitol featured live billboards with scantily dressed women snuggled into the cutout letters of the title. The gimmick, which became the logo for the film, was literally a traffic-stopper: the New York Police Department shut down the Capitol's living sign after the second night, and a judge in Cleveland forbade its use there. Notwithstanding MGM's publicity department, *The Hollywood Revue* didn't earn its huge grosses solely through lush hype. In a real way, it delivered the goods. No matter that many years after the fact it resembles early television. Audiences in 1929 were awed; it was the icing on the cake of *The Broadway Melody*. If it lacked sentimental appeal, it had acres of flash, some laughs, song and dance in profusion. And stars—some of the biggest, some heard here for the first time.[1] MGM sold it as a lavish theatrical presentation, with two-a-day road showings long before

1. The credits don't skirt the grandiose in announcing "With the following galaxy of stars": Masters of Ceremony, Conrad Nagel and Jack Benny; John Gilbert, Marion Davies, Norma Shearer, William Haines, Joan Crawford, Buster Keaton, Bessie Love, Marie Dressler, Ukulele Ike [Cliff Edwards], Charles King, Stan Laurel and Oliver Hardy, Polly Moran, Gus Edwards, Anita Page, [Karl] Dane and [George K.] Arthur, Nils Asther, Gwen Lee, The Brox Sisters, Albertina Rasch Ballet, Natova & Company, The Rounders. Lionel Barrymore's appearance is not credited, and Asther's bit, assisting Benny in introducing the finale, does not survive.

general release; and with its proscenium and pit orchestra and intermission medley, it behaves like a stage show much of the time, albeit one with a cast no theatrical producer could hope to match.

As the *ne plus ultra* of its form, *The Hollywood Revue* sets forth all the problems of these productions. Granted the inherently lumpy and uneven format, far too often is there the feeling of one act very arbitrarily following another without reason or pattern. Here, a lack of pace and proportion weakens the feeling of MGM pizzazz the film strives to present, although considering its scrappy evolution this is not surprising. Like the Fox *Follies* it was a committee project that made several sharp turns on its way to the screen. In December 1928, showman/songwriter Gus Edwards, hired by MGM to oversee its musical shorts, announced a six-reel *Movietone Revue*. This evolved, around the time of *Broadway Melody*, into a feature-length minstrel show titled *The Revue of Revues*, with MGM's musical people— Edwards, Charles King, Bessie Love, Cliff "Ukulele Ike" Edwards—and dances staged by Sammy Lee, directed by silent-film veteran Christy Cabanne. In the second week of April, with shooting almost completed, Irving Thalberg and producer Harry Rapf looked at the assembled footage and saw how clearly its origins showed through: it was a musical short subject that had just kept growing and, like the Fox *Follies*, lacked glamour and showmanship. Metro at half-mast would not be abided, so in venerable studio fashion the overhaul began. Cabanne's work seemed especially monotonous, so he was replaced by Charles Reisner, a competent director of silent comedy (Cabanne, who did about half the film, received no credit). It had already been decided to add star lustre in the form of a song and dance by Joan Crawford, and after Reisner came aboard, so did Buster Keaton. After the remainder was shot according to plan the tinkering continued. Marion Davies and Laurel and Hardy, working on other projects, were required to shoot their segments on the graveyard shift.[2] The star larder was raided one more time for two of the studio's biggest names, Norma Shearer and John Gilbert, and the final touch came just ten days before the premiere. "Singin' in the Rain" had already been spotted as the hit of the show, and late at night on June 10, 1929, a herd of MGM players went through a quick reprise of the Brown/Freed song for the Technicolor camera.

Leo the lion, the first celebrity on display in *The Hollywood Revue*, stamps the proceedings as MGM absolute, the crude recording giving his roar the sound of furniture dragged across linoleum. The girlie sign that caused such a ruckus at the premieres flashes by just after the credits, originally, but no longer in existing prints, with the young women reciting a credo for

---

2. Studio records show that Davies shot her number on May 25, 1929, from 6 P.M. to 6:45 A.M., which makes the disoriented quality of her performance a little more understandable.

all revue films that included the lines "It's a picture yet it isn't, for we're in the talkie age/And you're going to see exactly what you'd see upon the stage." The opening number bears this out with *Broadway Melody*-type photography: long takes of group formations from the equivalent of a mid-range orchestra seat. Just as one becomes accustomed to the static technique, a surprise: as the chorus struts in front of a high-contrast backdrop, the film stock alternates between negative and positive. What now seems a trite prank was a welcome treat for viewers so far denied visual magic by the talkies, and small camera tricks pop up throughout the whole show. Typical studio anonymities, Reisner and Cabanne could manage some visual interest in lieu of a personal style.

The first impression of *Hollywood Revue* is one of irredeemable tackiness, with dull photography and cardboard decor and second-rate material and performances. Too, its production history ensured a lack of structure and unity. The minstrel idea set up in the opening number goes away without explanation before the halfway point, and the second half sags dreadfully; a dead camera defeats Erté's exotic designs in a lavish "jewel" number, a dismally prolonged turn by an adagio troupe demonstrates what killed vaudeville, and a routine with Charles King, Gus Edwards, and Cliff Edwards long overstays its welcome. The emcees, Conrad Nagel and an improbably young Jack Benny, are disconcertingly unctuous, their banter filled with empty effusion and labored putdowns, and Benny's timing would never be as sharp onscreen as on radio or television. Here, along with the skinflint and violin jokes, he's oddly set forth as a lecher.[3] Yet with the dead wood there are occasional good—if self-amused—ideas. Of all the revues, this one takes the most pleasure in reminding the audience that it is a movie, specifically an MGM movie: a whole number is devoted to MGM star Lon Chaney,[4] there are in-jokes (Norma Shearer is joshed about husband Irving Thalberg), and even the technology of early sound comes in for kidding. Prerecording gives Conrad Nagel a mellifluous dubbed voice to sing "You Were Meant for Me" to Anita Page (which literally deflates Charles King), and Bessie Love wails, "These crazy sound effects have made a wreck of me." The assurance that made audiences go to see the film is still apparent. MGM was irresistibly proclaiming its status as the largest and richest movie factory in the world, flaunting its names and know-how. Only a few months earlier the studio had invented the

3. One of the women who slap him is Ann Dvorak, later an interesting lead actress in *Scarface* and at Warner Bros. In 1929–30 she was a charter member of the MGM chorus, and can be easily spotted in nearly all the studio's musicals.

4. "Lon Chaney's Going to Get You if You Don't Watch Out," an admonition sung by Gus Edwards to a bevy of nubile coeds. The moody star declined studio attempts to put him in the number, if only for a surprise gag at the end. Another conspicuous if understandable absence is that of Garbo; the studio tried, without success. The third major omission from the roster is Ramon Novarro, on hiatus at the time of production, studying music in Europe.

movie musical. Now, while continuing to aim for the largest possible audience, it was making its musicals bigger and brighter.

Due to its inclusion in MGM's musical retrospective/eulogy *That's Entertainment!*, the first star spot is probably the most famous moment in any of the revues. Joan Crawford, hailed as "the personification of youth and beauty and joy and happiness," sings and dances "Gotta Feelin' for You," assisted by the Biltmore Quartet and pianist Dave Snell. The sight is not soon forgotten: a painfully self-conscious Crawford gamely sings a "hot" song, then flails her way through an ungainly Charleston, arms flapping and feet stomping in movements redolent more of pest-control than Terpsichore. There is disturbing and unavoidable overlay here. All the later qualities connoting this ultimate driven movie star—the extremes of dress and makeup, the frightened and frightening determination to survive every trend, the mass approval achieved at untold personal price, the rigidity calling itself discipline—can be glimpsed in embryonic form lurking within the young girl seen in *The Hollywood Revue*. Only a few years past her days as a chorus hoofer, she is sweet-faced, a tad amateurish, and willing—needing—to please everyone. The studio used this stint as a trial balloon for future musical endeavors, and since audiences liked her and admired her guts, she sang and danced in several more films. Nevertheless, any success she achieved in this area came only through that iron resolve to attain, or feign, versatility. The voice lacked resonance and melody, the dancing was merely emphatic; Crawford was not a naturally gifted musical performer. As it is, she comes off better in *Hollywood Revue* than Marion Davies, who performs a sort-of song called "Tommy Atkins on Parade." Davies's sponsor William Randolph Hearst enjoyed seeing her in male attire, it is said, so she is done up as a cadet and flanked by a platoon of very tall palace guards. Striving for a gamine quality, Davies enters miniaturized through a tunnel of soldier's legs, and her discomfort soon becomes palpable, her voice quavering with terror and seeming inebriation, her tap dance perfunctory, the projection of anxiety precluding all else.

Since Crawford and Davies were not of music, their discomfort within its realm is comprehensible. But the new people dominating the film, whose business was music, are often uncomfortable without a live audience. Whether or not they're photogenic, they do not know how to play to the camera. This was the great unlearned lesson of the era, as Charles King demonstrates when he sings a dead-on-arrival item called "Your Mother and Mine." Other examples include Gus Edwards, cowriter of that and most of the songs, and Cliff Edwards (not related), whose wimpish persona and drab looks are not at all stimulating, despite his "Ukulele Ike" vogue and distinctive falsetto scat singing. (His more lasting fame, years later, was as the voice of Disney's Jiminy Cricket.) Among those taking more naturally to their chores is Marie Dressler, whose work here made an enormous impression on audiences and MGM brass. Shortly after her success in *The Hollywood Revue*, in some ways as a direct result of it, her career was sensationally reborn with *Anna Christie* and *Min and Bill*, and this large and homely woman outran Garbo as the most popular star in film. Here she shows why. "I'm the Queen" is supposed to be a song, but despite her years in musical comedy Dressler doesn't try to sing and doesn't need to. Instead, she uses multitudes of shtick, mugging imperiously, slamming it across. She shoots menacing glances at the chorus when it threatens to upstage her, slaps her shoulder when she catches it undulating to the hot-cha music, and has a whale of a time. Likewise Bessie Love, who later joins Dressler and Polly Moran (Benny characteristically introduces the trio as "five lovely girls") for some disorderly musical slapstick. Moran scores points with a takeoff on "Sonny Boy" so boisterous that it reportedly blew out a couple of microphones.[5] Dressler is here in her element, looking monstrous in bloomers, assisting in an deranged rendition of Offenbach's "Barcarolle" in which all the instruments fall apart. Laurel and Hardy, more accurately employed by Hal Roach (who released his shorts through MGM), were given a few hours to assemble bits and pieces of a sketch, lame by their standards but in this context a small riot: Hardy as incompetent magician, Laurel as inept assistant, with the presence of a large cake ensuring mayhem. "I faw down and go blop," Hardy reports when it's over. Buster Keaton's routine follows the "Tableaux of Jewels" that opens the second half. Neptune's court, shot with a blurry "underwater" effect, is the setting, and Keaton is the enticing sea-princess, performing a Salome dance similar to one from his early vaudeville days. The screwy exoticism is aided by his getup: veils, bangles, Louise Brooks bob, tin cups for breastplates, kitchen utensils dangling from his waist. The number, which finishes with a suicide by asp (a string of wieners), is too strange to be really funny and too far away from Keaton's deadpan norm. But in a curious way, it kids both the absurd excess of the preceding spectacle and the lavish exotica so dear to most revues. Plus, as a star showcase, it's a bridge to the sound era. Keaton is permitted to retain the silence so vital to his persona and is able as well to use his immense acrobatic skills to musical comedy ends.[6]

Nacio Herb Brown and Arthur Freed contributed only two of the production's fifteen new songs, and if their "Tommy Atkins" was a non-starter, their second song was a mammoth success. This actually wasn't the first time out for "Singin' in the Rain"; it had been written late in 1927 for *The*

5. "Sonny Boy" was kidded in several early talkies, as here and in Dressler's "I'm the Queen." Some targets are fair game.

6. Director Reisner had worked well with Keaton the previous year on *Steamboat Bill Jr.* Keaton's routine replaced a similar spot originally planned for Marie Dressler. Though it was not filmed, Dressler did pose for some stills on the "Tableaux of Jewels" set as a diaphanously clad Venus, invitingly posed on the half-shell.

Hollywood Music Box Revue, where it made little impression. Brown and Freed pulled it out again when *Hollywood Revue* came along, and how right they were. And though modern listeners used to Gene Kelly might not care for Cliff Edwards and his ukulele, it has *always* been a good song. Sammy Lee gives it a fitting staging, with playback technique enabling the use of real rain without intrusive splashing, as Edwards and the chorus cavort through a stylized park while raindrops reflect on the shiny stage floor. With the staging, the Brox Sisters' engaging close harmony, and Arthur Lange's musical arrangement, the immobility of the camera is completely sidestepped, and it remains an irresistible mix of period charm and history. Apart from its use in the great film that bears its title, this song ideally evokes a time and place—America, the halcyon days right before the Depression—and serves to epitomize the entire genre of the movie musical. *The Hollywood Revue* gives it a presentation worthy of both the music and the myth. While its other songs fade in comparison, "Lon Chaney" is affably amusing and "Low Down Rhythm" is especially snazzy, brightly sung by June Purcell with a ballet-tap specialty by *Broadway Melody* alumna Joyce Murray.

Unlike most Technicolor sequences, which tended toward irrelevant show, those in *Hollywood Revue* spotlight its prime merchandise.[7] Norma Shearer and John Gilbert do (as opposed to act) the balcony scene from *Romeo and Juliet*, then offer an instant Jazz Age replay—she tells him the old man's a bad hombre when he's loaded, Romeo exits on "I'm utsnay about ouyay!" It's sweet and silly how these major stars try bad Shakespeare and descend from their thrones with ill-fitting slang. In 1929, the idea of such an image switch in color was immensely appealing to the public, and even today it's poignant to see Gilbert looking fit and relaxed right before the plummet of his career. The other color sequence begins as a more conventional display. Charles King croons "Orange Blossom Time," ballerinas prance about in turquoise tutus and execute the first overhead shot in color, and lightbulbs flash amid the blossoms for a final tableau.[8] Most studios' revues would have ended on this note of crass splendor, but this is MGM. The scene shifts to a backdrop of Noah's Ark on Mount Ararat (possibly, a dig at Warners) and that scene added at the last minute. For a final chorus of "Singin' in the Rain" the camera pans across stars in rain slickers. Crawford, Davies, Benny, Keaton mute and glum, Love radi-

---

7. Warner Bros. also inferred that color was an added condiment to star power, as ads for John Barrymore's *General Crack* (1929) boasted. "Resplendent scenes in COLOR show you what he really looks like as he storms recklessly into the vortex of cyclonic romance and adventure." Indeed.

8. King's attentive and otherwise unidentified partner is one Myrtle McLaughlin. At the premiere, Grauman's ushers thoughtfully sprayed the audience with orange scent, a trick previously used in one of Irving Berlin's *Music Box Revues*.

ant, Dressler mugging beneath her umbrella. Treasurable, only at this studio at this time.

The phenomenon of *The Hollywood Revue* and its mainly positive critical response did not go unnoticed, for within a few weeks all the major studios announced their own revues. It seemed a godsend, foolproof formula. Buy some trappings and songs, put in all the contract players—can any of them sing or dance?—and hawk the studio and make a bundle besides. The fact that MGM practically made up its revue as it went along belied the instinctive flair of its production machinery. For all their potpourri, these shows didn't throw themselves together. A more damaging fact was that *Hollywood Revue* owed much of its success to a novelty factor which would be lacking in subsequent efforts. And, dangerously, the decision to produce more revues came while *The Hollywood Revue* was playing only at Grauman's, to an audience grounded in the industry, and the nationwide reaction to this unconventional sort of film was completely untested. These were hard lessons, and a few months later, Warner Bros. shot itself in the foot while learning them.

"The Advent of a New Event in Pictures" was the untoward slogan of Warners' revue, which was personally supervised by Jack Warner. *The Show of Shows* was shot mostly in August and September 1929 and opened at the end of November. At $800,000, nearly double the price of *Hollywood Revue*, it was (except for *Noah's Ark*) by far the most expensive Warner film to date. It was mostly in color and overloaded with famous names, scads of songs, and a battalion of dancers and chorus. It was the lengthiest, most densely packed of all the revues. And it was definitive proof that the revue would not work on film without a sense of style, a point of view, an ability to sort out what was good from what wasn't. With the exception of Al Jolson, Warners threw in everything it had, including the kitchen sink.[9] What was left out was what most of its product lacked at the time—complexion. For originality, Warners substituted budgetary largess; for cleverness, commotion; for tone, Vitaphone. Not only a recklessly obtrusive spectacle, a cinematic money pit, an ill-fitting collage of overproduced Vitaphone shorts, *The Show of Shows* was and is a monument to Warner Bros.' constant miscalculation of the public's taste and conception of musicals. It has no flavor, no perspective, no candor. It neither bears the weight of the musical's past nor carries implications for its future. And to add to it, it's only a movie in the sense that there were cameras shooting the stage show going on in front of them.

The inappropriate nature of *Show of Shows* as a whole can be gauged from some of the choices made by Warner, coproducer Darryl Zanuck, and

---

9. Actually a bathroom sink, but close enough. Jolson, not anxious to share the limelight with dozens of other stars, declined Warners' hefty offer. George Arliss and Marilyn Miller were other no-shows originally announced.

director John Adolfi, a flairless technician. Just as the studio had plunged into talkies in 1928 with all those arbitrarily part-talking efforts, here it dived deep without any real idea about what made a revue. *Show of Shows* lurches along aimlessly, a bad comedy routine followed by an irrelevant tableau, all in a sumptuous Technicolor buffet.[10] For all its shapelessness, *The Hollywood Revue* had given its audience gleaming moments tucked into the dross, for MGM's people had the ingrained awareness that even in a hodgepodge, stars are a studio's prime assets. They should be presented with care, to show the public what makes them particular and precious. *Show of Shows* doesn't do this. Its most crucial failure is its inability to give more than a few of its seventy-seven star performers anything distinctive to do, let alone play to strength. Nearly all of them are used indiscriminately, interchangeably: even a player as idiosyncratic as Beatrice Lillie is given nothing of interest.[11] Reflecting the turmoil in the studio's roster of contract players, the cast is a mélange of stage people and silent veterans. Most of them would be gone from the studio in a few months, superseded by the actors who gave Warners its distinctively urban look and sound: Cagney, Robinson, Blondell, and so forth. *Show of Shows*, then, is a jejune souvenir of Warner Bros. immediately prior to its becoming the studio familiar to viewers in the 1930s and today.

The first moments demonstrate perfectly what it's about and why it doesn't work. Without preface, it opens on the Reign of Terror—literally, as an aristocrat is guillotined and the rabble proclaims "On With the Show of Shows!" The French Revolution as metaphor for the sound revolution is a trifle heavyhanded when not done humorously, and when the aristocrat is H. B. Warner, who had portrayed Jesus for Cecil B. DeMille. Did Warners really think the decapitation of this particular actor would set the right tone? There is then a fade in to a long, long military number by the Pasadena Drum and Bugle Corps (the finest available talent, courtesy of Warner Bros.). The camerawork is even more stationary than in *Hollywood Revue*, using the proscenium to frame the action and shooting it from a considerable distance, with nothing resembling a closeup. Monte Blue, who leads

10. Mostly color, anyway. Despite Warners' intention to shoot it entirely in Technicolor, the process's cameras were in such intense demand in September 1929 that twenty of the revue's 128 minutes had to be shot in black and white.

11. Lillie, who appears only in a group recitation, did film another number, singing about going on a diet while the chorus boys around her reduced into midgets. This was cut from the final print and released as a separate Vitaphone short. Angered that she had not received additional compensation for a second film, Lillie sued Warners and lost.

Carmen's Habanera, as sung by diva Alice Gentle, was another *Show of Shows* casualty released as a short, as was a (second) number by boxer Georges Carpentier. This recycling process was also employed by MGM, who placed a couple of unused *Hollywood Revue* songs by the Brox Sisters in a short called *Gems of MGM*, and by Fox, who released excised footage from the *Movietone Follies* as *The Belle of Samoa*, with Lois Moran and Clark and McCullough.

the parade, makes no impression. In this movie, one star is the same as another.

But no one quite matches the Master of Ceremonies. Frank Fay had won fame in this capacity on the stage, so the choice to use him, deadly error as it may seem, had a logical base. How insufferably vain and fatuous he is; what unfunny jokes; such ponderously false geniality. Fay's contribution also includes a duet with comic Sid Silvers about bad breath, for heaven's sake, as well as an overheated torch solo, "Your Love Is All That I Crave," complete with Elvis-like spoken interlude—not as much as unintentionally funny. Incredibly, Fay was commended by many critics, reversing the usual 1929 scheme in which wise reviewers often outnumbered perceptive spectators. In this case audiences weren't fooled, and Warners' attempts to build Fay into a screen favorite met with resounding indifference. An irate theater owner in Texas reported that "about half my crowd took the trouble to . . . tell me that the picture would have been passable if he had been left out."

Show of Shows is so intent on giving the audience stars in the plural that it permits few solo performers to cut through its pageantry. Much of the cast is anonymous, for the lack of close-ups and the grainy photography sometimes makes faces indistinct. Additionally, most players are not introduced; it required an extra quarter to buy the printed program to figure out who anyone was. Of the few solos, it's unquestionably the raucous singing comedian Winnie Lightner who comes off best. Fresh from a huge triumph in *Gold Diggers of Broadway,* she had a roughhouse style that was too wearing to attain a permanent niche but here nearly pops off the screen. The woman loved to perform. She had fun doing it and had an exceptionally good voice, a strong soprano extending atop the belt region. "Pingo Pongo" is a lively novelty about cannibals that she socks over with a vengeance, and for the film's most celebrated and enjoyable moment, "Singin' in the Bathtub," she prances in an outsized bathroom with a line of male chorines dragged up as 1890s bathing beauties. As a sassy answer-back to Metro's song in the rain, it replaces that song's optimism with plain silliness, spark, and humor, as well as a freakish coda wherein the brutish wrestler-actor Bull Montana serenades Lightner with "You Were Meant for Me."[12] Other solo performers fare unevenly. Ted Lewis and his band make no impression in a blah pirate number, and both Irene Bordoni and Nick Lucas are treated unflatteringly by the camera, though Bordoni's assured sensuality provides a stray touch of elegance. The most bizarre musical moment apart

12. Studio correspondence reveals that MGM, displeased by the inclusion of one of its song hits and the burlesque of another, contemplated a lawsuit; Louis B. Mayer's enmity toward Warners was at its height in 1929. *Show of Shows* also tweaked *Hollywood Revue*'s ludicrous "Your Mother and Mine." Like "Sonny Boy," some songs are sitting ducks.

Chinese junk: Nick Lucas (far left) sings "Li Po Li" to Myrna Loy (far right) in *The Show of Shows*, while an overdressed chorus runs interference. *Photofest.*

from Bull Montana is provided by former middleweight champ Georges Carpentier, whom Warners briefly attempted to turn into an actor. He sings in a thin tenor that doesn't sound like it should belong to a prizefighter, then strips from tux to gym togs to lead chorus girls through exercises. As he's given no buildup or introduction, the element of surprise goes for nothing, and it becomes just another humdrum routine. With the *Carmen* aria excised, the sole attempt at "art" is John Barrymore's ballyhooed talkie debut: Gloucester's soliloquy from *Henry VI, Part III*. In his introduction Barrymore compares Crookback to Al Capone, but except for some succulently flavored syllables it offers little except a dead camera and a rare record of Barrymore in his prime. Nevertheless, this was the film's most rapturously received moment in 1929, doubtless because it was telling to see a talented performer working in his element.

Some of the absurdities in *Show of Shows* carry archaeological interest. "Sisters," introduced by Richard Barthelmess, features eight pairs of stars in songs and dances of different countries. Bedizened in stars and stripes, Dolores and Helene Costello move their lips while dubbed voices chime in; Shirley Mason and Viola Dana clog-dance amidst the tulips; Loretta Young and Sally Blane try a cancan. It's easy to smile at the inadequacy of the participants and their two-three-kick-turn steps, but that is beside the point. So is the fact that one of the sibling pairings is fictitious (Marion

Byron and Hariette Lake [Ann Sothern]). The format is a more basic problem: eight negligible variations on one theme is far too cumbersome. Larry Ceballos's staging, which slides cartoon scenery on and off to simulate each country, is silly, even childish, treating these grown women of film as participants in a Geography Day pageant, not as stars of an expensive motion picture.

Ominously, the exorbitant and heavily promoted "Chinese Fantasy" sequence is introduced by a barking Rin-Tin-Tin. As Nick Lucas sings and Myrna Loy dances, a large and outlandishly dressed chorus scampers about in ersatz Mysterious East decor to a song called "Li-Po-Li." Perhaps it's just as well that the staging and the song are entirely independent, for Al Bryan's lyrics operate on a rarefied plane of complete stupidity. Li-Po-Li is a renegade who steals oolong tea, currency, rice cakes, spice cakes, etc. (Note the innovative rhyme scheme.) Even putting aside the song's inherent offensiveness, it does not seem to have occurred to anyone that so ridiculous a piece might not work as a basis for a big number. Chorines twirl large parasols, soubrettes pop out of large jars, and Loy rubs Aladdin's lamp and gets a big cardboard genie. In a demented climax, the scenery flies up to reveal a large crosshatched system of ladders which the chorus spends several minutes climbing up and down while Louis Silvers's orchestra plays the blasted song over and over again and Lucas and Loy stand off on the side trying not to look too Occidental. The ineptitude, the waste of good money, is staggering. And yet . . . film preservation is a funny thing. *Show of Shows* had long been thought to exist only in fuzzy black and white prints, but one color reel finally resurfaced. It was, indeed, "Li-Po-Li," and although neither song nor staging is any better, the color itself is exceptionally attractive. Technicolor's strong points are stressed in the chorus's rich turquoises and golds, their red hats setting them off in their climb up and down those ladders. Suddenly the inanity is bearable, almost charming—which doesn't mean that this number should have happened in the first place. The finale, "Lady Luck," aptly summarizes the whole: endless, overstuffed with misused talent, static, pointless. Gauche, also, for Alexander Gray is made to sing the indelicate lyrics, "Don't give my hopes the razz." There follows an interminable assortment of dance specialties of every stripe. Onward they come without pause, all energy and no style, forcing one to yearn for the comparative minimalism of "Li-Po-Li." Finally, Betty Compson's entrance as the regal Lady is cause for exhausted relief, after which the biggest names in the show (and Frank Fay) stick their heads through star cutouts in a curtain while "Lady Luck" drones on some more—the focus finally resting on personalities instead of bounty.

With its implicit limitations, the revue was doomed in talkies, but even with a brighter prospect *Show of Shows* would have sped it to oblivion.

Figures told the story: the worldwide gross of *Hollywood Revue* was six times its cost; with *Show of Shows* it was far less than twice, barely enough to break even. And because of the hostility it engendered, especially outside larger cities, it was widely perceived as a flop, such epithets as "Lemon of Lemons" not being uncommon. Hollywood's revues were being killed off almost before they started, and several more were waiting in the wings.

Just before *Show of Shows* opened, *Sunny Side Up* had demonstrated that Fox could produce good musicals. Its new revue was not among them. While not a catastrophe on the order of *Show of Shows*, *Happy Days*, released in February 1930, has no bite. Like much of the surviving Fox work of the time, it is plagued by blandness, even anemia, the work of a company whose idea of imagination was to use someone like comic El Brendel over and over, always in the same role. At least *Happy Days* redressed the balance where name voltage was concerned, for unlike the *Movietone Follies* it had a sizable lineup: Janet Gaynor, Will Rogers, Charles Farrell, Victor McLaglen, Edmund Lowe, George Jessel, Warner Baxter, Ann Pennington, J. Harold Murray, Dixie Lee, George Olsen and Orchestra, and, to put Georges Carpentier in his place, Gentleman Jim Corbett. Perhaps not scintillating, yet workable. Unfortunately, there was a completely undistinguished and forgotten director, Benjamin Stoloff, and again an embryonic plot was clamped on. It was a frail pretext (with a working title of *New Orleans Frolic*) about Marjorie White keeping a showboat from ruin by cajoling a bunch of Fox performers into a gala minstrel show.

Aside from its cast, *Happy Days*'s only distinctive feature was also its most problematic. It was designed to provide a splendid launch for Fox's 70mm "Grandeur" process previously tried on *Movietone Follies* in one engagement. Weeks before the premiere, the industry was buzzing about a new film revolution. First sound, then color, now a screen as large as any stage and purported to give a feeling of three dimensions! Other studios checked in with their own wide processes, and several musicals were announced for the big new screen. In the event, *Happy Days* played in Grandeur in New York, Los Angeles, and, for some reason, Milan. The screen was immense, the sound was superior, but there seemed to be little imagination at work and less excitement. What showed in the final analysis was that less effort had been expended on the film than on the technical process. At any rate, most theater owners preferred to exhibit the normal-sized version of *Happy Days* shot simultaneously with the big one. The critics were indifferent, the financial returns moderate.

Happy Days (non-Grandeur version) survives as easily the most uninspired of the all-star revues. Not as ill-wrought as *Show of Shows*, it certainly lacks the varying degrees of sparkle that other studios' revues were able to muster. The musical staging, surprisingly credited to comic actor Walter Catlett, is undistinguished, and the attempt to tie the revue to a "plot" is

The cast of *Happy Days*, posed for the finale in a Grandeur-worthy configuration. From left, J. Harold Murray, "Whispering" Jack Smith, Gentleman Jim Corbett, El Brendel, Sharon Lynn, Paul Page, Victor McLaglen, Charles Farrell, Janet Gaynor, Edmund Lowe, Walter Catlett, David Rollins, Dixie Lee, Frank Albertson, William Collier Sr., Frank Richardson.

useless. All the story scenes has is Marjorie White's energy, and audiences would soon find her more visible than welcome, like many such performers in 1930. Not even the showboat setting has impact, at least not on a normal-sized screen. Most distressing, if not surprising, is the ill use to which much of the talent is put. Will Rogers, with his legendary outings in the Ziegfeld *Follies*, is relegated to a nondescript walk-on. Likewise Warner Baxter, obviously capable of doing more than a simple card trick. The songs, by the usual ragtag batch of composers, are unmemorable, which stymies Olsen and his band, one of the country's best at the time. Plus, by 1930 minstrel shows were becoming curios—outdated, colorful, questionable; witness the failure of Eddie Leonard's *Melody Lane*. Yet, as here, Hollywood would continue to stage minstrel acts into the 1940s, and the synthetic nostalgia indigenous to such re-creations was a hallmark of many later musicals made by 20th Century-Fox.

As with *Show of Shows* the acts are presented almost entirely in theatrical fashion, with few concessions to cinema and little reference to the participants' talents. The only performers to use their screen image are Victor McLaglen and Edmund Lowe, who kid their roles as rowdy marines in the Fox hits *What Price Glory* and *The Cock Eyed World*. Other numbers have moments of diversion or clever camera tricks, such as the bizarre "Snake Hips," expertly performed by Ann Pennington, which is enhanced by crane shots and a fetishistic air that seems particularly gamy for the staid Fox musical. "Crazy Feet," another dance number, is wittily introduced by a rising stage curtain contrived to resemble a trouser leg and is energetically danced by Dixie Lee, remembered today only because she gave up her career to marry Bing Crosby. Gaynor and Farrell's routine, a cloying young-love-in-bloom thing called "(We'll Build) a Little World All Our Own," is somewhat cinematic and also very hard to take, especially in a shot of them done up as infants, bonneted and encribbed. And so it goes. El Brendel does a comic minuet, Tom Patricola executes an eccentric dance, Marjorie White duets with Richard Keene on "A Diet of Love." Being neither dreadful nor outstanding, *Happy Days* thus epitomizes the Fox musical then and later.

If the final effect of *Happy Days* was ordinary, its very title soon carried ghastly irony. As it went into general release, cities across the country began to feel the effects of the stock market crash. Film receipts, along with those of other consumer goods, began to dwindle, and a mindless extravaganza called *Happy Days* seemed quite expendable. In addition, in March 1930 the Fox conglomerate (film corporation and theaters) was rocked by financial battles and threats of receivership. Rumors of overspending (things like Grandeur come to mind) and mismanagement shook the industry, and William Fox was paid $18 million to turn in his stock and sever his ties with the organization. In the hasty reorganization, it was quickly announced that Grandeur would be laid aside for awhile.

About the same time that *Happy Days* spread Grandeur across the Roxy's screen, revues were also emerging across the ocean. Following the successful launch of *The Hollywood Revue* in London, the British film industry, now trying its hand at musicals, mounted its own equivalent. British International Pictures' *Elstree Calling* opened in February 1930 to show how far-flung lay the influence of the Hollywood musical. A staple in English music halls and in the West End, the stage revue was here put into peculiarly Hollywoodish terms. *Elstree Calling* (the title refers to the location of the studio) is known today because of one credit line: "Sketches and other interpolated items by Alfred Hitchcock." As such, it's a quaint appendix to his career, and a few moments do evince his touch. The rest was directed by Adrian Brunel, with musical staging partly by André Charlot, whose trademarked revue style is detectable. Far more modest than its American counterparts, it also has a more novel format, being set up as a television broadcast—in 1930—from BIP's Elstree studio.[13] The overall tone is genial

13. The television-revue idea also had an aborted U.S. counterpart. In the fall of 1929 the Pathé studio announced its *International Television Revue*; as with many of the most grandiose musical plans, it was never made.

and lighthearted, more than was generally the case stateside. Most of the "Artistes in the Revue" (so billed) were old hands in variety such as Will Fyffe and Cicely Courtneidge, and most of the ensemble numbers are pale and shrilly sung copies of Hollywood. It's fascinating to see this intersection of America and Britain, the derivative colliding with the inimitable. The latter comes with soloists such as the boisterous singing comic Lily Morris and the legendary Harry Lauder, performances documenting theatrical traditions nearly extinct by 1930. The one American who shows up is hardly a typical Yankee: Anna May Wong, who figures in a nightmarish parody of the Mary Pickford-Douglas Fairbanks *Taming of the Shrew* film. The most direct link with American revues is four color sequences that demonstrate the superiority of U.S. technology at that point. It is not really photography at all, merely color stencilled onto black and white—early colorization, and no more effective than later efforts. With no greens or reds, the ashen salmony skin tones and muddy yellows make one yearn for the most limited two-color Technicolor, and the performers appear to be either haloed or boiling. *Elstree Calling* impressed neither the press nor the public; it had no influence whatever, and it was quickly forgotten.

With Warners, Fox, and England already checked in, more was on the way, as well as problems and delays that changed plans and occasionally made them fall apart. Besides its television extravaganza, Pathé also announced a screen version of Broadway's popular *Greenwich Village Follies*, planned in such a low key as to be entirely without stars or pageantry. When a few sane heads realized that no one at Pathé had the right flair, it was quietly scrapped. Radio Pictures (RKO) planned its *Radio Revels of 1929*, then *of 1930*, hopefully promising "Spectacle comparable to anything on stage or screen" and, ambitiously, "The first annual screen revue, to be presented yearly." These plans, vastly altered, resulted in *The Cuckoos* (1930), a musical comedy and not a revue by any stretch of the imagination.

Paramount, which announced its extravaganza in July 1929, continued to work on it into January. Audience response at previews prompted the addition of new numbers with more stars—Gary Cooper, Fay Wray, Jean Arthur, Richard Arlen, and others in one segment, Clara Bow in another. By release time in April, audience resistance to revues had already been noted. *The Show of Shows* had already damaged spectator goodwill, other musicals were drawing disappointing returns, and the indifferent response to *Happy Days* did nothing to help. So *Paramount on Parade* was carefully distanced from earlier entries: "Intimate as marriage . . . Good as Gold! Filmdom's favorites give a party on your screen! Not walking through it for the sake of their names, but each ACTING a real role, doing the stuff for which they are famous or startling you with delightfully new and different talents." The ploy worked: for the first time since *The Hollywood Revue*, a revue delivered on its promise, to much critical surprise. *Variety* observed:

Just when the industry is figuring studio revues are passe, the Zukor organization reintroduces the subject . . . with a picture that is in a class by itself. Real entertainment [and] the first production of this kind linking together with almost incredible smoothness achievements from the smallest technical detail to the greatest artistic endeavor.

Paramount on Parade did not have the high budget of the Warner revue nor Fox's technology, for all the good those did. It was marked instead by attributes that could be neither bought nor invented in the lab: finesse, a sense of humor, and, uniquely, a genuine understanding of what the studio and its players were about. Of all the revues, *Paramount on Parade* is the most genuinely up-front in telling where it came from and who brought it into being. Look at the title: Paramount was not just on display or exhibit—it was on *parade*. Pride, fanfare, celebration—this was the state of the studio, circa winter 1930. At this time, Paramount was beginning to assume the special character that would stamp its productions for much of the decade. Its best films of the early and middle 1930s behaved like no other studio's product. There was a soft glow in the photography, a casual Continental sophistication in the writing and playing, and, most of all, the highest authorial profile of any company, with some of the most distinctive directors in American cinema working at full strength: Ernst Lubitsch, Rouben Mamoulian, Josef von Sternberg, even Cecil B. DeMille all turned out work at Paramount that would not have been made anywhere else. Plus the star comics—the Marx Brothers, Mae West, and W. C. Fields—who had unusual dominion over their work, and ace writers such as Jules Furthman and Joseph and Herman Mankiewicz, witty and occasionally anarchic. The star roster was notable for its conjunction of the versatile with the unique: Maurice Chevalier, Marlene Dietrich, Nancy Carroll, Claudette Colbert, Fredric March, Gary Cooper, Sylvia Sidney, Charles Laughton, Miriam Hopkins, Cary Grant. *Paramount on Parade* is a curiously apt harbinger of all the good things the studio would achieve in the next few years. Small wonder that it has become a connoisseur's favorite among revues, probably more respected now than when it was made, and quite exceptional considering that as seen today it is a tepid reflection of its original form. The available prints are missing all the Technicolor sequences, approximately a quarter of the original footage, which had been much praised in 1930. Only one, the finale, is in current prints,[14] but in black

14. Four of the other five color sequences survive, without sound and in faded color; the stylish montage of theater ushers and production effects that originally opened the film seems to be completely lost. In the TV prints Gary Cooper, Fay Wray, and company come out in black and white to introduce their sequence, an antebellum hunt number, which then doesn't appear. However, even silent and in poor color it's the most sumptuous and elegant number in the film.

and white. Yet despite its deletions and blatant commercialism, it's a viewer-friendly charmer. It lacks the distended ennui of *Show of Shows*, the blandness of the Fox revues, or the tentativeness of *The Hollywood Revue*. And it's unpretentious in a way that Universal's *King of Jazz* would not be; it doesn't take itself too seriously, nor revues per se, nor Paramount, nor moviemaking in general.

Like some of the other revues, it had an overall supervisor. Elsie Janis, musical Jill-of-all trades and model for the talkie à clef *Mother Knows Best*, conceived the format and wrote songs and routines. Then the studio where director was frequently star made a Paramountean decision: eleven directors instead of one. Lubitsch, Edmund Goulding, Dorothy Arzner, Rowland V. Lee, Victor Schertzinger, Frank Tuttle, Edward Sutherland, and more.[15] The gesture is more impressive than the achievement, for little besides Lubitsch's scenes has a strong directorial profile. Yet its indication is that Paramount's priority for 1930 lay in establishing itself as a haven for individualists, preparing to soar as the producer of the most effortless and clever works in American cinema. The level was sustained for a few years until its curtailment by the onset of the newly enforced Production Code, which had little patience for the casually adult level of Paramount films.

Paramount on Parade also stresses personality more than any of the other revues, in both musical performers and the comedy players (though the Marx Brothers, originally announced, did not make it in). Jack Oakie, Skeets Gallagher, and Leon Errol serve as far more jocular hosts than Frank Fay, and the comedy refreshingly extends to the studio's dramatic performers, who spoof their established personae. Willliam Powell, Clive Brook, and Warner Oland, for example, send up their familiar roles of Philo Vance, Sherlock Holmes, and Dr. Fu Manchu in a sketch that has become a movie buffs' favorite. There's little of the condescension of the Metro and Warner stars, who too often seemed to grant audiences the boon of showing up. The musical program is the most varied of any of the revues, the songs well tailored to their performers: Chevalier's boulevardier, Helen Kane's boop-a-doop, Nancy Carroll's cooing sexiness, Buddy Rogers and Lillian Roth's cutesy romance, and the more pugnacious pairing of Zelma O'Neal and Jack Oakie. The clear headliner is Chevalier, who had transformed the Paramount musical with *The Love Parade*. His appearance is the most dominant star presence in any revue film, with three sequences directed by Lubitsch and the flattery of an imitation by the precocious moppet Mitzi Green. The extent of Chevalier's stamp can be seen in the finale, the one time a revue did not conclude with a gala reprise of stars and songs. It's

15. Goulding also appears onscreen, as does Ludwig Berger. Among the studio talent not appearing were Josef von Sternberg (shooting *The Blue Angel* in Germany) and George Cukor (still a New York-based novice). The only other mainstream American film to feature so lengthy a byline is also from Paramount: *If I Had a Million* (1932), with seven directors.

just Chevalier, leading apache chimney sweepers through Sam Coslow's "Sweepin' the Clouds Away." Scampering with chorines is outside the Chevalier norm, but the staging is attractive, the vaulting ebullience of the song contagious, and the final image—Chevalier looking triumphantly at the world below— an apt metaphor for this moment in his career. His other sequences are more typical of his and Lubitsch's style. "All I Want Is Just One Girl" finds him as a randy gendarme canvassing the park for fresh fare, and in the most Lubitschean segment he and Evelyn Brent demonstrate the origin of the apache dance. They spar *en boudoir,* bickering, shoving, ripping each other's garments to the strains of the familiar apache song. The scoring is alternately sly, boisterous, and conciliatory, pointing Brent's chic wounded dander against Chevalier's duplicitous caginess, trifling and captivating. Several slight nods were also made toward "serious" music, all filmed in color. Italian tenor Nino Martini warbled "Torna a Surriento," and Dennis King, fresh from *The Vagabond King,* roared out a florid pseudo-Russian apostrophe called "Nichavo! [Nothing]." In a lighter vein, Harry Green caroused as a Yiddish Escamillo in "I'm Isidore the Toreador," assisted by the statuesque Carmen of Kay Francis. Considering the early prominence of opera shorts, it's surprising that this burlesque Bizet was the only moment of opera to make the final cut of any of the studio revues.[16]

Given the slickness and the players' aptitude for their material, it's somewhat startling to encounter two examples of the Joan Crawford–Marion Davies I-bet-you-didn't-know-I-was-a-musical-performer ilk. This type of amateur-hour feigned versatility is not as prominent in the revues as one might think; besides Crawford and Davies, only Georges Carpentier had qualified as a genuine novelty thus far. Then emerged two surprising songsters from Paramount: Ruth Chatterton, the leading emotional actress in film, and Clara Bow, near the end of her reign as ultimate 1920s sex symbol. Despite the unaccustomed premises, they are aligned with their images. Chatterton's song is presented as a dramatic tour de force, wherein she is done up as a forlorn Parisian tart who accosts several doughboys (including an incongruous Fredric March) to sing "My Marine" with proficient technique and just enough voice. It's about as merry as John Barrymore's Shakespeare and nearly stops the film cold, though in 1930 audi-

---

16. Another Paramount singer, Jeanette MacDonald, had a curious connection with the film. While her scenes were not used in the English-language version she did host the Spanish version, which apparently does not survive. All told, there were four foreign-language versions, including Japanese. For the German version it was originally planned to have Lubitsch direct host wraparounds featuring new import Marlene Dietrich, in tuxedo. Too bad these plans fell apart.

In the foreign language department, Universal outdid Paramount by producing *King of Jazz* in nine foreign versions, including a German one hosted by Joseph Schildkraut and a Hungarian one hosted by Bela Lugosi.

ences were content to view it as an intriguing change of pace. Clara Bow was Paramount's most ill-treated actor as well as its most popular. Instead of expanding on her potential, the studio kept her bolted into the "It" image, and by the time of *Paramount on Parade* the Jazz Age was over and Bow's career was in trouble. Along with her mounting personal problems, the arrival of sound had diminished her confidence, and the occasional honk erupting from her pleasant Brooklyn contralto added few layers to her aura. Instead of boosting her self-respect or her material, the studio used music to forestall the inevitable. The singing Bow debuted as a last-minute addition to *Paramount on Parade,* performing "I'm True to the Navy Now"—Clara among sailors being a common motif. As an amateur she's not that bad, and while she didn't enjoy having her abilities stretched into such unfamiliar territory, with some training she might have been put to good use in musicals. Audience reaction was sufficiently favorable for her to sing in two more films *(True to the Navy,* "inspired" by her song, and *Love Among the Millionaires).* By then her health and her career were in deep decline. Paramount did little to alleviate any of it, and a year after presenting her as one of its prime luminaries, strutting gaily in *Paramount on Parade,* it terminated her contract.

If Paramount's revue was eminently typical of its studio, the last and best of the big studio pageants was in complete contradiction to the corporate forces that launched it. In the 1920s and the following four decades, Universal's output tended to be dominated by routine fodder, with its "A" pictures generally efficient and mostly unmemorable. But for all his paternalistic thrift, Uncle Carl Laemmle occasionally had the yen to splurge. He hired the most brilliant and extravagant director in Hollywood, Erich von Stroheim—and later approved his firing. He spent and made a great deal of money on Lon Chaney's *The Hunchback of Notre Dame* and *The Phantom of the Opera,* and there were also the tepid forays into Americana, *Uncle Tom's Cabin* and *Show Boat.* In 1929, Universal's new production head, Carl Laemmle Jr., determined to up the studio's ante with two films that could bring the studio more stature than ever. Wildly costly and totally dissimilar, they were shot concurrently in the winter and early spring of 1930. One was *All Quiet on the Western Front,* held by many to be the finest film Universal ever made. The other was a musical—not a musicalized drama like *Broadway,* but Universal's own revue, *King of Jazz.*

It's typical of the era that the first major revue to enter the planning stage was the last to appear. In October 1928, just after Universal began to look into musicals with *Melody of Love,* it signed bandleader Paul Whiteman, one of the biggest names in the business, to star in *The King of Jazz,* based on his life and career. It was one thing to hire Whiteman and orchestra to play stirring music and quite another to come up with a tenable property to put around them, for Whiteman was adamant about not appearing in some backstage melodrama where he would look totally ridiculous. Months elapsed, and the problems with the picture soon became an industry in-joke, as did the fact that Uncle Carl had paid Whiteman and his musicians a great deal of money to sit around idly.[17] Directors and scenarists passed through as if in a revolving door, and for Laemmle Sr. the expenditure of hundreds of thousands of dollars on an abortive project must have been galling. Finally, in September 1929, Universal made the same decision as other studios: *King of Jazz* would be a Whiteman-led all-star revue, directed by Paul Fejos, who had substituted outré spectacle for dramatic punch in *Broadway*. This was soon altered in a provocative fashion when the Laemmles engaged John Murray Anderson, whose name was synonymous with the Broadway revue at its most stylish. Attempts at a tandem Fejos/Anderson directorial arrangement evaporated with a Fejos tantrum, and Anderson, with no movie experience of any sort, was placed in charge of Universal's biggest film. Flush with the success of the past year's product, the Laemmles gave Anderson full access to the Universal exchequer. In addition to Whiteman's fees, major expenses included Technicolor used throughout, dozens of enormous sets, as much as $50,000 for rights to George Gershwin's "Rhapsody in Blue," and the world's largest wedding veil. The collision of Anderson's perfectionism with his lack of film experience made for a costly and prolonged shoot. Over twelve weeks, three times the schedule of most major musicals of the time, he constantly experimented with innovative photographic effects and with the lavish sets and costumes. All this, simultaneous with the costly *All Quiet on the Western Front*, may have made Uncle Carl look longingly back to the days of Von Stroheim. One of Anderson's more maddening tendencies was to shoot just about anything that struck his fancy, *then* devise the continuity of sequences, complete with rhythmic editing, in the cutting room. At the end of it the price tallied somewhere in the heart-stopping neighborhood between $1.5 and $2 million, making it the most expensive musical for some years to come, more costly than all but a small handful of pictures up to that time.

As an exemplar of its studio's style, *King of Jazz* is the exception proving the rule. As with the other isolated Universal films of high quality, it reflects its origins only in its director's ability to cut through the studio's workaday tradition to create something special. Laemmle was not always inclined to hire truly exceptional directors, yet somehow, as with Fejos, James Whale, and *All Quiet*'s Lewis Milestone, they turned up anyway. Even with Whiteman as the center of the show, with star billing unparal-

17. The deal had received a great deal of figurative and literal mileage from the hubbub surrounding Whiteman and band's journey to Hollywood in a gold-painted railroad car, courtesy of Old Gold cigarettes. Later, during the interminable delays in production, Whiteman and his group were able to use the car to make several short tours.

leled in any revue film, the dominant presence is John Murray Anderson. Hiring him was artistically astute if financially foolhardy, and the effect of the resulting work is that of the most elaborate stage spectacle filtered through a burgeoning cinematic intuition. With no one to tell Anderson that such-and-such could not be done, his staging and design and use of color and effects resemble those of no other film musical before or since.[18] *King of Jazz*, then, is an arresting hybrid embracing many of the best qualities of early-1930 stage and cinema, including good songs by a variety of composers and striking art direction by Herman Rosse that won an Academy Award. *King of Jazz* is in its way a glorious, unrepeatable stunt. Instead of the catchall concept of a studio strutting its wares, the revue is presented literally as a Whiteman scrapbook. By 1930 he was the best-known, if hardly the best, bandleader in the country—possibly the world. His sound was gently homogeneous, as middlebrow and unthreatening as his own bulkily genial presence; applying the word "jazz" to his whitebread style demonstrates the loose application of that term in the 1920s—the equivalent of "pop" today (cf. *The Jazz Singer*). The true musical quality came with some of his players: guitarist Eddie Lang, sax player Frankie Trumbauer, violinist Joe Venuti, and the legendary Bix Beiderbecke on cornet. All except Bix made it into the movie.

Surprises abound in *King of Jazz*, beginning with the opening segment: the first cartoon shot in color depicts Whiteman's journey to Africa to harness the elements of jazz. Setting aside some deplorable stereotypes the sequence is a delight, as is the subsequent introduction of the real-life Whiteman and band. After the musicians are shown in miniature, climbing out of Whiteman's valise, each instrumental section is presented in a solo vignette with bold composition and deliberately unreal color filters, looking as dazzling as it sounds. These first minutes are among the most imaginative in any musical, and if the production that follows them offers a somewhat bumpier ride, Anderson made enough right choices. The first, "Bridal Veil," features Jeanette Loff, a beautiful blonde with a clear soprano. It's one of revue's hoariest clichés—the specters of brides of the past parading by to inspire a bride of the present—yet is transformed through a presentation both tasteful and ostentatious. Ferde Grofé's scoring and Rosse's exquisite designs are as impressive today as in 1930, and the restrained use of color as devised by Anderson, Rosse, and chief cinematographer Hal Mohr is outstanding. The final tableau, Loff donning a veil the size of a football field, was milked to the hilt by Universal publicists. The hit song

18. Anderson later wrote that following *King of Jazz*, the Laemmles offered him a lucrative contract, but when they could not find the right follow-up property he returned to Broadway. In any case, Anderson received screen credit only two more times, devising water ballets for Esther Williams's aquatic star debut in *Bathing Beauty* (MGM 1944) and three-ring glitter for DeMille's *The Greatest Show on Earth* (Paramount 1952).

"It Happened in Monterey" is introduced by John Boles, recently tagged as the studio's biggest star, with Loff as an alluring, unlikely senorita. For all its bogus-Mexican excess the design is good, the color is rich and the lavishness assured. Boles's other big number is "Song of the Dawn," performed with a squadron of cowboys and notable for two reasons, one being the impressionistic color filters used on Boles's face; the other factor falls into the province of substantiated backstage gossip. Bing Crosby, a member of Whiteman's singing trio The Rhythm Boys, was to have been the soloist in this number, but a drunk-driving arrest prior to shooting derailed his main chance. Boles replaced him, and Bing made his film debut only as the most conspicuous Rhythm Boy.

Ever since Whiteman conducted the premiere of "Rhapsody in Blue" in 1924, the piece had come to connote the ideal melding of modern/classical and popular/jazz musical traditions. Not wanting merely to photograph the band playing the rhapsody, Anderson first set down a scenario depicting thoughts going through a listener's head while the piece is performed. The estimated budget for this fantasia was about $500,000, too much even for this film, though what finally emerged could surely not have cost all that much less. The sequence is wildly overdone, and its most effective section, the introduction, is also the simplest. Save for the opening cartoon it's also the only time that African music and traditions are cited for their contribution to American music. In a prelude to the rhapsody's opening clarinet solo, dancer Jacques Cartier, done up as a Zulu chief, performs in silhouette on an oversize drum, his movements at once ferocious and erotic. The rhapsody proper is less powerful. With Technicolor incapable of rendering blue accurately, Anderson and co-cinematographer Ray Rennahan manipulated lights and color filters to produce a compromise shade that's not quite right.[19] The central setpiece is an enormous "blue" grand piano with a platoon of keyboard players sitting at its monstrous keyboard and Whiteman and band set inside the piano where the strings would normally be. The soloist, often mistaken for Gershwin, is Roy Bargy, and while the performance is effective it's heavily cut and further marred by a barrage of overdone effects; a show which often totters precariously on the border of kitsch here spills over.

The less pretentious numbers offer more clearcut fun. "Happy Feet" and "A Bench in the Park" benefit from clever effects and the choreography of Russell Markert, who created the Rockettes a few years later. The dance highlight is "Ragamuffin Romeo," featuring some uncannily loose-limbed work from Don Rose and Marion Statler. As always in revues the comedy is wildly uneven, with a few blackouts featuring Universal players

19. The commercial videotape of *King of Jazz* has been color-corrected (not colorized) to produce an accurate blue tint in this and other scenes. The result, while attractive, completely misrepresents the film's original look.

Paul Whiteman, his orchestra, and multitudes of chorus, leaving no stone unturned in the "Melting Pot" finale of *King of Jazz*.

such as Laura La Plante, Slim Summerville, Glenn Tryon, and young Walter Brennan. A drunk routine by William Austin, in which he bemoans the goldfish he loved and lost, is so silly it's endearing, and so is a goofy barbershop quartet number graced by a audience sing-along portion with some of the lyrics helpfully printed in Hebrew.

Anderson surprised no one by dreaming up a killer finale, as large as *Show of Shows* and infinitely more palatable, based on a "Melting Pot" number he and Rosse had devised to open Boston's Metropolitan Theatre some years earlier.[20] Here, with the more specific "of Jazz" added, it depicts the musical aggregation that summons the definitive American sound, though once again a fine concept is diminished by no mention of the preeminent African-American influences. That aside, it's an exciting succession of sounds and images, song and dance of many (European) nations blended into a literal large pot. Viennese waltzes, a Highland Fling, "Santa Lucia," and so on are all stirred up by Whiteman, and out comes the American sound. Even in these diluted circumstances it's disappointing to find that the sound as played here is an antithesis of jazz, the Sousa march. Yet divorced from its connotations it's a fitting climax to a remarkable show. "Too much of a good thing," Mae West once said, in a rather different context, "can be wonderful."

King of Jazz premiered at the Roxy in New York on May 2, 1930, only three days after *All Quiet on the Western Front*, and with Whiteman and Gershwin himself in the onstage show. The one-two punch of Art (Erich Maria Remarque) and Dazzle (Whiteman/Anderson) did not quite realize the Laemmles' hopes. While *All Quiet* did achieve the desired impact, *King of Jazz* fell victim to both conditions and timing. It opened a scant ten days after *Paramount on Parade*, and while the success of that entry had seemed to curb some of the revue backlash, two in a row was pushing it. With so many musicals of inferior quality—a surfeit of *Shows of Shows*, not enough *Sunny Sides Up*—the public was feeling drained. Also, the fans who loved to listen to Whiteman did not necessarily feel compelled to see him, regardless of Anderson's care and craftsmanship. These factors were as fatal to *King of Jazz*'s financial chances as its prohibitive cost, and even some of the most laudatory reviews implied that the world was not holding its breath for one more filmed revue. This did not overstate the case, and neither did a pair of headlines in the trade press a few weeks later: *Variety*'s "Revue All Cold, Say Film Men," and *Billboard*'s "Picture Audience Turning Thumbs Down on Revues," articles directly resulting from *King of Jazz*'s vastly disappointing reception. Laemmle, while proud of the artistic result, took a bath in the neighborhood of $1 million; it was a case of too much too late.

With its combination of aesthetic quality and financial failure, *King of Jazz* took the early talkie to a pole exactly opposite that of one and two years earlier. The dilemma was obvious: audiences were beginning to demand the type of serious substance alien to most revues. With its unexpected-as-we-are procession of acts, *Hollywood Revue* worked only as a one-time stunt, and its receipts in some smaller communities, where film

20. Paramount, which owned the Metropolitan, produced a musical short of *The Melting Pot* at its Astoria studio in 1929.

without plot was incomprehensible, was disappointing. The relative success of *Paramount on Parade* was a deserved fluke, but *King of Jazz* proved that even the most finely wrought spectacle could fail if it was not perceived to have depth or purpose or individual personalities. The word "revue" was taboo by mid-1930; advertisements for such films as *The Cuckoos* explicitly stated "Not A Revue." In most ways, the Whiteman film brought the revue craze to its conclusion; yet there were some loose ends. Among them was Fox, which had planned to corner the 1930 revue market with such projects as *The London Revue* (to feature Beatrice Lillie and Gertrude Lawrence), *Melodies of 1930*, and *American Beauty Revue*. None of these got off the ground, but in July 1930, when musicals were nose-diving, there was released a picture variously called *Movietone Follies of 1930* or *New Movietone Follies of 1930* or some variant thereof. The unilluminating Benjamin Stoloff directed a cast including Marjorie White, Frank Richardson, and the ubiquitous El Brendel, and again there was the Fox lack of finesse, with an inert excuse for a backstage plot fronting a barrage of production numbers stacked up in the second half. In this one a nervy chorine (Miriam Segar) journeys to Southampton with her troupe and wins millionaire William Collier Jr. Former Ziegfeld beauty Noel Francis sang the modestly enjoyable "Cheer Up and Smile," and Marjorie White gave amusement with "I Want To Be a Talking Picture Queen"—Pirandellian wish-fulfillment set in a Fox Utopia called Movietonia. Apart from these the musical numbers were amateurish and the first half a total loss. Already anticipating the worst, Fox did its best to sell the picture as anything other than a revue. "Follies" in the title seemed a dead giveaway, and after considering renaming it *Movietonia*, the studio played to El Brendel's comedic strength. The *Follies* played San Francisco and Los Angeles as *Svenson's Wild Party* and in Minneapolis (whose Scandinavian community loved Brendel) as *Svenson's Big Night Out*. Under any title, public and critical reaction reached new heights of apathy. As if anyone cared, Fox had already announced plans to star Brendel in a 1931 installment; this time, needless to say, it didn't happen. While Fox musicals had advanced technically, their meager level of imagination had atrophied.

A far greater disaster was transpiring at the normally unflappable MGM. Late in 1929, the studio embarked on a massive project conceived originally as *The Hollywood Revue of 1930* and finally given the portentous handle *The March of Time*. The history of this cataclysmic enterprise is covered in Chapter Fourteen, and suffice it to say that the much-publicized demise of this star-crammed and totally misconceived undertaking well and truly sounded the death knell for musical revues. They were extinct by mid-1930, dying off faster and sooner than other movie musicals. Audiences preferred narrative, *Show of Shows* had been an abomination, and while not as prevalent as backstage or mammy films, revues were ultimately more wearing and confining. The form per se was not cinematic, there was little of what producers termed "heart appeal," and only through unusual effort was this inherent finiteness transcended by creativity or force of personality or sheer studio spirit. It's regrettable that the opposing forces were so inflexible, for in isolated moments the revues were first-rate. Freed of the need to use a plot as the reference point, gifted artists could proceed with heightened daring and wit. John Murray Anderson proved that.

The all-star revue did not figure conspicuously when musicals returned in 1933. Plans for a new *Fox Movietone Follies*, announced in mid-1933, evolved into 1934's *Stand Up and Cheer,* equal parts revue and Depression document. MGM's attempt to launch *The Hollywood Revue of 1933* transmogrified into the disastrous *Hollywood Party* (1934), which also had sort of a plot. For nearly a decade there was little else, then in the early forties the studios devised revues to boost wartime morale: *Star-Spangled Rhythm* (Paramount), *Thousands Cheer* (MGM), *Thank Your Lucky Stars* (Warners), all with backstage stories and with moments evoking the old house-party spirit, as when Bette Davis and Errol Flynn brought back the days of unwonted musical performers. Only one traditional revue, plotless and all-star, was produced by a major studio after 1930. MGM's *Ziegfeld Follies* (1946) was costly if unintended atonement for *The March of Time,* though despite the glitter and the talents of Minnelli and Astaire and Garland and everyone else, many found it regressive. Specters of *The Hollywood Revue* and *Show of Shows* hung a little too heavily, and this time no other studio jumped on the revue bandwagon.

A final, bizarre footnote: *Elstree Calling,* Britain's muddled homage to *The Hollywood Revue,* was, like most of its country's first musicals, a second-generation imitation of already derivative American styles. U.S. markets would normally have deemed such a piece unimportable, especially in the no-musicals-allowed dog days of late 1930. Nevertheless, after all the revue films had come and gone it was picked up by an imaginative New York exhibitor, cut to shreds, retitled *Hello Everybody,* and double billed with a rerelease of *The Birth of a Nation.* Griffith's classic, which also had quite a lot of footage removed, was outfitted with music and sound effects. No score was added to *Hello Everybody*—indeed, most of the cuts were evidently of musical numbers. Not that it mattered: the revamped work was of sufficient merit to rate few if any other engagements. On this resoundingly tinny note ended the era of the all-star revues.

CHAPTER 8

Broadway Babies

Variations on a theme:

On stage for the finale!

New York—the place we've dreamed 'n' talked about. Ain't it swell?

C'mon, put some snap into this number—last night you were all dyin' on your feet! [1]

Before being audible, lines comparable to these abounded on title cards in such self-explanatory silents as *An Affair of the Follies*, *The Song and Dance Man*, and *Broadway Nights*. Even the saintly Lillian Gish strutted about as *Diane of the Follies* back in 1916. There were many more, all featuring permutations of the same totemic backstage species: cocky hoofer, spunky soubrette, lascivious socialites of any gender, harried or lecherous producers, assorted menace and comic relief. The settings, too, were mainly standardized, with grimy dressing rooms as hotbeds of intrigue, shows with "Follies" almost invariably in the title, and dingy rooming houses and Park Avenue love nests to stand in as antithetical sites of romance sacred and profane. The zing and cadence of such tales did not always reproduce well silently, most piquantly with the addition of mute production numbers. Visuals had to carry the entire burden in these performances, which were often quite elaborate; recall that Paramount originally intended Florenz Ziegfeld's *Glorifying the American Girl* as a silent, Follies parades and all. MGM's *Pretty Ladies* (1925), featuring ZaSu Pitts as a Brice-like Follies comedian, included among its stage scenes a series of "turns" by actors

---

1. *The Great Gabbo*, *The Broadway Melody*, and *Gold Diggers of Broadway*, respectively.

replicating such Ziegfeld luminaries as Will Rogers and singer Frances White—the latter impersonated by a wildly out-of-character Norma Shearer. Among its other morsels were a winter carnival and quasi-Chinese procession, with chorines Myrna Loy (shades of "Li-Po-Li") and Lucille LeSueur (Joan Crawford).

Standard movie fare by 1929, backstage stories seemed to incarnate a particularly lurid candor, the purported truth beneath the artifice.[2] In reality they were simply glossy repackagings of the Protestant work ethic, preachments of virtue and talent rewarded, and proved to be the easiest, most elementary foundation for musicals. *The Jazz Singer* had been a slightly embellished backstager, as all its mammy descendants would be, and then came the ace style-setter. No one pretended that the plot of *The Broadway Melody* had not been seen before; the difference lay in newness, technique, and the startling overhaul given the clichés by Bessie Love's performance, the music, and the presence of sound. The mold was set, and in concrete. The second backstager, *Syncopation*, made the paucity of inspiration apparent. *Time* magazine, scanning the coming of sound with wry curiosity, plainly saw from *Syncopation* that backstage musicals would not offer a bounty of newfound thematic riches: "By this time even rural communities must find the [story] of a team of dancing partners . . . interesting only for its digressions." The procession continued over the ensuing months: *Close Harmony, Broadway, Fox Movietone Follies, Honky Tonk*. And *On With the Show!*, in some ways the ultimate backstage film, its behind-the-scenes atmosphere so much more immediate and convincing than any of its plot turns. While the market could undoubtedly bear sporadic entries after these, there had also been indications of other directions and possibilities: comedies with music *(Cocoanuts)*, romantic operettas *(The Desert Song)*, music dramas *(Hearts in Dixie)*. Nevertheless, the *Broadway Melody* syndrome, like Jolson's influence, was irresistibly seductive. By June of 1929, scores—literally—of backstage or related films were in various stages of planning or production. The inevitable question arises: What did the studios think they were doing?

The astonishing stream of backstage musicals in 1929 forms a concordance to the excesses and tumult of the era. At any other time it would be unthinkable that rival studios would scramble so fast to produce so much similar work. But—and Hollywood was trembling at the power of this particular "but"—these were desperate times, and rules and decorum had been thrown out. Fresh talent was far more accessible than fresh material, and it was infinitely less trouble to add new incidentals than to rethink and

---

2. They also continued in silents after sound came in. During that year silent films with no corresponding talkie version were produced for the many theatres not yet wired. One of them was Tiffany-Stahl's *Broadway Fever*, starring Sally O'Neil—released just before she proved, in *On With the Show!*, that she was indeed better seen than heard.

transform old formulas. All this is as much a part of the film industry as it is of politics. Yet there were some new wrinkles that portended disaster. The compressed time factor and rush to get the product out made for a most infelicitous clog, and the repetition divulged itself most blatantly in backstagers. With such convenient, lazy excuses for music, infinite variety was simply not part of the equation. The matrix was so narrow, in fact, that few of them even got into the "let's put on a show" of *On With the Show!* Instead, most of the plots were standard romantic triangles that could have fit into nearly any setting.

Taken as a whole, backstagers can seem numbingly repetitive, completely unleavened by imagination or grace; no wonder that audiences eventually took a walk. Modern viewers will likely want to do the same. While more palatable than mammy films, backstagers are just as standardized and less amusingly outrageous, with an uninflected sameness that makes them meld after a while. Who, after all, could distinguish between *Broadway Hoofer* and *Broadway Scandals*, both with the same leading man, or *Lord Byron of Broadway* and *Children of Pleasure*, both glossy MGM films with the same basic plot? Or all the interchangeable vehicles featuring tin-eared sexpot Alice White? Again, this is where we can see why audience favor eroded so much and so fast.

They do, on an individual basis, have moments. There are fair, occasionally memorable songs and performers, imaginative staging or design, and once in a while a few surprising seconds of depth or insight, accurate renderings of the high-pressure/low-class nature of theatrical life. Raucous humor crops up too, in sporadic bracing doses. "You toe dancers just get up on your toes tonight and give your heels a rest!" barks the stage manager in *Gold Diggers of Broadway*, as a reminder that chorus girls were popularly viewed as two small steps from the gutter. Those of finer sensitivities, beware: this is rough territory, and stereotypes of every stripe come crude and heavy. As one chorus boy in *Why Bring That Up?* (1929) is heard to exult, "And my new drapes are the most *gorgeous* shade of lavender!" Whatever else it may be, this side of the backstage binge is not boring.

The most important of these films quickly became archetypes, each with a host of imitators. Most obvious was the hoofer-heartbreak saga, set forth in the play *Burlesque* and in *The Broadway Melody*. Right behind that was the cabaret drama, often with gangster elements added, as in *Broadway*. Tin Pan Alley stories of struggling composers drew upon several sources: real-life models such as Irving Berlin, the opening scenes of *Broadway Melody*, several plays and novels. In such broad categories there was ample room for variation and overlap, plus such devices as changes of setting that range from college campuses to the circus, from Ireland to Hollywood. A few defy categorization. *Applause* and *The Blue Angel* transcended the genre, for with all their absorption in backstage minutiae, they are more properly designated "semi-musicals" and are discussed along with other crossover films in Chapter Fourteen.

Gold Diggers of Broadway crossed over in other ways. It would have been sprightly without songs, yet it was very much a backstage musical. Avery Hopwood's 1919 hit, which had starred Ina Claire on Broadway and Tallulah Bankhead in London, was titled simply *The Gold Diggers*—Warners Bros. tacked on the magic "Broadway" for 1929 appeal. The studio had already adapted the play for a 1923 silent directed by Harry Beaumont, with inveterate party girl Hope Hampton typecast in the lead. Hopwood worked along with scenarist Robert Lord for this remake, opening up the playgirls-on-the-make original to make excuses for the songs, many performed by pop balladeer Nick Lucas in an otherwise extraneous role. Somehow it all worked: here again was the showmanship and savvy that put Warner Bros. on top during the revolution. As with the Vitaphone premiere, as with *The Jazz Singer* and a few other moments of glory, the company produced a heat-seeking hit of a film perfectly calibrated to score immensely. It had none of the stiffness or archaisms of *The Desert Song*, the technological uncertainties of *The Singing Fool*, or the gaucheries of script and casting that marred *On With the Show!*, *Say It With Songs*, and so many others. In *Gold Diggers* all was confidence and clever packaging, each element part of an irresistible whole. Leading off was the best Technicolor yet seen, a collection of crowd-pleasing songs by Al Dubin and Joe Burke, and a snappy script that deftly balanced romance and gags. Roy Del Ruth cannily directed a well-integrated cast—Nancy Welford for ebullient mischief, Conway Tearle for stuffy urbanity, Lilyan Tashman for acidic finesse. Plus Nick Lucas, somewhat overused, and dancer Ann Pennington, somewhat underused.[3] And, hurtling through it all like a very noisy comet, Winnie Lightner.

Lightner's was the key triumph. Despite several Broadway stints—she introduced Gershwin's "Somebody Loves Me" in *George White's Scandals of 1924*—her trumpet voice and barrelhouse humor remained pure vaudeville, where she had trained. Sound shorts had shown her upfront style and zaftig physicality to be refreshing, if not at all subtle; her unabashed renditions of such items as "Where the Lollapaloozas Grow" ran her afoul of censor boards in several places. In *Gold Diggers*, her first feature, the role of the

3. Although *Gold Diggers of Broadway* can't be seen, its remake, *Gold Diggers of 1933*, is much with us, and the cast correspondence between 1929 and 1933 is as follows: Nancy Welford = Joan Blondell. Conway Tearle = Warren William. Winnie Lightner = Aline MacMahon. William Bakewell = Dick Powell. Helen Johnson = Ruby Keeler. Albert Gran = Guy Kibbee. Lilyan Tashman = Ginger Rogers. Nick Lucas and Ann Pennington, in otherwise superfluous roles, for Powell's song and Keeler's dance. One runner-up in 1929 was silent comic Constance Talmadge, who never appeared in talkies, and made what was reportedly a successful test for the Welford role—perhaps just not successful enough. For Broadway veteran Welford, this initial smash was not enough; her movie career quickly foundered.

raucous showgirl Mable gave her full scope: wisecracks, physical shtick, comic-vamping chubby old Albert Gran, blasting out character songs like "Mechanical Man." It was the first truly successful solo comedy performance of the sound era, a loud augury of all the hard-edged dialogue comics to follow over the next decade. Another prime magnet was Nick Lucas, or more specifically his performance of two song hits. "Painting the Clouds With Sunshine" is one of the classic smiling-through-tears ballads, and "Tip Toe Through the Tulips With Me," goofy as it is, somehow remains imperishable. Both were obviously spotted with an eye toward Technicolor, whose controlled yet splashy effect rated more plaudits than in *On With the Show!*, shot just weeks earlier. While most critics approved, this was more than anything else an audience picture, with ecstatic word of mouth, holdover engagements around the country and abroad through the fall and winter of 1929–30, and many customers returning for repeat viewings. When the final total was in, *Gold Diggers*'s $4 million gross put it right after *The Broadway Melody* in early musicals, and behind *The Singing Fool* in Warner films—a figure not exceeded at the studio until *Sergeant York* in 1941. It was a quintessential "feel good" picture; coming at the very end of the decade, its bright-hued mercenary optimism seemed to sum up the era for a large portion of the American public. This, ironically, just as the stock market was taking its dive.

All this success and social metaphor make it frustrating that, like much of the Warner and First National product of the transition years, *Gold Diggers of Broadway* is not known to survive in any form. As with other legendary lost titles, rumor has a projectionist in rural Montana (or wherever) retaining a print; all that verifiably exists are discs and one excerpt found in England in the late 1980s. The sound of Nick Lucas singing "Tulips" as the chorus clomps behind him sums up a whole era of upbeat zaniness; and the nine-minute clip is the entire last reel excluding the final minute. Nancy Welford and Conway Tearle wrap up the plot, there's a quick flash of Lightner gagging it up, and Welford goes onstage for the "Song of the Gold Diggers," followed by some acrobatic dance specialties. It recalls that relentless finale in *The Show of Shows*, yet it's more modest, quick and snappy. Del Ruth adds a striking high-angle shot of backstage bustle just before the curtain rises, the color is warm and attractive, and the footage flashes energy and vivacity far above the norm for 1929. There remain ninety minutes of *Gold Diggers of Broadway* that quite possibly will never be seen again; what does survive gives a glimpse of the high spirits that took the early backstage musical to its apogee.

A more somber source, *Burlesque,* pulled in more imitators than Hopwood's giddy comedy; the alcoholic Skid Johnson was a memorable anti-hero, at once funny, pathetic, and appalling. After multiple changes in cast, director, and venue, it was put under the supervision of Paramount producer David O. Selznick and shot in Hollywood in spring 1929. After much waffling Hal Skelly signed to repeat his Broadway performance as Skid, and to Barbara Stanwyck's disappointment Paramount stood by its decision to use Nancy Carroll as the faithful and feisty Bonny. Carroll's inexperience placed her at a disadvantage for some of the heavier dramatics, and when John Cromwell could not coax the performance out of her, his less tactful codirector Edward Sutherland wrung it out. Of the five new songs by Sam Coslow, Richard Whiting, and Leo Robin, the most notable was "True Blue Lou," a likably corny ballad which neatly distilled the plot's central predicament.[4] Afraid of small-town response to the title *Burlesque*, Paramount changed it to *The Dance of Life* (title courtesy of a then-daring sex study written by Havelock Ellis). Although the film was a success, it demonstrated another case of the *Broadway* syndrome, in which a host of imitators preceded a progenitive work to the screen. (And imitated afterward as well, including two official remakes: *Swing High, Swing Low* in 1937 and *When My Baby Smiles at Me* in 1948.) Today, the too-familiar story remains so, propped up irregularly by Carroll's strong performance and Skelly's uneven one. Of the songs only "True Blue Lou" works well, the Technicolor Follies scene being especially disappointing. Where *The Dance of Life* scores most is in evoking the seamy small time—grimy, devoid of magic, peopled with gross Beef Trust chorines and odious hangers-on—more authentically than any film of the time save *Applause*.

Another key saga of backstage heartbreak, *Glorifying the American Girl*, was also a Paramount production. Its plot was in some ways even more downbeat than *The Dance of Life*, its history more tortuous, its outcome less happy. In many ways this fascinating failure was 1929's musical equivalent of *Ishtar* or *Howard the Duck* and remains an unsettling experience for anyone who sees it for the first time. "Is this what they intended?" viewers invariably ask, and as with any major dud, the proper answer is no, not exactly. Long before it opened it had become a joke, an off-again/on-again white elephant which many thought would never see the light of day.

After Paramount's 1926 plan to use Florenz Ziegfeld's slogan on a silent spectacle was repeatedly postponed, the title resurfaced in 1928 as Paramount's first big talkie, then was abandoned again. With a musical craze rushing in around February 1929, the studio tried once more, still with scant idea of what its script should contain. What was easy enough to determine was that its central figure, predictably named Gloria, must embody the Ziegfeld ethos. For this the final choice was Mary Eaton, groomed by

---

4. With its tale of "a dame" who stuck unerringly with her abusive man, the song is a feminist's nightmare, "Frankie and Johnny" without the retribution. Of its many recordings Ethel Waters's was the best—perhaps because in real life Waters would never have taken the abuse Lou did.

(*above*) Backed by a living Technicolor palette, Nick Lucas and his trademark guitar serenade Ann Pennington and friends in *Gold Diggers of Broadway*. The song is "Painting the Clouds with Sunshine" and the time could only have been mid-1929. (*below*) A scene from *Glorifying the American Girl* which, while cut from the final print, gives a good indication of the script's bleak terrain. Here are Sarah Edwards (grasping), Mary Eaton (troubled), and Dan Healy (calculating).

Ziegfeld as the successor to his ultimate diva, Marilyn Miller. Like her predecessor, Eaton was a beautiful baby-doll blonde with ballet training and a small soprano voice that served adequately in *The Five O'Clock Girl* and other shows. All she lacked was Miller's unreproduceable charisma, for Eaton was not superstar material, just another pretty and hard-working performer. This she had demonstrated in *The Cocoanuts*, and a female lead in a Marx Brothers opus does not necessarily indicate one's ability to carry a Ziegfeldian musical drama—particularly one with some terminal problems.

Although J. P. McEvoy created Dixie Dugan, the archetypal stage-door flapper, little of his satiric wit came to bear on his scenario for *Glorifying the American Girl*. Somewhere along the line, it seems, all hands determined that the script should be less a gala homage to beauty and music than a downbeat parable admonishing those who aspire to any kind of fame. For Gloria, show business is a deliverance from a dreary department store job and an obnoxious leech of a mother. She seizes a chance to join a vaudeville act, only to discover that her new partner is even more of a creep than Mama, and when *Follies* stardom comes the price is high: the partner skims off most of her earnings, she loses the one man she cares for, and just Mama remains to supply hellish comfort. Going on for the finale she looks like every Ziegfeld myth rolled into one; but her song is a sad lament ("There Must Be Somebody Waiting for Me in Loveland"), and at the fadeout she takes her bow in abject misery. While this has an intriguing connotation—the *Follies* as Purgatory—the script lacked the courage of its downbeat convictions, playing less as a cohesive narrative than as a series of miniature crises dropped in between numbers. None of this deterred Paramount (Ziegfeld was involved only minimally) from spending a great deal of time and money. It was the first East Coast talkie to shoot outdoors, with locations at Grand Central Station and Manhasset, Long Island. Technicolor cameras were imported from the Coast for the revue scenes, with sets and costumes of glitzy *Follies* caliber, plus there were ballets staged by modern dance pioneer Ted Shawn.[5] After shooting wrapped in mid-June 1929, the assembled footage was found insufficient. It was first decided to add more color scenes, and when the cameras proved to be unavailable Paramount propped the story with star power in the persons of Eddie Cantor, Helen Morgan, and Rudy Vallee. Cantor, the only member of the trio to star in the *Follies*, revived one of his old sketches, Morgan reprised a song from *Applause*, which she had just filmed at Astoria, and Vallee contributed a fast

5. Since little or nothing in the choreography reflects Shawn's style, nor that of his partner Ruth St. Denis, his influence can perhaps be most felt with a number of men in the "Lorelei" and "Loveland" sequences who sport more muscles and less clothing than usual. Barely visible in both numbers (he's Adonis in "Loveland") is Johnny Weissmuller, already an Olympic champion but still three years away from Tarzan.

chorus of his theme "Vagabond Lover."[6] After this Paramount canceled a planned September opening for more recutting and tinkering.

By now it was an open secret in the industry that *Glorifying the American Girl* was a jinxed production, with a cost officially given as $350,000 but in actuality close to a million—much of it, apart from Ziegfeld's fee, spent on unused scripts. Paramount finally announced a New York premiere for November, then canceled it after a fiasco of a special preview. Its release ended up resembling that of lower-budget efforts that would bypass harmful New York reviews by playing most other cities first. In this case it was just as well. By the time of the New York run in early 1930, the critics had endured a four-year buildup, they had heard the bad reports, and only the Cantor sketch was exempted from their censure: "A very weak sister" *(American)*; "A series of Movietone shorts weakly strung together with an inept story" *(Evening Journal)*; "Feeble" *(Graphic)*; "Outmoded and dismally tiresome . . . . gasps pitifully for breath as it staggers along" *(Telegram)*; "The grace and pictorial beauty of Mr. Ziegfeld's stake is nowhere upon it" *(World)*. Plus a kiss-of-death *Photoplay* putdown: "Stone-cold turkey." Box office returns were predictably low, Mary Eaton's movie career was stopped dead, and Paramount's bookkeepers were compelled to charge the losses to "sound experimentation." The jinx continued to reverberate over the years, as the film slipped through the cracks into the netherworld of the public domain, resurfacing in prints of wretched quality to prove that even a bad movie is vandalized when rendered literally unwatchable and unlistenable. Fortunately Paramount had retained one complete print, and in 1987 this was preserved, in pristine and partly Technicolored splendor, by the UCLA Film and Television Archive

As it was in 1930, so it is today. *Glorifying the American Girl* remains a glittery wreck, a strange and sad fricassee of story lines and revue bits that collapses completely during its final reels. Apparently director Millard Webb (briefly married to Eaton) did not participate in much of the re-editing and reshooting, and the only stylish touch is an opening montage, set to the archetypal Ziegfeld anthem "A Pretty Girl Is Like a Melody," of working girls across the land streaming into New York to be glorified. Eaton, while never Sally O'Neil-style terrible, comes alive only during Gloria's *Follies* audition, when the steel becomes visible beneath the passive exterior and she snarls, "I've waited all my life for this opportunity and I'm not going to let it get away from me!" Otherwise she sings and dances decently, not enchantingly, and seems cold and blank. The rest of the

6. Vallee's visit to the Astoria lot, while brief, was not unmemorable. When his number wrapped, the egotistical singer expressed his appreciation to an unimpressed crew by handing out autographed photos. For weeks afterward, as an employee remembered, one had only to venture into any men's room in the studio to encounter one of the Vallee portraits, hanging in irreverently strategic places.

actors are obscure stage players (Edward Crandall, Olive Shea, Dan Healy), of whom only Sarah Edwards makes an impression as the monster mother. Helen Morgan's torchily neurasthenic "What Wouldn't I Do for That Man!" is the sole musical performance to rise above the lackluster, and the color sequences, garish and grainy, only hint at the pomp-and-marabou extravagance of a real *Follies*.[7] While Cantor's "Moe the Tailor" skit still brings laughs, the cumulative effect is pretty miserable. Yet even with all the waste there's something affecting about this sequined and pseudotragic Book of Job, perhaps because it now seems a tribute to the real-life Glorias who met untimely or unhappy ends—Anna Held, Lillian Lorraine, Olive Thomas, Marilyn Miller. And Mary Eaton.

For a title that could mean only one type of film in 1929, one might turn to First National's *Footlights and Fools*. Betty Murphy, a grief-and-greasepaint first cousin to Eaton's sad Gloria, wins stardom by turning herself into a naughty chanteuse named Fifi D'Auray. In addition to two identities she also has two men, a playboy and a ne'er-do-well gambler to whom she's secretly married. The latter robs the box office and goes to jail, the playboy leaves in disillusionment, and Betty/Fifi returns to *Sins of 1930* with divorce papers in hand. As written by Katherine Brush, past mistress of dimestore gloss, it was not an inspired story. But *Footlights and Fools* received an adrenaline boost from the casting, in a extravagant change of pace, of silent superstar Colleen Moore. One of the highest-paid performers of the time, she was the screen's first flapper and an expert comic, her trademark bangs-and-bob hairdo a fit frame for her hoydenish persona. By 1929 her career had begun to wane even as her biggest hit *(Lilac Time)* was in release, in part because Clara Bow had pilfered many of her fans by projecting real sexual heat to counter Moore's mere pep. Since she was versatile and had a passable voice, sound offered retrenchment. But producer-husband John McCormick was guiding her career into a standardized rut, and her first talkie, *Smiling Irish Eyes*, was an intense disappointment. A silly concoction best described as *Tin Pan Erin*, it gave her little to do other than act the winsome lass once more, pine after a songwriter (James Hall), and chase after a pig named Aloysius. While her charm survived the microphones intact and she sang well, those not put off aesthetically were offended ethnically. Irish-American groups denounced the film's stereotypic excesses, and after the first Dublin audience literally hooted it off the screen, it was banned outright in Ireland.

Casting about for a more palatable successor, Moore and McCormick decided to turn up the heat. Pulp that it was, Brush's story offered a challenge to which Moore responded energetically. Using Irene Bordoni and

7. The color was harshly criticized in many reviews, some of which took issue with the choppy way the *Follies* sequences cut between Technicolor onstage and black and white shots backstage and in the audience, to disorienting effect.

Anna Held as models, she cultivated a credible accent and an insinuating diseuse crooning style, and underwent a complete physical makeover, including scanty costumes. For leading men, McCormick borrowed two of Hollywood's new stage-trained actors, Paramount's Fredric March as the playboy and MGM's Raymond Hackett as the crook.

Footlights and Fools was released in October 1929 amid a heavy shower of publicity extolling "The NEW Colleen Moore!" Although one critic's sneering evaluation was "Ooh La La Begorrah," most observers enjoyed her suave change of pace. Alternately French-flirty and American-emotional, singing and cavorting through Technicolor chorus routines, she pulled it off with flair and assurance up to and including the downbeat ending. Despite these efforts, *Footlights and Fools* was considered too ordinary to compete at the box office with more consequential works. For Moore, earning a walloping $175,000 per film, it was nearly the end. First National was being absorbed into Warner Bros., and such high-priced talent as Moore and Corinne Griffith were no longer earning their keep. After *Footlights* she was off the screen for nearly four years, during which time she divorced McCormick. By the time she attempted to resuscitate her career she was too much of a back number to make a dent, so she moved on. *Footlights and Fools* does not survive, so her stint as a musical comedy star can remain only a distant and rather tantalizing memory.

If *Burlesque* was Ground Zero for 1929's musical explosion, *The Broadway Melody* was, at very least, Earth Parent. Its grosses, themes, methods all predetermined some close copies. The closest, unexpectedly, came from the source. In a self-defeating shortcut MGM cannibalized its biggest hit to provide material for most of its other musicals in the 1929–30 season. Usually Irving Thalberg was a shrewd judge of public taste, and the samenesses of the product could be disguised with gleam and colorful details. Not so with these. The Duncan Sisters, inspiration and first casting choice for *Broadway Melody*, had long since reached the top rungs of stardom in vaudeville and on Broadway with *Topsy and Eva*. The success of *Melody* was the greatest possible contrast to their own Hollywood failure with the 1927 silent *Topsy*, and, game to try again, they signed with MGM a few days after *Melody* opened. *Cotton and Silk*, the story concocted for them, was annoyingly familiar: the Hogan sisters—Rosetta as Casey is short and feisty, Vivian as Babe is dishy and dumb—score in vaudeville but split over pianist-songwriter James Dean (Lawrence Gray). The conflict between the Mahoneys in *Melody* was here so intensified as to become positively unpleasant. Another *Broadway Melody* holdover, the dreary Jed Prouty, was cast, with a breathtaking lack of appeal, as Rosetta Duncan's romantic interest. Given the abrasive tenor of the screenplay, it was ironic that just before its release late in 1929, the picture was retitled *It's a Great Life*. The reaction was consistent with that given to most vaudeville headliners: a drubbing by New York critics and a fair response in smaller towns, where Duncan fans turned out sufficiently to put their film into the credit column. And, again typically, there was no follow-up. The Duncans' only subsequent feature was MGM's aborted revue *The March of Time*, never seen by the public. Their stardom could not outlast the death of vaudeville. *It's a Great Life*, seen only rarely since 1930, is a shade more substantial than its reputation indicates. Technique had evolved extensively in the nine months since *Broadway Melody*, and veteran director Sam Wood, seldom a distinctive stylist, gives a fair pace to the opening reels. One startling moment comes when Babe has an attack of stage fright and a subjective camera zooms abruptly into the hostile audience. Soon after this the Duncan shtick takes over, all pushy and raucous, with heavy makeup and overlong routines that don't translate to film. Then there's that backstage bickering . . . and no Bessie Love in sight to inject some subtlety into the noise. Here we can see and hear how audiences grew weary of backstage movies. For reels and reels it goes on, Rosetta Duncan and Lawrence Gray yelling and trading insults until finally poor Vivian Duncan collapses into a coma. Only at MGM would delirium be an excuse to put a big Technicolor sequence into a small-time story, and here it is—Babe dreaming of stardom at the Palace in a brace of production numbers. "Hoosier Hop" is a gingham-and-gags barnyard stomp enhanced by overhead angles and crane shots, and "Sailing on a Sunbeam" features a surreal Art Deco sunburst, with chorus girls sliding down its bright rays. The Duncans' best moment comes with their song "I'm Following You," with close harmony on the first chorus and instrumental imitations on the second. Just two singers, no color or backstage racket, and a worthy glimpse of what vaudeville and stars like the Duncans meant to the American public.

About the same time, MGM was taking no chances on another backstager. Bessie Love and Charles King were reteamed as lovers in a theatrical setting, again with conflict and her ostentatiously sacrificing her happiness. "This one seems to have been run off on a stencil," a critic declared, though as variation they were placed in a company touring a Great War musical, *Goodbye Broadway*, sharing close quarters with assorted types: acerbic stage manager (Jack Benny), over-the-hill character woman (Marie Dressler), bibulous wardrobe mistress (Polly Moran), vamp (Nita Martan), effete chorus boy (George K. Arthur). After it was shot, previewed, and advertised as *The Road Show*, the studio had second thoughts and retitled it *Happy Days* after the one obvious hit in the score (Yellen and Ager's "Happy Days Are Here Again"). After Fox usurped that title, the third choice was *Chasing Rainbows*, and by the time it reached New York in March 1930 everyone was weary of backstage retreads. Surprisingly, it earned an excellent profit and fine reviews for Love and Dressler. But it was the last successful backstage musical for three years.

Chasing Rainbows makes for obvious comparison with its predecessor, and as with *It's a Great Life,* there are countless technical improvements. Charles Reisner's direction shows far more assurance than in *Hollywood Revue,* and the audience is made to care about these people and their show. King is better, if less sympathetic, than before, and Love is exemplary: only watch the subtle range of expressions crossing her face as she listens to King croon "Lucky Me and Lovable You." Dressler, with so-so material, is close to wondrous, with a drunk scene with Moran that audiences loved. Even Jack Benny stays in character. Yet nothing can hide the film's second-hand origins, and even those who liked *Chasing Rainbows* may have had mixed feelings; *The Broadway Melody* had by early 1930 become a legend, and so clear a copy seemed to dilute the memories excessively. As *Say It With Songs* proved, it wasn't fair to tamper with an audience's remembered goodwill.[8]

Bessie Love was caught in the same rut that hampered many talented players during the big-studio days. Having displayed great skill in one particular type of part, and lacking the clout to escape stereotyping, she was compelled to play the same role over and over. Forty years later she recalled, "I got a little fed up with doing all those musicals. Marie Dressler said she would spank me if I didn't stop them." It was Metro that needed the spanking. Immediately after Love finished shooting *Chasing Rainbows,* she was put into another backstage/masochistic role for the third time in less than a year.[9] This time there were, in effect, two Charles Kings, in the persons of Gus Van and Joe Schenck. Like so many others, Van and Schenck were fortyish vaudevillians who left the stage to crash movies. Their specialty was the comic ballad, sometimes in dialect, sung in distinctive harmony (baritone Van on melody, Schenck counterpointing above him in high tenor). After appearing in the *Follies* and on records they consolidated their fame with successful appearances in musical shorts for Vitaphone and Metro. Nowhere had they evidenced dramatic ability, which deterred MGM no more than it did any studio then hiring vaudevillians. So they were put into their own vehicle—and what else could these two play in but a backstage picture? And since it was MGM, Bessie Love would

8. Even today, *Chasing Rainbows* can't be judged objectively, for all of its Technicolor sequences seem to be lost. They included Love leading the chorus in "Everybody Tap," King's torchy "Love Ain't Nothin' but the Blues," and Dressler camping her way through "My Dynamic Personality." The most disappointing loss is the finale, King underscoring his reunion with Love with "Happy Days Are Here Again." It only survives in a brief snatch in the first reel. A huge hit, the song returned a couple of years later as the rallying cry of the Depression and the theme of the Democratic Party.

9. Not that this was her only work during that time: Love was MGM's busiest sound-film star in 1929. In addition to four musicals, she also found time to appear in *The Idle Rich* and *The Girl in the Show*—the latter, believe it or not, was a backstage comedy, not a musical. This was a lot of work, even for the sixty-plus-hour work week then in effect.

costar. Surprisingly, there were aspects of the result that weren't predictable. Shot as *Take It Big*, ultimately saddled with the incomprehensible title *They Learned About Women*, this was one peculiar musical.

To give MGM its due it did try for a different twist. The story of *They Learned About Women* was based on Waite Hoyt and Mickey Cochrane, major league players who toured in the off-season as a vaudeville duo. The dressing room was swapped for the locker room, V&S were cast as pitcher and catcher for the Blue Sox, and in place of large production numbers there was a great deal of baseball footage. Nevertheless, *Women* was a backstage movie trying to pretend it wasn't, with a spirit far closer to the Duncan Sisters than to the diamond. No matter that it was the talkies' first baseball story; it was the same as before, only more tiresome, a dreary backstage triangle with songs and a self-sacrificial Bessie Love. This time she gives up Schenck when he dallies with Mary Doran, and takes up with Van; when Schenck reforms, Van dutifully sends her back. Two doormats in one movie! Nor would anyone stake any claims on V&S's acting talent, for here were two middle-aged men trying to be romantic, and playing baseball to boot. Between their deficiencies, script problems, and the headaches of outdoor shooting, the film went through two directors (Jack Conway and Sam Wood) and over budget, winding up with one of MGM's longest shoots of the time. None of it did much good. The traditional jinx on baseball movies held, exacerbated by audience impatience with musicals and a misguided attempt to sell it as a drama. The pair's following could not stop their movie from ending up a fair-sized flop. Worse, while it was in release Schenck died of a heart attack at the age of thirty-nine.

With all respect to baseball fans, it can be said that the only worthwhile moments of *They Learned About Women* are musical. Van and Schenck do their accustomed close-harmony bit numerous times—including one ditty in Italian dialect, "An Old-Fashioned Guy," with some unthinkably offensive slurs—and Nina Mae McKinney, the bombshell from King Vidor's *Hallelujah!*, leads a big "Harlem Madness" number, wholly extraneous and pleasantly jazzy. The item for the archives, however, is "Ten Sweet Mammas," a beefcake and blues routine staged in the team's shower. With the likes of Van and Schenck and comic Benny Rubin clad in towels, this would not be termed a celebration of the male form; instead, it's a moment of energy and funky humor that stands out amid dreary and overlong surroundings.

The *Broadway Melody* bug also bit fledgling Columbia Pictures, whose first musical (started a week prior to *Song of Love*) was *Broadway Hoofer*, with a plot about as clever as its title: a small-time boy-girl act is disrupted when the boy is pursued by a temperamental diva. In true Columbia style the cast was pulled from newcomers (stage emcee Jack Egan) and affordable veterans (silent vamp Carmel Myers and the redoubtable Sally O'Neil), with ragtag songs and a few glitter-and-cardboard production numbers tossed in. The title was changed to the marginally grander *Broadway Scandals,* and the studio obtained some notice when CBS broadcast the film's tunes nationally as the premiere was in progress. None of this fooled critics into thinking that *Broadway Scandals* was anything but a cheap copy of a copy of *Broadway Melody;* Columbia's unsophisticated notion of big-time dazzle seemed particularly droll alongside the real thing, and O'Neil's musical gamine act (with borrowed voice) didn't convince anybody. It followed logically that *Broadway Scandals* performed best in the smallest communities, especially those not acquainted with big-time musicals.

A successor shot back-to-back with *Scandals* fared similarly, and since Jack Egan was again the lead, some had problems telling them apart. Not wishing to throw away a supposedly hot title, Columbia tried again with *Broadway Hoofer,* this time as the tale of a Broadway star who retires, incognita, to the sticks. On a lark she hooks up with a burlesque troupe and falls for its manager. This had the makings of an amusing premise, sort of a musical warmup for the runaway heiress comedies of the later 1930s, but at this time and studio was carried out with little distinction. Worse yet, it dismally wasted the talent of Broadway dancer Marie Saxon, whose valiant trouping and stylish self-possession made it quite obvious that she was much too good for either burlesque or a low-rent movie produced by a studio that knew nothing about musicals.

Although the Columbia musicals serve well to show the lower end of the backstage craze, there should be noted one other, incredible film. It may be recalled that at the dawn of cinema, Fort Lee, New Jersey, was briefly the movie capital of the world. While that changed soon enough the town continued to serve as the base for several minor companies. One of them, Rayart, produced features and shorts for small theaters. When sound came in, Rayart promptly hired bargain-basement talent to churn out musical shorts tailored to the most indiscriminate exhibitor. Then the Rayart hierarchy had an idea: let's keep going with one of the shorts and make our own backstage musical feature. Thus, in a few days in September 1929, there was produced in Fort Lee the seven-reel Raytone extravaganza *Howdy Broadway!,* allegedly featuring "several well known stars from the legitimate stage." Luminaries such as Tommy Christian and his Band and El-lalee Ruby, performing "Sophomore Strut," "Gazoozalum Gazoo," and the wrenching "Somebody's Sweetheart—Not Mine," were featured in a plot about a college band that makes good on Broadway. The entire budget likely did not exceed the cost of Bessie Love's sequined top hat in *Broadway Melody,* and this type of musical-at-any-cost madness shows how vigorous the public's yen for backstage films was perceived to be. It's been said that *Howdy Broadway!* was never released, which is easy to believe when confronted with the final result.[10] Believe it or not, it did play (obviously desperate) theaters well into 1930.

Performers were scarcely alone in experiencing trying times backstage. Songwriters also came in for their share, most often deserved, for they were nearly always depicted as louts whose heads are turned egotistically by sudden success. The stage precedents were mostly in nonmusical plays such as *Tin Pan Alley*, plus Eddie Kerns in *Broadway Melody*, selling his songs and inspiring envy among his cronies on the Alley. All told, there were not as many songwriter musicals as there could have been, and it was not quite as daunting an irruption as Hollywood's "composer biopic" binge in the 1940s. One was initially conceived as MGM's followup to *The Broadway Melody*. In late 1928 the studio announced that William Haines and Bessie Love would star in a musical based on Nell Martin's novel *Lord Byron of Broadway*. The oddly titled book traced the journey of an out-and-out heel and user, a tunesmith who lets no opportunity for material go unpassed. Broken romances are put into song, old love letters become song lyrics, and the death of his best friend serves as the base for a tear-jerking hit. Martin's story *à clef* was just mean and ironic enough to be diverting, an object lesson on the kind of nastiness which does indeed have its place in show business; it could have made a strong picture, perhaps without William Haines. By the time dozens of writers were done with it, most of Martin's acid had been neutralized. The leads were taken by stage players: bandleader/emcee Charles Kaley, ingenue Marion Shilling, and Ethelind Terry, Broadway's *Rio Rita*, all completely unknown to movie audiences, bland and pedestrian. So was the director, action-film specialist William Nigh, and when the dismayed producer Harry Rapf saw the result he called in Harry Beaumont to impart *Broadway Melody* punch to some extensive retakes. The little remaining ill will was toned down and the antihero given more of a comeuppance before his final atonement. When finally released, *Lord Byron of Broadway* quickly sank, with the observation made again and again how lackluster casting had undercut its effectiveness. The hit Brown/ Freed song "Should I?" and Cliff "Ukulele Ike" Edwards as the tragic buddy were insufficient bait for wary spectators. Nor did Technicolor help, though the fanciful "Woman in the Shoe" number still sports considerable charm. (The other color sequence was less useful—a kitschy Oriental ballet *cum* fire drill called "Blue Daughter of Heaven," so clumsily done that the overhead formations bend out of shape.)

Another songwriter opus followed shortly afterward and amounted nearly to a remake. *Children of Pleasure*—where did they get these titles?—was

10. Suffice it to say that *Howdy Broadway!* is the kind of effort that gives incompetence a bad name; the overall impression is that Ed Wood Jr. decided to put on a benefit in his garage. Best moment: one hapless dancer attempts a split and gets stuck midway, while the camera keeps rolling.

Backstager Flash—at MGM (bountiful) and at Columbia (shoestring): *(above)* Ethelind Terry in the Technicolor "Woman in the Shoe" number from *Lord Byron of Broadway*. *(below)* Jack Egan, Marie Saxon, and a hula kick line performing "Hawaiian Love Song" in *The Broadway Hoofer*.

adapted from the play *The Song Writer* by Crane Wilbur, who had also worked on *Lord Byron*. A standard triangle transplanted to Tin Pan Alley, it seemed to be based on Irving Berlin's marriage to socialite Ellin Mackay. Charles Kaley, again considered for the lead, was passed over in favor of Lawrence Gray, and costar Wynne Gibson soon became one of the best tough blondes in Depression cinema. Inspiration stopped about there, for the songs were only average and the director less so—the erratic, once-promising silent director Marshall Neilan, replaced once again by the reliable Harry Beaumont, this time midway into shooting. *Children of Pleasure* was a fast failure, a late entry in a played-out genre.[11]

Songwriting chicanery came to the fore at other studios as well. Pathé's *Red Hot Rhythm* featured Alan Hale as a chiseler making money off unknown composers by stealing good songs and charging to publish bad ones. This minor effort was an early credit for Leo McCarey, who soon went on to direct more important fare—*Duck Soup*, *The Awful Truth*, and so on. Fox's contribution to the songwriter division, *A Song of Kentucky*, was one of those early talkies trying to cover too many bases—Tin Pan Alley musical, love triangle, horse-racing yarn, symphonic romance—in its story of a Kentucky heiress (Lois Moran) and a New York songwriter (Joseph Wagstaff). The one notable idea was to use the composer's symphony to accompany flashbacks of his unhappy romance, but with an inane script and undistinguished music none of it worked.[12] In *Pointed Heels*, Paramount's disappointing holiday attraction for 1929, the songwriter was played by Phillips Holmes, a comely young actor without the driven authority to suggest a talented musician. In any case, *Pointed Heels* was dominated by the implacably urbane William Powell as a producer chasing after Holmes's wife, musical comedy star Fay Wray (who replaced Esther Ralson, who had replaced Clara Bow, who had replaced Mary Eaton in the role). Though Helen Kane and Richard "Skeets" Gallagher added songs and light relief, both were best taken in small doses. Besides Powell and some nice sets, *Pointed Heels* offered little.

Most backstage films discussed so far asserted that success and stardom were virtual guarantors of unhappiness. A less dire species of backstager intimated that a showbiz career could make life exciting and perhaps dangerous. Nightclubs were the setting, cabaret entertainers figured as protagonists, and gangsters and gunfire were seldom far away. The prototype was

11. Also rating a mention at MGM: Lewis Stone in *Wonder of Women* (1929), as a German concert pianist and classical composer with wanderlust and a faithful wife (Peggy Wood). Though given a tasteful presentation by director Clarence Brown, this one was a mite doleful for the masses. Plus it was only partly talkie, not the best idea for its subject matter.

12. Wagstaff, a stage juvenile of homely countenance, fared poorly in a medium where close-ups mattered as much as voice. One plainspoken exhibitor commented: "Lois Moran trying to express an enraptured deep feeling while this ugly bird is singing makes you think she is more likely suffering from acute appendicitis."

Broadway, and as with mammy films one musical personality (usually female) tended to dominate; ease in production was a salient factor. One performer in particular became closely identified with cabaret musicals, and if ambition were the sole criterion for superstardom Alice White would have enjoyed a long reign as queen of Hollywood. Her popularity, if that's the word, was not wholly inexplicable, for she was pert, very cute, and sexy. Starting as a studio stenographer, she nudged her way to a place before the camera, bleached her hair, and became First National's blonde equivalent of Clara Bow. After a success as Dixie Dugan in *Show Girl* (1928), she followed with a series of peppy minor films with predictable titles like *Hot Stuff, Naughty Baby,* and *Playing Around.* But she was no Bow, or Nancy Carroll either. She brought little authority to her acting, and undercut her sex appeal with a simpering coyness that makes her tough to watch today. (She was more successful years later in brassy supporting parts.) Short-lived as it was, her fame owed as much to her chutzpah as anything—except possibly the offscreen interest of her most frequent director, Mervyn Le-Roy. Certainly her musical ability was not responsible.

Broadway Babies, released in the early summer of 1929, was White's first all-talkie and her biggest hit, with ads bragging of "Honest-to-Ziegfeld songs and dances." It was a simple nightclub melodrama with songs, inspired by a couple of real-life stories, with Fred Kohler as the half-sympathetic mobster who pushes White (as Delight Foster) into stardom. Despite Kohler's good reviews and LeRoy's attempts at pre-*Little Caesar* grit and energy, it remained a star showcase. For modern viewers this translates as a truckload of misread lines and pouty pseudocuteness, plus some of the most amateurish musical performing in history. Visually White can make some moves that might pass for dancing, but all she can offer vocally is a childish soprano and erratic pitch. It remained so for several future vehicles, in which dialogue praising White's musical talent was disproved by the quality of her performances. For her next film, *The Girl from Woolworth's, The New York Graphic* attacked the star with graphic and near-libelous gusto: "A coarse, untalented young woman, who, 'tis said, has sex appeal galore."[13] And exhibitors wrote in to express irritation at her vocal efforts. "She can't sing," complained one Michigan theater manager. "Why do they kid those actors that they can sing?" They didn't, for long. White hastened the end of her starring career by indulging in a penchant for uncooperative behavior, including a salary dispute with her studio that cost her a big role (the lead in *No, No, Nanette*). When First National's contract stars were annexed by no-nonsense Warners, her fate was sealed. A couple of increasingly bad parts, then out.

13. In other words, who is she sleeping with? It might be noted that Mervyn LeRoy reshot most of *The Girl from Woolworth's* after the first version, directed by William Beaudine, turned out poorly. Beaudine retained screen credit.

Warners and First National, ultimately the haven for Cagney, Robinson, and Bogart, were also the source for most other underworld-set musicals. The grandmother of them all was released early in 1929: Texas Guinan in *Queen of the Nightclubs*. A melodrama with some comedy and a little music, it cashed in on Guinan's Prohibition notoriety without adding to either her reputation (she was horrendously photographed) or that of talkies (the reviews were equally bad). More viably, Billie Dove, Dorothy Mackaill, and Winnie Lightner each headlined one such venture. Dove, a *Follies* alumna whose beauty approached the mythic, starred in her one musical, *The Painted Angel*, late in 1929. Adapted from a Fannie Hurst story, it came and went as just another Dove picture, the star playing to her fans, and apparently she pulled off the musical interludes well enough. Likewise another *Follies* beauty, the British Dorothy Mackaill, who went through the mill in Michael Curtiz's Technicolor *Bright Lights* (1930). As a carnival dancer in provincial Africa, she was menaced by evil smuggler Noah Beery and eventually moved on to Broadway and, less plausibly, romance with Frank Fay. Besides Mackaill's way with the hula and the wisecrack, there was one good song in evidence, "Nobody Cares If I'm Blue." For Winnie Lightner, *She Couldn't Say No* (1930) was a stardom-bolstering reward for stealing *Gold Diggers of Broadway*. As Wild Winnie Harper, a bighearted if unlovely blues singer, she reached stardom, pined after mobster Chester Morris, and suffered when he chased after socialite Sally Eilers and got himself murdered. This was far more serious Lightner than usual, with torchy ballads alongside the usual roughhouse songs, and, in fact, more of her than many viewers wanted to see. Her attempts at pathos met with a divided response, and *Photoplay* sniped that "Winnie Lighter *should* have said NO." It turned out to be one of the studio's bigger successes of the year . . . but note that Lightner was never again called on to carry this type of story.

Had Warners opted to retain the services of its first musical funny lady, Fannie Brice, it might well have cast her in something similar to *She Couldn't Say No*. Excluding her bit in *Night Club*, Brice made no features for over a year after *My Man*. Still intending to go Hollywood, she signed for two pictures with United Artists producer Joseph Schenck and began work on a musical comedy-drama called *It's a Pleasure*. By the time it was released in February 1930, *It's a Pleasure* had been retitled *Be Yourself!* and her pact with Schenck had been dissolved in a flurry of animosity and litigation. In the event, while *Be Yourself!* was moderately successful, Brice's career as a movie star was over and her later film appearances few. While no gem, *Be Yourself!* preserves some prime moments of undiluted Fannie. Like *My Man*, the plot—a cabaret singer falls for a useless prizefighter (Robert Armstrong)—is too morose to suit her, and as with many United Artists films of the time, the presentation is as stodgy as it is drab. Yet Brice overcomes many of the liabilities. She cavorts in a mock ballet, sends up operetta with a screeching rendition of "A Heart That's Free," duels with Harry Green in Yiddish inflection, and leads a rather peculiar production number, "Kicking a Hole in the Sky," essentially as Fannie Semple McBrice, offering salvation to transgressors. The choicest scene, not surprisingly, involves Brice and a lighthearted song, Billy Rose's "Cooking Breakfast for the One I Love." Brice is in the kitchen, the dim Armstrong waits at the table, and the tenderness and the wisecracks intermingle brightly; an ordinary movie is elevated by a few special minutes.[14]

Another nightclub-set story was one of the sleepers of 1929. *Syncopation*, the first production under the new Radio Pictures (later RKO-Radio) trademark, had been produced by the FBO studio. The first true Radio production, shot on the former FBO lot in Hollywood, was *Street Girl*. 1929's busiest actress, Betty Compson, starred as an immigrant violinist who joins an all-male combo and wins all hearts. The plot really was just about that thin, and unreasonably stretched out to nine reels, but for the time, it worked. Instead of the usual backstage racket, *Street Girl* focused quietly on a few little people who want to play music and be happy. (Compson, incidentally, did her own playing.) The four Sidney Clare–Oscar Levant songs were presented modestly, with only one dance number ("Broken-Up Tune") in sight; even the indigenous wisecracking by Jack Oakie and Ned Sparks has a mellower hue. If it seems trivial, there's also a sweet warmth that spectators did not often find in the fall of 1929. Its gross, over a million dollars, was a boon to the fledgling studio, and in its own minor way *Street Girl* indicated some possible new paths.

Most backstage films tended to take the designation literally and deal with the world of live performance. A few times, the idea varied just enough to take audiences behind the cameras instead of the footlights. With its cross-referenced layers of self-glorification and self-laceration, film on film has always been an unsettled genre. The autobiographical spill-its-guts promise inherent in all backstage stories seems to multiply when film turns in on itself, and small wonder that audiences have been fascinated with the likes of *Sullivan's Travels*, *Sunset Boulevard*, *Singin' in the Rain*, *Day for Night*, *The Player*, and several versions of *A Star is Born*. Silent film had also occasionally looked in the mirror—King Vidor's *Show People*, James Cruze's *Hollywood*—so a peek behind talkiedom's magic processes would seem to be logical for the transition era. The first one announced was never made—Universal's *The Hollywood Melody*, intended to send up the current chaos. It likely would not have been any worse than *The Talk of Hollywood*, which paradoxically was a New York product. Conceived as a vehicle for dialect comic Nat Carr, it was thrown together by an independent and mis-

14. The star's recording of "Breakfast" has deservedly become a classic; it's surprising, yet sensible, to find out that some of her lines on the record are talk/sung in the film by Armstrong. ("Who the heck wants oatmeal sprinkled with lox?")

named company called Prudence Pictures and filmed in early May 1929 at RCA's Gramercy Studio in Manhattan. Carr, as mogul J. Pierpont Ginsburg, bumbles into talkie success by producing a feature of such ineptitude that it's mistaken for a comedy and scores a hit. Wishful thinking—even with some insider gags about microphones and recording, this was one of those disastrous early talkies where everything went wrong, including the music. Indeed, the only real laughs emanated unintentionally from the would-be Continental vocal stylings of the "alluring" Fay Marbé.[15] After intemperate trade ads boasted that *The Talk of Hollywood* "will shake the bellies of the world!," the mess sat on the shelf for many months; when finally released it was widely hailed as the worst talkie yet made. Its one unexpected survivor was writer-director Mark Sandrich; in later years, as he reaped plaudits for *Top Hat* and *Holiday Inn*, it's unlikely that he cared to reminisce about his first sound feature, *The Talk of Hollywood*.

Another behind-the-scenes musical, *Free and Easy* (MGM) contained some fair spoofing of the movies, along with an all-talking-singing-dancing Buster Keaton (for which see Chapter Eleven). Fox produced the operetta *Married in Hollywood*, discussed in Chapter Twelve, and also *Let's Go Places*, another showcase for the unphotogenic tenor Joseph Wagstaff. Originally titled *Hollywood Nights*, it could have been named *Evening in Death Valley* for all the use it made of its setting, with a weak mistaken-identity plot and badly done dance routines defusing its attempts to satirize talkie-making.

Show Girl in Hollywood, released in April of 1930, is the most interesting of the Hollywood-set musicals for reasons that have little to do with its star, Alice White. Her initial splash had been made as Dixie Dugan, so as a sequel J. P. McEvoy's mock-heroine moved to California, where lecherous moguls filled in for the Broadway wolves Dixie eternally fended off. There were appointments well above the White norm—large-scale numbers, some Technicolor, a competent cast—and they all unwittingly subverted the basic premise. Dixie, the script says, barges into Hollywood, defeats the opposition, and takes the country by storm. But White can't make this true, not with her inability to read lines and her woozy vocalizing. If that weren't enough, there was a genuine actor in the cast whose every scene pointed up the flimsiness of White's talent. Blanche Sweet had been one of D. W. Griffith's early stars in the teens and continued as a major name in the twenties in such films as *Anna Christie*. By 1929, despite her ability and intelligence, she was in the same boat as many contemporaries: too much the veteran to score in talkies and forced to support a younger performer. With a life-imitating resonance, Sweet was cast as Donny, a talented star

15. Her character's name, Adore Renee, was an obvious takeoff on MGM's Renee Adoree and gives an idea of the level of the satire. An enterprising if maladroit adventuress, Marbé later sued *Talk*'s producer for not coming up with a suitable follow-up vehicle tailored to her purported talents.

whose age—thirty-two—forces her over the Hollywood hill. "There's a Tear for Every Smile in Hollywood," she sings to Dixie, and Sweet turns pasteboard sentiment into genuine pathos.[16] Donny's suicide attempt is played and directed (by Mervyn LeRoy) with such dramatic understatement that the specter of Griffith suddenly uplifts a simpleminded comedy and subverts its attempts to cite White's "youth and freshness" as Hollywood's going commodity. No matter how much the script insists that the Dixie Dugans will inherit the movies, the juxtaposition between Sweet and White makes the greater truth quite clear. It also became clear when *Show Girl in Hollywood* opened to disappointing returns at about the same time White was dropped from her studio.

Aside from Blanche Sweet, the Hollywood caricatures are toothless and the sole merits in the film are documentary. There are shots of the First National lot just prior to its annexation by Warners, plugs for Vitaphone, and glimpses of Warner and First National stars, including Al Jolson (with Ruby Keeler) and Loretta Young. Most diverting is a seemingly accurate depiction of early sound shooting. As White and the chorus sing and dance "I've Got My Eye on You," there's a soup-to-nuts rundown of how it's done—three cameras in booths shooting simultaneously, the track laid down on the disc, and the final O.K. from the sound man. The number is captured complete in one take, as was standard with early Vitaphone, with live singing and an orchestra just off camera.[17] Such moments, and that one fine performance, alleviate what is otherwise just another backstage movie.

Having reached mammoth proportions by late 1929, the backstage profusion extended overseas. Europeans were starting to make their own musicals—and what they began with hardly needs stating. Britain's first two musicals turned up early in 1930. *Harmony Heaven* was a struggling-young-composer yarn so humbly appropriating all the clichés that it made *Rainbow Man* look like the farthest reaches of the avant-garde. *Raise the Roof* was far more jolly, a *Chasing Rainbows* without the angst and with some vigor and ingenuity in its musical numbers. Silent heroine Betty Balfour starred opposite a callow young Maurice Evans, and homegrown audiences reacted with reasonable enthusiasm. Germany's first (part-) talkie, *Because I Loved You* (*Dich hab' ich geliebt*, 1929), was technically assured and dramatically adequate, a success despite its overt resemblance to more lachrymose American efforts. As a New York critic observed, "Those clever Germans have been opening mail from Hollywood for they have not only chosen the

16. She's effective enough to make one forget that the song is a close copy of Fred Fisher's "There's a Broken Heart for Every Light on Broadway," though White undercuts its poignance by reacting with a blurted-out "Gee!"

17. According to production records for *Show Girl in Hollywood*, this was indeed how it was done. The musicians were hired individually for each number, and smaller ones such as Sweet's "Hollywood" required fewer players.

highly original backstage theme . . . but have added the little pal angle as well." Its derivative nature aside, the German sound-film industry was off to a strong and musical start.

Back home, audience nerves had begun to wear and the press was starting to take notice. A few scattered comments from that season:

June 1929:

> So persistent is the vogue for movies of backstage life, so continuous the presentation of the gallantries, loves and idylls of scene-shifters and ballet ladies, that we begin to long for something as esoteric as the true romance of an accountant.
>
> John McCarten, *New Yorker* (review of *On With the Show!*)

November 1929:

> The story is the usual backstage yarn that has been worked to a frazzle.
> *Film Daily* (review of *Why Bring That Up?*)

> About as good as all the other films which have portrayed brave troupers hiding their heartbreak.
>
> *New York Post* (review of *Footlights and Fools*)

January 1930:

> Nothing better demonstrates the never-say-die spirit (no matter how often misguided or blindly inspired they might be) of our Hollywood nabobs than their tenacious devotion to the song-and-dance productions. *The Broadway Melody* started it and caught the imagination of the world figuratively, but the majority of its would-be successors is so much clam chowder as compared to the caviar of the original.
>
> As if *Broadway Scandals* wasn't enough, the Columbia people now present the latest version of the lethal leg shows, vaguely titled *The Broadway Hoofer*.
>
> *Billboard* (review of *The Broadway Hoofer*)

The comments came to an irritated head in March:

> Witness the present Hollywood craze for plots dealing with stage life. Picture after picture has shown us the miraculous rise of an unknown vaudeville actor to stardom on Broadway. Why, you will ask, this persistent riding to death of a patently trivial subject? Because the public demands it? No, I am sure the reason is simply that Hollywood finds in stage life the easiest formula for making a song and dance show realistically plausible. . . . To make singing and dancing expressly cinematic . . . requires a little thinking and a little imagination, whereas aping the stage requires none.
>
> Alexander Bakshy, *The Nation* (review of *Happy Days*)

If [it] had been the first of the backstage productions it would have been a good picture. It isn't the first by goodness knows how many and that just about describes it.

Douglas Fox, *Exhibitor's Herald-World* (review of *Chasing Rainbows*)

If the public is not satiated with stories dealing with backstage life then the motion picture reviewers certainly should be. No doubt the public is beginning to feel just a little disgruntled with the numerous stories of this type that are being thrown at them.

Billboard (review of *Let's Go Places*)

An ominous headline atop the March 15 issue of *Billboard* told the rest of the story:

BACK-STAGE STORIES BANE TO EXHIBITORS

Ever since talking pictures found voice enough to sing and to record a rat-tat-tat of tap dancers on a hard-wood floor these backstage stories have been done and redone ad nauseam. At the start [they] were novelties, but now every inch of space has been covered. . . .

No doubt getting the urge from such stage successes as *Burlesque* and *Broadway*, the screen producers have overstepped all bounds and done the thing to death. . . . The exhibitors are beginning to cry halt and the box office is missing the jingle of the coin of the realm. . . . This back-stage cycle has been run to such an extent that a new pair of tires built on a different tread would not be amiss.

The outcry was as inevitable as it was justified. It also flew quite deliberately in the face of the remarkably favorable reception given a backstage musical that opened late in February. No question about it, *Puttin' on the Ritz* is one of the archetypal early musicals. Also, for a variety of reasons, it is one of the more frequently seen in subsequent years. Irving Berlin's endlessly revived title song gives it recognition-value lacking in most of its peers. Ditto one of its stars, Joan Bennett, who sustained a healthy career for over half a century. The rest has to do with vagaries of film distribution, which put the film on television in the early fifties and at sporadic intervals later on. Even its Technicolor sequence, "Alice in Wonderland," was put out in black-and-white prints for home viewing. And in all its incarnations, it has come to epitomize the popular view of the early musical—static, talky, sleazily sentimental, unsuitably cast, with amateurish and stagy song numbers. Unlike some of its fellows, this one—by and large—deserves the rap, which is why it's so startling to go back and see how well it was initially received.

Whatever else *Puttin' on the Ritz* may or may not be, it is *conventional*, and like many other musicals it emerged from a long and tangled and paradoxical web of production circumstances. Way back when *The Singing Fool* was on the soundstage and no one knew what a movie musical would be, United Artists producer Joseph Schenck began to delegate some of his decisions to his ambitious young cohort John Considine. The latter decided that he and Schenck should start work on the screen's first musical comedy, and in July they signed as a main player the self-styled "King of Broadway," Harry Richman. The child of immigrants, Richman was the kind of slick New York character who epitomized the fast-lane show world of the 1920s: titanically vain, energetic, street-smart, unscrupulous, inveterately lecherous. With his patent-leather style and nasal belt he rapidly achieved fame as a saloon singer, then went legit in the *Scandals*. He consolidated his fame by opening his own Manhattan nitery, Club Richman, holding court and singing to the rich and dangerous. Having preceded Al Jolson into films with an early appearance in a Lee De Forest short, he was now most willing to have the opportunity to outdo Jolson in features.

By September 1928 the project had achieved ceremonial proportions with an announcement that Irving Berlin would create script, words, and lyrics for *Say It With Music*, to star Richman in a saga of "the birth and evolution of the popular song as a part of America's modern civilization" and to be directed in New York by Alan Crosland, with Joe E. Brown heading the supporting cast. Then it fell apart. Scuttlebutt blamed Richman's on-camera charisma, alleged by some to be less than overwhelming. There had also been a pronounced failure, after dozens of tests, to find a costar; the most promising choice, Claudette Colbert, signed with Paramount instead. The project, postponed for nearly a year, finally began shooting in California in October 1929 under Edward Sloman. His direction of several quirky and unconventional silents did not particularly suit Richman's brassy hustle, and much of Berlin's work was discarded in favor of a story by producer Considine that welded bits of Richman's career to musty plot threads from every backstage movie ever made. Harry Raymond teams up with Dolores, a singer/songwriter, scores a hit, and opens his own club. Conceit sets in, he turns his back on Dolores and his cronies, and takes to drink. That one belt too many turns out to be bad booze, and in a burst of Old Testament retribution he is instantaneously struck blind. Dolores, meanwhile, becomes a Broadway star, and on her opening night the contrite crooner gropes his way to the theater for a tearful reunion.

Despite this nonsense, Irving Berlin remained anxious to incorporate movies into his power base. Retaining a stake in the production as a constant presence on the set, he found himself acting as a buffer to cushion the teenaged Bennett from Richman's take-no-prisoners ego. As for Richman, he went Hollywood with a vengeance. Slyly calculating the type of personal publicity to boost the picture and his own fame, he pursued and caught the most sensational star in pictures. His bicoastal affair with Clara Bow made international headlines of a sufficiently tawdry nature to damage her career and make him look like an overblown dimestore Lothario. Under these gamy conditions, United Artists' big backstager moved toward theaters. There had been false starts, production headaches, Richman's growing notoriety, bewildering title changes,[18] and a total, eyebrow-raising expenditure of about $800,000. When it opened in late February it must have seemed worth it, for it received the best reviews given any film of this type since *The Broadway Melody*. "Corking good picture. Richman great. . . . One of the best this season" *(Film Daily)*. "There isn't a wasted moment— no letdown from beginning to end" *(New York American)*. "Tuneful, strikingly staged and well acted" *(Herald-Tribune)*. "All-around swellest talkie singie of the backstage type to reach Broadway" *(Daily News)*. "Sets a standard which has not been approached since sound and color came to the screen" *(Post)*.[19] Outside urban areas, Richman's aura evaporated; many audiences didn't care what this pushy and plain-faced hoofer was doing with Clara Bow, and the alcoholism angle was often judged too fulsome. While receipts initially seemed to echo critical enthusiasm, the box office returns were ultimately a disappointment in light of the film's immense cost. Richman returned home, as had others, and it must have been a dent to his hubris when, months later, the best movie deal he could wangle was for two short subjects at Paramount, which then went sour when his demand for a two-reel format was countered by studio insistence that one reel was quite sufficient.

It's possible, if difficult, to see why *Puttin' on the Ritz* was so big in its day. New York considered Richman second only to Jolson as a pop troubadour, and the personal exploits that caused UA to dub him "The Idol of Broadway" gave him a romantic aura Jolson lacked. Crooning "There's Danger in Your Eyes, Cherie" and jauntily leading the title number, he was in his time and milieu the real thing; it's a quirk of history (and perhaps talent) that we can perceive it in Jolson but not in Richman. Another factor cited time and again was the splendor of the production—photography, sets, costumes, close-ups of the beautiful young Joan Bennett—and little of it translates across the decades. Bennett is palpably uncomfortable in a musical, especially in the "Alice in Wonderland" number. Supposedly it cements Dolores's fame, yet all Bennett does is skip here and there with dancing recreations of the Tenniel drawings; in monochrome, it's only a dim shadow of the Technicolor so well liked in 1930. Only in that wonder-

18. The final title did not come until late in production after it was clear that Berlin's song would be the hit of the show. Among the earlier titles: *Tin Pan Alley*, *The Song of Broadway*, *Play Boy*, *Broadway Vagabond*. Berlin's original title, *Say It With Music* (from his song hit) also turned up at the very end of his career, as the title of a never-made film project.

19. The praise extended to critics who normally had little truck with this type of diversion, such as *Time* and *The Nation*; both had earlier decried the movie musical's tendency to paint itself into pedantic corners. Not everyone was so taken, such as *Photoplay*: "Another backstage story. . . . Harry shows little in looks or acting, but you'll like his warbling."

ful title song, with the original ethnic-tinged lyrics Berlin later modified, is there the vibrancy of a big movie musical. Even with the proscenium setups and rabidly uncoordinated chorus dancing, something special is going on. Much of it, of course, has to do with Berlin's nervily syncopated tune and tinsel-and-grime lyrics. No surprise, also, that Richman is far more at home here than in scenes of romance, let alone pathos. Most memorable beside the song itself is the audacious set design—an urban back alley, clotheslines and telephone wires and cats, distant skyscrapers that sway to the music. Credited to production designer William Cameron Menzies, the set is actually the work of Robert Usher, one of those unbilled wizards whose work (here and at Paramount) gave Hollywood's golden age a good deal of its luster.

Richman's old rival also starred in a latecoming entry with a Berlin score, in some ways one of the more creative backstagers. One wouldn't think so on encountering the words "Al Jolson in *MAMMY*," but it wasn't what it seemed. This was the long-delayed *Mr. Bones*, once set as Jolson's first all-talkie. Had it been so, instead of the wretched *Say It With Songs*, the first leg of his movie career might have been more substantial. He finally got around to *Mammy* in the fall of 1929, after renegotiating his Warner contract. He had the studio over a barrel, and for *Mammy* was paid an unimaginable $500,000—much greater than the entire budget of most 1929 films, equivalent to far more than the ridiculously inflated star salaries of the 1980s and 1990s. Yet *Mammy* was not the standard one-man show. A melodramatic tale of a touring minstrel troupe, it actually required Jolson to interact with fellow performers in scenes he did not dominate, and for a while, under director Michael Curtiz and alongside his formidably hammy costar, Lowell Sherman, he gives something like a disciplined performance. Before the onset of excess—Jolson is framed on an attempted murder rap and goes on the lam—Curtiz manages a convincing and energetic simulation of the one-night stands and transience that constituted minstrel life. The opening scene, a minstrel parade during a rainstorm, shows how far Vitaphone's technique could be pushed by a resourceful hand, and an uproarious opera parody (originally in Technicolor) harkens to the looser, funnier Jolson of Broadway days. Berlin supplied him with two excellent songs: "Let Me Sing and I'm Happy" cuts straight to Jolson's essence, megalomania and all, and "(Across the Breakfast Table) Looking at You" presents him as, of all things, genuinely tender and restrained, far beyond "Sonny Boy" excesses. Because of its melodrama and Jolson's later obligatorily maudlin song to his mother (Louise Dresser), *Mammy* was judged as another piece of *Singing Fool* bathos, for which audience enthusiasm had already eroded. With Jolson's salary inflating the budget, *Mammy* was, with *Noah's Ark*, *General Crack*, and *Show of Shows*, one of Warners' most expensive productions and—ominously—the first Jolson picture to lose money.

Puttin' on the Ritz and *Mammy* only fed the growing aversion to backstage films and musicals in general. To the reasons usually given for their demise—overkill, redundancy, cloning—should be added the absurd way in which backstage conventions were forced, all seams showing, into other genres. A Western backstage musical, for instance—not a music-hall tale of the Old West but an off-kilter shotgun marriage like Tiffany's *Under Montana Skies* (1930). Or an uneasy mix of college and Tin Pan Alley: Fox's *Words and Music* (1929), assembled from spare parts from the *Movietone Follies*. Or soapy dramas like Pathé's *The Grand Parade* (1929) and *Swing High* (1930), respectively with minstrel and circus backgrounds, both with lachrymose Helen Twelvetrees and tenor (later cowboy star) Fred Scott, neither film properly integrating its setting with songs and heartbreak. Then there was *The Great Gabbo*.

How many ways can a good idea go wrong? Start with a high-profile writer and an original story with an offbeat protagonist, strong dramatic potential, and provocative psychological implications. Inject an ambitious director with a high reputation, operating as an independent and wanting to show the big boys. Add a talented egotist of a star, with public humiliation in his recent past, and a mediocre technical crew working under trying conditions. Most of all, envelop the whole in a decision to transform said dramatic story into an extravagant backstage musical. In a decade that provided few directors with a public identity, James Cruze was one of Hollywood's most recognized names. *The Covered Wagon* (1923) had made his reputation, followed by a mixed bag of work, the surefire *(Old Ironsides)* alongside the risky *(Beggar on Horseback)*, and by the advent of the sound era he had left Paramount to form James Cruze Productions. Resolving to make independent films with the quality and grossing power of big-studio product, he selected a Ben Hecht story, "The Rival Dummy," about a talented ventriloquist whose ego has long since gone over to the dark side. For Gabbo, his dummy Otto comes to be the receptacle and conduit for whatever finer feelings he retains. His loving and abused assistant Mary, who senses Gabbo's dual nature, is pushed away after she fumbles a cue. Time passes, and the now famous Gabbo is starring in a Manhattan revue. Mary is also on the bill as part of a song and dance team, and at Otto's prompting, Gabbo realizes what he's lost and determines to reclaim her. When he discovers that she's married her partner, Gabbo loses his marginal hold on reality, charges onstage during the finale, and ruins the show. After Mary attempts to comfort him he goes off with Otto as his name is removed from the marquee.

The story's potential was obvious, its aptitude for sound film even more so. How, after all, could silent film convey the thesis that Gabbo used speech as a pivot between art and life, between reason and madness? Cruze's second good idea was to hire the best of all possible Gabbos. Erich

Erich von Stroheim, with Otto, in quintessential form as *The Great Gabbo*.

von Stroheim had recently been fired as director of Gloria Swanson's *Queen Kelly*, and to the public his egomaniacal excesses were akin to those of the mad ventriloquist. The vision-obsessed perfectionism that created *Foolish Wives* and *Greed* and *The Merry Widow* made him, to audiences and industry, the prima donna director at its most acute. He was, it seemed, always being fired from his films, immersed in inconsequential details, the butt of employers' cracks about a "footage fetish." The type of genius that disregarded bosses and budgets was doomed in Hollywood, and after *Kelly* and the earlier financial disaster of *The Wedding March* Stroheim needed the money. *Gabbo* was the first time in many years he acted under another director, and the Teutonic rigidity he brought to the role made his crackup all the more pitiful. That forbidding appearance was ideal too, the cold visage and shaved head and monocle.

With story and star in place, Cruze veered wildly off course. As it was, screenwriter Hugh Herbert (the same one who burbled "Woo-woo!" endlessly through so many thirties and forties comedies) had watered down some of Hecht's better ideas. The story was set in a theater, the characters were performers: ergo, it would be a musical. Not just small numbers—a jingle for the dummy, a duet for Mary and her partner, or incidental flashes. Cruze wanted it big. After Stroheim's salary, the greatest expense went to a series of bloated production numbers that intruded upon the drama like elephants charging a lemonade stand. Twelve songs were commissioned, seven making it into the final cut; the energetic, often ill-advised Maurice Kusell was hired to stage them, and designer André-Ani, who had dressed Garbo, was enlisted to come up with ostentatious costumes. Then there was Multicolor for the requisite blue-and-orange shimmer. The time and expense and effort that might have made *Gabbo* a thoughtful work went, instead, into these *Follies*. For Mary, Cruze attempted to hire Broadway's Jeanette MacDonald, and when that did not work he turned to silent player Pauline Starke.[20] Shooting began with Stroheim and Starke in May 1929, only to be halted when Betty Compson, in private life Mrs. Cruze, became available and took over for Starke, who later sued. While Compson was dubbed with a MacDonald-like soprano (Stroheim's Otto voice was also dubbed), her vis-à-vis was an import from operetta, Don Douglas. Cruze's studio was too small for the grandiose musical numbers, so some shooting was done in a real theater—reportedly, the Los Angeles Shrine Auditorium. Cruze arranged to release *Gabbo* through Sono Art, home of Eddie Dowling, and the film received some of the most intense advertising ever given a non-major-company product. While some advance notice had already been made of Cruze's grand finale, featuring several nude women powdered up as living statues, the Broadway premiere topped it all—literally, with a living billboard derived from *Gabbo*'s most elaborate production number, "The Web of Love." For several days and nights scantily dressed spider cuties crawled about on a big web high above Broadway and 45th Street. This time, unlike the *Hollywood Revue* sign, the NYPD let it stay. Many critics were lenient as well, especially to Stroheim, and the trade press carried such comments as "Carries a great punch" *(Film Daily)*; "Right up in the front ranks . . . extraordinary . . . a great picture by any standard" *(Exhibitors Herald-World)*. Some even raved about the musical numbers, though others, such as *Photoplay*, observed that both the music and story suffered under their forced juxtaposition. The generic confusion cut so deep that some exhibitors, hard put to sell a picture that defied rational categorization, attempted to peddle it as all things to all people—Talking, Singing, Dancing, Tragedy, Everything. Ultimately *Gabbo* was counted a disappointment, too strange to compete with better packaged and less grainy big-studio product. Many were stumped as to what it meant, though few forgot the image of Stroheim and his dummy.[21]

20. MacDonald likely thanked her lucky stars until the end of her days that her film debut came not in *Gabbo* but a few weeks later in Ernst Lubitsch's *The Love Parade*. Given her later career, it might be commented that just because MacDonald missed the chance to work opposite Otto did not mean she'd never get another costar made of wood.

21. Unexpectedly, those images have also reverberated down the decades. The animated television sitcom *The Simpsons*, which habitually cast a wide net over pop culture in search of

The Great Gabbo is the strongest possible indictment of the wholesale musical virus infecting Hollywood in mid-1929. For most of its first half the urge is resisted; the one song used, Otto's little ditty "I'm Laughing," underscores Gabbo's ability to express his feelings only through the dummy. Despite a low-grade production (Cruze even skimped on lighting) and halting technique, there's an attempt at a meditation on life and show business far beyond the 1929 norm. Stroheim and Compson are notably more comfortable with dialogue than their director, and it's tempting to wonder what would have resulted if Stroheim had been permitted more input than just a few character touches. But once Gabbo and Mary and her husband Frank are at the theater it starts up. These are not just big point-less musical sequences—they are overtly obnoxious, Cruze and Kusell and André-Ani determined to bowl over an audience with grotesque design and gauche choreography. The numbers simply don't know when to stop, pil-ing on more choruses, more ratty variations on silly themes; Multicolor made them even more overbearing and perhaps more ludicrous. There are so many choice moments of outrage: a formally attired chorus in "Every Now and Then" exiting by getting down on all fours and crawling back-ward under the stage curtain, forming a lunatic fringe *vivant;* a preposterous ballet suddenly popping up in the middle of "I'm in Love With You"; garish spinning color wheels in "The New Step" that likely constituted someone's limp attempt at "color design"; ridiculous pseudo-Egyptian costumes for the finale that Gabbo wrecks. Only in Howard Jackson's pleasing musical arrangements is there any quality; borrowed from Fox, Jackson was doubtless relieved to return there for the infinitely superior *Sunny Side Up.*

Two sequences in particular form the mad extreme for the whole back-stage era. In "The Web of Love," music collides with offstage drama as Mary and Frank have it out in the middle of their adagio. For this, the Cruze team came up with High Concept—a gigantic spider web upon which various arachnid chorines pose, and there in the middle are Douglas and Compson, a spider and fly à la André-Ani. After singing of the inexora-bility of love, the pair comes down off the web—he with a noisy thud as he hits the floor—and starts a pas de deux, all leaps and catches and back-bends. Never have dance doubles been so obvious (Douglas's quadriceps suddenly quadruple in size), nor, as the pair bickers about Gabbo, has over-dubbing been done so clumsily. It's outrageous, incompetent, insane, and very, very funny, though poor Compson and Douglas (later a busy support-

---

targets, came up with a surprising one in a 1993 episode: a foul-tempered ventriloquist's dummy named Gabbo. The autobiographical overtones of the story also asserted themselves when Stroheim, haunted over the years by the story's relation to his own life, attempted to purchase the rights, only to discover that the property had already been acquired by Edgar Bergen, perhaps the most eminent ventriloquist ever.

ing actor) make a pitiable sight in their sequined insect suits. Originally there was an even worse number. "The Ga Ga Bird" was apparently removed after the initial engagements, ostensibly because of smeary color processing. Aesthetics may have played a larger role. The song itself was a sorry piece that made no sense in any context; to stage it, Kusell just had to go barnyard. Outsized insects are bad enough, but giant chickens? One lone "Ga Ga" vestige survives in the final print, in Stroheim's dementia/production number flashback montage just prior to the finale. Close inspection will reveal a few seconds of chorus girl chickens pecking around, complete with big webbed feet. Small wonder Gabbo goes crazy. Smaller wonder audiences stayed away.

Backstage stories would ever be a part of the musical equation—*42nd Street, On the Avenue, Babes in Arms, Kiss Me, Kate, The Band Wagon, Gypsy, Cabaret, A Chorus Line, Flashdance*—and the best of them transcended the genre's preset utilitarianism. Properly framed, the contrasting nature of on- and offstage performance could hold a beguilingly glitzy mirror to life, even in 1929. *The Broadway Melody*, through skill as well as novelty, had restored viewer faith in films; that trust, unhappily, would be systematically eroded as the follow-ups streamed in. Spectator allegiance was being twisted, miscued, abused. It had taken only *Show of Shows* to taint audience desire for revues. With backstagers it was sheer volume and repetition, plus the stockpiled misjudgment of form and content. *The Great Gabbo*, aberration that it is, shows the more blatant tendencies that gave musicals the death sentence. That so savvy a hand as James Cruze thought its musical chances were sound attests to the extent of the backstage mania; in its very ga ga bird extremity can be seen exactly what was going wrong. Having the musical form stretched to encompass so much so unsuitably shows how imprudent was Hollywood's skill in seizing upon and misappropriating the public's cravings. Soon enough both the good and the guilty would suffer.

CHAPTER 9

"With All Its Original Stage Enchantment"

Triumph and transition were equal partners in the musical theater of the 1920s. Established formulas and names still held sway, and the old guard reached its zenith with the operettas *Rose-Marie* and *The Vagabond King* and *The Desert Song*. Frivolity and star vehicles also dominated: *No, No, Nanette, Kid Boots, Good News*. Emerging alongside these were new concepts of how music and drama could be joined. A new generation of composers, lyricists, and writers—George and Ira Gershwin, Richard Rodgers, Lorenz Hart, Herbert Fields, Oscar Hammerstein II, Cole Porter—was beginning to take greater chances, as Jerome Kern had in the 1910s. Even when their work seemed the typical musical comedy of the era, it contained the seeds for later breaks from ingrained tradition. Gershwin's *Blue Monday Blues* (1922) was a trial run for *Porgy and Bess*; in *Dearest Enemy* (1925) and *Chee-Chee* (1928), Rodgers and Hart and librettist Fields increasingly strayed from conventional material and method. There was, above all, the success and influence of *Show Boat* to demonstrate the unique expressive language possible in American musical theater. Using sound film to transcribe this theater was one of the first suggested uses for the new medium, and the movies' bent for annexing stage properties would naturally increase with the addition of recorded dialogue. So it was that the first musical filmed with sound, *The Desert Song,* was about as close as possible to a literal transcription. But the procedure of literally transcribing stage musicals onto film rapidly went awry, as it was perceived that the dynamics of stage and film were sufficiently discrete to make for a strained transition. After the first crop of filmed shows in early 1930, critic Alexander Bakshy cited the "painful incongruity" of the situation in *The Nation:*

The conventions of musical comedy derive whatever meaning they have from being a frank entertainment on a stage that is physically connected with the audience. The characters suddenly breaking into song or forming themselves into dancing columns are never anything more than mere actors [and] the audience expects from them nothing more. It disregards the absurdities of the plot or the antics of the characters, because it never associates them with real life.

The screen imitators of musical comedy seem to be ignorant of this essential relationship between the actor and the spectator. They place their characters in perfectly natural surroundings, introduce them as perfectly normal people, and then make them behave as if they were escaped lunatics.

Something different was needed. Ingrained musical comedy conventions did not sit well on the big screen; it was a peculiar relationship in the early days, and it would ever be so. In the later 1930s and 1940s most Broadway-to-Hollywood adaptations were rendered almost unrecognizable, their songs removed or replaced and their books and characters rigorously laundered. The 1950s saw the age of the hard ticket, the musical as Event, the first time since 1930 that major musical films, almost all Broadway transfers, were marketed as reserved-seat attractions in almost exactly the same way as the original musicals. Rodgers and Hammerstein led the way here, maintaining rigid control even unto producing some of their own films. And until the late 1960s the grosses rolled in abundantly. Hollywood never stopped snapping up the most (and less) successful stage musicals for filming; yet how many made the transition to film with unalloyed success *in terms of being films?* All told, not very many. *My Fair Lady* or *Oklahoma!* or *West Side Story?* The jury, it might be said, is still out; somehow the specter of Thespis (or possibly David Belasco) pressed too heavily upon most of these movies, with their reverential tone and resolute formalism. Recall, then, comments made about the first of them, *The Desert Song:*

> The Warners, whether wisely or not remains to be seen, threw aside motion picture technique entirely. . . . If those who see it are willing to accept the picture for what it is, *The Desert Song,* by virtue of its music and optical appeal, is an attraction. That means, however, that what until now has been the accepted form of celluloid entertainment has to be forgotten, which is asking a good deal.
>
> Maurice D. Kann, *Film Daily*

> The libretto seems to obtrude itself more aggressively than it does on the stage, where we can often quite comfortably watch the spectacle and snugly ignore the spoken lines.
>
> John McCarten, *The New Yorker*

> Before musical plays are done into celluloid they must be completely
> rewritten, and their new producers must put far behind them the paint
> and canvas illusions of the stage.
>
> Creighton Peet, *New York Post*

Of course, a straight dose of *Desert Song* after years of silent film technique
would be a trifle intimidating to even the most stoic reviewer. Yet some of
these comments could apply to Broadway musicals filmed many decades
later. Speaking at least superficially, the more brash and dynamic and unpretentious the musical, the more smoothly it could move onto the screen.
The more serious or "elevated" its aspirations, the more rigidly it resisted
modification. Some of the early adaptations were rampantly faithful and
used the original stars. Others were mangled beyond recognition, sometimes to the good; and in some cases the distinctions between operetta and
musical comedy were blurred. This chapter deals with standard-issue musical comedies, as brought from Broadway to Hollywood. Operetta, that most
extreme and artificial of all types of narrative musicals, was in a class by
itself, and the rarefied and overwrought world of filmed operetta is covered
in Chapter Twelve.

As with backstage stories, there had already been a silent-film tradition
of adapted musical comedies, not with production numbers, but with the
properties felt to contain usable stories. Colleen Moore starred in *Sally* and
Irene, Eddie Cantor repeated his stage hit in *Kid Boots*, and MGM boosted
the careers of Constance Bennett, Joan Crawford, and Sally O'Neil by starring them as *Sally, Irene and Mary*. Come sound film and *The Desert Song*,
and the studios began to purchase Broadway's lyrical bounty. MGM was
among the earliest, and how odd that the first era of film musicals should
be bracketed by two of that studio's abortive Broadway adaptations, both
with Marion Davies. For better or worse, Davies is one of those historical
figures whose work and life will never be permitted to stand on their own
merits, for William Randolph Hearst, her protector, and Orson Welles, who
caricatured her as the woefully untalented second Mrs. Charles Foster
Kane, will always remain in her orbit. While Davies's artistic limitations
never descended to those of *Citizen Kane*'s Susan Alexander, her twenty
years in film produced not so much a cohesive body of work as a stream of
the public's consciousness. Name a leading trend between 1917 and 1937,
and there's likely to be one or more Davies films to correspond. She was,
sequentially, the frail wronged heroine à la Lillian Gish, the serene center
of spectacles and Ruritanian romances, the assertive flapper in the later
twenties, and so on.[1] Her fame, while genuine, was the kind that always

---

1. In the midst of these, she also contributed to the silent mini-fad of filming stage musicals. Contrary to popular belief, many of her MGM films were indeed (modest) profit earners;
one which was not was *The Red Mill* (1926), adapted from Victor Herbert's 1906 operetta and
directed pseudonymously by the scandal-ridden Roscoe "Fatty" Arbuckle.

followed custom, never set the style. Other stars changed with the times also, such as Davies's rivals Joan Crawford and Norma Shearer. But with them the public never sensed the gears shifting quite as loudly as with Davies and—particularly—with the Hearst publicity machinery. Stardom for its own sake, and for the sake of a control-freak tycoon, was just too synthetic, and never more so than when Hearst found a new trend for her: the infant musical. If it killed them both, he would make Davies the Marilyn Miller of movies.

In fall 1928, before filming began on *The Broadway Melody*, it was reported that MGM had purchased *The Five O'Clock Girl* as a vehicle for a talking-singing Davies. A moderate success in the 1927–28 Broadway season, it had featured Mary Eaton and Oscar Shaw, songs by Bert Kalmar and Harry Ruby, and a Cinderella plot that suited Hearst's vision to a T. For musical backup Davies was given Charles King, and the cast also included a handsome newcomer named Joel McCrea. Some weeks after shooting began in mid-December it became clear that a Davies catastrophe was imminent. While her vocal quality was adequate, her tendency to stammer was aggravated by the tension and technical difficulties, and it was mentioned that her singing was problematic (and would never be terribly good). If Davies appears flustered in *The Hollywood Revue*, shot five months later, imagine how her five o'clock girl must have looked. Hearst dreaded seeing his protégée shown in such an unflattering light, and MGM pulled the plug in mid-January, at a six-figure loss. Hollywood's first try at a traditional musical comedy was chalked up to experience and shelved.

It was through default as much as anything that Broadway's original *Five O'Clock Girl* and boy, Mary Eaton and Oscar Shaw, starred in the first Broadway musical comedy to reach the screen, *The Cocoanuts*, which ended up far less musical than it began and curiously was the only such adaptation filmed in New York in 1929. About this same time Warners and First National were leading the Hollywood companies in snapping up all the properties they could find. First on the soundstages was Warners' *Rainbow*, from a Vincent Youmans-Oscar Hammerstein II show that had been one of Broadway's most recent and celebrated flops. Retitled *Song of the West*, it did not reach the public until nearly a year later, by which time a promising musical drama had been transformed into a turgid Vitaphone operetta. This misbegotten project is discussed in Chapter Twelve.

More properly, the first age of the filmed Broadway musical begins with *Rio Rita*. One of 1929's most successful and well liked movies, it now requires a willing viewer to don a particularly rosy pair of specs to comprehend its impact. On Broadway in 1927, it was more notable as an event than as a work of popular culture, having been selected to open the Ziegfeld Theatre, the showman's Art Deco temple to himself and entertainment. Billed as a musical comedy, *Rita* was actually poised on the uncertain cusp between musical and operetta: *Rose-Marie* crossed with *The Desert Song* by way of the Cisco Kid. The usually easygoing Harry Tierney produced more grandiose songs than usual, the better to accommodate the Texas border setting, a chorus of Rangers, a bandit called "The Kinkajou," a man wrongly accused, and his sister, an inevitably beautiful and vocal young woman. Adding zing and accounting for the designation of musical comedy was a comic duo, scheming, shifty, and stupid. For these, Ziegfeld brought together solo comics Bert Wheeler and Robert Woolsey. Wheeler, who had appeared in Ziegfeld's 1924 *Follies*, was an accomplished singer-dancer with a junior-choirboy face; the bespectacled Woolsey, whose outsized cigar was never far away, countered Wheeler's ingenuous simplicity with a procession of smart-guy remarks. While they could not be termed inspired laugh-getters, they quickly became an established team. Due to their mischief, the lush production, and hummable songs, *Rio Rita* played for well over a year and was as logical a property as any for conversion to a musical film.

Rio Rita's transference was significant on several fronts. Principally, it was designed to give a jump start to a new company. As Radio Pictures was being put together in December 1928, studio head Joseph Schnitzer announced that one of its first steps was to acquire the rights to the show from Ziegfeld. Basically, *Rita* would serve Radio Pictures in the same fashion as it had the Ziegfeld Theatre, though not necessarily as the new studio's first production (a distinction that ultimately went to *Street Girl*). While Radio undertook to assemble a major sound-film facility virtually from scratch, *Rio Rita* had a fairly wobbly evolution. Wheeler and Woolsey were quickly hired to repeat their roles, and at first Broadway leads Ethelind Terry and J. Harold Murray were also considered. (Both did go to Hollywood that year, though not to Radio.) The choice for director went from *Syncopation*'s Bert Glennon, to silent comedy ace Malcolm St. Clair, and finally to Luther Reed, who was assisted by stage director Russell Mack. Reed, a former drama critic, had written and directed some undistinguished silent comedies (sample work: a 1926 item called *Honeymoon Hate*), and this would be his one moment of glory. John Boles, just done with *Song of the West*, was rapidly turning into the musical film's prime romantic lead and was the pick for ranger captain Jim Stewart.

Casting the title role was a greater challenge given an unexpected solution. While Radio busily started up its operation, it scored a coup: a genuine star to top off its roster of contract players. In 1928 Bebe Daniels had been fourth in an exhibitor poll of the highest-grossing film actresses—after Clara Bow, Colleen Moore, and Billie Dove. She had begun in her midteens in short comedies opposite Harold Lloyd, progressed to leads in some of Cecil B. DeMille's society dramas, and found her niche at Paramount in light farce. She had both spirit and an offbeat sensual prettiness that worked well in comedies whose titles told all—*Feel My Pulse, She's a Sheik,*

A Kiss in a Taxi. Came sound, and she was suddenly out. Considering her one of the dinosaurs, Paramount refused to so much as test her voice, and the furious Daniels bought out her contract and promptly signed with Radio, where former Paramount producer William LeBaron was production head. Instead of continuing with the same froth she had made in silents, she resolved to make her entry into sound a major attention-getter. She asked for the role of Rita, and Radio's skepticism was not necessarily diminished by her offer to take a salary cut in exchange for a share of profits. She was not known as a singer, but in the light of her fame and part-Spanish heritage, plus the pressure to get the film out as quickly as possible, she was cast. If nothing else her presence might have appeal as a stunt. With its outsized numbers and location work, this large-scale production was shot in twenty-four days—a feat even for the time—and to help cope with the mike-related rigors and extraneous noises Daniels's second cousin, Lee De Forest, visited the set to give pointers.[2] The final forty-minute stretch was shot in Technicolor, whose cameras were so tightly rationed that they were available only during the graveyard shift. Shooting would wrap around dawn, and as second lead Dorothy Lee quipped more than sixty years later, "I got to be good friends with the milkman."

Other musicals were in production at the same time as *Rio Rita*, for the studios were entering their one-track-mind phase. *Sunny Side Up, The Love Parade, Footlights and Fools, Married in Hollywood*, and, from Broadway, *Sally, Paris*, and *Little Johnny Jones*—quite a lot of work. *Rio Rita*, as the first to reach the public, was an unqualified smash: a paradigmatic event. As with *Gold Diggers of Broadway* the same season, it scored an immense, perfectly calibrated hit, well over $2 million. The show had retained its onstage glamour and found enhancement by outdoor photography the stage could not reproduce. Even exacting observers found a great deal to praise, and at year's end *Rio Rita* ended up high on many Ten Best lists. The greatest praise was reserved for Daniels, who won—from finicky New York critics—compliments an actor would kill for: "revelation—nothing less" (*American*); "superb" (*Mirror*); "astonishing" (*World*); "all the skill of a veteran" (*Herald-Tribune*); "meets the new demands amazingly well" (*Evening Graphic*). Despite the greatest length of any talkie so far—135 minutes—it played to turnaway crowds well into 1930. Boles, Wheeler and Woolsey, and Lee all shared the triumph, but the glory was reserved for Daniels and for Radio, in what would be the company's biggest hit until *King Kong*.

2. One of the more unwelcome sounds the mike picked up came from the fan Daniels carried in some scenes, which had to be rendered noiseless. Such experiences remained imbedded in the brain of assistant costumer Walter Plunkett, and more than twenty years later, when Plunkett designed the clothes for *Singin' in the Rain*, his memories, up to and including Bebe Daniels's fan, provided the source for some of the film's best jokes about early sound shooting.

The word "creaky" is never far from the mind while watching *Rio Rita* today. Often it seems only slightly advanced past *The Desert Song,* and with source material not as solid. Act and scene divisions are observed obstinately as actors and plot points lumber on and off the screen with wearying regularity; and the generic conventions become risible when writ so large: expository dialogue that would stop a bus, song cues and reprises seemingly dropped in from the fourth dimension, Wheeler and Woolsey's in-and-out comic relief, stereotyped characters, and some questionable ethnic overtones. Reed's direction is stodgy and flavorless, technical infelicities pop up without warning, and as staged by Pearl Eaton (Mary's sister), the production numbers never come to anything like cinematic life. Except for Boles and chorus in the outdoor-shot "Song of the Rangers," the proscenium is always implied. But look and listen hard, and enough of the 1929 magic comes through.[3] The location shooting clearly helped, Daniels and Boles al fresco playing out their romance with considerably more ardor than they could on a soundstage, and Boles shown and recorded to better advantage than in *The Desert Song.* Wheeler and Woolsey are a taste that many audiences will never wish to acquire, the kind of standardized Broadway comedy that can't bridge years and changing types of humor. Looked at objectively, some of their business still plays, and Wheeler was sufficiently skilled to pull off his songs and dances with brio. It's Daniels, at any rate, who carries the show. Her soprano will likely sound reedy and perhaps gurgling to modern ears, yet she clearly knows how to integrate singing into a cohesive dramatic performance, paying as much attention to the lyrics as to her spoken lines and not letting the stagy Spanish accent she adopts impede her effect. At times her mike fright and uncertainty with musical drama is apparent, yet she keeps on plowing through and takes Boles along with her. In their first scene, as she sings "River of My Dreams" in counterpoint to his "Rio Rita," the lyrical strength underlying this type of Broadway malarkey is readily felt, as is her absorption in the material and, at times, her exhilaration in showing up the S.O.B.s at Paramount and having the last laugh.

Few subsequent Broadway adaptations of the early years approached *Rio Rita*'s impact, which of course did not stop the studios from trying, Radio included: as *Rita* was premiering the studio was busy on *Hit the Deck*, adapted from the 1928 Broadway success. Excepting the Vincent Youmans songs "Sometimes I'm Happy" and "Hallelujah," there had been nothing particularly interesting about the show; its script, taken from the old play *Shore Leave*, was a drag (and would remain so for a second musical reworking, the Astaire-Rogers *Follow the Fleet*). With the ineffectual Luther

---

3. The prints generally available today are cut by about twenty minutes. At least some of the missing footage survives—Daniels and Boles lilting "If You're in Love, You'll Waltz," and Dorothy Lee leading the chorus in a quite incompetent performance of "The Kinkajou."

Reed again in charge, the film version of *Hit the Deck*, which opened in January 1930, fared mildly. The casting was particularly weak: Jack Oakie game but miscast as the hero and Broadway's Polly Walker a dim partner. The best contribution came from another stage performer, the large and large-voiced contralto Marguerita Padula, who led a black chorus in a vigorously staged "Hallelujah." Despite this and some Technicolor sequences *Hit the Deck* lacked the excitement necessary for a major impact, and this would happen with increasing frequency.

Of all the studios, First National seemed especially determined to partner Broadway with Hollywood. The company's schedule for 1929–30, its last as a separate organization divorced from Warners, was mainly given over to musical adaptations. Most of the properties had been purchased quickly, expensively, without undue discernment, and were filmed mostly the same way. With this type of assembly line work musicians and chorus might be shunted from one production to the next, sometimes on the same day. Individuality and creativity seemed to be lost in the shuffle, for with so much piling up at once the films seemed to blur together in a mass of production numbers and Vitaphone and Technicolor. *Little Johnny Jones* was the least important and the least successful. George M. Cohan's hard-sell writing and performing had dazzled crowds in 1904, as had "The Yankee Doodle Boy" and "Give My Regards to Broadway"; by late 1929 this flag-waving racetrack yarn (previously filmed by First National in 1923) had become archaic, a fact which neither updating nor new songs—standard practice at First National—could conceal. As Johnny, Eddie Buzzell lacked Cohan's manic edge and passionate sense of self, qualities without which *Little Johnny Jones* could not be revived. As a result, it ended up one of the least successful musicals of the time, its patriotic overtones faring especially poorly in the lucrative foreign market.[4] After this weak start Buzzell quickly moved on to short subjects and eventually to the director's chair.

Paris was the first Broadway adaptation to reach the public in the wake of *Rio Rita*, opening less than a year after its Broadway run. The show's main claim had been as the definitive vehicle for Irene Bordoni, whose rolling eyes, pursed lips, and assured vocal and comic technique had made her the successor to Sarah Bernhardt as America's favorite Frenchwoman. *Paris* was something of a departure for a big Broadway musical, employing only one setting and lacking large numbers or a traditional chorus. Instead, there was risqué comedy and some sharp songs, including, and this is its greatest significance in retrospect, the earliest examples of the mature Cole Porter style. This was not his first show, but "Let's Do It (Let's Fall in Love)" and others gave the first full demonstration of his gifts. By the time

---

4. In Ottawa, *Motion Picture News* reported, it was withdrawn after only one performance, and the exhibitor then placed ads apologizing for its poor quality—a particularly dire fate in a country ordinarily quite tolerant of American work.

it reached the screen, however, there was far more Bordoni than Porter. Only two of the original songs remained—Porter's "Don't Look at Me That Way," and E. Ray Goetz's title song.[5] The rest was given over to new work by house regulars Al Bryan and Ed Ward, perpetrators of "Li-Po-Li" and others. Even "Let's Do It" was cut to give way to the gauche Bryan/ Ward likes of "Miss Wonderful" and "I'm a Little Negative (Looking for a Positive)." The play's chic intimacy was further diminished by the interpolation of that 1929 bugaboo, Technicolor revue scenes, which did not necessarily enhance either Bordoni's personality or that of her leading man, London revue star Jack Buchanan. While successful, *Paris* on the screen was by no means a killer. Bordoni was not well known in much of the country, Buchanan less so, and First National did little to promote them in a way that attracted huge crowds. A sizable share of the gross came from overseas, where both stars had fans of long standing. "Long standing" indeed: while *Paris* no longer exists to support this view, Bordoni's concurrent stint in *Show of Shows* suggests that her brand of artifice showed too plainly on the screen. Her youthful vivacity was effected too obviously, the coquettish sensuality applied too knowingly, the comedy playing too calculated. She sounds fine on the Vitaphone discs, but like the skirts of her famous theatrical gowns, it was all too big for the screen and for most American audiences. Most of the best reviews, in fact, went to a supporting player, Louise Closser Hale, in her stage role of the frigid Boston Brahmin who attempts to steer her son (Jason Robards) clear of Bordoni's wiles. Hale stayed on in Hollywood to serve as one of those wonderful character actors whose work adds so much to early thirties cinema. (She can be seen near her best in *Shanghai Express* and *Dinner at Eight*.) Unlike Bordoni she had no entrenched image to support, no youthful illusion to maintain. It makes quite a difference.

But youth was very much at the heart of another First National "Big Lady" show shot concurrently with *Paris*. This time it was as big a hit on the screen as on Broadway nearly a decade earlier. Even audiences who had never seen a live musical had heard of Marilyn Miller, the most popular woman on Broadway in the 1920s. *Sally* was as closely aligned with her as any legendary star-show combo: Joseph Jefferson and *Rip Van Winkle*, Maude Adams and *Peter Pan*, down to Yul Brynner in *The King and I* and beyond. The other name intimately linked with Miller was Florenz Ziegfeld. He had not exactly made her a star, for she had started out in vaudeville at age six and made Broadway at sixteen, in *The Passing Show of 1914*. Her fame grew, founded on a mix of blonde beauty, exuberant dance

5. As with nearly all Broadway shows in those years, the *Paris* score was written by several hands, and at least one Porter gem hadn't made it to opening night—"Let's Misbehave." Goetz, also a producer, had a long list of credits and in private life was (as it were) Mr. Bordoni.

(*above*) Irene Bordoni, exuding ooh-la-la in the company of as stagy a chorus grouping as one could ask for, in *Paris*. (*below*) Alexander Gray and Marilyn Miller, looking for the silver lining in *Sally*.

skills, and a fiercely blindered concentration on her career. Ziegfeld glorified her in his 1918 and 1919 *Follies*, and Broadway teemed with rumors of their affair.[6] *Sally*, in 1920, was a defining event in both their careers. The plot was the purest Cinderella gossamer, in part a steal from the 1919 hit *Irene*, and with Miller and Ziegfeld and Jerome Kern it was magic. As a Greenwich Village slavey who makes good in the Follies and finds the right millionaire, singing "Wild Rose" and "Look For the Silver Lining," pirouetting daintily through Victor Herbert's Butterfly Ballet and hoofing it up in jazzier numbers, Miller was an authentic American heroine, the ideal postwar sweetheart. The show ran nearly two years, by which time the Miller-Ziegfeld relationship had reached toxic proportions. For Ziegfeld rival Charles Dillingham she starred as *Sunny* (1925), also with a fine Kern score. (Prior to this she tested other waters with a revival of *Peter Pan*—she was too feminine, with not enough vocal variety.) Though *Sunny* was almost as big a hit as *Sally*, Miller's Broadway luck soon began to dwindle. Back with Ziegfeld for *Rosalie* (1928), she fared only moderately. Her fame had peaked, and while the beauty with which she tripped across a stage tended to conceal her circumscribed acting and vocal skills, she was limited and she knew it. Movie musicals offered a lucrative new option, and in April 1929 she signed with First National to revive her greatest moment of glory. Aware of her fame and worth, she negotiated a whopping $100,000 salary—twice what the studio had paid Bordoni for *Paris*. Stars' earnings were not nearly as publicized in 1929 as they are today, yet Miller's fee for *Sally* was widely aired, even promoted. Studio publicists proclaimed her the highest-paid star of all time—"$1,000 per hour for 100 hours work!" An arbitrary and inauthentic deduction, yet cushy advance notice for a legend making a film debut. Another aspect of her renown soon asserted itself as well when it was observed that she was spending a great deal of time in closed-door dressing-room conferences with Jack L. Warner.

Sally was more prestigious than *Paris* and considerably more costly. Technicolor was employed throughout (the third and last such talkie to open in 1929), and a fair part of the budget went for some enormous sets and for the power it took to light them, which at times could drive the soundstage temperature up to an unconscionable 135 degrees. Kern's score fared a little better than Cole Porter's: "Silver Lining" was imperishable, the title song sweetly appropriate, and "Wild Rose" too catchy to lose. The new songs (by Al Dubin and Joe Burke) were less interesting. The support-

6. He was at the time married to Billie Burke, who—as always—persevered and stuck it out. (Miller fared less well, going on to a disastrous marriage to Mary Pickford's wastrel and reportedly syphilitic brother Jack.) Not the least of Ziegfeld's contributions to Miller's career was to change the spelling of her first name (Mary Lynn), which in its final form seemed to capture the combined glamour and comfy darlingness that was her star image. It was the name of this blonde Marilyn which, years later, was the source and inspiration for another MM who became even more famous.

ing cast was also mostly new—Joe E. Brown (in the role created on Broadway by Leon Errol), former Keystone Kop Ford Sterling, T. Roy Barnes, and the invaluably snappy Pert Kelton.[7] Broadway baritone Alexander Gray, who had played the romantic lead opposite Miller on tour, was cast in the film at her request and quickly became the Warners/First National musical mainstay, with six films in less than a year. Gray was the operetta stalwart at its most basic: fine to hear, attractive to look at, and, in an earnest way, stiff as a board.

Sally opened in New York just before Christmas 1929, to modified rapture. The beloved old show seemed creaky on the screen, the elapsed decade and a close-up camera making it seem, more than ever, a marshmallow weighing ten tons. Yet Miller's Cinderella alchemy survived the transfer: the star emerged as the auteur, and *Sally* went on to score an enormous hit in the U.S. and abroad. Miller starred—at greatly increased salary—in another re-created Broadway hit, *Sunny*, then returned to Broadway. She came back for Warners' *Her Majesty, Love*, which effectively ended her film career. Broadway was always her main venue anyway, and despite her waning vogue she scored one final coup—the aptly titled *As Thousands Cheer* (1933)—before dying astonishingly young in 1936.

The movies' penchant for playing havoc with stage legends was perceived even before Sarah Bernhardt strode her way peculiarly through *Queen Elizabeth* in 1912. Given what is known of Marilyn Miller's art—her voice was not terribly attractive, her beauty and appeal were of the sort that bloom early and fade fast, she had a battery of mechanical tricks to rival the best—it would be easy to number her among the many who lost out when placed onto the screen. Certainly nothing in *Sunny* or *Her Majesty, Love* disputes this. *Sally*, the one film to offer a conclusive argument one way or another, was seen by only a handful of people in the six decades following its release. It was not lost, merely unavailable. Writers wishing to discuss Marilyn Miller's contribution to the early musical had to rely on reachable (and not always reliable) evidence and inference, including stills from *Sally* that show a heavily rouged and fairly hard-looking star. So it's generally read that Miller didn't work out in the movies, that she was too old or stylized or self-conscious to implant her fairy-princess magic onto film. Thus, when it did reach a larger audience around 1990, *Sally* had a few surprises to deal out—enough, at least, to bridge the years and make the legend comprehensible. The dim black-and-white copies of *Sally* that survived exacerbate the obvious faults—the unimaginative photography, formula-bound script, a miscast Joe E. Brown, and at first Miller herself.

---

7. Errol had already played his role in Colleen Moore's 1925 silent *Sally*. Barnes, almost totally unknown today, was a proficient comedian on the stage and in silents. He's now remembered, if not by name, for one indelible talkie moment: the pesky salesman searching for Karl LaFong in W. C. Fields's *It's a Gift*.

Director John Francis Dillon gives her a unique star entrance—the first glimpse of her is a close-up of the darting feet—after which she confirms fears that this myth should have been left undisturbed. Her speaking voice gurglingly recalls Irene Dunne at her most dithery, the Technicolor makeup seen in monochrome gives her the look of an overpainted figurine, and the famous smile seems goofily unrelenting when seen close up. At age thirty-one she's trying to play about sixteen, and the strain shows. Her singing voice also fulfills negative expectations. Her one try at recording, a test pressing of *Rosalie* songs, was not released. Understandably: "Look for the Silver Lining" is almost painful, Miller flatting notes and scooping intervals like there's no tomorrow.[8] Finally, after about half an hour of stale plot, she begins to dance and comes alive, and one comprehends. "All I Want to Do Do Do Is Dance," she sings, and truer words were never put in any musical.

Miller was not technically flawless by any means; her arms sometimes flail in ungainly fashion, sometimes her posture is oddly stooped, and her tap work is too determined to be effortless. These liabilities she overcomes with two hallmarks of the irreplaceable performer: she seems to love what she's doing, and she makes it impossible and unnecessary to look anywhere in the frame except at her. The best of her work is probably the most eloquent dance on film until the rise of Fred Astaire. A knockabout duet with Joe E. Brown to "Silver Lining" is wholly delightful, clearly communicating optimism through dance, joy through one gifted performer's elated interaction with another. The "Butterfly Ballet" that seals Sally's stardom is overstuffed and stagy, shot mostly in the usual proscenium mode. Yet when Miller emerges from a floral cocoon she redeems it, and a precious and seemingly irretrievable slice of theater history is preserved as if in amber, even in the surviving drab black-and-white prints that render most of *Sally* even more fragile and tattered.

Since the Fates are sometimes beneficent, around the time that *Sally* was beginning to play at film archives and revival houses, three minutes of its original Technicolor surfaced. As with *Gold Diggers of Broadway* the discovery was made in England, presumably a fine spot for collectors to nurture a fondness for early musicals. The footage comprised most of the "Wild Rose" song and dance—in fact the best number in the film, Miller as an

___

8. It's especially unfortunate next to Gray's big baritone, and they both have the affected sort of stage diction that overlays the "ooh" vowel sound with a distracting umlaut ("Whene'er a cloud appears in the blö"). Considering Miller's singing, how extremely ironic it is that when it came time for someone to portray her in MGM's stodgy Jerome Kern "biography," *Till the Clouds Roll By* (1946), the selection was Judy Garland. One of the worst singers in musicals portrayed by one of the best, though the need for high star voltage in the role was understandable. However, when it came time for a full-length Miller biopic, Warner's insipid *Look for the Silver Lining* (1949), she was played by June Haver, whose charisma quotient was far lower than that of either Miller or Garland.

elegant flapper cavorting with chorus boys at a Long Island estate. (This is the huge set that became so unbearably hot during shooting, which makes the performers' high spirits all the more remarkable.) In color she looks far more youthful, with a wild rose bloom that's very appealing, and Dillon and dance director Larry Ceballos had the right instinct about how to shoot it. The camera follows Miller as she dashes madly about the set, spinning, throwing off high kicks with abandon—there's probably more energy in this scene than in any other film made that year. It's the same type of full-figure dance photography that Astaire would later demand, and as a coupling of performer and medium it's precisely what musical films were and are supposed to be about. Miller finishes with a grand flourish, flinging roses at her admirers; across all these decades, the admiration is still warranted.

In the Broadway of the 1920s, *Sally* and *Paris* were prime examples of star showcases, the book musical as gem-like setting for the gifts of one compelling performer.[9] Another type of show was propelled by an ensemble cast, along with a situation-rich script and often with an especially strong score. *No, No, Nanette* was the exemplar here. While its Broadway run in 1925 was not extraordinarily long, it also ran with vast success in Chicago, in London, and on tour. The very title seemed to evoke precisely the giddiness of an entire era, and two of Vincent Youmans's songs—"Tea for Two" and "I Want to Be Happy"—became instant standards. First National paid $75,000 for the rights, intending it as the capstone of its efforts to establish Alice White as a major musical star. The thought of White pouting her way through "Tea for Two" is worthy of a substantial cringe, and in any case this gaffe was averted when White's salary dispute with the studio cost her the role of Nanette and, ultimately, any chance at top stardom. Her replacement, Bernice Claire, had the far more authentic credentials of roles on Broadway and on tour. Alexander Gray, already cast as *Nanette*'s juvenile lead, brought her to First National's attention much as Marilyn Miller had done with him for *Sally*. With an Alice White Nanette, much of the music would have been simplified; Claire's skilled coloratura made for exactly the opposite consideration. She was also a fetching actress and with *Nanette*'s release at the outset of 1930 was commended as a welcome find.

No, No, Nanette is one of the more tantalizing of the lost early musicals, a case study in how Broadway properties were being treated in 1929 Hollywood. As with *Paris*, the contours of a sparkling show coarsened noticeably with filming. The story was altered to accommodate a generic backstage

9. One example that narrowly missed filming was *Treasure Girl*. The show had been one of the surprising failures of the 1928–29 season—doubly surprising because it had featured Gertrude Lawrence singing a Gershwin score. Pathé, which otherwise made no major musicals, bought the property, only to shelve it early in 1930 after months of work.

plot, with juvenile lead Tom (Gray) as a composer and Nanette as star of his show. While some of the stage shenanigans concerning Bible publisher Jimmy Smith (Lucien Littlefield) remained, they took a back seat to big revue numbers completely unrelated to the script. In *Nanette* the alteration was made more conspicuous by the shifting of all the musical chores to the two young lovers instead of dividing the songs among the entire cast, as on Broadway. This partition of musical and comedy made for a lopsided effect, as the *New York Herald-Tribune* perceived:

> [By] placing the musical numbers at the beginning and end of the picture and . . . making them fit in with some fantastic plot about the production of a show . . . the outdated narrative, deprived of the salvation of song cues, was forced to wander on aimlessly to a tedious conclusion, and all of the frailties of its formula were cruelly exposed.

Nor was the situation helped by the now standard practice of eliminating nearly all the original songs. Only the two biggest hits remained, with "Tea for Two" in a quick run-through right after the credits. The remainder of the sprightly score was shunted aside in favor of "King of the Air," "Dance of the Wooden Shoes" and other non-Youmans nonentities, most of them tinny excuses for overstuffed production concepts—here an aviator number, there tulips and windmills, and so on—in Technicolor, which jarred with the black-and-white plot scenes. With its very title sufficient bait for most filmgoers, *Nanette* scored a sizable success. Still, its cumulative effect was disappointing, and it made little attempt to address the question of how properties of this type should be transferred.

A month after *Nanette*, Gray and Claire were at it again with First National's *Spring Is Here*, originally announced for the less lyrical team of Douglas Fairbanks Jr. and Loretta Young. This was the first Richard Rodgers/Lorenz Hart musical to reach the screen, albeit not one of their more distinguished efforts: a standard triangle romance (Gray, Claire, and Lawrence Gray), with daffy sideline characters and fine songs, including "Yours Sincerely" and the sumptuous "With a Song in My Heart," the latter sung, unconventionally, by the suitor who loses out. This was an unpretentious black-and-white production, and that modesty turned out to be its biggest asset apart from the score—though, as usual, only three of the songs remained.[10] The novelty in the new songs was that one became a hit— "Cryin' for the Carolines," sung by the Brox Sisters; obviously a lyric Lorenz Hart would never have written. *Spring Is Here* was, in one critic's

---

10. "With a Song in My Heart," "Yours Sincerely," and the title song, which is not the familiar Rodgers and Hart song of the same name, but a breezy item fully titled "Spring Is Here in Person." In the Hasty Post-Production Department, it can be noted that the opening credits give the composer's name as "Richard Rogers."

words, "just a light frappe," an enjoyable show with pleasant people and a couple of great songs. Lawrence Gray's skimpily nasal tenor does no favors to "With a Song in My Heart," so it was providential that Alexander Gray was given the chance at the very end of the movie to pour his baritone into those rapturous phrases, with Claire soaring over him in blissful counterpoint. This, unfortunately, was not enough to make a hit. A few months earlier it might have been noticed; by May 1930, and even with its moderate cost, *Spring Is Here* lost money.

Buddy DeSylva, Lew Brown, and Ray Henderson were archetypal Broadway craftsmen whose shows were among the most successful and audience-pleasing of the late twenties. Not for them the daring of Gershwin, the innovation of Rodgers and Hart, the racy élan of Porter, or the lyricism of Kern. Instead, they were solid pros who knew their audiences, on Broadway and on film. Three of their biggest hits, all hinging on sports themes, came to the screen just a few months apart. In *Hold Everything* it was boxing, in *Good News* college football, and in *Follow Thru* golf. Despite the glut of musicals around mid-spring 1930, these fared well onscreen and at the box office. Improved technique, more attentive casting, and smoother grained production concepts all contributed. *Good News* had been the biggest hit on Broadway, and along with *No, No, Nanette* it became one of the cornerstones of twenties musicals. Rah-rah hijinks have never been rendered in more definitive form: zippy coeds, dumb jocks, a climactic big game, and "The Varsity Drag." This show ranked with *Broadway* as one of the era's most borrowed-from hits, and by the time MGM filmed it other studios had already put out copies *(College Love, Sweetie, Sunny Skies)*. As *Photoplay* put it: "This one, like the pardon from the governor, arrived too late." As *Good News* reached theaters in late summer 1930, musicals were on the critical list. The producers had already sensed this, for some of the songs were cut before shooting and in final editing. "Just Imagine" and "Lucky in Love" were gone entirely, while "The Best Things in Life Are Free" was reduced to a quick run-through. The rest worked well enough for *Good News* to pull its weight and earn a profit—fortunately for MGM, who reportedly paid $200,000 for the rights. The show is now most familiar through the 1947 MGM remake, in which color and postwar energy filled in for the original Jazz Age dash, and even by 1930 it must be conceded that some of the Broadway zest had begun to pall. These are some of the oldest-looking collegians in the history of education, and the antics of comic Gus Shy (in his Broadway role) often try the patience and the stomach. Another Broadway holdover, Mary Lawler, makes a particularly drab ingenue. But there's much to enjoy. Bessie Love, cast for once in a nonmasochistic role, happily gives herself over to pratfalls and comic dances, and the "Varsity Drag" and title numbers are led by an energetic brunette named Dorothy McNulty, who later changed her hair color and her name (to Penny Singleton) to star in a long series of *Blondie* movies.[11] "The Varsity Drag," particularly, is a capstone of twenties tomfoolery and one of the most exhilarating sequences in early sound cinema. Its basically theatrical staging is overlaid with vigorously cinematic touches—sharp editing, fluid camerawork, even animation and special effects. Blackboard drawings come to life, floors start to burn up from the frenzy, and McNulty finally collapses into a convenient wheelchair. In a way, this number sums up that first musical era: a sizable amount of silliness, some rough edges, and a whiff of greasepaint, plus a great deal of vitality, a dollop of imagination, and a willingness to take chances.

Comedy came to the fore in Warners' *Hold Everything*, a reasonably successful blend of prizefighting, music, vulgarity, and Technicolor. Joe E. Brown starred as the inept boxer Gink Schiner, the same role that had won Broadway fame for the sublime Bert Lahr; while Lahr accused Brown of plagiarizing some of his mannerisms, Brown scored well enough on his own merits, including some acrobatically comic ring sequences. As Gink's girlfriend Toots, Winnie Lightner was noisier than ever, and with Brown completely outshone nominal romantic leads Sally O'Neil and Georges Carpentier, the latter sparring better than he sang or acted. Except for "You're the Cream in My Coffee," the songs, old and new, were not exceptional, though brought into the plot more organically than in *No, No, Nanette* or *Paris*. Laughs counted for more to the film's sizable audiences, and Brown was launched on a successful starring career.

Follow Thru came late in the day: September 1930, when films were being shorn of music and audiences were staying away. Even with Technicolor, Buddy Rogers, Nancy Carroll, and "Button Up Your Overcoat," this would not be the film to stem the tide. It went out as a standard Paramount programmer without immense ballyhoo, got so-so reviews, did satisfactory business, was soon forgotten, and survived in a battered print and a negative retained by the Technicolor Corporation.[12] Sixty years after the fact, *Follow Thru* emerged—in a sparkling new print from the UCLA Film and Television Archive—as one of the breeziest and most genial of early musicals. *Rio Rita*'s stiff formality here gives way to smooth technique, and while golf is as uninspiring as ever on film there's quite a bit of benignly

11. She had already played the role in the Chicago company. There are other interesting people in the *Good News* cast—Lola Lane as "the other coed"; Delmer Daves, later a prolific director; Ann Dvorak, leading the chorus once again; Buster Crabbe, a real-life sports hero in a momentary appearance as a student; and midget Harry Earles, who costarred in *Freaks* and *The Unholy Three*, here spotted briefly and memorably in "The Varsity Drag."

12. It was a contractual stipulation that all Technicolor negatives would be housed on the company's premises. In the mid-1950s, with the two-color process completely obsolete, the company began systematically to destroy its negatives from the twenties and early thirties . . . yet for some reason *Follow Thru* was spared.

"I Want to be Bad," zings Zelma O'Neal to her imps in *Follow Thru*, and who would doubt it? At least two hallmarks of 1930 production style are in evidence: heavy Technicolor makeup, and the seams of a hastily thrown-together set.

trivial fun. Carroll's red hair and green eyes made her perfect for early Technicolor, and though she saw this role as a demotion she and Rogers make as sweet a team as ever appeared in a medium-grade musical; "(We'd Be) A Peach of a Pair" they sing, and are. The secondary pair is just as good: Jack Haley and Zelma O'Neal, holdovers from the original production and an ideal matchup—he simpy and sarcastic, she foghorned and feisty. Their "creator" rendition of "Overcoat" evokes its era as giddily as "Varsity Drag," which O'Neal had also introduced on Broadway; "I Want to Be Bad," the only conventional production number, is better still. O'Neal literally raises hell, with devil chorines and music so hot that flames blast from the instruments, until a heavenly fire brigade comes down to cool things off. Silly and captivating, *Follow Thru* is the last of its breed, the kind of entertainment that the Depression rendered extinct.

Fun as *Follow Thru* is, critics took quite a different tack when discussing it in 1930. "I Want to Be Bad" was viewed as extraneous and foolish, the regulation plot was seen as an obstruction, and the color produced a yawn. Audiences were becoming as hostile as the press, which makes the relatively good showing of *Follow Thru* all the more surprising. Other latecomers fared far less well. For *Sunny*, Marilyn Miller cashed in on her earlier hit with an astronomical $225,000 salary; by release time in November 1930 much of the music was cut, leaving a mostly nondancing Miller in black and white trying too hard to be giddy in comedy. The public generally stayed away. Likewise Al Jolson in *Big Boy,* his only early Warner film to be adapted from one of his Broadway hits. (The title referred to a race horse, not to the star; Jolson, wearing blackface throughout, played a stable hand who turns jockey.) There was less bathos than in any previous Jolson film, but he had worn out his welcome, and the meager gross of *Big Boy* could not possibly recoup his immense salary. Radio had an even bigger flop. *Leathernecking* downgraded Rodgers and Hart's *Present Arms* into a ill-fitting blend of service comedy and musical numbers, featuring the equally mismatched duo of Eddie Foy Jr., completely at sea, and stage soprano Irene Dunne, ditto.[13] Another second-rank Rodgers and Hart show, *Heads Up,* fared marginally better at Paramount's Astoria studio. This bland tale of Coast Guardsmen and rum runners called time out for one impressive moment: Buddy Rogers and chorus in a near-Expressionistic staging of the lovely "A Ship Without a Sail."

The worst fates were reserved for *Great Day* and *Rosalie.* The latter, Marion Davies's second try at the Broadway big league, was every bit as unfortunate as *The Five O'Clock Girl.* The Marilyn Miller stage show had been earmarked for Davies back in 1928 and its filming postponed more times than *Glorifying the American Girl.* Production finally started up in the fall of 1930 only to be cancelled almost immediately, in part because Davies had no desire to tempt the fates with a full-blown musical outing. After another brief try in 1932, it was an additional five years before *Rosalie* made it to the screen, as a vehicle for the more tenable song-and-dance talents of Eleanor Powell. *Great Day* fared still more ignominiously. Vincent Youmans's 1929 musical play had had problems of its own, including an obtuse script that sank even such songs as "More Than You Know" and "Without a Song." MGM, who had backed the show, proceeded with the film version in August 1930, with Joan Crawford in the lead role. Trade ads promised "Stunning Joan as a Southern heiress, wild and wonderful, in a grand romance" directed by Harry Pollard, viewed as a Southern specialist after *Uncle Tom's Cabin* and *Show Boat.* Shooting got under way just as studios were beginning to yank musicals off their schedules and continued for about two weeks until it was abruptly halted for "story revision." Forever after, Crawford claimed responsibility for the shutdown, saying that she had gone to Louis B. Mayer and pleaded with him not to make her play a baby-doll singing ingenue with a honeysuckle accent. And, she continued, since Mayer always knew what was good for her career he realized that the footage was terrible and stopped filming. A good story, but likely not too

---

13. This was an improbable start to a distinguished career; later on Dunne preferred to regard *Cimarron* (1931) as her first film and profess to wish that *Leathernecking* never happened.

accurate, for Crawford would not have had the power to shut down a film singlehandedly. Most likely the MGM powers, already stung by *The March of Time* and other disasters, had already started considering this musical one too many, and with major script problems to boot; if Crawford did go to Mayer it only served to reinforce their view that Broadway musicals on the screen were dead, and she would not be the performer to engineer their renaissance.

With all the abortions and disasters of late 1930, it's remarkable—another of those strange paradoxes peppering the era—that one of the year's biggest hits came out at this time as both a musical and a Broadway adaptation. A literal one, very expensive and in Technicolor, which had lately been taking quite a rap. Despite all the seeming minuses, *Whoopee!* scored as solidly with audiences as it did with critics, and it survives today as the summation of filmed musical comedy, vintage 1930.

It's not too difficult to divine why *Whoopee!* succeeded at such a dark time, for it was founded on a propitious intersection of talents: the theatrical savvy of Florenz Ziegfeld, Samuel Goldwyn's film know-how, audacious dance staging by Busby Berkeley, and ace musical comedian Eddie Cantor. Adapted from Owen Davis's play *The Nervous Wreck*, Ziegfeld's 1928 show (without a final exclamation point) starred Cantor as a terminal hypochondriac on the loose at an Arizona dude ranch. The plot did not make inordinate sense, likewise a romantic subplot involving an heiress and a handsome half-breed. (True to current prejudices, he's revealed to be white and the union is sanctified.) It allowed for all sorts of trappings, up to and including live horses and a beauty parade, Indian maids à la Ziegfeld. The show's success could not offset Ziegfeld's recent heavy losses, so despite the letdown of *Glorifying the American Girl*, he entered into a coproducing agreement with Sam Goldwyn to film *Whoopee*. Goldwyn was solidly established as the industry's most successful independent producer, each film an expensive rhinestone sparkler made with the best taste money could buy. In the silent era he had produced a profitable series of romances, and as sound dawned he saw the new kind of escapism offered by musicals. Eventually he cornered the market on frilly, emptyheaded, star-driven musical comedies, in which his stable of Goldwyn Girls offered prominent support. *Whoopee!* was the first, and rarely again would the formula work so well. Besides Ziegfeld and Cantor, Goldwyn snagged other Broadway participants: most of the cast, conductor George Olsen,[14] and designer John Hark-

14. Olsen was married to Ethel Shutta, who repeated her stage role for the movie; a few weeks after the show opened, Olsen and Ziegfeld had a massive falling-out and Olsen left the pit. Fortunately, he was convinced to participate in the film version, and the dash and verve of his stage-band forces give *Whoopee!* a unique, compact, wholly inimitable sound.

Eleanor Hunt, who had been a Ziegfeld showgirl in the original production, was promoted to ingenue lead for the film, though it wasn't a role that would make any sort of impression.

rider. In the usual 1930 tradition, most of the original score was jettisoned in favor of new songs. The most conspicuous loss was "Love Me or Leave Me," sung onstage by Ruth Etting (in a completely immaterial role); also gone were most of the lyrics for the show's other hit, "Makin' Whoopee," for which new and somewhat denatured lines were substituted.

If the Broadway *Whoopee* had been a Cantor vehicle par excellence, the Hollywood version was slanted even more in his favor, with full star treatment and a salary of $100,000 plus 10 per cent of the gross. The popeyed manic-neurotic with the Jewish wisecracks and ringing tenor dominated everything; it's the essence of the star comic style so popular on Broadway until the 1950s. Routines, gags, and specialty numbers all drop in from nowhere to allow for the Cantor bag of tricks. He wants to do one of his blackface numbers? *Voilà*—get him corked up for "My Baby Just Cares for Me." He wants to throw in some of his sketch-comedy shtick? He's playing a hypochondriac here, so he can riff on about operations and surgical scars. And on and on. Cantor's comedy was the factor most responsible for *Whoopee!*'s hit with the public, his domination so vast that the rest of the show was seen as a setting for his gags. Today *Whoopee!* seems a quintessential musical comedy; in 1930 it was judged (per *Motion Picture News*):

> Not a filmusical *[sic]* comedy as the screen has previously known this type of entertainment [but] strictly a comedy with plenty of gags and laugh situations and sequences—with a slight auxiliary story to hold things together logically. . . .

A few months earlier, the Marx Brothers' *Animal Crackers*, with nearly all its Broadway score removed, had been a big hit for Paramount. *Whoopee!*, a far more lavish display piece, was viewed in precisely the same terms: a comedy with songs. The lush Goldwyn production with its $1.5 million-plus budget, the Technicolor, the ensemble numbers, were all secondary. Audiences in autumn 1930 wanted to laugh, needed to; Cantor—however much an acquired taste today—answered the call. He became an instant movie star and with Goldwyn and Berkeley promptly began work on more of the same.

Berkeley had not been a part of the original show, and it was apparently Cantor's idea to engage him; Ziegfeld probably had little say in the matter, for he was discovering that nobody would ever be permitted to "co-produce" with his autocratic partner. While Berkeley had already assumed full directorial status on Broadway, he was hired only for the dances. The nominal director, Thornton Freeland, had been engaged on the basis of his indifferent work on *Be Yourself!*, and his staging (it must be so called) of *Whoopee!*'s plot scenes was pedantic. Not so Berkeley; from the opening "Cowboy" number something special is clearly going on. The blocking of the dancers is stagy, certainly not anything new, but the camera intrudes in a way it had not done before. The focal point for the sequence was the lens, not a theater spectator's perspective, so the formations are constantly framed in abstract terms comprehensible only when seen on projected film. Meaningless on stage, they become geometric lyricism under the gaze of Berkeley's camera. It's the culmination of the instinct that prompted Harry Beaumont and Sammy Lee to zero in on Joyce Murray's tapping feet in *The Broadway Melody;* dance, on film, operates on a different plane. By no means does "Cowboy" come near the baroque arabesques of vintage Berkeley; yet he was clearly born for the musical film and even in this earliest work can be seen as an irresistible catalyst bridging the gap between Broadway and movie magic. "Cowboy" is notable for another reason, too: the petite and vivacious young woman who sings the opening chorus and crowns Berkeley's first overhead shot is the thirteen-year-old Betty Grable. She had arrived in Hollywood several months earlier, first appearing in the chorus of *Let's Go Places*. Berkeley and Goldwyn obviously saw something in her: she can also be seen in the wedding procession scene and, grinning impishly, in "Stetson." A promising start for someone so young, though her stardom would not be cemented for another decade. This charter roster of Goldwyn Girls features several other future names: Virginia Bruce and Claire Dodd, both prominent in thirties cinema, and Ernestine Mahoney, later known as Jean Howard, a popular figure in movieland society.

"Stetson," exuberantly led by Ethel Shutta, is more explicit in forecasting the later Berkeley style. The sequential close-ups of attractive women points to one of the director's great contradictions: his deployment of massed dancers could seem dehumanized, even fascist objectification, people reduced to their mathematical/formational possibilities. Yet clearly he loved his "girls" enough to give them closeups, treat them as objects of beauty, and give his massed fantasies a human edge. Ziegfeld loved women too, and *Whoopee!'s* "eleven o'clock number" is one of the master's most extreme flights of fancy: the showgirl/Indian parade that stopped the show in New York is if anything more spectacular on film. Harkrider seems to have used every feather in California to make the headdresses for this scene, which epitomizes the major traits of *Whoopee!* on film: the vast precedence given to spectacle over sense, the very casual racial callousness, and the salient quality of total artificiality. No al fresco naturalism, such as *Rio Rita's* haciendas or *Follow Thru's* golf greens. Except for a few shots *Whoopee!* was filmed entirely in patently stagy settings under brilliantly painted green-and-mauve Technicolor skies. It was the same basic aesthetic that Warners had used on *The Desert Song,* with an enormous upswing in assurance and a far greater quota of laughs.

Despite its grosses, *Whoopee!* was not a repeatable stunt. Indeed, it was the exception that reinforced accepted instincts about the problematic road linking stage and screen. Back at square one, the ads for Warners' *The*

Desert Song had bragged, "With all its original Stage Enchantment." Precisely—and, *Whoopee!* or not, this just wouldn't play. The later Goldwyn/ Cantor/Berkeley films were original creations, and there would be few successful adaptations of Broadway musicals for many years after *Whoopee!* In its own brassy way, *Whoopee!* was a dead end. Yet, withall, it ended its era on a high note and survives robustly as a prime piece of Broadway under glass. Over the subsequent decades of Broadway-to-Hollywood projects, many better shows would have to settle for less than this bright-hued jumble of nonsense and expertise.

CHAPTER 10

Just Imagine

From the very beginning, original content—the term "original" is of course staggeringly relative—was a cornerstone of musical film. The earliest instinct in the spring of 1928 had been to look to Broadway for ready-made material, yet Jolson's films, *My Man, The Broadway Melody, Syncopation, On With the Show!,* and *Gold Diggers of Broadway,* were originals, and after *Rio Rita* and its stepchildren started the procession of adaptations, such work continued. Although these films lacked the familiar titles and ace songs of stage hits, they retained obvious pertinence. Even when the cost of script treatments and rewrites ran into five digits, these would not reach the numbers spent to acquire a *No, No, Nanette* or a *Good News.* The question of songs was not as vital as it seemed, either, considering the wholesale elimination of most Broadway tunes going west. Original material offered a modicum of potential for cinematic life, the sense that these songs and characters and situations were based in celluloid independence rather than stage constriction. It was hardly true on a regular basis, yet some of the early originals were among the most interesting films of the time, and the most successful.

Just as *Rio Rita* became the prototype for adaptations, a concurrent film opening in early October 1929 led the way for the originals. In producing *Sunny Side Up* William Fox took several gambles. One was to commission, in December 1928, an integrated musical comedy, scenario and songs, from the successful Broadway team of DeSylva, Brown and Henderson. It was decided that this would serve as the all-talkie debut of Janet Gaynor, just emerging as Fox's leading star; since she specialized in winsomely resilient underdogs it took little resourcefulness to effect a *Sally*-type story about a Yorkville tenement girl who grabs for the brass ring of Southampton soci-

245

ety. It suited Gaynor as much as it did the rampant optimism of the late 1920s, and Gaynor's traditional leading man, Charles Farrell, took the plunge with her. Neither was a singer in any accepted sense, so their songs were made to conform to limited vocal ranges.[1]

In some film projects it can be clear early on that a surefire hit is in the making, for which reason unwavering self-confidence seems to color the work and ability of everyone involved. *Sunny Side Up* was perhaps the prime example of this in the early talkie age, and Janet Gaynor and director David Butler were particularly affected. With only moderate resources and little training, Gaynor pulled off something approaching a tour de force. Hard work and ambition had much to with it, and so did instinct and affinity. The role of Molly O'Day was similar to many Gaynor played during her career, and it seems that the actor and the ethos of the role were pretty congruent. If Gaynor was a shrewd woman, she was also an innocent; her performances in *Seventh Heaven, Sunrise, State Fair*, and *A Star is Born* were convincing because she believed in them wholeheartedly, lies and all. The performer centering *Sunny Side Up* clearly buys into the Cinderella myth to the point where she can stare straight into the camera and sing "I'm a dreamer, aren't we all?" with the most unshakable conviction this side of Jolson. No matter that her singing voice sounds like that of a cartoon character, and that Charles Farrell, the object of her dreams, combines the looks of Adonis with the voice and manner of a complete dimwit. Under the right circumstances, sincerity can triumph over skill.

Not even the most skilled or self-convinced artists could propel a whole show without assistance, and in this Gaynor had good fortune and good backup. David Butler, a former actor recently turned director, ended up making a career out of light-headed fare: vehicles for Shirley Temple, Bob Hope, Doris Day. Butler is the kind of efficient, expeditious technician who never rates a retrospective. Yet his work on *Sunny Side Up* is more than that, from that famous opening shot of the camera roaming around the tenement, picking up a cacophony of urban sounds and images. While a good script clearly makes a difference, Butler puts some of his own vigor into such set pieces as the Yorkville block party and (study in contrasts) the Southampton soiree. The clash of classes is at the heart of *Sunny Side Up*, and at Fox such a conflict would naturally be much softer grained than at Warners in the early thirties, or even in MGM's Joan Crawford shopgirl romances. But Butler directs his actors well, he keeps things moving, and he makes much and graceful use of outdoor shooting; even when the film goes on about twenty minutes too long the proceedings seldom flag. A few

1. Farrell's lack of musical aptitude was so obvious that there were second thoughts about using him. Among the alternates considered was Hugh Trevor, a Radio player who was as tall as Farrell, nearly as handsome, and with a better voice. Yet such casting would have eliminated the a priori magic borne by the Gaynor-Farrell team.

pre-Production Code moments, especially, remain in the memory: a feminist handing out birth-control leaflets is razzed by a tenement mom with a litter of kids; a very young Jackie Cooper tries to recite "The Village Smithy" at the block party while squirming to get to the bathroom; and Marjorie White, as Molly's sensible best friend, goads her into action with a pointed "What the hell are ya cryin' about?"

DeSylva, Brown and Henderson's score, like their script, was not bottom-line extraordinary. Yet it equaled their Broadway work, and the team's dominion over the project ensured that the script and music bonded unusually well. One of the charms of *Sunny Side Up* is its unaffected intimacy, with songs mostly arising from situations to illuminate the characters and their motives. The title song fixes on Molly's optimism, while "If I Had a Talking Picture of You" is as right for Molly and Jack as it is for Gaynor and Farrell and, by extension, as the unofficial anthem of the early sound era.[2] "You've Got Me Pullin' Petals off of Daisies" is a screwy love song for the secondary couple (White and Frank Richardson) in the same vein as "Button Up Your Overcoat" and benefits from Seymour Felix's energetic staging. "Aren't We All," the most interesting of the songs, carries emotional depth beyond Hollywood or Broadway norms. Rarely do romanticism and rueful awareness mingle so well to express both one's need to dream and the awareness that disappointments await. It climaxes memorably with an ascent and crescendo that finally explode—"He's ideal, but then, he isn't real and I'm a fool!"—after which these hard facts are resigned into a gentle amen: ". . . but aren't we all?"

With all *Sunny Side Up*'s good points, its most celebrated moment—and sole large production number—can, with spartan restraint, only be termed a lulu. "Turn On the Heat," led by Sharon Lynn, is a paean to Eskimo sex and fiery tropical love staged by Felix with one eye on Freud and the other on a chorus of marginally talented young women who writhe through the proceedings with little coordination and absolutely no inhibition. The outrageous result is a delightful precursor of the Busby Berkeley extravaganzas of 1933–35 which gave ingenuity and vigor similarly rampant precedence over taste. (Berkeley is also heralded by the bananas that sprout up near the end of the number, just as suggestively as in the master's psychosexual Carmen Miranda nightmare "The Lady in the Tutti Frutti Hat" in *The Gang's All Here*.) The staging, if far more kinetic than most early numbers, is not particularly cinematic, yet vigor takes more forms than just moving the camera. "Turn on the Heat" is wonderful mainly because no one concerned felt any need to hold back or any constraint—not from

2. There is one excruciating moment when Gaynor-Farrell reprise "Talking Picture" at the charity show. She's too cute, he's too coy, and their thin little voices sound almost exactly like the Meglin Kiddies—who, dressed as grownups, toddle out for a rather awesome second chorus. Rarely has infanticide felt this justifiable.

This lobby card from *Sunny Side Up* is fairly representative of the film as a whole: corn overlayed with a great deal of charm. Left to right are Charles Farrell, Janet Gaynor (twice), Marjorie White, El Brendel, Frank Richardson.

sound men judging what wouldn't work, or from the Hays Office, or from innate finer feelings, or even from the studio Fire Marshall. They got up and did it, all energy and jubilant trashiness. And when audiences today roll in the aisle upon witnessing it, the laughter is more in appreciation than derision. "The hottest girls in the world are Eskimos," Lynn sings, and you'd better believe it.

Like a couple of the other smash hits of 1929, *Sunny Side Up* elicited good, not overwhelming, reviews. The financial figures told a different story—a gross of $3.5 million, holdover engagements, and long runs in small towns heretofore resistant to some of the big musicals. The success owed as much to musical know-how as to the Gaynor appeal, and it was hardly surprising that all the studios were soon busy with their own non-backstage original musicals, Fox included. As if to demonstrate how hard it had been to bring off *Sunny Side Up* its director and stars were at it again a few months later with *High Society Blues*. This weak dose of syrup can only be called the worst kind of early talkie: rigid, overlong, uneventful. In contrast to *Sunny Side Up*'s integrated musical comedy, *High Society Blues* is neither fish nor fowl, just some songs dropped into a tedious romance about a clash between oafish new money (his family) and snobbish old (hers). No DB&H script or songs this time, and no help from Butler's regressive direction. Farrell, carrying more of the burden this time, was more ineffectual and nasal than ever, and not even the irrevocably haughty presence of Hedda Hopper as her mother could make Gaynor convincing as a socialite. Despite a few references to the Crash, this type of poor little millionaire fantasy would have been jeered off the screen a year later. Nevertheless, the star duo was still riding high on the strength of *Sunny Side Up* and had just topped newspaper polls of favorite performers in New York and Chicago. Even for such retrograde junk as *High Society Blues*, the public turned out in droves, professing to swoon at the sight (if not sound) of Farrell serenading Gaynor with a ukulele and playing minstrel to her lady in a fairy-tale flashback. It could hardly be, however, that many didn't see this as a major comedown. Gaynor certainly did, and promptly went on strike for better roles.

Before *Sunny Side Up* established ground rules for filmed musical comedy there had already begun an onrush of college football musicals, obviously prompted by Broadway's *Good News*. The first of these was Universal's *College Love*, the most profitable were MGM's *So This Is College* and Paramount's *Sweetie*, and the worst was Tiffany's *Sunny Skies*, which featured comic Benny Rubin as a nebbishy student who receives a blood transfusion from the class hero. A few surprising collegians (and musical performers) turned up in these—Robert Montgomery and Elliott Nugent in *So This Is College*, Loretta Young and Douglas Fairbanks Jr. in First National's *The Forward Pass*, and, in *Sweetie*, Nancy Carroll as a chorus girl who somehow inherits a university. The last-named at least had moments of diversion courtesy of Jack Oakie and Helen Kane. He hammed through a rousing "Alma Mammy," she booped through "He's So Unusual." Otherwise, college life was no more inspired in 1929 than on later Hollywood campuses.

Marion Davies's long-delayed sound entrée (except for *The Hollywood Revue*) came with *Marianne*, released about the same time as *Sunny Side Up*. That this turned out one of the fresher and more appealing entertainments of its season is somewhat remarkable, considering its tumultuous Hearstian evolution. After the fiasco of *The Five O'Clock Girl*, Hearst determined that a more film-oriented property might be suitable for Davies's first bout with talkies. He commissioned a lighter replay of *The Big Parade*, with Marion as a peppery mam'selle sparring with doughboys stationed near her farm. Since Hearst still envisioned his paramour as a musical sweetheart, *Marianne* was given an abundant overlay of songs, some of them rendered by Davies in a thick accent, Paris via Culver City.[3] For musical backup there was the resistible Broadway veteran Oscar Shaw, who had just appeared in *The Cocoanuts*. With Davies still terrified of sound, the silent version of

---

3. The accent actually seems to have been an unexpected boon; Davies was so occupied with maintaining the French intonation that she was distracted from her chronic stammer.

A *Marianne* no audience heard: Oscar Shaw sings to Marion Davies in the first, aborted version, released only as a silent.

Marianne was shot first; even that was a chore, Hearst's incessant meddling being no boon to anyone involved. By the time it came time to shoot the talking *Marianne,* the entire cast (save Davies) had been replaced, and, peculiarly, Shaw was moved out in favor of a Hollywood regular, Lawrence Gray. While Gray's musical experience was minimal, he had a passable tenor voice and, more importantly, was far more at ease before the camera. Both he and Davies won fine albeit somewhat surprised reviews, and despite its cost *Marianne* garnered a small profit—one of the last Davies pictures to do so. It survives well, if not so much as a musical as a demonstration of the studios' ability to bounce back from technical hardship. It shares with *Sunny Side Up* an excessive running time and, more importantly, a minimum of the more odious attributes of early talkies. Much of the quality comes from the direction of Robert Z. Leonard, a silent veteran and one of MGM's prime workhorses (*The Divorcée, The Great Ziegfeld* and *Ziegfeld Girl, Maytime, Pride and Prejudice*). There is a great deal of location shooting, some complicated camera movement, and a general air of vitality; the performers, Davies included, are clearly not intimidated by the microphone. In some of her silents Davies had evinced a gift for mimicry; here she shines with imitations of Sarah Bernhardt and (somewhat anachronistically) Maurice Chevalier. The heavy accent actually suits her voice pretty well, and she and Gray duetting on the hit "Just You, Just Me" offers one of the more fetching moments of that year.

It's one of those strange ongoing ironies of the time that Davies, with minimal musical aptitude, would fare well in *Marianne*, while the infinitely more suitable Gertrude Lawrence came to grief in a concurrent Great War musical, *The Battle of Paris*. Here was the film for which *Photoplay* coined the term "floperetta." Lawrence, following her stage success in *Charlot's Revue* and *Oh, Kay!* and the less popular *Treasure Girl*, would have seemed a natural, and had already done well on film in one of the earliest Movietone shorts. But her first starring vehicle was a cataclysm. Indeed, Paramount's Astoria lot was a fairly unhappy place in the summer of 1929. On the downstairs stage, Rouben Mamoulian was waging ongoing battle with a recalcitrant crew to make *Applause* something more than a standard backstage drama; and upstairs, on the studio's main stage, Robert Florey was coping bleakly with a futile script and a prima donna without a proper showcase. The film's working title, *The Gay Lady*, was an emphatic misnomer, for even with Lawrence and costar Charlie Ruggles striving valiantly, there were no laughs to be had, and precious little entertainment. Florey unsuccessfully attempted to remove himself from the project, and Paramount was so unhappy with the result that it held up release for a number of months, after which *The Battle of Paris* died a quick theatrical death. Gertrude Lawrence was many things to many audiences, but a Parisian gamine she was not, especially in circumstances the *Billboard* critic termed "the strangest mixture that Paramount has ever offered to the dear public." Another casualty was Cole Porter, in his inauspicious film debut. Lawrence singing Porter sounds tempting—as indeed it would be in the 1933 London show *Nymph Errant*—but neither artist was working here at anything like peak capacity. Only in "They All Fall in Love" is there a glint of Porter wit and Lawrence glow.

A pair of lesser calamities concocted on the West Coast gave fair demonstration of the perils involved in trying to assemble original musical comedies under the most routine assembly-line circumstances. *Tanned Legs* rolled out of the Radio plant in the late autumn of '29, although this tale of monkey business at a Florida resort had been designed as a summertime entertainment and, as with some others, had been started as a straight comedy. After some days' shooting on location at Laguna Beach, RKO brass—probably in answer to rumors of Fox's work on *Sunny Side Up*—decided to scrap the cast (except leading lady June Clyde) and director, and add music. Too bad the plot wasn't scrapped as well, for an inviting theme à la *The Cocoanuts* collapsed upon a pile of unconnected plots and one final ridiculous burst of melodrama. The opening credits of the film bear the legend "An original musical play," but there was little imagination involved in delegating Oscar Levant and Sidney Clare to stuff in a bale of inferior songs barely connected with the plot or characters. This is generic filmmaking at its most barren, and astute observers were quick to perceive that such work did credit to neither the new musical film or to the new studio. Allen Kearns, later the leading man in Broadway's *Girl Crazy*, was displayed to notably poor advantage, and Ann Pennington, for whom this was quite a comedown after *Gold Diggers of Broadway*, was unloaded into a nothing sideline role, with much of her screen time shunted aside in favor of the juvenile hero, a role for which Joel McCrea had been originally mentioned. It went instead, in a radical case of trading down, to Arthur Lake. His whining persists even when he sings, and the script is so badly put together that he isn't allowed to come to the rescue of the beleaguered heroine (Clyde). Instead, he remains an adjunct, as useless and obnoxious as is *Tanned Legs* in toto.

Director Marshall Neilan had been for a brief time a golden boy in American cinema, showing enormous promise in several films with Mary Pickford and others. By 1929 it had all faded in a smog of alcohol and self-destructive behavior, but even after *Tanned Legs*, fledgling Radio was willing to give him another chance. Of all inappropriate things, he was given another original musical, a star vehicle centering on a performer who needed every iota of help he could scrounge. While Rudy Vallee in *The Vagabond Lover* was certainly a promising concept for millions of crooner-mad women, as a film it was a turkey. Again there was a nothing script, not another mammy story (for which thanks) but some gibberish about a bandleader and his group turned loose on Newport society. It was a minor miracle that *The Vagabond Lover* ever made it out at all, due not to Vallee but to a huge fire at Consolidated Film Labs in Hollywood, which was first feared to have destroyed the film. Perhaps only the good parts were lost, though enough was salvaged to release the film a few weeks after *Tanned Legs*. Any hopes Vallee had of screen stardom were quickly dashed in catastrophic reviews that left only his singing unscathed. It was, by consensus, an absolutely hopeless performance, and particularly stagnant next to that of Marie Dressler, cast as a gorgonesque dowager and stealing scenes wholesale. Whatever comic possibilities Preston Sturges and others later found in Vallee were nowhere to be found here, and Neilan couldn't even photograph him properly. Critics reacted with more hostility than they had even to Ted Lewis, with cracks such as "Buck teeth weren't made as an aid to heart throbs and a wooden expression is seldom conducive to emotional fervor" *(Exhibitor's Herald-World)*. And, "For gosh sakes sing, Annie" *(Photoplay)*. After the core Vallee fans had their fill, *The Vagabond Lover* instantly died at the box office, and angry exhibitors wrote in to place the blame wholly on Rudy.

While few of the other original musicals of that boomtown fall and winter of 1929–30 were as ill-wrought as the Neilan twins or *The Battle of Paris*, an insufficient number were worthy of the standard set by *Sunny Side Up*.

Promotional tie-ins were not uncommon in 1930, but the one for *Tanned Legs*, as run in the July issue of *Photoplay*, takes the cake.

Honey was typical, and another reason why Nancy Carroll chafed at Paramount's bent for casting her in musical froth. *Come Out of the Kitchen*, a popular stage farce in the mid-teens, had been filmed as a Paramount silent in 1919, then dusted off for Carroll and other musically inclined contractees. It came out in spring 1930 and served its purposes adequately, yet it's another of those clear indicators that musical conventions were being misunderstood. The play, about an impoverished heiress who rents out her mansion and poses as the maid, was a decent foundation for light musical romance. But once again there was no thought given to what truly makes a musical comedy flow organically, or how to pace and integrate musical sequences. This last problem, which had hobbled Paramount's campus musical *Sweetie*, would be a mistake made time and again in the studio's original musical comedies. The first song in *Honey* comes more than half an hour into a 73-minute film, after reams of dry exposition, and such ungainly proportions conspire to strand a game cast. All the timeworn ingredients are here: the heroine's song of romantic aspiration ("In My Little Hope Chest"), which she tearfully reprises after her dreams have crumbled; the comedy/rhythm number for the second leads (Skeets Gallagher and Lillian Roth, singing "I Don't Need Atmosphere"), and so on. This was musical painting-by-numbers, as audiences were beginning to observe. Small wonder that the one truly worthwhile moment in *Honey* bears no relation to plot or character: Sam Coslow's rousing "Sing You Sinners," an obvious homage to "Hallelujah!" in *Hit the Deck*, is given a powerhouse run-through by a black choir in a revival scene. For the second chorus Mitzi Green, so obnoxious through most of *Honey*, shows that child performers can be appealing under the proper circumstances. Then Lillian Roth comes out for a third chorus that permits a one-minute glimpse of something magical: a talented performer allowed to do what she does best. Suddenly free of the constraints of miscasting to which Paramount often subjected her, Roth belts and shimmies with immense verve, totally basking in the joy of the moment. The drab plot then resumes and wraps up fairly quickly, and an ordinary movie ends—but there's been one sublime moment.

Paramount tried other original musical comedies during 1930 with mixed results. *Safety in Numbers* was a Buddy Rogers showcase par excellence, the star's dimples flashing brighter than ever as he romped about as an heir on the loose in Manhattan who finds himself chaperoned by a trio of wiseacre chorines. Plainly, this was an event fashioned solely for the fans, a still-sizable group who duly ate it up—especially when Buddy sang the lovely "My Future Just Passed" to Kathryn Crawford.[4] Another star vehicle fared

---

4. Another item of interest in *Safety in Numbers*: a young Carole Lombard, in the first of her rare musical outings, as one of Buddy's protectors. The brittle screwball persona was still some years off, and it's a somewhat abashed Lombard who undertakes to get through a chorus of "(Young Man,) You Appeal to Me" without actually singing one note.

less well at the time, though it holds up a shade better today. Clara Bow, in her declining days at the studio, strayed into Janet Gaynor territory for *Love Among the Millionaires*, as a railroad-yard gamine who finds the right rich man in modest and sweet Stanley Smith. She certainly tried hard and her singing had improved since *Paramount on Parade*, but it was another one of the studio throwaways that gave her neither proper treatment nor attention. And most 1930 spectators, starting to tire of "It" and some unsavory offscreen publicity, preferred the noisy antics of Mitzi Green as Bow's sister. Precocious as ever, Green offered some of her famous impersonations, including a fairly sharp takeoff on Bow herself—not the most alert or generous gesture to be made by a studio hoping to prop up a waning, insecure star. *Let's Go Native* was far happier, in fact one of the brighter musical comedies of 1930 to come from Paramount or anywhere else. Despite the presence of Jack Oakie, Jeanette MacDonald, and (in support) Kay Francis, this was no star vehicle. A fast and often funny ensemble piece, it contained good songs and almost no sense whatever; the latter was the likely reason for Paramount's holding up its release for six months. The unhinged plot embraced an impoverished heiress (MacDonald), a smart-mouthed Brooklyn cabbie named Voltaire McGinnis (Oakie), a shipwreck, several mistaken identities, and a desert island with a self-appointed king (Skeets Gallagher). It was sheer malarkey, played with bounce and directed by Leo McCarey with some of the affinity toward musical anarchy he later brought to *Duck Soup*. The characters occasionally invent the most ridiculous song cues to give themselves excuses to sing, Oakie socks over a frisky piece called "Joe Jazz," and even Kay Francis gets into the spirit by doing her own singing, in a higher and more attractive voice than might be expected. For MacDonald, then beginning to show signs of prima donna imperiousness, this was not a happy occasion, yet she was pro enough to enter into the spirit of it with enthusiasm and even wear her native grass skirt as if she meant it. Not a major film by any means, *Let's Go Native* is one of those clever pieces of fluff that, by the fall of 1930, was getting lost in the shuffle.

After *Sunny Side Up*, nearly all the Fox studio's musical output remained bland and ordinary—the revues, *High Society Blues*, *Let's Go Places*, and the Sue Carol trifles *The Big Party* and *The Golden Calf*. Yet there were major and minor exceptions to the dullness. The latter was *Women Everywhere*, one of those completely forgotten titles that somehow survived. It rates at least a footnote as the only musical directed by Alexander Korda, and one of his last films before returning to England for more sterling work. *Women Everywhere* was a catchall that managed to comprise gunrunners, shady Algerian dives, the Foreign Legion, battle scenes, eight songs, and Fifi D'Orsay, who struts her stuff at a cabaret memorably named The Squinting Cat. As a bid for *Desert Song*-type allure, it was a showcase for Broadway's

J. Harold Murray, who swaggered acceptably and sang well, though after an hour or so the combination of his bravura and D'Orsay's perpetual esprit grew wearying. This type of generic cross-pollenization was a good example of the lengths to which producers of the time would go to accommodate musical forms.

DeSylva, Brown and Henderson, remaining under contract to Fox after *Sunny Side Up,* spent the first part of 1930 at work on something which, though originally intended for Gaynor and Farrell, was notably unlike their earlier work and probably a bit mad. They took their cue from, of all things, Fritz Lang's *Metropolis,* with its fabulous and naïve look at life in the future, its bizarre designs and fearful anticipation of the erosion of individual rights. Not even the bolder Broadway experiments of the twenties had tackled a subject as offbeat as science fiction, and the team's script, set in the New York City of 1980, had any number of fascinating touches. People bear serial numbers instead of names (albeit preceded by name-sounding letter prefixes such as LN and J), meals come in pills, marriages must be government-sanctioned, and interplanetary flight is becoming a reality. And Prohibition is still in effect. Careening through it all is a fugitive from 1930, a nitwit awakened after a fifty-year coma. Future shock was indeed a great peg on which to hinge the story, titled *Just Imagine* after one of the songs in *Good News,* yet the idea went a trifle awry by the time it was all done, after various decisions in casting and production assured that this most intriguing of early musical concepts would be given the proven Fox homogenization. Janet Gaynor, fuming over the inadequacy of *High Society Blues,* dropped out of the running early on to begin a strike for more money and a greater say in scripts. With her gone, the role of LN-18 lost its individual contours, though at one point Ruby Keeler was suggested. The final choice was the newest Fox ingenue, a teenaged colleen named Maureen O'Sullivan. Charles Farrell, busy struggling through Fox's production of *Liliom,* would have clearly been lost in some of J-21's more ambitious vocal moments, and the role went to John Garrick, a stalwart and stoic British baritone just returned to Fox after a dreadful operetta outing at United Artists called *The Lottery Bride.* The most defining casting choice was for Single-O, the refugee from 1930. The character was originally named Hermann Schultz, so obviously a German or Jewish dialect comic was intended. But Fox's comedian of choice just then was El Brendel, whose comedy dialect was Swedish. Schultz was changed to Swensen, and ample time given to Brendel's yumpin' yimminy witticisms. It's startling to realize how popular Brendel was in 1930—galling, too, when one considers the silent clowns whose fame he preempted. Perhaps the novelty of sound gave his Scandinavian inflections a freshness now beyond recall. Just sit through a Brendel performance today—any Brendel performance—and try to laugh. His clown's demeanor is not backed by anything remotely resembling humor, and his jokes are either senseless or wore out their welcome around the time of Charlemagne. This, amazingly, is the same comic *Motion Picture* magazine crowned, in its review of *The Big Party*, "the most irresistible man on the screen." Yet in *Just Imagine* it couldn't be more apparent that this Rip Van Winkle brings none of the delight of Woody Allen's *Sleeper*.

Just Imagine was a godsend to the Fox publicity department, who enfolded its shooting in a cloak of ostentatious secrecy. When some extremely tantalizing publicity stills were leaked out, it was clear that this was something far out of the Fox mainstream. Novelty, in fact, was its strongest point, for by release time, November 1930, selling it as a musical would not have been an astute way to recoup an investment of $1.1 million. Curiosity and Brendel sold it, and it finally did well enough. Later it passed into legend and, like Single-O, dropped out for nearly half a century. Those incredible stills of the special-effects New York skyline, all gleaming Art Deco fantasies and clean lines, made *Just Imagine* one of the most tempting of lost films; when it finally did resurface around 1970, disappointment was inevitable. First there was Brendel to contend with, and the name Single-O seemed to approximate the character's IQ and appeal far too well. And there are other faults. The score is a mediocre far cry from the joys of *Sunny Side Up;* only "Never Swat a Fly" has the requisite air of dazed humor. And the standard musical comedy conventions are far too prosaic for such a tale, with the obligatory serious and comic couples (O'Sullivan with Garrick, the inevitable Marjorie White with Frank Albertson) and soggy ballads for the hero to deliver on cue. The production values, too, seem skimped apart from Stephen Goosson's stunning skyline model, which is milked for everything it's worth. There are some bare sets, not enough witty touches, an insufficient futuristic glow. The flight to Mars that should be such a highlight ends up being virtually thrown away, with undistinguished special effects and a climactic revolt that's badly staged and edited. Most disappointing, perhaps, is David Butler's direction; this is the work of the Butler of *High Society Blues*, the same faceless helmsman who turned out all the innocuous star vehicles in later years; certainly there's little of the zip and crane shots and compositional care of *Sunny Side Up*. With all this, *Just Imagine* seems flat as a board when seen on television or in private screenings. The presence of an audience, though, ignites some of the original spark. Perhaps it's communal enthusiasm or mass psychology, maybe a shared delight in seeing the throwaway futuristic gags—such as the warm-air hand dryer—that were indeed prophetic. The climactic revolt on Mars seems to acquire more excitement, and Joyzelle Joyner, as the Queen of Mars and her evil twin, is certainly an arresting presence in any case.[5] Her burly and effeminate attendant even inspires a good line out of El Brendel: "She's not the queen, *he* is!" Seen with an audience, Brendel does seem just a little funnier. So *Just Imagine* is a uncommon piece, a curious mix of the drab and the fantastic, a stab at unaccustomed material eons before the likes of *The Rocky Horror Show*, and it could only have been made at one time in the history of film.

So could an even more outlandish curiosity that opened just prior to *Just Imagine*. For all its futuristic gewgaws, *Just Imagine* was at heart just another DeSylva, Brown and Henderson show, *Hold Everything 1980*. But the mere idea of a musical comedy directed by Cecil B. DeMille is enough to make the sensitivities flinch and the imagination wander to the possibilities lying in store when *King of Kings* meets *King of Jazz*. Certainly there could be some of the bizarre qualities and spectacle missing in *Just Imagine*. To see how this master of philistine showmanship coped with the musical form, it's necessary to turn to MGM, where other efforts at original musical comedy had not been exceptional: *So This Is College*, a *Follow Thru* manqué called *Love in the Rough*, and a throwaway for Joan Crawford, *Montana Moon*.[6] DeMille joined Metro's directorial roster just as sound dawned, following a long career at Paramount and a stint in independent production. As well known for "daring" society romances as for spectacles, he threw both styles into his MGM debut, *Dynamite*. His experiences with Dorothy Parker on *Dynamite*'s theme song have already been recounted, and long before that film reached its audience he began to consider the role of music in his second talkie. In typical style, DeMille announced a contest to award $1,000 for the best story idea, and though no suggestion proved usable he was struck by the number of entries that mentioned operatic themes. He loved opera, and certainly there's a Wagnerian sensibility at work in his epics, with their message-laden theatricality and blatant set pieces. With opera out of the question for his next project, DeMille managed to pass over operetta and move straight to musical comedy. The plot, concocted by his longtime associate and former mistress Jeanie Macpherson, was a fantastic combination of *Die Fledermaus* and DeMille's 1920 *Why Change Your Wife?*, with *The Guardsman* tossed in for good measure. A dull socialite (Kay Johnson) wins back her straying husband (Reginald Denny) from a

5. An exotic actress-dancer usually billed by her first name only, she's one of those bizarre fringe performers who could only turn up in early thirties cinema. She made her most vivid impression in Cecil B. DeMille's *The Sign of the Cross* (1932) performing "The Naked Moon," which might best be described as DeMille's version of lesbian performance art. In the recently restored uncut print, it proves to be one of his most over-the-top stunts, leaving no jaw undropped.

6. *Love in the Rough*, which costarred Robert Montgomery and Dorothy Jordan, did feature a bright score by Jimmy McHugh and Dorothy Fields, including the zippy "I'm Doin' That Thing" and "Go Home and Tell Your Mother." Montgomery, it might be added, came up surprisingly well as a song-and-dance man.

gold digger (Lillian Roth) by masquerading as, literally, the vamp from hell. Not at just any costume ball: at a futuristic blowout on a dirigible, which eventually crashes . . . after which there's a happy ending. It played every bit as incredibly as it sounds, and with songs (by Herbert Stothart, Clifford Grey, Elsie Janis, and Jack King). DeMille called it *Madam Satan*.[7]

As written, *Madam Satan* could have passed for a stage musical. Even the blimp sequence could have been a simple affair, as a similar scene in *Just Imagine* had been. Nor does the first half bode well, its bedroom-farce shenanigans staged so lamely as to indicate that DeMille had no sense of humor whatever. He's so ill-at-ease with songs, so awkward with setting up cues that Johnson's maid (Elsa Petersen) is talking to her one moment and singing to her the next, without graceful elision. But the director's deepest grained affinities eventually took over, and the masquerade ball that forms the second half of *Madam Satan* is one of the great examples of weirdness in American pop cinema: a twilight zone wherein musical comedy meets disaster epic, all designed and costumed (by Adrian) with the farthest out Art Deco affectation. Not until Stanley Kubrick's *Full Metal Jacket* would a film so bluntly change its tone at midpoint. There's music all over that doomed blimp: the party guests sing "The Cat Walk" as, yes, they scamper along catwalks to climb aboard, assisted by chorus girls in cat suits; Roland Young conducts a musical "Girl Auction"; Kay Johnson, in a costume whose décolletage appears to plunge down to her knees, leads the men in an operetta-style apostrophe, "Meet Madame"; and, most famously, a futuristic "Ballet Électrique" passes all description. It would have to be fabulous to redeem that lethal first hour, and it is. And DeMille caps it all with a Zeppelin crash that still impresses—not just the effects themselves, which are quite good, but the details and the way the scene builds and builds. Are there enough parachutes? Will Denny go down with the ship? How does someone wearing outsized pheasant plumage parachute to safety?[8] None of it works because the music is particularly good (it's not) or because DeMille could deal gracefully with musical staging (he couldn't). It's that cocky damn-the-torpedoes DeMille spark that pushes it on. As he does in even his silliest pseudo-historical opuses, he goes for the hard sell with conviction and flair and force, and darned if he doesn't make it work. In 1930 and now, *Madam Satan* may be an aberration, but it is assuredly not a cheat. It delivers on the spectacle, more so than in much of DeMille's work, and has unexpected vigor on the musical end as well.

7. Title courtesy of a 1914 silent that DeMille had remembered; in both cases the less suave "Madam" spelling was used.

8. Answered in order: (1) No, so (2) Denny dives off the Zep just before it plunges into the City Reservoir; and (3) with most of her feathers intact, Lillian Roth parachutes through the roof of a men's Turkish bath, to her and the viewers' delight. Other escapees fare less well: Roland Young lands inside the lion's den at the zoo, and a many-armed Balinese idol touches down on a flock of understandably startled Harlem crapshooters.

No other film could ever be mistaken for *Madam Satan*. Here, Reginald Denny evaluates the relative merits of Lillian Roth and Kay Johnson as Roland Young helps out. (Tyler Brooke, visible just above Denny's extended arm, was later memorable as the composer in *Love Me Tonight*.)

Johnson takes to her vamp songs with unaccustomed dash, and Roth's fleshy impertinence finds far more ease in lewd Trixie than as a debutante in *Honey*.[9] Even Reginald Denny acquits himself as he waltzes Johnson through "All I Know Is You're in My Arms."

Considering the technical logistics and special effects, it's remarkable that DeMille brought *Madam Satan* smoothly through production nine days ahead of schedule. Not cheaply, however: at just under a million dollars, it was Metro's most expensive film of the year and its costliest musical until Lubitsch's *The Merry Widow* in 1934. Because musicals were dead by the time of its release, it was sold on the basis of sex and spectacle, with De-Mille's as the only star name emblazoning marquees. Critics, along with their traditional condescension toward DeMille, were perturbed by its strange mix of genres and styles, and audiences in smaller towns reacted with dazed confusion. It didn't seem to be *about* anything, and its opulent frivolity lacked the more linear comic attractions of *Just Imagine* and *Whoopee!* Unlike them *Madam Satan* turned out to be a major flop, for which

9. Her "Low Down" song early on is particularly zingy—not least because of one cheeky couplet in the chorus: "Bach and Chopin/Can't give me what jazz can." The rhyming is quaint, to put it nicely, yet Roth socks it over.

MGM posted a $400,000 loss. After one more disaster *(The Squaw Man)*, DeMille returned to Paramount and more accustomed material. No more musicals for this director.

The Depression had begun to alter the national mood irretrievably while *Madam Satan* was still in production; by the time it reached theaters it was obsolete, and this type of free-form hallucination would never again be seen on the American screen. One of the distinctive traits of early musicals, in fact, was their tendency to treat the medium as a collage of found objects, jamming the most ordinary conventions alongside some truly lunatic notions. This presented itself, in various incarnations, as *The Great Gabbo*, *Just Imagine*, *Is Everybody Happy?*, and many more. How fitting that *Madam Satan*, the utmost example of the trend, winds up with that well-staged blimp wreck; in one clean sweep this scene now seems to embody the end of the Jazz Age, the collapse of American prosperity, the death throes of early musicals, and, most literally, the flop of this last baroque gasp of twenties frivolity. Cecil B. DeMille's use of metaphor was usually painfully literal and obvious. This one, ironically, he never intended.

CHAPTER 11

The
Cuckoos

Having attained the highest and purest form of development in all silent film, comedy came to be the area most affected by the arrival of sound. Adventures, westerns, romances, and other genres could be recast less drastically, for it was in comedy where silence had resided most unconditionally. The expressively mimetic world molded by Chaplin, Keaton, Harold Lloyd, and their cohorts, in which vaudeville, circus, ballet, and body language commingled and slapstick could rise to the level of poetry, all crashed down in 1929 in a burst of noise and a sea of stage comics and verbal gags. Visual comedy continued and always would, yet changes came fast and dizzying in just what would be effected to make a film audience laugh. Verbal humor was suddenly a blank check, the revered art of silent title-writing vanished, and for some artists the damage was terminal. Others somehow found their own way—Chaplin was powerful enough to remain implacably mute for years, and Lloyd and Stan Laurel were among those forging connections between their art and verbal communication. The upheaval, regardless of its resolution, was immense, and the timeless and universal world of film comedy gave way to something more specific, more beholden to time and place and nationality.[1]

The situation was compounded by the newcomers with stage credentials and, most often, some musical ability. On Broadway and in vaudeville the

---

1. The pacing changed also, in ways detectable and not. As Walter Kerr observed in *The Silent Clowns*, the hand-cranked cameras used to shoot silent comedies could have their speed altered at will, contributing immensely to the desired visual effect of a gag: what, after all, would silent comedy be without a speeded-up camera? In sound-film shooting this was no longer possible, and a uniform camera speed could add dead weight to a snail-paced talkie comedy.

unreal worlds of comedy and music coexisted readily—Broadway entertainment had, in fact, been built on this foundation since the days of Harrigan and Hart. That, and early sound cinema's marked propensity for reckoning everything in musical terms, made film's linking of music and comedy a prearranged conclusion. The transition was uneasy for participants and audiences alike, and as sound comedy was finding its bearings the musical film formed a pro tem battleground upon which stage and cinema performers struggled to determine what types of humor would work with audiences and to what extent music could factor into the equation.

Early-talkie comedy musicals are a ramshackle bunch: Broadway adaptations with stage players, screen originals with film people, crossover titles that aren't quite musicals and aren't quite anything else. Even operetta can be touched upon. What distinguishes them from musical comedy à la *Good News* is the extent to which they depend on a central comic as a driving force, as on Broadway. Until the 1960s the star comic—"top banana" being the eminently appropriate appellation—was a staple in the musical theater, from the Weber and Fields extravaganzas of the 1890s, through Fred Stone, Eddie Cantor, and Bert Lahr, to Jackie Gleason, Phil Silvers, and Zero Mostel. There was Fannie Brice, too, and Beatrice Lillie and Nancy Walker. They weren't "musical performers" on the order of Marilyn Miller or Jack Buchanan, though most of them were proficient in song and dance. Rather, they were clowns whose talents could be uniquely heightened through musical means, either in revue or in an absurd plot that gave full vent to their special silliness. Seldom were their vehicles on Broadway's cutting edge, although Victor Moore did figure memorably in the Gershwins' *Of Thee I Sing* in 1931. More commonly, they were high-grade bread and butter fare, ideal for theater parties and for built-in New York audiences, often with "specialized" cultural humor. Like their more seriously lyrical sisters and brothers, most of the Broadway and vaudeville comics went west in 1929, or, at least, some blocks east to Astoria. A few stayed on, but most ran true to form and returned to the stage after an outing or two. The Marx Brothers bonded with film, musical or not, immediately, yet such master clowns as Bert Lahr took a while to get a sense of movie comedy's different scale. Triple takes to bring a stage audience to tears of laughter could weigh a ton when not properly modulated for the camera.

The cultural aspects of many of these comics figure prominently, for Hollywood comedy from 1929 to mid-1934 did not avoid ethnic diversity. It was not handled in any sensitive "correct" manner, to be sure, but decidedly with more bite and edge than in subsequent years. Much of the diminution had to do with the enforcement of the Production Code, while some was tied to the decline of vaudeville and "dialect" comedy forms. Most homogenization came as a perceived need to cater to the largest common denominator, usually read White Anglo-Saxon Christian. The Eddie Cantor seen in the "Moe the Tailor" sketch in *Glorifying the American Girl* is far more based in Jewish comedic traditions than in any of his later films; that was how, in large part, Broadway knew him. His film work became steadily standardized, and it's both fitting and ironic that this was done at the behest of Sam Goldwyn (né Gelbfisz), whose polished and utterly whitebread productions often seemed to act as attrition for his roots. It's worth noting that Goldwyn later applied the Cantor treatment even more stringently to Danny Kaye, whose anglicization included a cosmetic makeover. But the early years saw ethnic humor in full array, with all the attendant joys and woes of such treatment, and this carried forth into the musicals in which these comics appeared. The various brands of humor of these performers have been and ever will be discussed in other quarters and other books. (Count the number of books on the Marxes alone.) It's the music, and the various ways in which the comics channelled their personas into it, which belongs to this chapter. While commonly overlooked as a part of the total package, it often served as the bridge upon which comedy performers moved from stage to film, or from silence to sound, and it frequently amplified comedic content and timing in ways in which straight verbal or visual comedy could not.

Cantor is once more the touchstone here, for while his films were more out-and-out musicals than most of the others' he spans every aspect of the formula. Cantor was the essence of all-round top banana. His persona was such that he could—with stretching and suitable digression—participate in a plot; he had jokes and asides to spare; his ethnic references managed to span both Jewish humor and blackface, as Jolson's did; he was sufficiently limber to do sight gags; his looks ("Banjo Eyes") and affect (those jittery clapping hands) could produce instantaneous recognition and many imitators; and his singing and dancing both extended beyond the proficient to the uniquely treasurable. All this came to play for the first time on film in *Whoopee!*, and his performance takes to an extreme what earlier comedians did or attempted to do in musical cinema. Cantor's plots were compelled to find the most casual excuse for an uptempo ballad, usually in blackface. *Whoopee!*'s "My Baby Just Cares for Me" comes, basically, out of nowhere, in such fashion to make the maid's song in *Madam Satan* sound eminently logical. Yet it played. The smash of *Whoopee!* owed less to Ziegfeld showgirls or Technicolor than it did to Cantor fighting off Ethel Shutta's advances or going on about his surgical scars or suddenly bursting into a unrelated song about a nonexistent "baby."

A number of the stage performers who could sidle into musical mode first implied the possibilities in short subjects. For Cantor, Joe E. Brown, Bert Lahr, George Burns and Gracie Allen, plus Milton Berle and Bob Hope and Danny Kaye later on, the shorts were a proving ground and a screen test. Others took an immediate plunge into features, as demonstrated most successfully by the Marx Brothers in *The Cocoanuts*. Here at very least was a demonstration of how funny Broadway clowns could be while busily laying waste to a tired musical comedy plot. No one was deluded into thinking that the film's vast success had anything to do with Mary Eaton or even Irving Berlin; it was the Marxes who brought in the customers and demonstrated the potential of audibly filmed comedy. Not at all surprisingly, the brothers made a return trip to Astoria a year later for the film version of *Animal Crackers*, the show in which they had been appearing at night while shooting *Cocoanuts*. Their second film was an even bigger hit, in fact Paramount's top grosser of 1930, replenishing the coffers after such disappointments as *Glorifying the American Girl* and *The Vagabond King*. In an increasingly grim year, it was just what audiences wanted—one New York showing clocked in 388 laughs.

Indifferently directed by Victor Heerman and edited with rudimentary incompetence, *Animal Crackers* is hemmed in every bit as much as its predecessor by plotting and stagebound treatment. With most of the score cut, its status as a musical is tenuous. Yet the archaic ensembles of *Cocoanuts* are in truth not too greatly missed here, and the laughter usually drowns out the creaks and moans of the laborious art-theft plot and the textured theatricality—as when, most conspicuously, a thunderstorm rolls in at one point and, sure enough, a stagehand rattles a sheet of tin somewhere behind the set. Viewing *Animal Crackers* alongside *Cocoanuts* gives the false impression that cinematic technique, at least by Astoria standards, had not advanced appreciably in the fifteen months separating the two films. What had changed, and for the better, was the Marxes' and Margaret Dumont's ease before the camera. Groucho, as Captain Horatio Spaulding, is in full charge, running on about shooting an elephant in his pajamas and all the rest. In this patently artificial environment the brothers thrive, Groucho furnishing his own theatricality by riffing in "asides" à la O'Neill's *Strange Interlude*.[2] And the subsidiary romantic plot with Lillian Roth and Hal Thompson fits in better, since Roth's vivacity matches up with the brothers more genially than Mary Eaton's doll-like hauteur. The musical action, skimped as it is, gives the Marxes far more scope and opportunity. "Hooray for Captain Spaulding" is to their canon as the Triumphal Scene from *Aïda* is to Verdi's, and small wonder that it became Groucho's signature. His "Hello, I must be going" verse distills Marxian logic better than any book-length discourse.[3] For years *Animal Crackers* was the least-seen Marx pic-

2. A close listen to Groucho's stream-of-consciousness ruminations also uncovers a movie in-joke: a totally nonlinear reference to *"The Trial of Mary Dugan*, with sound!"

3. It will be noticed in the song that one line in an exchange between Groucho and Margaret Dumont seems to be spliced out. This was done, alas, by order of the Breen Office—successor to the Hays Office—when *Animal Crackers* was rereleased. Dumont exults, "He is the only white man/Who's covered every acre," after which the censor cut Groucho's leering retort, "I think I'll try to make her!" Several other lines were cut as well.

ture; reissued theatrically in the mid-1970s, it proved funnier than any number of that decade's comedies. It also reinforced some viewers' conceptions of the primitive nature of early movie musicals. The truth is, of course, that *Animal Crackers* is no more typical of early musical cinema than it was, on Broadway, a standard-issue musical comedy. Like the Marx Brothers themselves, comparisons are useless.

Paramount, the Marxes' first haven in the movie industry, was Hollywood's comedy center for the first half of the 1930s, and its most distinctive output swung wildly between two poles. On the one hand there were the Marxes and their cohorts, cultivating a comedy aesthetic that amounted virtually to institutionalized anarchy. Logic and social strictures were defiled with breathtaking diffidence, with music and song often serving as the final iconoclastic garnish. At the other extreme was the work of Ernst Lubitsch and his imitators, all sly nuance and Continental flair. Maurice Chevalier, uncrowned ruler of this province, shuttled between light operetta and more straightforward comedies with music during his Paramount tenure. Seldom has a film performer hoisted insouciant charm to this level. Chevalier's rapport with audiences was the stuff of myth: in nearly all his Paramount films he will address the camera—therefore the spectator—in a direct way few other performers could emulate, much less carry off. His best films were the operettas for Lubitsch and Rouben Mamoulian, yet the comedies also succeeded for a while. The first of them, *The Big Pond* (1930), was especially popular. Adapted from a Broadway comedy, this tale of assimilation and chewing-gum-factory intrigue had originally been planned to spotlight the quite different talents of Charlie Ruggles. When Paramount desired a more informal follow-up to the posh *Love Parade*, it was quickly retooled (by Preston Sturges, among others) to allow for Chevalier and songs. The latter provided Chevalier with one of his exponential hits, "You Brought a New Kind of Love to Me" (a.k.a. "If the Nightingales Could Sing Like You"). As with other overused theme songs it was reprised endlessly throughout *The Big Pond*, once as a duet for Chevalier and his elegant costar Claudette Colbert, and straightaway joined "Louise" in the repertory of Chevalier mimics, most memorably by the Marx Brothers in *Monkey Business* (1931).[4]

Another Paramount comedy-music combo, the first after *The Cocoanuts*, was a far cry—from taste, certainly, and even more from later accepted forms of humor. A comic duo calling itself "The Two Black Crows" would, by definition, be a temporal phenomenon, steeped in stereotypes long since discredited. George Moran and Charles E. Mack were vaudeville

4. Given *The Big Pond*'s plot—an immigrant making good in America—it's ironic that Chevalier's ostensibly all-American costar was almost as French as he. Colbert, who had lived in the U.S. since age eight, spoke French fluently and proved it by appearing with Chevalier in *La Grande Mare*, the French-language version of *The Big Pond*.

stars who had crossed over to Broadway revues, radio, and—most note-worthy at the time—a successful batch of phonograph records. Their rou-tines, obviously an offshoot of the minstrel tradition, contained enough lazy drawling to sink a battleship, and this type of humor was still viable for many white Americans. (*Variety* once observed that the team's popularity extended to some black audiences as well.) After many decades, the rea-sons for their success may seem mysterious. In other practitioners of racially insensitive humor there can often be divined reasons for success, compre-hension if not acceptance or appreciation. Not so with Moran and Mack; seen and heard today, they are not broad enough to be outrageous, just two men with minstrel makeup telling stories. The stereotypes, as obvious and unseemly as could be, just lie there—blackface for its own sake, with-out reference to vitality or humor, much less humanity. Yet the perceived national taste in early 1929 was another matter entirely, and it was felt that Moran and Mack rated a feature. Shot under the title *Backstage Blues*, it was obviously designed to sing and dance, though since the Moran-Mack oeuvre did not encompass such talents the production numbers were frag-mentary and unnecessary, precisely antithetical to a reasoned concept of comic musical. The film, finally titled *Why Bring That Up?* after one of the team's catchphrases, compounded the offense by deriving its plot from the mammy stories—a successful blackface pair is split asunder by a worthless vamp (Evelyn Brent), and a full quota of remorse is followed by a ridicu-lous finale in which Mack rouses Moran from a coma by reciting lines from one of their routines. (Their dramatic power in this and other scenes, it should be stated, was on the same level as the hilarity of their comic mo-ments.) Except for a few sharply realized glimpses of backstage bustle, director George Abbott was sadly at sea with this mess, which is virtually incompatible with his work as Broadway's most respected pro. With the team's popularity, *Why Bring That Up?* was a major success, even breaking attendance records in some cities, and perhaps this heightened attention was the cause of the pair's falling-out. Mack returned to Paramount in 1930 with a new Moran (Bert Swor) for *Anybody's War*, neither a musical nor (in effect) a comedy. Later on the original Moran returned for the team's final work—a few short subjects, a final abominable feature (Mack Sennett's *Hypnotized* in 1932), and, ultimately, oblivion.

Apart from the issue of social irresponsibility, *Why Bring That Up?* was exactly the wrong type of comedy musical, a film thrice divided against itself. Perhaps it made sense to cast Moran and Mack as themselves, white actors who don the cork for their onstage routines. And the backstage ma-nia of mid-1929 was so hard to resist that some music was likely inevitable. But to make the music and the comedy mutually exclusive, and employ a melodramatic plot as the unifying thread, was totally self-defeating. In *Ani-mal Crackers*, if not in *The Cocoanuts*, the Marxes show how comedians and music may illuminate each other; in *Why Bring That Up?*, everything sticks out like a sore thumb. It's worth noting that one of the reasons for the decline of The Two Black Crows was the meteoric ascension, late in 1929, of *The Amos 'n' Andy Show* on CBS Radio. The comedy of Freeman Gosden and Charles Correll was sharper and faster than Moran and Mack, and their supporting characters (Kingfish, Madame Queen, et al.) offered support worthy of Restoration comedy. Movie attendance began taking a conspicuous dive on nights when the program was on and, fittingly, Radio Pictures was the studio that decided to bridge the gap, paying Gosden and Correll a mammoth $250,000 plus percentage to take the movie plunge. Originally their film was planned as a musical, with Bert Kalmar and Harry Ruby providing songs and script on the order of their earlier Broadway success, *Animal Crackers*. The result was *Check and Double Check* (also taken from a catchphrase), released in the autumn of 1930 with even less music than the film version of *Animal Crackers*. Little remained of the original musical conception except a few quick shots of Duke Ellington's orchestra, woefully wasted, plus one evergreen song, "Three Little Words." That *Check and Double Check* was a dolefully unfunny farrago was almost beside the point; it rapidly became the highest grossing film of the year—a freak hit that opened everywhere to immense crowds, then tapered off precipitously after the fans had their fill.

Another team featured by Radio, Bert Wheeler and Robert Woolsey, were in some ways the converse of Amos 'n' Andy and The Two Black Crows. They had been paired, somewhat synthetically, to fit into the overall schema of Ziegfeld's *Rio Rita*, and the teaming worked well enough to hold through a successful film career until Woolsey's death in 1938. No social or ethnic underpinnings in operation here, merely two clowns—one sly, one naif, both vastly dependent on their writers. Their material was preposterously uneven, and watching them today with an audience is an illuminating experience. Once in a while there'll be a genuinely funny gag or bit of physical comedy, followed by a procession of puns and routines so deficient as to rate not even a groan. Audiences have been known to sit in total silence, and critics during the pair's glory years often felt the same way. Box office response was another matter, and after the success of *Rio Rita* it was preordained that Radio would give them their own showcase. Wheeler's musical abilities had been well presented in *Rio Rita*, and the team's first starring film turned out to be one of the few full-scale comedy musicals of the time. Ultimately titled *The Cuckoos*, it underwent a peculiar odyssey that encompassed the musical subgenres of revue, Broadway adaptation, and operetta. In the revue-conscious days of mid-1929 Radio Pictures engaged Bert Kalmar and Harry Ruby to create *Radio Revels*, to be set in a radio station and feature most of the studio's talent plus a host of stars connected with the parent company RCA. Around the time that *Show of Shows* put revues at a disadvantage, Radio began to alter its plans; the broadcast idea was laid to rest, and Kalmar and Ruby adapted their show *The Ramblers* for screen use. On Broadway in 1928 it had been a disappointment, with a Ruritanian setting and operetta doings—Gypsies, kidnappings, etc.—blending somewhat uneasily with Kalmar and Ruby's vernacular style and uncomplicatedly nice songs. For film use they toned down some of the fantasy, dropped songs and added new ones (including the endearingly simple "I Love You So Much"), and built up the comedy roles for Wheeler and Woolsey. Still titled *Radio Revels*, it was put into production in early 1930 under the direction of Paul Sloane, working on far less literal fare than *Hearts in Dixie* and far more at ease with the romantic and melodramatic portions of the script. To help out with the comedy Radio engaged Roscoe Arbuckle—the same "Fatty" whose career as a top silent clown had ended brusquely in a hail of scandal and false charges. When he could get work as a director, he used the ironic pseudonym William B. Goodrich, a twist on "Will B. Good," though for *The Cuckoos* he received no credit at all. Arbuckle's influence on *The Cuckoos* probably connects with the upturn in the number of visual gags given to Wheeler and Woolsey. The highlighting of their roles, in the title as well as in the script, enforces the concept of *The Cuckoos* as a comedy musical, though technically it remained a filmed Broadway show. Most of the traditional components were there, including ensemble dances, stagebound sets, romance set to music ("All Alone Monday"), and Technicolor sequences. At first glance none of this meshes especially well with the increased accent on comedy, as provided by Wheeler, Woolsey, and their perennial foil Dorothy Lee. Yet the note of giddy artifice is somehow sustained, unto Lee hectically "Dancing the Devil Away" in one color sequence, and a lunatic Gilbert-and-Sullivanish "farewell" ensemble shot under a brilliantly green Technicolor sky. Musical as it indisputably is, *The Cuckoos* was advertised to emphasize comedy and the fact that it was not a revue, the studio perhaps being worried about the former *Radio Revels* tag. The comedy audience did turn out in force, and *The Cuckoos* was a sizable hit. So was Wheeler and Woolsey's next vehicle after supporting Bebe Daniels in *Dixiana*. *Half Shot at Sunrise* was far more comedy than musical, with a World War background, yet its best moments were once again musical, including a ballet trio for Woolsey, the seductive Leni Stengel, and a lawn sprinkler. After that, the pair followed Hollywood's lead and generally stayed away from music for several years.

A far rougher Broadway team, Olsen and Johnson, maintained an off-and-on affiliation with film. Unapologetic veterans of the school of hard knocks, they were the spiritual fathers of Abbott and Costello, and best known for their anarchic Broadway vaudeville ("revue" is too formal for these two) *Hellzapoppin'*. Though their major film work came later, Ole

Olsen (taller, slightly more savvy) and Chick Johnson (rounder and dumber) were present for the end of the first musical rush in 1930. Elmer Rice's comedy-drama *See Naples and Die* somehow became the basis for an unsavory concoction from Warner Bros. with the hopefully naughty title *Oh Sailor Behave!* Charles King, his MGM career winding down, played the romantic lead, with Broadway singer Irene Delroy in the role created in the play by Claudette Colbert. Olsen and Johnson were shoehorned in along with five undistinguished songs, and under any title audiences saw Naples and died. This was one of Warner's least successful musicals of 1930, though some unfamiliar with the team's onstage shtick found them moderately amusing. Warners next cast them in another musical show, this time a bona fide Broadway extravaganza, Cole Porter's *Fifty Million Frenchmen*. For more on this peculiar project, see Chapter Fourteen.

Film's best-loved comedy team touched on musical matters only sporadically. Laurel and Hardy's first two sound features, *The Hollywood Revue* and *The Rogue Song*, were extremely musical, and "the boys'" participation in both was specifically intended as non-musical extenuation. While this remained consistent later on, through *The Devil's Brother*, *Babes in Toyland*, and *The Bohemian Girl*, their first starring feature shows how nicely music could fit into Laurel and Hardy's sunnily unbalanced world. *Pardon Us* (1931), a parody of MGM's prison drama *The Big House*, was a short subject that somehow grew to feature length. The padding showed most conspicuously in an interlude when the pair go on the lam, don blackface, and find work on a plantation. This makes no particular sense even by this team's standards, nor does the song they contribute at this point. "Lazy Moon," a nearly forgotten ballad from 1903, is sung by Hardy in a sweet high tenor, and danced by Laurel with deftly flat-footed breeziness. There's nothing else like it in the team's work until several wonderful moments in *Way Out West* six years later, and it distills much that is gentle and lovable about Laurel and Hardy.

Most of the solo comedians in early talkies were holdovers from the silents, and with a few exceptions it took some years for genuine dialogue humor—a comic performer interacting with a supporting cast instead of a partner—to settle in as the preferred mode of film comedy. Prior to that, in this period of tumult in film and in the nation, El Brendel was briefly considered the most popular comedian in pictures. What this says about audience inclinations in 1930 is debatable—part of his popularity was undoubtedly due to a lack of competitors, at least in features. Joe E. Brown and Eddie Cantor were not yet established, and comedy teams and formerly silent clowns making the changeover were essentially in another category. So there was Brendel, with his Scandinavianisms and general air of inept buoyancy, attracting attention in *Sunny Side Up* and starring in *Just Imagine* as well as such forgotten musicals as *The Golden Calf* and *The Big*

Party. His usual contribution would be a spoof dance, often joined to a hybrid hayseed-Nordic ballad. Little of this holds up any better than his comedy routines, although his lewd writhing to "I Feel a Certain Feeling Coming On" in *Movietone Follies of 1930* rates a passing frisson.

More viable musical contributions from solo comics sometimes came from unexpected sources. Buster Keaton, for example. His silence a fortress against a burdensome universe, this most impassive of clowns seemed the utter antithesis of audibility. He had, however, traded in his cherished independence for an MGM contract just before sound came, an act he later viewed as the worst mistake of his life. The Metro mentality was a indifferent to Keaton's genius as it was unsympathetic to his personal problems, and after a good start there he descended quickly, ultimately enduring the ignominy of an imposed teaming with Jimmy Durante. On the way down he was placed oddly and not unsuccessfully into musical mode. His dance in *The Hollywood Revue* had been the bridge on which he shifted gears; his full entrance into talkies came some months later with *Free and Easy* (1930). This was another entry in the Hollywood-takes-a-tuneful-look-at-itself genre, with Keaton as a boob named Elmer Butz who stumbles into movies and becomes a star while losing Anita Page to matinee idol Robert Montgomery. If nothing else *Free and Easy* demonstrated that sound per se need not defeat a great mute clown. Keaton's sandpaper baritone sounded like it could belong only to this elegant-featured melancholy stoic, yet the uses to which the voice was put were questionable.[5] While *Free and Easy* was not as ill suited as his later MGM films, it was clearly a comedown. The problem lay partly in craftsmanship; despite some beautifully timed moments there is an overall feeling of ragged routine all too common after the first anxious months of sound. Particularly in editing and continuity, Hollywood production in general fell prey to sloppiness, the drive to do it taking precedence over the capability for more polish. More serious, and indicative of Keaton's problems with a large studio, is the way in which *Free and Easy* misunderstands and finally mangles his screen image. Instead of the resolute unsentimentality of *The Navigator* or *The General* he's turned into an object of pity, scoring public triumph and private heartbreak. It's almost a replay of *Glorifying the American Girl*, and it works just about as well. At the very end Keaton literally becomes Pagliacci, his clown makeup the thinnest veneer over a broken heart. Seeing a great artist so debased is enough to make one turn away from the screen in embarrassment.

Nevertheless, *Free and Easy* has more interest than most comedy musicals. Some of it is pure history: there are copious glimpses of life on the

---

5. Foreign audiences got to hear him also, for there was a Spanish version of *Free and Easy* with (except for him) an alternate cast. He spoke his lines phonetically, with somewhat uneasy charm.

MGM lot, vintage December 1929, with cameo appearances (DeMille, William Haines, Jackie Coogan) and some credible on-set views of camera blimps and live orchestras accompanying musical numbers. While early-talkie Hollywood is perhaps too glaring a setting for Keaton (he worked better in the surreal silent-movie-within-a-movie scenes in *Sherlock Jr.*), he copes well with such scenes as Elmer's first film appearance, a comprimario role with one line—"The queen has swooned"—that he mispronounces for take after take, and his strange screen test, in which he is pummelled by a succession of large women. Stranger still are the musical numbers, eccentric to the point of parody. Montgomery, with a strangulated dubbed tenor, is seen in several scenes of an absurd Viennese operetta, and the production number that makes Elmer a star is a bewildering mix of good and bad things, the latter including some of the worst chorus dancing this side of *The Great Gabbo*. Yet Keaton shines—and his casting in a musical starts to make sense—in two extended sequences. A comic ballet with the massively indomitable Trixie Friganza is a small gem of misbegotten grace and knockabout lyricism, and Keaton's rendition of the title song is one of the authentic delights of the era—he sings and dances like a veteran and bounces about in a marionette bit with acrobatic dexterity. No, it's not quintessential or perhaps even good Keaton. But it is, in some ways, quality movie musical. Even when on unfamiliar and potentially unwelcome turf, Keaton was pro enough to extend himself, find the means to connect with the music, and make it work. While not the smash he later claimed, *Free and Easy* was enough of a success to prove his viability in talkies, at least for a while. Likewise *Doughboys*, which followed several months later. This time Keaton served mainly as a comedian, leaving the infrequent musical sequences to others.

Comparatively few of the leading comics in the late silent era were women, and none had reached the level of a Chaplin or Keaton. Colleen Moore and Bebe Daniels were regarded less as comic players than all-round talents, a perceived versatility which also made their transition to musicals more plausible. Constance Talmadge, perhaps the most popular woman in silent comedy, never made a sound film after her *Gold Diggers of Broadway* audition. The situation seemed briefly to change as sound came in, when several leading comic women were permitted feature-length showcases. Despite the burden of trite plotting in *My Man*, Fannie Brice had indicated some of the possibilities, and others followed. One early arrival was Charlotte Greenwood. The Broadway veteran with the mile-long legs and astronomically high kicks had appeared in a few silents as well as a stream of Broadway comedies, revues and musicals. In addition to dance skills she had a ringing soprano and a unique ability to project vigorous common sense and pixilated whimsy simultaneously. In 1929 Warners filmed her in one of her musical stage successes, *So Long Letty*, which was transferred onto the screen as a bedroom farce with a handful of incidental songs and few opportunities for Greenwoodian acrobatics. In voice and manner she was a natural for talkies, albeit too eccentric to play leading roles when rules of age and category were reinstated after the early years of sound. Her prime movie fame came years later, when she served long and well as one of the few non-interchangeable constituents in the 1940s Fox musicals. Winnie Lightner, a musical comic of vastly dissimilar stripe, suffered much the same fate as Greenwood, without the later-career follow-up. After *Gold Diggers of Broadway* her one chance to carry a big comedy musical came in mid-1930 with Warners' *The Life of the Party*. This was intended as big-scale foolishness, with Lightner supported by an expansive Technicolor production, romantic leads from the musical stage (Jack Whiting and Irene Delroy), strong comic support (Charles Butterworth and Charles Judels), tailor-made songs, even a fashion show. But Warners, fearful of the dwindling interest in musicals, cut some of the music during production and most of the remainder afterward. Lightner was left with only one song—appropriately named "Poison Ivy"—and *The Life of the Party* played out as a raucous gold-digger farce that occasionally paused to cue in songs that never came. Yet Lightner lived up to her billing as "The Princess of Pep" and made it one of Warner's few outright successes in the fall of 1930.

In a more conventional heroine mode there was Marion Davies, who—had she been more in control of her career—might have flourished as one of comedy's elite. Her primary gifts, Hearst's intentions to the contrary, had always been as a laugh-getter. She had good timing, she was a fine mimic, and the sense of fun she brought to her personal life also translated into her performances. When she was permitted to flex her comedic muscles in her later silents—*Tillie the Toiler, The Patsy, Show People*—the results were first class. *Marianne* had also showed this side of Davies, though its World War plot and some dramatic conflict later on mitigated against the effect. Her second full talkie, *Not So Dumb*, showed her well in command of sound comedy, and after a few attempts at *The Five O'Clock Girl* and *Rosalie* she extended her forte into a semimusical context with Harry Beaumont's *The Florodora Girl*. One of the Broadway stage's earlier examples of a smash British import, *Florodora* was also one of the first examples of a long run achieved on the strength of one hit song—the double sextet "Tell Me Pretty Maiden." By the late '20s the show's very name was sufficient to summon forth a whole era, and Florodora sequences had been used in *My Man, Show of Shows*, and *It's a Great Life*. *The Florodora Girl*, originally titled *The Gay Nineties*, sounds similar to the nostalgia-drenched extravaganzas of the 1940s, yet was actually less a musical than a light comedy with incidental songs that grew too serious in its later reels. Except for a pretty Technicolor finale re-creating the sextet, the music was present less for its own sake than to provide atmospheric upholstery. The costumes and romance typified Hearst's view of Davies as a sentimental heroine, yet she was also permitted to participate in some lighthearted comedy. As one of the legendary sextet pursued by millionaire Lawrence Gray, Davies radiated impish sparkle and all-around good cheer and also, to quote Louella Parsons, never looked lovelier. With a stronger script or a firmer musical setting she might have scored decisively. However, script problems and Hearstian meddling sent *The Florodora Girl* over schedule and budget, and its grosses were curtailed when the estate of *Florodora* composer Leslie Stuart sued MGM for infringement of copyright, after which many exhibitors canceled their bookings. The film's ultimate failure marked the start of Davies's decline, and her performances soon became increasingly desperate—not so much attempts at acting as efforts to mollify her powerful and stubborn protector.

By the early fall of 1930 it was clear that musicals of all kinds were not succeeding, and several Broadway clowns who arrived onscreen late in the year would encounter various degrees of demusicalization. Joe E. Brown followed his success in *Hold Everything* with Mervyn Leroy's *Top Speed*, from a moderate Broadway success of the year before. With most of its Kalmar-Ruby score cut it became far more a comedy vehicle than the play had been, and Brown's career as Warner Bros.' head funnyman was cemented for a number of years. A 1928 Broadway hit, *Rain or Shine*, had been carried energetically by Joe Cook, whose versatility caused him to be dubbed "The One-Man Vaudeville." Cook repeated his stage role two years later in a straight comedy version of *Rain or Shine* directed by the emerging Frank Capra. The show's undistinguished score was completely excised, reportedly to Capra's relief. Song cues and musical performances mattered far less to him than the aspects of can-do Americana that *Rain or Shine* shares with much of his later work.

Another much-loved Broadway clown was Ed Wynn, The Perfect Fool—so he was billed, and so went the title of one of his biggest shows. He had puttered across the screen to minimal effect in some silents: a mute Ed Wynn worked about as well on the screen as a mute Caruso had, and with a comparable lack of success. For the talking screen Wynn was engaged by Paramount to appear in a toned-down reworking of his 1927 hit *Manhattan Mary*. DeSylva, Brown, and Henderson's score was almost entirely cut (one song remained, plus two by other hands), and with a less musical title, *Follow the Leader*, the film showcased Wynn's flubdub eccentricity and trademarked procession of zany inventions. Until he gave several outstanding dramatic performances late in life, Wynn was not a performer to integrate into any kind of plot, even as silly a one as *Follow the Leader*.[6] So the

6. He shot *Follow the Leader* in the daytime while starring in Ziegfeld's *Simple Simon* on Broadway at night. Chances are he may not have known from one show to the next what role he was playing . . . not that it mattered.

film stopped cold on numerous occasions to allow him to dither, honk, and go through his routines. Seen today, *Follow the Leader*, with its spartan made-in-Astoria technique, resembles outtakes from a Wynn *Colgate Comedy Hour* television appearance of the 1950s—same material, same flat visuals, same Wynn. When he's not onscreen the show is monopolized by Lou Holtz, a charter member of the Harry Green–Benny Rubin school of inflection. Between these two, a pair of young women in the cast are kept mostly in abeyance—Ginger Rogers, as the ingenue, and Ethel Merman, making her feature debut in a small role. Except for Merman's blared rendition of "Satan's Holiday," there's little to be seen of their later personalities, although their appearances in *Follow the Leader* rates a historical note: when shooting at Astoria (Merman's hometown) concluded, they both went straight into the Gershwins' *Girl Crazy*. Ed Wynn also went back to Broadway and would not have a successful film for nearly thirty years.

A worse fate greeted the most individual of female comics . . . literally a lady clown, given her marriage to Sir Robert Peel. Beatrice Lillie was such an original that it's surprising that the American film industry gave her several chances at this time. She was an established name on Broadway and in London, but this was not comedy as Winnie Lightner practiced it. Lillie's art saw comedy as an elegantly contained madness: straight-faced, cool, campily decorous long before anyone knew what camp was. The fairies at the bottom of her garden were far too subtly delineated to appeal to the wider span of American filmgoers, and her litigious clash with Warner Bros. could have been predicted. A happier alliance seemed imminent when she signed with Fox, who announced a Lillie-headlined revue. When that came to naught she was put in a full-fledged comic musical, *Are You There?* With Lady Peel center ring as Shirley Travis, London private detective extraordinaire, who journeys to a country manor to unravel a vaguely nefarious plot, it was conceived as a Lillie circus, with an amiably disconnected storyline and the opportunity for various disguises and uniquely Lillie situations. It sounds like, conservatively speaking, a hoot, and perhaps in some ways it was; yet the fey stylization of Lillie's insanity was badly at odds with the painfully literal hominess prevalent in Fox musicals, and the offhand direction of Hamilton MacFadden was not the technique to bridge the gap. When assembled, *Are You There?* resembled a messy cross between *Animal Crackers* (Lillie has a Captain Spaulding-like grand entrance) and a standard El Brendel outing, punctuated by bizarre production numbers and a general air of futility. Fox kept it on the shelf for some months, then cut out half the music. A few test showings drew a response of utter perplexity, such as the comment in *Motion Picture News* that "the average audience won't know whether they went supersubtle on this, or just muffed the works. It's supposed to be funny . . . but between preparation and the cutting room something missed fire and the results show it." Finally, and

Bea in clover: Lady Peel inciting the hunting chorus in *Are You There?*

contrary to some reports, Fox released *Are You There?* in Lillie's native country (Canada), in her adopted country (England), and at last very briefly to a number of American theaters, where it elicited the most meager response imaginable.

Not until its "rediscovery" nearly forty years later could *Are You There?* draw anything like a lucid reaction from a reasonable audience, and not surprisingly opinions varied wildly.[7] Some saw it as a reclaimed gem, an ideal habitat for the Lillie carnival; others, particularly those not disposed toward 1930 moviemaking in general, found it a misfire. Perhaps it's most rationally viewed as something in between—an interesting try with some amusing moments that doesn't and can't come off. More importantly, it's a signal example and an extreme case of an early sound film attempting to come to terms with a unique clown in a musical context. That the attempt ultimately fails is due to the same factor that stunted a number of potentially good early musicals: none of the creative personnel could come up with a cohesive production concept, let alone one allotting free rein to Beatrice Lillie's composed eccentricity. Yet for everything that goes wrong

7. Part of the wildness came from Lillie herself, when she appeared at a Museum of Modern Art screening early in the 1970s to rather scandalous effect. See Kenneth Anger's *Hollywood Babylon II* for details.

there's at least the willingness to try for something off center. Had just one other person on the project had Lillie's gifts or proclivities toward stylish zaniness, the film would have coalesced better, even if very few audiences in 1930 could have appreciated it. As it is, both the tone and Lillie's efforts to connect with the script and the audience vary from moment to moment. Skittering through an assortment of disguises and situations, she appears variously as a Confucian sage, the terminally aristocratic Lady Diana Drummond, and a rowdy Cockney nurse who wreaks havoc upon the lusciously venal Olga Baclanova.[8] Yet even in the slapstick moments that occasionally arise, Lillie seems distanced from the proceedings beyond her usual air of containment, apparently telegraphing the awareness that the material is unworthy of her. The musical sequences that remain are of little help. The opening, "Lady Detectives," with its constantly changing sets and musical style, obviously had some time and money lavished on it, yet its attempts at chichi drollery send off misfires in every direction. Likewise the climactic "Bagdad Daddies," in which Lillie is sent into flight, Peter Pan-like, for no good reason. Only "Queen of the Hunt Am I" exhibits anything like vintage Bea. Following a fox hunt that looks toward both *Love Me Tonight* and *Auntie Mame*, Lillie extols herself in mock-operetta style, complete with choral refrain and roulades. For just a couple of minutes we can glimpse the nature of her talent, and what kind of film *Are You There?* might have been.

In its chaotic assault on conflicted comedic styles, *Are You There?* could only fit in an age that also spawned *Madam Satan* and *The Great Gabbo*. A few years later, as times changed, Paramount brought the comedy musical to a summit: *Million Dollar Legs, Duck Soup, International House,* the early Mae West pictures. Nor would such work ever be entirely absent from film for several decades afterward; later conspicuous practitioners included the Ritz Brothers, Bob Hope in and out of the "Road" pictures, Martha Raye, hayseed prima donna Judy Canova, Danny Kaye, Donald O'Connor, and, in a final sensational heyday in the 1950s, Dean Martin and Jerry Lewis. In most cases, comedy and music were not permitted a facile coexistence. Musical performers in comedies were brought in as "specialty" artists or part of a more serious romantic plot, and comedians were around solely for laughs. The days when Groucho Marx could ratify his comic might with "Hooray for Captain Spaulding" or Buster Keaton would lead a chorus through "Free and Easy" were mostly extinct. Genres began to reaffirm their boundaries without the maniacal crossover potential of the first two years of sound. It was a more orderly, situation this way and probably inevitable. And, yes, the films often remained funny.

8. It must be admitted that the contrast between Lillie's starchy Cockney and Baclanova's sensual Slav offers a few chuckles, and perhaps some gratitude that early musical comedy could occasionally get this strange.

CHAPTER 12

Of Viennese Nights and Golden Dawns

Russia—the waning days of the tsars. (*Chorus*—"Prayer," *after Tchaikovsky*) Chafing against imperial oppression, the beautiful peasant Anuita, known as The Flame (Bernice Claire), evades the Cossack troops of handsome Prince Volodya (Alexander Gray) and incites the populace to revolution by lifting her voice in the militant "Song of the Flame." Fellow revolutionary Konstantin (Noah Beery) eyes Anuita with increasing lust, provoking jealousy in his lover Natasha (Alice Gentle). Nicholas II is promptly overthrown, the national fervor—exacerbated by Natasha's rousing "Liberty Song"—simmers, and Prince Volodya longs for the old days ("Petrograd"). Disenchanted with Konstantin's brutal treatment of the populace and his lustful overtures (*reprise:* "Song of the Flame"), Anuita returns to her own Polish village, where the sprightly Grusha (Inez Courtney) sings the gay "The Goose Hangs High" in celebration of the Harvest Festival. Volodya decamps to the same village, and he and Anuita cast aside their political differences to fall in love (*duet:* "When Love Calls"). Konstantin, meanwhile, revels in his new-found power and in the joys of vodka ("One Little Drink"), ceasing his carousing long enough to arrest Volodya. The prince, his execution imminent, sings the "Cossack Love Song." Distraught, Anuita formulates a plan to buy his freedom by offering herself to Konstantin. Natasha is both enraged (*reprise:* "Liberty Song") and embittered ("Passing Fancy"). When Anuita's ruse is discovered she is thrown into prison (*reprise:* "Song of the Flame"); Volodya disguises himself and attempts to free her, but is captured and jailed (*duet reprise:* "Cossack Love Song"). Before they can be executed, Natasha realizes that nothing will be gained through this carnage and has Konstantin arrested by his troops (*reprise:* "Liberty Song"). Offered a final request as he is led to his execution, he asks again for "One Little Drink." Politically redeemed, personally crushed, Natasha

278

decides to "Wander Away," and the newly freed Anuita and Volodya celebrate as the chorus joyfully reprises "The Goose Hangs High."

All this in seventy-one crowded Technicolor minutes. Such is *Song of the Flame,* adapted from a 1925 Broadway operetta and released by First National in May 1930. It was neither the best nor worst of Hollywood's early operettas, the most or least successful, nor, incredibly, the most absurd.[1] It was, however, the most densely packed, musically and theatrically, thus rendering even more inane its occasional references to politics and history. As such, it epitomizes Hollywood's early attempts to harness operetta—that most exotic and daunting stepcousin of musical comedy.

The high profile operetta assumed in the early days of sound has no sustained parallel in American film history. In 1930 operettas seemed to be everywhere, with blossom-scented (or, as above, borscht-flavored) passions surging in a vehement and incrementally unwelcome tide across the American screen. There is nothing else in film history to resemble the florid pomp and stiffly observed conventions of these movies, and the excesses and artifice of the worst of them—*Golden Dawn* and *Lottery Bride*—transcend comprehension. Somehow they manage to be alien to both film and stage, belonging instead to some bizarre stylized Ruritania where people are replaced by lyrical automatons, conflicts give rise to rhapsodic outbursts, and choruses chime in as if by rote. This could never comprise a serviceable aesthetic for an American mass audience, but for a time producers left such considerations unaddressed. The saga of operettas in 1929–30 is as grandiose and ultimately absurd as any plot rejected by Rudolf Friml or Sigmund Romberg. And for all the moments of ennui and lunacy, there was contained in these delusionary arabesques the occasional moment of imagination or authentic grandeur.

OPENING CHORUS

The twenties had been a diamond decade for operetta on the stage: *The Desert Song, Rose-Marie, The New Moon,* and constant revivals of beloved warhorses such as *The Merry Widow* and the works of Victor Herbert. In an America seeking workable forms of popular amusement, operetta seemed a good bet—far less daunting than opera, yet offering a semblance of culture in its trained voices and lyrical eloquence and big choruses. Without quite achieving grand opera's splendid overkill, operetta did maintain its own roster of excesses, in which suspension of disbelief could lapse into a moratorium on sense. Characters burst into song at the damnedest times, and

1. A further improbability is that George Gershwin was one of the composers who worked on the score. Only one of his songs was used in the film version, and both show and film are likely his most esoteric credit.

choruses seemed to have the knack of offering endless exposition. With this, and despite its European roots, there was operetta's appeal, which was far more egalitarian than opera. Broadway's operettas were always in English, and the tendency to advance the plot through dialogue cut through much of opera's "lofty" nature. These plots, along with the character motivations, were prototypic and easy to absorb; for all the exotic locales and courtly rigmarole, they were basically boy meets girl, with subplot and gewgaw filling in for character development. The best of them, the most permanent, had sufficient fine music to compensate for the emotive simplicity. Six decades and more after the fact, no audience attends the occasional revival of *The Desert Song* to revel in the story of Pierre and Margot; it does it to hear "One Alone" and "The Riff Song."

Stage audiences sought and found in these works a luscious escapism equal to the appeal of the movies. The silent screen, concurrently, adapted some operettas to surprisingly reasonable effect. Erich von Stroheim inverted the Viennese lilt of *The Merry Widow* into a more neurotic and passionate constituent for MGM in 1925, and two years later Ernst Lubitsch refashioned *The Student Prince* with wit and grace. Even Rose-Marie turned up, in the unlikely if passable person of Joan Crawford, and as she mutely inflamed the hearts of the Canadian Northwest in early 1928, studios began to ponder the move to sound. Operetta was one of the earliest options contemplated, more so than informal musical comedy, and among the first candidates were an MGM remake of *The Merry Widow*, with Lehar melodies subbing for Stroheim fetish, and a sound version of the venerable *Maytime* at Paramount.

Notwithstanding the delays attendant to its genesis, *The Desert Song* was the first film operetta by a wide margin, and while many of its reviews may not have augured similar ventures, its grosses assuredly did. Still, perhaps some studio executives might have paid a trifle less attention to the money and a little more heed to Carlotta King's blank expression, which intimated much about the problems that could befall operettas on the screen. Warners, of course, heeded it least of all, and in cahoots with First National acted with the greatest dispatch. In the saga of the screen operetta these two companies shape up as the villain—or perhaps the buffoon. They indiscriminately purchased several stage operettas of little distinction, commissioned new works, and dusted off a few older titles already filmed silent. Yet—it's a leitmotif running through these chapters—their timing was off again.

Several other studios' productions beat the Warner operettas to the screen; as with revues, each studio approached operetta differently and with vast gradations of competence. The lure of the genre—melodic appeal, familiar titles, romance, stage prestige—clearly outweighed the more practical exigencies. While there was no way to truly gauge how operetta's standard components might transfer, surely a bit more thought might have been diverted there. The unsubtleties of characterization and inanities of plotting were not deemed especially problematic, for they were equaled any day by Hollywood's norm. But the peculiarly stylized manner in which operetta dealt its cards seemed incompatible with big screen methodology. Conveying plot points through serious music ensured that operettas tended to place their songs far more ponderously than in most musical comedy. In *Good News* and its fellows, lead-ins to songs were mostly light, often self-mocking, funny, and fun. In *The Desert Song* and *New Moon* they were often deadly serious. Passion and politics alike might be portrayed in the same rhapsodic key—*Song of the Flame* was the ultimate example—deliberately unreal, meant to be seen and heard from yards away in a theater. The closer the camera, the more ludicrous it could be and, with stage-trained operetta stars, could look. Pop singers with an easy style or surefire Jolsonesque bravado might work on film, yet a close-up camera could zoom in, laser-like, on any number of the infelicities to which operetta people seemed markedly prone. It was the Marion Talley syndrome all over again—a performer succeeding or not through combined physical appeal, theatrical savvy, training, and plain luck. None of this, however, stopped the operettas from blooming onto the screen in a steady stream from mid-1929 on, all their lilting overabundance completely intact.

FOX: SCHMALTZ AND SHAMROCKS

The first operetta after *The Desert Song* to make it onto American screens came, unexpectedly, from Fox. Having hired more stage performers than any other studio in 1929, Fox put many of them to work on an uneasy blend of hokum and pizazz called *Married in Hollywood*. This had been a genuine Viennese operetta, produced there (with its English title) in 1928, with music by master operettist Oscar Straus. As liberally adapted by Fox, its plot concerned an American singer (Norma Terris) touring with a troupe in a Balkan principality, who falls in love with the crown prince (J. Harold Murray). His family objects, deports her, and promptly there's the standard postage-stamp revolution beloved of operetta librettists. The prince somehow turns up in Hollywood and finds work as an extra in a film that, naturally enough, stars his lost and now famous love. In a final Multicolor sequence, they play out the operetta's title on the set of her latest movie.[2]

2. The Multicolor finale is the only part of *Married in Hollywood* currently available for viewing. Along with invaluable glimpses of the Fox lot as it appeared in the summer of 1929, it furnishes proof of director Marcel Silver's faulty sense of showmanship, being entirely prosaic in tone, with almost no music—a curious and unsatisfying note upon which to end a large-scale musical romance.

Such a plot gives an idea of what film operetta portended. How literally to present such a story, how seamlessly to fold songs into it, how to determine if the tone should be one of straight romance or spoof—Fox was not the studio to address such issues. Despite the expense and effort, *Married in Hollywood* was a disappointment, released as an ordinary programmer instead of the planned "special." Casting, as it often would be, was part of the problem. Performers who tackled their stage roles with fervent conviction could look grotesque on the screen, and those attempting to scale down looked merely stolid. While the two stars of *Married in Hollywood* had firm stage credentials (Terris with *Show Boat*, Murray with *Rio Rita*) and won some good reviews, they lacked the finesse to make an audience respond to the intricate triviality of such a story. Murray's propensity for hammy bombast has been noted in a previous chapter, and Terris's capable singing was insufficient compensation for a sharp-featured and wintry manner in no way reminiscent of customary romantic film heroines. The pair returned a few months later in a follow-up: a musical version, obviously prompted by *Show Boat*, of Booth Tarkington's archaic *Cameo Kirby*. *Time* put it best: "Unintentional[ly] . . . one of the most hilarious burlesques of Mississippi River fiction ever written." Terris hied back to Broadway, and Murray soon followed.

Another Fox project did achieve, despite many faults, some of the stature lacking in *Married in Hollywood*. While *Song O' My Heart* had the lachrymose plot and rudimentary characters of a glorified mammy story, its center was occupied by a singer of vocal entitlement far beyond even operetta's privileged realm. John McCormack is popularly remembered as the ultimate Irish tenor, with all attendant stereotypes: beefy appearance, ringing high notes grasped at every opportunity, interminable encores of "Mother Machree" and "I Hear You Calling Me." But there was vast artistry, too, and classical training that enabled him to bring the same beauty to "Molly Malone" as to Mozart. As with a select few—Caruso, Melchior, and Callas most conspicuously—his work remains a benchmark of style, his recordings studied and replayed many years after his death. Such artistry did not come cheaply, and, after interminable negotiations with Fox, McCormack emerged with a Jolsonesque fee of half a million dollars and an extraordinary amount of publicity proclaiming this debut the catalyst to merge sound film with Art. Nor, except for the dreary script, did the studio skimp on other aspects of the production. Frank Borzage, Fox's prize director, took Grandeur cameras to the Ould Sod for location shooting, and an entire Irish village was constructed on the Fox back lot. While in Dublin, Borzage searched for a fresh-faced ingenue to carry the subsidiary romance and found a pretty and inexperienced eighteen-year-old named Maureen O'Sullivan. For her, *Song O' My Heart* would mark the beginning of a six-decade career.

A premiere timed to coincide with St. Patrick's Day 1930 aided *Song O'My Heart* in stirring up uncommon attention. Its tattered story of lost love and its stereotypes only a cut above *Mother's Boy* paled beside the irresistible chance it gave mass audiences to feast on McCormack. His eleven songs (from "Plaisir d'Amour" to "Little Boy Blue") and genial presence were the film's only justification, and fortunately the script asked little more of him than to show pain, joy, or concern at appropriate moments. Apart from him the film was and remains endlessly dismal, and watchable only as a document of a great singer in his prime; except for a few lush visuals, its bathos stumps even Borzage's skill. Business in 1930 was mixed, for the less Irish the population the lower the grosses, and the much-touted Grandeur version was almost never shown. As with *Mammy*, the immense salary at the heart of its budget guaranteed that *Song O' My Heart* would earn a minimal profit at best, and that Fox would not pick up McCormack's option for a second film.[3]

MGM: STOUTHEARTED STARS

In 1929 Metro-Goldwyn-Mayer was still a few years away from its mythic slogan "More Stars than there are in Heaven," but the empowering concept was present and carried over to the Metro operettas. John McCormack's acquiescence to talkies was considered one of two elevating events in the 1929–30 musical season. The other concerned a homegrown opera star, at the time—especially in the male division—a rare breed in the United States. Few had risen more meteorically than Lawrence Tibbett, a baritone from Bakersfield who did journeyman singing for some years before suddenly attracting massive attention at the Metropolitan Opera in 1925. There was ample fodder here for the publicity machinery: a certifiably all-American guy with a voice, alternately caressing and stentorian, that was one in a million. While not handsome, he cut an impressive figure onstage, lithe, swaggering, far more exciting than most of the foreign competition and with solid dramatic instincts. Of all top-rung opera stars, Tibbett was the most obvious candidate for movie stardom and duly signed with MGM in mid-1929. Early options weighed for Tibbett included a filmed *Pagliacci* (presumably with the tenor lead of Canio transposed down) and an operetta version of *Cyrano de Bergerac*. The final choice, while more prosaic, was still

3. To keep McCormack happy during his California sojourn, Fox had rewarded him with a prime badge of superstardom: a huge bungalow-dressing room. Later, the unoccupied building became a focal point for infighting among covetous studio employees, and was eventually turned into offices for the wardrobe and hairdressing departments.

Fox's attempt with another tenor, (Don) José Mojica, was considerably less propitious. *One Mad Kiss* (1930) was a bandito operetta of such catastrophic quality that it narrowly avoided being shelved permanently. Only the Spanish-language version did well, in South American countries as well as Mojica's native Mexico.

a stretch for MGM: an adaptation of Franz Lehar's 1912 operetta *Gypsy Love* (*Zigeunerliebe*), eventually retitled *The Rogue Song*.

Little of the Lehar of *Merry Widow* vintage was brought to bear on MGM's reworking of *Gypsy Love*. Scenarist John Colton, best known for the Broadway shockers *Rain* and *The Shanghai Gesture*, reworked the story into a stentorian and occasionally sadistic yarn of a bandit chief in imperial Russia who abducts a haughty princess out of revenge and inevitably falls in love with her.[4] To the adapted Lehar score was added new music by Herbert Stothart, a prominent stage composer (cowriter of *Song of the Flame* among others) beginning a lengthy tenure at MGM, and the songs were all Tibbett's—no other soloists were allowed. The bizarre choice for director was Lionel Barrymore, who had moved behind the camera after *The Lion and the Mouse* and recently won plaudits for MGM's *Madame X*—praise due far less to his stagily leaden style than to Ruth Chatterton's skillful acting and, possibly, the prestige attending his name and experience. The decision to assign him *The Rogue Song* (replacing Robert Z. Leonard, still busy on *Marianne*) seems to have hinged on his affinity, as an actor, for full-blown melodrama, in which this script was liberally steeped. Tibbett and the Music Department, it was felt, would take care of the rest. This was belied by some fairly grim rushes loaded with Barrymore bombast, Tibbett lustiness, and no trace of humor or lightness. Four weeks after *The Rogue Song* began shooting on August 27, 1929, production supervisor Paul Bern and the MGM hierarchy saw the need for drastic recarpentering and hurriedly borrowed Stan Laurel and Oliver Hardy from the Hal Roach studio to supply slapstick relief as Tibbett's most inept aides.[5]

As the studio's first all-Technicolor production and an agent for Tibbett's authority, *The Rogue Song* received more attention than any other MGM film of early 1930 save *Anna Christie* ("Garbo Talks!"). The acclaim was almost all Tibbett's, with bounteous praise coming from nearly every domestic and foreign corner. That the voice recorded well was no surprise; what startled was the exuberance with which he seized the screen, which seemed particularly hot alongside the alabaster inertia of his costar Catherine Dale Owen. Tibbett was no McCormack or Martinelli, standing still to

4. It was common at the time to come out with novelizations of major movies, usually illustrated with stills. That for *The Rogue Song*, published by the A. L. Burt Company, was written by a young MGM scribe, Val Lewton, who went on to a far different career—producing a classic series of horror movies (*Cat People*, *The Seventh Victim*, etc.) at RKO.

5. The team's contribution to *The Rogue Song* has been the matter of some dispute. It's been alleged, for example, that their roles were written and their scenes shot after the rest of the filming had concluded. No: the production records for *Rogue Song* show that they started on September 27, 1929, days before shooting was slated to wrap, and their participation sent the schedule ten days over the original estimate. They worked out their bits on a vacant stage while Barrymore shot with the main crew elsewhere, and spent only two days in work with Tibbett or any other cast members. The remainder of their scenes were conceived independently and spliced into the main story piecemeal.

open his mouth and do it all with the voice. Instead, he strode around the stagy MGM sets, grimacing and gesticulating in a manner just restrained enough to avoid hamminess, adding lustre to the trite script and routine score. One scene that drew particular discussion had a bound and bare-chested Tibbett bellowing out "When I'm Looking At You" to a rapt Owen while being flogged: seldom did operetta get kinky, and with him violence could be channeled into vocal conviction. His presence and the reviews were sufficient to make *The Rogue Song* the most prestigious of all the oper-etta films, though when the financial returns were posted MGM saw a loss. Part of it was due to Tibbett's high salary guarantee, more to that crucial audience outside major urban centers. The aura of culture Tibbett's ap-pearance implied was intimidating and finally alienating to the sizable bloc of viewers who went to *The Rogue Song* for Laurel and Hardy more than for Tibbett, then felt cheated. The film's financial loss placed it in the same "worthy try" category as such later money-losing stabs at Metro culture as *Romeo and Juliet* and *The Good Earth*, and Tibbett's option was renewed to give him a conspicuous, if briefly held, spot in the studio constellation.

The most famous of lost film musicals, *The Rogue Song* is known, with a fair amount of irony, as "the lost Laurel and Hardy feature." Some of its effect can be divined from surviving evidence. Tibbett's singing, heard on the discs and concurrent commercial records, is stunning, simply one of the best voices ever captured on a sound track. What he's given to sing is less inspiring, for the Lehar and Stothart melodies are trifling and rather dull for an artist who towered as Verdi's Iago and Simon Boccanegra. And the lack of proportion is more crucial than in *Song O' My Heart*, which was clearly a McCormack concert plopped into a rickety story. Giving Tibbett all the *Rogue Song* music (save for a ballet scene) exposes the plot and other characters as the faceless contrivances they are; even a star dominating his vehicle needs ballast.[6] Between this and the autonomy of the Laurel and Hardy bits, it could read as an unthinking exercise in Brechtian alienation. The one existing fragment does give (along with L&H's "What fur coat?" gag with a bear in a dark cave) evidence of surface excitement, including an invigorating shot of Tibbett standing tall and macho in the face of gale-force winds. Unfortunately, most of the screenplay is far less thrilling, and Barrymore, in his short-lived hiatus from on-camera scene-stealing, was hardly the director to provide the right sense of proportion. Though the Technicolor was reckoned the best to date, the reliance on painted exteri-ors and stagy groupings tended to act as a stiffening agent; the cumulative effect apparently was one of Tibbett and Laurel and Hardy cavorting in a wax museum. *The Rogue Song,* if it ever reappears, will likely never be

6. Regarding Tibbett's musical dominance, a later equivalent would be Judy Garland in *A Star Is Born*, where the monopoly was diluted with assets not available to Tibbett—focused direction, a powerful costar, and a subtle screenplay.

Flogged yet still vocal, Lawrence Tibbett holds forth in *The Rogue Song. Photofest.*

judged a recovered gem, nor even the best of early operettas. But the sight and sound of Tibbett in full cry would doubtless make an impact.

Tibbett's personal success was enough for MGM to try out a second American opera star. Grace Moore's career, while not at Tibbett's level, did exemplify American enterprise in its tastiest form. Talent plus ambition and shrewdly deployed allure propelled her from Tennessee church choirs to Broadway and onto the stage of the Metropolitan. There, without Tibbett's supreme vocal endowment, she proved his equal in the ability to be irresistible onstage. It was a not a matter of great looks or transcendent expertise, but rather the precise thing missing from a Marion Talley: the ability to maintain a charismatic poise that balanced musical phrasing with physical presence—part artistic instinct and part hard work. It formed the core of Moore's career. She made people want to see her as well as listen to her, and as with Geraldine Farrar and certain others, both visual and aural elements were needed to grasp her appeal. MGM attempted to bolster Moore's chances with a Tibbett-like debut, casting her as the most legendary of divas, Jenny Lind. She was given an elaborate production, new songs by Herbert Stothart, and the most extended opera interludes yet seen in feature films. Lightning did not strike twice. The dull script, centered upon the star's romance with an impresario (Reginald Denny), was based more on Lind mythology than on factual incidents, and its sole dynamic moment was a bout of stage fright that caused her to faint dead away in the middle of *Norma*'s "Casta Diva." Wallace Beery also popped up as P. T. Barnum, for no good reason. Dowdily made up and unsympathetically photographed (and thus inadvertently reflecting the real Jenny Lind), Moore seemed self-conscious and subdued, a world away from Tibbett's fiery charisma. Metro, seeing the lame result, tried to heat up the proceedings by insinuating sex appeal where there was none. The working title *Jenny Lind* gave way to *The Soul Kiss* and finally to *A Lady's Morals*—a label intimating a "daring" quality as missing from the script as it was from Lind's life. Predictably, the film died a thousand deaths at the box office upon its release in the fall of 1930.

Only Moore's singing escaped unscathed, and MGM, a great place for star match-ups, tried again. TIBBETT AND MOORE IN *THE NEW MOON* sounded surefire: a sumptuous Sigmund Romberg banquet, with the best voices in cinema's aerie lifted in "Lover, Come Back to Me," "One Kiss," and "Stouthearted Men." The Broadway book and colonial New Orleans setting were jettisoned in favor of a plot scanning suspiciously like *Rogue Song of the Flame*—a romance between a Russian princess and a lieutenant in the Empire's declining years. It was this very ordinary script, incessantly tinkered with and rewritten, that caused *New Moon* to go far over schedule and budget. (Some bouts of operatic temperament, it may be assumed, also factored in.) This was September 1930 and operettas had been crashing at the box office for months, yet Metro persevered. The sound of those two voices in tandem was an irresistible prospect, and when *New Moon* opened at the end of the year the notices were glowing. While much of it was arid and stodgy, the musical excitement created by Tibbett and Moore was genuine, and for a few weeks it was thought that this one film could be the salvation of the dying operetta. Not so, for the production difficulties had skyrocketed *New Moon*'s cost well beyond that of *Rogue Song*, and business was considerably less, especially in those smaller towns. Instead of

(*above*) The attempts at sexiness implicit in titling the Jenny Lind story *A Lady's Morals* naturally extended to the advertising. Grace Moore is here rendered more sultry and attractive than she ever looks in the film. (*below*) He's effusive, she's interested, and much skirmishing lies ahead. Maurice Chevalier sings "My Love Parade" to Jeanette MacDonald in *The Love Parade*.

saving operettas it confirmed their demise; MGM let Moore go and placed Tibbett in different fare.

MGM also made operettas with in-house talent. After Ramon Novarro's unexpected hit with "Pagan Love Song," he requested time off from his contract to study voice, and it was alleged that a thrilling operatic voice was being prepared for a major European career. Not unexpectedly, Novarro as opera singer remained chiefly an onscreen entity, courtesy of several pieces that trod gingerly between operetta and tuneful romance. *Devil May Care* (1929), Novarro's talkie debut, was a slickly produced tale of the Napoleonic era based on a 19th century comedy, with an attractive Herbert Stothart score. Novarro carried it to respectful reviews and ample financial success, and came up with more of the same in 1930. A zippier modern yarn, *In Gay Madrid,* was followed by *Call of the Flesh,* the most dramatically and musically serious of the trio. This was another sexed-up title (formerly *Singer of Seville*), and Novarro directed as well as starred in the French and Spanish versions and cowrote one of its songs, "Lonely." In addition to fielding some heavy drama, he turned up in several operatic excerpts that found him in over his head in a way such as few stars are permitted to be revealed.[7] Several problems were becoming evident. Though a number of critics and viewers professed to admire Novarro in sound films, his voice and deportment were, particularly in operetta's lush environs, what can be termed "light" . . . and which mean-minded observers might deem "archly effeminate." His speech projected sweetness, not machismo, and his soft-grained tenor and clipped Mexican accent seemed a tad tenuous for the heroic grand manner of musical drama. Irving Thalberg and other MGM executives presumably realized this, for in all three musicals Novarro was given Dorothy Jordan as a romantic interest. A pretty soubrette with a shrill soprano, Jordan seemed to be in every other MGM film made in the early thirties, almost always to unmemorable effect. She was the least intimidating of costars, and in *Devil May Care* she and Novarro belie the title's dynamic promise by comporting themselves like Bo Peep and Boy Blue—while a more mature and sensuous singer, Marion Harris, is shunted aside with little to do. This treatment was evidently deemed necessary for Novarro to sustain the illusion; a while later, alongside Garbo in *Mata Hari,* he seemed less a lover than a nephew. As with another gay actor on the MGM roster, William Haines, Novarro was demoted from the ranks when his image was seen—and heard—to lack an aura of conventionally forceful heterosexuality.

7. In its original release *Call of the Flesh* featured Novarro in an overwrought Technicolor performance of "Vesti la Giubba" which was, admittedly, well reviewed in 1930. Current prints contain an alternate black and white number, equally *agitato:* "Ah fuyez, douce image" from *Manon.* It's Novarro vs. Massenet, and both lose; the star's struggle with the upper reaches of the aria recalls the recordings of Florence Foster Jenkins.

The contribution to operetta by the most continental of Hollywood studios was quantitatively sparse—only three films in 1929–30—yet represented some of the highest-grade filmmaking in those years. While most studios assigned their operettas to faceless hirelings or ill-suited technicians, Paramount had Ernst Lubitsch. Star power was in evidence also, in the ambrosial persons of Maurice Chevalier and Jeanette MacDonald; nevertheless, it was the director who had the winning hand here. His arrival at Paramount coincided with the onset of sound, and he was clearly ripe for new challenges. In Germany he had been commended for both spectacles (*Madame Dubarry, Sumurun*) and comedies (*The Doll, The Oyster Princess*), and his first Hollywood outing had been contentious: *Rosita* (1923) was more costume epic than comedy, and still more a duel of wills and wits between Lubitsch and producer-star Mary Pickford. From that he moved to Warner Bros., a somewhat unexpected roost from where he proceeded to give the Hollywood community a series of lessons in how to make screen comedy a stylish combination of wit, innuendo, artful photography, and careful design. Nearer the end of the silent era he reverted to heavier fare with John Barrymore's *Tempest* and *Eternal Love*, and his verve and success declined noticeably. Sound revived his inventiveness. Partly through instinct and experience, perhaps partly through his early work under Max Reinhardt, he remade the infant sound cinema into a silky interweaving of dialogue, music and lyrics, and visuals. The saucy point of view that had earlier caused so much notice was not diminished by being made audible and melodic; indeed, Lubitsch might be considered the first to truly set film to music.

The Love Parade, his first sound film, was also the first operetta written directly for the screen. Neither of those reasons accounts for its place in the history books. Nor, on balance, does its plot, adapted from the Leon Xanrof–Jules Chancel play *The Prince Consort*. It was set in the same environs—Paris and a mythical kingdom (Sylvania)—that had served the genre from *The Merry Widow* on down. The difference lay in the director's point of view, which suffused every aspect of the project. The key to Lubitsch's triumph with *The Love Parade* was his ability to preserve the conventions of operetta while never taking any of them too seriously. Dialogue, music, performances—all were refracted through his chronic inability to see the battle of the sexes as anything other than a cause for mockery. In *The Student Prince* Lubitsch had sobered up sufficiently to view a prince's conflict between love and duty as a romantic tragedy. By the time of *The Love Parade* the champagne was flowing again, and the romance between a queen and a rakish nobleman can only be seen as a comic battle royal with bluntly sexual overtones. MacDonald's Queen Louise is too intent on duty and Chevalier's Count Alfred too knowingly randy for their arranged union to be anything other than an invitation to collision. "The queen is always right!" sings her loyal maid (Lillian Roth). Perhaps so, yet when her husband starts to feel neglected he engineers a full-fledged revolt, to which the queen must inevitably capitulate. She loves Sylvania, but she's passionate about Alfred, the "Dream Lover" she had sung about so rapturously early in the movie. The victory, true to Lubitsch's chauvinism, is tipped in favor of the male—but at least it comes after he's been humbled somewhat, as in his aria of sexual frustration "Nobody's Using It Now."

Can it be possible that this film, flashing beams of wit and irony in every direction, was shot at the same time as *Married in Hollywood* and *Golden Dawn*? After scores of imitators and pretenders the wink and sparkle remain unmistakable, even as the occasional early-sound longueur shows through. The director's stamp clearly lies on the fluid and witty camerawork, almost entirely unshackled from the confines of the booth, recalling his skill in silents as well as his preoccupation with opened and unopened doors. The camera in *The Love Parade* alludes to things too naughty for dialogue, or avoids things too blatant to be seen; neither way is it blunt or indelicate— this is Lubitsch's governing aesthetic. There's also his skill with performers.[8] The film was a vested triumph for Chevalier, whose impudence— liberated from the confines of *Innocents of Paris*—matched that of Lubitsch. If his roguishness occasionally seems too calculated to modern observers, the skill and charm remain genuine and overwhelming. MacDonald is perhaps even more remarkable, blooming as few performers do in a first film. It's a different MacDonald than that found in her Nelson Eddy films: a little heavier, a shade plainer, more sensual, less arch.[9] Contrast her poise with that of a concurrent film novice, Norma Terris in *Married in Hollywood*. Some of the difference lies in performer's instinct and material, and the rest in the disparity between two continental directors, Marcel Silver and Ernst Lubitsch. Both women had the training and the credentials, but where Terris was pinched and guarded, MacDonald was glowing and candid—as in the famous scene of the queen's meeting with her cabinet. An arranged marriage, she's told, is inevitable, and the prospects for a worthy catch none too good. Nonsense, she protests, she deserves the best man going, and to prove it lifts up one side of her skirt. "In all of Sylvania," MacDonald boasts, "there's only one leg as good as this one." Then she

8. One performer unable to avail herself of the Lubitsch touch was a young extra named Jean Harlow, who's easily recognizable in a theater box near the end of the film.

9. MacDonald's rather generous jawline required that she be carefully lit and photographed and that she direct her chin downward. Obviously she and Paramount's cameramen learned their lessons quickly: *The Vagabond King*, shot immediately following *The Love Parade*, shows a conspicuously more photogenic MacDonald.

exposes the other leg: "And that's it!" Imagine any other actress in any other operetta comporting herself with this degree of cheek.

Music is as essential to *The Love Parade* as innuendo, and the first full operetta score written for film is as charming as it is apt. Victor Schert-zinger's music (he was also a capable director) and Clifford Grey's words mesh so closely with script and direction that it's amazing to find one 1929 critic densely complaining that the songs should have been "introduced logically." For the songs do precisely that, laying out character development, romance, conflict, comedy—it's all here, and as ideally suited to Chevalier's slyly confidential boulevard style, singing directly to the camera, as to MacDonald's soaring lyric soprano. His valet, Lupino Lane, and her maid, Lillian Roth, also net appropriate songs, and even Chevalier's dog is given a chorus of "Paris, Stay the Same." MacDonald's "Dream Lover" is the preeminent treat, a sinuous waltz of such appeal that it turned up as background scoring in Paramount pictures for decades after-ward. (Surprisingly, it did not remain in MacDonald's repertoire, though the lesser "March of the Grenadiers" did.)

Like *The Broadway Melody*, *The Love Parade* was an epochal event. It made sound film suddenly seem worthy of intelligent adults, placing the sparkle and wit of fine stage comedies adjacent to a well-preserved sense of cinematic gaiety. The reviews were outstanding, the box office returns gratifying, and industry validation came with six Academy Award nomina-tions, then a record number.[10] There was also some unwelcome fallout regarding the sophisticated fashion in which Lubitsch scored his points. Even Middle America was able to figure out that the women Chevalier was singing about in "Paris, Stay the Same" were whores, plain and simple, and censor boards in several states made numerous cuts. Given Lubitsch's taste, such things seem ridiculous—yet the protests relating to the film's light treatment of sex and marriage greatly fanned flames that led, in 1930, to the formation of the Production Code, which would not be rigorously enforced for another four years.[11]

Jeanette MacDonald and Lillian Roth were shunted postehaste into Para-mount's second operetta, which had started while *The Love Parade* was still shooting. *The Vagabond King*, released in February 1930, was in many ways the antithesis of Lubitsch's style: an adapted stage work, a more traditional operetta score, and solemn to the point of ponderousness. Boudoir sparring

10. No winners, however. The categories were picture, director, actor, cinematography, art direction, sound. Chevalier was also up that year for *The Big Pond* (the Academy used to allow such things); a fellow nominee was Lawrence Tibbett for *The Rogue Song*.

11. Much of the protesting was done by small, tightly organized church groups in several areas, who rained angry letters down on the Hays Office. Everything old is new again: these were quite similar to the conservative factions which, purporting to represent a majority of Americans, let loose the self-styled media/moral watchdogs of the 1980s and 1990s.

was exchanged for pageantry and a fancifully depicted historical character, rogue poet François Villon. The source material was not the small bit known about Villon's life, but a perennially popular stage drama from 1901, *If I Were King*. The fancy of playwright Justin Huntly McCarthy, carried forward to the operetta, was that Villon, as victim of an elaborate prank by the insidious Louis XI, is made king for a day and stirs his rabble cohort to rout the attacking Burgundians. Romance, as provided by the two women who love Villon, was secondary and far removed from Lubitsch's erotic sheen. Katherine (MacDonald) is a saint, Huguette (Roth) a streetwalker, and in the 1925 Broadway original the difference was calibrated by their defining songs. One gets the exalted "Some Day," the other "Love for Sale" (pre–Cole Porter, and not used in the movie). The show was pervaded with theatrical spectacle: tapestry-like sets, lofty fifteenth-century headdresses, enormous choruses of courtiers and commoners, skullduggery and redemption. Most of all there was a luminous score by Rudolf Friml, fresh from the triumphant *Rose-Marie*. That show had revealed the classically trained actor Dennis King to be a vigorous singing leading man, thus beginning a long tradition in which the British theater has given unexpected bounty to the American musical stage. The role of Villon was intended as a tour de force, and King responded with overpowering relish.

By 1929 the story was familiar and perhaps old hat to moviegoers. The play had been filmed in 1920, and in 1927 John Barrymore starred in a variant, *The Beloved Rogue*. But to a studio anxious to make an inroad in filmed operetta, *The Vagabond King* was greatly tempting. After some interest by Warner Bros. the property was acquired by Paramount, who decided to go all out. As often occurred at this studio, the choice of director would be crucial in determining the character of the project. That choice, Ludwig Berger, was another of the émigré directors so esteemed in Hollywood around this time. While he had not yet directed a sound film, Berger's background was intriguing: a Ph.D. in musicology, extensive theater experience that included many collaborations with Max Reinhardt, some opera and ballet, and finally some sumptuous German silents such as *Cinderella* (1923) and *The Waltz Dream* (1925). With his trained ear and discriminating eye, he surely seemed like an intelligent choice for a musical spectacle, one whose dangerously high budget of $1.25 million included Technicolor, the services of Dennis King, and some enormous sets. With Teutonic expedition, Berger set about making as personal an imprint on *The Vagabond King* as Lubitsch did in *The Love Parade*. He worked closely with Technicolor's Natalie Kalmus to engineer what might be termed the first comprehensive color scheme in any film, the tints employed less for splash than to intensify drama and serve as emotional metaphor. After filming was done and Berger was on holiday, Paramount's executives deemed some of his work too stately and ordered about a week's worth of retakes, including the battle montage at the climax of the film. Reportedly, these were directed by no less a hand than Ernst Lubitsch.

When it premiered in February 1930, *The Vagabond King* was touted as Paramount's most prestigious film in years, yet the expected triumph did not quite materialize. The power of the original play was missed, and audiences outside the largest cities, already put off by the inflated ticket prices demanded by the studio's Publix theater chain, found it too formal. It also had the misfortune of playing most places only a couple of weeks after *The Rogue Song,* and many similarities were noted. While Paramount had the more polished film, MGM had the more charismatic star, for Dennis King proved a disappointment. His handsome baritone, for all its power and effect, lacked some of Tibbett's sovereign authority, and too often he seemed to mistake the Paramount soundstage for the Casino Theatre. The gesticulating and the fustian speeches seemed to illuminate François Villon less than they did a star's need for aggrandizement. Then there was his tendency to hog the camera. Jeanette MacDonald, herself no stranger to wiles and temperament, was given a full dose of King's tricks when, while shooting "Only a Rose," he edged the front end of his profile into camera range during some of her solo passages. Forever after she remained scornful of the scene she dubbed "Only a Nose." King's option with Paramount was not picked up; nor, after one more film, was that of Ludwig Berger.

The divided reaction given *The Vagabond King* in 1930 still holds. "Impressive" is the word that comes instantly to mind, and for operetta's luxuriant claim upon the senses that's only half a loaf. The overall dramatic mood is one of cool bombast instead of warm passion, and for that much of the blame can be divided between King and Berger, the calculated magnetism of the former fitting in too well with the latter's unbending technique. There's no spontaneity or sparkle—Lillian Roth, who could conceivably have provided some, flounders in a role written to accentuate carnality and sacrifice, qualities over her head and beyond her years. MacDonald, who looks ravishing and sounds it, too, is allowed little of the spirit of her Queen Louise. Besides the songs, her role permits no more than a display of loving and haughty gazes and an occasional glimpse of regal spunk. The one performer who makes the drama work is the canny veteran O. P. Heggie, who plays Louis XI—magnetically—as a crabby opportunist, every palsied gesture and vocal tic personifying his kingdom's moral decay.

Despite its stultifying pomp, *The Vagabond King* cannot dismissed as merely an ornate ceremonial procession. If Berger is to be blamed for the drama, he must also be credited for the stunning look and sound. The musical presentation is outstanding, the Paramount chorus and orchestra going on all cylinders, yet it's the design that is most special. For nearly sixty years *The Vagabond King* was seen, if at all, in black and white prints. They might as well have run it without sound: as UCLA's preservation print finally made clear, color is the heart of Berger's achievement. His Paris is a sinister, shadow-drenched place, with a conspirator lurking in every fetid cranny to spy on Villon's harangues. Then, when he is suddenly transported to the palace, the visuals change to a series of exquisite tableaux in rich greens and golds, inspired by tapestries and illuminated manuscripts. Berger's stylized mise-en-scène mixes two-dimensional backdrops, startling lighting effects, and color splashes that propel the drama far more compellingly than Dennis King's bombast. The final battle scenes, a riotous montage of fiery hues, are terrifically effective. Formalized as they are, Berger's visuals are thoroughly self-referential: at one point MacDonald looks through a telescope to gaze upon a vista that's quite obviously a painting. Moments like this puzzled audiences in 1930; while staginess was one thing, artifice raised to this level of sophistication was unsettling and finally distancing. *The Vagabond King*, ultimately, was a rather splendid house divided against itself, and for its merit could not possibly have been the smash Paramount intended. It was as unique as *The Love Parade*, albeit not in a way to signal viable cinema. Like another director's Technicolor vision, *King of Jazz*, it remains a striking anomaly.

A Lubitsch follow-up to *The Love Parade* was inevitable, and while *The Vagabond King* was being launched plans started on a new operetta for Lubitsch, Chevalier, and MacDonald, eventually titled *Monte Carlo*. Chevalier, preferring to embark on a concert tour after more than a year of nonstop moviemaking, soon dropped out. His replacement was Jack Buchanan, a major star in London musicals and revues and familiar to American moviegoers who'd seen him opposite Irene Bordoni in *Paris*. He and MacDonald were given a group of outstanding songs and a production as elaborate as *The Love Parade*. Screenwriter Ernest Vajda borrowed his central conceit from *Monsieur Beaucaire:* on her wedding day, a countess flees a marriage to a ridiculous prince in favor of excitement and fortune in Monte Carlo, and meets a count . . . who, smitten with her, hires on incognito as her hairdresser. During a performance of a *Beaucaire* operetta, she realizes the truth. It was even fluffier than *Love Parade*, more reliant on situation and the hoary ploy of mistaken identity, and by the time of *Monte Carlo*'s release in September 1930 it seemed out-of-step with audience tastes, which had already reached the satiation point where musicals were concerned. In addition, there was a rather giddy frivolity about *Monte Carlo* which, coupled with the plot's preoccupation with gambling, sat ill upon spectators beginning to feel a financial and emotional crunch. Lubitsch's ability to wed music to image and innuendo was as suave as ever, and more technically polished, but while parts of *Monte Carlo* surpassed *The Love Parade*, it remains a less consistent work. Probably Chevalier could have cut through and made it a hit, and, watching Buchanan's rather brittle performance, it's hard not to dream of Maurice. A self-satisfied manner and adenoidal

voice—no matter how accomplished the performer—are not what are required to carry this plot and counterbalance Jeanette MacDonald's erotic
hauteur. The best moments, in fact, are those that precede Buchanan's
entrance. The Lubitsch touch is in full bloom in the opening sequence, the
hellish wedding procession that MacDonald so wisely flees. As a torrential
downpour erupts, overstuffed guests scurry into church beneath a banner
that reads, "Happy is the bride the sun shines on." Just so, and when it
turns out there's no bride the idiotic groom announces that he'll recapture
her—to which the chorus offers in approbation, "He's a simp, he's a simp,
he's a simple-hearted soul!" MacDonald, meanwhile, has hied to a de-
parting train clad in chinchilla coat and scanties, abandoning herself to an
adventurous future. "Beyond the blue horizon waits a beautiful day," she
sings, and Lubitsch the innovator syncs the noise of the train engine and
wheels to the propulsive rhythm of the song to fulfill an expression of unbridled optimism. It's the only well-remembered scene in *Monte Carlo*, and
despite abundant glimmers in the remaining eighty minutes there is notably less sparkle than in *The Love Parade*. There are some marvelous and
assured moments, but *Monte Carlo* often feels less like an operetta than a
too-ordinary musical comedy. In 1930, critics were so pleased to get another spray of Lubitschian perfume that they overlooked most of the flaws
and commended Buchanan. Audiences felt otherwise; at any rate, and despite her own fine performance, MacDonald was dropped by Paramount
before *Monte Carlo* opened. It's likely, though, that she knew she'd be
returning to Paramount, to Lubitsch, and to filmed operetta.

0 FOR THREE: UNIVERSAL, RADIO, AND UNITED ARTISTS

All three Paramount operettas made vigorously ambitious attempts to rec-
oncile stage and cinema, and if the success rate varied the skill and talent
were unquestionable. To appreciate the achievement, consider the work of
other studios who approached operetta with less than fully wrought entitlement, mainly with distressing results. Neither Universal, Radio, nor United
Artists had personnel equipped to finesse the genre's special needs, which
did not deter them from going ahead with ill-advised projects. Arthur Hammerstein (Oscar II's uncle) was an old hand at producing inflated operetta
on Broadway, with such entries as *Song of the Flame* and *Golden Dawn*. His
simultaneous entry into and exit from film was UA's *The Lottery Bride*, a
calamity of impressive proportions. There were some worthy participants
here, including Jeanette MacDonald, Joe E. Brown, and composer Rudolf
Friml, all of them at the mercy of a boneheaded script that somehow managed to encompass a Norwegian dance marathon, an arranged marriage to
a mail-order bride, a criminal on the lam, and a last-minute Arctic rescue
by Zeppelin. Perhaps the most unfortunate aspect of this project was that

it was not made at MGM, where such mishaps would be aborted before release; surely the fact that an angry Friml left midway through filming should have sent up flares. Yet Hammerstein persisted, springing for expensive retakes after preview audiences hooted in derision. Neither he nor his incompetent director, Paul Stein, had the vaguest notion of what they were doing, and by the time *Lottery Bride* trudged onto screens it was December 1930, when far better operetta films were flopping. If Hammerstein's time on Broadway was past, it had never existed in Hollywood. Soon after *Lottery Bride* opened to an epically dreadful reception, he declared bankruptcy.

While it would seem that Uncle Carl Laemmle would not permit such disaster to visit upon his studio, Universal did make its own ill-advised stab at full-strength operetta. Alongside its most important films of early 1930, *All Quiet on the Western Front* and *King of Jazz*, the studio released *Captain of the Guards*, an uncommonly appalling pastiche of costume spectacle and music drama. Ostensibly recounting the story of Rouget de Lisle and the beginnings of the French Revolution, this film—shot as *La Marseillaise*—had about as much concern with fact as *Song of the Flame* had with Lenin. The historical licenses traditionally associated with both operetta and Hollywood here commingled stratospherically: the revolution, Houston Branch's scenario averred, came as a side effect of the romance between de Lisle (John Boles) and a village lass (Laura La Plante, unhappily miscast and badly dubbed). She becomes a virulent revolutionary ("The Torch") to avenge her father's death and is tossed into the Bastille—which is then stormed for the sole purpose of uniting these two musical lovers. Director Paul Fejos railed against these offenses, fought with supervising producer Junior Laemmle, and was finally replaced by John S. Robertson, who reshot nearly all Fejos's footage. Fejos requested that his name be removed from the credits, and the little of his that remains—a banquet sequence and the excitingly composed battle scenes—comprise the only moments of quality. There had also been a shot at culture in the Laemmles' choice of cosongwriter. Charles Wakefield Cadman was an esteemed composer specializing in romanticized depictions of Native American themes such as the opera *Shanewis*. How this qualified him for a French Revolution operetta is not clear, but a famous composer is a famous composer; in any case Cadman's undistinguished songs for *Captain of the Guards* made no impact. When the film finally emerged, months over schedule and many thousands over budget, critics scoffed and the public stayed away. For French-speaking audiences, the offense was such that it was decided not to exhibit the film in France under any circumstances.

The basic premise behind Radio's one operetta was far sounder. Bebe Daniels's triumph in *Rio Rita* was the kind to spawn follow-ups, and it was planned that she star as Carmen opposite the Don José of John Boles.

Opera was deemed, as ever, beyond Hollywood's grasp, and Daniels moved on to *Love Comes Along,* a modest romance with music that adhered to the *Rio Rita* formula. Wishing a bigger-league successor, Radio turned to *Rita*'s creators for something comparable. The result was *Dixiana,* a moonlight-and-Mardi Gras concoction in which antebellum New Orleans stood in for *Rita*'s border town. *Dixiana* featured the same Daniels (as a tempestuous beauty disputed), the same composers and director, the same Wheeler and Woolsey and Dorothy Lee. Technicolor once again, a large budget, and—until the last minute—plans to shoot it in a widescreen process. With Boles unavailable, and with *Dixiana*'s demanding score tipping the vocal balance in favor of operetta, Radio turned up a second-string Tibbett in Everett Marshall, whose firm baritone and adequately dashing manner had won approval at the Metropolitan Opera and elsewhere. Marshall, however, lacked Tibbett's ease before the camera, let alone his magnetism. Bebe Daniels, already unhappy about the so-so score and her own pasteboard role, quickly perceived that Marshall would not exude the proper romantic aura and that *Dixiana* would not work out well. The fall of 1930 was the worst possible time for this type of ornate escapism, and despite some flattering reviews *Dixiana* lost a great deal of money for the studio. It survives—attractively so, in UCLA's meticulous restoration—as a treatise on the state of musical affairs circa autumn 1930. Technically quite accomplished, it demonstrates the progress in the nine months since *Rio Rita,* with some of the best Technicolor surviving from that era.[12] But *Dixiana*'s ultimate message is one of technique without substance. Production gloss, fake magnolias, and ruffled pantalettes are insufficient camouflage for undeveloped characters and ill-knit storylines. Devices that might work onstage are disaffecting on the screen. Dixiana, for example—who is she and why should an audience care about her? We never learn, and Daniels, burdened with a sorghum accent and no motivation, is forced to cash in on the goodwill she acquired as Rio Rita. Wheeler and Woolsey's connection with the central plot is tenuous to the point of nonexistence, and their routines—one supposedly involving a chamber pot—are abrasive and interminable. Dorothy Lee's character turns up in mid-film without explicable reason. The Everett Marshall problem, too, is formidable. His attempts at Southern-aristocrat swagger are undercut by a nose and mouth that don't seem to belong on the same face and are bisected by a repellent pencil-line moustache. Donning a clown suit for Mardi Gras, he seems less Pagli-

12. The color sequence acquires added resonance as the film debut, in a tap specialty, of Bill "Bojangles" Robinson. The UCLA restoration of *Dixiana* was also a reclamation. For many years it had been (like *The Cuckoos*) available on television without its color scenes, which formed its final twenty-one minutes. Home audiences were quite baffled by a story that stopped before its conclusion, as well as a Bojangles who received billing but never showed up.

acci than Bozo, and the haplessness reaches a sublime level in one tense scene when a fly is seen lighting on his face, twice. The voice is another story, and Marshall tries to sell this score like it's Puccini. But save for "Mr. and Mrs. Sippi," sung over the credits, the songs are oddly lacking. The Marshall-Daniels grand duet, "A Tear, A Kiss, A Sigh," has a droopy melody and lyrics out of a sub-bottom drawer. Daniels's first, startling entrance, popping out of a giant egg as part of a stage spectacle, is sabotaged by her song, "I Am Your Baby Now," which has a prettily tangoesque rhythm but is structured so poorly that it ends just as the audience is preparing to hear the refrain. The supposedly gala title song, too, is merely pedestrian. Perhaps it was due as much to the product as to the changing market that *Dixiana*'s ads deceptively implied a sex-filled spectacle, with artwork suggesting that Daniels is being raped. It didn't work, and the studio never again approached such musical precincts.

WARNERS AND FIRST NATIONAL, AND MELODY AND MADNESS

The ultimate collapse of the operetta boom owed to a series of crucial miscalculations. Paramount's Continental artists were prone to overestimate American spectators' affinity for sophisticated fare. MGM erred on the side of gravity, with insufficient lightness to make its operettas accessible. Fox trafficked in unsound material and casting. *Captain of the Guard* proved that Universal was all-around incapable. None of these gaffes and misjudgments, however, can compare to what transpired at Warner Bros. and First National, the studio conglomerate that killed film operetta, then paid and paid.

One way or another, economics cut to the heart of it. Warners, in 1929, was experiencing an influx of cash unlike anything the industry had seen. The company's gross profits for the year 1928–29 were $35 million, up 300 percent from the previous year. This was the big time; yet, as much of the studio's work demonstrated, its soul and ethos remained low budget. Not that the studio didn't attempt to compensate for its inherently proletariat status by spending money: in the latter half of 1929 Warner Bros., and its newly acquired associate First National, behaved like the most boorish nouveau-riche plutocrats. *The Show of Shows* was the most garish single example of this crass overspending, but there was much more. Inflated salaries, expensive properties, and production excesses caused Warner film budgets for 1929–30 to zoom up to twice the previous year's figure. At least a couple of the Warners, priding themselves on being big-time nickel-and-dimers, began to be concerned, justifiably. The company was soon paying an awful toll for its miscalculations, and would likely have done so regardless of the stock market crash. Even if attendance had remained unaffected by the crash and retained the high figure of late 1929, audiences would not have stood for the Warner/FN bill of fare. It was totally out of step with national taste, and with what other studios were producing. In 1930 there were innumerable examples: big-budget comedies without laughs *(A Soldier's Plaything)*, misfired costume spectacles *(Captain Thunder)*, expensive vehicles for fading stars *(The Lash, Back Pay)*, and many more. But the operettas stood out, even in this overfed group. They were costly and time-consuming, they required special promotion that the studio's press corps was not equipped to handle, and, nearly without exception, they were horrendous money-losers.

The colossal misjudgment at the heart of the Warners operetta splurge seems to be rooted in the Vitaphone shorts, where trained voices were sometimes lifted in excerpts from works such as *Maytime*. It sounded so attractive, and operettas were so well liked anyway, that it likely seemed that full-length operetta could naturally carry over to film. It duly did with *The Desert Song,* and despite that film's delayed release and legal difficulties, Warners felt vindicated by its immense success. What they did not perceive was that the most powerful aspect of that success was novelty. Few reviews had neglected to comment on this fact, but more than most studios Warners did not operate to please critics. It did make stabs toward better notices in 1929–30 with "elevated" vehicles for George Arliss and John Barrymore, and with all those operettas—which, whether brought from Broadway or commissioned anew, generally seemed to emanate from some misbegotten intersection lying between Vienna and Burbank.

The first to make it onto the soundstage demonstrated exactly what the Warner approach would be. *Rainbow* on Broadway was neither operetta nor standard-issue musical comedy. The first important post-*Show Boat* attempt to combine Americana with a cogent musical program, it died a fast death—for reasons more technical than artistic—soon after its opening in November 1928. In addition to its rich and varied score by Vincent Youmans and Oscar Hammerstein II, the show intelligently attempted to portray conflicts and relationships far beyond the likes of *The New Moon* or *No, No, Nanette.* Its Gold Rush/covered wagon/army camp atmosphere was ready-made for screen scope, and by turning a misfire into an onscreen hit, Hollywood, as symbolized by Warners, could have showed Broadway. That it ultimately did not demonstrates why operetta became an albatross; in this case it began by dwarfing a few good choices with some dazzlingly wrong ones. In the former category were Technicolor, John Boles, Joe E. Brown, and Broadway pro Vivienne Segal;[13] there was also the forward-looking decision to take Vitaphone out of doors for the first time. Warners and Western

13. However much sense it made to cast Segal, she was added only as a last-minute replacement. Lila Lee, not a singer by any stretch of the imagination, was originally signed for the role.

Electric had developed a remote system, connecting the microphones to soundproof trucks, that enabled the company to trek up to Lone Pine, two hundred miles north of Hollywood in the Sierra Nevada Mountains. Unfortunately, this company was led by Ray Enright, a mediocre contract director with no demonstrable affinity for musical staging. Additionally, Warners had started the standard procedure of replacing much of the original score with mediocre new songs. All the mistreatment rapidly transformed *Rainbow* from a flawed, ambitious musical drama into an insipid operetta entitled *Song of the West*. The title change was itself illuminating, exchanging the evocative for the banal; *Show Boat*, given the same working over, might have been turned into *Mississippi Serenade*.

Under any title, *Song of the West* was a nonstarter, and matters did not improve after shooting finished in June 1929. Following some miserable previews Warners shortened it by two reels, removing some of the operetta content if not improving the quality. More delays set in as a result of backups at the Technicolor plant, which also affected such Warner films as *Under a Texas Moon* and *Golden Dawn*. Originally intended as one of the prime Warner entries for autumn 1929, *Song of the West* did not open until mid-March 1930, by which time some infinitely more accomplished operettas had opened. Alongside *The Love Parade* and *The Vagabond King* it seemed dated, ludicrous, and skimpy, with weak recording and stiff performances. It was an especially unhappy feature debut for Segal, and only Joe E. Brown (in Charlie Ruggles's stage role) was exempted from the brickbats. The New York press, having appreciated *Rainbow*, was unusually severe, none more so than the *Herald-Tribune*, which employed such stingers as "slovenly, ugly, clumsy and generally dull . . . tragically unworthy of its brilliant, if unlucky original." Given its ingrained weaknesses and delayed release, the film performed rather well at the box office—a respectable worldwide gross of $920,000—though it ultimately did film operetta a great disservice.

Warners retained Vivienne Segal's services, and a month after *Song of the West* wrapped Segal and director Enright were in a re-created African village on Warners' back lot struggling with the aberration that was *Golden Dawn*. The title has popped up occasionally in these pages, usually in a derogatory context. With just cause: here was the great folly of the age, winning the Technicolor booby prize of the first musical wave. Warners' lack of connection with the American public reached its nadir here, and the film survives to tell the whole sorry tale. On the Broadway stage, in 1928, it had already been something of a disappointment despite some important names, including composers Emmerich Kalman, Herbert Stothart, and Robert Stolz, producer Arthur Hammerstein, lyricist Oscar Hammerstein II, librettist Otto Harbach. Like *Rio Rita* it had opened a Broadway showman's temple to himself—Hammerstein's Theatre, later the Ed Sullivan—but in the age of *Show Boat* it was an anachronism. The standard exotic setting, Dutch East Africa, acted as a backdrop for a ludicrously straightfaced tale: Dawn, a (supposed) native girl, is so favored by the gods that she was spared the indignity of being born black, and her romance with a British officer is complicated by her duties to her people and the machinations of a monstrous villain. A host of white actors done up as natives, attempting serious performances in a Viennese-style operetta, was too eccentric a brew to make a major impact.[14] The show ran for nearly six months, and likely would never have been heard from again if it had not been for Warners, who somehow determined that *Golden Dawn* was ideal film material.

Words can be such paltry objects—too much so, certainly, to convey the bejeweled horror that is *Golden Dawn*. An earnest attempt was made by professional bon vivant and part-time critic Lucius Beebe when he reviewed it in the *Herald-Tribune*. "Reason," he declared, "totters at the thought that any one could have conceived in seriousness such a definitive catalogue of vulgarity, witlessness, and utterly pathetic and preposterous nonsense." Such outrage, however righteous, could only be insufficient. If it were one whit less ludicrous, it would be one of the most offensively racist films ever made; as it is, completely bereft of taste, finesse, aesthetic faculty, or simple good sense, it's an unparalleled exercise in unconscious humor. This is the mad inverse of the *Great Gabbo* coin, distending an operetta's traditional boundaries to embrace unsifted and unsuitable content. In Technicolor, the blatant unreality was accentuated; the surviving black and white copies heighten the insane collision of stagy decorum and racially inflammatory melodrama. There simply has never been anything like it.

Warners' cast for *Golden Dawn* was as bizarre an assemblage as any in history. Poor Vivienne Segal, forced to wear a blonde wig, skimpy sarong, and leopard skin while trilling a gay waltz called "My Bwana"; Walter Woolf, trying to be stalwart as the British officer-hero;[15] Alice Gentle as Dawn's vindictive mother Mooda, light years from grand opera with her fervent rendition of "Africa Smiles No More"; Lupino Lane and Dick Henderson, ace British comics endeavoring to be jolly; Helen Kanesque soubrette Marion Byron; and, above all, Noah Beery. Perhaps Otto Harbach

14. One cast member not in blackface, as an Australian POW, was young Archie Leach—Cary Grant in his first featured American role.

15. Later, after attaching the surname King, he performed memorably as the Marx Bros.' nemesis in *A Night at the Opera*, by any measure a happier experience than *Golden Dawn*. In 1932, long after all parties had done their best to forget *Dawn*, Woolf sued Warners for the salary of a second, unmade film for which he'd been contracted. The studio countersued for a half-million dollars, claiming that Woolf was in poor voice when he made *Dawn*, thus spoiling its box office chances. This was tantamount to blaming Frigidaire for the sinking of the *Titanic*.

Never before, never again: The excesses of *Golden Dawn* may have seemed to preclude the possibility of a dramatic climax, yet here it is, with Walter Woolf, Nigel de Brulier, Noah Beery, the god Mulunghu, and a wincing Vivienne Segal. Woolf is preparing to issue a fearsome edict to de Brulier: "I warn you, Hasmali, if you go through with this sacrifice, you'll be responsible to the British government!" *Photofest.*

saw *The Emperor Jones,* ate heavily, fell asleep, and had unthinkably bad dreams. Little else can account for Beery's role and performance as Shep Keyes, the self-crowned tyrant who terrorizes the Africans, antagonizes the British, and pants for Dawn. Wearing badly applied dark makeup, sporting a Kingfish-like accent, stomping about and cracking his whip as he growls the sadomasochistic "Whip Song"—he is utterly spectacular, in a way as to make orthodox notions of bad acting, even in operetta, wilt in comparison. Enright's direction is far less sanguine, mainly a matter of parking the camera and hoping for the best, but Walter Anthony's screenplay rises indelibly to the event.[16] This is the most barefaced involuntary camp imaginable, piling on one absurdity after another, alternating songs like "Jungle Bungalow" with exchanges such as:

> *Segal* Why is Bwana angry?
> *Woolf* This is no laughing matter, Dawn!

16. It even lapses into illiteracy when a portentous title card announces that "There was no joy among the natives; A draught was destroying them." Since there is no beer or wind in sight, we must assume the word intended was "drought."

Or so he thinks, as it continues, without letup, through Dawn's betrothal to the idol Mulunghu in a haphazardly choreographed scene (the supposedly fearsome god, whose music cue bears the title "Mulunghu Thabu," resembles a giant troll doll), and on to Shep's comeuppance, in which Beery caps his performance, and indeed sums up the entire experience, by yelping, "I'se afraid! I'se afraid!"

Golden Dawn was withheld from release for many months, due partly to delays at Technicolor and also to concern over its quality, which even Warners could tell was lacking. After a few trims (including Segal's rendition of "Jungle Shadows"), it was released with ads that amplified the melodrama and ignored the music. "Africa's Cruelest Whip-Man! He takes what he wants by brute force! . . . Smashing drama of a primitive and passionate people!" Except for a brave few in the trade press, critics were dismayed; the financial returns were awful, and in the South nearly nonexistent: Warners, fearing that *Dawn*'s miscegenative overtones would prompt reprisals, pulled it from release in eleven states. While it's mesmerizing to think of the saga of *Golden Dawn* climaxing with Ku Klux Klan-generated protests, there were apparently no incidents.

After this, the focus shifted to First National. By this point the two studios were sufficiently aligned to pool their resources for the simultaneous production of two expensive operettas, *Song of the Flame* and *Bride of the Regiment*. *Flame*'s assault on Russian history has already been noted; *Bride* took an old operetta, *The Lady in Ermine*, and fitted a new score to its tale of a nobleman's wife who defeats an enemy army by tricking the rogue general into thinking he's seduced her. The casts were drawn from the studios' operetta stalwarts: Vivienne Segal, Alexander Gray, Bernice Claire, Alice Gentle, Noah Beery, Walter Pidgeon, Lupino Lane, and nonsingers Myrna Loy and Louise Fazenda. The inept Ray Enright, who was to have directed *Flame*, was detained with the problem-plagued *Song of the West* and replaced by Alan Crosland.[17] *Song of the Flame* was the more prestigious, with Crosland's staging and use of color given special approval; *Bride of the Regiment* ran into censorship trouble in some areas and drew large crowds only in Chicago, where it played as an "Adults Only" attraction. Both films were pompously solemn pageants substituting tunes and Technicolor for logic and dramatic incisiveness; with astonishing illogic, it was felt appropriate to open them only a week apart in May 1930, with *Golden Dawn* following a few weeks later. Audiences were being driven away.

Good sense had clearly deserted Warners and First National with their

17. Crosland had his own problems on *Song of the Flame*. On November 18, 1929, character actor Sheppard "Shep" Camp sustained massive injuries after falling from a horse during the filming of one scene, and died two days later. His completed work was used in the final cut, with his unshot scenes being given to a new character played by Lloyd Hamilton.

operettas. Yet something approaching good taste was starting to set in. In 1929 Sigmund Romberg was firmly entrenched as the dean of operetta composers, a position inherited from Victor Herbert and maintained through *The Student Prince, The Desert Song,* and *The New Moon.* Similarly, Oscar Hammerstein II was ranked as Broadway's leading writer of librettos and lyrics, earned through distinguished collaboration with Romberg, Jerome Kern, and others. (He also had to share responsibility for *Golden Dawn.*) Warners, at the height of its buy-all phase, offered Romberg and Hammerstein lofty sums to create operettas directly for the screen, the first of which was *Viennese Nights.* About the same time the studio dusted off an ancient David Belasco play, *Sweet Kitty Bellairs,* as operetta source material. First National, meanwhile, began work on the first Victor Herbert musical of the sound era, *Mlle. Modiste.* Once again it was too much at once, with all three shot within a few weeks of each other in February-April 1930, and all costarring the busy Walter Pidgeon. By the time the films were ready for release that fall there was outright hostility for musicals in general and Technicolor operettas in particular, and without star names or other strong inducements they could not possibly return their cost. Warners did try hard with *Viennese Nights,* giving it a strong push in opening roadshow engagements, proclaiming it as "Made without regard to Hollywood precedent, Hollywood formula or Hollywood tradition!" But with a domestic gross on the level of *Golden Dawn,* it was a bust. *Sweet Kitty Bellairs* fared worse yet, not even rating first runs in many cities. *Mlle. Modiste* was previewed as *Toast of the Legion*—surely too close to *Bride of the Regiment*—and finally retitled *Kiss Me Again,* after its enduring hit song. The studio hoped that by waiting nearly a year to release it there would be an upswing in musical fortunes. However, in the Depression-ridden winter of 1931, alongside gangster pictures and stark dramas, *Kiss Me Again* could not have seemed less germane.

The irony in the poor showing of all three films is obvious: after bungling screen operetta for so long, Warners/First National finally got it right. Each of this well-made trio is devoid of the assembly-line pall infesting earlier works. *Viennese Nights* is solid and poignant, *Sweet Kitty Bellairs* is a dashing romp, and *Kiss Me Again* is vivacious and bright. As the doomed lovers of *Viennese Nights,* Vivienne Segal and Alexander Gray are so affecting that their occasional woodenness is overruled by their voices, conviction, and faith in the material. No *Golden Dawn,* this: Romberg and Hammerstein's score includes "You Will Remember Vienna" and "I Bring a Love Song," and is set in a *Student Prince/Maytime* tale of a love affair thwarted yet somehow imperishable. It was schmaltz, unquestionably, and occasionally heavy going, but Alan Crosland's inventive deployment of sound and visuals gives the stagy plot moments of cinematic beauty: a military parade fluidly shot outdoors; a romantic scene, half in shadow, of Segal listening to Gray play his violin; Gray's dementia upon realizing Segal has left him, evoked through a subjective camera whirling around in multiple exposure; the shrill invective of Gray's ghastly wife giving way to his memories of Segal's beautiful soprano. The Technicolor design is subdued and elegant—Romberg and Hammerstein's contract gave them approval over every set and costume—and the supporting cast competent, including Bela Lugosi in a bit. Along with the feeling that MGM saw it before making *Maytime* in 1937, the final impression is that all hands concerned cared a great deal about what they were doing. This was rare in 1930, rarer still in a Warner musical, and it makes *Viennese Nights* special.

Although *Kiss Me Again* was designed to showcase Bernice Claire, she was long gone from the studio by the time of its release. Fluidly photographed by Lee Garmes, *Kiss Me Again* is proficient light-romantic filmmaking whose ample humor compensates for the occasional creak in the old plot. Claire is properly fetching as the shopgirl who makes good and renders the title song with full diva allure, while Pidgeon makes a sturdy romantic partner. There's also the sight and sound of venerable character actor Claude Gillingwater, who rants his way delightfully through "I Want What I Want When I Want It." Herbert's songs were augmented with a few adequate new ones, including "Make-Believe Ladies' Man," which features the memorable sight of Warners' busiest actor, Frank McHugh, set upon by a group of fashion models who deck him out in drag. Sweet, pretty, and beguiling, it's a film out of step for its time, and more accomplished than many slicker later works.

Of the three late operettas *Sweet Kitty Bellairs* scored the most resounding and predictable failure. It had no stars, a title recognizable only to aficionados of theater lore, and a powdered-wig-and-breeches setting hopelessly ill-tuned to late 1930. One wonders who Warners reckoned its target audience to be. Few, surely, other than the small group of literate filmgoers not deterred from operetta by the likes of *Song of the West* and *Captain of the Guard*. In a respectful review, *Variety* correctly tagged its chances: "This frothy pastel-shaded comedy has about as much punch for the screen public as ice cream in winter." Just so—the domestic gross was woefully low, the foreign gross (there was minimal overseas marketing) almost nil. It was immediately forgotten, leading lady Claudia Dell moved to supporting roles, and prints survived only in black and white. What a surprise, then, to encounter such an unmitigated treat: a Dresden figurine of a movie, brittle, beautifully detailed, totally artificial. While the setting is Bath, in 1793, no one attempts an English accent. It's a fantasy—a masque, even— and it's no coincidence that at the end masks are quite literally removed. The plot encompasses mistaken identities, duels, intercepted love letters, true love, and gout, and the form duplicates an eighteenth-century ballad opera complete with pastiche songs and rhymed couplets. Who could envision Warners producing something so posh? High comedy and slapstick, bedroom farce and adventure, operetta and musical spoof—all are deftly balanced by director Alfred E. Green, who sustains the sixty-three-minute charade with near-Lubitschean skill, and the songs—by the uncelebrated Walter O'Keefe and Robert Emmett Dolan—serve the material with immensely idiomatic tact. Instead of generic Tin Pan Alleydom, here are pieces such as "Pump Song" and "Peggy's Leg," which could not possibly be removed from the context. Stylistically the music recalls Gilbert and Sullivan as much as it does "The Beggar's Opera," and ordinarily prosaic actors such as Ernest Torrence and Lionel Belmore bound into their vocal chores with Pinaforesque bravado. As the sweetly minxish Kitty, Claudia Dell compensates for the vocal endowment of a Jeanette MacDonald (the ideal Kitty) by conferring blonde radiance and coquettish moxie. In the annals of musicals, as in the annals of Warner Bros., *Sweet Kitty Bellairs* is a minor entry and perhaps merely a footnote. At the time it lacked the prestige of *Viennese Nights* or *New Moon*, and is too fragile to hold up today as a rediscovered masterwork. Yet it shows how far Hollywood had come in the eighteen months separating it from *The Desert Song*, how much had been learned and assimilated. It played on American screens at the most inapt time imaginable—yet survives far better than most of its better-known contemporaries.

For every operetta that came out—and, invariably, failed—in mid-to-late 1930, several were planned and not made, or abandoned, or postponed. One of the leading casualties of these never-weres was the inanimate (if rich-voiced) Carlotta King, who signed with MGM in mid-1929 and spent months preparing for a production of *Rose-Marie* that was never filmed. Other near-misses at Metro included *Naughty Marietta* and *The Merry Widow;* the latter, first announced for Grace Moore and either Lawrence Tibbett or Reginald Denny, was later slated for Jeanette MacDonald. It was even announced, in October 1930, that MacDonald, Maurice Chevalier, and Ernst Lubitsch would all go to MGM to make *The Merry Widow*. They did indeed, but not for nearly four years. Among the Warner operettas never made were *Danube Love Song*, commissioned from Oscar Straus, and *Maytime*. Universal, unchastened by the thud of *Captain of the Guard*, planned two more operettas for John Boles, *The Love Cavalier* and *Gypsy Love Song*. Radio's elaborate part-Technicolor production of Victor Herbert's *Babes in Toyland*, planned as a Christmas offering for 1930, was scrapped at the very last minute; the cast was to have included Irene Dunne, Everett Marshall, Wheeler and Woolsey, Dorothy Lee, Edna May Oliver, and Ned Sparks. Also planned for Marshall and either Dunne or Bebe Daniels was an ersatz-

Rose-Marie piece called *Heart of the Rockies*, terminated at about the same time. The reasons given were always the same: musicals were dying, operettas most of all.

A number of comments were made, in the latter part of 1930, about operetta being simply over the head of most film audiences. While it's hard to envision deeming *Golden Dawn* too intelligent for anyone, the sentiment is understandable—but not quite accurate. Some of them were successful, and there would be popular ones later on. Perhaps they were considered beyond spectators because often they seemed devoid of humanity. Audiences could weep with Bessie Love, laugh with Eddie Cantor, and swoon as John Boles waltzed with Bebe Daniels. But what of some of the others—Russian revolutions, a posturing François Villon, songs of the West, and lottery brides of the regiment? They did not seem to be what was needed, these processions of well-trained vocalizing mannequins, parodying history and imitating life on overextended budgets, with thoughtlessly conceived scripts and inattentive casting. By the late fall of 1930, as it was staging a major premiere for its new original operetta, Warner Bros. knew that operetta on film was dying, and that, good as it was, *Viennese Nights* would not likely alter the situation. So, for many knowing observers at the time, this pretty and sad story of lovely things gone wrong could only have had a valedictory air. It still does, and at its very end two ghostly figures walk off as Romberg's music swells. Then the music dies. You will remember Vienna.

CHAPTER 13

Is It a Musical?

If the human voice had been a drug in 1929, Hollywood would have been hellbent on taking a monumental overdose. The films of the first full year of sound were full of talk, full of noise, full of song, and in this time preceding the overt and unstated formalization of boundaries for musical film, no excuse was too illogical or perfunctory to introduce music to movies. In theme tunes or through inane plot pretexts, as long as the texture of musicals was still in flux, songs could be worked in anywhere. In the comedies already discussed, it seemed a relatively automatic gesture; less so was the use of music as a compliant tool to dress up an otherwise barren drama. Few major films in 1929, *Disraeli* and *Madame X* being the most prominent exceptions, avoided the temptation entirely, and the result was a bewildering twilight area of generic crossover. Films that weren't outright musicals on the order of *On With the Show!* or *The Love Parade* might skirt the line narrowly with a great deal of music and singing that might or might not be purely incidental. Sometimes, when done to capitalize expendably on the gimmick of sound, it only contributed to the growing saturation; other times it was employed with creativity and foresight, cutting straight to the heart of making sound film work and demonstrating how resourceful directors could transform overused devices. And in some cases music could be used in curious, often persuasive ways to enhance the allure of a star or the appeal of an unpromising story.

To casual observers of 1929 and 1930 cinema, the opportunistic use of music in many dramas may seem quaint to the point of gaucherie. It's often unnecessary, it contributes nothing to the mood, it can detract from the action, it hardly furthers characterization. But it was initially felt to fill the public's craving, and it did sell sheet music. In an ordinary 1930 marital drama called *Young Man of Manhattan*, a very young Ginger Rogers comes on in mid-film. She interacts a bit with other actors and then, for no great reason, begins to sing "I Got 'It' (But It Don't Do Me No Good)." The catchy song, which brought Rogers some early attention, has nothing to do with her portrayal of a flapper on the make, let alone the central conflict between Norman Foster and Claudette Colbert. *Our Blushing Brides* (MGM 1930), featured Joan Crawford in one of her first shopgirl-Cinderella roles, as a department store mannequin tangling with society. Given Crawford's public and the studio's bent, a fashion-show sequence would be expected; yet even for MGM this one went more than the distance. Albertina Rasch, who was usually busy creating Technicolor ballet sequences, made a full-fledged spectacle of it, a riot of chiffon drapery, fluid gestures, and sculptural posing. Only in Hollywood, and it stopped the film cold.[1] Lower-budget offerings could be intrusively musical as well, such as *Party Girl*, an exploitation drama released by Tiffany in January 1930. Tainted-but-true heroine Jeanette Loff, contemplating her love for Douglas Fairbanks Jr., happens to pass a piano—so she sits down to play and sing "Oh, How I Adore You." While possibly true to character, such an radical plummet in verisimilitude, which might pass in a regular musical, seemed especially jarring in a hot exposé. But by that time such interpolations had become commonplace. Theme songs also remained, and any film with even casual reference to a nightclub or theater would, it seemed, be compelled to pay a visit. Seldom were the songs in the background, or the simple affairs they would be in forties *films noirs*. Instead, the narrative would come to a complete stop for an extraneous bit of song and dance and often a chorus routine with a few leg shots.

Fox's *The Cock Eyed World* is a good example of songs used in an extensive yet expendable fashion to enhance a film's box office potential. Raoul Walsh's *What Price Glory* (1927) had proved that profane stage dialogue could be just as potent on the silent screen, especially when mouthed by Victor McLaglen and Edmund Lowe as Sergeants Flagg and Quirt, whose macho horseplay will not be impeded by something so trivial as war. For the sequel Walsh took them to Russia and, via Coney Island, to a Central American uprising, all with barracks songs and pop ballads for sonic flavoring. Unquestionably one of 1929's most fluid productions, it demonstrated how a strong director could make sound film pay off. It's also, today, a coarse and wearisome gust of Walshian misogyny and empty heroics, which no amount of technique could possibly make palatable. Between the blustery banter, the endless pseudo-profanity, and the interminably used ex-

1. Semi-musicals were familiar territory for Crawford at that time. Her first starring sound film (*The Hollywood Revue* doesn't count) was *Untamed* (MGM 1929), another of the what-is-its of the year. As a tropical wildcat named Bingo, Crawford sang "Chant of the Jungle" in the first reel and later duetted with Robert Montgomery.

change "Sez you?"—"Sez me!," this is the noisiest of early talkies, its music only adding to the din without softening its corrosive sexism. Not too surprisingly, it made an obscene amount of money. One hit like this can offset the losses of a dozen *Hallelujah*s; then as now, worthy intentions mean far less at the box office than lusty posturing.

Also in the macho domain, it began to be noted how music could raise the temperature on the Western front. Although horse operas took an inevitable dip in 1929, several films paved the way for such later balladeers as Gene Autry and Roy Rogers. Designed as Warner Bros.' answer to *In Old Arizona*, *Under a Texas Moon* was the last word in crossover: semi-Western, semi-musical, semi-comedy/adventure. Its only 100 percent aspect was Technicolor, and as with *Song of the West*, delays in making prints held up its release for many months. In the starring role of the Cisco-like rogue who can't leave the ladies alone, Monte Blue was replaced just prior to shooting (May 1929) by the most improbable of banditos: Frank Fay in his film debut, with a black mustache and dyed hair, serenading such fiery senoritas as the pan-ethnic Myrna Loy. By the time *Under a Texas Moon* was released, *Show of Shows* had come and gone and another Fay outing was not necessarily to be seen as a cause for rapture. Nevertheless, *Under a Texas Moon* fared better with critics and in theaters than many of the big musicals hitting at the same time. Some of it was due to the novelty and to a perceived lightness in tone, also to attractive uses of both music and color. Through some Murphy's Law of film preservation, this most immaterial of the Warners Technicolor movies is the one which survives in the best condition. Sure enough, the cumulative effect of *Under a Texas Moon* is one of generic confusion. Taking a comic-opera tone, with a musical-comedy star in a *Rio Rita*-like setting rendered in prettily unreal hues and an occasional break for Spanish-tinged melodies, it adds incidents alternately farcical and melodramatic, and direction (by Michael Curtiz) that does not seem able to assemble it all into a cohesive whole.

In contrast with the perfunctory or improper uses of music in other crossover films are the two most analyzed and studied works of early American sound cinema. King Vidor's *Hallelujah!* and Rouben Mamoulian's *Applause* were sustained attempts at a poetic synthesis of sound and image, directed toward amplifying and expanding upon their (wildly disparate) subject matter. Unlike Ernst Lubitsch, who also held forceful sway over the content and character of his first sound film, Vidor and Mamoulian reached somewhat farther than their grasp. But there's far more than simply the grandeur of failure in both films, and greater talent and ambition than can be defeated by naïve material or technical inadequacy.

Unlike many directors working in 1928, King Vidor insisted on choosing his stories whenever possible, and after his smashing success with *The Big Parade* (1925), MGM was willing to cede this perquisite some of the time.

The Crowd (1928) was one of the most resolutely personal of big-studio silent films, and Vidor and MGM were rewarded with rapturous reviews plus a small profit. After serving Marion Davies well with two comedies, *The Patsy* and *Show People*, Vidor decided to move ahead with another special project just as MGM was beginning to address the issue of sound. The Texas-born director had long been considering the idea of a story of life among Southern people of color, for which he could draw upon childhood memories of revival meetings and mass baptisms. Although a prosperous all-black film industry was then in operation, Vidor's idea was not one to warm the hearts of MGM executives. (This also helps to indicate why, over the following years, there was a shamefully insufficient number of black artists appearing in musicals.) That he was given the green light for such a story is due to several converging factors. One was his reputation, which included his ability to wring lucrative films out of sometimes unpromising material. Another was the fact that the promise of a soundtrack made the subject seem more attractive: spirituals and other traditional melodies might carry immense appeal for many audiences. A third factor—for which Vidor must be taken at his word—lay in his belief in the material, which was so strong that he offered to make the film off salary. The classic comeback to this offer came from company president Nicholas Schenck: "If that's the way you feel about it, I'll let you make a picture about whores!" [2]

Prostitution was only a hinted-at incidental in Vidor's stirringly titled story, which concerned one man's journey from the cotton field to the pulpit, on to sin and retribution and, ultimately, redemption. It was clearly conceived as an epic of the race, with the director's earnest intentions filling in as best as possible for his ultimate inability to comprehend the hearts and minds and souls of the people he was trying to depict. By October 1928 Vidor was completing casting in Chicago and New York. With Paul Robeson unavailable for the central role of Zeke, he settled on Daniel L. Haynes, recently in a Robeson role on Broadway—Joe in *Show Boat*. As the contrasting women in Zeke's life, Vidor picked Texas blues singer Victoria Spivey as the innocent Missy Rose, and Harlem dancer Honey Brown as Chick, the saloon girl whose quest for salvation leads to Zeke's downfall. Vidor spent four weeks shooting exteriors in and around Memphis, and when MGM's sound truck did not arrive on time, he filmed silent, resolving to dub in the dialogue after the fact. When work resumed on the MGM lot Honey Brown was replaced by Nina Mae McKinney, a seventeen-year-old alumna of the chorus of *Blackbirds of 1928*. Vidor shot and shot, Fox's hastily conceived "homage" *Hearts in Dixie* came and went, and *Hallelujah!*'s status moved from part to all-talking. To shore up its commercial

2. Vidor retold this story so often that it has passed into myth. Perhaps it's true . . . then again, as Vidor's films conclusively prove, he was an *awfully* good storyteller.

chances, but over Vidor's wishes, MGM commissioned two new songs from Irving Berlin. The 77–day shooting schedule was one of the longest the studio had seen, and post-production work sprawled over a nightmarish six months. Without access to sound Moviolas or other yet-to-be-invented equipment, Vidor had to approximate the synchronization of a complex music-and-dialogue track to the many scenes shot silent.

When *Hallelujah!* finally opened in August 1929, the reaction was variously elated and suspicious. It was most positive in the urban North, where it did well in both black and white theaters. For many spectators and critics it was apparent that this was likely the first talkie made with the same eye toward artistry as such ambitious late silents as *The Crowd* and *Sunrise*; the simplicity of *Hearts in Dixie* here gave way to a serious look at religion, temptation, and resilience. In New York, where it played simultaneously on Broadway and in Harlem, *Variety* ran reviews based on the response of both audiences. Many of the spectators in Harlem, it observed, reacted to the most dramatic moments with what appeared to be uproarious laughter . . . evidently not from derision, but from intense satisfaction. Yet *Hearts in Dixie* did remove some of the edge from *Hallelujah!*'s box office potential, and the triumph was further compromised by some of the resistance feared by MGM executives. This was, by definition, a difficult film to market, and many exhibitors reacted with an unsavory combination of bigotry and greed. Those managing nonsegregated theaters alleged that white patrons would be deterred from attending by too great a number of black spectators, and theater chains in the South refused point-blank to book it. The ban finally fell, early in 1930, after bookings in Jacksonville and New Orleans. Many European audiences were captivated as well, and here and abroad even those who sensed the unwitting white-liberal patronizing beneath Vidor's good intentions were mesmerized by his forceful images and the use of music to probe emotional truths too fervent for spoken words. The performances were mesmerizing, too; Nina Mae McKinney became the first woman of her race given a long-term contract with a Hollywood studio. But the reaction among many white audiences, especially in small towns, ranged from boredom to confusion and, in a few cases, hostility. This was not so much due to overt prejudice, though there was also that, as to an unwillingness to be challenged. It was one thing to laugh along at Stepin Fetchit, and quite another to be drawn into the story of Brother Zekiel and his fall from grace. Given MGM's financial health at the time, and Irving Thalberg's affinity for quality work, the modest loss incurred by *Hallelujah!* was more than offset by its achievement and enduring reputation.

Music is more at the heart of *Hallelujah!* than in more overt musical fare. As with so much in this film, intention and ambition exceed the ultimate achievement, technically and artistically. Vidor's musical choices were not always suitable—an early shot of cotton-pickers singing "Old Folks at Home" is a painful example—yet, at its best, the use of spirituals and traditional songs, as conducted strongly by Eva Jessye, is direct and potent. The major set-pieces of the baptism and revival sequences startle even today with their frenzied vocal outpourings, and even smaller moments used vocal cadences in arresting ways—Zeke's "Cannonball Express" sermon, with its rhythmic blend of speech and song, Mammy's gospel wail upon discovering her sons are missing, Chick's absent-minded crooning of "St. Louis Blues" when she decides to betray Zeke. Much of it must be taken on faith, for the sound and synchronization clearly indicate all the technical problems that beset Vidor, and even the much-cited chase through the swamp is compromised by the use of speeded-up silent film. Yet the boldness of Vidor's imagery offers constant compensation, as does the emotional directness of the actors. Not too surprisingly, Nina Mae McKinney makes the strongest impact, with her impudent sexuality and raspy self-assurance; she can still bring down the house when, after beating her pimp senseless with a poker, she barks, "That's what I'll do to anyone who stands in *my* path to glory!" Singing and dancing "Swanee Shuffle" in a low-down dive, she registers with the same force, if not artistry, as Vidor's first inspiration for the role, Ethel Waters; and the production's rough edges also help the other Berlin song (Haynes's "Waiting at the End of the Road") to fit into the musical program without seeming too jarring. *Hallelujah!* is no more free from dishonesty or condescension than it is from melodrama, and few things date worse than stereotypical pandering or, for that matter, primitive technique. What can survive, as it does here, is a director's powerful and sincere vision.[3]

Applause was the polar opposite of *Hallelujah!*, its urban expressionism replacing Vidor's rural poetry, and with subject matter—a backstage melodrama—well in keeping with 1929 norms. But there was much in common: a director even more bullheaded than Vidor, with uncompromising vision and unconventional methodology; a sustained and somewhat self-conscious drive for artistry far beyond the conventional parameters of early sound cinema; and the awareness that music and song could add depth as well as entertainment. Born in Russian Georgia, Rouben Mamoulian had trained at the Moscow Art Theater and, after coming to America in 1923, spent an extended time directing opera at the American Opera Theater in Rochester. His breakthrough came with his first Broadway show, DuBose Heyward's *Porgy* in 1927, a show whose subject matter and approach helped

---

3. Almost unique among early sound films, it was given a theatrical reissue. In 1939, MGM dusted it off, cut out about nine minutes of inertia and questionable material, and spruced it up with new credits and intertitles. These changes were understandable, but *Hallelujah!* is now a somewhat different film.

crystallize some of King Vidor's ideas for *Hallelujah!* Mamoulian's impressionistic application of music and nonliteral sound was widely applauded, and by the time Paramount came calling in 1929 he had directed several more shows and was ready to try out some new ideas in sound cinema. After spending several weeks at the Astoria studio watching other directors, he then, as he later recalled with symptomatic bravado, "decided to do the exact opposite." His assignment was not particularly inspiring, for Beth Brown's novel *Applause* was a tawdry backstage tale that mixed mother love with seamy burlesque types. But Mamoulian had enough to work with. Not for him the rigid photography and stilted posturing of early-sound dramas. His *Applause* would be a flamboyant collage of mobile camerawork and overlappingly textured sound. Astoria, far away from the prosaic tendencies of Paramount's West Coast studio, was a fit place for his experiments, and also gave him access to some interesting New York talent. For Kitty, the burlesque queen who sinks lower and lower, the initial choice had been Mae West: one of the more jarring "what ifs" in film lore. The more tenable final pick was torch singer Helen Morgan, just finishing a sensational run as Julie in *Show Boat*. Her acting talent was mainly intuitive, and the pathetic vulnerability and self-destructiveness seen in her performance were as much autobiography as they were Beth Brown or Mamoulian. She had no actor's vanity, either; Morgan barely batted an eye when called upon to look like a hideous bloated wreck twice her age.

Mamoulian and the crew fought every step of the way. He pushed, he insisted, and sometimes they acceded. Other times they sabotaged him, a few of their gaffes being allowed into the final cut. There was no frame of reference, in June of 1929, for the kind of camera mobility Mamoulian was demanding, and his insistence on a two-channel soundtrack (Morgan singing on one, her daughter praying on the other) seemed beyond imagining. Annoyed and bullied, the crew came up with the contemptuous nickname *Applesauce*, and as if the technical barriers were not bad enough in the studio, Mamoulian hauled the company out to a number of New York locations, including Pennsylvania Station and the Times Square subway stop. Not only was the director's method alienating to many, his vision seemed nearly horrific: Helen Morgan in a matted blonde wig and vile clothes, the most misshapen chorus girls this side of a freak show, a burlesque-show audience jammed with bald leering baboons. It was, almost, *Deglorifying the American Girl*. And it was mostly brilliant. To their credit, Paramount's executives could clearly see what Mamoulian was up to, and they let him do it his way. After *Applause* opened in New York in October, the critics were mainly astonished. Such sordid material—which seemed even more so with dialogue—and so excitingly made, so far beyond any other backstage film. Mamoulian could do no wrong . . . for about three weeks.

When the financial reports came in, and many of the outlying reviews, the calls from Paramount suddenly stopped. He went back to the stage for another year.

The initial sensation of *Applause* was forgotten for several decades, just as many historians attempted to treat 1929 as a year which produced technology devoid of artistry. Finally, just as Mamoulian's film career was coming to an untimely halt, *Applause* began to make the rounds and the history books. Perhaps it can be thought of, with a slight stretch, as an earlier equivalent of *Citizen Kane*—the conception of one person (a film neophyte) suffusing every frame, a sustained reach for greatness, an occasional clutch at straws, and most particularly the drive to push visuals and sound beyond conventional representation. Nowhere else in early sound cinema will there be found this type of dynamic editing and ruthless application of montage, constantly adding depth and significance to shallow and hackneyed dialogue and situations. *Applause* is no musical, for all its setting and moments onstage and snatches of Helen Morgan song, but music is crucial to its texture. "What Wouldn't I Do for That Man!" becomes the most poignant of torch songs when applied to Morgan's love for the seamy slicker (Fuller Mellish) who uses her; and "Give Your Baby Lots of Loving" carries an affecting double edge when used both as a burlesque routine and as a heartfelt lullaby. At times *Applause* doesn't work: when Beth Brown's melodrama comes to the fore, or some of the supporting actors overdo it, or the mechanics clash with Mamoulian's vision. Yet it is never less than startling, and how it looked to most people in 1929 can only be imagined.[4] At times beautiful, often pretentious and arty, frequently primitive, sometimes unintelligible—it tries for so much more than most conventional films that it can't help but be flawed.

Applause was by far the most distinguished of a sizable group of dramas in 1929 that fed upon the mania for backstage stories without entering into full musical territory. *New York Nights* (United Artists), *Jazz Heaven* (Radio), and *The Melody Man* (Columbia) all had songwriter-heroes, and *Behind the Makeup* (Paramount) featured Hal Skelly in another *Dance of Life*-type yarn.[5] Given the wholesale attitude toward musicalization, some producers showed restraint in not going fully musical, although ancillary songs were always present. On occasion, backstage settings also turned up to fortify the allure of silent stars, invariably women, making uneasy talking appearances. The worst of these was actually billed as "All Talking—Singing—Dancing," though its music was incidental and its quality less than negligi-

4. Some preferred to jeer, as with *Photoplay*'s "This is a curious one. . . . A confusing job." Others, in the trade press and in outlying regions, declared their disgust with sordid subject matter treated in such a full-strength manner.

5. *The Melody Man* had also been a crossover-type show on Broadway in 1924, a drama with some songs by Rodgers and Hart. Columbia dropped these and added one forgettable new ditty.

ble. Mae Murray, the most extravagantly unreal of stars, was a nonplayer in Hollywood by 1929. Her pouty affectations and self-gratifying posing mesmerized crowds for years, most spectacularly in *The Merry Widow* (1925), until finally her propensity for temperament and self-delusion became wearing offscreen and on. A tour in vaudeville enabled her to bask in the adulation of a live audience and offered recourse against her blackballing by Louis B. Mayer, and eventually the talkies beckoned. Tiffany Pictures, a safe haven for the fallen, starred her in *Peacock Alley*, reworked from one of her silent hits. Overweight, overaged, petrified of the microphone, Murray laboriously attempted to recite lines and impersonate a nightclub dancer torn between two men. The desperation even seeped into some of the ads: "The Orchid of the Screen in Her Greatest and Most Gorgeous Offering. . . . A superb voice . . . . She's younger, more charming than ever!" Matters were not helped by attempts to underscore Murray's "versatility" with a badly dubbed song and a flashy Technicolor sequence in which she tangoed and impersonated a toreador and a bull. "Watch my feet!" she squeals.[6] The filming, not too surprisingly, had been a nightmare for all parties, and the only vestige of *Peacock Alley* after its disastrous run lay in a stream of legal animosity between Murray and Tiffany.

For Corinne Griffith, whose stardom in silents was founded almost wholly on her beauty, a comedown in talkies was seen as an elementary progression. Alexander Korda's *Lilies of the Field* (1930) her first all-talkie, was in some ways an upgraded equivalent to *Peacock Alley*—a story of a socialite who strays and pays, with nightclub sequences mixed in. The salient features of Griffith's performance were, in order: lovingly diffused close-ups, fancy poses in knockout gowns, nasal speech, a game try at tap dancing, and a feebler attempt to sing. The only interest in *Lilies of the Field* came from its Mechanical Ballet, a bizarre riot of Moderne and Deco notions that climaxed with the striking image of Griffith as a living autohood ornament. Financially, *Lilies* was a fiasco, and Griffith soon retired with (for a while) far more grace and equanimity than Mae Murray.[7] Even stranger was the case of serial queen Ruth Roland. She attempted to move from thrills to musical drama with *Reno* (Sono Art 1930), a minor yarn of motherhood and divorce that came to a halt on several occasions to permit Roland to prove that she sang better than she spoke.

6. The sequence, for which Xavier Cugat leads the orchestra, survives as an indelible record of Mae Murray's mislaid star complex. Her overripe figure unattractively revealed by a scanty costume, she scampers about like a hyperactive adolescent; it's almost as if Norma Desmond had been permitted to make *Salome*.

7. Since *Lilies of the Field* is a lost film, it would seem that its ballet sequence is only a memory. Not quite: a few moments of it survive in *The Tenderfoot*, a 1932 Joe E. Brown comedy. At one point Brown goes to a Broadway show and is entranced by the dancers and spectacle. What he's seeing is clips from *Lilies*, complete with precision-machinery chorus girls and dancing robots.

Crossover, Good and Bad: *(above)* Gloria Swanson and a hit song in *The Trespasser. (below)* Mae Murray, her face and waistline heavily retouched, struts her stuff in the Technicolor sequence in *Peacock Alley,* with Xavier Cugat's band in the background.

In most of these star sorties, musical sequences were misused to feign non-existent expertise. With Gloria Swanson the ploy was both legitimate and successful. Her silent stardom had been almost as florid as Mae Murray's, but under all her excesses lay the substance to back up the style. Near the end of the silent era she proved herself as *Sadie Thompson*, after which she planned to top Murray's *Merry Widow* by starring in an even more fabulous piece of Stroheim decadence. With her newly acquired professional and personal associate, Joseph P. Kennedy, she started production on *Queen Kelly*, one of the legendary debacles in American cinema. The saga is mostly well known—Stroheim spending Swanson's money like water, the uncompleted script developing along ever-stranger paths, and his termination when Swanson found his newest ideas too fetid to contemplate ("There's a madman in charge!"). The less-known aspect of the *Kelly* story was that by the time production began in fall 1928, it was slated as a part-talkie with music. As a silent it would have been outdated, and Swanson was determined to use sound to show just how versatile she was. She could sing. No Janet Gaynor make-do or Ruth Chatterton act-through-the-music here: this was a vibrant and exciting soprano. After Stroheim departed in mid-January 1929, Kennedy considered adding more music to *Kelly*, perhaps making it all-talking, but after some months the project was abandoned.

At her lowest professional ebb to date, Swanson and writer-director Edmund Goulding quickly went to work on a simple soap opera, *The Trespasser*, designed to introduce her to talkies in the most sympathetic possible way. As with Corinne Griffith and other silent heroines who deigned to sing, music did not necessarily fit well into a plot about a wronged woman battling to keep custody of her child. But Swanson knew how to form bridges from drama to song. When her character in *The Trespasser* began to succumb to romance, Swanson went to the piano and began "Love, Your Spell is Everywhere," written by Goulding and Elsie Janis to Swanson's vocal specifications. The song's rhapsodic melody set off her brazen upper range, and despite its stilted lyrics, it seemed true to the moment, possibly to the character, and certainly to an astute and talented star who knew a great deal about showmanship. Along with a compellingly pointed natural timbre, her musical performing had a rapt fervor—a naturalistic grand manner, if such is possible, centered firmly on illuminating both text and melody. She comprehended music far more when it was placed in a dramatic context, which is why her singing works better on film than on record.[8]

8. She also, when focusing on giving a performance, was less prone to go off-pitch, which sometimes happened on her records. Her second song from *The Trespasser*, Toselli's "Serenade," almost falls apart in its recorded version; in spite of her opulent tone, Swanson sounds as if she's sight-reading. Likewise the sensuous "Come to Me" from *Indiscreet;* she sings it twice in the film, both times with far more urgency than on her recording. The only one of her first six talkies in which she did not sing was *Tonight or Never* (Goldwyn/UA 1931)—in which, ironically, she played an opera star.

Her triumphant sound debut past her, Swanson, with proper guidance, should have moved on to more successes. But Kennedy, whose drive and ambition far eclipsed his abilities as a producer, still had *Queen Kelly* on the brain. While he was attempting to set up a deal to coproduce *Kelly* with MGM, he told the press, with characteristic brashness, that the project was being reconfigured as a Swanson operetta, with a score by Franz Lehar. Imaginative aggressiveness did not breed fact, however, and soon angry denials issued from the composer in Vienna: Kennedy had bought one song from him, and that was all there would be. *Queen Kelly* in sound was shelved, and for Swanson's second talkie, *What a Widow!*, Kennedy commissioned three songs from Vincent Youmans. Though audiences still loved Swanson and applauded her singing, a trifling piece of slapstick about empty-headed socialites seemed, in the bleak autumn of 1930, as out of step as a film could be. Likewise *Indiscreet* (UA 1931), which featured the final collaboration of DeSylva, Brown and Henderson. The discernment which made *The Trespasser* so right had vanished; that film had helped establish a major trend toward confessional soap operas, and had she done another one Swanson would have been better off than she was in empty comedies playing characters named Tamarind. The Depression rendered such doings high-handed and oppressive, the musical end of her allure now meant little, and the Kennedy partnership was up in smoke. Swanson was directionless, and despite some game tries, she would not resume her place on the cutting edge until *Sunset Boulevard*.

The Murrays, the Griffiths, even the Swansons were all displaced by a new breed, the most conspicuous of whom founded an entire career in an area where drama and music converged. With a background in cabaret and musical theater as much as in drama, Marlene Dietrich had the credentials to span genres with ease. She also had Josef von Sternberg, the American director who traveled to Germany and selected her for *The Blue Angel* (UFA 1930). Again, as with *Applause*, the backstage drama became a zone of distress, an axis for the tawdriness of the whole world. And Dietrich, as the cabaret queen Lola-Lola, stole the film away from its nominal star, Emil Jannings. The look, the legs, the impudence, the coarse sexuality all played major roles in the theft, perhaps the singing most of all. Sternberg was always more comfortable with visuals than with dialogue, but his instincts for the presentation of music were as valid as they were, on occasion, outrageous. Dietrich reclining on a barrel, one leg cocked across the other as she doffed her top hat, or straddling a chair, or mooning her greedy spectators in frilly panties—the images were startling, irrevocable, the most overtly sexual yet connected with musical performance. So were Frederick Hollander's songs, both in German and in translation. "Falling in Love Again" means something quite different from the German "From Head to Foot I'm Made for Love": one slice of romantic irony swapped for another.[9] Either way, and along with "Lola" and "This Evening Children (I Gotta Get a Man)," it defined Dietrich.

American stardom, after this, was no surprise, although the persona and the musical style changed a great deal. Weight loss and different lighting soon brought the archetypal hollow-cheeked Marlene look, and the strident soprano heard in "Lola" dropped an octave to the familiar sensual basso. *Morocco* (Paramount 1930), her American debut, permanently altered the rules for stars doing musical crossover. Again cast as a cabaret artist, Dietrich was now a bruised fatalist instead of a man-eating hussy, the sexuality of her songs overlaid with a new sly elegance. The erotic tension between star and director—however torturous its offscreen manifestation—propelled Sternberg to deal with musical matters with inventive audacity. In top hat and tails, Dietrich growls out a lament to dead love ("Quand l'amour meurt") as if it were an anthem of defiance, then pulls off a career-making coup by taking a flower from a spectator—female—whom she then thanks with a kiss on the lips. Between this and the brash wantonness of her subsequent "What Am I Bid for My Apples?" movie audiences were in a vastly different nightclub from the one where, a few months earlier, Alice White chirped "Ooh-ooh, I've Got My Eye on You-ooh." For years afterward nightclub singers in films, sometimes in real life too, would bear the Sternberg/Dietrich stamp. Ballads became huskier, lighting more painstaking, and languor was treated as a style instead of a passing attitude. Pola Negri's comeback try, *A Woman Commands* (RKO 1932), is a good example, showing more craft and flair in its one song number (Nacio Herb Brown's "Paradise") than in the whole rest of the dismal movie. Dietrich's (and formerly Negri's) home lot of Paramount was the epicenter for this type of treatment, and whether they could sing, like Claudette Colbert, or not, like Miriam Hopkins, or else were Tallulah Bankhead, few Paramount players escaped the consequences. The original always outdid the pretenders. After putting music to dramatic ends with Dietrich's *Dishonored* (1931) and *Shanghai Express* (1932), Sternberg put her in bona fide production numbers in *Blonde Venus* (1932). If the sheer simian and Freudian scandalousness of "Hot Voodoo" exceeds its aesthetic effect, perhaps that is what Sternberg wanted. In any case, next to this piece of sensory overload, even good musical films could momentarily appear dull and dowdy.

Morocco was far more a harbinger than *Under a Texas Moon* would be, and after 1930, music became more standardized in rapid order. 1931 was the most sonically arid year in sound-film history, with not even underscoring permitted in most cases, after which dramas and musicals gradually began to align their priorities. 1934, where this chronicle concludes, saw the

9. In the concurrent (and inferior) English version of *Der Blaue Engel*, Dietrich adds an odd variant during one chorus of "Falling in Love Again," when "What am I to do?" becomes "What's a girl to do?" She never did it that way again.

genres gradually begin to assert themselves in ossified form. Either a film was a musical or it wasn't, and it would be advertised as such; the taste of the moviegoing public was by now sufficiently regimented to accept what it was given on that basis. Seldom would there be the crossover lure of 1929, when advertising would hawk a drama as being "Spiced with snappy ballads" or other such confused ploys. More and more, consumers knew what they were getting, generically if not qualitatively. Filmgoing, under such circumstances, became safer and more predictable. Whether that was a good thing was left up to the individual viewer; those remembering *Applause* or *Hallelujah!*, or Gloria Swanson's vocal *coup de théâtre*, might have had cause for nostalgia.

CHAPTER 14

The March of Time

FLOPS OF 1930—Musicals Take The Lead
Film Daily headline, July 1, 1930

Question often asked the exhibitor by patrons is: "Is it a musical?"
If it is, there's a drop-off.
Variety, July 9, 1930

They are as sick that surfeit with too much, as they that starve with nothing.
The Merchant of Venice, Act I

Some crises are by their nature unavoidable, and when they set in, the resultant inevitability seems uncommonly dour. Eternal heralds of "I told you so" hardly cushion the shock and denial of those affected. Proponents recede, fingers point, and devastation reigns. Laws of gravity need not apply here, for all concerned react by overreacting.

Popular history's tendency to seek out anything that can be labeled "The First" was noted early in this story. Just as frequent is the quick-fix search, when disaster strikes, for simple and easily identifiable causes. It is perhaps inevitable, then, that the sudden death of the early musical remains probably its best-known aspect. Given the unending search for easy reasons, the same excuse is always cited: oversaturation. Everything, save quality, in too great a volume. And, as a glimpse at Chapters Eight or Twelve will suggest, the proliferation of backstage stories and operettas passed all comprehension. Nevertheless, satiation is only the most obvious component of the debacle. Other causes are more complex, and with ramifications far denser. Neither quantity nor even quality was totally to blame for the startling rancor with which spectators turned their backs.

323

At the outset of 1930 the picture had looked uncannily bright, even more so for musicals than for the industry as a whole. As far as could be detected, Black Friday had only a slight effect on film company stocks, and grosses and attendance were at record highs. The gamble of sound had paid off more sensationally than anyone could have imagined, and both studios and audiences seemed happy. Soundstages were operating at peak capacity, film budgets were being raised significantly, and studio schedules for the coming season were jammed with musicals of every description. By one journalist's count there were as many as three hundred songwriters and lyricists working in Hollywood; the Roosevelt Hotel, where most of them lived or congregated, had the air of a western branch of Tin Pan Alley. The trains were running east as well as west, for many newcomers were obviously not working out, yet there seemed to be a future of titanic promise. *Sunny Side Up* and *Gold Diggers of Broadway* and *Rio Rita* were drawing huge crowds, and bigger guns were being readied for the new year—*King of Jazz, Puttin' on the Ritz, The Hollywood Revue of 1930*—plus a run of operettas and Broadway adaptations. Making them more expensive seemed justifiable: after lucrative dreck like *Mother's Boy*, it followed that pictures many times superior and more costly would do that much better. All the studios felt that way and continued, with nearly manic diligence, to make better and more musicals.

In the midst of the overproduction, there had been at least one dire omen. *Syncopation* and *Mother's Boy*, among other musicals, had been produced at Pathé's New York studio, on Park Avenue at 134th Street. On the morning of December 10, 1929, during production of the musical short *The Black and White Revue*, the studio was destroyed by a flash fire. The casualties were appalling—ten dead, including dancers and crew members, and eighteen injured: perhaps the worst disaster in the history of film production. It was quickly determined that a piece of sizzling carbon from an arc lamp had fallen onto the flimsy (and nonfireproofed) scenery, causing it to go up almost immediately, after which there were delays in calling the Fire Department and evacuating the building. Scapegoats were eventually found in Pathé's executive wing, and the company's inadequate attempts at damage control hastened its imminent decline and ultimately its absorption into Radio Pictures. Carelessness was obviously a key factor of the tragedy, and the New York Fire Department began to take notice of the hazardous conditions under which studios in the city were operating. Production in and around New York quickly tapered off, and soon only two major outfits were in operation—the Vitaphone studio in Brooklyn, which was exclusively devoted to shorts, and Paramount's Astoria plant. That the Pathé fire had hinged on the production of a musical was not irrelevant. The haste and expedition with which musical features and shorts were being fabricated, here crossing over into criminal negligence, indicated the force-feed nature of the desperation. There had been so many intemperate follies amid the tumult: the hapless malfeasance of *Golden Dawn*, the cheapjack stupidity of *Howdy Broadway!*, the disastrous ill-planning of *Glorifying the American Girl*. And adding immensely to the level of stultification was the production of an endless array of musical shorts. When journalists predicted many more musicals for 1930, many also included the assertion that more substantial work would be needed.

The improvements did indeed come. Technique advanced rapidly, many performers and scripts became more suitable, and the governing aesthetic seemed to be progressing adequately. But by April gross receipts, so massive just four months earlier, started to slip precipitously. Exhibitors began to complain, and early in the month a *Motion Picture News* editorial carried the startling word that "The Musicals Strike Some Sour Notes."

> Speculating over the reason for the failure of musicals [at] the cash register, the inevitable conclusion is that the producer himself is to blame. The copycat tactics which have prevailed in this industry . . . unloosened on the market near and far melodic films in such a flood that it was inevitably apparent the public would tire of them. Just like those courtroom sagas of some months ago . . . . Everybody had them and it wasn't very long before the imitators found the negatives as well as headaches on their chests.

But was the problem sheer volume? In backstage films, unquestionably. Between the full musicals and the crossovers, that genre was played out. And the year-end overcrowding had also been excessive, Broadway adaptations joining with backstagers to put a stranglehold on the market. The effect was akin to a virus—because of a growing mistrust of backstage stories, anything with songs became more and more suspect. Yet note that most of these films fared exceptionally well through the winter of 1929–30; even something as derivative as *It's a Great Life* earned a profit. It was not until March, and *Puttin' on the Ritz*, that the impatience graph had skyrocketed. Much of the overcrowding came with smaller theaters often given to running films only one night. With the block bookings required by some distributors, they occasionally were compelled to play two or more musicals in the space of a week—too much for a one-theater small town.

The American film audience is a beast of many heads, and in early 1930 it was beginning to be turned in upon itself. After over a year of sound the public had finally begun to take the technology for granted. Not that the country could not still be jolted by a sound-related phenomenon: "Garbo Talks! in *Anna Christie*," as orchestrated by the MGM publicity department in March 1930, remains one of the great media events. Generally, however, sound was no longer a novelty, and as most spectators resumed evaluating film on the basis of content and merit it was increasingly clear that audiences were becoming polarized by the medium. Talkies were less universal, more specific than silents, and provoked more vested reaction from the spectator. And these responses were split along some clear-cut American lines: urban against rural, north against south—and, less seriously, east vs. west.[1] The implications here are fairly clear regarding the disparity in the spectators' backgrounds, realm of experience, and, in many cases, levels of education. Also, critically, the extent to which audiences were acclimated to live theater. It cannot be taken for granted that spoken drama—and "stage diction"—would have been automatically accepted by the entire filmgoing public. Radio's influence was not yet pervasive in this area, and regional accents and dialects in some places were sufficiently strong to reduce the appeal of many sound films and talking performers. Silents, relying on pantomime and action, had been far more egalitarian.

Musicals were an inevitable victim of this culture clash, and the problem lay not so much in bulk as in perceived unsuitability. On one hand, the codified system of artificialities structuring musical comedy could seem elusive and alienating to audiences not accustomed to them. "Characters bursting into song" or similar words turn up frequently in mid-1930 articles analyzing the collapse of the musical market, as the conventions of integrated music began after a time to strain the credulity of spectators lacking the frame of reference to accept them. Yet these less sophisticated viewers were frequently the ones to whom the studios directed their work. It had first been noticed with the the most deliberately artificial of the musicals, the revues. For all its stunt appeal and big grosses in the cities, *The Hollywood Revue* fared indifferently in small towns. It was so alien to traditional filmmaking that audiences drawn in by the star names were exasperated by the rigidity with which it ignored nearly every known rule of cinema. And this was not clear until six months after its premiere, for until then it played only in big cities, not in general release. Following right on top of that was *Show of Shows*, which likely did more damage than any other single film to taint the public's affection for musicals. As with *Say It With Songs*, spectators felt betrayed, and matters were not improved by *Happy Days*. Before the spring it was already concluded that revue on film was dead. Legend has it that by late 1930 films were being advertised with the proviso "This is NOT a Musical!" There is some evidence of this, but it's mainly rooted in the curse of revues. In March and April of 1930, such films as *Chasing Rainbows* and *The Cuckoos* did carry a tagline in their advertising saying, "Not a Revue."

1. Note, for instance, an observation from a little later on. *Motion Picture Herald*, reviewing the 1933 Fox musical *My Weakness*, noted that it had drawn large crowds at Radio City Music Hall. Then it added: "In certain communities in the hinterland, a large attendance at a New York Theatre may have the effect of an adverse reaction along the lines of 'if New York liked it, we will not.'"

Audiences, then, were unwilling to stretch their affinities to encompass plotless processions of songs and dances and gags. The other realm toward which they remained unbending was operetta, and with *The Rogue Song* and *The Vagabond King* it was the same as with revues—good in cities, less in those impatient little burgs all too resistant to claims of "culture." As the grosses for such films as *The Vagabond King* made clear, a musical could do turnaway hard-ticket business in a big city and not draw flies in small towns. The quandary could be doubly defeating with a film such as *Song of the West*. While its subject matter and treatment would appeal to the less polished film public, the operetta format and use of "class" singers would only make such crowds restless—and the exact opposite held in urban centers. Exhibitor hostility soon increased, fed by the excessive rental charges imposed on operettas by the distributors. *Vagabond King* and *Song O' My Heart* each cost over a million, and there were high tariffs for works as unsatisfactory as *Golden Dawn* and *Captain of the Guards*. This meant narrower windows of profit, and often higher ticket prices. So exhibitors fanned, and sometimes exaggerated, the flames of musical discontent. Their letters to the trade journals were filled with invective aimed at the film exchanges who overcharged for operettas and other expensive musicals, which then did no better business than pictures that had cost the exhibitor a great deal less. It became increasingly easy for theater owners, and then spectators, to shun these bombastic static pageants in favor of melodramas and low comedies.[2] Only a small number of musicals in 1930 could bridge that gap; few filmmakers had arrived at the proper set of compromises through which musicals could find a semblance of across-the-board popularity. Given the high cost of producing a big musical, this spelled financial disaster.

There was also the problem with color. In the wake of *On With the Show!*, most of the major studios signed contracts with Technicolor, which promptly bore fruit in the form of *Sally*, *The Rogue Song*, and so forth. Most people were happy, until the growing discontent with musicals began to coincide with a large batch of hastily processed prints from Herbert Kalmus's new Technicolor plant. Spectators might be willing to accept the limited spectrum and often unimaginative color schemes, but they would not countenance eyestrain. Between insufficient illumination, grain flecks the size of soccer balls, and—worst of all—blurred "fringing" caused by improperly aligned matrices, color became a literal headache. For studios, too, who had spent millions on prints whose delayed manufacture meant

2. A bizarre related excuse was offered by scores of exhibitors starting in the summer of 1930: the rise of miniature golf, considered a fresh novelty after audiences became accustomed to talkies. Some showmen attempted to fight it directly by installing miniature courses in their parking lots—a harbinger of dish night and other stunts deemed necessary to draw in Depression crowds.

that their release was pushed back and that now were generating outright hostility. When the complaints began coming in, Kalmus quickly took the defensive to claim that the problem was not so much Technicolor's as it was the studios', who ruined his process by relegating it to poorly designed and badly written musicals. What he did not announce publicly was that he was very much aware of the system's inadequacies, as well as the slip-shod quality of its current product.[3] He had already begun work on perfecting a three-color full-spectrum process, which would not come until 1932, and not in live-action films until late 1933. As the demand began to subside, the quality improved noticeably, as with *Whoopee!* and *Sweet Kitty Bellairs*. But not even the success of *Whoopee!* could stem the antipathy, which was such that a growing number of advertisements omitted any mention of color. The situation had become the exact opposite of a year earlier, when music and color had buoyed each other up.[4]

In mid-1929, musicals seemed a giddy reflection of the national mood—but one year later, while the movies remained flighty, the country was embarking on a long night of despair. The more severe impact of the Depression was still some time off, yet already there was beginning in many areas a creeping sobriety that seemed incompatible with musicals. Assuming a wary stance, a large portion of the public was not yet prepared to treat musicals as blues-chasing escapism. Once their novelty began to wear off, the inherent artificiality and frivolity of musicals demanded a suspension of disbelief most spectators were not willing or able to provide. In contrast, sex was selling. Despite the formulation of the Production Code in April 1930, prostitution and unwed-mother stories were paying off. Spurred by the success of Fox's *Common Clay* in the early fall of 1930, the industry began directing its attention to the primrose path. Gangster films, too, which had taken a dip in 1929, were about to make a comeback with *Little Caesar* (Warners/First National). This type of bleak sensationalism seemed far more in sync with the dominant temper than *New Moon* or *Sweet Kitty Bellairs*.

The studios, of course, had not foreseen the retreat in the American audience's capacity to accept escapist entertainment. The rapidity with which the shift occurred was so pronounced that, in mid-1930, the bottom promptly dropped out of the market. Film stocks had begun to recover fairly well from the stock market crash, but the sudden plunge in receipts

3. Demand for Technicolor was so great in early 1930 that the company's facilities were forced to expand as the processing work continued. Later, lab technicians would tell horror stories about attempting to do meticulously detailed work while riveters' guns blasted away nearby. No wonder some of the films looked so bad.

4. Another technical process taking an even more severe dive than color was widescreen film. Besides adding enormous expense to exhibitors, it made little impression on audiences. Most films received little or no exhibition in their wide versions; it would be twenty-plus years for that idea's time to come.

around that same time made for disaster. The fate of the motion picture industry during the early Depression is well known—Paramount and Fox tottering on the edge of receivership, Warner Bros. cutting everything (save executive salaries) to the bone, and only MGM staying afloat with some degree of poised profit making. The extent to which the collapse of the musical field accounted for these disasters cannot be underestimated. It was a terrible price to pay for joining that greedy bandwagon and losing touch with the public—and Warner Bros., which seldom did things in half-way measures, suffered the worst of all. The company had invested more, had made bigger plans, and, with its penny-wise/pound-foolish production schedule, had timed its musical releases farthest ahead. The results of all this were rendered in a vivid splash of red ink, which by 1931 indicated a net loss of $8 million.

The extent of the damage was such that instead of engendering mere indifference, musicals began to elicit outright hostility. The press, acting as a bellwether, told the story. *Photoplay*, reviewing *Leathernecking:* "In spite of a lot of things, they're still making musical romances." *Billboard* on the Denver run of *Sweet Kitty Bellairs*—"Exquisite coloring and picture a year late." *Variety* on the Pittsburgh run of *Bride of the Regiment:* "Typical operetta flop, hardly getting a terrible $6,000. Another operetta and how this burg hates them." A Kansas theater owner reporting on *Dixiana:* "A big flop. . . . Everett Marshall is a squawkie singer just like Dennis King." And an exhibitor in Ohio, offering some blunt criticism of *Show of Shows:* "A better title for me would be The Lemon of Lemons. Just three nights of empty seats. Even those few who saw it complained about it." The gripes continued, and by autumn 1930 the success of the few musicals doing good business was ascribed anywhere else. With *Whoopee!* and *Animal Crackers* it was comedy, with *Just Imagine* it was novelty and El Brendel, with *Madam Satan* (in its profitable first weeks) it was DeMille and sex. Otherwise the situation was dire.

The studios reacted to the crisis with the dazed rigor of a lapsed teetotaler attempting to vanquish the first hangover. As they had when sound came in, the film companies purged their rosters, this time of any talent with even a remotely musical tinge. The chorus people were cut first, then the musicians and actors, plus those pesky over-confident songwriters, whose departure would save the studios an estimated $100,000 per week. Day after day, the trade press reported the people whose contracts were terminated or bought out or not renewed—dance director Dave Bennett, Charles King, Jeanette MacDonald, Bessie Love, Claudia Dell, Carlotta King. MGM cut its music department by about 90 percent. Buddy Rogers was demoted from star to featured player. Months before *Viennese Nights* and *Kiss Me Again* opened, Alexander Gray and Bernice Claire were back onstage, singing their movie songs to live audiences.

In addition to the turnover in personnel, there were some hasty substitutions made in studio plans. There were no backstage films on the drawing board for the 1930–31 production season, and few Broadway adaptations. There were, however, a large number of operettas; the plans had obviously been made shortly after the beginning of the year, before the bombs started falling. In the summer of 1930, they were quickly removed. The shift in public taste can be demonstrated by a hasty substitution made by Radio Pictures. *Babes in Toyland* was taken off the 1930–31 schedule, and *Bachelor Apartment* was quickly added: no more Victor Herbert, lots more sex. Radio also canceled *Heart of the Rockies*, set to star the now highly undesirable Everett Marshall. The very titles of such films sound inappropriate when contrasted with current fare that was bringing in healthy returns: *Min and Bill* (rowdy schmaltz), *The Big House* (crime), and *Office Wife* (sex).

By aborting musical projects at or near the last minute, the studios were losing many thousands already spent on rights, scripts, and music. But it was far worse with projects already completed or well into production. With millions of dollars tied up, all hands attempted some ornate maneuvering to recoup as much as possible. As usual, the studio of excess suffered the worst and scrambled the most. Executives at Warner Bros., home of delayed-release patterns and chronic misjudgment of audience taste, believed (and hoped) that the national aversion to musicals would subside after a few months. *Bright Lights*, the Technicolor backstager with Dorothy Mackaill and Frank Fay, was shot in December 1929 and January 1930, opening in Los Angeles the following July. With its subject matter completely out of vogue, Warners decided to hold up its release in most places 2znfor another seven months. *Kiss Me Again* was treated similarly, and in neither case did the elapsed time improve the financial chances. With less overt musicals, Warners adopted a slash-and-burn policy: as much music was removed as could be without rendering the films completely incoherent. *The Life of the Party* and three Joe E. Brown pictures—*Top Speed, Going Wild*, and *Sit Tight*—were all restructured both during production and in the editing room to expunge offensive material. As a result, audiences were confronted with a host of musical comedy players (Bernice Claire, Irene Delroy, Jack Whiting, Paul Gregory, Claudia Dell) employed for almost anything except their vocal talents, and occasionally being glimpsed setting up cues for songs that did not follow. Since some of these performers had little to offer apart from their singing the move was aesthetically questionable, yet financially sound: these four comedies were among the few films to bring in profits to the studio during a very grim season.

A less happy fate befell *Fifty Million Frenchmen*, one of the authentic curiosities of the era. In 1929 Warners, with an eye toward filming, had backed the Broadway version—thus becoming the first studio to fully bankroll a live play. It was one of the company's more prudent investments that year, for audiences were delighted at the first full flowering of the Cole Porter style. "You Do Something to Me," the racy "I'm Unlucky at Gambling," and gamy "The Tale of the Oyster" all offered far more diversion than the book, which was the usual jumble about some not-so-innocents on the loose in Paris. But by the time Warners filmed the show the script had become a significant concern. Having planned to film the show as a big-scale musical, Warners sprang for a costly production and a cast filled with stage players—William Gaxton, Claudia Dell, Helen Broderick, Olsen and Johnson. But this was August of 1930, the same month that MGM scrapped *Great Day* and *The March of Time* and Radio terminated *Babes in Toyland*. Few things could have seemed less inviting than a fancy Technicolor musical comedy. So it was out with the songs, every last note, and in with more scenes for Olsen and Johnson. Between them and the insertion of some Sennett-like slapstick, *Fifty Million Frenchmen* became an intemperately rowdy comedy prone to moments of outright smuttiness, with insufficient leavening from the use of Porter's music as background scoring. Disguising it as a comedy was useless, for this show without its songs was less than zero; there was some critical comment that music, however alienating to current audiences, might have helped. Nor did Olsen and Johnson's earlier flop with *Oh Sailor Behave!* help; despite audiences' affinity for low comedy in 1931, *Fifty Million Frenchmen* died at the box office.

Demusicalization would also befall the best-trained voice in movies. Lawrence Tibbett's third MGM film was specifically designed to highlight his nonsinging abilities, although the presence of several songs was considered *de rigeur*. In *The Southerner* he was cast as an aristocratic ne'er-do-well who returns to the family plantation in time to stir up a ruckus. Despite Tibbett's game attempts at creating a raffish character, the story was not particularly well developed, and Harry Pollard—assigned this after the *Great Day* debacle—directed with a wonted heavy hand. It was clearly a letdown after the previous Tibbett films, and was judged as such when it opened regionally in February 1931. MGM, sensing the need for damage control, withdrew the film and attempted to give it Biblical resonance by changing its title to *The Prodigal*. It also shortened it by one reel, and in deference to the times the cuts were not of Pollard-induced inertia but of Tibbett's vocalizing: two songs ("The Glory Road" and "Life Is a Dream") were deleted, leaving little more than Tibbett's strong rendition of "Without a Song," which had been salvaged from *Great Day*. The questionable judgment of the deletions did not prevent *The Prodigal* from losing a sizable portion of its relatively moderate cost.

In addition to buying and investing in shows, Warner Bros. had also begun to pay for the services of many of the best composers and lyricists in musical comedy. In June 1929, the studio signed Sigmund Romberg and

Oscar Hammerstein II to a long-term contract for one film a year and continued the streak over the next months with the acquisition of Rodgers and Hart, and then Jerome Kern and lyricist Otto Harbach. The initial result of these investments was *Viennese Nights*, which upon its completion in March 1930 seemed to hold all the promise in the world. Came the dawn, and Warners had high-priced talent working on properties which, by mid-1931, no one would want. The most ignoble fate was reserved for Kern, by 1930 the most reputable composer in musical theater. Engaged to create the next Alexander Gray-Bernice Claire piece, he and Harbach created *Call of the East*, an unlikely Great War operetta that somehow bridged the gap between *Rose-Marie* and *The Dawn Patrol*. By production time some of the score was curtailed, and Gray and Claire were replaced by Jack Whiting and Irene Delroy. With a new title, *Men of the Sky*, and further musical deletions, it finally went into release in June 1931. Just enough music remained—two songs plus a few vagrant strains—to indicate what it had once been. But with nice musical comedy actors unable to carry serious drama and meaning absolutely nothing at the box office, and without any sort of clear-cut appeal, *Men of the Sky* ended up one of the biggest critical and popular flops in a year ridden with them. Its production cost, $462,000, had been comparatively high, due partly to Kern's fee; the total worldwide gross was, pathetically, less than half that sum.

After the prestige and fine reviews given *Viennese Nights*, Romberg and Hammerstein were given somewhat more respectful treatment. But their second Warner light opera was in some ways as inappropriate as the concurrent *Men of the Sky*. Directed by Alan Crosland, *Children of Dreams* was set in rural California and told of the lives and loves of itinerant fruit-pickers, one of whom becomes a singing star. That such a subject was given the green light was tribute solely to the songwriters' stature and clout. This time the public, in the summer of 1931, was permitted to get a full-strength musical; there were ten songs, plus frequent reprises, over a nine-reel length, the music so abundant that some scenes gave the impression of being through-composed light opera. Once again the cast was topped by stage players—Paul Gregory, Margaret Schilling—with no identification value, and the sight of contemporary poverty-stricken people bursting into rhapsodic apostrophe ("If I Had a Girl," "That Rare Romance," etc.) at routine intervals seemed, to Depression audiences, an offensive spectacle. *Photoplay*'s barometric postmortem was typical: "Another reason why the box-office turned thumbs down on musicals." Few were surprised that the reviews and returns were nearly as deficient as those of *Men of the Sky*.

Rodgers and Hart and librettist Herbert Fields came up with a vehicle for Marilyn Miller tentatively titled *Sweethearts*. Far more modest than the usual Miller fare, it offered a *Sunny Side Up* situation in reverse: the romance of a fluffy socialite with a hunky construction worker. Miller, perhaps sensing less opportunity than in her usual showcases, opted to film *Sunny* instead. Her role went to another musical comedy player, Ona Munson, while the construction man came from the Hollywood ranks in the unfailingly pleasant person of Ben Lyon. Given the blatantly un-Rodgers-and-Hartesque title *The Hot Heiress,* it was shot some weeks prior to *Fifty Million Frenchmen,* and, faring a little better than Cole Porter, the songwriters saw three of their songs make the final cut. Carefully billed as a comedy, *The Hot Heiress* found little favor following its release in March 1931. It seemed too gossamer-trivial and, once again, insensitive to the national mood. Nor, without the likes of "With a Song in My Heart," was the deliberately artless score the sort to draw attention. But this good-natured little romance with songs survives well and, like *Sweet Kitty Bellairs,* shows the intractable Warner Bros. style loosening up to accommodate unaccustomed material. The opening scene is particularly spirited, Rodgers's score blaring out a jangle of urban dissonance as director Clarence Badger zeroes in on a skyscraper in progress. After a few moments of banter with buddy Tom Dugan, Lyon launches into "Nobody Loves a Riveter but His Mother." Without preamble or conventional lead-in, the moment seems calculated to produce a small and amusing jolt, and Lyon's likably untrained voice matches the proletarian casualness of Hart's lyric. As with *Spring Is Here,* there's a thin plot and agreeable characters, and both Lyon and Munson are appropriately winning.[5] Even some professed foes of musicals admitted that *The Hot Heiress* benefited from its songs, though few audiences cared to find out.

Other studios handled the situation differently. Universal, where Uncle Carl Laemmle was bemoaning the $1 million-plus loss on *King of Jazz,* moved completely out of musicals without a second thought. Radio, likewise: Wheeler and Woolsey were just as popular in straight comedies that cost less and earned more than *Dixiana.* Paramount, Fox, and Goldwyn all had major participants who might overcome the hostility. With Chevalier and Lubitsch, Paramount felt able to proceed with *The Smiling Lieutenant,* and Fox, with Gaynor and Farrell on hand and the recent acquisition of George and Ira Gershwin, could move ahead with *Delicious.* Goldwyn, with Eddie Cantor and Busby Berkeley, felt the most secure.[6] But he too had a major flop at the end of 1930. In charisma if not disposition, Evelyn Laye was British operetta's equivalent of Marilyn Miller. Her radiant beauty,

5. Attractive as Munson was, her work here and in other Warner films made little impact. Eight years later everyone sat up when a painted and padded Munson played Hollywood's ultimate madam—Belle Watling in *Gone With the Wind.*

6. Berkeley, marking time between the annual Cantor-Goldwyn spectacles, pulled some occasional odd jobs during this lean period. Among them was a comic production number for Mary Pickford's unsuccessful *Kiki* (1931) and a routine for Universal's *Grand Hotel*-in-a-nightclub, *Night World* (1932). The latter (set to "Who's Your Little Who-zis?") offers a thumbnail Berkeley compendium, overhead shots and all.

The wrong people, the wrong time: The look and sound of Evelyn Laye and John Boles seemed to bear out the title *One Heavenly Night,* but the box-office figures told a different story.

innate grace, and luminous soprano would have seemed, at the beginning of the year, to be the answer to a movie producer's prayer. Goldwyn promptly signed her (at $50,000) to star opposite the immutable John Boles in an original operetta cobbled by some odd hands: story by novelist Louis Bromfield, script by dramatist Sidney Howard, and music by—this sounds like parody—the American/Austrian combination of Nacio Herb Brown and Bruno Gransichstaedten. As shooting progressed, Goldwyn's minions labored to find both the right tone and the right title. The former was never achieved; the piece, about a flower-seller's romance with a prince, moved randomly from serious Viennese to light spoof to brittle comedy to wearisome slapstick. Its climax was a wild scene of Laye and Boles hurling operatic imprecations at each other during a driving rainstorm. The title, after many changes (including *Moonlight Madness* and *Queen of Scandal*), became the noncommittal *One Heavenly Night.* Alongside the contemporaneous *Lottery Bride,* it looked and sounded pretty good: Laye cast her patented spell, Boles pulled his weight, and the Goldwyn gloss, including some handsome photography by Lee Garmes, was well in evidence. But even with more sex than operettas usually contained, it was a film totally discordant with its time, and that rainstorm scene, so enjoyably over-the-top when seen today, drew heavy critical derision. The public stayed away, and grosses were so non-heavenly as to be among the worst Goldwyn ever had. His next release, the grim *Street Scene,* seemed far more appropriate. Goldwyn, arch purveyor of big musicals, never came near anything like operetta again—at least not until *Porgy and Bess,* nearly thirty years later . . . which then finished off his career.

Goldwyn's fellow United Artists producer, Joseph Schenck, had a rougher time. His experience with Harry Richman had not deterred him from either musicals or Broadway egotists, and as Al Jolson's contentious association with Warners was winding down, Schenck offered him a staggering deal: four films at half a million each, the first to be *Sons o' Guns,* a mediocre Broadway musical acquired at the unwisely high fee of $110,000. After several months, with Jolson's movie stardom in even greater trouble than movie musicals, Schenck's coup began to feel less dazzling. He finally shelved *Sons o' Guns* and later sold it to Warner Bros. (who filmed it nonmusically in 1936). By the time Jolson did make a film for Schenck, it was two years later, and by that time the idea of paying him—or any performer— $500,000 to appear in a musical seemed a daft, anachronistic, and unwelcome reminder of intemperate times.

Schenck, it must be observed, was never averse to pursuing big names. His Broadway prospects not particularly bright at the moment, Irving Berlin was more eager than ever to follow the comparatively disappointing *Puttin' on the Ritz* with a movie triumph. While Berlin's script ideas for *Ritz* had gone unused, he was able to sell Schenck and UA on a package that included his own story, eight songs, and his services as supervisor. Harry Richman had overshadowed his first try, and this time Berlin was determined to do it himself. His none-too-original story detailed the stormy romance, in New York and aboard a transatlantic cruise, of a Wall Street bigwig and a famous aviatrix; love wins out even as he's wiped out by the Crash. With its essentially dizzy Jazz Age story tempered by somber post-Black Friday touches, this tale required no carbon tests to date it as early-to-mid-1930. Berlin titled it *Lucky Break,* then *Reaching for the Moon,* and for the aviatrix he signed one of Hollywood's most prominent musical women, Bebe Daniels. Both Lawrence Gray and Broadway's Jack Whiting were mentioned for the male lead, and after Ruby Keeler was ruled out, the second female lead went to Paramount's Ginger Rogers. Although Busby Berkeley was announced to stage the dances, the job soon passed into the less sparkling hands of Maurice *(The Great Gabbo)* Kusell. Then, in June 1930, the tone of the project was altered decisively when Douglas Fairbanks, one of the founding fathers of United Artists, stepped into the role of the Wall Street man. The screen's most popular swashbuckler was then heading toward his fifties and obviously in search of a change in direction; this was his first modern-dress role in a decade. He had no vocal talent whatsoever, which meant reconfiguring some of the musical chores, and suddenly *Reaching for the Moon* was subtly changing from a Berlin show to a

Fairbanks romp. Berlin, while recognizing the financial soundness of this casting, was not particularly pleased—and became less so with the work of writer-director Edmund Goulding, with whom he felt no rapport.

By the time *Reaching for the Moon* went before the cameras in September 1930, the budget had escalated to $1.1 million, including high fees for Fairbanks, Berlin, UA overhead, and some enormous Moderne sets by William Cameron Menzies. No Ginger Rogers, however—she had departed for New York, and her role went to June MacCloy. Despite ongoing audience aversion, the film was shot and initially previewed as a musical, with six Berlin songs, mostly for Daniels and the belter MacCloy, and one reportedly sung by Fairbanks. Then Schenck had second thoughts; few musicals had drawn more than flies over the past few months, and the odd combination of Fairbanks-Daniels-Berlin seemed unlikely to revive the glory days of *Rio Rita*. So all but one song was cut—not even Berlin's attractive title song was spared—and *Reaching for the Moon* became a straight romantic comedy. The sole musical survivor was the indifferent "When the Folks High-Up Do the Mean Low-Down," sung by Daniels, MacCloy, Bing Crosby, and shipboard chorus; despite the vaunted Berlin touch, it sounded like nothing more than a discard from the latest Alice White picture. The deletions only heightened the story's disjointedness and changes in tone—here a giddy romp, there a serious romance, there an opportunity for Fairbanks to show that he was still in physical trim. Despite a critical response that was equally uneven, *Reaching for the Moon*, though it could not possibly recoup its ruinously high cost, was not as drastic a money-loser as *Madam Satan* or *New Moon*. The public still liked Fairbanks—although, as with fellow UA stars Mary Pickford and Gloria Swanson, he was hastening the passing of his vogue by losing touch with the tastes of a still-loyal audience. Beyond that, and with its production problems well known within the industry, *Reaching for the Moon* soon became a symbol of what had happened to musicals. For Berlin, it remained one of the most unpleasant and ignominious experiences in a very long life, and in later years he would become incensed at the very mention of the title.

Along with the early sound era's biggest single triumph, *The Broadway Melody*, Metro-Goldwyn-Mayer was also responsible for some of its major fiascoes, but managed to keep its mistakes more private than other studios. Elsewhere, the iffy product would, however unwillingly, be eventually released. Paramount sneaked out *Night Club*, Fox declined to shelve *One Mad Kiss* and *Are You There?*, and Warners—even apart from *Golden Dawn*—often seemed to turn a blind eye to quality control. At "Retake Valley" in Culver City, the situation was handled differently. Much of it had to do with Irving Thalberg's drive toward "quality," as spelled out in the company manifesto furled around Leo's mane: "Ars Gratia Artis." In this case, Art for Art's Sake might be best interpreted as genteel middlebrow pretension.

The literary adaptations, the wan stabs toward "class" such as *A Lady's Morals*—these represented the countenance Thalberg preferred to give the world. Not that much of MGM's work of that time has a cultured air; this studio could tickle and tease *(Our Blushing Brides, Those Three French Girls)* with the best of them. Yet even when it trafficked in garbage, there was always something silk-purse and self-possessed about the Metro product. It had the biggest and best-funded production system going, and even its less prestigious output bespoke a lion's mark of superiority. The craftsmen and committees retooled the films incessantly, with more rewrites and retakes than anywhere else; there was a more intensive round of sneak previews as well, the better to determine just what was needed. Keep making it better, Thalberg would order, and don't be afraid to spend.

Some of the Metro philosophy has already entered these pages, mostly in a positive vein: the fine-tuning that made *The Broadway Melody* more special; the overhaul that put star shimmer into *The Hollywood Revue*; the quest for balance that accounted for Laurel and Hardy's presence in *The Rogue Song*. Also, the reshoot mania that accounted for two-director credits on *Lord Byron of Broadway* and *They Learned About Women* and steered them clear of outright calamity. The result of much of this work is obvious: MGM films generally had a less individual stamp than the finer work of other studios. Unless a director had the clout of Vidor or DeMille, his signature would give way to the high-gloss and frequently stilted buff job Metro seemed to give nearly every production. The dismaying ineptitude of a *Captain of the Guard* would be invariably averted at MGM; but rarely would a Lubitsch or even a Ludwig Berger have the opportunity to realize a personal vision.

More than the retakes that could stave off disaster, the MGM ethos came most conspicuously into play with the projects that were, in the end, totally abandoned. Any other company making *The Five O'Clock Girl* would have muddled through to the end. Perhaps there would be some heavy cutting and a retake or two, then a release that avoided major critics as long as possible; with a big star's name atop the marquee, and the announcement that it was a musical, it would likely have gotten by in a mid-1929 market. Yet even without the presence of William Randolph Hearst, MGM would not have done it, and it happened again this way with *Rosalie* and *Great Day*.[7] Once again, another studio would have seen them through to the end

7. Another Joan Crawford project a few months after *Great Day* was also treated drastically, in this case a salvage job that saved the picture. When *Complete Surrender* fared poorly at previews, Thalberg determined that the problem was star chemistry. So leading man John Mack Brown was replaced by the up-and-coming Clark Gable, and as *Laughing Sinners* the heavily reshot film was a financial success. (And, as footnotes to a footnote, Crawford did sing and dance in it, and the working title of the film, *Torch Song*, would figure again in Crawford's "musical" career.)

and, as Warners did with *Bright Lights* and *Kiss Me Again*, perhaps hold up the release to try for a more receptive audience later on. Metro simply pulled the plug and wrote them off, its finances being nearly as secure as its reputation was germane. Never was this more conspicuous than in the case of its most infamous nonstarter, *The Hollywood Revue of 1930*—retitled, with ominous prescience, *The March of Time*.

It began in August of 1929. *The Hollywood Revue of 1929* was doing turnaway business in reserved-seat engagements in large cities . . . ergo, filmed revues were the next leading trend. *Show of Shows*, *Paramount on Parade* and *Happy Days* were in various stages of planning or shooting, and the question of what to do with Paul Whiteman had been answered by making *King of Jazz* an extravaganza without a plot. There had been scattered rash declarations and predictions that movie revues might work—as they had on Broadway with the *Follies*, *Scandals*, and *Vanities*—as annual events. Fox was proposing a 1930 *Movietone Follies*, and Radio claimed that its *Revels* would become a yearly occurrence. MGM producer Harry Rapf, counting the returns from *Hollywood Revue*, had a similar thought. And while far less a visionary than an efficient studio hack, he began to conceive something different. Most MGM producers had specialties; Rapf's was lower-class schmaltz. While others concentrated on Garbo and Eugene O'Neill, Rapf turned out bread-and-butter hokum that consistently made money. Given his affinities, it's not too surprising that he maintained an acute nostalgia for the golden age of music hall entertainment—the days of Weber and Fields, Lillian Russell, Fay Templeton—and resolved to pay film tribute to those years with an overwhelming pageant ultimately titled *The March of Time*. Although Russell was gone, Rapf signed up Weber, Fields, and Templeton, along with some other veterans—DeWolfe Hopper, Louis Mann, Josephine Sabel, Barney Fagan, plus one already at the studio, Marie Dressler. Since few of those names meant much to 1930 film audiences, Rapf and director Charles Reisner expanded the concept to form, in effect, a one-film encapsulation of the whole of show business. For the past, the vaudeville people; for the present, a jazzier assembly of current MGM players; for the future, some of Gus Edwards's kid acts.[8] Accordingly, the vets filmed their songs and routines in late 1929 and early 1930. Weber and Fields revived their pool hall sketch, Louis Mann did his famous chicken routine, Dressler romped as an ingenue in a spoof melodrama, Templeton performed "My Dusky Dixie Rose," and the Albertina Rasch dancers appeared in massive re-creations of old-time Hippodrome spectacles. Reisner then started on the newer material, which included a light touch of class with Ramon Novarro's rendition of Messager's "Long Ago in Alcala,"

---

8. For a time the project bore the title *Just Kids*, referring both to the Edwards small-fry and, with unbearable cuteness, to the more venerable participants.

Disaster in the Making—*The March of Time: (above)* An ingenueish Marie Dressler cavorts with William Collier Sr. in a comedy sketch, while Joe Weber and Lew Fields look on. *(below)* Shooting the "Lock Step" number in Technicolor on MGM's extra-high new Stage Six. The Dodge Sisters are center stage, with Austin "Skin" Young on the right. (This number did reach the public on two occasions: in a 1934 MGM short, *Jailbirds of Paradise,* and in a clip in *That's Entertainment, Part 3* in 1994.)

Raquel Torres posing prettily in a clock number, and—where much of the money was spent—some enormous production numbers, mostly in Technicolor. One featured a giant violin and an offscreen Bing Crosby singing "Poor Little G-String," a huge prison set acted as a backdrop for a dance routine called "The Lock Step," and, biggest of all, a flock of showgirls formed a "living fan" approximately the size of Montana. Spectacular, no question about it, and shot by Reisner with almost no imagination or feel for cinema. This was after all not that uncommon early in 1930, but *The March of Time*'s most fatal flaw was that for all its "concept" it lacked organization. Except for the resolutely unexciting "old-timers" footage, it seemed to have even less point than *Show of Shows*.

The timing here was acutely pertinent. By February 1930, as shooting finished, it was beginning to look like trouble. Reisner promptly sent a rather desperate memo to Rapf stating that since revues were clearly dead, he would pump some story values into the picture. Instead, he shot more songs and sketches, featuring Cliff Edwards, Benny Rubin, Polly Moran, and the Duncan Sisters, and also considered numbers with Charles King and Lawrence Tibbett. The "future" segment with Edwards's kids was dropped, replaced by a routine by the Myers-White dog troupe (cf. *Dogway Melody* in Chapter Three). Months went by, and as the tinkering continued it became clear that such confusion was embarrassingly non-Metro. It had worked on *Hollywood Revue*, but this was a year later. Instead of hurriedly releasing the thing and accepting the consequences, the studio tried, without luck, to make it something better or, more unrealistic still, something other than what it immutably was. By early summer the industry was buzzing with rumors of a total failure, and with a much-quoted and very high price tag attached: over $750,000. After halfheartedly placing *The March of Time* on its fall release schedule, Metro shelved it.

While it was too late for damage control, MGM had already begun salvage operations. With a big overseas market and an extensive program of foreign-language versions, the studio cobbled together *Wir Schalten um auf Hollywood! (We Broadcast [from] Hollywood)*, a lighthearted tour of the film capital by German musical comedian Paul Morgan, that made ample stops for *March of Time* production numbers.[9] After this it was decided to build Technicolor short subjects around swatches of the revue. Thus, *The Devil's Cabaret*, a two-reel comedy featuring Eddie Buzzell, came to a halt for the Rasch ballerinas to execute a static "Devil Ballet." Through sentiment as much as financial considerations, Rapf still desired all that footage to be up on the screen. Beginning in September 1930, he began to run *The March of*

9. This all-but-unknown film also featured Adolphe Menjou in a major supporting role and newly shot cameo appearances by John Gilbert and Joan Crawford. While the title does not appear in the screen credits of either star, they each performed (in English) in a comic scene opposite Morgan.

Time for a succession of studio writers, then commissioned them to write a screenplay around the numbers. A massive pile of scripts began to accumulate, mostly bearing the titles *Toast of the Town* or *It's Gotta Be Big!*, and still nothing workable could be assembled to dispose of Rapf's unlucky revue. The practice continued for three years, and it soon grew to be a dark joke among the Metro scribes that any bright and unsuspecting new kid in the department would be lured by Rapf into the screening room to see his unreleased masterpiece, seduced into thinking that he or she might be the chosen one to solve the dilemma of *The March of Time* and save the studio. (Among the unsuccessful aspirants were Donald Ogden Stewart, director Karl Brown, and songwriter Clifford Grey.) A solution was not reached until mid-1933, and then it was hardly spectacular: *Broadway to Hollywood*, discussed in Chapter Sixteen.

The August 20 issue of weekly *Variety* carried three relevant articles. One announced the shelving of *The March of Time*, the other two concerned the demise of *Babes in Toyland* and *Great Day*. Nothing could have better epitomized the disastrous state of the art than these three events, coming all at one time. Three days later, *Billboard* clinched it with a front-page story under banner headlines:

MUSICAL FILMS ARE TABOO

SONG WRITERS RETURNING EAST IN GREAT NUMBERS

Cry of exhibitors that productions with music . . . are drug on market heeded by screen moguls . . . .

The only films named in the article were the Broadway musicals that deleted all their songs—*Fifty Million Frenchmen* and *Rain or Shine*. But titles weren't necessary; everyone knew. The red ink continued over the next months with the losses incurred by *Viennese Nights*, *New Moon*, *Madam Satan*, and *One Heavenly Night*, among others, and exhibitor resistance continued to mount. Perhaps in reaction, films in late 1930 and through 1931 became progressively dour, their tone reflecting the plunging grosses and slashed budgets and salaries. Theme songs were out, and background scoring was still too identified with musicals to be permissible. The genre had played itself out, as Warner Bros. found out with *Kiss Me Again* and *Children of Dreams*. And it seemed that the pendulum was in no hurry to swing back.

CHAPTER 15

Voices in the Wilderness

After 1931 had concluded, *Variety* labeled it "The worst year financially in the history of pictures [and] also, virtually, the worst annum in the existence of almost every other industry." There was none of the publication's usual hyperbole here. The Depression was in full force, and the film industry—from studios down to exhibitors—felt it and saw it reflected in the tone and quality of the films. Only a few films dealt with the crisis directly—*Reaching for the Moon* was one—yet most of the rest clearly seemed driven by cheerlessness. The escapism imparted by American film during the early Depression was, perhaps, the least frivolous it has ever been. A fusion of financial negativity, technical uncertainty, and aesthetic doubt prompted the movie industry to reckon the average American spectator in search of hard-edged fare. Traditional diversionary genres—Westerns, adventures, costume stories—were virtually nonoperational, and many comedies were often coarse and rough. The gangster film, earlier judged to be dead, staged a loud return, and horror films began a lurid and often violent cycle. Seldom, too, had sex and degradation been so prominent: 1931 was the year audiences were startled to see the fanatically wholesome Janet Gaynor play the most dissolute junkie in Shanghai in *The Man Who Came Back.*

Musicals maintained their status from late in 1930: they were nearly nonexistent, and all but a few of the small number of musicals released in 1931 were leftovers from the previous year—*Kiss Me Again, Children of Dreams, New Moon, Bright Lights, One Heavenly Night*—which all did poorly. The moratorium had bred contempt, and both industry and public antipathy seemed to continue. Not all felt the demise to be permanent, for many insiders did believe that musicals would stage a return. "When they can be well done" was the standard condescending platitude, as if some of the earlier musicals hadn't been. Each new musical in 1931 was carefully observed to see if it would be the next *Broadway Melody*, to bring back the trend with a bang. Several of the 1931 and early 1932 musicals did achieve financial success, but with the industry's current Depression blues plus the memory of those late-coming musical failures, there was immense resistance. Each of the successes during this dry period was given an alibi, some reason why it succeeded besides or despite the fact that it was a musical. The public, for the most part, was not given the chance to judge whether musicals should be staging a comeback. Yet overseas the popularity of American musicals had abated far less. The saturation had not been as intense, and, Depression or not, escapism and frivolity were accepted with far greater equanimity in foreign climes, such as the remainder of the Americas, Europe, and much of the rest of the world as well. *Viennese Nights*, for example, was the top-grossing film in Australia in 1931, with a record-breaking run at Sydney's Prince Edward Theatre, and the popularity of Jeanette MacDonald and Maurice Chevalier extended to China, where they ranked high on a list of most popular stars early in 1933.

Just as significant a phenomenon was the launching of the European movie musical even as the American variety was dying. The earliest efforts tended blandly to repeat stateside conventions, and then some French and German artists began to find their own way. René Clair's conversion to the merits of sound, as partly prompted by *The Broadway Melody*, has already been mentioned. By late 1929 he had created *Sous les Toits de Paris (Under the Roofs of Paris)*, which made it clear that the painfully literal nature of so many American sound films would have no place here. Clair interwined the visual rhythms of silent film with the new element of sound, and the result blends so seamlessly that it's often difficult to tell if the music is propelling the visual or vice versa. The more prosaic reaches of plot and dialogue did not matter very much, for Clair's world ran on music and image. He expanded his ideas over the following years in *Le Million* (1931), with its captivating sung dialogue, and on to the social satire, simultaneously penetrating and benevolent, of *A Nous la Liberté* (1932). So pervasive was the effect of these three films that for years afterward, whenever actors or objects in films were seen to move in a rhythmic or percussive fashion, or whenever a camera's movements seemed timed to music, the director was "doing a René Clair." Innovation, as it often does, became cliché—which makes it all the more impressive that Clair's films retain their freshness.

Clair was the predominant, virtually sole force in French musical cinema for some years. In Germany, a number of directors expanded the country's deep-rooted traditions of operetta and *singspiel* onto film with resource and a singular combination of allusive wit and Teutonic ponderousness. The first major international success (*The Blue Angel* was a unique exception) was

Geza von Bolvary's *Zwei Herzen im Dreivierteltakt* (*Two Hearts in Waltz Time,* 1930), which in its technically crude way managed to evoke genuine lyricism with far more panache than did the likes of *Song of the West.* It soon attracted attention in German-American communities and on the burgeoning art-house circuit, running a solid year in one New York theater. The musical remained alive, then, for certain audiences and for creative hands versed in lyrical tradition, and German studios exploded into a musical boom as forcefully as the U.S. had in 1929. The creative roster included directors Erik Charell, Willy Forst, and Wilhelm Thiele, and writers Walter Reisch and Billy Wilder. Among performers, Richard Tauber found film much more conducive to his musical style than had another much-loved tenor, John McCormack, and more traditional stars emerged in Hans Jaray, Willy Fritsch, British émigré Lilian Harvey, and Renate Müller. *Dr. Caligari* and films by Lang, Murnau, and Lubitsch had in earlier years imparted the might of German filmmaking. The country's musicals indicated that the creative tradition was being upheld. In more frivolous quarters, admittedly, yet with unquestioned style and uncommon substance. After *Zwei Herzen,* other German musicals began making the international rounds, often in concurrently filmed versions in French and English. One of the most distinctive, and least successful abroad, was G. W. Pabst's mordant reworking of Weill and Brecht's *Die Dreigroschenoper* (*The Three-Penny Opera,* 1931). It was too caustic for American audiences, who preferred Charell's *Der Kongress Dantz* (*Congress Dances,* 1931), with its sumptuous fairy-tale setting and plot overlaid with innuendo and satire worthy of Lubitsch, and with rhythmically conceived sequences derived from René Clair.

England found some of its bearings through the German product after a somewhat rocky start with weak imitations of American work.[1] *Sunshine Susie* (1931) was a British-produced version of Wilhelm Thiele's *Die Privatsekretärin* (1931), a light tale of a secretary's romance with her boss. As directed by Victor Saville with a full battery of graceful and witty touches, it surpassed the original and became an unexpected and fitting hit. The effervescent Renate Müller, who had also played the title role in the German, French, and Italian versions, scored particularly strongly with "Today I Feel So Happy" (Paul Abraham and Desmond Carter), as big a hit in Britain as "Happy Days Are Here Again" had been across the ocean. Saville, already working out some of the dynamics of sound in earlier works, obviously communed with both the letter and spirit of the Lubitsch and Clair films, and his absurdly low (by Hollywood criteria) budget, $150,000,

---

1. Besides the backstage musicals and *Elstree Calling,* another early British effort reflecting American trends was *The Loves of Robert Burns,* one of 1930's major failures. The stalwart tenor Joseph Hislop portrayed Burns in a soapy fiction that seemed to combine the worst elements of *Song O' My Heart* and *A Lady's Morals.*

went less for production values and inflated salaries than for genuine cleverness and authentically spirited entertainment such as Hollywood had seldom attained since the beginning of sound. Without major stars or prestigious collaborators, Saville created a small and unmistakable gem, and he soon followed it with a delightful series of films—*Evergreen, First a Girl*, etc.—showcasing the first major star to emerge from British musical cinema, Jessie Matthews.

The unbridled ebullience of *Sunshine Susie* was in the greatest contrast imaginable to the mood in the United States in 1931, both in life and on film, and in such an environment few in the industry were inclined to delve into similarly light—let alone musical—material. The first musical placed in production after the official demise of the cycle, *The Smiling Lieutenant*, was the work of Ernst Lubitsch, whose prestige and clout were such that he could choose his own projects. *Lieutenant* was a stepchild of *The Love Parade*, with a full operetta as source material—Oscar Straus's *The Waltz Dream*, which Lubitsch had originally intended to film in 1925 when he was at Warner Bros. At that time his claim on the property was usurped by UFA in Germany, who released a silent *Waltz Dream* directed by Ludwig Berger. Lubitsch, retaining his fondness for the project, decided in the fall of 1930 to star Maurice Chevalier in a remake that would have the benefit of Straus's lustrous score. That musicals were considered obsolete mattered less to him than the opportunity to reteam with Chevalier, and the combined lure of this pair was sufficient grounds for Paramount to sanction a costly and ostensibly risky project. Filmed in January-March 1931, *The Smiling Lieutenant* was the most ambitious project at the Astoria studio since the mid-twenties, studio flackery proclaiming it the first million-dollar talkie made by its eastern division—though, unofficially, *Glorifying the American Girl* had exceeded that figure. Since Jeanette MacDonald had signed a contract with Fox, the director cast two less vocal stage performers who had made films at Astoria. Claudette Colbert was cast as Franzi, the musician who catches the eye of Chevalier's Niki, and Miriam Hopkins as Anna, the wallflower princess who blossoms after her arranged marriage to Niki. Lubitsch, possibly with a wary eye directed toward the financial fate of recent operettas, decided to forgo the more serious lyrical outpourings of the genre and use Straus's waltz "While Hearts Are Singing" solely as an instrumental, except for a moment when Colbert recited the lyrics. Most of the remainder of the stage score was jettisoned, and Straus wrote several new songs (lyrics by Clifford Grey) specifically to advance character and situation. "Toujours L'amour in the Army" was the standard Chevalier-singing-his-libido-directly-to-the-camera entry; "Breakfast Table Love" portrayed Niki's affair with Franzi in lines such as "You bring passion to the prunes"; and the cheeky mistress gave advice to the dowdy bride in "Jazz Up Your Lingerie."

Any financial risk was promptly indemnified as soon as *The Smiling Lieutenant* opened in New York in late May to turnaway crowds and enthusiastic notices. The response was repeated in urban areas around the nation—indeed, around the world, particularly in French-speaking countries that received the three stars in the concurrently produced *Le Lieutenant souriant*. At a time when the film industry's overall financial figures showed a ruinous decline from those of the previous year, Lubitsch and Chevalier were invincible, and year-end reports showed *The Smiling Lieutenant* as one of the top moneymakers, and Paramount's biggest-grossing film, of 1931. The only resistance came in smaller communities, where foreign actors, Continental wit, and affably frank sexuality were regarded with suspicion or distaste.[2] Otherwise the film's success was total and comprehensible: there were simply no works of wit or allusion—or musical humor—to compete with it. But the success was seen as a tribute to the strength of the Chevalier-Lubitsch partnership, not as a bucking of the apathy toward movie musicals.

As the result of an ongoing copyright dispute that had raged since the time of the silent-film version, *The Smiling Lieutenant* was completely out of circulation for many years, eventually rumored to be a lost film. As in many such cases, (a) it was merely unavailable, perhaps a bit misplaced, and (b) legend incremented the merits of an unknown quantity. When it resurfaced, the general elation was tinged with the inevitable letdown. Some of the disappointment pertained to technique. Lubitsch was indeed expanding his mastery of sound-film methodology beyond the occasional missteps of *The Love Parade* and *Monte Carlo*, with more camera movement and background scoring than nearly any other 1931 film. The use of visual metaphor, too, was in full bloom: one shot of breakfast cooking was all that Lubitsch needed to convey the information that Niki and Franzi have commenced their affair. Still, he could not completely neutralize the stiffness and sense of confinement endemic to films shot in the New York studio.[3] Plus, more than *The Love Parade*, the barometer of social attitudes in the intervening decades relocated *Lieutenant*'s bedroom politics into highly suspect climes. Franzi, the intelligent and self-reliant leader of an all-female orchestra (The Viennese Swallows), is made to renounce her

2. One Lubitschean exchange in particular was a likely thorn in the side of some xenophobic viewers. The Hopkins character tells her father (George Barbier) that if she isn't permitted to marry the lieutenant she'll resort to extraordinary measures—marry an American. The King is, of course, shocked.

3. Déjà vu was a hallmark of the Astoria style, for close quarters and managerial considerations dictated that the same sets be reused from one film to the next. The key incident in *The Smiling Lieutenant*—the ceremonial parade where Hopkins believes Chevalier's smile is directed at her instead of Colbert—is played out on the same street on the Astoria back lot (now a parking lot) that had previously witnessed scenes from *The Battle of Paris* and *Applause*.

Lubitsch did manage to surmount the studio crimp in one witty transitional shot of a train, in which he heightened the story's fairy-tale nature by having a flagrantly unreal toy train tootle through a painted countryside.

claim on the man she loves with the line intended to set the kiss of death upon independent women: "Girls who start with breakfast don't usually stay for supper." Men, naturally, need not labor under such strictures, although despite Chevalier's mastery, Niki may now seem less imperturbable scamp than irresponsible louse. The performances of Colbert and Hopkins are so good, in fact, as to undercut the likely intentions; both characters deserve better than they get from Niki or Lubitsch. Yet withal, and especially in a grim year, the many felicities of *The Smiling Lieutenant* overwhelm most of its flaws.

Palmy Days was the inevitable rematch, in black and white, between the *Whoopee!* team of Samuel Goldwyn, Eddie Cantor, and Busby Berkeley, and it owed its success to the same recipe that prompted Lubitsch and Chevalier: bankable star in foolproof formula. The title, ironically sideswiping the current national situation, referred to a ring of bogus spiritualists for which Cantor served as an unwitting front man, and more than *Whoopee!*, *Palmy Days* configured the design of Cantor's later vehicles. He would play a character named Eddie who bumbles into some dangerous or larcenous situation and by dint of his own hyperactivity emerges victorious, while a secondary love plot lurked barely detectable in the background and music acts as garnish. Cantor, his radio popularity burgeoning, was bolstered by a salary increase that now earned him $175,000 per film and 15 percent of the gross,[4] and Goldwyn's post-*Whoopee!* confidence in Cantor's drawing power was such that the budget for *Palmy Days* staggered into seven figures. Ads blared it to the world: "Looks like a million! Costs what it looks like!" The brashness of the ploy, and of the film, worked as well with the public as it had with *Whoopee!* and even more profitably in some cities. Once again a public otherwise uninterested in songs and dances was willing to traverse musical environs suitably garnished with laughs, largess, and Goldwyn Girls. In the gloom of autumn in 1931 this was a combination uniquely suited, in the words of one critic, "to help President Hoover relieve any one of their *[sic]* feeling of depression." With only three major song sequences, *Palmy Days* assumes its musical mantle cautiously, albeit unquestionably, and any non-Cantor element takes a determined back seat. This includes the estimable Charlotte Greenwood, plus George Raft as a hood, yet before the star takes over, Berkeley is permitted a dynamite opening. In the gymnasium of a surreally outsized Goldwyn bakery, Greenwood leads the Goldwyn Girls through the bluntly titled "Bend Down, Sister." "Ham and eggs," Greenwood chimes, "should always be outside looking in," and Berkeley stages this tribute to diet and exercise with unerring randiness, progressive cinematic ingenuity, and a healthy portion of

---

4. Along with his heavy broadcast schedule and personal appearances, Cantor had also co-written a movie script for a fellow comedian. *Mr. Lemon of Orange*, an El Brendel vehicle par excellence, had been released by Fox in March 1931.

cleavage. Of the other songs the prime entry was "Yes, Yes (My Baby Said Yes, Yes)," soon a Cantor standard, with Con Conrad and Cliff Friend's reiterated music and lyrics—"Swanson, she's jealous of Swanson/And not only Swanson, but Clara Bow!"—tallying smartly with Cantor's manic edge.

The Cantor formula seemed as bankable as any during the uncertain autumn of 1931, so MGM attempted an imitation *Whoopee!* with another Broadway star-clown. The studio secured the rights to the Broadway musical *Flying High* and the services of its star Bert Lahr, then spent nearly a year avoiding musicals entirely. Finally, as Busby Berkeley and Charlotte Greenwood were finishing up *Palmy Days* in the late summer of 1931, MGM engaged them and proceeded with *Flying High*. The show had been another DeSylva, Brown and Henderson item keyed to a current fad— here, stunt flying—and its ramshackle book and mild score played second fiddle to Lahr's antics. Metro hands reworked the script, replaced all but the title song, and placed Greenwood in the role played on Broadway by her precise physical opposite, Kate Smith. Under director Charles Reisner it remained a Lahr show, no question about it, with much of the hubbub circling around his screwy "aerocopter" invention. Between the star and Berkeley's two big numbers, *Flying High* was well reviewed when it opened in December—but, even with a budget far less than the Cantor films, it lost a great deal of money. This was mainly due, one way or another, to Lahr. Apart from one Vitaphone short he was unknown to the larger film-going public, and his technique could seem overpowering to unaccustomed eyes and ears. Incontestably superior to Cantor as a clown, he lacked his rival's camera savvy, for a style formed from bluster somehow transferred to movies less well than one based on high-strung tics. Perhaps it was true, as later stated, that Lahr had to wait for a nonhuman role—the Cowardly Lion—to find the proper channel onto film. In *Flying High*, solo and in conjunction with Greenwood or Charles Winninger, he's performing to the balcony, his reactions and takes broad enough for a truck to drive through. Busby Berkeley, on the other hand, seemed to be growing more cinematic. Deprived of the Goldwyn vulgarity and some of the Goldwyn budget, he started to explore other tricks, as in "Happy Landing," where he paid tribute to aviation by having the chorus form the words "Byrd" and "Lindy" for the benefit of the overhead camera. In contrast to Reisner, whose direction of *Flying High* maintained the stiff artificiality of earlier MGM musicals, Berkeley was clearly pushing for mobility and composition, and his work comprises *Flying High*'s main significance.

At the same time it attempted to join the Cantor sweepstakes, MGM also tried again with Lawrence Tibbett, whose film days were clearly numbered. After the failure of *The Southerner/The Prodigal*, a battery of writers created *The Cuban Love Song*, a reworking of the *Madame Butterfly* plot with the emphasis shifted to the man's role. It juggled romance, comedy, tragedy, and music in fairly attractive proportions, with the star as a marine stationed in Havana who becomes involved with a fiery peanut vendor, portrayed with wonted salsa by Lupe Velez. Her occupation cued Tibbett's rendition of the current hit song "The Peanut Vendor," trick photography enabled him to sing the title song in a duet with himself, and he bore up as well in comic byplay with Jimmy Durante as he did in the numerous love scenes. *The Cuban Love Song*, despite some mixed reviews, did in fact bring the studio a profit—the only one of its Tibbett films to do so. His stardom, however, seemed more manageable on the stage of the Metropolitan Opera than at MGM, and this was his last film for the company.

Marilyn Miller was equally out of temper with a nonmusical time, and the fact that Warner Bros. announced her for three films for its 1931–32 season was perhaps due to considerations less professional than personal—i.e., Jack Warner. In the event, only one film was made. *Her Majesty, Love* was the first of a series of American films that owed more to the emerging German musical cinema than to any domestic trends. It was a literal and in some scenes shot-for-shot remake of a German film *(Ihre Majestät die Liebe)* directed by Joe May and released earlier that year, a Cinderella yarn with music about a barmaid and a millionaire. At this time and at this studio, such gossamer would not easily transfer onto American celluloid, and under the supervision of director William Dieterle it took on an unbecoming grimness. Miller, given no opportunity to do any of the things she did best, seemed even stranger than she had in *Sunny*, and somewhat ill-matched with the uncomfortably cast Ben Lyon. The music, while attractive, was used in such a way as to appear beside the point, and only W. C. Fields, in his talking-feature debut, emerged with credit as Miller's loopy father, playing with an off-and-on Viennese accent and wrecking a society banquet with one of his juggling routines. While not a financial disaster on the order of *Children of Dreams*, *Her Majesty, Love* was by no means a success, and its showing was used to demonstrate that audiences in early 1932 were not yet ready for a return to musical fare. A concurrent Warner offering, *Manhattan Parade*, was marginally more successful though similarly odd. Early on it had been planned as a musical, with components assembled from successes past: Winnie Lightner, a theatrical setting, vaudevillians Smith and Dale, and an elaborate Technicolor paint job. By the time it was released it had no music apart from Harold Arlen's "I Love a Parade" over the credits, and a subdued nonsinging Lightner was indeed a puzzlement. Like *Her Majesty, Love*, *Manhattan Parade* was an example of the uncertainty besetting its studio at a crucial point in its existence.

The final major musical to open in 1931 was simultaneously the most predictable and the least expected. Without managing to attain any kind of reasonable entity, it somehow merged utter conventionality with a daring as rare for the genre as for Fox Films. In August 1928 the studio had hinted that it was reaching a deal with George Gershwin to write the score for a Movietone musical comedy. Four years after *Rhapsody in Blue* and months before the first movie musicals, Fox's willingness to engage such a talent was a positive harbinger at an equivocal time. When the deal fell through, Fox signed the more conventional DeSylva, Brown and Henderson, though it remained tempted by the idea of a Gershwin musical. He finally did sign with Fox in 1930, to be paid $100,000 to write an original musical comedy with his lyricist brother Ira and librettist Guy Bolton. The possibilities could have been immeasurable, but in the early fall of 1930 Fox wanted something bankable. Paramount had Chevalier/Lubitsch, Goldwyn had Cantor, and at Fox there was Janet Gaynor and Charles Farrell, neither doing as well without the other and Farrell hopelessly lost in sound film without his partner. As sophisticates snickered and critical impatience began to heat up, the larger public remained captivated with them to the extent of making such tripe as *High Society Blues* and *The Man Who Came Back* major successes. Bolton, constricted by the nothing-succeeds-like-success ethic and the needs of a collective dramatic range well this side of the Lunts, could do no better than take the basic outlines of *Sunny Side Up*, El Brendel included, and funnel them through Ellis Island. Gaynor, struggling with a Highland brogue, was cast as a winsome Scottish immigrant (Heather, no less) who meets a polo-playing Prince Charming (Farrell) on the boat coming over and narrowly misses deportation before the course of true love runs smooth. Such additional complications as arose came from a young Russian composer and Farrell's socialite fiancée.[5]

Gershwin's initial instinct was to take the money and run; Hollywood night life, even in the iffy closing weeks of 1930, bore considerably more appeal than coming up with tunes for actors who didn't sing very well. "Blah Blah Blah" had, in fact, already been tried out, with different lyrics, in the Ziegfeld flop *Show Girl* and in the aborted *East is West*. Another song, "Delicious," gave the film its title in place of the provisional *Skylines*. Gershwin reserved the major portion of his gifts for two set-pieces unlike anything tried in film up to that point. The first, a dream sequence, neatly posited an immigrant's optimism in operetta style: Gaynor welcomed off the boat by the press, by Mr. Ellis (of the Island Ellises), and finally by a rather sexy Miss Liberty herself. While it seems slightly curtailed—Fox was likely leery of the content—the scene clearly shows a composer and lyricist working to expand a conventional form beyond ordinary literal bounds, and Gaynor's determined artlessness comes off nicely in a fantasy

5. The Russian was portrayed by Raul Roulien, a native of Rio de Janeiro; this particular immigration saga was not the occasion for ethnic verisimilitude. The casting of the socialite was particularly insensitive. Earlier in 1931 Virginia Cherrill had glowed as the blind flower-seller in Chaplin's *City Lights*—and here she was as a haughty creep.

Scottish immigrant Heather (Janet Gaynor) is welcomed to the New World by a uniquely American octet in the Gershwins' dream sequence from *Delicious*.

setting. The second sequence brought forth the concert-hall Gershwin in the form of "New York Rhapsody." Gaynor flees from the police into an Expressionistic nightmare Manhattan, alone in a big city of looming shadows and off-angle compositions, alternately soothed and prodded by Gershwin's bluesy outbursts. The piece worked extremely well, and later, as the Second Rhapsody, it became a standard concert work a couple of rungs below "Rhapsody in Blue." Gershwin would not work again in film until nearly six years later, near the end of his brief life, and never on a score for a dramatic film. *Delicious* is the closest he came and, for its comparative unimportance in his canon, it intimates tempting potential he never realized.

So thirteen or so minutes of *Delicious* lived up to the promise movie musicals had intimated from the beginning. That part was imaginative and accomplished, combined stage enterprise with film resource, and like *Sunny Side Up* inspired director David Butler to work way above his norm. Unfortunately, there remained about an hour and a half of film far closer to *High Society Blues* than to *Of Thee I Sing*, the show to which Gershwin turned his attention after leaving Hollywood early in 1931. Without his presence the Fox creed took over, and as with most films of its year *Delicious* is unduly heavy, the work of filmmakers who defeated the technical limitations of sound yet remained artistically pent up. It contains the long pauses and arid stretches of works of the previous two years, and without background scoring—think of the opportunity lost here—and with full doses of El Brendel's humor, it seems singularly joyless. Farrell's limited screen time (with nothing to sing) inspires gratitude, but with only four songs apart from the two major set-pieces the music is skimped and, in context, not particularly impressive. Fox was nevertheless so certain of its chances that the advertisements mentioned the music prominently. It had been many months since songs were felt to aid a film's appeal, however much the name Gershwin was subsidiary to those of Gaynor and Farrell. Because of the stars and the notable lack of competitive "family" entertainment at the time, *Delicious* made a strong showing as Fox's Christmas attraction for 1931. ("Encourage this clean picture by attending it," directed *Photoplay*.) Although Gershwin's name bought Fox some pleasing P.R. in big cities, *Delicious* would have been a success with music by anybody, or by nobody at all.

The final tally at year's end, not counting holdovers and hangovers from 1930, was three unequivocal hits, all with proven stars and formulas; two failures; and *The Cuban Love Song*, which was less of a success than it was a nonflop. Contrasts with the preceding two years, as well as the current boom in Europe, could not have been more stark, and nothing indicated a less occluded situation anytime soon. Theaters were going dark, budgets and salaries continued to plunge, and so did grosses and attendance. In 1930, average weekly film attendance had reached a record 110 million, up from 65 million in 1928; by 1932 the figure was down to 60 million. This seemed to few in the industry as a time to consider bold musical moves, and so the small amount of ground held in 1931 would be timorously maintained in 1932. Paramount had Chevalier and Goldwyn his annual Cantor extravaganza. The rest were silent. MGM and Warners, each burned by failure, saw no need to try again; and Fox could put Gaynor and Farrell into other fare and make just as much money.

With Radio Pictures, presently RKO-Radio, the decision to try the company's first musical since *Leathernecking* was prompted in some ways by simple expedience. In March 1931 Radio purchased the rights to the Gershwins' *Girl Crazy* for $33,000, contemplating going the *Fifty Million Frenchmen* route and removing the score entirely—though if ever a score had made a show, it was here. "I Got Rhythm" and "Embraceable You" and Ethel Merman's epochal Broadway debut were far more important to the show's success than its regressively trivial modern-Wild West plot. However, regressive trivia was not totally out of line with Radio's leading comedy stars, and the *Girl Crazy* plot was reworked just enough to allow for Wheeler and Woolsey instead of the stage's Willie Howard. What remained of the score was relegated to a position well behind the team's antics and those of Mitzi Green. The Gershwins contributed a new song, "You've Got What Gets Me," for Wheeler and Dorothy Lee, and an enterprising starlet named Kitty Kelly took Merman's role. With four songs and a hectic script, the insecurity of intention—comedy or musical?—showed up clearly, and *Girl Crazy* was so decisively rejected by preview audiences that RKO's new production head, David O. Selznick, ordered massive reshooting.[6] The film was essentially an ordinary programmer, but with the additional work its cost shot to about $700,000, on a level with *Delicious* and *Grand Hotel.* Under such economics *Girl Crazy* could not hope to succeed, and Wheeler and Woolsey moved back to the more accustomed comedic environs of *Hold 'em Jail.* Around the same time RKO also failed to find an audience for an outstanding foreign import, for the European success of *Sunshine Susie* was not repeated when it was retitled *The Office Girl* and given a wide American release. In a nonmusical season and without stars or other commercial lures, this was hardly a surprise.

Production problems also figured in a far more illustrious early-1932 musical, Paramount's *One Hour With You.* This was the first of two Chevalier musicals announced for the 1931–32 season; the other was *Love Me Tonight,* and to costar in both of them Jeanette MacDonald was recalled to Paramount. The *Smiling Lieutenant* forces were again assembled—composer Oscar Straus, writer Samson Raphaelson, and Ernst Lubitsch—with the production planned this time for Hollywood. The difference was that Lubitsch would not direct *One Hour With You.* He was, in the early fall of 1931, hard at work on a stark drama, *The Man I Killed,* and would not be done before *One Hour With You* commenced. Although his duties on the latter picture would thus be only supervisory, he had already determined that it would bear his stamp if not his signature and for subject matter had gone back to his early Warner Bros. period. *The Marriage Circle,* adapted from Lothar Schmidt's play *Only a Dream,* had been his first American success, and its five-sided roundelay of marital suspicion and intimated adultery was forward, funny, and obviously well suited to musical treatment. As *The Man I Killed* proceeded, Lubitsch collaborated closely with Raphaelson on the script for *One Hour With You,* and while Leo Robin wrote all the lyrics, *Monte Carlo*'s Richard Whiting wrote additional tunes to supplement those by Straus. The somewhat unenviable job of directing such a prearranged package went to George Cukor, a stage director who had begun to amass solid film credits. While recognizing his dominion over the production to be not unlimited, Cukor also saw it as a prestigious opportunity. Shooting began late in November 1931, and after a week Lubitsch demanded a con-

---

6. With the original director (William A. Seiter) unavailable, the retakes were supervised by Norman Taurog. Busby Berkeley, then at RKO to direct the native dances for *Bird of Paradise,* helped restage the "I Got Rhythm" sequence. As was most common with retakes, even extensive ones, neither man received credit—at least until eleven years later. Berkeley, hired by MGM to direct the remake of *Girl Crazy* with Mickey Rooney and Judy Garland, was fired after shooting "I Got Rhythm," for which he retained screen credit, and on the remainder of the film was replaced by Taurog.

ference with Cukor and production head B. P. Schulberg. In the most reasonable-sounding of tones, Schulberg told Cukor that this was, essentially, a Lubitsch production and that Lubitsch (finishing up *The Man I Killed*) would spend an increasing amount of time on the set. When Cukor assented, Schulberg commended him for sportsmanlike conduct. What the director probably did not know was that both Raphaelson and Chevalier had felt his concern with seemingly trivial details to slow down the pace and miss the comedic point. Some of this seems to hint of conspiracy and, given Cukor, possibly of well-concealed homophobia as well. At any rate, for the remainder of the 44–day schedule, in both English and French versions, Lubitsch and Cukor worked in uneasy tandem on both rehearsal and shooting. Ads were released naming Cukor as director, and that was the onscreen credit at the first preview on February 9, 1932, along with, in much larger letters, "An Ernst Lubitsch Production," and also "Personally Supervised by Ernst Lubitsch." Two days after the preview, Schulberg asked Cukor to remove his name from the credits, averring that if he did not Lubitsch would have his own name taken off. Lubitsch, clearly playing hardball, knew that *One Hour With You* was most identifiable as his own work and that, with contract negotiations coming up, it would do him well to be identified with a hit—which *The Man I Killed* was proving not to be. Cukor refused the change, Schulberg made threats, and the result was a lawsuit in which Cukor attempted to block the premiere of *One Hour With You* until the matter was resolved. The out-of-court settlement finally reached superficially favored Lubitsch: he was given full director credit, with "Assisted by George Cukor" in smaller letters.[7] Cukor, granted release from his Paramount contract, moved to what proved a more hospitable berth at RKO, and began a long string of successes—and no more musicals for over two decades.

Little or nothing in *One Hour With You* betrays the artistic and emotional tensions of its creation, and, approached with no background knowledge, it would immediately seem the logical successor to Lubitsch's three earlier comedy operettas. So historically it is claimed for him, a flattering entry on one's résumé under any circumstances. Particularly in its first two-thirds it seems virtually effortless, gliding casually between straight dialogue, rhymed-and-rhythmed speech, and songs that arise out of situation even more suavely than in *Smiling Lieutenant*. The cinematic fourth wall is penetrated with increasing insolence, Chevalier addressing the audience directly and singing to the camera with a conspirator's confidentiality. He and Mac-Donald work with prodigious dexterity, and Genevieve Tobin, Charlie Ruggles, and Roland Young beguilingly fill out the central quintet. The

7. Lubitsch's victory was even greater in some surviving prints of *One Hour With You*, which don't mention Cukor at all.

glum solemnity hobbling *Delicious* is nowhere to be found, courtesy of rich photography and a witty background score as filled with innuendo as anything said or done upon the screen. The fleet moments of sadness or sincerity underlying portions of *Smiling Lieutenant* are completely gone: this is intended solely as a devastatingly polished romp and an etude in cinematic fluidity, Paramount Champagne vintage December 1931. *One Hour With You* exists to charm and mildly titillate its audiences, not move them; and this is exactly what happened in the spring of 1932. Even with a $1.1 million production cost, it was a major success in the U.S. and abroad, where the slightly more risqué *Une Heure près de toi* scored particularly well. Lubitsch was content to bask in the credit, and Cukor was satisfied to move to more accustomed ground. In later years he happily ascribed to the opinion that it was a Lubitsch-only film. "I may," he said, "have shot some of what you see in the film. . . . All I remember is I behaved extremely well in this awkward situation." And: "If you think you can detect what I did in it, you're imagining things."[8] Quite a contrast to the words in the affidavit accompanying his suit, where Cukor constantly refers to how much he did without Lubitsch's presence. Regardless of his protestations of reticence, Cukor would not have let the filming go by without imprinting the finished product, "Lubitsch touch" or not. So perhaps *One Hour With You* is best termed *both* a Lubitsch film and an imitation Lubitsch film, a genre popular in the twenties and starting up again early in 1932. It can be bracketed by *The Smiling Lieutenant* and *Trouble in Paradise* in the Lubitsch canon, and at the same time by *Girls About Town* and *Our Betters* in Cukor's. It also showed Paramount, and a few observant others, how a well-done musical could hold its own critically and popularly even when lawsuits were lurking in the background.

This Is the Night, produced at Paramount just after *One Hour With You*, was less a musical than a comedy musically conceived, and it straddled its genres with greater aplomb than *Girl Crazy* or *Her Majesty, Love*. As with many of Lubitsch's properties, it started as a European play. *Pouche*, by Rene Peter and Henri Falk, had been imported by *Gold Diggers* playwright Avery Hopwood and adapted as *Naughty Cinderella*, a straight comedy starring Irene Bordoni. A bedroom farce with interlocked layers of mistaken identity and casual adultery, this was the precise type of lightly sexy pseudo-Continental semi-Lubitsch fare the movies were willing to address starting in late 1931. While *Her Majesty, Love* had made timorous stabs in that direction, Paramount was the only studio at the time truly capable of the grace, technical expertise, and elegant smut that could make such comedies work, with or without music. Despite this *This Is the Night* (working

8. He was also not averse to taking shots at the perceived lack of depth in Lubitsch's work: "Lubitsch's pictures were brilliant," Cukor said, "but they lacked feeling. . . . [He] never constructed his pictures to get you involved, he didn't want to."

title: *He Met a French Girl*) was somewhat peculiarly assembled. Director Frank Tuttle had shown no subtlety or lyric bent in *Sweetie* or *Love Among the Millionaires*, and the cast seemed a trifle odd. Lily Damita was at that point a Gabor-like star, more famous for her fame than any achievement, and not nearly as skilled as Bordoni. Opposite her, as a devastating Casanova, was Roland Young, an immensely deft comic actor with no detectable sex appeal whatever. The script called for Damita and Thelma Todd to prefer Young to Cary Grant, which surely strained as much credulity in 1932 as it does today. But Grant was a movie neophyte with only one bad short subject *(Singapore Sue)* to his credit; his raw exuberance, which would take some years to refine, was well suited to the role of Todd's Olympic-athlete husband. He pays more attention to his javelin than to his wife, from which it may be safely construed that the script never skirted double entendre for very long. A running gag had Todd's dress constantly being torn off her, and the plot was set in Paris and a never-never Venice, places where audiences could expect Cinderella to be naughty.

Of ill-fitting materials are good movies sometimes made. *This Is the Night*, released in April 1932, is an unmitigated delight, and as musical as a non-musical can get. Paramount did try to bill it as "a new type of screen musical romance," an impression fostered by credits and fadeout set over an orchestra in a pit. But this is deceiving. A film in which none of the principals sing (Grant does have a few lines of boisterous recitative in his opening scene), and which makes its major points through dialogue and pantomime, is no musical. When a gondolier (Donald Novis) sings the title song in Italian, Roland Young can only recite the words in translation for Damita's benefit. Yet the music seems to be almost always there, cushioning or commenting. In many scenes there is the kind of wraparound score contained in *One Hour With You*, and, most importantly, Tuttle had obviously been making a close study of the work of René Clair. Several sequences, particularly "Madame Has Lost Her Dress," are presented with metronomically coordinated music and image, with such Clair techniques as rapid-fire rhythmic editing and passing lyrics from one person to the next. Apart from an interminable drunk scene with Young and Charlie Ruggles the sparkle does not flag, and at best it seems more fluent, even more fun, than the rather calculated *One Hour With You*. While the rest of the actors are predictably good, Lily Damita is surprising. She had just played the Genevieve Tobin role in the French version of *One Hour With You*, so perhaps her work with Lubitsch (and Cukor) accounts for the quality of her work in *This is the Night*, which is an infinite improvement on the wooden (or, in *The Cock Eyed World*, trashy) performances she usually gave. As the little movie extra paid to pose as Young's wife, she manages to keep sex appeal and innocence operating on a simultaneous basis, and the result is as charming as anything Lubitsch ever directed. With lesser stars than *One*

Hour With You, and a far-lower-profile director, *This Is the Night* did not attract inordinate attention or great box office returns, and is generally remembered only as Cary Grant's first feature. But its more immediate importance was its indication, along with *One Hour With You,* that Paramount was interested in exploring more possibilities related to music in film. The ultimate realization of those possibilities was closer than anyone could have guessed.

It seems hard to believe, at least on the surface, that a film as luminous as *Love Me Tonight* could come out of such a dark period in movies. A *Variety* headline of May 1931, "Old Man Gloom's Around," was as pertinent to the aesthetic disposition of film as to its financial status, and things had seemed to get only worse over the succeeding twelve months. Paramount's films were no less grim or sordid than those of any other studio, nor extraordinarily higher in overall excellence. The workaday Paramount program pictures were generally unimaginative, and the studio had an insulting bent for squandering its extraordinary roster of contract players on wearisome dross. It was, nevertheless, a relatively stable haven for some strikingly individual artists. Not that Adolph Zukor and B. P. Schulberg and the rest of the brass were of greater discernment or taste than the Mayers or the Warners. It was only that they had reached their determination of what made a well-realized—ergo, financially successful—film, and this was to give a markedly gifted or unique talent creative control far above the norm. In the American film industry, this constituted taking chances. Whether the talent was Lubitsch, Josef von Sternberg, Rouben Mamoulian, or the Marx Brothers, the effects on the screen and at the box office, even in the dog days of 1931–32, were generally gratifying. The Lubitsch-Cukor *One Hour With You* intrigues showed the extent to which Paramount recognized the potency of the directorial force, and the studio had even gone so far as to hire Sergei Eisenstein, although the gaps had been too wide to bridge in that instance. For Mamoulian the freedom translated mainly into technical and developmental carte blanche. Nearly one and a half years after he had filmed *Applause* he returned to Paramount, this time on the West Coast. With his second film, *City Streets,* there was financial success as well as narrative and technical daring, and when assigned Paramount's entry in the new cycle of horror films, he managed to give *Dr. Jekyll and Mr. Hyde* everything in the book, including a few new pages in the creative use of nonobjective sound. His first three films were all melodramas of sex and emotional or physical violence. For his fourth, he was given *Love Me Tonight,* the next Chevalier picture, which had earlier been slated for Harry D'Arrast or Lubitsch.

Leopold Marchand and Paul Armont's play *Le Tailleur au Chateau* was the engaging tale of a poor tailor who, when he travels to a castle to collect on an unpaid bill, is mistaken for a baron. He goes along with the ruse to win payment and the heart of the beautiful young princess who lives there, but when he counsels the princess on a riding habit for the impending fox hunt, his familiarity with costume gives away the deception and he is ejected. Through a ruse concocted by an urchin named Kiki whom he'd earlier befriended, he and the princess are eventually reconciled. Such a plot was sufficiently frivolous to have fit into the Warners-First National-Alexander Gray-Bernice Claire program of early 1930, and it would obviously depend greatly, two years later, on gifted hands. Richard Rodgers and Lorenz Hart, in their first film work since *The Hot Heiress*, began crafting a nine-song score measured to Chevalier-MacDonald's vocal requirements, after which Mamoulian signed on, fresh from outstanding reviews for *Dr. Jekyll*. He immediately began exercising the same prerogatives that had engendered such strong feelings on the set of *Applause*. The script had the kernel of a good idea, Mamoulian felt, and to get it right he went through a fair portion of Paramount's writing staff. One change made was the elimination of the feisty-cute Kiki, a role for which Robert Coogan (Jackie's kid brother) had been slated. The starting date was pushed back several times, and while the two stars sat waiting and drawing salary, the budget soared past one million dollars.[9] The meticulous planning extended to all areas of production, including the supporting cast. Likely not through design, this summation of early musicals was cast with names whose work formed, more than any cast outside the revue films, a retrospective for the entire history of the genre thus far: Charlie Ruggles *(The Battle of Paris, The Smiling Lieutenant, One Hour With You)*, Charles Butterworth *(The Life of the Party)*, Myrna Loy *(The Jazz Singer, The Desert Song, Bride of the Regiment)*, Joseph Cawthorn *(Street Girl, Dixiana)*, Robert Greig *(Animal Crackers)*, Mary Doran *(Lucky Boy, Broadway Melody)*, Bert Roach *(No, No, Nanette, Song of the Flame, Viennese Nights)*, Tyler Brooke *(Madam Satan)*, Marion Byron *(Broadway Babies, Golden Dawn, Children of Dreams)*, Edgar Norton *(Sweet Kitty Bellairs)*, George Davis *(Broadway, Devil May Care)*.

The film musical is seldom considered a personal category of filmmaking in the sense of authorship, the individual dominance on which some critics base the auteur theory. Astaire supervised the tenor and creation of some of his films, Kelly some of his, also Berkeley in varying manifestations, plus such directors as Clair, Minnelli, and a few others. More often, the splintery collaborative nature of the musical seems to preclude, often deliberately so, the preeminence of one specific force or presence around which all other elements gather. Yet with this fuzzy criterion as a starting point there are instances in these first five years where the governing force is more assertive. A few star presences shaped the films to an almost unparal-

---

9. As with *Glorifying the American Girl*, scripts were a major item, salaries another, and a third was paying off European theaters Chevalier had scheduled to play, then was forced to cancel when the shooting schedule was moved back.

leled extent—Jolson, particularly in *The Singing Fool*, and Marilyn Miller in *Sally* come readily to mind, both more intrinsic centering forces than their putative directors. More conventionally, a director came to the fore with Lubitsch, John Murray Anderson, and Ludwig Berger, whose films for better or worse were the realizations of a single concept that infused every aspect of the project. Rouben Mamoulian had already demonstrated this absolutism. On the stage it had become apparent that his directorial complexion relied on a deliberate, often self-consciously stylized intersection of the visual and the sonic. In film this translated as technical innovation geared to aesthetic ends. *Applause*, in the final analysis, was far less a portrait of human disintegration than a relentless defiance of the constriction of sound-film technology. And so his work would continue over the subsequent six years, each component of film isolated and probed to determine the point where method and art might meet, might sometimes *become* each other.[10]

Love Me Tonight was conceived not so much as a film with music as music itself put on film, with the textbook elements of melody, harmony, rhythm and texture laid out either in sequence or in conjunction. The intention is clear from the first frames, the celebrated opening sequence modeled after a scene the director had created for the stage play *Porgy*. Dawn in Paris, and the city begins its day with an audible stir: church bells, a chimney noisily expelling puffs of smoke, street workers starting to their tasks—all in a synthesized rhythm of sound, image, and montage. As with Harry Beaumont in the first minutes of *The Broadway Melody*, or David Butler in *Sunny Side Up*, and with far more assurance, Mamoulian is clearly stretching. Pushing actually, making film go as far as it can, expanding audiences' perceptions . . . at which point the self-conscious artistry of the moment is slashed by Chevalier's first line—"Beautiful morning sound of Paris, you are far too noisy for me!"—after which he bangs his window shut.

So it continues for the whole enchanted film, every scene finding a new way to advance the story, music and image minutely calibrated yet with exuberant lightness. The technique in *Love Me Tonight*, while as conspicuous as it is deliberate, is neither ponderous nor existent for its own sake. It serves, instead, to tell this bewitching fairy tale of a princess and a poor man, who just happen to be named Jeanette and Maurice. Mamoulian's achievement, as well as those of Chevalier and MacDonald, Rodgers and

10. After 1935 and his pioneering work in three-color Technicolor on *Becky Sharp*, Mamoulian's career is traditionally adjudged to have spiraled downward. "[His] tragedy is that of the innovator who runs out of innovations" was the assessment handed down by auteurist Andrew Sarris. That's true only in part: just as much of the perceived decline was due to a pandemic homogenization overtaking American moviemaking after 1934, much of it a caution-beset reaction to the newly enforced Production Code and the fear of church and moral groups. In Mamoulian's case this meant less interesting material, more rigorously enforced supervision from the studio overlords, and circumscribed technique.

Hart, C. Aubrey Smith and Myrna Loy and the other actors and technicians, can be dissected, analyzed, and catalogued in a fashion reaching to the most abstract discourse in the farthest reaches of theory or criticism. The ~ssence of *Love Me Tonight,* however, is not easily captured, and the enforced distance of a critic or historian must at some point give way to simple statements. *Love Me Tonight* is a wonderful film, one of the two or three greatest musicals ever made, and Rodgers and Hart's score is one of the finest ever written for motion pictures.[11] Every song and joke, each camera trick and unexpected sound effect works just as intended—which means just as Mamoulian intended. The man didn't write "Mimi" or instruct Chevalier in the finer points of projecting sly verve while singing it; nor did he teach Jeanette MacDonald how to phrase "Isn't It Romantic?" with such elegant abandon. But his is the final responsibility for combining everything into such an ecstatic unity. For critics who call *Love Me Tonight* "imitation Lubitsch" or "too Rene Clair"—they could toss in a mention of *Congress Dances* also—yes, the influences of other works are felt. How could they not be; specifically, how could anyone have made a romantic musical comedy *cum* operetta featuring Chevalier and MacDonald and not have the specter of Lubitsch be detectable? What is important is that Mamoulian acknowledges his sources, borrows a bit, and then moves beyond them. Chevalier and MacDonald develop deeper characterizations than in their previous films, chiefly because the slyness and sexual skirmishes are coupled for the first time with genuine romance. When, in the title song, they finally do sing a romantic duet, Mamoulian eschews the conventional two-shot in most musicals, two stars standing nose-to-nose singing "I Love You!" Instead, he deduces the true mystery and intangibility of love by splitting the screen in two, showing Chevalier and MacDonald asleep and dreaming of each other in duet. Isn't it romantic?

Each scene reflects the same caring skill. "Isn't It Romantic?" owes both to René Clair and to the source cited by Mamoulian, a fairy tale in which a piece of embroidery made by a princess is borne by the wind across many lands until it reaches her one true love. And the way the song's lyrics are passed from one person to the next is ironically balanced in the penultimate sequence, "The Son of a Gun Is Nothing but a Tailor," in which Maurice is reviled by everyone in the castle from the lord to the basest menial. Mamoulian goes so far as to recall early silent Westerns to make his final set piece, Jeanette racing on horseback to stop the train and reclaim Maurice, as exciting as it is funny.

11. "Mimi," "Isn't It Romantic?," and "Lover" all entered the standard repertory, the latter pair with the more generalized lyrics Hart was compelled to write for their published versions. "Lover," one of the archetypal Rodgers waltzes, was the slowest to find popular acceptance.

Magic time: The leading actors in *Love Me Tonight* pose for a group shot on the set. From left, C. Aubrey Smith, Charles Ruggles, Maurice Chevalier, Myrna Loy, Jeanette MacDonald, Charles Butterworth, Elizabeth Patterson, Blanche Frederici, Ethel Griffies.

Such is the level of self-fulfillment in *Love Me Tonight*—intemperate observers may be tempted to invoke the word "perfection"—that it can today be accepted, appreciated, adored by those inclined, even after suffering the ignominy of several cuts. As with a number of other early-thirties films *(Mata Hari, King Kong, Arrowsmith, The Sign of the Cross),* these were made to reflect the more sedate moral tone imposed upon the film industry following the establishment of the Legion of Decency and the strengthened enforcement of the Production Code in mid-1934. When *Love Me Tonight* was reissued late in 1949, the following four deletions were made; a complete print is not, so far, known to exist.

> 1. "A Woman Needs Something Like That," a Rodgers-Hart tune talk-sung to Jeanette by the Doctor (Joseph Cawthorn) after he examines her and concludes that she's not wasted away, just wasted. "A door bell needs tinkling," he goes on, "a flower needs sprinkling, and a woman needs something like that."

> 2. An exchange in which Valentine (Loy) informs Butterworth and Ruggles that she will liven up the houseguests' outing by taking them to see the Virgin's Spring.

> *Ruggles*   What is it, a new dame?
>   *Loy*   No, no, it's a spring of water. The Spring of the Virgin.
> *Ruggles*   Oh!
> *Butterworth*   I didn't know there was one in the neighborhood.

3. A second exchange about the Virgin's Spring a few moments later between Loy and Chevalier when he first enters the castle. She offers to show it to him privately—"Tonight, if there's a moon!"

4. Loy's rendition of "Mimi" in the series of "Mimi"s sung by the residents of the castle. Hers was second, between C. Aubrey Smith and Ruggles, sung in bed *en* [semi-transparent] *negligée*, with a knowing chuckle at "You've got me sad and dreamy."

However ridiculous it seems that such harmless material was considered objectionable, it's more daunting still to note that in 1937, when Paramount considered reissuing *Love Me Tonight* to capitalize on MacDonald's MGM-Nelson Eddy popularity, it was told by Production Code czar Joseph Breen that it would do well to "reconsider" the idea. *Love Me Tonight* then had to wait another twelve years for its Code-mandated vandalization. Let the search for the complete version continue.

Love Me Tonight premiered at the Rivoli Theatre in New York on August 11, 1932, four months after *One Hour With You* opened. With only the peripheral *This Is the Night* and the minor *Girl Crazy* in the interim, this translated as the lowest quota of musicals in release since 1928. *Love Me Tonight* was seen in some quarters as the spur for a renaissance. The critical reaction was among the most positive given any film since sound had come in, and initially the box office response was equally affirmative; Chevalier's legions plus the reviews brought in large crowds in urban centers and abroad. It was not the failure legend has sometimes said. But it was too specialized, or perhaps just too special, to win sufficient audiences in outlying regions, which meant that *Love Me Tonight* lost money while a film of comparable cost and wider appeal, *Palmy Days,* made a profit. This was particularly alarming to Paramount, then approaching a tottering financial state. It seems less so today in light of the result.

For the remainder of 1932, Paramount had already planned a number of films with varying degrees of lyric content, and though it remained the only studio operating on so active a basis, the stir caused by *Love Me Tonight* contributed to an awareness of impending change.[12] *Million Dollar Legs,* Paramount's demented tribute to the 1932 Los Angeles Olympics, was in production at the same time as *Love Me Tonight,* and the juxtaposition of these two unconventional works says much about a studio willing, in 1932,

12. Fox and Warners were also beginning to lay plans. MGM considered going fully musical with the Marion Davies backstager *Blondie of the Follies,* released in September, then retreated from the idea. All that was left were some quick moments onstage and a comedy song by Jimmy Durante.

to reject the safe path. Far from being an ordinary farce, *Million Dollar Legs* was Dada, a conglomeration of silent-comedy gags, free-association verbal humor, and nonlinear narrative that played out like an immense and often very funny non sequitur, with music as part of the general barrage. For indecipherable plot purposes, Jack Oakie was provoked on several occasions to pick up his ukulele and sing the national anthem of Klopstockia, the sub-Ruritania where most of the action was set. The anthem, as it happened, was Richard Whiting's title song to *One Hour With You*, fitted out with gibberish lyrics, and the incongruity between the song's past association and its present incarnation ("Woof blugel jig") was a fair indication of what was going on in the mind of scenarist Joseph Mankiewicz. Gibberish of a different sort was prompted by the entrance in mid-film of Lyda Roberti, a Polish singer and comedian fresh from Broadway. As the terminally irresistible spy Mata Machree, she vaunted her prowess in a song that came out, more or less, "Ees torrrific wann Eyee git chott." Comedy and music were suddenly coexisting again, and would also do so a few months later in the Marx Brothers' *Horse Feathers*, with two songs by Kalmar and Ruby. "Everyone Says 'I Love You,'" the brothers sing to Thelma Todd, and the insipidly sweet lyrics suddenly read as riotously accusatory double-entendres.

In a more overtly musical vein Paramount put two films into production in July 1932 that can, in hindsight, be seen as the bridge between the closing first era of musicals and the dawning second. Rodgers and Hart continued their association with the studio by producing the score for *The Phantom President*, another film designed to capitalize on a national event. In this case it was the presidential campaign and election, and the studio's iconoclastic daring showed through once again. For *The Phantom President*, far from being a Yankee Doodle rouser, was an acidic and startlingly prescient look at the political process in all its mendacious splendor. Warner Bros. had done something similar earlier that year with *The Dark Horse*, but only Paramount, and only in 1932, would set it to music. The presidential candidate, T. K. Blair, is an eager cog in his party's corrupt machine but, less happily for his handlers, he's also a desiccated boor with less charisma than a dish of brussels sprouts. The political puppet masters are stumped until they meet Pete Varney, a powerhouse medicine-show huckster who is a dead ringer for their candidate. Blair is put under wraps, Varney is hired to headline the campaign as a more dynamic Blair, and the complications ensue predictably. Except for the obligatory love interest the details were consistently cynical, as in one shot where director Norman Taurog dissolves from one horse's rear, a real one, to another, equally real—a windbag politician in mid-speech.

Casting from strength, Paramount reached beyond its Jack Oakie-Stuart Erwin contract roster and signed a genuine legend. His years of major

Broadway stardom some years past, George M. Cohan remained synonymous with the frenzied flag-waving that *The Phantom President* both en-
dorsed and kidded. He had also been putting out feelers to the talkies for
several years, having done a couple of silents earlier on. The choice was
more right than anyone except Pirandello could have dreamed, for Cohan
was both Blair and Varney. The exuberant big-hearted born-on-the-Fourth-
of-July (he wasn't, actually) hoofer was the exhaustively fostered public
image; thanks to Jimmy Cagney, it remained so long after his death. The
private Cohan, and the one who made his presence known on the set of
The Phantom President, was a hyper-megalomaniacal churl given to chronic
and graphic fits of displeasure over anything deemed beyond his control.
No interviews, no cooperation, and it was all exacerbated, if such was possible, by Cohan's growing awareness that Jimmy Durante, as his sidekick,
was stealing (or being handed) much of the film. Somehow Rodgers and
Hart were not so distracted by this that they did not produce an interesting
score. Their work for *The Phantom President* is inevitably minor alongside
Love Me Tonight's score, and much of it did not make it into the final cut,
yet their touch is unmistakable. "The Country Needs a Man," a prologue
added as an afterthought, brings back the rhymed dialogue of *One Hour
With You* and *Love Me Tonight,* as portraits of presidents past rouse themselves into decrying the current situation with an implied depth of political
criticism unthinkable in the tamer Hollywood of two years later. "Somebody Ought to Wave a Flag" is Cohan absolute, dancing at age fifty-four
with the vitality of a youngster, shot by Taurog from an iconically respectful high angle;[13] "Give Her a Kiss" pulls out the Paramount bag of tricks
as a chorus of birds and frogs encourage Cohan to do the natural thing with
Claudette Colbert; and the mammoth convention sequence brings back the
rhymed dialogue, with masses of chanting constituents grouped and edited
to build feverishly. Not all of *Phantom President* works so well, and as much
of its unevenness must be ascribed to uncertainty of intention as to Cohan's
tantrums. Handing Durante much of the film—his schtick seemed far
fresher in 1932—meant cutting into the musical presentation. Nevertheless, the accomplishment was sufficiently creditable to maintain Paramount's high average and draw good reviews and crowds during the political season. When the election and the big-city engagements ended, so did
business. It was far from the disaster later alleged by Richard Rodgers, who
claimed it to be even less popular than Hoover, but matters were not
helped by Cohan's badmouthing the whole affair to anyone within earshot,
including the press. Hollywood, he declaimed, was the bunk; his only sub-

13. Since Cohan is more familiar to modern audiences through his film biography, it can
be stated that Jimmy Cagney obviously modeled a great deal of his dancing on the original,
yet without submerging his own personality. The result is one unique performer's tribute to
another, as Fred Astaire also did in *Swing Time* with "Bojangles of Harlem."

sequent feature was a little-seen adaptation of his play *Gambling*. Regardless of his opinions, *The Phantom President* paid his legend more rounded tribute than he would ever realize.

The other Paramount musical in the fall of 1932 phased the studio's lyrical aesthetic into different areas. Coincident, and not entirely coincidental, with the fall of the movie musical was the rise of radio. Convenience, accessibility, cost, and addictiveness were all factors in radio's heightened popularity after 1930, and any ostensibly "free" entertainment would be its own justification during the worst of the Depression. The film industry, beginning in the late 1920s, had been aware of the threat of radio and reacted by keeping radio's presence in early talkies to a minimum while exploiting the medium as a vehicle to promote its product. Radio settings and stories turned up only rarely, as in *Say It With Songs*, and considering the number of possibilities, the omission was obvious.[14] Given Paramount's adventurousness during 1932, it was not surprising that this was the studio to break the ban, with an adaptation of William Manley's 1931 play *Wild Waves*, a modest comedy about romantic and professional doings in a financially troubled radio station. By the time it went before the cameras in the summer of 1932 it had been retitled *The Big Broadcast*, with guest appearances by many of the most popular singers and orchestras in radio. It was, in a way, a reversal of the curiosity value of the early sound era; audiences knew and loved the voices and would now be introduced to the faces that accompanied them. However, the most important voice in *The Big Broadcast* was attached to a face many moviegoers already knew. Following his appearances in *King of Jazz* and *Reaching for the Moon*, as well as his nonappearance (as it were) in *The March of Time*, Bing Crosby had left the Whiteman orchestra to work as a single. He sang again in Paramount's *Confessions of a Coed* (1931), then scored mightily with a three-tiered media barrage: his own program on CBS radio; a succession of hit records; and a popular series of two-reel comedies for Mack Sennett. The shorts gave him the opportunity to sing his hits to movie audiences and work at delivering dialogue and relaxing before the camera. By the summer of 1932 Paramount was ready with a contract, and Crosby was ready to act in features. *The Big Broadcast*, though it gave top billing to Stuart Erwin, was carefully fashioned as a star debut. The irresponsible radio singer in the script was renamed Bing Crosby and, tapping into the "crooner" publicity, played up as a mercurial and egotistical ladykiller with a melancholy streak, who's also a nice guy with a voice in a million.

The advertising for *The Big Broadcast* made its objective clear—"Names! Names! Names! All the leading stars of the air"—and to that end Para-

14. Radio did begin to occupy the screen around 1931 when, with increasing frequency, characters would enter a room, turn on the radio, and immediately have background music that would not jar an audience's diegetic sensitivities.

mount reactivated its Astoria studio, which had closed in March 1932, to take advantage of New York's radio industry. Kate Smith, The Boswell Sisters, The Street Singer (Arthur Tracy), The Mills Brothers, and Cab Calloway and his orchestra all filmed specialty numbers, while Guy Lombardo's band, originally scheduled, was replaced by the Vincent Lopez group. Crosby sang the surefire "Please" and "Here Lies Love," the latter also performed by Arthur Tracy.[15] The essentially trivial four-sided-romantic triangle plot (Crosby, Erwin, Leila Hyams, and Sharon Lynn), was given more than its worth by director Frank Tuttle, wittily scored and with a Paramountean air indicating that it mattered more than simply as a dowdy pretext for the singers. Most enjoyable were the visual touches and trick photography—Cab Calloway's microphone jumping along with his swinging beat, a cat sliding under a door, time literally standing still—all of which made the implication that film could equal radio for aural entertainment and then surpass it with stimulating visuals. The singers all delivered as advertised—the Boswells swinging on "Crazy People," Calloway tweaking the drug culture with "Kickin' the Gong Around," Kate Smith in lavish voice for "It Was So Beautiful," which had been written for *Blondie of the Follies* and then used only as background score. And Crosby was a clear natural, with an effortless presence and casual virility not yet congealed into his later ultrarelaxed mien.

The success of *The Big Broadcast* charted a graph nearly apposite to Paramount's earlier musicals in 1932. It did only average business in larger cities, where radio stars often made live appearances, sometimes in movie houses; but returns from smaller communities where the singers had never been seen were vast. The demographic message was duly heeded: sophistication brings fine reviews, costs a great deal, and fares poorly in the sticks, while something geared to a wider audience will cost less and do better. The key for the wider audience was, in this case, radio, until then a comforting if elusive force in the American home; by simultaneously demystifying and exalting radio and its stars, and thus making *The Big Broadcast* a hit, Paramount seemed to have stumbled upon the egalitarian slant needed to bring back musical films. A corner was, unknowingly, being turned.

Radio fame had also worked to the good for Samuel Goldwyn, for it kept Eddie Cantor popular in between his annual film appearances. *The Kid from Spain* operated on the same principles as *Whoopee* and *Palmy Days*—an oversized budget ($1.4 million), Cantor loosed upon an improbable setting (a never-never Mexico), offbeat romantic interest (Lyda Roberti), an irrelevant romantic subplot (Ruth Hall and a uniquely miscast Robert Young, pretending to be Hispanic), and Busby Berkeley in increasingly cinematic

---

15. The only radio stars present in nonmusical mode were cast, in their feature film debuts, as the beleagured station manager and his disconnected secretary, and were sedately billed in the credits as George N. Burns and Grace Allen.

fettle. As in the previous two Cantor films, Betty Grable again led off the Goldwyn Girls, whose number included two other blondes of note. One, Toby Wing, was presently the quintessential Hollywood chorus girl; the other was Paulette Goddard, who reached stardom after she darkened her hair and became associated with Charlie Chaplin.[16] Cantor's centerpiece this time was a bullfight where he impersonated a matador, a situation in which his standard hysteria was extremely appropriate. Berkeley, meanwhile, pushed for more sex and novelty in his routines, including a water ballet in which the Goldwyn Girls swam into formation (while wearing pumps) for the benefit of his overhead camera. With massive publicity and reserved-seat runs in large cities, *The Kid from Spain* was the most popular Cantor film to date. It would have been so even if a new musical season was not approaching, yet alongside *The Big Broadcast* and *The Phantom President* it contributed to the perception that a formerly discredited film cycle was starting to revive. This impression was enhanced by the knowledge of some inside information. Fox, impressed with *Congress Dances*, had engaged its star, Lilian Harvey, as well as the leading man of its French version, Henri Garat. Later, the studio would sign the film's director, Erik Charell. Another coming development made it seem, at a glance, like 1928 again: Al Jolson was back making movies.

Jolson's film, *Hallelujah, I'm a Bum*, was the final musical of 1932. Though it did not open until the following January it belongs inextricably to the first era of musical filmmaking that otherwise concluded with *Love Me Tonight* and *The Phantom President*; in many ways it saw the era to its close.[17] It was again a Rodgers and Hart project, albeit without Paramount's suavity and in some ways even more troubled than the Cohan film. And it is one of those uncommon works that virtually demands a thesis: from ambitiously visionary concept through argumentatively muddled creation to fascinating, compromised outcome, it seems to enclose the full spectrum of the American moviemaking ethos—Art vs. Entertainment, Commerce vs. Idealism, the Orson Welleses vs. the Cecil B. DeMilles.

It began in fiscal urgency. Al Jolson had not made a film since *Big Boy* in 1930, at which point he appeared to have used up his movie popularity. This was becoming obvious just as he signed a four-film/$2 million contract with Joseph Schenck at United Artists. When his debut with that company, *Sons o' Guns*, was tabled, he starred on Broadway in the modest success *The Wonder Bar* and took salary advances from UA that totalled over $800,000. With this much money and no film, the anxious Schenck turned

---

16. Unverifiable reports also mention a teenaged Jane Wyman as part of the chorus. Possible—yet try to find her.

17. *The Kid from Spain*, for all its success and Berkeley prowess, was not so explicitly a product of its time, for Sam Goldwyn's musicals spent nearly thirty years doing the same thing to the same effect.

to a recent UA arrival, Lewis Milestone. The director of *All Quiet on the Western Front* had signed with Schenck to direct or closely supervise four films, but when he could not produce a workable idea for Jolson, he moved ahead instead with *Rain*. Finally Schenck engaged some major creators: Ben Hecht to write an original story, S. N. Behrman to write the script, Rodgers and Hart for music, lyrics, and a great deal of rhymed dialogue. The intention was for a new-style Jolson beyond the old mammy excesses, and it was decided to Americanize the *Love Me Tonight* concept and make it simultaneously fantastic—a full-scale operetta structure—and socially relevant—subject matter dealing with the Depression, unemployment, and homelessness. The title was *The New Yorker,* and Jolson would play Bumper, mayor of the Central Park bums, so liked and respected that he's on easy terms with the city's real mayor. The latter quarrels with his mistress, and when she attempts to drown herself in Central Park Lake, Bumper rescues her. Since she now has amnesia they fall in love, and to support her, Bumper and his sidekick Acorn get real jobs. When he discovers her identity he returns her to the mayor and goes back to the park.

The plot is appealing and also precarious. To balance whimsy, social commentary, and a conventional love triangle in any context would require enormous control and assurance. With Al Jolson and an ambitious vernacular/folk opera structure it could be impossible. This is likely the reason director Harry D'Arrast dropped out just before filming began in July. His replacement was Chester Erskin (he later added a final "e"), a stage director and associate of Milestone. Milestone himself, having finished *Rain*, stayed in close supervision. Soon enough, despite good reports on Erskin's work, the situation began to resemble that of Cukor and Lubitsch on *One Hour With You*. Jolson was no great balm on the set either, deciding he didn't like Erskin, going off to the racetrack whenever possible (whence much of his salary would remain), and doing his best to supplant Rodgers and Hart's carefully assembled score with some more traditional showstoppers (samples: "Color Line" and "Five Cents in My Pocket.").[18] Erskin apparently did his best under the various trying circumstances, but the rough cut of *The New Yorker* served to confirm all the apprehensions. Milestone, abandoning all "supervisory" pretense, took full control of a massive retake schedule. Roland Young, who had played the mayor, was now ill and/or unavailable, which necessitated still more shooting with his replacement, Frank Morgan. The title, meanwhile, moved from *The New Yorker* to *Happy Go Lucky* to *The Optimist* and finally to *Hallelujah, I'm a Bum*, with

18. On-the-set home movies of *Hallelujah, I'm a Bum* show the Jolson temperament in fair fettle as he begins to lose all semblance of patience with costar Harry Langdon, who goes up in his lines for take after take.

Milestone listed as director and Erskin's name nowhere to be found.[19] By the time everything was done the cost of an essentially intimate musical parable had risen past $1.1 million. Jolson's salary was the main burden, and the rewrites and overages took care of the rest. Only an Eddie Cantor could have made such a sum retrievable, and by the end of 1932 Jolson was not his equal at the box office.

United Artists likely did itself no favors with its advertising campaign for *Hallelujah, I'm a Bum*. Besides the title itself—a striking, evocative, and appropriate tag virtually guaranteed to keep an early-1933 audience away— UA played up the rhymed dialogue as the greatest innovation to hit the screen since sound.

> The Man Who Started It All Now Starts It All Over Again!
>
> He amazed you with The First Talkie Ever Made! Now he'll thrill you with this—The First Picture Ever Done in "Rhythmic Dialogue!"
>
> It moves moves moves in rhythm with your Heart!
>
> **Unlike anything you've ever seen before**

Rhymed—or rhythmed—dialogue had already been heard from the screen in German as well as English, and in any case the audience response to *Hallelujah, I'm a Bum* was disastrous. The Jolson fans that did turn out were confused by his restraint and alienated by the fancy rhymes, and others stayed away. Critical response was extremely mixed, and not even the urban centers that had embraced the innovations of the previous two Rodgers and Hart films accepted it. This, plus the brassy competition of *The Kid from Spain* and the new Warner Bros. offering *42nd Street*, sealed its fate.

After so much fiasco, perhaps it's justifiable that history has treated *Hallelujah, I'm a Bum* with respect and approval. So much of it is different (start with Jolson's casting, proceed to the subject matter) and so much daring (the rhymed dialogue, a fairly even-handed view of race relations, Harry Langdon as a Communist who refers to police on horseback as "Hoover's Cossacks") that it should be a masterpiece. But it's not; it's a fascinating collection of ideas, some brilliant and many mundane, that try to coalesce and can't. The startling vigor of Jolson's scenes with his fellow bums, which form the core and glory of the movie, are balanced out by the more ordinary Jolson-Morgan-Madge Evans love triangle. And the fragmentary presentation of the songs seems less deliberately offhand than roughly curtailed. Jolson gets through about one line of the chorus of "I Gotta Get

19. He was, however, to be seen in the final cut. He appears as the photographer taking the picture of Frank Morgan. Richard Rodgers plays his assistant, and Lorenz Hart turns up later as the bank teller who won't cash a five dollar check.

Back to New York" before Milestone cuts away, and he's barely permitted a full chorus of the exquisite "You Are Too Beautiful," previously used as underscoring for much of the film. *Love Me Tonight* succeeded because its songs and fanciful concept could be kept consistent with its fairy-tale plot. In *Hallelujah, I'm A Bum* the elements don't converge—whimsy scrapes up against liberal social commentary, conceptual daring alternates with pulp romance. This, plus the splintered authorship—Hecht, Behrman, Rodgers and Hart, Jolson, Schenck, Milestone, Erskin—is a pretty fair guarantor of a broad reach and an inadequate grasp. This particular Emperor does have clothes, but they are too small and insufficiently well knit.

With *Love Me Tonight*, the first era of musical films had reached its climax. That Jolson should then bring that age to its close is one of those rare symmetries that history, in its generosity, sometimes bestows. 1933 would be a different era, and yet it began as the first one had: with Warner Bros., and with a backstage film that would change many minds about movies with songs and dances.

Plus ça change . . .

CHAPTER 16

1933: "We're in the Money"

Franklin Roosevelt was elected president on November 8, 1932. By the time of his inauguration four months later, the national mood had turned a perceptible corner. The economy was no more prosperous, unemployment was not lessened, yet for the first time in nearly three years confidence began to seem a rational option. Film, as always, served as a barometer to measure the change. Attendance had already begun to rise in some areas; production was recovering from its lowest point in fifteen years; and both technical assurance and overall quality seemed on a marked upswing. This converged neatly with the country's growing willingness to turn its back on the Depression, and the result was a new vein of escapist entertainment. After its product glumly reflected the national mood for several years, the film industry began to foster the notion that things were indeed starting to get better. In the course of this the long-shunned musical suddenly rose as a phoenix-like emblem of defiant optimism. One film became the symbol of national renewal, and just as with the one film that had epitomized the coming of sound, it came from Warner Bros. The studio, it is related, singlehandedly brought back musicals with *42nd Street*—and once again the tale is one of those convenient corner-cutters beloved of popular history. Given an iconic force as powerful as *42nd Street* it's an easy generalization to make, and while there's obviously much more to the story, give credit where it's due: Warner Bros. did deliver as promised, then returned to the showmanship of the early Vitaphone days to bind it up in a glossy package of mythmaking that has lasted for many decades.

Warner Bros., by 1932, had renounced all claims on making movies for the ages. It had been hit harder than many studios by the Depression because it had invested more after the coming of sound. In reclaiming commercial efficacy both the character and the methodology of the Warners and First National films (the distinction between the companies existed now for fiscal reasons) were altered drastically. Through accident as well as calculation, Warners had changed enormously since the days of *Show of Shows* and *Is Everybody Happy?* Budgets and salaries were cut, shooting schedules minimized, and the stockpile production system greatly modified. Employees were machines, not artists, as Jack Warner acknowledged in July 1932 when he handed down an edict denying actors any contractual say in scripts or roles. The times were felt to call for the measures, and in the process there vanished the feeling that a lowbrow studio was trying to raise its sights merely by increasing its budgets. Between the Depression and corporate rigor and a group of resourceful employees, the Warner profile had manifested: noisily urban, proletariat, cynical, aggressive. This was the studio that could produce witheringly nasty political satires *(The Dark Horse)*, unflinching social documents *(Wild Boys of the Road, Heroes for Sale)*, brutal gangster stories *(The Public Enemy)*, and sundry low-life melodramas *(The Strange Love of Molly Louvain, Two Seconds)*. Musicals did not seem to fit into this equation, or into a studio ethos that had changed radically since *Golden Dawn*. Warners went even beyond the stringent non-musicality of the other studios in 1931 and 1932; *Her Majesty, Love* owed more to contractual and personal alliances with Marilyn Miller than to any Paramount-like desire to explore possibilities. The only other concession, *Crooner* (1932), used its few songs to satirize the public's idolization of Rudy Vallee. No one had to remind Warners that musicals were expensive, time-consuming, and required performers and creative people beyond the standard contract list. That they were out of fashion was an excellent excuse to avoid them completely and move on to another hard-edged low-cost drama.

Unless . . . a musical could be given an edge, be made to seem something other than a procession of pointless numbers framed by an irrelevant plot. Many musicals in 1929–30 had been more than this, of course, yet this negative view had been nurtured by the low grosses and hostile exhibitor reports from two years earlier and echoed the popular perception of musicals in 1932. The situation began to ease around the time of *Love Me Tonight,* and other studios gradually began to address music-related possibilities. For Warners, the success of such an endeavor rested on how well the project could conform to the studio's emergent identity.

Warners was always on the lookout for material, whether from books, magazines, headlines, or in imitation of other companies' product. In the summer of 1932, some months prior to its official publication date, Bradford Ropes's novel *42nd Street* came to the attention of the Warners story department. While leaving much to be desired from a literary standpoint, it offered intriguing incidents, barbed plot twists, and a barrel of flinty wisecracks. Perhaps most distinctive was the way Ropes used a confined situation to bring together a diverse group of characters. This, to Warners story readers, was a grabber, for ever since *Grand Hotel* opened to spectacular effect the previous April, the studios had been searching for similarly interactionary narratives into which could be placed a marquee full of recognizable names. Perhaps the cast would not be quite as all-star as *Grand Hotel*'s MGM-prime lineup, but it would have enough appeal to draw in audiences. The crux at which the *42nd Street* plots met perhaps gave some pause: it was backstage, centered on the production of a musical comedy, *Pretty Lady*. Backstage was just what producers wanted to avoid; it was the type of musical most associated with bringing the genre to a premature demise. And yet the astringency with which Ropes sketched his characters and fashioned their tart dialogue seemed congruent with the 1932 Warner temperament. Cheaply cynical, poorly developed, couched in tedious banalities—yet *42nd Street* had an edge, an unsmiling urban vibrancy that could work. Ropes, in fact, dived further into show-business grit than Warners could allow, for one of the novel's central relationships was the love-and-money affair between *Pretty Lady*'s director, Julian Marsh, and its juvenile lead, Billy Lawler. And Billy, while none too sympathetic, paled alongside the two main women characters. Dorothy Brock is an over-the-hill nymphomaniac forced to relinquish the lead in *Pretty Lady* when she is injured in a drunken fall. Her replacement, Peggy Sawyer, is a sweet chorine; as soon as *Pretty Lady* becomes a hit, she turns into the most formidable ogress this side of Lady Macbeth. The other characters are portrayed with equal tact and sympathy—*Pretty Lady* could as easily be called *Chamber of Dread*.

Optioning the book, Warners set writers to it and began planning its equivalent of a *Grand Hotel* cast. The evolution of the casting choices reveals how calculation and fate can combine to give a film its precise texture.

42ND STREET			
Character	*Original/Alternate Casting Choice*		*Final Choice*
Julian Marsh	Warren William	Richard Barthelmess	Warner Baxter
Dorothy Brock	Kay Francis	Ruth Chatterton	Bebe Daniels
Peggy Sawyer	Loretta Young		Ruby Keeler
Billy Lawler			Dick Powell
Pat Denning			George Brent
"Anytime Annie" Lowell	Joan Blondell		Ginger Rogers
Lorraine Fleming	Glenda Farrell		Una Merkel
Andy Lee	Frank McHugh		George E. Stone

That a nonmusical performer such as Loretta Young was considered indicates insecurity regarding how far to go with the music. *42nd Street* could have been made a straight drama, with brief parenthetical onstage flashes to limn *Pretty Lady*'s progression from out-of-town uncertainty to Broadway smash. But, and it seems that production head Darryl Zanuck was largely responsible, it was decided to make it a semimusical, with three specific choices that bore enormously on the final product. Lyricist Al Dubin and composer Harry Warren had worked separately for Warners in the past and proved an ideal team. Busby Berkeley, just finishing *The Kid from Spain*, had been drawing good notices ever since *Whoopee!* Ruby Keeler had abandoned show business after marrying Al Jolson, and her casting as Peggy Sawyer was seen as somewhat of a comeback.

It was bold, although not extraordinarily so, to give the project such a definite musical profile; it was, after all, well known that other studios beside Paramount had musical ideas in various stages of development. So putting these specific contours into a *Grand Hotel* context was as logical as it was adventurous. Keeler was already in California, in fact, because Jolson was shooting *Hallelujah, I'm a Bum* at United Artists. In any case, *42nd Street* was not put into production surreptitiously, as some accounts have asserted, for such a thing would not have been possible under the Warners' eagle eye. It was, simply, a later addition to the studio's program for the 1932–33 season, which was already set to include such titles as *20,000 Years in Sing Sing, I Am a Fugitive from a Chain Gang*, and *Central Park* (also, at one point, another musical—the Technicolor operetta *Maytime*, later cancelled). *42nd Street* was added to the roster early in August and whisked toward production in exemplary house style. The rights to the book were formally purchased on August 15, still prior to publication, for a nominal $6,000. Less than six weeks later, just as the package was assembled and ready to roll, an ill-timed bout with tonsillitis forced Mervyn LeRoy out of the director's chair and into Cedars of Lebanon Hospital. His last-minute replacement was Lloyd Bacon, of *The Singing Fool, Gold Diggers of Broadway*, and many others, who began shooting on September 28. The filming of the dramatic and musical sequences remained discrete and partly concurrent. Bacon shot the plot scenes in thirty-two days, finishing on November 3. Berkeley started on October 18; "Young and Healthy" and "Shuffle Off to Buffalo" were each shot in three days, and for the complex title number the company worked eleven days straight (including Sunday) and wrapped on November 15. The final production cost, $439,000, was low in comparison with the Goldwyn extravaganzas, yet high for Warners—more than double the cost of an average Warner film for 1932, and more than the company had spent on any production since 1931's *The Mad Genius* and *The Last Flight*, both money-losers. The rough cut of *42nd Street* showed that the money was well spent, and before the year was out the legend had started: Warners, who had started musicals back in the stone age, was going to revive them bigtime. "Biggest Screen Event Since Birth of Vitaphone" ran one of the taglines. *42nd Street* would have been a financial success under nearly any circumstances; through a dazzling synchrony of ballyhoo, timing, and social upheaval, it became a sensation.

First there was the film itself. While it was still in production, Warners proclaimed *42nd Street* as "The 1932 Version of *Gold Diggers of Broadway*," which was not inaccurate. It had the shrewd state-of-the-art crafting—this time including the new Western Electric Wide Range Recording—and precise dovetailing of form and content to elicit maximum response. Warners' emergent urban drive channeled so well into the backstage ambiance that the basic storyline, which harkened back to *On With the Show!*, was transformed and uplifted. Some of Ropes's more expendable characters were excised, some of the motivations and incidents inevitably softened, yet there was an urgency about the narrative and an almost melancholy energy that somehow made the backstage film seem fresh all over again.[1] Ropes's original wisecracks helped set the tone, and one of them, Andy's assessment of Anytime Annie, was adapted into one of the script's best-known lines: "She only said no once, and then she didn't hear the question!" The hardness of such dialogue, its startling combination of the lewd and the sassy, is a leitmotif throughout *42nd Street:* "It must've been tough on your mother not having any children!" *(Regarding a haughty chorine who lists her address as Park Avenue):* "And is her homework tough!" "In a star, it's temperament . . . In a chorus girl, it's just bad taste!" *(Star, to assembled detractors):* "What is this? Target practice?" "You got the *busiest* hands!" The speed with which the script was readied dictated last-minute modifications, which enabled some of the sass taken out of the book to be put back on-site as filming went along with scores of dialogue changes pencilled into the shooting script. These included such lines as Annie's acid retort to a stage manager's appeal to put more emotion into a song. "Whaddaya want me to do, bite my nails?" Ginger Rogers demands, with tone and look sufficient to decimate an army.

The dialogue's flint is echoed in performances that run on Depression angst: Warner Baxter's driven director, broken and depleted in a remarkable final shot,[2] Bebe Daniels's insecure diva, Ginger Rogers and Una Merkel as sluttish, good-natured chorines. Balanced against these were the character of Peggy Sawyer—vastly softened from the novel's smiler-with-a-knife—and the performance of Ruby Keeler, which jointly accounted for a major part of the film's success. She may strike the latter-day uninitiated

1. The Julian Marsh-Billy Lawler liaison was, inevitably, omitted from the script, and Billy finds more conventional happiness with Peggy Sawyer. Aside from his poor health, Marsh's personal life remains something of a mystery. A possible allusion to his original situation comes when he asks Andy to accompany him home for some needed company.

2. As filmed, Baxter overhears the praise directed to everyone except him and muses ironically, "Just another show!" The line was cut, and Baxter was left to reflect on his accomplishment in silent, perhaps more effective, gloom.

as across-the-board incompetent. The line readings—there's no question of characterization—are misjudged, the voice grating in speech and abradant in song, the posture and mien gawky and self-conscious. Her primary identity (apart from Jolson), as a tap dancer, may surprise viewers confronted with flailing arms, leaden footwork, and the fact that the top of her head is more visible than her face—she's staring down at those feet to make sure they do her bidding.[3] This opacity as a performer, however, was offset by an artless projection of total innocence and vulnerability. This is what separates Keeler from the Sally O'Neils and Alice Whites of earlier musicals, and it hit audiences at precisely the right moment. She was sweet, she was good, she worked hard and was rewarded. That famous desperate speech Marsh gives to Peggy just before she goes onstage—"You're going out there a youngster, but you've got to come back a star!"—has passed beyond camp into folklore, encapsulating a myth Depression spectators were ready to believe. And despite her blank expression as she listens to Baxter deliver the line, it applied to Keeler as much as to Peggy Sawyer. "A most astounding film debutante," said the Boston *Evening American*; "Hail Queen Ruby!" gushed a viewer in a letter to *Photoplay*. As Dorothy Brock, Bebe Daniels was crisply authoritative in her satin pajamas singing "You're Getting to Be a Habit With Me." Singing and tapping the title song, Keeler seemed to be trying much harder; ergo, she and Peggy deserved to succeed, to take up the mantle Daniels and Brock seemed to renounce. Brock surrendered because she was ready to quit a drunken and insincere rat race; Daniels capitulated because, as became apparent in 1933, the revived movie musical would make few slots available to its former monarchs.

Dick Powell, Busby Berkeley, Al Dubin, and Harry Warren all benefited nearly as much as Keeler. Powell was a new-style male ingenue for musicals, and the difference can be seen by contrasting his performance of "Young and Healthy" with that of Clarence Nordstrom in "Shuffle Off to Buffalo." Nordstrom is overripe, phlegmatic, consciously cute—the Charles King type at its least potent. Powell is aggressively young and healthy, leering visually at Toby Wing and audibly with his brash tenor—and somehow retains the innocence to warrant Keeler's adoration. And Dubin and Warren's songs, brash and robust, did not clash with the dramatic action as in earlier backstagers. The arching outbursts of "Young and Healthy" and the ricky-tick ribaldry of "Shuffle Off to Buffalo" seemed entirely suited to a milieu where shows are born of sweat and desperation, and the title song's syncopation and game lyrics evoke more of the real Broadway than either the screenplay or Ropes's novel. *42nd Street* has come to represent

3. Her heavy-footed technique, which seems absurd to those accustomed to the more stirring likes of Eleanor Powell or Ann Miller, is actually part of a different style of show dancing now obsolete. Instead of metal taps the shoes had wood soles, producing more sound the harder they were banged down. Marilyn Miller does the same kind of tap in *Sally*.

the Busby Berkeley style at its most basic—yet while obviously a milestone for him much of it was not a departure. "Young and Healthy" was obviously cued by his work on *Flying High* and *The Kid from Spain*, and "Shuffle Off to Buffalo" achieved its raffish effects solely through means possible on any stage. The breakthrough came with the title number, with its crane shots (including that final wobbly move up the skyscraper toward Powell and Keeler) and lurid details that showed Berkeley moving beyond the Goldwyn girlie-show narcissism. By exercising full license to stage numbers not possible in any theater, Berkeley gave musical film a fresh complexion. Logic—even dance—were far less considerations than spectacle and excitement, as propelled by a special energy that made escapism seem urgent and even relevant.

The release of *42nd Street* was skillfully aligned with Roosevelt's recent victory. Warner films were politically conscious, in the sense that they mirrored the convictions of those setting company policy, and the Warners were passionately pro-Roosevelt. By proclaiming *42nd Street* "The Inauguration of a New Deal in Entertainment" the edge was blurred between politics and entertainment—something which Roosevelt himself, and his successors, would learn to do with increasing skill. And just as he intended the New Deal to bring the American public prosperity, Warners brought it *42nd Street*—in effect, brought it Hollywood. In conjunction with General Electric, Warners sponsored a cross-country trainload of glitz called The *42nd Street* Special ("The Greatest Ride Since Paul Revere"), which hit major centers between Los Angeles and New York in late February and early March 1933. Powell, Keeler, Rogers, and Guy Kibbee were already working on a follow-up backstage musical, so the only *42nd Street* participants on the junket were supporting actor Lyle Talbot and several of the chorines (paid a whopping $25 per week for their participation), plus Tom Mix and his horse, Bette Davis, Joe E. Brown, Glenda Farrell, Preston Foster, Laura La Plante, and Leo Carrillo.[4] The train was timed to hit Washington on the day of the Inauguration, with the stars participating in the parade and festivities, and in other cities its arrival coincided with the opening of *42nd Street*. The film drew turnaway crowds, as did others in the weeks around the Inauguration: *Cavalcade, State Fair, King Kong, She Done Him Wrong*. Just one musical amid a crop of big films, but the incalculably smart publicity helped give the perception that musicals were back.

The impact of *42nd Street* was immediate, enormous, and worldwide, its

4. The trip proved a boon for Davis, whose career at Warners had not been phenomenal so far. She received a bale of "Local Girl Makes Good" publicity during the Boston stopover, and Warner ads later alleged that "The *42nd Street* Special Made Her Famous." Many years later she recalled the hatred and resentment on the Depression-weary faces of those greeting the Hollywood visitors. They were likely unaware that the actors were working eighteen-hour days promoting G.E. products as well as Warner films, and that Mix's horse was being better treated than any of the actors.

final gross of $2.26 million more profit than Warners had seen since *Gold Diggers of Broadway*.[5] Such success both hastened the return of the musical and altered its contour—neither, necessarily, for the better. For *42nd Street* was more imitable than any musical seen on the screen in three years, and its influence reestablished formulas that people like Lubitsch and Mamoulian had eradicated. *Variety*'s review, terming it *The Broadway Melody of 1933*, was more accurate than anyone could have thought, as a preponderant number of successful musicals for many years afterward would one way or another be direct successors of *42nd Street*. Backstage atmosphere again, contemporary tone if not time period, and Berkeleyesque numbers were the staples—and nearly all lacking *42nd Street*'s enterprise, vigor, and wit. Their balance sheets, however, ensured that such would soon be the most prominent road taken. It was the summer of 1929 all over again: the number of musicals released in 1933 was twice the combined total of the previous two years. They were split between those that cloned *42nd Street* and those, mostly planned at the end of 1932, that drew on earlier models. The latter, following more inventive paths, would taper off precipitously after the middle of 1933. That year, and 1934, are the beginning and the end, the culmination, rebirth, and in some ways untimely conclusion of much of musical films' potential. When formulas became clearer cut, there seemed less and less reason to stretch.

42nd Street's unerring tap into the upswinging national mood tended to obscure the pronounced failure of two major musicals that opened a few weeks earlier. Both were, in different ways, products of the earlier era of the musical, so the timing was relevant. One was *Hallelujah, I'm a Bum*, and the irony of Jolson failing at the moment of his wife's triumph was lost on few observers.[6] The other failure, *Hello, Everybody!*, was ostensibly in new post-*Big Broadcast* mode, a radio star front and center. Suddenly radio-conscious, Paramount had found that Ed Wynn's on-air fame made *Follow the Leader* more successful in an early-1933 release than it was in 1930. With *Hello, Everybody!* the studio attempted to pour old wine into a newer bottle, unknowingly recalling the time when ill-suited singers were dumped into dramatic stories and permitted to founder. The singer in this case was Kate Smith, which means that "Biggest Star in Radio" jokes lumber off the tongue with tiresome ease. The fact is by late 1932 the stocky

5. It was only the tenth Warner/First National film to go over the $2 million mark, at the time an unofficial superhit threshold, and eight of the the ten were musicals. In descending order: *The Singing Fool, Gold Diggers of Broadway, The Desert Song, The Jazz Singer, On With the Show!, Noah's Ark, 42nd Street, Say It with Songs, Sally, Lilac Time*.

6. Nor, it can be assumed, did it go unnoticed in the Jolson household, though he was reportedly proud of his wife's film success. After the marriage ended the sweet-tempered Keeler preferred to keep comparatively mum about the experience. Inklings of the nature of the relationship did, however, surface on occasion. One latter-day quote: "He was the world's greatest entertainer. He used to tell me so every day."

(above) The new backstager: *42nd Street*'s supporting actors were responsible for a great deal of its impact. Here, a monocled Ginger Rogers (as Anytime Annie) parries with George E. Stone and Una Merkel. *(below)* Kate Smith with manager Ted Collins in *Hello, Everybody!* The thoughts lurking behind her tight-lipped expression can only be imagined.

"Song Bird of the South" was a major and much-liked presence in millions of American homes, and Paramount's logic in signing her is not indecipherable. It was then in the process of making a star of Bing Crosby, and if the ample Smith seems like far less malleable material for movies, it should be remembered that Marie Dressler was then ahead of Garbo, and Gaynor and Crawford and Dietrich, in most lists of top stars. The problem was not necessarily one of weight, though Smith's trial run in *The Big Broadcast* may have unsettled many audiences with photography and costuming that almost seemed calculated to maximize her bulk. Nevertheless, if she was capable of turning a funny/endearing personality to the camera, and if Paramount was able to place said personality into a congruent script, her plush singing would carry the rest.

That none of this came to pass was due to both star and studio. Smith herself had been the butt of enough fat jokes onstage and off to have developed a fierce shell notably at odds with her on-the-air sunniness, and her retinue, headed by manager Ted Collins, helped make the moat wider still. She rejected Paramount's story ideas and songs right and left until the studio came up with a yarn by tear-jerker novelist Fannie Hurst. No laughs or looseness, just Kate as a farm girl who sings her unselfish heart out and becomes a radio star after the man she loves opts for her sister. A staff of Paramount writers worked hard to put these sweepings into filmable form as Smith and handlers warily scouted for anything that might not conform to the image. It was titled after her radio catchphrase, and in a last-minute change the lead character's name was made Kate Smith, and her manager named (and played by) Ted Collins. While not a particularly expensive film apart from her salary—later reports alleging that it cost over a million seem improbable—it was given a fair amount of care and attention, apparently in all the wrong areas. Making Smith a martyr to love with a beautiful sylph of a sister (Sally Blane, far closer in looks to her real sister, Loretta Young), giving her mostly mediocre songs to sing—including a whopper called "Pickaninnies' Heaven"—and putting her in sleeveless housedresses: none of this implied a star's enhancement. Most surprising, at least in hindsight, was Smith's on-camera presence—abashed, recessive, self-conscious, light years from the hearty confidence exuded on television years later. She seemed at ease only in some of the songs and during her amusing dance routine to "Dinah," where she showed off some steps picked up during vaudeville days. Whether *Hello, Everybody!* would have been successful had it and she been any better is debatable. The jokes on many minds were indeed made, and instead of doing poor business it did next to none, with record low grosses reported in city after city.[7]

7. *Variety* reported that one particularly rude exhibitor tried to drum up business by circulating *Hello, Everybody!* handbills with diet tips printed on the back.

Fortunately for Paramount, a less expensive film with songs that was shot at the same time drew mammoth returns which more than offset the losses. Mae West, annoyed by the attention given Smith, found immense placation when *She Done Him Wrong* proved an instantaneous smash. (Later, superstitiously regarding the title *Hello, Everybody!* as a jinx, West refused its utterance in her presence.) This outsized divinity clearly did have the stuff for film, and took care to make sure that the package included that nasal growl she called singing; her raunchy renditions of "A Guy What Takes His Time" and "I Wonder Where My Easy Rider's Gone" distilled her personality as well as any of her barrage of innuendoes.

Two of the first films to cash in on the new post-*42nd Street* boom had been important parts of the first wave. Goldwyn reissued *Whoopee!,* and Carl Laemmle finally made a dent in the million-dollar loss of *King of Jazz*. As with *Follow the Leader,* returns were excellent, in the case of *King of Jazz* (which Laemmle cut by several reels and restructured) better in many areas than in 1930. Universal also scored with an import, which like *Sunshine Susie* was an English version of a German success. *Be Mine Tonight* (formerly *Das Lied einer Nacht*) starred the attractive Polish tenor Jan Kiepura, and a well-planned ad campaign trading on the public craving for musicals made it a sleeper hit. Paramount tried to continue the Chevalier magic with *Bedtime Story* and *The Way to Love,* both romantic comedies with music. The grosses on *Love Me Tonight* implied that Chevalier was slipping, and instead of acceding to his pleas for a change of pace or shoring him with a strong story, his studio slashed the budgets and pared down the music. *Bedtime Story* was a dangerous portent in that most of the public paid less heed to Chevalier than to Baby LeRoy, an ineffably pleasant infant with an inborn affinity for the camera. *The Way to Love* won its greatest attention during production, when Sylvia Sidney rebelled and walked off the set after some days of shooting. She was replaced by Ann Dvorak, and *The Way to Love* became the first certifiable Chevalier turkey and his last Paramount film for many years.

As comedy musicals reemerged, they tended to mirror the more positive scattershot qualities of earlier years. Laurel and Hardy's *The Devil's Brother* reversed the *Rogue Song* ratio by giving them the most footage and relegating the musical and romantic portions of Auber's *Fra Diavolo* to second place. Since Dennis King's singing bandit was as florid as his François Villon, the tension between the slapstick and the serious was sufficiently palpable to make for higher highs and lower lows than most L&H features. Wheeler and Woolsey, who had maintained their popularity in mainly nonlyric precincts, ventured afield with two vehicles in the spring of 1933. They left RKO for Columbia to film *So This Is Africa,* with two songs by Kalmar and Ruby as well as an unusually large quota of bawdy humor. It proved that blue jokes were an odd choice for these two, who fared much better on their home lot with the more overtly musical *Diplomaniacs*. Sporting craziness far above the Wheeler-Woolsey norm, it fit precisely (and chronologically) between *Million Dollar Legs* and *Duck Soup* on the cracker-factory continuum, its resemblance to the Paramount Dada partly due to the contribution of *Legs*'s scenarist, Joseph L. Mankiewicz. Wheeler and Woolsey's material rarely had any point of reference beyond its own corniness, yet in just over an hour *Diplomaniacs* kidded global politics, U.S. policies, operetta, and any number of other topics with admirable celerity. Movie musicals got it too, in a dandy parody of *Love Me Tonight* and in a Berkeley-prompted production number that somehow merged Pig Latin with *Whoopee!*-style Indian maidens. *Diplomaniacs* gave the team a fair success after the disappointments of *Girl Crazy* and *So This Is Africa,* and also helped director William A. Seiter to regroup after *Hello, Everybody!*

The distance between *Diplomaniacs* and *Duck Soup* must unavoidably be that between Wheeler and Woolsey and the Marx Brothers, i.e., between professional competence and transcendent madness. *Duck Soup*, their fifth assault on film and Zeppo's farewell, is the Marxist connoisseur's dream, for many the team's finest moment. The staid sanity usually targeted by the Marxes appeared here in the form of the ultimate insanity—war—and as the empty politics that foolishly attempt to rule the world.[8] The amusement of a *Diplomaniacs* is transformed into a wondrous array of lunacy with the aid of co-writers Kalmar and Ruby, who also did the inspired score. The musical formality of *Cocoanuts* long gone, *Duck Soup* forces the Marxes' mad cinema to confront operetta-style stiffness. Its music is almost entirely ceremonial—Groucho's grand entrance, the hymn to Freedonia, the epic "The Country's Going to War"—and with straightfaced solemnity equates the atrophied pomp of traditional operetta with the insincere pomposity of diplomacy. The concerted choruses, the troupes of ballerinas sprinkling petals, the reckless unreality that shotgun-mates warfare with lyricism à la *Song of the Flame:* all are the stock of operetta that *Duck Soup* assaults with dazzlingly concentrated force. Contrary to legend, the initial response from critics was at worst mixed and from audiences excellent, albeit less so in smaller communities than earlier Marx epics. Only its outsized cost, bred of a lengthy shooting schedule, retakes, and much unused footage (the first cut ran almost two hours) caused it to be seen as a failure, severing the Marxes' association with Paramount.

8. *Duck Soup* was irreverent from first gasp onward. Its first working title was *Ooh, La La,* and when asked what that meant the Marxes replied that the title was self-explanatory. The insanity extended to the ad campaign, which was designed to encompass a range of phenomena. Photos of the brothers in costume for *Duck Soup*'s final war scenes were given such captions as "Maedchen in Uniform?" and "I Surrender, Dear!" Then, just before it opened, the town of Fredonia, N.Y., protested the use of its name (with an extra "e") as the moniker for the deranged Ruritania where most of the film was set. The Marxes' response: "Change the name of your town. It's hurting our picture."

While *Duck Soup* flayed operetta's excesses, Fox was attempting to find a useful American equivalent to the European successes in that form. *Congress Dances* and *Love Me Tonight* were the inspiration here, works of sagacious finesse being emulated by a studio whose leading lights were Will Rogers and Janet Gaynor, as well as Charles Farrell and El Brendel. Fox attempted to bridge the gap by importing some of the original Continental creators, with mixed results. When an adaptation of Noël Coward's *Bitter Sweet* did not work out, Fox produced *Adorable*, the first large scale American musical released after *42nd Street*. It was a slightly Americanized version of *Ihre Hoheit Befielt (Her Highness Commands)*, the French version of which had starred Lilian Harvey and Henri Garat, both veterans of *Congress Dances* recently signed with Fox.[9] Although Harvey was hailed as Fox's new musical star, Janet Gaynor was cast opposite Garat in *Adorable*. The choice was simultaneously comprehensible and erratic. Gaynor, pushing hard on the princess-incognita adorableness, could not find a center of balance to interact with Garat; the resultant off-center chemistry between Foxy hominess and Gallic suavity set up friction no amount of production or music could assuage. Perhaps the original choice for director, Erich von Stroheim, might have heightened the dark edges in the story and in Gaynor's persona. When studio politics prompted Stroheim's removal from this as well as the already completed *Walking Down Broadway* (which was largely reshot), he was superseded by William Dieterle. In *Her Majesty, Love* Dieterle had been unable to blend Continental froth with American crust, and *Adorable*, despite some fanciful sprinklings, turned out the same type of stale meringue—Gaynor's first failure in many years. In hindsight its only distinction, besides as an exemplar of the failed *Love Me Tonight* school, is as Billy Wilder's first American credit, as cowriter of the original German film.

With *It's Great to Be Alive* Fox went offbeat with a musical comedy with operetta overtones, sequences of rhyming dialogue, and a fantastic *Just Imagine*-ish plot dealing with the last man on earth on the loose in a planet filled with women. It had originally been done at Fox in a Spanish version expressly for the foreign market, which had turned out well enough to be refilmed in English in more elaborate form, with a screenplay by Arthur Kober. It was a good attempt, at a studio generally unequipped for ornate caprice, and with a less than inspired choice for the planet's last remaining man. Raul Roulien, midway between his stints between playing a Russian in *Delicious* and (more plausibly) a Brazilian in *Flying Down to Rio*, lacked the Chevalieresque élan needed to anchor such a risqué trifle, at least in its English version, and the level of humor was too often exemplified by the name of the character portrayed by Edna May Oliver: Dr. Prodwell.

9. Harvey appeared in the German, French, and English versions of *Congress Dances*, Garat in the French version only. Upon his arrival in Hollywood his name was Anglicized to Henry.

Without star names, and with its musical whimsy butting up against its moments of low humor in uneven fashion, *It's Great to Be Alive* fared poorly.

Similar miscalculations set in with Lilian Harvey, whose appeal in European cinema, especially *Congress Dances*, did not survive the transatlantic journey unimpaired. An inconsistent performer, Harvey often crossed the line from the charmingly elfin to the tiresomely fey, and—like some other imports—was not unfailingly photogenic. A cunning director and sympathetic cameraman could steer her beguilingly clear of her usual affectations; otherwise she was a questionable prospect, and Fox did her no favors with her first American film. The very title *My Lips Betray* portends operetta kitsch at its acme, and the potential was realized by adding John Boles at his most fatuous as costar and mixing in a sugary Continental setting and dull score. The concoction was virtually indigestible, and Fox opted to shelve *My Lips Betray* temporarily and rush Harvey into a contemporary musical comedy. While clearly a trifle, *My Weakness*—as befits a movie framed by an appearance by Harry Langdon as Cupid—had moments of genuine sparkle and was clearly a better showcase for Harvey than *My Lips Betray*. As a frumpy chambermaid made over by Lew Ayres and a harem of charm specialists, Harvey kept the preciousness to a minimum, displaying both good comic timing and a gorgeous lithe ballerina's body. Harvey's come-hither song to the bemused Charles Butterworth, "Gather Lip Rouge While You May," remains both strange and charming, and the *Love Me Tonight* tradition continued with sparkle in another musical number. As Ayres and Harvey kiss for the first time, all the bric-a-brac in the room comes alive to serve as Greek chorus. Figurines, what-nots, and movie magazine covers (Clara Bow's has a Brooklyn accent) warn them "You Can Be Had—Be Careful!" With music and lyrics by B. G. DeSylva, Leo Robin, and Richard Whiting, and direction by an on-form David Butler, the sequence balances sex ("You can be had" was a Mae West catch-line), humor, and fantasy in optimal quantities: this one scene in this pleasant smidgen of a movie is just about an ideal demonstration of how clearly a musical could be given an individual and wholly filmic syntax. After another year or so, with generic constriction and the imposition of the Production Code, such cherishable moments would be largely gone. Though "Be Careful" was singled out for special notice, *My Weakness* fared indifferently. *My Lips Betray*, finally released some weeks later, did worse. In the year of Ruby Keeler, Lilian Harvey could not fit in.

Except for Wheeler and Woolsey, RKO had studiously avoided any musical impulses since the time of *Dixiana*.[10] This changed in November 1932

---

10. As Warners did with *Manhattan Parade*, the company produced a Technicolor backstage comedy, *Fannie Foley Herself* (1931), that managed to completely sidestep the issues of song and dance.

when producer Lou Brock mounted an ambitious three-reel musical. Ostensibly a showcase for bandleader Phil Harris, *So This is Harris* was designed to test spectator tolerance for both shorts and features by coupling a full musical program with a volley of camera tricks derived from René Clair and from several of Paramount's musicals. Mark Sandrich, his directorial skills honed considerably since *The Talk of Hollywood*, worked with the studio's special effects wing to give *Harris* visual flair all but unknown in a short subject; and upon its release *Harris* was given more attention than any live-action short since the days of *George Bernard Shaw*.[11] This, coupled with the concurrent hit of *42nd Street*, prompted RKO to upgrade Brock and Sandrich to features. The result was *Melody Cruise*, released simultaneously with Warner Bros.' second musical spectacular, *Gold Diggers of 1933*, in mid-June. Again there were camera tricks both funny and inventive, including (courtesy of special effects artisan Linwood Dunn, fresh from *King Kong*) the most creative use of optical wipes in any film to date. Plus rhymed dialogue, ingenious editing, and Mamoulianesque bystanders who manage to make constant, giddy comment on each turn of the plot. The stylish presentation made it doubly unfortunate that *Melody Cruise* was, like the ballet on ice with which it inexplicably climaxed, all flash and no substance. Even in the cellophane arena of musical escapism its script was notably devoid of character, conflict, and incident, and directed by Sandrich in a fashion that betrayed a lack of feature-film experience. Leading man Phil Harris was an additional liability, his Harry Richman-on-cornpone personality set off far less well than in *So This Is Harris*. Either Ben Lyon or Nelson Eddy, both candidates for the role, would have done better. In spite of Harris, *Melody Cruise* scored well with a public newly attentive to musicals, and Brock was soon at work on a similar and more ambitious project, *Flying Down to Rio*.

With or without *42nd Street*, Bing Crosby's success in *The Big Broadcast* and his ongoing popularity as a radio star made additional film appearances inevitable. Still somewhat dubious about his dramatic capabilities, Paramount cast him in *College Humor* in the secondary role of a university professor given to lecturing his classes on the niceties of delivering a ballad. "Learn to Croon" became a hit, as did "Down the Old Ox Road," which he sang as the culmination of an "Isn't It Romantic?"-inspired sequence, university types passing the lyrics on until they reach Crosby on his balcony. Despite Jack Oakie's starring role as a typically overaged Hollywood collegiate, Crosby's was the name that brought in the crowds and made *College Humor* one of the leading contributors to Paramount's mid-year rescue from receivership.

11. *So This Is Harris* was one of two shorts in 1933 that greatly helped to promote the return of musical features. The other: Disney's sensational *The Three Little Pigs*, buoyed by the smash hit song "Who's Afraid of the Big Bad Wolf?"

Paramount's other savior, Mae West, had polarized the nation with *She Done Him Wrong*. On the one hand were the millions who roared at her lewd cracks and gasped gleefully as she assumed the role of sexual conqueror. It was to these hoards, as well as exhibitors still uncertain of her appeal, that Paramount aimed some of its most blatant promotion—one *Variety* ad focused firmly on West's cleavage to proclaim "The Bull's Eye of Lusty Entertainment." The other side comprised slowly coalescing groups of churchgoers and moral watchdogs, for whom West was the most loathsome trollop since Potiphar's wife. She confirmed their direst fears by letting loose her second starring vehicle, *I'm No Angel*, in October 1933. In addition to being a virtual deification of West—playing a lion-tamer whose specialty seemed to be the human kind—it raised the stakes on her musical acumen. The response to her songs in *She Done Him Wrong* motivated her to pay special attention to the program for *I'm No Angel*. "I Found a New Way to Go to Town" and "They Call Me Sister Honky Tonk," two of her *Angel* songs, were as racy as they sound; consider, then, that among the song titles she rejected for the film were "Walking the Streets" and "I Don't Want to Do That." *I'm No Angel* was, to no one's surprise, as big a hit as *She Done Him Wrong*, and West quickly set to writing a third sexual epic that would give even greater scope to the musical sequences.

MGM's lyrical plans, laid prior to the advent of *42nd Street*, reflected the same European and operetta trends as those of Fox. Besides its ongoing attempts to resurrect *The Merry Widow*, the company announced a musical version of Thorne Smith's novel *Turnabout*. This tale of gender exchange ultimately gave way to another risqué fantasy, *I Married an Angel*. Janos Vaszary's comedy, successfully produced in Budapest *(Angyalt Vettem Felesegul)* in 1932, was a satire both naïve and racy about a winsome seraph who descends to earth, marries a dissolute mortal, and becomes quite corrupted. It sounded like a Lubitsch film, and the director did consider it for Miriam Hopkins; in the end MGM acquired it for its new singing contract players, Jeanette MacDonald and stage baritone Nelson Eddy. Two other new arrivals at Metro were Rodgers and Hart, who began work on *Angel*'s screenplay and songs early in 1933. The difficulty in translating Vaszary's naughty conceit was far greater than merely the distance between Hungarian and English, and Rodgers and Hart were so unsure of the material that they tried the trick of jettisoning the fantasy and making the lead role an aviatrix merely mistaken for an angel. Later they attempted to stick to the original story, but despite rhyming dialogue similar to *Hallelujah, I'm a Bum*, and scattered bright moments and pleasant songs, their efforts were unsuccessful. Other writers followed, equally ineffectively, and by this time most of MGM's musical attention was being directed to backstage musicals. *I Married an Angel* was put on the shelf, MacDonald put in another Continental-toned musical, *The Cat and the Fiddle*, and Eddy kept generally in abeyance until he was paired with MacDonald late in 1934 for *Naughty Marietta*. Had the company persevered more with the original script, an *I Married an Angel* released in late 1933 might have been a spicy, memorable event.[12]

That MGM did not work harder on original treatments of musical fantasies is attributable to a phenomenon which can be labeled The *42nd Street* Virus, which set the tone for all but a handful of the most successful musicals in 1933 and the next decade. It was naturally analogous to the *Broadway Melody* outbreak of mid-1929, and backstage films of 1933 and 1934 often seemed to constitute a *Chasing Rainbows*-redux. The clichés were upgraded, to be sure, the technique far more polished, yet the intrinsic features remained: the unknown finding audience favor, the rigors of putting on the show, the temptations of Park Avenue, the faithful lover and screwy sidekick. *42nd Street* raised the ante by inspiring its own set of dramatic and musical clichés. Busby Berkeley's style, in particular, was ripe for imitation, and film after backstage film tried to emulate or outdo the master's spectacles. Overhead formations, sequential shots of chorus girls, odd angles, mass groupings, all duplicated over and over. The window of creativity often seemed more limited than in earlier years, when the models had been stage spectacles with a bit of *Broadway Melody* thrown in, neither of them copied as assiduously as the Berkeley pieces. The clones never matched the original, for Berkeley's imitators erroneously believed that sheer lavish clutter—instead of structurally ordered processions of images—was the key to his touch. So the most ironic component of *42nd Street*'s deserved success was that in recreating the musical it formed a new, narrower set of matrices. While *Love Me Tonight* indicated that musicals could be made with invention and daring, the flop of *Adorable* and MGM's inability to negotiate *I Married an Angel* prompted the inference that "different" or European models might not work in a revived environment. The "New Deal in Entertainment," which made such efforts seem faded and futile, was packaged so stylishly that its conventional core was temporarily obscured. At the end of 1933, it was obvious that a pileup of backstagers had started. But this time it did not abate. Its details slickly varied, the backstage film maintained its equilibrium for the next twenty or so years.

12. MGM tried again with *I Married an Angel* just prior to *Marietta*'s release. However, the intervening sixteen months had seen the rise of the Catholic Legion of Decency and the strengthening of the Production Code. This was, then, not the time for a tale of an angel explicitly losing both divinity and virginity, and Code czar Joe Breen responded lividly to the *I Married an Angel* script: "Aside and apart from the basic plot of this story, page after page of the dialogue is vulgarly offensive and profane." With such opposition, MGM permitted Rodgers and Hart to rework the material for Broadway's far more permissive climes, and it was successfully produced in 1938. Only one of the original movie songs (the title song) was used. The play was then extensively laundered and filmed, finally, with MacDonald and Eddy in 1942.

Why didn't audiences get fed up, as they had in 1930? Mostly because they had changed, and so had their viewing habits. The spring of 1933 was a time of immense anticipation, triggered by Roosevelt's election and the daring with which he closed the nation's banks one day after his inauguration. The Depression could now seem, if not less severe, less unendurable. A note of hope was sounding, and the nation's box offices—which accepted IOUs during the bank holiday—reaped the benefits before almost any other industry. Film's potential for escapist uplift became more clear than it had been in years, and the innate sunniness of the musical, which seemed inane and irrelevant in 1930, was suddenly the ideal conduit for a nation's optimism. Even with radio's intrusion, film grosses began to ascend to their 1929 levels. Another change in film spectatorship during 1933 concerned the perception of genres as a series of cycles. After mid-1930, when musicals died, there were numerous references to the passing of the "musical cycle," which was replaced by the renewed gangster cycle *(Little Caesar, The Public Enemy)*, the horror cycle *(Dracula, Frankenstein)*, and so on. The return of musicals in 1933 coincided, in fact, with a jungle cycle, led by *Tarzan, the Ape Man* and *King Kong*. But by early 1934 it was obvious that spectator habits, and producers' perceptions of their audiences, had changed. When *42nd Street* opened, Jack Warner stated that his company would produce two musicals, no more; the memory of the 1930 balance sheets was likely ringing in his brain. Just a few months later that idea changed, when it became obvious that musicals and other film staples were no longer considered transient phenomena, in for a burst of popularity and then gone. This as much as anything explains musicals' ability to maintain their hold on public affection over the ensuing decades. While cycles did (and do) remain, changes in spectatorship around 1933 helped to establish more permanent networks of genres and audience preferences. It also signified the impending demise of the earlier generic jumble responsible for *The Great Gabbo* and *Madam Satan*. Musicals would not be mistaken for anything else, and the standardization would be progressively obvious with the presence of much fake Berkeley and a shallow well from which to draw ideas.

Jack Warner held to his promise to quickly follow the lead of *42nd Street*. The studio released two (not one) more backstage spectacles in the subsequent six months, beating most of the imitators with time to spare. The first, in the works long before *42nd Street* opened, was a remake of *Gold Diggers of Broadway* originally called *High Life*. Its final title, *Gold Diggers of 1933*, neatly mixed nostalgia and modernism. Many of the *42nd Street* people were again present, along with two—Joan Blondell and director Mervyn LeRoy—who had narrowly missed out the first time. *42nd Street* had alluded to the Depression, reflected it in its mixture of hope and cynicism; the new *Gold Diggers* was positively immersed in Depression references from its first frames. "The long-lost dollar has come back to the fold," sings Ginger Rogers, and as she launches into "We're in the Money" Busby Berkeley dangles wry wish-fulfillment before cash-poor audiences.[13] The number *is* money, tons of it, used as decor and hats and boas and G-strings, with only barely implicit irony. For the second chorus Berkeley and Rogers manage to filter national optimism through the most trivial of pop phenomena—Rogers does it in Pig Latin, prattling "Ereway inhay the oneymay" while Berkeley pulls the camera in so close that her features distort. The giddiness, and the number, are curtailed posthaste with the arrival of the sheriff and his men, come to close the show for nonpayment of bills. Reality has intruded.

If ever soaking the rich seemed justifiable, it's in *Gold Diggers of 1933*, although Rogers (as Fay Fortune) is the one true gold digger in sight. The others—Keeler, Blondell, Aline MacMahon—just want to get along and get in a show, surviving meanwhile on hope, wisecracks, and stolen milk. Eventually Hopwood's millionaires vs. chorines plot overpowers the Depression references, even as the fresh lines remain. In Winnie Lightner's old role, MacMahon replaces rowdy pratfalls with acerbic chutzpah; "If that's the wolf," she says, hearing a knock at the door, "we'll eat him!" The far less sanguine Keeler reiterated her claims as the backstager's least worldly madonna, and Busby Berkeley reiterated his as the musical's most audacious and cinema-minded force. "Pettin' in the Park" is one of the best-known distillations of his rowdiest impulses: an atmosphere of unconfined randiness; midget Billy Barty (just a child himself) as an unruly voyeuristic baby; and the famous fadeout on Dick Powell taking a can opener to the back of Keeler's tin bathing suit. "The Shadow Waltz" is the first of Berkeley's romantic roundelays, in which a waltz or similar melody would repeat ad infinitum as background for permutations of girls and camera angles. For this one Berkeley pushed for more and more odd shots, placing the camera sideways against a mirror to show dancers and their reflections gliding from the top to bottom of the film frame instead of side to side. It also has the unforgettable neon violins, with visible extension cords, that were to prove near-fatal when an earthquake hit the set on March 10, 1933. In addition to toppling the studio's water tower, the quake came close to frying a few of Berkeley's electrified enchantresses. The Depression resumes the foreground in the finale, a bitter tribute to FDR's "forgotten man," the war veteran fallen on rugged times. It was a situation on the minds of millions of Americans, especially in the wake of the vets' Bonus Army March on Washington in May 1932 to obtain their service pensions

13. Commonly known as "We're In the Money," the song's proper name is "The Gold Diggers Song." This came just before publication, in the light of the huge sales of *42nd Street* sheet music. The presence of a title song was seen to always help sales, and inasmuch as *Gold Diggers* did not have a title tune, "We're in the Money" was retitled to qualify.

early. National feeling toward them was divided, prompting Joan Blondell to open the song "Remember My Forgotten Man" with "I don't know if he deserves a bit of sympathy." Aside from a captious immediacy unheard of in musicals, Al Dubin's lyric also had a fair quota of schmaltz ("Once he used to love me," etc.), yet Berkeley's images send it bounding from kitsch sentimentality to populist document: streetwalkers, tenements, transitions of men parading off to war to trudging through trenches to standing on breadlines. The final shot, an army of the homeless reaching toward Blondell's hooker as if for salvation, while soldier silhouettes march impassively overhead, is so powerful as to remove any questions regarding taste or the propriety of concluding a frivolous entertainment with such a scene. Indeed, prior to the first preview Jack Warner and supervisor Hal Wallis ordered that it replace "Pettin' in the Park" in the closing spot so as to end the movie on that extraordinary last shot. It couldn't, they rightly figured, be topped.

The notices and reception for *Gold Diggers of 1933* were equal to those of *42nd Street,* and the financial returns considerably more gratifying. Costing the same as its predecessor, it grossed nearly a million dollars more, almost in a league with the previous *Gold Diggers.* Once more a follow-up was already in the works, for which a grateful Jack Warner gave Busby Berkeley carte blanche. In this third offering the Depression was less in evidence than backstage atmosphere, though not the environment framing *42nd Street.* Instead, it was the theater of the Depression phenomenon of prologues, live spectacles performed onstage in large movie houses between features. In a flush time such things would not have been feasible or necessary, but desperate theater owners were willing to spring for the prologues to draw in the audiences. The leading producer of these tab shows was the Fanchon and Marco outfit, which specialized in such scaled-down versions of Broadway hits as the *Sally* company in which Mary Eaton toured in 1932. As was well known, Fanchon and Marco's work was the inspiration for the third big Warner musical of 1933, at first titled *Prologue* and ultimately named *Footlight Parade.* Its cast was led by the most dominant star presence since the days of Jolson and Lightner. For the millions unaware of James Cagney's years as a vaudeville hoofer, *Footlight Parade* was an immense surprise; until then he had merely been known as the screen's nerviest tough guy. Otherwise the cast of Warners backstage specialists was as before, although Dick Powell was originally sidelined by pneumonia. His announced replacement was Stanley Smith *(Sweetie, King of Jazz, Good News)* until it became clear that audiences would accept only Powell opposite Ruby Keeler. Warners then postponed his scenes until his at least partial recovery. Lloyd Bacon was back as director, although Busby Berkeley's participation was compromised by conflicting obligations that caused him to leave *Footlight Parade* early to return to Sam Goldwyn for *Roman Scandals*. The (little) remaining work was completed by a veteran of an earlier era, Larry Ceballos.

Jimmy Cagney's energizing staccato makes *Footlight Parade* likely the fastest-moving of all musical films, as well as the most asymmetrical. The three giant Berkeley numbers come bang-bang in succession right near the end, bigger and longer than the comparable setup in *42nd Street*. Here, then, is the complete opposite of the "organically" integrated musical comedy favored on Broadway and film after the early 1940s, yet for all its lack of proportion *Footlight Parade* is so snappy that a question of balance becomes superfluous. Cagney and Blondell fight and love their way through the first hour, pitching cracks right and left as a volley of subplots whizz by. "As long as there are sidewalks," Blondell informs perfidious gold digger Claire Dodd, "you've got a job!" Then Berkeley takes over, at first vapidly with "Honeymoon Hotel," which is little more than an anemic "Shuffle Off to Buffalo" minus the charm. The other two are far better, with the "Shanghai Lil" finale bearing more narrative structure than in any musical sequence up to that time. Perhaps there is too much: by trying for too many striking images Berkeley lets it become disjointed, lurching from Cagney prowling an opium den to a sailors' brawl to a Cagney-Keeler tap meet to the patented overhead effects. These, as it happens, are some of his most delirious formations, what with a smiling President Roosevelt and the National Recovery Administration's "We Do Our Part" eagle belching gunfire from every feather. While much of "Shanghai Lil" is captivating and Cagney is terrific, it lacks the concentration of "Forgotten Man" or the number just preceding it, "By a Waterfall." And Keeler, whose haphazard grace usually coupled well with Berkeley's impulses, is hampered by all sorts of things: her buildup as a fabulous temptress to rival Princess Turandot, the sickly attempts to make her look and sound Chinese ("I miss you velly much a long time," she chirps to Cagney), and her juxtaposition to a tap dancer of genuine skill and idiosyncrasy. "By a Waterfall" presents her in less challenged mode, required simply to give "yoo-hoo" response to Powell's tenor calls and lead Berkeley's troupe through the most staggering water ballet in the history of liquid. If *Footlight Parade* contained nothing else of merit this number would have been sufficient to make it a hit. One of the defining moments in Berkeley's work, it has nothing to do with dance, almost nothing to do with song, and centers totally on visual flair and the ability to intrigue with new compositional permutations. Audiences had never seen anything like it, except in a few shots in *The Kid from Spain* where Berkeley was clearly warming up for this. Neither taste nor logic was a factor by any means in this interminable series of simpering half-naked women, wearing silly rubber bathing caps meant to represent hair, gamboling through an astounding variety of aquacade formations, all in a sequence ostensibly taking place on the stage of a movie theater. Forget the musical's usual suspension of logic; here was fabulous spectacle for its own sake alone and in abundance beyond the compasses of most Depression dreamers. Give Berkeley credit: he knew how to build a number, how to keep topping himself with more spectacle, more outrageous shots of crotches and thighs, all the way through. It's carried off without a hitch, without so much as one droplet splashing on the lens. And his waterlogged lovelies manage the ordeal with finesse, a somewhat uncomfortable-looking Keeler included. (The only exception is one befuddled chorine who briefly goes astray during one of the "snake" formations.) None of the Berkeley imitators, in 1933 or the years to follow, could replicate his brash grandeur; and few backstage films would ever equal *Footlight Parade*'s cocky momentum.

Gold Diggers of 1933 opened in mid-June, *Footlight Parade* in late September. In the interim, the copies began to issue forth. The first, *Moonlight and Pretzels*, opened in August, and a more earnest *homage* to *42nd Street* can scarcely be conceived. Not so much in its plot, which diverges from its model at most junctures, as in its eagerness to tap into the newfound appreciation for the backstage film. So anxious is *Moonlight and Pretzels* to please its viewers that it succeeds in spite of itself. It is—the wording is quite deliberate—terribly wonderful, and seldom have so many inadequacies been so dire and irrelevant all at the same time.

A film as strange as *Moonlight and Pretzels* would naturally have an odd production history, and this one begins with a pair of undistinguished New York-based producers, William Rowland and Monte Brice. The quick smash of *42nd Street* prompted them to plan an equivalent, this time with none of that California artifice. Broadway would be their oyster in a made-in-New-York backstage musical soaked in atmosphere, authenticity, and stage talent. To finance it they contacted Carl Laemmle, who had viewed the return of the musical with some interest and was about to reissue *King of Jazz*. The plan was sufficiently solid for him to authorize a whoppingly low budget of $100,000 and appoint his son-in-law, Stanley Bergerman, to supervise it. Also traveling east for the extravaganza was Karl Freund, who would share directorial chores with Brice. An outstanding cinematographer, Freund had recently directed his first film, *The Mummy*, though his skill with atmospheric horror mattered less to Uncle Carl than his ability to plow through the shoot with no wasted time or cash. Universal's Lew Ayres was originally scheduled for the lead, a brash songwriter who goes places, but when both he and Dick Powell proved unavailable, Broadway actor Roger Pryor was hired. The only Hollywood names in the cast were Mary Brian and Leo Carrillo—plus "guest appearances" by reminders of the past, Alexander Gray and Bernice Claire, who had returned to New York and varied stage work with stints in Vitaphone shorts filmed in Brook-

The Busby Berkeley Style, Counterfeit and Genuine: *(above)* Alexander Gray and chorus eulogize the stock market crash in a cramped (if resourceful) tableau from "Dusty Shoes," staged by Bobby Connolly for *Moonlight and Pretzels*. *(below)* A blonde Ruby Keeler and an enthusiastic troupe of Berkeley lovelies wax lyrical in one of the non-electrified moments of "The Shadow Waltz" in *Gold Diggers of 1933*. *Photofest*.

lyn.[14] The songs came from two divergent quarters. Herman Hupfeld was a composer-lyricist with credits ranging from "When Yuba Plays the Rumba on the Tuba" to "As Time Goes By," and Jay Gorney (composer) and E. Y. (Yip) Harburg (lyrics) had unforgettably set the Depression into song with "Brother, Can You Spare a Dime" and earlier had written "What Wouldn't I Do for That Man!" for Helen Morgan in *Applause*. Bobby Connolly, staging the musical numbers, did his best to duplicate the Berkeley style in cramped quarters on a shoestring budget. The most money was put into the ersatz-"Forgotten Man" finale, "Dusty Shoes," filled with effects quite deliberately stolen from *Gold Diggers of 1933*.[15]

Under the wry working title *Shoot the Works, Moonlight and Pretzels* was shot in eighteen days in June 1933 at the Astoria studio, with location work at the Casino (formerly Earl Carroll) Theatre. Astoria, undergoing a brief renaissance, was being leased to all comers, and *Moonlight and Pretzels* was preceded by *The Emperor Jones* and *Midnight*. Universal did far better than with its earlier musical cash-in, *Melody of Love*, for *Moonlight and Pretzels* repaid its meager investment many times over. Its great success is comparable to *Syncopation* in 1929, coming in early on a new trend ahead of glossier projects, sold with unerring accuracy to a music-hungry market. The reviews were mostly good, and several of its songs quickly became hits. Even its very title was an inducement, literally tapping into the beer garden craze sweeping the country as the first leg of Repeal. The public was avid for just the type of amusement it proffered: hard-boiled laughs, a supposed insider view of show-biz magic, catchy tunes that made light of the Depression, and (as billing boasted) "50 Famous Show Girls." It was seemingly not dissimilar to the Warner-Berkeley pieces—yet it had some major differences. Of all musical films made after 1932, this one is the closest to the first pioneering musicals in its enterprising try-anything-once spirit and intentions, and in the fashion by which its creators' reach far exceeds their grasp. The plain fact is that except for some of its music, nothing in *Moon-*

14. Many of Gray and Claire's shorts were in Warner's "Broadway Brevities" series. The cinematic equivalent of Fanchon-Marco tab shows, they were retitled two- (or three-) reel remakes of past movie musicals. Claire recreated her Anuita for *Flame Song* and with Gray sped through *The Red Shadow*. Others included *Silver Lining (Sally), Fifi (Kiss Me Again), Yours Sincerely (Spring Is Here)*, and *Paree, Paree (Fifty Million Frenchmen)*. Other familiar names in the Brevities: J. Harold Murray, Vivienne Segal, Stanley Smith, Nancy Welford, and a debonair young Bob Hope in *Paree, Paree*.

Gray and Claire's presence in *Moonlight and Pretzels* was part of an unofficial rite of passage by which several leading lights of the old musicals made final token appearances in the new. Other examples include Winnie Lightner in *Dancing Lady*, Vivienne Segal in *The Cat and the Fiddle*, plus the near-misses of Stanley Smith in *Footlight Parade* and Alice Gentle, originally set to sing the "Carioca" in *Flying Down to Rio* and then replaced by Etta Moten.

15. Gorney's spacious music and Alexander Gray's resonant baritone imply that "Dusty Shoes" will reach toward social relevance. The lyrics, however, include the singer's punning imprecation to his footwear: "You and I, we'll build up our soles again." Harburg, when he wanted to, could be something of a wag.

light and Pretzels is especially good, and the script device of an untalented dancer (Mary Brian) who doesn't make good is echoed by the film itself. No one is photogenic, none of the performances outstanding, and both the script and the staging of the numbers seem intent on maximal gaucherie. The inadvertent sabotage of traditional musical gloss is quite startling: a camera pans across the chorus girls' legs to reveal that some of them have scuffed shoes; grotesquely bumptious choreography in the title song turns a gay romp into yahoo purgatory; singer Lillian Miles, trying hard for dramatic effect in "Dusty Shoes," shrieks an accusatory "We're *rotten!*" at the camera, as if the audience in toto were responsible for the Depression. Miles is also answerable for that weirdly avaricious rub-fingers-together gesture during "Are You Makin' Any Money?" that, once seen, is never forgotten. So it goes, and therein lies its spell. Few mainstream films seem so totally nourished by sheer nerve, without reference to skill or talent or money; the putative script takes a back seat, and the overt text of *Moonlight and Pretzels* becomes its attempts to succeed without stumbling. What a movie!

MGM's first attempt to cash in on the new backstage craze had motives more ulterior than the usual commercial impulses. While the company had been weathering the Depression better than its rivals, it had retained a persistent blot of red ink called *The March of Time*. Except for its German incarnation and the short *The Devil's Cabaret*, Harry Rapf's revue sat on the shelf in mute defiance of all the writers who tried to turn its tangle of sketches and spectacle into a lucid entertainment. Finally, in January 1933, Moss Hart succeeded where his predecessors had not, devising a story that chronicled the evolution of American entertainment through the story of one show business family, with time along the way to sample sequences culled from *March of Time*. In revered studio fashion, Hart's ideas were set upon by another battery of writers, including Bradford Ropes, recently signed with the studio to give its new backstage stories a *42nd Street* zing. The cast for the new sections included Alice Brady and Frank Morgan as prototypic vaudevillians, and Jackie Cooper, Mickey Rooney, Russell Hardie, and Eddie Quillan as their son and grandson, young and grownup. While the concept was sound, and Brady and Morgan excellent, the plot was listless and disjointed—dozens of writers to make a script this poor?— and the old footage fit in so badly that it was cut to only four minutes. The original title seemed to court disaster, so it was released in September 1933 as *Broadway to Hollywood*. Few were unaware of its roots, particularly during the brief Technicolor "March of Time" sequence coming midway through. Audiences turned out, for whatever reasons, in modest numbers, hardly enough to offset a production cost that had risen to nearly a million dollars. MGM posted half that as a loss, put a few leftover Technicolor *March of Time* numbers into some shorts featuring the Three Stooges (these included *Nertsery Rhymes* and *Jailbirds of Paradise*), then finally said goodbye to the whole misbegotten escapade. Unbelievably, even as the ghosts of *March of Time* were being laid to rest, the studio was mounting another revue without form or cohesion. *The Hollywood Revue of 1933*, not released until the following year as *Hollywood Party* (and discussed in the next chapter), proved that some important and expensive lessons had not been absorbed.

Perhaps it was the toil of *The March of Time/Broadway to Hollywood* that caused MGM to remain backstage, far from the fantasy of *I Married an Angel*. Bradford Ropes followed *42nd Street* with another show business novel bearing the self-explanatory title *Stage Mother*, and the studio filmed it as a semimusical just after *Broadway to Hollywood*. Brown and Freed supplied a couple of new songs (including "Beautiful Girl," originally meant for *Dancing Lady*), and Alice Brady was again cast as a greasepaint matriarch, with Maureen O'Sullivan as her overpowered daughter. There was certainly a great deal more marrow here than in *Broadway to Hollywood*, as well as a more credible theatrical environment supplied by director Charles Brabin. Ropes obviously relished making this mama a paragon of her detested species, and Brady played it all the way down—pushing, blackmailing, pimping, wrecking lives; this creature was a worthy if soft-soaped forebear of Mama Rose in *Gypsy*. Given greater care and planned as more of an all-out musical, *Stage Mother* could have been one of the central works in its division. Unfortunately it was somewhat undercut by its make-do intentions, as with the casting of O'Sullivan, obviously not in musical trim, and in the most glaring use of a dance double since *The Great Gabbo*.

MGM spent far more effort and money on its other musicals of that season, *Dancing Lady* and *Going Hollywood*, which both recalled the musical's salad days in their attempts to give a diva's allure some needed prop-up. As first conceived, and as a novel serialized in the *Saturday Evening Post*, *Dancing Lady* was another entry in the through-the-years style to which the studio seemed drawn, recounting the career of a tough Hoboken hoofer named Janie who rises from vaudeville to Broadway and down again, through mob ties, marriage to a socialite, and ultimate happiness with her old vaudeville partner. The character's most striking attribute was her single-minded concentration on her career, viz., to dance is to work is to exist. This tied in uncannily, almost biographically, with MGM's most driven star, Joan Crawford, and the property was tagged for her as early as March 1932. A year later, as work on the *Dancing Lady* script was under way, Crawford needed a boost. She had tried to accentuate her versatility in the interim by playing Sadie Thompson in *Rain* and an English aristocrat in *Today We Live*, with unsatisfactory results on both fronts. *Dancing Lady* was intended as a sleek recoup, combining Crawford's *Our Dancing Daughters* hoyden with her sensual sufferer from *Possessed*. The standard procession of Metro writers followed (including Moss Hart, John Howard Lawson, and Anita Loos, all uncredited) and only after several months' work was the script coupled to the *42nd Street* blueprint. Janie was turned into a feistier sister to Ruby Keeler's Peggy Sawyer, and Patch Gallagher was changed from a scrappy vaudevillian into a Julian Marsh-style wizard of theater. The seedier aspects of the novel and the earlier scripts were reduced to Janie's one stint in a downtown burlesque emporium, her downfall was eliminated, and her problems inevitably smoothed into a gouache of MGM gloss that permitted none of the pulse of *42nd Street* or the inside dirt of *Stage Mother*. David O. Selznick, recently arrived at MGM, knew and cared far more about producing dramas than he did about making musicals fly, and Clark Gable, cast as Patch very nearly at gunpoint, was perhaps the most unwilling and unsuited participant in any 1933 musical. Production was held up to await his return from an extended vacation, followed by a serious infection, followed by tonsillitis, and when he finally did show up (collapsing on the set at least once) he delivered one of his least sanguine performances.[16]

In MGM's best corporate style, *Dancing Lady* was assembled and reassembled by many hands, including dance directors Sammy Lee and LeRoy Prinz and songwriters Brown and Freed and Rodgers and Hart, the latter with one of their least infectious works, "That's the Rhythm of the Day." The one hit to emerge, "Everything I Have is Yours" (Burton Lane and Harold Adamson), was given to Art Jarrett to sing after it became obvious that Crawford couldn't handle it. Nor was her dancing up to the promise of the script. Her authority had increased since *Hollywood Revue*, but not her skill; dance, as rendered by her emphatic feet and thrashing arms, became a grim mandate. The one real dancer on hand was Fred Astaire. He had been considered for the role of Patch when the character was still a hoofer, and when that was changed he signed with RKO. With Astaire's first film, *Flying Down to Rio*, not shooting for some weeks, Selznick borrowed him to play himself and partner Crawford. The bit could have been done by anyone, though while it cramped his creative impulses the experience helped him to adjust to on-camera performing. Another movie novice checking in briefly was Nelson Eddy, previously in about seven frames of *Broadway to Hollywood*. With *I Married an Angel* on hold, MGM was trying to figure out what to do with him.

A Crawford-Gable romance would have fared extremely well under any circumstances in late 1933. Titling that romance *Dancing Lady* and implying

16. During the various delays Lee Tracy, William Gargan, and Russell Hardie were considered as replacements. Gable's behavior was a main factor in MGM's decision to lend his services to Columbia for *Night Bus*, which he regarded as even more insulting than *Dancing Lady*. He upgraded his view when *Night Bus* was retitled *It Happened One Night* and became a nearly instant classic.

musical bounty made it a smash, in fact the model of the MGM commercial hit. (Pertinent figures: negative cost, $923,000; domestic gross, $1,490,000; foreign gross: $916,000; profit: $744,000. The grosses are closely comparable to those of *42nd Street* and *Footlight Parade*.) The film's main significances were, in fact, financial, aside from serving as early exposure for Astaire, Eddy, and the Three Stooges, as well as a farewell for Winnie Lightner. But there was no ruling point of view—least of all from director Robert Z. Leonard—to mesh the song and dance with the studio gloss and Crawford's determined-tenement-Cinderella formula. A great deal of musical footage, including a futuristic robot sequence called "The Go-Go-Go," was shot and then discarded, likely due to a lack of cohesion, plus Crawford's deficient brio. (Some of the scenes went into MGM's musical morgue, the Three Stooges shorts.) As a result, the climactic production numbers are rather a mess, shinily expensive without any of Berkeley's focus. Here, then, was a demonstration that a musical film, even one with abundant financial success, needed more than money and star potency to account for its existence. Having reaffirmed her popularity without augmenting her versatility, Crawford made no more overt musicals until *Torch Song* in 1953. That film, in some ways an inadvertent sequel to *Dancing Lady*, shows how twenty years of fear and drive could harden Janie (and Crawford) into the most ossified star imaginable.

Unlike Crawford, Marion Davies was a star only through reluctance, and her reappearance as a musical participant in 1933 was another Hearst ploy to keep her fame looking fresh-minted. Early in the year a few songs were inserted to positive effect into Davies's *Peg O' My Heart*, from the old Broadway chestnut. Hearst, encouraged, put her in a new-style backstager partly influenced by her best silent comedy, *Show People*, and her costar was film's most popular new singer, Bing Crosby. *Going Hollywood* was the result, a promising musical comedy that dissipated its effect through script uncertainty, unfelt direction by Raoul Walsh, and Davies's own disinterest. Three years after *The Florodora Girl* she looked about twenty years older and twenty pounds heavier—half of it makeup—and her glazed lassitude sat oddly on her role as a schoolteacher who hies to Hollywood and becomes a star. His assurance waxing with each film, Crosby partnered her as well as possible, and was rewarded with one of Brown and Freed's best scores. "We'll Make Hay When the Sun Shines" and "After Sundown" were good (the latter in unfortunately truncated form) and "Temptation," sung to Fifi D'Orsay in a Tijuana dive near the end of the film, was dynamite. A drunken paean to lust and self-loathing is about the last thing one associates with Crosby, yet before his screen personality smoothed into its accustomed placidity he was capable of projecting heat and danger. The more famous he got the less these were evident, and Crosby's utter relaxation is a great part of the reason that his musicals, over thirty years, were probably the most conventional, least daring of any star's. It was easier to go through the same tropes and use other time to hit the recording studio or the radio station, the golf course or the racetrack. A consummate predictability soon set the pace for Paramount's musicals, since Crosby rarely went to other studios after *Going Hollywood,* and seldom would the studio regain its spirit and daring. No more *Love Me Tonight*s, not even many *Let's Go Native*s. As for *Going Hollywood,* aside from Crosby's songs and a fairly nifty title number set in Grand Central Station, it was no great shakes. Its laughs were too intermittent (except from Patsy Kelly and Ned Sparks) and its star chemistry anemic—plus as an insider piece it had none of the spark of a coeval MGM offering, *Bombshell,* whose candid satire of stardom would not have sat well with Hearst. *Going Hollywood*'s overblown numbers shot its cost up to the level of *Dancing Lady,* and not even Crosby's standing and the traditionally strong Christmas trade prevented it from posting one of MGM's more notable losses for the time.

Some of the inside-Hollywood spark *Going Hollywood* missed was present in Paramount's *Sitting Pretty,* a far more modest piece which had opened a month earlier. It was, in fact, one of the more agreeable musicals to deal with movies, less through penetrating wit or satire than through a general air of good cheer, fine songs (by film newcomers Mack Gordon and Harry Revel), and an ingratiating cast. Jack Oakie and Jack Haley played Tin Pan Alley types who hitchhike into Hollywood to take advantage of the musical renaissance and encounter Ginger Rogers, an extra, and Thelma Todd, a star. It was all in unpretentious and brightly played fun, with a space near the end for a budgetary blowout for the score's hit tune, "Did You Ever See a Dream Walking," performed by Rogers, Art Jarrett, and a flock of seemingly unclad young women waving ostrich fans in the best Sally Rand style. Sub-Berkeley perhaps, yet, like the entire film, entirely congenial.

Just prior to *Sitting Pretty,* Jack Oakie had costarred with Bing Crosby (before *Going Hollywood*) in *Too Much Harmony.* The only Paramount release of 1933 except for the independently made *Take a Chance* to directly reflect the *42nd Street* backstage effect, it featured Crosby as a Broadway star who discovers an act (Oakie and Skeets Gallagher) in the sticks and brings it to New York.[17] The similarities in the story and the cast to Paramount's first musical, *Close Harmony,* were not a coincidence, for *Too Much Harmony* was intended as something of an updated sequel; Harry Green was also on hand, and Nancy Carroll had been mentioned at one time for a lead. (Buddy Rogers, his career in eclipse, was on the East Coast shooting *Take a Chance.*) Rarely in 1933 did new musicals design to look to their past in so specific a fashion, for the trend had already started to treat the first

17. The uninspired story represented some of the lower end of the oeuvre of Joseph L. Mankiewicz. Years later, he would have far more trenchant things to say about backstage life with *All About Eve.*

musical wave in the manner of a despised relative just arrived from the old country on a cattle boat, whose very presence embarrasses the rest of the family. The shininess of *Footlight Parade* and its like made the earlier efforts seem all the more frowzy, and since the films were seldom revived, the legend of their expendability grew and grew. *Too Much Harmony* was itself no great shakes, as such typifying the main impulses of Paramount musicals for years to come. Crosby, by now coming away from every film with at least two hit songs, delivered on "Thanks" and with his recording of "Black Moonlight," sung in the film, in a particularly lurid staging, by Kitty Kelly.

The only 1933 film to revive the Broadway musical adaptation, *Take a Chance*, seemed no different from its fellow musicals. A thinly—in this case inanely—plotted backstage story about a pair of carnival hucksters (James Dunn and Cliff Edwards) who connive to put on a show, its calling card on Broadway had been Ethel Merman's rendition of "Eadie Was a Lady." For the movie Lillian Roth performed it in such a fashion to imply that she had memorized every inflection of Merman's recording.[18] Shot independently at Astoria by the dauntless Brice-Rowland team, it was a follow-up of sorts to *Moonlight and Pretzels*, on a doubled budget but with significantly less entertainment. The tactless charm of *Pretzels* was replaced with mere klutziness and a brassily disjointed script that sank to such hopeless sub-*42nd Street* ploys as having unknowns go on for stars injured by falling sandbags. Perhaps the worst miscalculation was Bobby Connolly's elaborate staging of "It's Only a Paper Moon." That the song, salvaged from a flop play called *The Great Magoo*, was good enough to become a hit and a standard owed little to Connolly. His concept, for no sane reason, had Buddy Rogers and June Knight traveling from Coney Island to Renaissance Venice, where a duel is fought over her honor. This was hardly "Paper Moon," and in a field with more attractive competition, *Take a Chance* fared indifferently.

Another weak (if profitable) backstage musical that added to the growing glut was *Broadway Thru a Keyhole*, released in November by United Artists as one of the first productions of Darryl Zanuck's Twentieth Century Pictures. The voyeurism implied by the title was not unwitting, for *Keyhole*'s chief selling point was its author, columnist Walter Winchell. His percussive reportage of news and innuendo had already prompted several films, and for his first screen story he zeroed in on seminal dish: Al Jolson's romance with Ruby Keeler while she was under the protection of underworld figure Johnny "Irish" Costello. Winchell piously protested that his story had nothing to do with the Jolsons, so of course everyone knew who the movie was about long before it started shooting; the resemblances were so

---

18. Roth replaced Ginger Rogers, whose adept mimicry might have begat an even more detailed Merman impersonation.

deliberate, in fact, that Texas Guinan was cast as, essentially, herself—Keeler's former employer.[19] Jolson finally confronted Winchell in a very public place (the Hollywood Stadium) and decked him. Far from pressing charges, the columnist was ecstatic—this was some of the strongest pre-opening publicity imaginable, and in defending his wife's honor so publicly Jolson gave his own flagging standing a lift as well. The box office was also boosted by ghoul interest related to Guinan's death the week it opened. After this, *Keyhole* itself was decidedly anticlimactic, its promise of lowdown dispelled by awkward dramatics and some of the weakest musical presentation seen since 1929. As Keeler, Constance Cummings was a talented dramatic actress with such little affinity for song and dance that her visible discomfort spoke Pirandellian volumes on the perils of miscasting. The Jolson role was none too complimentary—a bandleader-singer-violinist with severe hypochondria—yet was cast from strength with Russ Columbo, Crosby's leading rival as an airwave heartthrob. This was one of his few film appearances prior to his early death, and despite the role and the unattractive circumstances, his potential is unmistakable. Ideally it would have been displayed in something more palatable than *Broadway Thru a Keyhole,* which exploited the backstage genre without enhancing it.

Radio's backstage possibilities having been demonstrated in *The Big Broadcast,* airwave luminaries predictably trooped out during 1933 for guest spots or showcases. *Hello, Everybody!* was an epic failure, and dialect comic Jack Pearl, known on the air as Baron Munchhausen, did little better with MGM's *Meet the Baron,* a comedy with music that reiterated David O. Selznick's lack of empathy with musical production. Paramount's *International House* was far better, a bizarre cross between *Million Dollar Legs* and *The Big Broadcast* that somehow incorporated radio stars (sample: Cab Calloway's "Reefer Man") in a sort of *Grand Hotel* plot set in Wu Hu, China. It managed to fit in a large production number, as did, stranger still, Universal's *Myrt and Marge,* a noncommittal transference of a popular radio show, and an occasion little happier than *Check and Double Check.*

The film that made the most solid use of radio ties was Paramount's *Torch Singer.* Like *Stage Mother* (and, in the Stone Age, *The Trespasser*), it put music into a soap opera plot, in this case the unwed mother theme common in the early thirties. This was wedded to a minor radio phenomenon, New York's "Lullaby Lady," who talked and sang to kids several nights a week, to produce a yarn about a young singer who gives up her baby, reaches saloon stardom, then stumbles into a job as radio's "Aunt Sally," all the while trying to track down her daughter. This was more

19. There were other pieces of scandal casting as well. Paul Kelly, who played the gangster-protector, had served jail time (after a sensational trial) for the beating death of his lover's husband. Peggy Hopkins Joyce, past mistress of cafe society, divorce, and tabloid headlines, was also originally to be in the film, but illness forced her out.

farfetched a plot than usual, but there was implacable conviction at its center. While Claudette Colbert had dabbled in musicals before, this was her first and only full-length challenge, made just prior to her three-tiered grasp on genuine stardom in 1934—*It Happened One Night, Cleopatra, Imitation of Life. Torch Singer* gives a more varied Colbert than any other film, from farce to tragedy and all points between, including music. Her voice, not a conventionally attractive instrument, was split between a Dietrich moan on the bottom and a plangent fruity soprano on top, and Leo Robin and Ralph Rainger had to carefully tailor the four songs to her idiosyncratic range. The dramatic instincts stoking her vocalism, however, were outstanding, as she sold her songs unerringly through vocal and physical expression, stance, and gesture, making as convincing a motherly lullaby lady as she was a sensual cabaret queen belting out "Mama's waiting for you." In spite of her skill, *Torch Singer* was soon forgotten, and except for an occasional tune from Irene Dunne the woman's picture and the musical would seldom meet again. But Colbert's performance remains the real thing, generic crossover at its most rewarding and the kind of tour de force few performers attempt.

The Christmas attractions in 1933 cinemas supported the verity that musicals were not only back, they were agreeable compensation for not being able to afford large gifts. *Dancing Lady* and *Going Hollywood* were the holi-

Claudette Colbert, not quite upstaged by her Travis Banton gown, sings "It's a Long, Dark Night" in *Torch Singer*. Ralph Rainger, who collaborated on the song with lyricist Leo Robin, is at the piano.

Eddie Cantor, *Roman Scandals* incarnation, keeping young and beautiful with a trio of Goldwyn Girls. On the right is Barbara Pepper; on the left, Lucille Ball.

day offerings reflecting the dominant *42nd Street* ethos; two others indicated where musicals had been and where they were going. *Roman Scandals* was the annual Cantor-Goldwyn pageant, and like all its predecessors had a high price tag ($1.1 million), good and bad jokes, and a blinding array of young women posing through Busby Berkeley numbers. It was perhaps the high point of Cantor's movie career, the most assured blending of his stage principles with Goldwyn's bent for glossy professionalism. While *Whoopee!* had been more adventurous in its way, *Roman Scandals* was the most proficient Cantor film and frequently the funniest, partly because its writers (including George S. Kaufman and Robert E. Sherwood) forged a good premise. Cantor's movie comedy was usually based in incongruity, an urban hysteric placed into some outlandish setting—a dude ranch, a bakery, Mexico and bullfighting. The success of DeMille's *The Sign of the Cross* early in 1933 sparked the idea for the most fanciful milieu yet—ancient Rome. When George Bernard Shaw refused to sell Goldwyn the rights to *Androcles and the Lion*, the producer commissioned a modern story with an ancient flashback à la *Noah's Ark*. In this case it was *Just Imagine* in reverse: a well-meaning modern boob who dreams himself in ancient Rome and discovers that political corruption is nothing new. The puns and cracks were in full bloom, as in Cantor's realization that he's going to be executed:

"I haven't been born yet! It wouldn't only be murder—it would be birth control!" There were few problems putting music into this, including one number for singing star Ruth Etting, making her feature debut after dozens of shorts. After his epic year at Warners, Busby Berkeley returned for his final job with Goldwyn and produced work both striking and uneven, implying his discontent with the producer and his annoyance at being taken off *Footlight Parade*.[20] His most insolent sequence in *Roman Scandals* is "No More Love," a miniature drama set in a slave market, with one beautiful young victim who dies after being forced to dance for the leering baboons who bid on her. It makes some explicit links between sex and sadism, but more than "Shanghai Lil," its narrative drive is too skimped and abrupt to encompass the flood of images Berkeley intently delivers. These include that famous line of Goldwyn Girls chained to the wall, apparently nude except for blonde Godiva wigs. The effect is one of unpleasant beauty, Berkeley's adoration of the female form straying into exploitation. One of the naked women—she's in the third close-up—is Lucille Ball, a New York model making her film debut. Though there had been some dispute about hiring her, someone obviously liked her; she gets a line of dialogue leading into the "Build a Little Home" number early on, she undresses again for the "Keep Young and Beautiful" sequence, and was selected for the cover of the *Roman Scandals* campaign book sent to exhibitors—demurely clad in her wig and a smile, she poses alongside Cantor in his toga and blackface.[21] *Roman Scandals* reaped abundant profits, yet for all its gleam it seemed a little old-fashioned alongside such newer models as *Dancing Lady* and *Flying Down to Rio*. The lavish top banana extravaganzas still prominent on the stage were beginning to lose impetus onscreen, victims of the drive toward standardization that would hobble musical film conspicuously. Not that these imminent changes were all negative: Fred Astaire was in the wings at RKO.

The best known of the numerous legends that have sprung up around Astaire's entering film is the one about that cosmically myopic producer who reputedly looked at Astaire's screen test and reported, "Can't act. Can't sing. Balding. Can dance a little." Anecdotally irresistible, and likely untrue. Circa 1929, when Astaire and his sister Adele were Broadway's favored dance team, they tested for Paramount at the request of Astoria producer Walter Wanger. Astaire loathed the test and the way he looked in it,

20. Between script delays and a guaranteed Christmas opening, *Roman Scandals* was shot on an unusually tight schedule, three units often working simultaneously: Frank Tuttle directing the plot scenes; Berkeley with the musical numbers; and Ralph Cedar on the climactic chariot chase. The haste shows in moments of awkward editing and bumpy continuity.

21. After completing her chores Ball went to Twentieth Century for a non-musical bit in *Broadway Thru a Keyhole*, then another showgirl stint in *Moulin Rouge*. She resumed her Goldwyn Girl identity the next year for Cantor's *Kid Millions*.

and Wanger's proposed film version of the Astaires' stage hit *Funny Face* soon fell through. The pair returned to the stage until Adele Astaire retired in 1932, and as a solo Astaire starred in Cole Porter's *Gay Divorce*. Then he began to contemplate a change. In early 1933 he was approached informally by several film studios resuming musical production. He finally signed with RKO, which was likely intent on finding a new musical lead after Phil Harris's uninspiring showing in *Melody Cruise*. By the time the contract was drawn up, RKO had begun to plan its second major musical of the year. *Melody Cruise* had applied flash and music to a shipboard setting; producer Lou Brock's follow-up, *Flying Down to Rio*, would do the same in the air. Part of this had to do with the burgeoning appeal of Latin American themes and rhythms (pre-Good Neighbor Policy), and part with production head Merian C. Cooper—a major stockholder in Pan American Airways. An aviation theme set in an exotic locale was especially novel after the recent eruption of backstage stories, and although the plot was a standard romantic triangle, its details were flashy and fresh. Dolores Del Rio, Gene Raymond, and Raul Roulien were the lead trio, with Astaire placed in comic-musical support. First choice for the role opposite him was Dorothy Jordan, who ultimately declined it in favor of marrying Merian C. Cooper; presumably she would have given Astaire the same lightweight partnering she had given Ramon Novarro. A more serious contender for the role was the brassy Pert Kelton, whose raucous cheek is hard to envision opposite Astaire's then-callow demeanor. Perhaps Kelton was removed for fear she could not partner him in the dance sequence being planned. Her replacement, Ginger Rogers, had no problems in that sphere, and had already appeared successfully in the year's biggest musical hits, *42nd Street* and *Gold Diggers of 1933*. Years earlier Astaire had coached her for a dance in *Girl Crazy* on Broadway, and they knew each other well; their rapport, in dialogue as in dance, was obvious to all. Immediately after finishing *Flying Down to Rio*, Rogers went to Paramount for *Sitting Pretty* and Astaire sailed for London to perform *Gay Divorce* in the West End. Neither was aware how much one frivolous and showy movie would merge their identities and alter their careers.

Modern viewers approaching *Flying Down to Rio* expecting typical Astaire-Rogers fare are invariably mystified. Far less time is spent on them than on the shallow love triangle (for which they serve as Greek chorus), and they only dance two quick choruses in the mammoth "Carioca" number. The more conspicuous prominence of *Flying Down to Rio*, as seen in 1933, is its exuberant doffing of many of the musical conventions of its time, partly though not exclusively with the help of its subsidiary couple. In some ways *Rio* is still a displaced backstager; most of the songs are done "in performance," with Rogers as a sassy band singer and Astaire a wisecracking accordionist. Yet its heart is closer to romantic adventure than to *Pretty Lady*. Intoxicated on technology, both aviation and moviemaking, it expands on the "original musical" tendency of 1932–33 with the aid of some post-*42nd Street* sass. It's a *Melody Cruise* that works. Vincent Youmans's songs, with witty lyrics by Gus Kahn and Edward Eliscu, are among the best in any film thus far, and for the negligibility of their roles Rogers and Astaire are showcased quite well, more appealingly so than Del Rio and Raymond. Rogers, in a see-through dress, sings "Music Makes Me" in a tone both jaunty and suggestive, her face in animated rapport with the lyrics. Astaire, given no songs or dances for a while and commended to a sidekick part, takes longer to make a positive impression. He finally comes into his own with some deft comic business and a dazzlingly brief tap solo to "Music Makes Me," plus his one duet with Rogers.

Even with Astaire and Rogers, the primary energies of *Flying Down to Rio* are concentrated in its two big numbers, "Carioca" and the title song. The latter is quite unforgettable, not necessarily because of its peppery rhythm or the smart way Astaire sings it but because of Brock and Cooper's *coup de grace:* a flock of skimpily dressed chorus girls executing precision formations on the wings of airplanes supposedly flying high over Rio de Janeiro. In place of the formal cohesion of Berkeley's best numbers, dance directors Dave Gould and Hermes Pan intertwined giddiness and danger, including one chorine falling from a plane and narrowly escaping death. Absurdity raised to such a height, at the service of a trivial musical comedy plot, becomes its own escapist justification, in a way a culmination of all the silly fun stunts that movie musicals had tried to do up to that point— *Madam Satan*'s blimp, *Just Imagine*'s Martian ballet, maybe even that idiotic spider web in *The Great Gabbo*.

"Carioca," on the other hand, looked to the future, less through its rather haphazard ensembles than through those two short duets from Astaire and Rogers. Solo dancers had previously made an impression in film and so had groups, but dance couples had been rare. Perhaps the most memorable instance had been the knockabout tandem for Marilyn Miller and Joe E. Brown in *Sally;* otherwise Miller and other soloists in early years worked without conspicuous partners. Astaire's first movie assignment was, in fact, an early example of a film-dance couple, although shepherding Joan Crawford through the *Dancing Lady* routines could not be reckoned an auspicious foreword to a brave new dance world. That came with Rogers, not just for what they did together (which in "Carioca" was not that much) but for the joyous way they seemed to connect on the dance floor. While dance had served sundry functions in film, it had seldom represented the elated collusion seen when Astaire and Rogers begin. He had worked on this type of teamwork with his sister for years, and Rogers was on a sufficiently hip wavelength to catch on quickly. There is one brief moment of "Carioca" when Astaire and Rogers become a team: in the "Two heads together are better than one" section, their eyes meet for perhaps two seconds, and it's suddenly all there. Two dancers—one great, the other outstanding—have become one unit. That's what audiences saw as *Flying Down to Rio* made the rounds around Christmas 1933 and New Year's 1934, and that unit coupled with the novel trimmings made it a hit. Its significance to the Astaire-Rogers canon is based more on hindsight: mainly that, with her assistance, he was seen as the cause for *Rio's* favorable response and high grosses, prompting RKO to star them together in the true beginning of the Astaire-Rogers pictures, *The Gay Divorcée*.

The resurgence of musicals in 1933 had been as startling, and in some ways as intemperate, as their advent four years earlier, and so powerful as to make another burnout seem imminent. On the surface, there were potent resemblances to the earlier era: the songwriters were coming back, budgets were going up, and many of the films were beginning to have an air of interchangeability. Fox, for example, had three backstage stories in production simultaneously—*Fox Follies, Bottoms Up, George White's Scandals*—with their supervisors in a race to see which one could be released first. But the dynamics had changed since 1929, and so had the industry. 1933 had been a buffer year, the new and old coexisting and, as in *Flying Down to Rio*, intermingling. In 1934 it would all change.

CHAPTER 17

1934: The Past as Prologue

When the film industry's commerce and art were uprooted in 1928, technology was the central agent for its transformation. Six years later, when there were changes of almost equal weight, the considerations were chiefly moral. Whether it wanted to or not, whether it needed to or not, Hollywood would be cleaning itself up in 1934. For the most part, this did not entail altering the tone of its business practices or the moralities of its inhabitants. Instead, it involved the movie community's changing the face it showed to the world through its films. And, among many other things, its musicals would never again be the same.

The musicals that were revived in 1933 were altered permanently the following year. The rise of the Legion of Decency and the new teeth given the Production Code were leading causes for the change, along with the new currents and viewer preferences being made increasingly obvious. The effect was to diminish the musical film overall, channelling much of its earlier potential into a province of fail-safe conventionality. That might perhaps seem an odd statement given the new trends of 1934–35: the rise of the Astaire-Rogers dance musical, the return of opera stars, the resurgence of the operetta—all areas in which the musical was establishing an identity. Yet except for the originality of Fred Astaire's concept of story told through dance there was little new; at the same time there was an unmistakable diminution, a petrification of formula and theme that the musical would rigidly observe for much of the rest of its existence. A few impressive gains were countered by much that would not be recaptured, from the exhilarating codification of genre that made *The Broadway Melody* a seminal event, to the rapturous invention of *Love Me Tonight*, to the fierce energy of *42nd Street*. Many other things would not be missed, of course, yet even many of the mad gaffes of the early years had a certain baroque grandeur that could be viewed with some interest—more, possibly, than the slicker pre-set packaging after 1934. In 1929 and 1930 producers of musicals scrambled to define their formulas; by 1935 they had found them or had them imposed. Players and protocol were pretty much in position and the musical's niche prescribed. Backstagers, reestablished as the preponderant musical trend, became bigger and brassier to compensate for the loss of that extra layer of sexy grit. Thematic material for production numbers softened—no more "Pettin' in the Park"—and dance costumes showed less skin. Lubitsch-style romantic comedies with music became virtually extinct after 1934, through changing tastes and through fear of sex. Paramount's *She Loves Me Not*, released in September after the Code was established, was instructive. Miriam Hopkins played a dancer hiding from gangsters in a boys' dorm, with Bing Crosby as a bemused professor. Where there would have been innuendo galore a year earlier, there was now cleaner rowdy fun, plus Crosby crooning the decorous "Love in Bloom."[1] Something on the order of "Jazz Up Your Lingerie" was no longer feasible, and the final marks of the old erotic style transmogrified into the safer precincts of the Astaire-Rogers films.

There was, first of all, the Code. What had started as a well-intentioned drive to expunge some of film's baser urges ended up a classic case of baby thrown out with bath water. There's no question that to reflect the national temper and draw the crowds, studios went much farther in the early thirties than ever before. American film seldom seemed so willing to exploit the profitable possibilities of the seamy side.[2] Neither prone nor immune to treatment of this sort, musicals simply became franker along with other types of film. It was especially obvious by late 1933, with candid references to prostitution and promiscuity in musicals, gay and lesbian characters spotted with some prominence, occasional drug references, and a great deal of female flesh permitted in production numbers. Spurred by but not exclusively part of the Roman Catholic Church, various groups were becoming increasingly irate about film's influence on youth and general morality. Just why this happened, and how much of it was related to the Depression or distrust of Roosevelt or resentment over the end of Prohibition, is a matter

1. The college campus was clearly one way in which the Paramount musical would escape run-ins with Code-unfriendly subject matter. *College Rhythm*, which opened some weeks after *She Loves Me* Not, was a good example and more energetic than many. The impenetrable diction and high spirits of Lyda Roberti (memorably singing the title song and "Take a Number from One to Ten") were most welcome in an increasingly diluted environment.

2. The coming of the Code, and the films it bridled, deserves far greater coverage than this chapter can give it, or than it has gotten elsewhere so far. As a weak substitute, herewith the best-known films of 1932–33 considered responsible for bringing about all the fuss: *Scarface, Red-Headed Woman, The Story of Temple Drake, Baby Face, Convention City, She Done Him Wrong,* and *I'm No Angel*. There are many others, but these are the prototypes.

of some speculation. What is a fact, indisputably, is that while musicals fared among the worst from the subsequent strictures, few of them had been seen as undue contributors to the epidemic that caused the purge in the first place. There were, nevertheless, some musical-related incidents by which Code czar Joe Breen asserted his new power with remarkable pettiness.

The Code had been drawn up in 1930 by the MPPDA—the Hays Office—as a reaction to what was viewed as excessive permissiveness in late-twenties films. Along with some celestial pronouncements regarding the moral principles of art (i.e., "Wrong entertainment lowers the whole living condition and moral ideals of a race"), it laid out a set of guidelines at once specific and vague to govern the subject matter and details of mainstream American films. Among its many precepts:

> No plot shall present evil alluringly.

> Seduction and rape should never be treated as comedy.

> Impure love, the love which society has always regarded as wrong and which has been banned by divine law, must not be presented in such a way as to arouse passion or morbid curiosity on the part of the audience.

> The fact that the nude or semi-nude body may be beautiful does not make its use in the films moral.

For all the high-minded flummery, the Code was not really enforceable for its first four years. Will Hays's minions inspected every script and pored over each song lyric, yet the studios disregarded the suggested changes whenever possible. Hays was livid, for example, about the lesbian dance in *The Sign of the Cross,* yet could not turn push to shove when DeMille refused to cut it. The only real power came from individual censor boards, the most severe being those in Pennsylvania and Ohio, as well as Chicago, where the toughest crime film could hardly equal activity seen on the street on any given day.

Occasionally the studios relented to Hays, especially when he threatened bans and blackballs, as when Warner Bros. was obliged to reshoot much of *Baby Face* (1933) after a boycott was implied. This, however, was an extreme case, and films continued to deal in gamy material while Hays and the moralists seethed. In mid-1933, their patience was running short, and a *Variety* headline announced an impending "DEADLINE FOR FILM DIRT." By the beginning of 1934 the studios had started to pull back a bit. Warners, preparing *Dames,* was well aware that Busby Berkeley's girl-filled spectacles could be a target for cleanup. Berkeley had planned to go all out for one number in which Joan Blondell would sing some lead-pipe double entendres about a cat and a little white mouse, up to and including an invitation to "come up and see my pussy sometime." Then production supervisor Hal Wallis heard about it, and on March 19 sent Berkeley a memo saying, in effect, Drop it.

The Catholic Church, meanwhile, had started to fan its own flames, and by April 1934 the Church's Episcopal Committee on Motion Pictures had formed the Legion of Decency. Other churches joined in to threaten a boycott, which the film industry—then in a recovery—could not countenance. The choice ultimately lay between the boycott, the threat of government intervention, or Hays. Thus was the Code finally given power, effective July 1, 1934. To enforce the Production Code Administration, Hays appointed Joseph I. Breen, his New York assistant and a former newspaperman. Alternately patriot, prude, bigot, and bully, Breen brought all these to bear on his Code-mandated duties with terrible force, and changed the complexion of film swiftly and decisively for decades. Moralists and church leaders promoting the ideals of the Legion of Decency were ecstatic; people in the industry were publicly supportive and privately annoyed; moviegoers seemed, on the whole, oblivious. The presumed dirt had not affected many of them too directly, and the new cleaner films did not strike them as any less valid. Attendance continued to rise, as it had before there was a Legion of Decency.

Musicals had not come in for any special censure on the hit lists of the Legion or the Code, except for one special case which sped the Legion to its appointed rounds all the sooner. Had the Legion of Decency fixed on no other goal, the defeat of Mae West would have been sufficient for the moralists. With the immense profits on *She Done Him Wrong* and *I'm No Angel*, she seemed an invincible, and therefore more irresistible, target. Early in 1934 she started work on *It Ain't No Sin*, a title calculated to raise the crusaders' hackles. It was planned as West's lushest vehicle yet, with elaborate musical numbers—one had her posing as various erotic icons, including the Statue of Liberty—and an appearance by Duke Ellington and his orchestra. Once again West placed herself in the role of sexual subjugator, a St. Louis gal on the loose in red-hot New Orleans, taking all comers and purring the carnally nostalgic "My Old Flame." The premiere of *It Ain't No Sin* was set for June 1934 in censor-ridden Chicago, the better for West to validate her primacy. Trembling into action, the Legion forced the premiere to be canceled and the film to be put back into production for laundering. West was forced to shoot a scene in which she married the leading man (Roger Pryor), and unwillingly acceded to a number of cuts and trims. The title had to go as well and, her rage equalling her egotism, West suggested that it just go out under her name *sans* title. Eventually it was released as *Belle of the Nineties*, and the enforced dilution of West's powers continued through the remainder of the decade.

Otherwise, a few musicals were cited in the first list of films banned for members of the Legion—*Wonder Bar, Hips Hips Hooray*, and the semimusical *Bolero, Palooka,* and *Fashions of 1934.* A few months earlier there would have been more, but modifications were already underway. Nevertheless, along with Paramount's concurrent *Murder at the Vanities,* the five films cited exemplify the kind of material being targeted by the Legion and the Hays Office. *Hips Hips Hooray* was bawdier in title than in content, a comedy with music about the cosmetics industry that gave Wheeler and Woolsey a stylish presentation they had not often enjoyed. Under director Mark Sandrich the duo seemed smoother and funnier, especially in a gracefully goofy mock pas de quatre (W&W, Dorothy Lee, and Thelma Todd) that is a team highpoint. There was a notably good song as well, "Just Keep on Doin' What You're Doin'," originally written by Kalmar and Ruby for *Duck Soup.* Such minor smut as the Legion divined was far more palatable than the smeary innuendo of *So This is Africa,* and involved a few spicy lines and the opener, "Keep Romance Alive," sung by Ruth Etting to a host of RKO lovelies in a variety of undress.

Palooka (UA) and *Bolero* (Paramount) had, at least in conception, a little more sin at their cores. The former, part of film's intermittent fascination with comic strips, featured Stuart Erwin as the nitwit boxer and Jimmy Durante as his trainer. The songs were incidental, and so was the sex, as supplied by Lupe Velez as a flammable temptress in a remarkably engineered low-cut gown. *Bolero,* one of those periodic dramas with a dance background, was based on a real character. Maurice (one name only) was an exhibition ballroom dancer with a well-discussed gigolo past, and rumors of his fast-lane life brought special excitement to his performances. George Raft, whose past had color of its own, might have seemed the ideal lead for *Bolero.* Yet his dance skills leaned far more to Charleston than sensuality, necessitating obvious doubles for him and Carole Lombard in the febrile dances LeRoy Prinz staged to Ravel's music. Raft's charisma off the dance floor was equally unsound, rendering even more puerile the film's aspiration to erotic epic. *Bolero,* then, was more tease than anything else, and only delivered the goods in one scene: Sally Rand, at the height of her notoriety, performing her fan dance. "Legend" is a fair word to use here, for Rand purveyed her feathery brand of voluptuous kitsch over six decades. In *Bolero,* with two huge fans, no apparent garments, and Debussy's "Claire de Lune," she gives a fair demonstration of what the fuss was about.

Rand's popularity was felt in a number of other dance numbers with fans in 1933 and 1934. Busby Berkeley, who usually started trends, followed on this one, after *Sitting Pretty.* But for Warner's *Fashions of 1934,* his first film of the year, Berkeley produced a feather number to stagger the ages. The film was a curious throwback to the earlier "Is it a musical?" days, ostensibly a light comedy about the rag trade with William Powell as a debonair con who lifts designs from the fanciest couture houses in Paris. Powell's attempts at snappy banter were somewhat obstructed by a tinny script and by the tense, miscast presence of Bette Davis as his sleek vis-à-vis, enfolded in so many layers of extrinsic glamour that she seemed imported from another planet. While a Berkeley spectacle was the film's only reason for being (except for a procession of swank Orry-Kelly gowns), it was fitted in only through several unconvincing turns of script. The number's lack of connection with fashion was seemingly irrelevant; Berkeley and his bosses wanted to do it with feathers, so there was a subplot about Hugh Herbert raising ostriches. Fortunately, "Spin a Little Web of Dreams" was very nearly worth the whole tiresome movie, Berkeley on the loose amid barely clad human harps and a rather extraordinary all-woman all-feather crew of galley slaves to row Venus's barge. The director's erotic fixations had never seemed so blatant before, the harps coming in for special attention as Exhibit A of Berkeley's bent toward dehumanized objectification. The Legion of Decency had flagged *Fashions of 1934* for some suggestive moments in the script, yet the fetishism of its spectacle, as injected extraneously into an otherwise indifferent film, is what now appears so disruptive.

After that gaudy sidetrip Berkeley moved to his next large-scale Warner musical, which was also something of a departure. *Wonder Bar* had an exceptionally checkered history: an intimate musical play from Germany (*Wunderbar*, 1930), liberally adapted to serve as Al Jolson's Broadway comeback (*The Wonder Bar*, 1931), discussed as a screen comeback for George Jessel and Norma Talmadge (1932), after which Jolson bought the rights himself and attempted to have it filmed as the second entry on his United Artists contract (early 1933), then sold the rights and his services to Warner Bros.[3] Jolson's return to his original studio was inevitable. His wife was there; he and the Warners knew (sometimes acrimoniously) how to deal with each other; and that eternal legend of "The First Star of Talking Pictures" could be milked optimally by all parties. *Wonder Bar*, too, made sense as a Warner property, diluting Jolson's dominance in a multistory structure for which *Variety* used the verb Grandhotel to describe the script treatment. Jolson's Paris nightclub served as the arena for love, comedy, adultery, and violence, retaining a Lloyd Bacon-directed backstage milieu and the opportunities for Busby Berkeley's spectacular numbers. The original cast announcements for *Wonder Bar* were up to all-star specifications— Jolson, Kay Francis, Joan Blondell, Adolphe Menjou, Aline MacMahon, Dick Powell, Ann Dvorak, Bette Davis, Glenda Farrell, Pat O'Brien. By

---

3. He had first attempted to sell the package to MGM, which declined. Given the performance of *Hallelujah, I'm a Bum*, Jolson returned to his first home on notably diminished ground: he was paid $21,000 for the stage rights, a salary of $29,000, plus 10 percent of the gross over $800,000. Through either negotiation or error, his stature was also diminished in his billing: though top-billed onscreen, he was listed fourth in most print ads and on the sheet music.

In moods ranging from serene to dour, the stars of *Wonder Bar* (Cortez, Del Rio, Jolson, Francis, Powell) toast the health of the Warner Bros. Publicity Department.

November 1933, Blondell had been replaced by Fifi D'Orsay, Menjou by Warren William, MacMahon by Ruth Donnelly, Dvorak by Dolores Del Rio, and O'Brien by Ricardo Cortez. (Davis was most likely an alternate for the Francis part.) Just as filming started, William stepped out and Henry Kolker came in, Farrell's role was taken by Merna Kennedy, and Kay Francis (busy on another film) was first replaced by Genevieve Tobin, then came back in.

Of all the Warner Bros. musicals, *Wonder Bar* is the most elaborately provocative, filtering the *42nd Street* aura through a Continental tone considerably more credible than that in *Fashions of 1934*, with a complicated system of interlocked illicit affairs that have caused its plot to be dubbed a "ménage a l'infini." Very nearly so, for instead of concerning itself with getting a show produced, this film had its mind firmly on lust. Kolker is married to Francis, who is being unfaithful with Cortez, who is loved by Del Rio, who is loved by Jolson and Powell; meanwhile, two nouveau-riche couples from Schenectady (Guy Kibbee and Ruth Donnelly, Hugh Herbert and Louise Fazenda) are bent on finding paid romance away from the conjugal hearth. (A gigolo slips Fazenda the message "You have such a kind face; you remind me of my mother.") The periphery is equally charged, memorably with a couple on the dance floor who are cut in by a young man . . . who then dances off with the other man. Jolson, leering from the sidelines, lisps the comment, "Boys will be boys—woo!" Violence erupts as well—Del Rio stabs the detestable Cortez during the performance, after which Jolson covers the crime by stashing the corpse in an auto and encouraging its suicidal owner to drive off a cliff. All this while a nightclub show goes on, with songs for Jolson and Powell, dances for Del Rio and Cortez, and two Berkeley extravaganzas. "Don't Say Goodnight" is a waltz staged amid large moving columns with dancers in black masks, the graceful and Freudian mixed in equal portions, and with a whale of a climax as the back walls of the stage fly up to reveal mirrors, filling the screen with dancers multiplied to infinity. Berkeley's second number, "Goin' to Heaven on a Mule," has been cast by posterity in a rare role: the most insensitive sequence in the history of musical cinema. Jolson was the single most overwhelming star force in any Berkeley spectacle, and it was not unforseeable that his presence could mean trouble; blackface was essential to his star image, and Berkeley proceeded to set it off in a large-scale demonstration of the least generous impulses in American entertainment. Here is blackface raised to Olympus—not the casual racism of Jolson's solos or of minstrel shows or even Moran and Mack, but a monstrous lexicon of "darkie heaven" stereotypes, Jolson encountering every conceivable racist joke in the Pearly Gates: Uncle Tom, fried chicken, crap shooting, and a giant watermelon out of which gangling Hal LeRoy tap dances.[4] The song itself (Warren and Dubin) is meandering and unseemly, the staging elaborately coarse, the whole sequence a blot on Berkeley's career and an ugly asterisk that has limited *Wonder Bar*'s circulation for years.

Aside from that one brush with musical notoriety, which ostensibly would not have been affected by the Production Code, *Wonder Bar* plays as a moving violation of every Code stricture except nudity and drug use. Most startling is its treatment of murder. Cortez and Del Rio perform a sado-masochistic tango, excitingly scored and edited, whose explicit linking of sex and violence includes a couple of closeups of Cortez cracking a whip across Del Rio's beautiful face.[5] When she stabs him as the dance ends, Bacon shows the blood on the dance floor, yet all the sympathy remains with her, and afterward another character's suicide is ruthlessly appropriated to give her a happy ending and a new lover. Stylish and unsettling, *Wonder Bar* is a fascinating excursion into odd musical impulses that would soon vanish permanently.

Paramount's *Murder at the Vanities*, released three months later, shared many of *Wonder Bar*'s qualities: a suavely lurid combination of backstage

---

4. At one point also, stereotype multiplies against itself to produce a "sissy" angel (Eddie Foy Jr.) who measures Jolson for his new wings.

5. Jolson's introduction is equally notable: "He whips her with a whip . . . but she loves it!" Listed in the program as "Tango Del Rio," the dance was directed by Bacon, not Berkeley, and choreographed by José Fernandez.

atmosphere, musical numbers, sex, and mayhem, adapted from a moderately successful show with a new score, and more like Warners than Paramount in its procession of hard-edged wisecracks. On Broadway in 1933, it had featured two film people, Olga Baclanova and Bela Lugosi; on film, the leads were taken by two stage performers, Kitty Carlisle and Danish matinee idol Carl Brisson, who had already appeared in films in Europe. The plot was a fairly standard whodunit, with a theater atmosphere—opening night of Earl Carroll's *Vanities* revue—as an unusually ripe environment for suspects and red herrings. Music and mystery are balanced in fair proportion for most of its length, until the accumulated weight of production numbers and clues makes it begin to sag around the three-quarter point. As with *Wonder Bar*, there is illicit sex and a view of murder as wholly justifiable when it rids humankind of an objectionable person, and in several scenes the film's two corpses are treated nonchalantly, somewhat like furniture. Yet the most flagrant portions of *Murder at the Vanities* lie in its musical sequences. Carroll's shows were traditionally the bawdiest revues on Broadway, and as staged by Larry Ceballos and director Mitchell Leisen the movie numbers retain his theatrical perspective and carnal excess. They also, unlike *Wonder Bar*, brought forth a song hit, the quintessential tribute to Repeal: "Cocktails for Two." Except for a brief and dynamic appearance by Duke Ellington and his orchestra, the other numbers keep their attention centered fully on sex, with such scenes as a giant dressing table filled with nudes, a conveyor belt of undressed women clamoring to become Carroll showgirls, and a herd of cowgirls trussed up on their backs with their legs spread open. Another Sally Rand-type feather number, "Live and Love Tonight," puts its skin to less exploitative means, with Carlisle and Brisson stranded on a desert island surrounded by an ocean of blonde fan-wavers. The best-known sequence is "Marahuana," in which Gertrude Michael moans her desire to be soothed by the caress of sweet marijuana and live in fantasy. The song is explicit enough, but Leisen punctuates it by raising the curtain behind Michael to reveal huge cacti out of a Freudian desert, atop which sit giant flowers with nude women in their centers. At the very end of the song a blunt connection is made between sex and violence by having the first murder victim discovered up in the flies when blood drips onto the breast of one of the showgirls.

While hardly the smash of *Wonder Bar*, *Murder at the Vanities* was considered an enjoyably second-rank entertainment, its nudity and violence and "Marahuana" bothering few people at the time. (A few state censors did, however, cut a "Nuts to you" line and a song lyric referring to "dirty hosannas." But six weeks after it opened *Murder at the Vanities* would have been difficult to produce in its same form, and six months later would have been impossible. The inveterate bluenose Joe Breen finally caught up with "Marahuana" the following year when it was brought to his attention by a member of the U.S. State Department's Commission of Narcotics. The last thing Breen wanted was to look incompetent before high officials, and when the complaint came in he fumed. Though the domestic run of *Murder at the Vanities* was long finished and it was showing only in a few foreign countries, "Marahuana" was immediately excised from all prints. This was the type of incident that crimped musicals further and further: the more infractions found, even a year after the fact, the tighter the MPAA resolved to control their content.[6]

Other musicals in early 1934 were less blatant in conception, mostly in reflection of the approaching Code. In *Moulin Rouge,* produced by Darryl Zanuck's new Twentieth Century Pictures, Constance Bennett essayed a double role and introduced the disenchanted "Boulevard of Broken Dreams." Warner's *Twenty Million Sweethearts* was a popular radio musical with Dick Powell and Ginger Rogers in modest musical circumstances that were in calculated contrast to the Berkeley epics. Paramount's *We're Not Dressing* was a shade more rambunctious, a musical update of Barrie's *The Admirable Crichton* that permitted Bing Crosby and Ethel Merman to sing, Carole Lombard to look attractive, and Burns and Allen to be the screwiest of several people stranded on a desert island.

MGM's *Hollywood Party* was less fortunate than these, a closing vestige of the first school of musical filmmaking: planned with hasty uncertainty, shot in disarray, edited and re-edited in apprehension. Just as he laid *The March of Time* to rest producer Harry Rapf was handed a great deal of money to do the same thing all over again. *The Hollywood Revue of 1933* was to star a choice buffet of contract talent: Jimmy Durante, Joan Crawford, Jean Harlow, Ted Healy and the Three Stooges, Marie Dressler, Clark Gable, Laurel and Hardy, Johnny Weissmuller, and Mickey Mouse. It was determined that there should be the pretense of a plot, so there arose a few narrative threads about Durante, the Weissmuller-like star of "Schnarzan" movies, throwing a massively hectic party. Soon retitled *Hollywood Party*, it made sense only as an excuse for musical sequences and comic specialties, and once again there was less structure than there were ideas for numbers, with but vague notions of how the two might be linked. Concurrent with their attempts on *I Married an Angel*, Rodgers and Hart contributed script ideas and twenty songs, including two different title numbers. "I'm One of the Boys" would give Marie Dressler an opportunity to cavort in Dietrichesque trousers, and "Dreams of Hollywood" was an extended sequence for Jean Harlow. As a studio switchboard operator with a yen to become a star, Harlow would sing "Prayer," which Rodgers tai-

6. *Murder at the Vanities* also ran afoul of television when the Paramount films were put into syndication in 1958. *Vanities* had a few runs, until the nudity and the drug song raised a few hackles. Then it was withdrawn for over a decade, resurfacing as a cult film in revival houses and spawning a Bette Midler recording of "Marahuana."

lored to her scant range. Crawford's stint was far gamier—"Black Diamond," Joan in high-yellowface and Adrian gowns as a sensual Harlemite who sleeps her way to stardom in Paris cabarets, comparing herself to a diamond that's not white, yet still good enough for a night.[7]

Without a cohesive script, production started in August 1933. Edmund Goulding had already been replaced as director by Russell Mack, who was then followed by Richard Boleslavsky. Chilling reminiscences of *The March of Time* came teeming: ideas for star spots tossed in and thrown out with manic zeal; large-scale numbers shot without regard to shape or structure; a cast list that changed daily. Many of the production notes from *Hollywood Party*—conferences, outlines, script fragments—survive, revealing a big film in a great deal of trouble. Boleslavsky, veteran of the Moscow Art Theatre and student of Stanislavsky, was completely at sea, especially with the comedy scenes that were constantly being added to try to give the thing some shape. Meanwhile, George Stevens directed Laurel and Hardy's scenes independently, their tenuous link with the proceedings recalling *The Rogue Song*.[8] Sometime in the fall, there was planned a literal spoof of "Shuffle Off to Buffalo" called "Fly Away to Ioway," Durante and Polly Moran cavorting à la Keeler and Nordstrom through a blimp that splits open in the manner of Berkeley's train. Rodgers and Hart wrote the song, and the number was shot, then discarded. Weissmuller, whose image and romance with Lupe Velez came in for ribbing, worked on a water ballet with "By a Waterfall"-style chorines that was not used. A deal with Walt Disney produced one bit that did come off as planned, Mickey Mouse appearing at the party and introducing a Technicolor *Silly Symphony*, "Hot Chocolate Soldiers" (words and music by Brown and Freed in "Painted Doll" mold). Boleslavsky finally left the production and was replaced variously by Allan Dwan, Roy Rowland, Charles Reisner (*March of Time* again), and probably a few others. Running gags began to circulate of how everyone's fingerprints were on *Hollywood Party* and no one wanted to take the credit—or blame. Work continued off and on through the winter, mostly with "plot" scenes, and finally songwriter and studio publicist Howard Dietz was called in from New York to find cohesion in the miles of film.

7. Plans for all three of these star appearances were scrapped in October 1933, when *Hollywood Party* was well into production. "Black Diamond" was mercifully relegated to the scrap heap, although Crawford gave a chilling latter-day hint in her dark-faced "Two-Faced Woman" sequence in *Torch Song*. Rodgers and Hart recycled "Prayer" as another mediocre offering, "The Bad in Every Man," sung to little effect by Shirley Ross in MGM's *Manhattan Melodrama*. They were lucky the third time: with another set of lyrics and no film to support it, the tune became the perennial "Blue Moon."

8. Since *Hollywood Party* was released without director credit, it does not appear in Stevens's filmography. The Laurel and Hardy scenes, which he directed and co-wrote, form perhaps 10 percent of the finished film in its American version. The British prints, about 7½ minutes longer, detailed the boys' exploits on their lion farm. For their ardent English constituency, their brief appearance in the American version had obviously not been enough.

Lilian Harvey and the Piccoli Marionettes in the nightmare sequence of *I Am Suzanne!*
With Frederick Hollander's moody score, Harvey's edgily fey demeanor, and a host of
psychological implications, this is the type of number doomed to extinction in Hollywood after 1934.

By May, the costs had exceeded those of *Going Hollywood* and *Dancing
Lady*, and it was decided that no more could be done.

One of MGM's costliest projects of the season, *Hollywood Party* was
given an ominously second-rung release minus director credit, and as with
Broadway to Hollywood, insiders were diverted by playing connect-the-dots
between the footage and the stories of how bad shooting had gone. For
exhibitors and plain folks it was without point or reason, funny and spectacular in spots yet unnervingly incoherent, and its loss of half a million dollars
reflected all the trouble. *Hollywood Party* is in fact fun, in its peculiar way.
The egg-breaking scene with Laurel and Hardy and Lupe Velez has become a classic of ovate magnificence, and Durante and Polly Moran are
acceptable in moderate doses. Mickey Mouse does a wonderful Durante
impression, and the main surviving production number—Frances Williams
and switchboard chorines in the title song—remains giddily enjoyable. Yet
there's no avoiding the catch-all incoherence, the Baron Munchhausens and
Robert Youngs and Three Stooges popping up without reason or cause, the
total lack of structure and the lunges to make the script and music coalesce.
The anarchy of *Million Dollar Legs* and *Duck Soup* had formal underpinnings; this has desperation and memories of vaudeville. Five years into its

existence, the musical film no longer had the loose codes and casual rules to permit such an aberration.

The fiasco of *Hollywood Party* was perhaps the most conspicuous case of the old giving way to the new in the 1934 musical. It happened again and again in less drastic ways at all the studios, as in cases where the Lubitsch/ *Love Me Tonight* romp of romance and Continental wit was marked for extinction in the face of low grosses and a growing perception that New Deal audiences were increasingly xenophobic. Lilian Harvey's final Fox musical (she came back in 1935 for a nonmusical) was *I Am Suzanne!*, which premiered at the end of 1933 and opened wide in mid-January. This was a true original, conceived by songwriter Jay Gorney (credited to others due to contractual pledges) about a lame ballerina and the dour puppeteer (Gene Raymond) who re-creates the world for her through his marionettes—this almost twenty years before MGM's *Lili*. Daring, occasionally neurotic, far more whimsical and imaginative than this studio's norm, *I Am Suzanne!* was European in setting and tone, in its luscious photography and its score by *Blue Angel* expatriate Frederick Hollander. Harvey finally achieved the captivating grace of her German films, and Gene Raymond, Leslie Banks (as Suzanne's Svengali), and some outstanding marionettes were equally effective—but American audiences were already being weaned toward more literal fare. *I Am Suzanne!* seemed far too silky for its time and studio, both already concentrating on more prosaic backstagers. Immediately after playing Suzanne, Harvey was to have gone into Fox's *George White Scandals* with Rudy Vallee. Preferring to return to Europe, she was replaced by Vallee's protégée, band singer Alice Faye.

The *Scandals* typified the new Fox musical along with two other brassy backstagers simultaneously in production. *Bottoms Up* was an amiable Hollywood story with a non-singing Spencer Tracy; *Stand Up and Cheer* was a sibling of *Hollywood Party,* having started life as the *Fox Movietone Follies of 1933*, then merely *Fox Follies*. As with its eponymous predecessors, it was to be an all-star revue with a modest backstage plot, this one supplied by Will Rogers and interestingly topical. Prompted by Roosevelt's creation of the N.R.A., Rogers envisioned a new cabinet post, a Secretary of Amusement empowered to laugh the nation out of the Depression. He would, predictably, be assisted in these efforts by an array of Fox stars, including Spencer Tracy, Warner Baxter, Sid Silvers, Clara Bow, John Boles, Lew Ayres, Lilian Harvey, El Brendel, Janet Gaynor, and James Dunn. When Rogers decided not to play the Secretary role himself it went to Baxter, in a retread of his Julian Marsh. Boles and Dunn were also added, as were Stepin Fetchit, Aunt Jemima, and a few others. No Harvey or Gaynor or Bow, or even Brendel, but there was a five-year-old veteran of musical shorts and a few features. Whatever the speculation, six decades later, on why Shirley Temple became such a big star so quickly, let it first be said that there had been nothing like her in previous musical films. She wasn't precocious like Mitzi Green, or an infant darling like Davey Lee. She was, simply, an adorable little girl who phrased her songs with instinctive charm and danced like a pro. Next to the jejune adult performers in *Stand Up and Cheer*, her performance of "Baby, Take a Bow" was a breath of fresh air. The film needed all the help it could get, for despite all its fascinating Depression references it was a dispiriting throwback to the first era of dispensable Fox musicals. Talent and style were in far less evidence than money, and Sammy Lee's dance direction filtered Busby Berkeley scope through *High Society Blues* inanity. The songs were not bad, yet not even the spellbinding combination of epic denial and fascist fervor underscoring its "We're Out of the Red" finale seemed to inspire much enthusiasm. Perhaps, then, it was the lackluster nature of her surroundings that made Temple stand out more charismatically. Certainly the Fox management knew it, for in early January 1934, after the *Follies* was in production only three weeks, the buildup had begun.[9] Fox spread the word that Temple was the bright attraction of its new revue and gave her third billing, and when the film opened late in April the critics and public gave her the most attention. Given the burgeoning search for wholesome material, the timing could not have been better; in just a few months, Temple was rating over-the-title billing and codifying one aspect of "family entertainment" for many years.

Even prior to its 1935 merger with Twentieth Century Pictures, Fox had started to banish the more interesting trends and Continental flavor in its musicals following two last costly efforts in 1934. *Caravan* was the unhappy result of the studio's acquisition of *Congress Dances* director Erik Charell. There were, in this overstuffed and underpowered demi-operetta, strong parallels with earlier musicals: a Hollywood newcomer given free rein to create a visually stunning pageant *(King of Jazz, Vagabond King)*; a musical concept given to nonsinging leads (Charles Boyer, Loretta Young, Jean Parker, Phillips Holmes), forcing the songs to subsidiary, mostly choral placements *(This Is the Night)*; and, ignominiously, a Gypsy-marries-countess plot both insubstantial and inane *(Bride of the Regiment, One Heavenly Night*, and many others). Charell's absorption in sumptuous imagery somehow precluded pace and dramatic sense, and the compensation of *Congress Dances*-style wit was nowhere evident. Such a high-priced debacle was the precise type of barometric indicator that producers seek out. It was gorgeous; it had a great deal of music in a Continental setting; there was no backstage song and dance—and the public soundly rejected it. So

9. It was not titled *Stand Up and Cheer* until February, after shooting completed. The stated reason for the change was that Warners' *Fashions of 1934* played some places as *Fashion Follies of 1934* to ensure that audiences knew it as a semi-musical instead of a fashion show. Fox, reckoning the Follies tag was now played out, cried foul and changed their title.

it was seen to follow logically that the public wanted more *George White's Scandals*, with Alice Faye shimmying to "Nasty Man," and fewer *Caravan*s, with Gypsies singing while Loretta Young and Charles Boyer gazed soulfully at each other. Charell, it was perceived, did not take to American film production, and the disaster of *Caravan* (and possibly the nature of his abilities) was such that he never directed a film again, in America or Europe.

While the failure of Fox's *Music In the Air* was less comprehensible than that of *Caravan*, it also sealed the fate of Continental-flavored musicals. It had, at least, an American pedigree, a successful Jerome Kern operetta/musical comedy that ran successfully on Broadway in 1932. However, its creators were mainly from German cinema—Erich Pommer, producer of exceptional successes from *Metropolis* and *The Blue Angel* to *Congress Dances*; director Joe May, who worked in operetta before moving to film in 1912; and young Billy (spelled here Billie) Wilder, his wit already in evidence in a number of screenplays. The Kern show operated as somewhat of a *Moonlight and Pretzels* in Bavaria—a pair of village babes venture into the big city woods of Munich and land in the clutches of the operetta world's leading lights, a lyricist-leading man and a relentlessly self-dramatizing diva. The point of the script was that home is simpler and nicer—a basic theme in Hollywood for the rest of the decade (cf. *The Wizard of Oz*), and particularly engaging here when set to such attractive Kern melodies as "I've Told Ev'ry Little Star" and "The Song Is You."[10] Material that might have cloyed unbearably in other hands was loaded with touches alternately bumptious and sly, Fox's German team spoofing both the oompah hominess of the village and the self-absorption of the city dwellers. The latter found definitive countenance in the performances of John Boles and particularly of Gloria Swanson, singing and posturing with orotund, over-the-top intensity in her only full musical. The character's megalomaniacal careerism and rapacious pursuit of a younger man so clearly foreshadow Norma Desmond that it now seems irrelevant that fifteen years later Swanson was not Billy Wilder's first choice for *Sunset Boulevard*. One sequence in particular forms the core of *Music in the Air*—Boles and Swanson manically turning a music publisher's office into a miniature palladium to offer an impromptu enactment of their upcoming show, in precisely the same fashion that Judy Garland essayed a production-number-on-a-dime in *A Star is Born*. It's uproariously droll, operetta's conventional excesses fully observed as Boles spoofs his earlier roles with zest and Swanson enacts the tainted ingenue with hectic glamour. The elegant swagger of such scenes made *Music in the*

10. "The Song Is You," one of Kern's most rhapsodic fabrications, unfortunately was heard only as an instrumental. John Boles sang it to June Lang in a dressing-room scene deleted before the film opened.

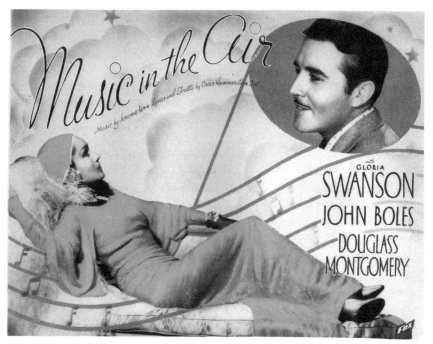

Swanson and Boles advertising *Music in the Air*. Music and lyrics are all very fine, but a diva's allure will invariably assume first place.

Air, despite its standardized plot, seem too sophisticated for a mass audience beginning to dote on Shirley Temple.

The failure of *Music in the Air* came toward the end of 1934, after the Code had come in and the old musical guard had faded. But a similar Kern show had fared disappointingly at the outset of the year. The brief renaissance of adaptations of Broadway shows was, in fact, almost exclusively devoted to Jerome Kern, and most of his shows—even *Show Boat*—were backstagers of one sort or another. *The Cat and the Fiddle* was also set in a European world of songwriters, dedicated musicians, and temperamental stage stars, and this time Kern's lyrical surge was expressed through "The Night Was Made for Love" as well as "She Didn't Say Yes" and "The Breeze Kissed Her Hair." MGM purchased the show early in 1933 for its first musical star, Ramon Novarro, and its newest, Jeanette MacDonald. She was being groomed as a new favorite, he was being returned to musicals after several years of miscasting. With the problems befalling *I Married an Angel*, this was to be MacDonald's MGM debut and, partly at the prompting of Louis B. Mayer, was prepared with inordinate care. The airy final result betrays none of the incessant rewrites and intensive retakes that shot *Cat*'s production cost to nearly twice its original budget. As singer-songwriters who quarrel and love from Brussels to Paris, Novarro and Mac-Donald play with verve and finesse, his androgynous edges balanced by her Paramount crispness. There is also the imposing support of Frank Morgan, Charles Butterworth, and Vivienne Segal—the latter, in her last film, clearly relegated to support, yet still in fine voice.[11] As directed by William K. Howard, *The Cat and the Fiddle* is considerable, charming ado about very little, and quite possibly the closest a backstage musical came to being a Lubitsch-style souffle. Only in the final onstage sequences does the effort show, and these were the most fussed-over portions of the film. After Howard left the production, Sam Wood directed a new set of operetta scenes that seem both heavy and disjointed, including a finale in the new three-color Technicolor process. Though it had been used in cartoons for over a year, this was the process's first application in a live-action film, and while it now captured blues and yellows with fidelity, it gave MacDonald's and Novarro's faces a look of strident unreality. The process, despite Herbert Kalmus's ballyhoo, was not quite perfected, and the last-minute decision to use it here rendered *Cat*'s finale more jarring than iridescent. The film opened in February to fine reviews and initially good business, but it soon became clear that Novarro no longer retained box office clout and MacDonald did not yet possess it. The decline of both Novarro and Continental sparkle did not abate, and despite its merit *The Cat and the Fiddle* was soon forgotten.

With *I Married an Angel* on hold, Jeanette MacDonald was then given the prize title role in MGM's longest-delayed musical, *The Merry Widow*. Along with Maurice Chevalier and Ernst Lubitsch she had been mentioned off and on for the film since late 1930, along with many others. In 1933 Irving Thalberg determined that its time had come, and though Chevalier and Lubitsch were set, MacDonald was not. Grace Moore was another leading choice, and other announced candidates ranged from the lackluster (stage star Peggy Wood) to the intriguing (Gloria Swanson) to the rococo (Joan Crawford). Finally it went to MacDonald, and Thalberg, now working as an MGM producer instead of production head, determined that the Paramount touch, however much it cost to import, would be the ideal setting for Lehar's warhorse.

Finance was indeed one of the preeminent constituents of *The Merry Widow*, which by the time it was done shooting in July 1934 was the most expensive musical yet made, its cost greater than any MGM film since the studio's first production, *Ben-Hur*. Along with the unstinting production, there were clever new lyrics by Lorenz Hart and expansive (sometimes

---

11. Some later claims had Segal as the victim of a MacDonald-ordered cabal that trimmed down Segal's role of a sensual, temperamental diva. The precise quote, unverifiable and possibly untrue, hints at the steel-beneath-gossamer nature of operettadom that *Music in the Air* spoofed. MacDonald to Segal: "Hello, Viv, have you seen your part? It stinks!"

inflated) orchestrations by Herbert Stothart—all calculated to dwarf any previous operetta. There was also unusual vigilance from the Hays Office, though the Code was not yet enforceable. Part of the reason for the attention was Lubitsch's reputation for innuendo, which was deemed out-of-step in a chastened time; the rest of this concern was apparently a vendetta. Several months earlier, when the Hays Office attempted to make numerous cuts in Metro's *Queen Christina*, Thalberg appealed the ruling to arbiters and won the case. Hays and Breen neither forgot nor forgave and, their power on an upswing, were glad to make a test case out of the biggest studio's biggest film. During production the Hays Office badgered Thalberg with requests for changes, many of which were ignored. By release time Thalberg had agreed to do a few retakes and cut the saucier moments of the cancan at Maxim's. Anything else, he said, would be too expensive. So *The Merry Widow* opened in mid-October 1934 and was universally acclaimed as a sumptuous delight, with director and stars well on form. Nine days after the premiere, Breen sent a memo to Hays:

> The picture as it now stands is . . . definitely bawdy and offensively—in spots—suggestive. . . . We made a mistake in approving this picture as it now is. . . . Possibly I should have insisted upon the deletions which we repeatedly urged upon Mr. Thalberg and which for one reason or another we agreed to waive.

He proceeded to list the cuts that should be made, and these were forwarded on to Thalberg. The outraged producer pleaded that the film would be rendered jumpy and incoherent by the cuts, but this time the Code had the power. MGM sent detailed instructions to all its exchanges to make twelve deletions in each distribution print of *The Merry Widow*; these ranged from single words (two feet of film) to dialogue exchanges (twenty-six feet), as well as a shot of Minna Gombell removing from her leg a garter bearing the legend "Many Happy Returns." Compared with Lubitsch's previous operettas, as well as many musicals produced less than a year before, the disputed material was wholly innocuous, little of it more than remotely suggestive; yet this is how the Code was predisposed to function, and these were the strictures under which film would operate for the ensuing three decades.[12]

The controversy, such as it was, had little bearing on the box office fate of *The Merry Widow*. Chevalier's domestic popularity had been eroding since

12. Another germane example: a reissue of *The Cat and the Fiddle* planned for 1937, when Jeanette MacDonald's popularity was at a peak. Three years earlier, the Hays Office had passed the film without a qualm, even making the unusual gesture of sending MGM a letter commending the film's artistry. By 1937, his power in place and his mindset in a completely different cast, Breen wrote Mayer that the film presented an "immoral relationship [MacDonald and Novarro living together] with[out] any of the proper compensatory moral values." Reissue plans were hastily canceled.

Bedtime Story, and neither MacDonald nor Lubitsch had the fame to float a $1.6 million enterprise into the profit column. MGM, however, had planned wisely, for there was a simultaneous version shot in French, along with special versions prepared for the British and Belgian markets that necessarily eliminated Lubitsch's jibes at the monarchy.[13] The stars and the title carried far more weight overseas, and since the foreign grosses were double the American returns, *The Merry Widow* posted only a modest loss. Chevalier and MacDonald, who had never been particularly happy playing opposite each other, were reportedly relieved that this would be their last film together. Perhaps fittingly, this *Merry Widow* has always been somewhat controversial, both adored and disliked. The problem is less the Production Code (since MGM did not cut the negative, all the deletions have been restored) than the collision between Paramount and MGM. The latter studio's bent toward blunt pomp occasionally seems to put a chokehold on Lubitsch's attempt at roguish sparkle, and the result is a film that goes in and out of focus as it changes its tone. While MacDonald and Chevalier are both fine, they often seem inhibited by the teeming seriousness of Metro's million-dollar production values. Chevalier's days as an American leading man were nearly over, and for MacDonald *The Merry Widow* signaled her transition to the Nelson Eddy years, in which her prima donna status would be accented at the expense of some of her comedic élan.

Another change in direction was heralded by Warners' next Berkeley film, *Dames*. On the surface it seemed to be the same as before, certainly with the same stars: Powell, Keeler, Blondell, Kibbee, Herbert, plus ZaSu Pitts, who didn't constitute too great a stretch. But some of the previous snap was missing. It had originally been conceived as a remake of *No, No, Nanette* with new songs, and that film's plot had been one of its weaker points. Even with only a few vestiges of *Nanette* remaining in the script, *Dames* was a comedown from any standpoint except Berkeley's. The characters were either outlandishly stupid or unnervingly venal, the plot trivial and vapid, and Ray Enright's direction characteristically faceless and without *Golden Dawn*'s odious glories. With the approaching clampdown of the Code, and even apart from the deletion of the no-no Blondell song, the Warner musical was losing its guts. As *Fashions of 1934* had demonstrated, Berkeley's ornate sprees needed some kind of offset. It was not just the numbers that had set Warners musicals apart from the imitators in 1933–34. It was the nervous energy of *42nd Street*, the wisecracks of *Gold Diggers* and *Footlight Parade*, the sensationalism of *Wonder Bar*. None of them played merely as stage waits before and between the numbers. Beginning with *Dames* and the Code, they did. "I Only Have Eyes for You," Berke-

13. For the British and the Belgian versions, the buffoonishly cuckolded King Achmed of the American version (played by George Barbier) was turned into a general, and "King Maximilian" was referred to but not shown.

ley's meditation on the infinity of Ruby Keeler's charms, and Blondell's rowdy "The Girl at the Ironing Board," and especially the phantasmagoric title number, are all so much more compelling than the script that a creeping ingratitude sets in. After finding its stride, the backstage musical was forcibly regressing to a late-1929 triviality. The grosses on *Dames* were notably lower than those of its predecessors, and Warners acceded to the trend toward "family" entertainment by putting Powell and Keeler in the insipid and numbingly popular *Flirtation Walk*, released in November. He was a West Point cadet, she a campus belle, and "Pettin' in the Park" was a distant, pleasantly raunchy, memory.

The changes in direction were felt in other areas as well. The small companies, then in a state of transition, offered their own reflections of big-studio trends with titles such as *Rainbow over Broadway* (Chesterfield) and *King Kelly of the USA* (Monogram). *Transatlantic Merry-Go-Round* (United Artists) tried for some of the same excitement as *Wonder Bar*, with a *Grand-Hotel*-on-the-ocean murder plot featuring Jack Benny and Nancy Carroll. But with an inadequately thought-out structure and indifferent musical program it collapsed, a victim of confused intentions. Eddie Cantor's *Kid Millions* was given the same ballyhoo as his previous annual bashes for Goldwyn, yet fared less well. Between his familiarity on radio and his frenzied persona, Cantor was wearing out the public, and working with a whitewashed script, he seemed less entertaining than usual. Apart from the genial astringency of Ethel Merman, as a moll posing as Cantor's mother, the only distinction in *Kid Millions* lay in its finale. Lacking Berkeley and now unable to show Goldwyn Girl flesh, the producer attempted to compensate by employing another type of spectacle: the new Technicolor, far better modulated than that in *The Cat and the Fiddle*.[14] At once crass and endearing, the sequence has Cantor opening a huge ice cream factory for kids to gorge themselves free of charge. Depression dreams did not come more downright than this, especially in a post-Code time when it was necessary to substitute ice cream for more adult indulgences.

By the end of 1934 the new path was clear, as set by the Code and film grosses as well as by several major new stars. The rise of Shirley Temple, especially propitious in the year of the Code, has been noted. The renaissance of Grace Moore was possibly less predictable, for if the diva was all-American her repertoire assuredly was not. Her emergence as a star in 1934 was a more daring stroke than her first attempt four years earlier, when any kind of musical performer was fair game. After recovering from her film

14. The three-strip process had also been used for a sequence in *The House of Rothschild* prior to its "formal" launch in the much-ballyhooed two-reeler *La Cucaracha*, released by RKO. It had, previously and unofficially, turned up in other 1934 musical shorts, such as Warners' *What! No Men?*, a bizarre cowboy-and-Indians charade with El Brendel and Wini Shaw.

setback with stage success, Moore returned to MGM in 1933 to dicker for the lead in *The Merry Widow*. Legend has consistently held that she lost the role when Irving Thalberg deemed her overweight; the more plausible truth is that she had not been considered the top candidate for the Widow since her two flops in 1930, and that three years later she was likely in the running only as an alternate to Jeanette MacDonald. In any case, when it was clear Moore would not be Metro's Widow, she accepted an offer to star in a film for Columbia Pictures. Quite a step down, yet several Columbia productions were attracting major attention in 1933 *(The Bitter Tea of General Yen, Lady for a Day, Man's Castle)*, and it was reckoned the most promising of the minor studios. Just as Moore signed with the studio in November 1933 it was shooting its breakthrough hit—*Night Bus*, later retitled *It Happened One Night*—as well as its first musical since 1930, *Let's Fall in Love*.[15] *One Night of Love* was as much a departure for Hollywood as for Columbia, being the first attempt to spotlight opera in a feature film since Moore's own lamentable *A Lady's Morals*.

Instead of fictional biography, the plot of *One Night of Love* was a mix of Cinderella, *Tosca*, and Ruby Keeler—an American singer goes to Italy to study with a temperamental genius and finds love and stardom. At a small studio, Moore was given prima donna attention she would never have received at MGM, with such niceties as a conductor (Pietro Cimini) who allowed her Carmen to yank the tempo of the Habanera without mercy. More than anything, it benefited from technology greatly improved since Moore's previous film work. Her lack of conventional beauty—she had a goofy look from some angles, rather like comic Joan Davis—was neatly disguised by a shimmer of soft focus and attentive angles and hairdress, and her spinto soprano was floated on a cushion of careful miking and plush recording not available in 1930. It gave her the glamorous look and sound she could create on stage but had not been able to bring to film. Her Tennessee pluck was shrewdly deployed to dilute the audience-threatening grandness, and director Victor Schertzinger was able to cloak most of her dramatic limitations and, on the side, co-author an alluring title song. Released in September 1934, *One Night of Love* was a triumph for "Miss Grace Moore," as she was billed. Her "Sempre libera" and "Ciribiribin" were rapturous, and her Butterfly (the Entrance and "Un bel di," both performed uncut) genuinely world-class. True to such prestige events, the grosses were far more impressive in larger cities than elsewhere, yet re-

---

15. A modest spoof of the Garbo mania rampant in early-thirties Hollywood, *Let's Fall in Love* is most notable for its classic title song (Harold Arlen and Ted Koehler) and for bringing fame to Ann Sothern. As Hariette Lake, she had appeared briefly in *Show of Shows*, *Song of the West*, and *Doughboys* before landing a Broadway lead in Rodgers and Hart's *America's Sweetheart*. She changed her name on the advice of studio head Harry Cohn and occasionally dabbled in musicals over a long career.

mained sufficient for rival studios to scramble about for their own photogenic opera stars.

It was relatively easy for studios to devise equivalent Temples and Moores of both genders. Fred Astaire's appeal, never mind his skill, was not reproduceable, and in the company of Ginger Rogers, co-choreographer Hermes Pan, producer Pandro Berman, and director Mark Sandrich, he made RKO a haven for the finest musical impulses in film for the rest of the decade. Apart from the advent of Astaire, RKO's role in the musical resurgence had been spotty and mainly technological, as in producer Lou Brock's camera tricks for *So This Is Harris*, *Melody Cruise*, and *Flying Down to Rio*. In the first of these the novelty and style was sufficient, especially in a short subject; in the second, the visual magic could not deflect from weaknesses in all other areas; in the third there was a superior score, the Carioca and the airplane stunts, and indications of new directions from Astaire. Yet Brock still seemed to view musicals in 1929 terms, with technique and content forming at best a coincidental relationship. This became woefully obvious with the release in September 1934 of *Down to Their Last Yacht*, a costly and completely irrational extravaganza about indigent millionaires and lustful South Sea islanders. The excesses of a *Madam Satan* appeared tactful alongside this dotty excuse for a musical, which climaxed with an enormous "South Sea Bolero" that suggested an unholy union between Busby Berkeley and Margaret Mead. *Yacht* was a calamity on the order of *Show of Shows*, misusing some musical conventions and ignorant of many others. Both critics and audiences reacted with disdain, and Brock was soon out of RKO; yet before that last fiasco he had served Wheeler and Woolsey well with a period spoof titled *Cockeyed Cavaliers*, directed by Mark Sandrich. One exhilarating musical sequence in mid-film was worth any number of misfired puns: a frisky hunting song that climaxed with a 360° pan around Noah Beery and chorus, and unlike the tricks in *Melody Cruise*, this one enhanced its context. Sandrich was judged a fitting match for Fred Astaire's impulses on how screen musicals could be rethought in dance terms, and the new director-star team embarked on *The Gay Divorcée*.

Cole Porter's *Gay Divorce* had been Astaire's final Broadway outing before his defection to Hollywood, as well as his first work without his sister Adele. Although the reviews were not impressive, Astaire proved his worth as a solo performer, and after he finished work on *Flying Down to Rio* he went to London for a revised, this time critically applauded, version of the show. By May, when he returned to RKO, producer Berman had purchased *Gay Divorce*, and the influences of the Production Code Administration were being felt. A light treatment of divorce and co-respondents was not a property to find favor at a time when the Catholic Church was threatening boycotts, yet RKO was permitted to retain the story's essential outlines as long as they skirted innuendo. There was also a self-imposed new title, indicating that while a person having a divorce might find joy, the act itself remains painful. Other casualties included twelve of Porter's songs, leaving only his "Night and Day" alongside the unPorterish "Let's K-nock K-neez" and the more satisfactory "A Needle in a Haystack" and "The Continental." After the reaction to *Flying Down to Rio,* the selection of Ginger Rogers to costar was inevitable as well as fortunate: the heightened refinement necessary to play opposite Astaire fit well with Rogers's promotion from tartish supporting roles no longer permitted by the Code.[16] The unreality of *The Gay Divorcée*'s plot and setting had already been foreshadowed in *Melody Cruise,* with its frivolously unsentimental air and Art Deco trappings, and with the addition of more viable content—especially Astaire's dancing—there was suddenly a new type of musical. His natural reserve as well as his stage roles opposite his sister had made Astaire uncomfortable with the idea of romantic acting, and he was not a trained actor in any case. All his affinities were defined in terms of musicality: dancer, singer, instrumentalist, composer. These, then, were what made sense to him to carry the plots of his films. Romantic pursuit and attainment, elated insouciance, rejection and even loss, were presented in Astaire's films most often as a song followed by a dance. This becomes clear early in *The Gay Divorcée* with "A Needle in a Haystack," in which he sings of his need to see Rogers again after their first accidental meeting, then dances around his living room with elegant abandon. No wasted movements, nothing superfluous in his resolve, almost despite himself, to go out and look for the woman of his dreams; his dance gives more dimension to the moment than multiple pages of exposition.

The giant production number "The Continental" is the most expansive sequence in *The Gay Divorcée,* and to corroborate the regained strength of musicals in 1934, it was given the first Academy Award for Best Song.[17] But in this new-wrought musical form the group dances and exhaustive permutations in "The Continental" matter far less than Astaire and Rogers's first romantic duet, "Night and Day." To Cole Porter's luxurious melody they dance out an overture to seduction followed by uncertainty and finally acquiescence. That this number spelled out sexual consummation in the most tasteful terms imaginable was not remarked on at the time, and perhaps not even Astaire knew he was doing it, although surely his unconscious did. He was also, at the same time, defeating the absurd strictures of the Production Code through the most exquisite of

16. Two roles between *Flying Down to Rio* and *The Gay Divorcée* chart the progression. In Warners' *Upper World* she was a nightclub dancer (i.e., stripper), shimmying to "Shake Your Powder Puff." Then, in *Twenty Million Sweethearts,* she was elevated to a more demure heroine. By the time of *The Gay Divorcée* she was well past her "Anytime Annie" days.

17. The Oscar for musical score, also new that year, went to *One Night of Love.* Both it and *The Gay Divorcée* were also up for Best Picture. So was *Flirtation Walk,* possibly for being Warners' self-congratulatory attempt to clean up musicals.

Fadeout: Fred and Ginger in *The Gay Divorcée*, finishing their "Night and Day" dance and commencing a new age for musical film. *Photofest*.

means. Months earlier, he and Rogers seemed to dance The Carioca with conspiratorial joy. Here, working as a unit, the partnership comes together to give movie musicals a sparkling, special depth.[18]

18. It was probably at the behest of Mark Sandrich that "Night and Day" was shot Berkeley style, as it were, with a series of fairly short takes edited together. By his next film, Astaire had taken over, and his duets with Rogers were shot in the longest possible takes, usually two shots maximum (as opposed to twelve for "Night and Day")—a purity of form that unintentionally harkened to the long takes necessary in early sound films.

As demonstrated in *The Gay Divorcée,* such quality was new, yet in other guises the resonance had been present in favored pockets from the very beginning. It had been seen and heard as early as 1926, when Giovanni Martinelli confronted audiences with the sight and sound of a clown's despair, and in 1927, with Al Jolson defining himself during "Blue Skies" and "My Mammy." It went on through Bessie Love breaking down in her dressing room, Ethel Waters torching "Am I Blue?," Marilyn Miller paving the way for Astaire's dance innovations, and Maurice Chevalier's complaint that nobody's using it now. And with Mamoulian and Berkeley and other gifted directors and songwriters and artists it continued on through to 1934. It was small moments sometimes—Lillian Roth rocking to "Sing You Sinners"—and sometimes entire films. There are those who reckon *The Gay Divorcée* the true beginning of musicals; what constitutes a beginning? The unity and cohesion Fred Astaire brought to musicals was both new and always present. Musicals are not so straitjacketed that they require one channel of expression, one level upon which to succeed. They had, to greater and lesser extent, been succeeding all along. Through baby-step technical improvements and faint glimmers of originality, through producers' incomprehension and audiences' apathy, past crass commercialism and baseless prudery, there had been evolution and advancement. The arrival of Astaire and his creations was fortunate, for by that time there was much diminution occurring in many other areas. The old had died, and for better and worse, the new had taken over. Musicals found a circumscribed niche as never before, and all ahead was safe, professionally assured, and kept within unthreatening bounds. No more Vitaphone or two-color Technicolor or booby-prize Webs of Love. And certainly there were no remnants of a stage mother currying a dance teacher's favor by offering to fix him up with new boyfriends, as Alice Brady had done. Nothing remained, either, of a director answering the question "Isn't It Romantic?" by creating a visual symphony. In a time when recent memories were too painful for reflection, the old musicals were easy to leave behind. America had changed, and so had its movies. By the end of 1934 that first song was over, and there would be no encore.

Epilogue

As 1934 gave way to 1935, the lessons had been learned and the direction was resolved. The new trends were clearly set, with less paradox and more consistency—and no room amidst the professionalism for the experiments and excesses of earlier times. Astaire and Rogers were the axis for film dance—they were then preparing *Roberta*—and despite the occasional imitators would remain preeminent for the balance of the decade. The brassy Fox style—presently Twentieth Century-Fox—was well in place. Alice Faye was beginning to find her way, and *George White's 1935 Scandals* introduced a new solo dancer, Eleanor Powell, who would render tap dance on film with ruthless brio. Shirley Temple was beginning to assume her position atop popularity charts, sometimes with the help of song and dance and perhaps most memorably in its most unpretentious incarnation: her staircase dance with Bill Robinson in *The Little Colonel*, her first film of the year. At Paramount the Crosby vehicles continued, an increasingly laid-back Bing singing attractively languid ballads without apparent effort or involvement. MGM was preparing to relaunch operetta with *Naughty Marietta*, in which Jeanette MacDonald in her post-Lubitsch post-Code incarnation would no longer be merely a connoisseur's delight; with Nelson Eddy on hand instead of Chevalier, there was no question about dominant personalities. Chevalier himself gave one last demonstration of his powers, in a dual role in Twentieth Century's imitation-Berkeley *Folies Bergère*, then was gone. Unreasonable demands and salary requirements figured in his departure, but surely the massive shift in tastes mattered even more.

At Warners, Busby Berkeley was finally given a feature film to direct: *Gold Diggers of 1935*, implacably escapist and with some of the energy and almost none of the edge of its predecessors. No more Depression references were allowed, although Berkeley did fly with the greatest of all his achievements, "Lullaby of Broadway." An inexorable urban nightmare, it was also the crowning paradox in Berkeley's career—the dance director who cared little about choreography here rose to the occasion with some of the finest group dance ever put on film, after which his work tapered off pointedly. The other Warner musical people continued in accepted mode—Powell and Keeler, and the fading if game Jolson—as the studio's musicals increasingly lost their snap. Universal made an impressive showing with the remake of *Show Boat* in 1936, but then retreated into pedantic musical linotype, alleviated only by the fresh-faced soprano earnestness of Deanna Durbin. Grace Moore's unforeseen hit with *One Night of Love* meant that Columbia had a new musical star (*Love Me Forever* was her vehicle for 1935) and that all the other studios would try out opera singers once again—Lily Pons, Nino Martini, Jan Kiepura, Gladys Swarthout, James Melton, and, to close the circle of this entire narrative, Marion Talley.

Little of this sounds necessarily dissimilar to what was going on in the musical film for the previous year and a half. But in their relentless drive toward genericization the films themselves made the differences markedly clear. Production standards, even in lower-budget entries, had reached a level of formidable efficiency. Photography and recording, design and musical arrangements, dance direction and performances—all were as the components of the most minutely crafted watch, and frequently with the mechanical aspect so implied. The polish and gloss and accomplishment were generally far greater, the songs often vastly so, and there would be few of the miscalculations of the earlier films—but some of the adventure of the medium would never return. With few glitches and little apparent effort newer musicals seemed to glide past like Sonja Henie, the ice skater whose interchangeable vehicles epitomized the commercial work of the later 1930s. The tension between form and content was completely eased out, the conventions became effortlessly accessible, there was no call or need for iconoclasm or, often, depth. The Production Code had in any case made many quests for alternative qualities seem unfeasible, not specifically because these qualities hinged on sex, but because the Code's condemnation of darker fare made standard content seem the most efficacious route. Expansion into new areas, or upon possibilities considered and tried in 1930 or 1932, was for the most part more trouble than it seemed worth.

Musicals, then, became bigger and narrower. In 1936 MGM produced the first musical since *The Broadway Melody* to win the Best Picture Oscar— *The Great Ziegfeld*, in which the showman's darker and more intriguing sides mattered almost not at all, and MGM's drive for blockbuster magnificence mattered completely. Soon afterward the studio took screen operetta to its zenith with the MacDonald-Eddy *Maytime*, a post-Code *Viennese Nights* of awesome proficiency. Other companies had their own prototypes and their own hits, and the genre settled effortlessly into a mold of stereotypical finesse, and generally of one escapist dimension. They had the energy and the professionalism, but they were indisputably less enterprising. Occasionally there were some surprises, such as Paramount's attempts at putting a Brecht-Weill score into *You and Me* (1938), or director Julien Duvivier's enlivening Metro's *The Great Waltz* (1938) with a rhapsodic camera. And there were the occasional moments of glory—Disney's first animated features and *The Wizard of Oz*, as well as appearances from Bill Robinson and Fats Waller and Louis Armstrong to show how shamefully other aspects of American entertainment were being neglected.

The later changes and periods of luster are well known: some conscious Broadway and Hollywood efforts to elevate musical forms and textures, the Arthur Freed unit at MGM, the various glories of Garland, Kelly, Minnelli, Astaire, Grable, Hayworth, and so forth. In this time when the musical seemed, on occasion, to assume its full powers, its first years seemed almost biblically remote. Certainly no one cared, even when *Singin' in the Rain* was released, to point out the groundbreaking work of the early efforts. Perhaps this was only enhanced when, in the 1950s, many of the first musicals began turning up on television. Without a frame of reference they seemed more than slightly daft, and even next to TV variety shows appeared archaic and inept.[1] A few legends were maintained—Jolson, Chevalier, a few of the Berkeley films—and the remainder receded into the realm of trivia and esoterica. The relentless maw of popular art found easy discards here, and camp-seekers took care of the rest.

Given the vagaries of the public's taste, it may beggar belief to hold to a contention that these creaky old confections still matter. On the surface, the only message they seem to disclose is of how incredibly far we've come since. But look hard, past the monolithic presentation and stolid methodology. Look at the times in these films that people seem to strive, seem to take chances, attempting and often failing to attain new forms of communication. Look at the directors who refused to take no for an answer, who tried to fuse stage and cinema into a lucid composite. And listen, past those prickly old soundtracks, to the great singers and musicians, and to the poor ones as well. Their songs, for better and otherwise, still come drifting through the dark toward us, conveying the enterprise and adventure, the

---

1. Their sale to television at this time ensured their survival, at least in 16mm format. Unfortunately, especially in the case of the Warner Bros. musicals, the sole surviving copies of the early Technicolor musicals were transferred onto black-and-white stock only and then junked. There were not yet the facilities to do the work in color, the demands of television at the time were exclusively monochrome, and the old Vitaphone prints were deemed obsolete. So out with the history.

ineptitude and imitation, the grandeur and folly, the commerce and art. Without them film would have been the poorer. We, the audience, would be the poorer. And on those occasions when some of their initial splendor shines through once more, we are permitted to retrieve vestiges of our past, when song and dance somehow mattered immensely, and when our own lives and perceptions seemed unutterably more innocent.

A Selective Discography:
The First Musicals on Record

Given the popularity of early movie musicals, a profusion of related phonograph records would have been foreseeable. The expected items by dance bands and popular vocalists were augmented by many records more closely related to the films, performed by cast members. While the likes of Chevalier and Tucker were naturals for this sort of tie-in, there were also the Lawrence Grays, Noah Beerys, and Lupe Velezes—film actors making rare (often one-time-only) stabs at recording. With a few exceptions, the list that follows includes most of the original-film-cast performers who, between 1927 and 1934, made studio recordings related to their films. (The exceptions include such related discs as the Chevalier *Movietone Follies* side and John Boles's two sides from *Cameo Kirby*.) There are some odd gaps, for what was recorded often depended on the studio or performer's contractual associations; also, a tremendous drop-off began in mid-1930, when the Depression hit the recording industry as hard as it hit everything else. Among the cuts included are those (often in English) from foreign musicals discussed in the text, and also the foreign-language versions occasionally made by stars of American-produced films.

Although some of these have been rereleased on LP or compact disc, the label numbers refer only to the original 78-rpm issues (or, in a few cases, recordings made and not released until much later—i.e., Joan Crawford's "How Long Will It Last?"). Following this discography is a short list of the more pertinent LP or CD recordings or compilations.

A. ORIGINAL 78 RECORDINGS

Abbreviations:	Record Labels	Countries
Br: Brunswick	HMV: His Master's Voice	F = France; G = Germany;
Col: Columbia	Par: Parlophone	UK = United Kingdom
Dec: Decca	Vic: Victor	N/r: recording not released
El: Electrola	Voc: Vocalion	at the time

Film Title/Artist/Song Title	Label/Record Number
Applause Helen Morgan 　What Wouldn't I Do for That Man	Vic 22149
Barbarian, The (1933) Ramon Novarro (in 1936) 　Love Songs of the Nile	HMV [UK] C-2778
Be Mine Tonight Jan Kiepura 　Tell Me Tonight/La Danza	Par [UK] RO 20201
Be Yourself Fannie Brice 　Cooking Breakfast for the One I Love/When a Woman 　　Loves a Man	Vic 22310
Bedtime Story, A (In French: *Monsieur Bebe*) Maurice Chevalier 　J'ai d'la Veine/Printemps dans les Squar's à Paris	Vic 150091
Belle of the Nineties Duke Ellington and Orchestra 　Troubled Waters/My Old Flame	Vic 24651
Big Pond, The Maurice Chevalier 　Livin' in the Sunlight, Lovin' in the Moonlight/ 　　You Brought a New Kind of Love to Me 　Paris, Je t'aime D'Amour/Vous etes mon nouveau 　　bonheur	Vic 22405 Vic 22415
Big Broadcast, The Bing Crosby 　Please 　Here Lies Love Donald Novis 　Trees Arthur Tracy 　Here Lies Love	 Br 6394 Br 6406 Br 6538 Dec [UK] F-3495
Blue Angel, The Marlene Dietrich 　Falling in Love Again/Lola 　Ich bin von Kopf bis Fuβ auf Liebe eingestelt/ 　　Nimm dich in archt vor blonden Frau'n 　Blonde Women 　Ich bin die fesche Lola/Kinder, heut'abend da such'ich 　　mir was aus 　This Evening Children	 Vic 22592 El [G] EG-1170 HMV [UK] B-3524 El [G] EG-1802 El [n/r]

Bolero
Ralph Rainger, Nat Finston and Paramount Studio
  Orchestra
    Raftero   Vic 24515

Broadway Melody, The
Charles King
  The Broadway Melody/The Wedding of the
    Painted Doll   Vic 21964
  You Were Meant for Me/Love Boat   Vic 21965

Broadway Thru a Keyhole
Abe Lyman and Orchestra
  You're My Past, Present and Future   Br 6672
  Doin' the Uptown Lowdown/ When You Were A Girl
    on a Scooter and I Was A Boy on a Bike   Br 6674

Call of the Flesh
Ramon Novarro (in 1935)
  Lonely   HMV [UK] C-2778

Cameo Kirby
John Boles
  After a Million Dreams/Romance   Vic 22230

Captain of the Guard
John Boles
  You, You Alone/For You   Vic 22373

Cat and the Fiddle, The
Jeanette MacDonald
  Try to Forget   Vic 24754

Chasing Rainbows
Charles King
  Happy Days are Here Again/Love Ain't Nothin' but
    the Blues   Br 4615
  Everybody Tap/Lucky Me, Lovable You   Br 4616

Check and Double Check
Duke Ellington and Orchestra
  Three Little Words (w/Rhythm Boys)/Ring Dem Bells
    (w/Cootie Williams)   Vic 22528
  Three Little Words/Old Man Blues   Vic 23022

Cheer Up and Smile (1930)
Whispering Jack Smith
  Where Can You Be?/You May Not Like It (But It's a
    Great Idea)   Vic 22443

Children of Pleasure
Lawrence Gray
  Leave It That Way/The Whole Darned Thing's
    For You   Br 4775

College Coach (1933)
Dick Powell
  Lonely Lane   Br 6685

College Humor
Bing Crosby
  Moonstruck/Learn to Croon   Br 6594
  Down the Old Ox Road   Br 6601

College Rhythm
Jack Oakie
  College Rhythm/Take a Number from One to Ten   Melotone M-13236
Lyda Roberti
  College Rhythm/Take a Number from One to Ten   Col 2967-D
Lanny Ross
  Stay as Sweet as You Are/Let's Give Three Cheers
    for Love   Br 7318

Congress Dances
Henri Garat
  Serait-ce un reve?/Ville d'amour   Polydor [F] 522122
Lilian Harvey
  Just Once for All Time   Par [UK] R-1088

Cuban Love Song
Lawrence Tibbett
  Cuban Love Song/Tramps at Sea   Vic 1550

Dance of Life, The
Ethel Waters
  True Blue Lou   Col 1871-D

Dangerous Nan McGrew (1930)
Helen Kane
  Dangerous Nan McGrew/I Owe You   Vic 22407

Devil May Care
Ruth Etting
  The Shepherd's Serenade/Charming   Col 2066-D
Ramon Novarro (in 1936)
  The Shepherd's Serenade/Charming   HMV [UK] C-2778

Dixiana
Everett Marshall
  Mr. and Mrs. Sippi/Goodbye Old Pals   Vic 22471

Doughboys
Cliff Edwards
  Sing (A Happy Little Thing)   Col 2235-D

Flirtation Walk
Dick Powell
  Flirtation Walk/Mr. and Mrs. Is the Name   Br 7328

Flying Down to Rio
Fred Astaire
  Flying Down to Rio/Music Makes Me   Col 2912-D

Footlight Parade
Dick Powell
  By a Waterfall/Honeymoon Hotel   Br 6667
  Ah, the Moon Is Here   Dec [UK] 3772

Fox Movietone Follies of 1929
Maurice Chevalier
  That's You, Baby   Vic 21927

Gift of Gab (1934)
Gene Austin
  Blue Sky Avenue   Vic 24725
Ruth Etting
  Talkin' to Myself/Tomorrow—Who Cares?   Col 2954-D
Ethel Waters
  Ain't Gonna Sin No More   Dec 141

Going Hollywood
Bing Crosby
  After Sundown/Beautiful Girl   Br 6694
  Temptation/We'll Make Hay While the Sun Shines   Br 6695

Gold Diggers of Broadway
Nick Lucas
  Tip Toe Through the Tulips With Me/Painting the
    Clouds With Sunshine   Br 4418

Gold Diggers of 1933
Dick Powell
  The Gold Diggers' Song/I've Got to Sing a Torch Song   Perfect 12919
  Pettin' in the Park/Shadow Waltz   Perfect 12920

Golden Dawn
Noah Beery
  Whip Song   Br 4828

Great Gabbo, The
Earl Burtnett's Biltmore Trio
  The Web of Love/I'm in Love With You   Br 4511

Hallelujah
Daniel L. Haynes and Dixie Jubilee Singers
   Waiting at the End of the Road   Vic 22097
Ethel Waters
   Waiting at the End of the Road   Col 1933-D

Hallelujah, I'm A Bum
Al Jolson
   You Are Too Beautiful/Hallelujah, I'm A Bum   Br 6500

Happy Days
George Olsen and Orchestra
   I'm on a Diet of Love/Mona   Vic 22259

Heads Up
Helen Kane
   My Man Is on the Make   Vic 22475
   If I Knew You Better/Readin' Ritin' Rhythm   Vic 22520

Hello, Everybody!
Kate Smith
   My Queen of Lullaby Land/Twenty Million People   Br 6496
   Moon Song/Pickaninnies' Heaven   Br 6497

Here Is My Heart [1934]
Bing Crosby
   With Every Breath I Take   Dec 309
   June in January/Love Is Just Around the Corner   Dec 310

Hips Hips Hooray
Ruth Etting
   Keep Romance Alive/Tired of It All   Br 6721

Hold Everything
Al Jolson
   When the Little Red Roses Get the Blues for You Br 4722

Hollywood Revue of 1929
Cliff Edwards
   Singin' in the Rain/Orange Blossom Time   Col 1869-D
Nick Lucas
   Your Mother and Mine   Br 4378

Honky Tonk
Sophie Tucker
   I'm Doin' What I'm Doin' for Love/
     Feathering a Nest (for a Little Bluebird)   Vic 21993
   He's a Good Man to Have Around/
     I'm the Last of the Red-Hot Mommas   Vic 21994
   I Don't Want to Get Thin   Vic 21995
   Some of These Days   Vic 22049

Ihre Hoheit Befiehlt (Her Highness Commands)
Lilian Harvey and Willy Fritsch
  You Brought Me Love   Par [UK] R-1179
Lilian Harvey and Henri Garat
  Love Was Smuggled Into My House/
    Don't Ask How, Don't Ask Where   Dec [UK] PO-5013

I'm No Angel
Mae West
  I'm No Angel/I Found a New Way to Go to Town   Br 6675
  I Want You—I Need You/They Call Me Sister
    Honky Tonk   Br 6676

Indiscreet
Gloria Swanson
  Come to Me/If You Haven't Got Love   Br 6127

Innocents of Paris
Maurice Chevalier
  It's a Habit of Mine/On Top of the World Alone   Vic 22007
  Valentine/Les Ananas   Vic 22093
  Wait 'til You See Ma Cherie/Louise   Vic 21918

International House
Baby Rose Marie
  My Bluebird's Singin' the Blues   Br 6570

Is Everybody Happy?
Ted Lewis and Orchestra
  I'm the Medicine Man for the Blues/Wouldn't It
    Be Wonderful   Col 1882-D
  In the Land of Jazz   Col [UK] CB-5

It's A Great Life
Duncan Sisters
  I'm Following You/Hoosier Hop   Vic 22269
Lawrence Gray
  I'm Following You/Sailing on a Sunbeam   Br 4631

Jazz Singer, The
Al Jolson
  Mother, I Still Have You   Br 3719
  My Mammy/Dirty Hands, Dirty Face   Br 3912

Kid from Spain, The
Eddie Cantor
  What a Perfect Combination/Look What You've Done   Col 2723-D

Kid Millions
Eddie Cantor
  An Earful of Music/Mandy   Rex [UK] 8390
  Okay, Toots/When My Ship Comes In   Rex [UK] 8391

Ethel Merman
   An Earful of Music   Br 6995

King of Jazz
John Boles
   It Happened in Monterey/Song of the Dawn   Vic 22372
Grace Hayes
   My Lover/I Like to Do Things for You   Vic 22388
The Rhythm Boys
   A Bench in the Park   Col 2223-D
   So the Bluebirds and the Blackbirds Got Together   Col 1819-D
Paul Whiteman and Orchestra
   It Happened in Monterey (w/Johnny Fulton)/
      Song of the Dawn (w/Bing Crosby and chorus)   Col 2163-D
   Happy Feet (w/Rhythm Boys)/A Bench in the Park (w/
      Brox Sisters and Rhythm Boys)   Col 2164-D
   I Like to Do Things for You (w/Rhythm Boys)/
      Ragamuffin Romeo (w/Jeanie Lang)   Col 2170-D

Lady of the Pavements [1929]
Lupe Velez
   Where Is the Song of Songs for Me?   Vic 21932

Lord Byron of Broadway
Charles Kaley
   Should I?/A Bundle of Old Love Letters   Br 4718

Love Comes Along
Bebe Daniels
   Night Winds/Until Love Comes Along   Vic 22283

Love Me Tonight
Maurice Chevalier
   Mimi/The Poor Apache   Vic 24063
   Mimi/Je suis un méchant   Vic 24066
Jeanette MacDonald
   Love Me Tonight/Isn't It Romantic?   Vic 24067
   Veux tu m'aimer?/N'est-ce pas poétique?   Vic 24068

Love Parade, The
Maurice Chevalier
   My Love Parade/Nobody's Using It Now   Vic 22285
   Paris, Stay the Same   Vic 22294
   Mon cocktail d'amour/Personne ne s'en maintenant   Vic 22368
   Paris, je t'aime d'amour   Vic 22415
Jeanette MacDonald
   Dream Lover/March of the Grenadiers   Vic 22247

Loves of Robert Burns, The
Joseph Hislop

Loch Lomond/Ye Banks and Braes of Bonnie Doon/
    Bonnie Mary of Argyle   HMV [UK] B-3264
    Annie Laurie/Afton Waters   HMV [UK] B-3265

Lucky Boy
George Jessel
    My Mother's Eyes   Vic 21852

Lucky in Love (1929)
Morton Downey
    Love is a Dreamer/When They Sing the Wearin'
        of the Green   Vic 21940

Mammy
Al Jolson
    Let Me Sing and I'm Happy/Looking at You   Br 4721
    To My Mammy   Br 4722

March of Time, The
Charles King
    Here Comes the Sun (not filmed)   Br 4849
Ramon Novarro (in 1936)
    Long Ago in Alcala   HMV [UK] B-8426

Marianne
Cliff Edwards
    Just You, Just Me/Hang On to Me   Col 1907-D

Merry Widow, The
Jeanette MacDonald
    I Love You So (Merry Widow Waltz)/Vilia   Vic 24729
    Tonight Will Teach Me to Forget   Vic 24754

Montana Moon
Cliff Edwards
    The Moon Is Low   Col 2169-D

Morocco
Marlene Dietrich
    Give Me the Man/Quand l'amour meurt   El [G] EG-2275

Mother's Boy
Morton Downey
    I'll Always Be Mother's Boy/There'll Always Be
        You and I   Vic 21940
    There's a Place in the Sun For You/The World Is
        Yours and Mine   Vic 21958

Monte Carlo
Jeanette MacDonald
    Beyond the Blue Horizon/Always in All Ways   Vic 22514

Moulin Rouge
Boswell Sisters
   Song of Surrender/Coffee in the Morning and Kisses
      at Night   Br 6733

Murder at the Vanities
Carl Brisson
   Cocktails for Two/Live and Love Tonight   Br 6887
Duke Ellington and Orchestra
   Ebony Rhapsody   Vic 24622

My Man
Fannie Brice
   I'd Rather Be Blue/
   If You Want the Rainbow (You Must Have the Rain)   Vic 21815

New Moon
Lawrence Tibbett
   Lover, Come Back to Me/Wanting You   Vic 1506

Nothing But the Truth (1929)
Helen Kane
   Do Something   Vic 21917

Oh Sailor Behave!
Charles King
   Love Comes in the Moonlight/Highway to Heaven   Br 4840
   Leave a Little Smile   Br 4849

On With the Show!
Ethel Waters
   Am I Blue?/Birmingham Bertha   Col 1837-D

One Hour With You
Maurice Chevalier
   What Would You Do?/Oh! That Mitzi   Vic 22941
   Qu'auriez-vous fait?/Oh! Cette Mitzi   Vic 22944
Jeanette MacDonald
   One Hour With You/We Will Always Be Sweethearts   Vic 24013
   Un heure pres de toi/Coeur contre coeur   Vic 24019
Donald Novis
   One Hour With You   Vic 22971

One Night of Love
Grace Moore
   One Night of Love/Ciribirin   Br 6994

Operator 13 (1934)
Mills Brothers
   Jungle Fever   Br 6785
   Sleepy Head   Br 6913

Pagan, The
Ramon Novarro (in 1936)
   Pagan Love Song   HMV [UK]C-2778

Palmy Days
Eddie Cantor
   There's Nothing Too Good for my Baby   Vic 22851

Paramount on Parade
Maurice Chevalier
   Sweepin' the Clouds Away/All I Want Is Just One Girl   Vic 22378
Dennis King
   Nichavo!   Vic 22263
Charles "Buddy" Rogers
   Sweepin' the Clouds Away/Anytime's the Time to
      Fall in Love   Col 2143-D

Paris
Irene Bordoni
   My Lover/I Wonder What Is Really in His Mind   Col 1983-D

Perfect Understanding (1933)
Gloria Swanson
   I Love You So Much That I Hate You/Ich Liebe Dich,
   My Dear   HMV[UK] B-4357

Pointed Heels
Helen Kane
   I Have to Have You/Ain'tcha?   Vic 22192

Possessed (1931)
Joan Crawford, Gus Arnheim and Orchestra
   How Long Will It Last?   Vic [n/r]

Prodigal, The
Lawrence Tibbett
   Without a Song/Life Is a Dream   Vic 1507

Puttin' on the Ritz
Fred Astaire
   Puttin' on the Ritz   Col [UK] DB-96
Harry Richmond
   Puttin' On The Ritz/There's Danger in Your Eyes,
      Cherie   Br 4677
   With You/Singin' a Vagabond Song   Br 4678

Ramona
Dolores Del Rio
   Ramona   Vic 4053

Rio Rita
Bebe Daniels
  You're Always in my Arms (But Only in my Dreams)/
    If You're in Love, You'll Waltz   Vic 22132

Rogue Song, The
Lawrence Tibbett
  The Rogue Song/The Narrative   Vic 1446
  When I'm Looking at You/The White Dove   Vic 1447

Roman Scandals
Ruth Etting
  No More Love/Build a Little Home   Br 6697

Sadie McKee (1934)
Gene Austin
  All I Do Is Dream of You   Vic 24663

Safety in Numbers
Charles "Buddy" Rogers
  My Future Just Passed/I'd Like to Be a Bee in
    Your Boudoir   Col 2183-D

Say It With Songs
Al Jolson
  I'm in Seventh Heaven/Little Pal   Br 4400
  Used to You/Why Can't You?   Br 4401
  One Sweet Kiss   Br 4402

She Done Him Wrong
Mae West
  I Wonder Where My Easy Rider's Gone/A Guy What
    Takes His Time   Br 6495

She Loves Me Not
Bing Crosby
  Straight from the Shoulder (Right from the Heart)/
  Love in Bloom   Br 6936
  I'm Hummin' (I'm Whistlin', I'm Singin')   Br 6953

Show of Shows, The
Irene Bordoni
  Just an Hour of Love   Col 2027-D
Ted Lewis and Orchestra
  Lady Luck   Col 1999-D

Singing Fool, The
Al Jolson
  Sonny Boy/There's a Rainbow 'Round My Shoulder   Br 4033

So This Is College
Cliff Edwards
  Sophomore Prom   Col 1907-D

Song o' My Heart
John McCormack
   Ireland, Mother Ireland/The Rose of Tralee   Vic 1452
   I Feel You Near Me/A Pair of Blue Eyes   Vic 1453
   Little Boy Blue   Vic 1458

Song of the Flame
Noah Beery
   One Little Drink   Br 4828

Song of Love, The
Belle Baker
   I'm Walking With the Moonbeams (Talking to
      the Stars)/Take Everything But You   Br 4558
   I'll Still Go On Loving You   Br 4624

Song of the West
John Boles
   West Wind/The One Girl   Vic 2229

Sunny Skies
Benny Rubin
   The Laughing Song   Br 4798

Sunshine Susie
Renate Müller
   Today I Feel So Happy/Just Because I Lost My
      Heart to You   Col [UK] DB-687

Sweetie
Helen Kane
   He's So Unusual   Vic 22080

Syncopation
Morton Downey
   I'll Always Be in Love with You/My Inspiration Is You   Vic 21860
Fred Waring's Pennsylvanians
   Jericho/I'll Always Be in Love with You   Col 1907-D

Take a Chance
Cliff Edwards
   It's Only a Paper Moon/Night Owl   Voc 2587
   Come Up and See Me Sometime   Voc [n/r]

They Learned About Women
Van and Schenck
   Does My Baby Love/Dougherty Is the Name   Vic 22352

Too Much Harmony
Bing Crosby
   Thanks/Black Moonlight   Br 6643
   The Day You Came Along   Br 6644

Transatlantic Merry-Go-Round
Boswell Sisters
  Rock and Roll/If I Had a Million Dollars   Br 7302

Trespasser, The
Gloria Swanson
  Love, Your Spell Is Everywhere/Serenade   Vic 22079

Twenty Million Sweethearts
Ted Fio Rito and Orchestra with Dick Powell
  Fair and Warmer   Br 6859
Dick Powell
  I'll String Along with You   Br 6793

Vagabond King, The
Dennis King
  If I Were King   Vic 22263

Vagabond Lover, The
Rudy Vallee
  Heigh Ho, Everybody, Heigh Ho   Vic 22029
  I'll Always Be Reminded of You/A Little Kiss Each
    Morning   Vic 22193
  I Love You, Believe Me, I Love You/If You Were the
    Only Girl in the World   Vic 22227

Wagon Master, The (1929)
Ken Maynard
  Lone Star Trail   Col 2310-D

Wake Up and Dream (1934)
Russ Columbo
  Too Beautiful for Words   Dec [UK] F-5405
  When You're in Love/Let's Pretend There's a Moon Br 6972

Way Out West (1930)
Cliff Edwards
  Singing a Song to the Stars   Col 2235-D

Way to Love, The
Maurice Chevalier
  C'est en flamant dans les rues de Paris   HMV [UK] B-7146
  Pres de vous/Un peu plus, un peu moins   HMV [UK] B-7161

We're Not Dressing
Bing Crosby
  Love Thy Neighbor   Br 6852
  May I?/She Reminds Me of You   Br 6853
  Good Night, Lovely Little Lady/Once in a Blue Moon Br 6854

Wolf Song (1929)
Lupe Velez
   Mi amado   Vic 21932

Woman Commands, A
Pola Negri
   Paradis (Paradise)   [French recording]

Women Everywhere
J. Harold Murray
   Beware of Love/Smile Legionnaire   Br 4836

Wonder Bar
Dick Powell
   Why Do I Dream Those Dreams?/Wonder Bar   Br 6792
   Don't Say Goodnight   Br 6793

Wonder of Women
Peggy Wood
   At Close of Day   HMV [UK] B-3282

B. LPS AND COMPACT DISCS

Film Star Parade	Living Era [UK] CD AJA 5020
(Cuts by Daniels, Buddy Rogers, Swanson, etc.)	
Hollywood Sings	Living Era [UK] CD AJA 5011
(Studio cuts and sound track excerpts by Swanson, King, Richman, etc.)	
Hollywood Sings	Pro-Arte CDD 509
(Studio cuts and radio transcripts by Dietrich, Colbert, West, etc.)	
Hooray for Hollywood: Unforgettable Movie Hits	Conifer [CD] [UK] TQ 157
(Cuts by Dietrich, Crawford, Novarro, Swanson, etc.)	
Legends of the Musical Stage	Take Two [LP] TT 104
Cuts from Vitaphone discs (*My Man, Gold Diggers of Broadway*, etc.)	
Lost Films: Trailers from the First Years of Sound	Take Two [LP] TT 110
Soundtracks of Vitaphone discs of trailers (*Gold Diggers, No, No, Nanette*, etc.)	
"Makin' Whoopee"	Conifer [CD] [UK] TQ 132
(Cuts by Buddy Rogers, Jolson, Boles, etc.)	

Movie Musicals 1927 to 1936	BBC [UK] CD 654
(Cuts by Jolson, MacDonald, Chevalier, Cliff Edwards, etc.)	
Rodgers and Hart's *Hollywood Party*	Beginners Productions [UK] [LP] BRP 2
1982 Recording of R&H's mostly unused score	
Sing Before Breakfast: Songs From the Great Talking Picture Musicals 1929–1939 (1990–91 Recordings from *My Weakness, Moonlight and Pretzels, Safety in Numbers,* etc.)	Shadowland/Rialto [CD] SLRR 9101
Stars of the Silver Silver Screen 1929–1930 (Cuts by Tucker, Jessel, Boles, Daniels, Swanson, etc.)	RCA Victor LPV-538
Why Ever Did They? Hollywood Stars at the Microphone (Cuts by Novarro, Berry, Velez, Del Rio, Swanson)	Pearl [UK] Past CD 9735

Notes on Lost Films

By definition, a list such as this is incomplete and evanescent, as well as inherently inaccurate. The films listed below, nearly all discussed or mentioned in the text, are currently, as best as can be determined, not known to exist. But as happens time and again, fragments and entire features have been known to resurface, and some of these titles may well exist in private hands, in mislabeled film cans in studio vaults, or in previously uncontactable foreign archives. This appendix, therefore, is set down both to heighten awareness of the erosion of our fragmentary film heritage, and to spur the intrepid toward possible reclamations. Anyone discovering the existence of any of these lost titles should contact one of the major film archives, such as UCLA or the Library of Congress.

A. TOTAL LOSSES

These films are considered lost, in (or nearly so) their entirety. For many of them the Vitaphone discs have resurfaced, often in private hands. (A few titles sometimes thought lost have been left off this list due to unconfirmed—if strongly held—reports of their survival.)

The Air Circus	*Fox Movietone Follies of 1929*
The Big Party	*The Girl from Woolworth's*
Bride of the Regiment	*Gold Diggers of Broadway*
Cameo Kirby	*Happy Days* (Grandeur version)
Chauve-Souris	*Hold Everything*
College Love	*The Home Towners*
Convention City	*Honky Tonk*
Fannie Foley Herself	*Is Everybody Happy?*
Footlights and Fools	*Let's Go Places*
The Forward Pass	*Lilies of the Field*

Little Johnny Jones	*The Patriot*
Love, Live and Laugh	*The Perfect Crime*
Melody Lane	*Queen of the Nightclubs*
The Melody of Love	*Red Hot Rhythm*
Mother Knows Best	*The Rogue Song*
My Man	*Smiling Irish Eyes*
Napoleon's Barber	*A Song of Kentucky*
No, No, Nanette	*Song o' My Heart* (Grandeur version)
Not Quite Decent	*Song of the Flame*
On Trial	*State Street Sadie*
One Mad Kiss	*Tenderloin*
The Painted Angel	*The Terror*
Paris	*Women They Talk About*

B. BLACK AND WHITE SURVIVORS

The following features, originally shot in color (or, where marked (S), with color sequences) survive only (or, as with *Sally* and *Show of Shows*, mostly) in black and white.

Bright Lights	*Manhattan Parade*
The Broadway Melody (S)	*On With the Show!*
The Dance of Life (S)	*Paramount on Parade* (finale)
The Desert Song (S)	*Puttin' on the Ritz* (S)
Fifty Million Frenchmen	*Sally*
Golden Dawn	*Show Girl in Hollywood* (S)
The Great Gabbo (S)	*The Show of Shows* (nearly all-color)
Kiss Me Again	*Song of the West*
The Life of the Party	*Sunny Side Up* (S)
The Lottery Bride (S)	*Sweet Kitty Bellairs*
Mammy (S)	

C. MISCELLANEOUS LOSSES

These films survive, in greater or lesser degree, fragmentarily. (C) indicates that the original color sequences are completely lost. The other losses are listed as appropriate.

Animal Crackers (edited reissue version survives)
Call of the Flesh (C)
Chasing Rainbows (C)
Glorious Betsy (soundtrack lost)
The Golden Calf (several reels lost)
Good News (C)
The Great Gabbo ("Ga Ga Bird" number lost)
Hallelujah (edited reissue version survives)
Horse Feathers (edited reissue version survives)

The Hollywood Revue of 1929 (opening recitation missing)
Leathernecking (C)
The Lion and the Mouse (soundtrack lost)
Love Me Tonight (edited reissue version survives)
The March of Time (portions survive)
Noah's Ark (shortened version survives)
Paramount on Parade (opening reel lost, plus soundtrack for several numbers)
Pretty Ladies (C)
Rio Rita (edited reissue version survives)
Say It With Songs (songs deleted from first reel)
Show Boat (shortened version survives only, without soundtrack)
The Singing Fool ("The Spaniard Who Blighted My Life")
So This Is Africa (censored version survives)
Syncopation (several reels lost)

Notes on Sources

Unless otherwise indicated, all film costs and grosses cited in the text are derived from the Warner Bros. Collection, University of Southern California (for Warners and First National films) and from the Eddie Mannix Collection, Margaret Herrick Library, Academy of Motion Picture Arts and Sciences (for MGM films).

Source abbreviations are as follows:

USC/WB   Warner Bros. Collection, University of Southern California
USC/MGM   Metro-Goldwyn Mayer Collection, University of Southern California
USC/Fox   Twentieth Century-Fox Collection, University of Southern California
NYPL   Performing Arts Research Center, The New York Public Library at Lincoln Center
AMPAS/MH   Margaret Herrick Library, Academy of Motion Picture Arts and Sciences

CHAPTER ONE

Kinetophones—Viola Dana: Interviewed for *Hollywood* documentary series (Thames Television, 1980); Harry Beaumont: "Film Plays Then and Now," *The New York Times*, February 10, 1929.

Chauve Souris—Variety, April 30, 1930; also, Bert Granet Oral History, American Museum of the Moving Image, Astoria, N.Y.

Vitaphone—"Her voice was far from attractive": *Photoplay*, October 1926. "Whether the Vitaphone is any better": Roy Chartier, *Billboard*, August 14, 1926. "It may be only a relatively short time": Mordaunt Hall, *The New York Times*, August 15, 1926. It averaged $23,000: *Variety*, April 27, 1927. "Almost precisely as the most extravagant booker": "Second Vitaphone Show Causes Much Discussion," *Billboard*, October 16, 1926.

Movietone—Fox Film Corporation had bought a significant interest: *Billboard*, October 16, 1929. Harry Lauder: Alexander Walker, *The Shattered Silents* (New York: William Morrow, 1979), p. 23; Ruby Keeler: Miles Kreuger to author.

Vitaphone's third outing—"Monotonous similarity": Sime, *Variety*, March 30, 1927. "[She] is caused": *The New Yorker*, February 12, 1927. Several theaters terminated their contracts: *Variety*, July 20, 1927.

The Jazz Singer—The chief source for this chronology is Robert L. Carringer's introduction to *The Jazz Singer* screenplay (University of Wisconsin Press, 1979), must reading for those interested in the sound revolution. The many differences between the final script and the finished film illuminate the collaborative, sometimes improvisatory nature of the filmmaking process, even in mainstream productions. "Jessel has a contract": *Variety*, May 25, 1927. "My Mammy," "It All Depends on You" and "Blue Skies": Vitaphone Production Reports, USC/WB. "I had a simple . . .": quoted in Carringer, p. 20. "Speaking pictures": *Variety*, November 30, 1927.

CHAPTER TWO

Tenderloin—"The players sound . . .": Chester E. Durgin, *Long Island Press*, August 14, 1928.

Glorious Betsy—"My God . . .": Conrad Nagel, quoted in *The Real Tinsel*, ed. Bernard Rosenberg and Harry Silverstein (New York: Macmillan, 1970), p. 184

Polls showed that . . . no one wished silents to go away: *Variety*, December 12, 1928, and January 30, 1929.

Lights of New York—"Hokumed junk . . .": *Variety*, July 11, 1928.

George Bernard Shaw—"That white whiskered lad . . .": *Variety*, June 27, 1928.

The Singing Fool—Premiere: *Film Daily*, September 20, 1928, and other reports. Exhibitors played Jolson's commercial recordings: *Variety* described the process in its August 8, 1928, issue, in connection with a Jersey City showing of *The Jazz Singer*. Exhibitor letters later reported that it was also done in connection with *The Singing Fool*. "Great entertainment": Roy Chartier, *Billboard*, September 29, 1928. "The Spaniard Who Blighted My Life": *The Singing Fool* music/legal files, USC/WB.

Technical inadequacies—*Noah's Ark:* Richard Koszarski, "On the Record: Seeing and Hearing the Vitaphone" in *The Dawn of Sound*, ed. Mary Lea Bandy (New York: Museum of Modern Art, 1989), p. 21. "On Saturday . . .": Mordaunt Hall, *The New York Times*, January 28, 1929. In Des Moines: "Talkers for Blind," *Variety*, February 20, 1929.

The Melody of Love—*Variety*, September 19 and December 22, 1928, among other accounts. "It is as if . . .": quoted in digest of *Melody of Love* reviews, *Film Daily*, October 30, 1928. "Most of the talking . . .": Edwards, *Variety*, October 17, 1928. "Sooner or later . . .": Sid, *Variety*, October 31, 1928.

Warners announced it would make no more all-talking films: *Variety*, December 19, 1928.

"PICTURES' MOST SENSATIONAL YEAR": *Variety*, January 2, 1929.

CHAPTER THREE

"The novelty of sound": Michael Wilmington, *Los Angeles Times*, February 18, 1990.

The Broadway Melody—Most of the recounting of its production derives from scripts and story and production notes, USC/MGM. Tests for leading man: *Variety* reported on October 10, 1928, that after fifty tests there was still no decision. "I had done . . .": Bessie Love, quoted in John Kobal, *Gotta Sing, Gotta Dance* (London: Hamlyn, 1971), p. 39. Pair of silk bloomers . . . : Louis Bull, "Unwanted Sounds Cause Humorous Talkie Trouble," *New York Graphic*, April 11, 1929. "At the time . . .": Love, in Kobal, p. 39. Page's hysteria: "Anita's Hysterics," *Variety*, November 7, 1928. "Coffin on wheels": Harry Beaumont, quoted in *Exhibitors Herald-World*, February 16, 1929. Stagehand in stocking feet: Bull, "Unwanted Sounds." Cut in "s": Ibid. "AS EXPECTED": *The New York Times*, February 11, 1929. "Fair faces and wild slang": Mordaunt Hall, *The New York Times*, February 17, 1929. "For anyone . . ." and ensuing quotes: René Clair, "The Art of Sound," in *Film Sound: Theory and Practice*, ed. Elisabeth Weis and John Belton (New York: Columbia University Press, 1985), pp. 92–95. Superimposed subtitles: *New York Herald-Tribune*, September 1, 1929; *Variety*, September 25, 1929. "The possibilities . . .": Sid, *Variety*, February 13, 1929. "The faces of the players . . .": Hugh Castle, "The Talkie Melody," *Close Up*, September 1929.

CHAPTER FOUR

"It was the night . . .": William Haines, quoted in Bob Thomas, *Thalberg: Life and Legend* (New York: Doubleday, 1969), p. 146.

Making of *The Desert Song*—Carlotta King's casting: *The Desert Song* program book. Legal obstacles: *Variety*, October 24, 1928, and February 20, 1929; *Billboard*, February 16, 1929. "There can be no permanent place . . ." Land, *Variety*, February 13, 1929.

Show Boat—A work as significant as this deserves its own book, and such is happily the case. Miles Kreuger's *Show Boat: The Story of a Classic American Musical* (rev. ed., New York: Da Capo Press, 1990) gives the most detailed possible history of *Show Boat* on stage and film.

Hearts in Dixie—"Balconies are liable . . .": Sid, *Variety*, March 6, 1929.

Syncopation—"A nance interior decorator": Bige, *Variety*, April 10, 1929.

Release of *The Desert Song*—"It is an interesting . . .": Mordaunt Hall, *The New York Times*, May 2, 1929.

Broadway—Cathedral of St. John the Divine: *Billboard*, June 8, 1929.

Fox Movietone Follies of 1929—Script drafts, USC/Fox. Jackie Cooper: interviewed in Hollywood, August 31, 1990. $750,000: *Variety*, December 12, 1928.

On With the Show!—"One imagines . . .": Mordaunt Hall, *The New York Times*, May 29, 1929. "The conversation consists . . .": *Photoplay*, August 1929.

Songs—All Warner productions would feature theme songs: Warners carried the announcement in press campaign books for several 1929 productions, including *On With the Show!* Audience overfamiliarity with stage songs: See "Aged Bordoni Songs," *Variety*, February 27, 1929. Top-selling songs in September 1928: *Variety*, September 26, 1928. Hal Roach and Thelma Todd: See *Billboard*, "Recording Clause in Film Contract," May 4, 1929. "Never before . . .": Jerry Hoffman, "Westward the Course of Tin-Pan Alley," *Photoplay*, September 1929. "The principal [song] . . ." John S. Cohen Jr., *The New York Sun*, December 26, 1931, quoted in *Photoplay*, March 1932. "Though all the orchestras . . .": Maurice Fenton, "Do-Re-Mi-Fa-Sol!" *Photoplay*, December 1929.

Sound processes—Warner films would be available with sound-on-film: *Variety*, May 28, 1930.

Photography—Rouben Mamoulian: Among the more extensive of the numerous chronicles of the making of *Applause* are the Mamoulian interview for *Sight and Sound*, reprinted in Charles Higham and Joel Greenberg, *The Celluloid Muse: Hollywood Directors Speak* (Chicago: Henry Regnery, 1971), and the interview with Mamoulian videotaped for The American Museum of the Moving Image. "Photography seems dead . . .": Land, *Variety*, May 29, 1929. "Helene Costello . . .": *Variety*, July 11, 1928. "Six months ago . . .": James R. Quirk, "Close-Ups and Long-Shots," *Photoplay*, May 1930. "The finest to date": *Photoplay*, March 1930. "The Technicolor work . . .": *Harrison's Reports*, January 11, 1930.

Performers—"The producers assembled . . .": *The New Movie*, March 1930.

Voice (and dance) doubles—"When you hear . . .": Mark Larkin, "The Truth About Voice Doubling," *Photoplay*, July 1929. *Mata Hari: Variety*, November 3, 1931.

CHAPTER SIX

"Having used up . . .": Sime, *Variety*, December 26, 1928.

Lucky Boy—An account of the filming of the sound sequences appeared in *Exhibitors Herald-World* on December 1, 1928.

The Rainbow Man—"Seldom has the screen . . .": quoted in digest of *The Rainbow Man* reviews, *Film Daily*, April 21, 1929. Far East tour: See "Talkie Roadshow for Orient," *Billboard*, September 21, 1929.

Innocents of Paris—"It is rather . . .": Peter Vischer, *Exhibitors Herald-World*, May 4, 1929.

Mother's Boy—See *Exhibitors Herald-World*, May 18, 1929, reporting on the problems attending the seating of critics at the opening.

Melody Lane—"Here we go again . . .": *Motion Picture*, October 1929.

Say It With Songs—"Zanuck probably couldn't . . .": *Exhibitors Herald-World*, October 19, 1929. Audience disillusionment with Jolson's sob-story style is reflected in many of the reviews. Songs deleted prior to the first TV runs: *Say It With Songs* music/legal correspondence, USC/WB

Blaze O' Glory—"Here is a production . . .": Jack Alicoate, *Film Daily*, December 31, 1929. Laudatory comments: See *Film Daily*, January 21, 1930. Father James

J. Halligan (Church of the Holy Name, New Rochelle) commented that *Blaze O'* *Glory* was "A wonderful, clean talkie [with] fine human interest and true military flavor."

CHAPTER SEVEN

The Hollywood Revue—Production reports, USC/MGM. "It's a picture . . .": *The Hollywood Revue of 1929* dialogue cutting continuity, NYPL.

The Show of Shows—"About half my crowd . . .": *Exhibitors Herald-World*, August 2, 1930.

Paramount On Parade—Dialogue Cutting Continuity: AMPAS/MH. "Just when the industry . . .": Waly, *Variety*, April 23, 1930.

King of Jazz—See John Murray Anderson's autobiography (as told to Hugh Abercrombie Anderson), *Out Without My Rubbers* (New York: Library Publishers, 1954), pp. 118–127.

"Revue All Cold . . .": *Variety*, May 14, 1930.

"Picture Audience Turning . . .": *Billboard*, June 14, 1930.

CHAPTER EIGHT

"By this time . . .": *Time*, April 22, 1929.

Gold Diggers of Broadway—See James Seymour, introduction to *Gold Diggers of 1933* screenplay (Madison: University of Wisconsin, 1980). Constance Talmadge: James R. Quirk, "Close-Ups and Long-Shots," *Photoplay*, June 1929.

Glorifying the American Girl—Reports of this project appeared in the trade press from 1926 on. Among the most detailed are those in *Exhibitors Herald-World* on May 18, 1929, and June 8, 1929, and a blind (but obvious) item in *Variety* on November 27, 1929. Rudy Vallee's visit to Astoria: Bert Granet Oral History, American Museum of the Moving Image. Reviews: see the digest of critical comments in *Film Daily*, February 9, 1930; also, *Photoplay*, January 1930. "Sound experimentation": *Variety*, November 27, 1929.

Smiling Irish Eyes—The controversy surrounding this film, and the protests by the United Irish Societies and various other groups, were covered in the Irish-American press in September 1929 and (after the Dublin fiasco) in February 1930. The relevant articles may be found in the Colleen Moore scrapbooks, AMPAS/MH.

Footlights and Fools: New York Telegraph, November 17, 1929.

Chasing Rainbows—"This one seems . . .": Douglas Fox, *Exhibitors Herald-World*, March 1, 1930.

"I got a little fed up . . .": Bessie Love, quoted in Kobal, *Gotta Sing Gotta Dance*, p. 40.

Howdy Broadway!—"Several well known stars . . .": *Exhibitors Herald-World*, October 12, 1929. Played well into 1930: In *Exhibitors Herald-World* on June 21, 1930, an Indiana exhibitor averred that *Howdy Broadway* "is not up to [the] standard set with other productions of this type."

A Song of Kentucky—"Lois Moran trying . . .": *Exhibitors Herald-World*, March 22, 1930.

Alice White—"She is a coarse . . .": quoted in digest of reviews of *The Girl from Woolworth's, Motion Picture News*, December 28, 1929. "She can't sing . . .": *Exhibitors Herald-World*, June 28, 1930. In the September 20 issue an exhibitor said of White in *Sweet Mama:* "Why make this girl sing? She can't and why insist? Poor singing queers all the pictures. You can't kid the public and make them like it."

She Couldn't Say No—"Winnie Lightner *should* . . .": *Photoplay*, May 1930.

Show Girl in Hollywood—Production records, USC/WB.

"Those clever Germans . . .": Jack Alicoate, *Film Daily*, January 30, 1930.

"So persistent . . .": *The New Yorker*, June 8, 1929. "The story is . . .": *Film Daily*, October 13, 1929. "About as good . . .": *New York Post*, quoted in digest of *Footlights and Fools* reviews, *Film Daily*, November 19, 1929. "Nothing better demonstrates . . .": *Billboard*, January 25, 1930. "Witness the present . . .": *The Nation*, March 5, 1930. "If [it] had been . . .": *Exhibitors Herald-World*, March 1, 1930. "If the public . . .": *Billboard*, March 8,1930.

Puttin' on the Ritz—"The birth and evolution . . .": *Exhibitors Herald-World*, September 1, 1928. $800,000: *Variety*, July 16, 1930. "Corking good picture . . .": Arthur W. Eddy, *Film Daily*, February 16, 1930; other review quotes reprinted in *Film Daily*, February 26 and March 7, 1930. "Another backstage story . . .": *Photoplay*, April 1930. Robert Usher: Michael Webb, "Robert Usher: Imagining Movies," *Architectural Digest*, April 1992. Usher's set sketches for *Puttin' on the Ritz* and *Be Yourself* have been preserved by the Museum of Modern Art Film Department.

The Great Gabbo—Hugh Herbert: The July 13, 1929 issue of *Exhibitors Herald-World* printed an on-set photograph of Herbert with Betty Compson. Jeanette MacDonald: *Variety*, May 8, 1929. Cruze's grand finale: *Variety*, June 19, 1929. "Carries a great punch . . .": *Film Daily*, September 15, 1929. "Right up in the front . . .": *Exhibitors Herald-World*, September 13, 1929. "Extraordinary . . .": *Exhibitors Herald-World*, September 21, 1929. "A great picture . . .": *Exhibitors Herald-World*, December 21, 1929. Stroheim's attempts to purchase the rights: See Richard Koszarski, *The Man You Loved to Hate: Erich von Stroheim and Hollywood* (New York: Oxford University Press, 1983), p. 232. Smeary color processing: *Variety*, September 18, 1929.

CHAPTER NINE

"The conventions . . .": "Screen Musical Comedy, Alexander Bakshy, *The Nation*, February 5, 1930.

"The Warners . . .": *Film Daily*, May 2, 1929; "The libretto . . .": *The New Yorker*, May 11, 1929; "Before musical plays . . ." quoted in digest of *Desert Song* reviews, *Film Daily*, July 1, 1929.

The Five O'Clock Girl—*Motion Picture News*, January 5, 1929; *Variety*, January 16 and 23, 1929; *Billboard*, March 2, 1929.

Rio Rita—See Bebe Daniels's account of the production in Kobal, *Gotta Sing Gotta Dance*, pp. 27–33. The exhibitor poll in which she placed fourth was reported in *Exhibitors Herald-World*, December 29, 1928. Placing ahead of Daniels were Clara

Bow, Colleen Moore, and Billie Dove. Walter Plunkett: Interviewed in Kobal, *Gotta Sing Gotta Dance*, pp. 33–36, and in David Chierichetti, *Hollywood Costume Design* (New York: Harmony Books, 1976), pp. 42–43. "I got to be . . .": Dorothy Lee, interviewed in Hollywood, September 1, 1991. The greatest praise was reserved for Daniels: all quotes reprinted in *Rio Rita* trade ads in *Film Daily*, October 8 and October 29, 1929.

Little Johnny Jones—Ottawa cancellation: *Motion Picture News*, April 5, 1930.

Sally—"$1,000 per hour . . .": the figure was cited in *Photoplay*, October 1929, among other places. Jack L. Warner: Bob Thomas, *Clown Prince of Hollywood: The Antic Life and Times of Jack L. Warner* (New York: McGraw-Hill, 1990), pp. 69–71. 135 degrees: *Variety*, July 24, 1929; also mentioned (and exaggerated) in the *Sally* program.

No, No, Nanette—"[By] placing the music . . .": quoted in digest of *No, No, Nanette* reviews, *Film Daily*, February 4, 1930.

Spring is Here—"Just a light frappe . . .": *Film Daily*, July 20, 1930.

Good News—"This one, like the pardon . . .": *Photoplay*, August 1930.

Sunny—$225,000 salary: budget sheets for *Sunny*, USC/WB.

Great Day—"Story revision . . .": *Variety*, August 20, 1930.

Whoopee—"Not a filmusical . . .": Walter R. Greene, *Motion Picture News*, July 12, 1930.

CHAPTER TEN

Sunny Side Up—Hugh Trevor: *Motion Picture News*, June 8, 1929. $3.5 million: Aubry Solomon: *Twentieth Century-Fox: A Corporate and Financial History* (Metuchen, N.J.: Scarecrow Press, 1988), p. 10.

High Society Blues—Janet Gaynor's reaction to this film was recounted in Harriet Parsons, "Janet Goes to War!," *Photoplay*, August 1930, pp. 38+.

The Battle of Paris—"The strangest mixture . . .": James F. Lundy, *Billboard*, February 8, 1930.

Tanned Legs—Reports of the aborted first production are given in *Exhibitors Herald-World*, July 27, 1929, and August 3, 1929, and Variety, August 7, 1929.

The Vagabond Lover—"Buck teeth . . .": Douglas Fox, *Exhibitors Herald-World*, December 7, 1929. "For gosh sakes . . .": *Photoplay*, December 1929.

Just Imagine—Ruby Keeler: *Variety*, June 11, 1930. Hermann Schultz: DeSylva, Brown and Henderson script dated May 7, 1930, with none of Brendel's Scandinavian shtick, in USC/Fox. "The most irresistible man . . .": "El Steals Another," *Motion Picture*, May 1930. $1.1 million: Solomon, *Twentieth Century-Fox*, p. 238.

Madam Satan—Production reports, USC/MGM. DeMille's contest: *Exhibitors Herald-World*, February 23, 1929.

CHAPTER ELEVEN

Check and Double Check—Freak hit: *Variety*, December 10, 1930, reported that the gross would reach between $2.3 and $2.6 million, on an initial investment of about $1.1 million. The reason for the high production cost, beside Gosden and Correll's high guarantee, was that Radio Pictures was "obligated to assume the additional expense of keeping the two boys on the air during the making on the Coast," which ran to about $15,000 per week.

The Cuckoos—Roscoe Arbuckle: See *Variety*, January 29, 1930, and March 5, 1930. Arbuckle reportedly directed many of Wheeler and Woolsey's scenes and devised a number of gags.

The Florodora Girl—Lawsuit: see *Billboard*, July 26, 1930, and *Variety*, April 19, 1932.

Are You There?—"The average audience . . .": Red [Maurice] Kann, *Motion Picture News*, November 29, 1930.

CHAPTER TWELVE

Song O' My Heart—McCormack's salary: *Billboard*, May 4, 1929, and *Variety*, September 10, 1930; the latter article stated that McCormack was asking $650,000 for a second film.

The Rogue Song: production records and Dialogue Cutting Continuity, USC/MGM.

The Love Parade—"Introduced logically . . .": Maurice Kann, "Chevalier's Second," *Motion Picture News*, September 28, 1929. Protests from church groups: Letters and reports in the MPAA (formerly MPPDA, or Hays Office) file on *The Love Parade*, AMPAS/MHL. The film was extensively cut in Pennsylvania, with a number of cuts also in Ohio and Chicago.

The Vagabond King—$1.25 million: *Variety*, September 25, 1929; earlier it had been reported that the film rights alone had cost $200,000, and Dennis King's salary was given as $8,500 per week. Natalie Kalmus: See interview in *Exhibitors Herald-World*, November 9, 1929. Retakes by Ernst Lubitsch: *Variety*, December 25, 1929.

Captain of the Guards—See the report on the Fejos-Junior Laemmle contretemps in *Motion Picture News*, March 29, 1930. Ban in France: *Variety*, April 16, 1930.

Dixiana—See Bebe Daniels, interview in Kobal, *Gotta Sing Gotta Dance*, p. 33.

Song of the West—Lila Lee: Contract dated March 6, 1929, USC/WB. "Slovenly, ugly . . .": quoted in digest of *Song of the West* reviews, *Film Daily*, March 11, 1930.

Golden Dawn—"Reason totters . . .": Lucius Beebe, *New York Herald-Tribune*, July 26, 1930. Woolf-Warners suit: *Film Daily*, March 2, 1932, and *Variety*, March 8, 1932. Ban in the South: "*Golden Dawn* Pulled in South; Race Angle," *Motion Picture News*, August 2, 1930.

Viennese Nights—Romberg and Hammerstein's contract: Some of the particulars were listed in *Time*'s review of December 8, 1930.

Sweet Kitty Bellairs—"This frothy pastel-shaded comedy . . .": Rush, *Variety*, September 10, 1930.

The Merry Widow—*Variety*, October 22, 1930.

Decline of operettas: See "Musicals and Operettas," *Variety*, June 25, 1930, and remarks in city-by-city grosses for such films as *Bride of the Regiment*. (See also Chapter Fourteen.)

CHAPTER THIRTEEN

The Cock Eyed World—An obscene amount of money: In *Twentieth Century Fox: A Corporate and Financial History*, Aubry Solomon gives the gross as $2.7 million.

Hallelujah!—"If that's the way . . .": King Vidor, *A Tree Is a Tree* (New York: Harcourt, Brace, 1952), p. 176. *Variety* ran reviews: August 28, 1929. Land saw *Hallelujah!* at the Embassy, and Mark viewed it at the Lafayette in Harlem. Ban in the South: *Variety*, January 15, 1930.

Applause—"Decided to do the exact opposite . . .": Rouben Mamoulian, *Sight and Sound* interview reprinted in Higham and Greenberg, *The Celluloid Muse*, p. 130. Mae West: *Variety*, April 10, 1929. "*Applesauce*": See accounts of the making of *Applause* in *Exhibitors Herald-World*, July 13, July 20, August 10, and August 24, 1929. "This is a curious one . . .": *Photoplay*, January 1930.

Peacock Alley—Legal animosity: *Variety*, March 12, 1930; *Motion Picture News*, March 22, 1930, *Exhibitors Herald-World*, March 22, 1930. Murray sued Tiffany for $1.75 million, charging that her "professional reputation was damaged by the way *Peacock Alley* was produced." The suit was later dropped. A letter by a Texas exhibitor to *Exhibitors Herald-World* (May 3) cracked: "If Mae Murray hadn't sued Tiffany for making this somebody else would."

Gloria Swanson and *The Trespasser*—A deal to coproduce *Kelly:* Joseph P. Kennedy, [unsent] telegram to E. B. Derr of Pathé, January 8, 1930. (Memo mentions that matter was discussed instead by telephone.) Pathé Film Exchange General Matters File, AMPAS/MHL. Franz Lehar: *Film Daily*, January 7 and February 23, 1930; *Exhibitors Herald-World*, February 15, 1930; *Variety*, April 9, 1930. Audiences on Swanson's singing: Transcriptions of preview card comments on *What a Widow!* (Pathé General Matters File, AMPAS/MHL) reveal that while most spectators were disappointed in the film nearly everyone was highly enthusiastic about her vocal performance.

CHAPTER FOURTEEN

As many as three hundred songwriters: "Dropping of Song Writers Saves $100,000 Weekly," *Billboard*, December 6, 1930.

"Speculating over the reason . . .": "The Musicals Strike Some Sour Notes," editorial by Maurice Kann, *Motion Picture News*, April 5, 1930.

"In certain communities . . .": Aaronson, *Motion Picture Herald*, September 30, 1933.

"Characters bursting into song . . .": See "Theme Songs Within Reason or Producers Will Cut 'Em," *Billboard*, May 31, 1930, and "Picture Audiences Turning 'Thumbs Down' on Revues," *Billboard*, June 14, 1930.

Technicolor—Expansion of the company's facilities: "What? Color in the Movies Again?," *Fortune*, October 1934.

"In spite of a lot . . .": *Photoplay*, October 1930. "Exquisite coloring . . .": *Billboard*, August 23, 1930. "Typical operetta flop . . .": *Variety*, July 9, 1930. "A big flop . . .": *Exhibitors Herald-World*, December 20, 1930. "A better title for me . . .": *Exhibitors Herald-World*, April 26, 1930.

The Southerner/The Prodigal—Dialogue cutting continuities of *The Southerner* (dated February 2, 1931) and *The Prodigal* (March 7, 1931) reveal the cuts made (USC/MGM).

Children of Dreams—"Another reason . . .": *Photoplay*, April 1931.

$1 million-plus loss on *King of Jazz:* See "$1,000,000 'Jazz' Loss and 'Abie' Suit in 'U's' Drop of 2 Million," *Motion Picture Herald*, March 21, 1931. Universal's net loss for 1930 was $2,047,821, and it was stated that the loss on *King of Jazz* would have been greater were it not for the strong European response.

Jolson-Schenck deal: "Al and Joe," *Motion Picture News*, October 25, 1930.

Reaching for the Moon—Lucky Break: Motion Picture News, May 10, 1930. Ruby Keeler: *Variety*, May 28, 1930. Ginger Rogers: *Film Daily*, June 15 and June 29, 1930. $1.1 million: Scott Eyman, *Mary Pickford: America's Sweetheart* (New York: Donald I. Fine, 1990), p. 204. Six Berlin songs: One of these ["Do You Believe Your Eyes (Or Do You Believe Your Baby)"] was performed at a Berlin tribute at Symphony Space in New York in 1994. One song reportedly sung by Fairbanks: *Variety*, June 28, 1930. Berlin would become incensed: Laurence Bergreen, *As Thousands Cheer: The Life of Irving Berlin* (New York: Viking, 1990), p. 532.

The March of Time—The chief source of information is the production file, including memos and script fragments, USC/MGM. *Wir Schatten Um auf Hollywood!* . . . *The Devil's Cabaret:* Dialogue cutting continuities, USC/MGM; also, *Variety*, November 5 and 19, 1930. A massive pile of scripts: *Broadway to Hollywood* script files, USC/MGM. A dark joke: The USC *Broadway to Hollywood* files contain a *March of Time* parody by Lew Lipton, with contributions by Moss Hart, dated December 1932. Done in the form of a scenario, it concerns a writer (Donald Ogden Stewart) who tries to break the *March of Time* jinx and finally does so by having Jimmy Durante supply ridiculous narration over the original numbers. It turns out to be a dream; *The March of Time* survives unconquered.

"MUSICAL FILMS ARE TABOO": *Billboard*, August 23, 1930.

CHAPTER FIFTEEN

Viennese Nights in Australia: *Film Daily*, August 9, 1931.

The Smiling Lieutenant—Paramount's biggest-grossing film: "1931 Survey of Film Leaders," *Variety*, January 5, 1932.

Palmy Days—Cantor's salary increase: *Variety*, November 5, 1930. "To help President Hoover": *Motion Picture Herald*, September 5, 1931.

Delicious—Show Girl . . . East is West: Edward Jablonski, *Gershwin* (New York: Doubleday, 1987), p. 206. "Encourage this clean picture . . .": *Photoplay*, February 1932.

Girl Crazy—Norman Taurog: *Variety*, February 2, 1932; Busby Berkeley: *Variety*, February 16, 1932. $700,000: *Variety*, March 1, 1932.

One Hour With You—Much of the information regarding the George Cukor situation is from Cukor's notarized deposition (February 17, 1932) to the Supreme Court, New York County, in the matter of Cukor vs. Paramount Pictures. Also, an exhibit in the suit—a Lubitsch memo to Cukor dated February 12, 1932. (Both in the Cukor Collection, AMPAS/MHL.) $1.1 million: The *Film Daily* report of Paramount's receivership difficulties (February 1, 1933) lists the official cost of *One Hour With You* as $1,135,000. "I may have shot . . ." and subsequent quotes: George Cukor, interviewed in Carlos Clarens, *Cukor* (London: Secker & Warburg, 1976), pp. 129–130.

"Old Man Gloom's Around": *Variety*, May 20, 1931.

Love Me Tonight—Robert Coogan: *Film Daily*, January 6, 1932. Over a million dollars: *Variety*, May 31, 1932. "[His] tragedy is that of . . .": Andrew Sarris, *The American Cinema* (New York: E. P. Dutton, 1968), p. 160. A fairy tale: Rouben Mamoulian, *Sight and Sound* interview reprinted in Higham and Greenberg, *The Celluloid Muse*, p. 136. Four deletions were made . . ."Reconsider": MPAA file on *Love Me Tonight*, AMPAS/MHL.

The Phantom President—George M. Cohan: See *Variety*, October 11, 1932, and January 10, 1933; also, Richard Rodgers, *Musical Stages: An Autobiography* (New York: Random House, 1975), p. 154.

The Big Broadcast—Script drafts, AMPAS/MH. The demographic message: See *Variety*, November 8, 1932.

Hallelujah, I'm a Bum—Salary advances: *Variety*, April 19, 1932. Harry D'Arrast . . . Chester Erskin: *Variety*, July 12 and August 2, 1932; *Film Daily*, July 13 and August 12, 1932. "Color Line" and "Five Cents in My Pocket": *Variety*, August 30, 1932. Milestone . . . took full control: *Variety*, December 13, 1932; *Film Daily*, December 15, 1932. In his unpublished memoirs (Lewis Milestone collection, AMPAS/MHL) Milestone states that he took over from Harry D'Arrast at the last minute, and does not mention Erskin.

CHAPTER SIXTEEN

42nd Street—Production notes, USC/WB. Bradford Ropes's novel: See Rocco Fumenti, Introduction to *42nd Street* screenplay (Madison: University of Wisconsin, 1980). Casting choices: production notes and also *Motion Picture*, March 1933; *Film Daily*, August 24, September 1 and September 19, 1932. The *42nd Street* Special: Bette Davis recalled the tour in several television interviews in the late 1970s; she also discussed it in her autobiography, *The Lonely Life* (New York: G. P. Putnam's Sons, 1962), in which her account is somewhat less acrid than in later years. *Variety*'s review: Abel, *Variety*, March 14, 1933.

"He was the world's greatest . . .": Ruby Keeler apparently used this line (in several variants) a few times, once to an audience at a New York film tribute in 1984.

Hello, Everybody!—Kate Smith rejected Paramount's story ideas: *Variety*, September 13, 1932. The lead character's name: The screenplay drafts and script for *Hello, Everybody!* (Paramount Collection, AMPAS/MHL) all show the character's name as Kate Beverly. Handbills with diet tips: *Variety*, February 14, 1933.

She Done Him Wrong—Mae West on *Hello, Everybody!:* George Eels and Stanley Musgrove, *Mae West* (New York: William Morrow, 1982), p. 122.

Duck Soup—"Change the name of your town . . .": *Film Daily*, October 26, 1933. The first cut: *Variety*, October 31, 1933, which recounted the extreme secrecy under which *Duck Soup* was previewed, and also stated that forty-five minutes had been deleted.

Delicious—Erich von Stroheim: *Variety*, August 16, October 10, and November 29, 1932.

I'm No Angel—"The Bull's Eye": *Variety*, January 31, 1933. Among the titles she rejected: *Variety*, April 11, 1933.

I Married an Angel: Play and film scripts, song lyrics, and notes, USC/MGM. "Aside and apart . . .": Joseph I. Breen, letter of February 2, 1935, to Louis B. Mayer, *I Married an Angel* MPAA file, AMPAS/MHL. Earlier, Rodgers and Hart had submitted for approval the lyrics of the following songs: "We're Together Again," "I'm Thru With Saying I'm Thru," "Tell Me I Know How to Love," "I Married an Angel," "The First Thing I Know," "Come a Little Closer."

Jack Warner stated . . . two musicals: "Only 2 Musicals at WB to Avoid Cycle Repetition," *Variety*, January 31, 1933.

Gold Diggers of 1933—"Forgotten Man" moved to finale: *Variety*, May 30, 1933.

Footlight Parade—Stanley Smith: *Variety*, June 20 and July 11, 1933; *Film Daily*, July 6, 1933. Berkeley and Ceballos: *Variety*, June 20 and August 15, 1933.

Moonlight and Pretzels—$100,000 budget: "Cheaper Films Made East," *Variety*, July 4, 1933, also *Variety*, July 11, 1933.

The March of Time and *Broadway to Hollywood*—Script files and production notes, USC/MGM.

Dancing Lady—USC/MGM; see also Ronald Haver's account of the production in *David O. Selznick's Hollywood* (New York: Alfred A. Knopf, 1980), pp. 136–148.

Too Much Harmony—Sequel to *Close Harmony: Variety*, April 18, 1933.

Flying Down to Rio—Pert Kelton: *Film Daily*, July 18, 1933; *Variety*, July 18, 1933.

CHAPTER SEVENTEEN

"Wrong entertainment . . .": The Motion Picture Production Code of 1930, reprinted in *The Movies in Our Midst*, ed. Gerald Mast, pp. 321–333.

"DEADLINE FOR FILM DIRT": *Variety*, June 13, 1933.

Dames song for Joan Blondell: *Dames* production notes and Hal Wallis memo to Busby Berkeley (March 19, 1934), USC/WB.

It Ain't No Sin/Belle of the Nineties—West suggestion to drop the title: *Variety*, July 3, 1934.

The Legion of Decency—A few musicals were cited: Notes from the first meeting of the Legion of Decency (Detroit, May 13, 1934), in *Wonder Bar* MPAA file, AMPAS/MHL.

Wonder Bar—Al Jolson: *Wonder Bar* contract (June 29, 1933), USC/WB. Grandhotel: *Variety*, November 7, 1933. Original cast announcements: *Wonder Bar* production records, USC/ WB, also *Variety*, August 1, 1933, and Warner Bros. trade ad in *Variety*, August 8, 1933. "Ménage à l'infini": Program notes, "Warner Bros. Before the Code" series, Film Forum 2, New York City, 1994. A few state censors . . . Joe Breen: MPAA file on *Murder at the Vanities*, AMPAS/MHL.

Hollywood Party—Script files and production notes, USC/MGM; also, Henry Jenkins, *What Made Pistachio Nuts? Early Sound Comedy and the Vaudeville Aesthetic* (New York: Columbia University Press, 1992), pp. 107–128.

I Am Suzanne!—Jay Gorney: Letter of November 14, 1933 from Jesse L. Lasky (producer of *I Am Suzanne!*) to Gorney explaining why he was contractually bound to give the *Suzanne* writing credit to Rowland Lee and Edwin Justus Mayer. Courtesy Mrs. Sandra Gorney.

Stand Up and Cheer—Scripts and notes, USC/Fox. Title change: *Variety*, February 27, 1934.

The Cat and the Fiddle—Scripts and production notes, USC/MGM; also, MPAA file, AMPAS/MHL.

The Merry Widow—Candidates for the title role: See *Film Daily*, September 19, 1933, *Variety*, January 30 and March 13, 1934. The Hays Office: MPAA file on *The Merry Widow*, AMPAS/MHL. "The picture as it now stands . . ." Joseph I. Breen memo to Will H. Hays, October 22, 1934, AMPAS/MHL. "Immoral relationship . . .": Joseph I. Breen, letter of April 19, 1937 to Louis B. Mayer, AMPAS/MHL.

Dames—Remake of *No, No, Nanette: Dames* script file and production records, USC/WB.

Selected Bibliography

Many of the areas considered in these pages have been touched upon in segments of the extensive film literature. However, the only previous book solely devoted to this same era of musical film is the compendium of articles on musicals taken from issues of *Photoplay* between 1926 and early 1933. Other works have covered the various aspects of the period with widely diverse degrees of depth, comprehension, and accuracy. Similarly, the birth of sound per se, particularly its aesthetic ramifications, has received noticeably scant treatment, although the Walker and Geduld books are recommended. As channels for further investigation, the sources listed below run the gamut from essential reference to esoteric curiosity, from the scholarly to the near-obsolete to the gossipy. In some the illustrations, not the text, carry the primary value; a few can only be viewed as essential.

A. BOOKS ON MUSICAL FILM

Altman, Rick. *The American Film Musical.* Bloomington: Indiana University Press, 1987.

——, ed. *Genre: The Musical; A Reader.* London: Routledge & Kegan Paul, 1981.

Burton, Jack. *The Blue Book of Hollywood Musicals.* Watkins Glen, N.Y.: Century House, 1953.

Carringer, Robert L., ed. *The Jazz Singer.* University of Wisconsin Press, 1979.

Delamater, Jerome. *Dance in the Hollywood Musical.* Ann Arbor: U.M.I. Research Press, 1978.

Feuer, Jane. *The Hollywood Musical.* Bloomington: Indiana University Press, 1982.

Fordin, Hugh. *The World of Entertainment: Hollywood's Greatest Musicals.* Garden City, N.Y.: Doubleday, 1975.

Fumento, Rocco, ed. *42nd Street.* Madison: University of Wisconsin Press, 1980.

Harris, Steve. *Film, Television and Stage Music on Phonograph Records: A Discography.* Jefferson, N.C.: McFarland & Company, 1988.

Hirschhorn, Clive. *The Hollywood Musical*. New York: Crown, 1981.

Kobal, John. *Gotta Sing Gotta Dance. A Pictorial History of Film Musicals*. London: Hamlyn, 1971; rev. ed., London: Spring Books, 1983.

Kreuger, Miles, ed. *The Movie Musical from Vitaphone to 42nd Street: As Reported in a Great Fan Magazine*. New York: Dover, 1975.

Mast, Gerald. *Can't Help Singin': The American Musical on Stage and Screen*. Woodstock, N.Y.: The Overlook Press, 1987.

McVay, Douglas. *The Musical Film*. New York: Barnes, 1967.

Mordden, Ethan. *The Hollywood Musical*. New York: St. Martin's Press, 1981.

Raymond, Jack. *Show Music on Record*. Washington: Smithsonian Institution Press, 1992.

Sennett, Ted. *Hollywood Musicals*. New York: Harry N. Abrams, 1981.

Seymour, James, ed. *Gold Diggers of 1933*. Madison: University of Wisconsin Press, 1980.

Springer, John. *All Talking! All Singing! All Dancing!* New York: Citadel, 1966.

Stern, Lee Edward. *The Movie Musical*. New York: Pyramid, 1974.

Vallance, Tom. *The American Musical*. New York: Barnes, 1970.

B. OTHER WORKS ON FILM

Balio, Tino, ed. *The American Film Industry*. Madison: The University of Wisconsin Press, 1976.

Bandy, Mary Lea, ed. *American Moviemakers: The Dawn of Sound*. New York: Museum of Modern Art, 1989.

Bergman, Andrew. *We're in the Money: Depression America and Its Films*. New York: New York University Press, 1971.

Bordwell, David, Staiger, Janet, and Thompson, Kristin. *The Classical Hollywood Cinema: Film Style and Mode of Production to 1960*. New York: Columbia University Press, 1985.

Dooley, Roger. *From Scarface to Scarlett: American Films in the 1930s*. New York: Harcourt Brace Jovanovich, 1979.

Geduld, Harry M. *The Birth of the Talkies: From Edison to Jolson*. Bloomington: Indiana University Press, 1975.

Higham, Charles. *Warner Brothers*. New York: Charles Scribner's Sons, 1975.

———, and Greenberg, Joel. *The Celluloid Muse: Hollywood Directors Speak*. Chicago: Henry Regnery, 1971.

Hirschhorn, Clive. *The Warner Bros. Story*. New York: Crown, 1979.

Jacobs, Lewis. *The Rise of the American Film: A Critical History*. New York: Harcourt, Brace & Co., 1939.

Jenkins, Henry. *What Made Pistachio Nuts? Early Sound Comedy and the Vaudeville Aesthetic*. New York, Columbia University Press, 1992.

Jewell, Richard B., and Harbin, Vernon. *The RKO Story*. New York: Arlington House, 1982.

Katz, Ephraim. *The Film Encyclopedia*. New York: Harper & Row, 1979.

Limbacher, James L. *Four Aspects of Film*. New York: Brussel & Brussel, 1968.

Mast, Gerald, ed. *The Movies in Our Midst: Documents in the Cultural History of Film in America*. Chicago: University of Chicago Press, 1982.

Rosenberg, Bernard, and Silverstein, Harry, eds. *The Real Tinsel*. New York: Macmillan, 1970.

Sklar, Robert. *Movie-Made America: A Cultural History of American Movies*. New York: Vintage Books, 1975.

Solomon, Aubry. *Twentieth Century-Fox: A Corporate and Financial History* (Metuchen, N.J.: Scarecrow Press, 1988.

Walker, Alexander. *The Shattered Silents: How the Talkies Came to Stay*. New York: William Morrow and Company, 1979.

Weis, Elisabeth, and Belton, John, eds. *Film Sound: Theory and Practice*. New York: Columbia University Press, 1985.

C. BIOGRAPHIES AND AUTOBIOGRAPHIES

Anderson, John Murray, and Anderson, Hugh Abercrombie. *Out Without My Rubbers*. New York: Library Publishers, 1954.

Behr, Edward. *Thank Heaven for Little Girls: The True Story of Maurice Chevalier's Life and Times*. London: Hutchinson, 1993.

Berg, A. Scott. *Goldwyn: A Biography*. New York: Alfred A. Knopf, 1989.

Bergreen, Laurence. *As Thousands Cheer: The Life of Irving Berlin*. New York: Viking, 1990.

Cantor, Eddie, and Ardmore, Jane Kesner. *Take My Life*. Garden City: Doubleday, 1957.

Clarens, Carlos. *Cukor*. London: Secker & Warburg, 1976.

Croce, Arlene. *The Fred Astaire and Ginger Rogers Book*. New York: Galahad Books, 1972.

DeMille, Cecil B. *The Autobiography of Cecil B. DeMille*, ed. Donald Hayne. Englewood Cliffs, N.J.: Prentice-Hall, 1959.

Goldman, Herbert G. *Jolson: The Legend Comes to Life*. New York: Oxford University Press, 1988.

Harris, Warren G. *The Other Marilyn: A Biography of Marilyn Miller*. New York: Arbor House, 1985.

Haver, Ronald. *David O. Selznick's Hollywood*. New York: Alfred A. Knopf, 1980.

Jablonski, Edward. *Gershwin*. New York: Doubleday, 1987.

Jessel, George. *The World I Lived In*. Chicago: Henry Regnery, 1975.

Knowles, Eleanor. *The Films of Jeanette MacDonald and Nelson Eddy*. New York: Barnes, 1974.

Koszarski, Richard. *The Man You Loved to Hate: Erich von Stroheim and Hollywood*. New York: Oxford University Press, 1983.

Kostilibas-Davis, James, and Loy, Myrna. *Myrna Loy: Being and Becoming*. New York: Alfred A. Knopf, 1987.

Love, Bessie. *From Hollywood with Love*. London: Elm Tree Press, 1978.

McGilligan, Patrick. *George Cukor: A Double Life*. New York: St. Martin's Press, 1991.

Milne, Tom. *Mamoulian*. London: Thames & Hudson, 1969.

Mueller, John. *Astaire Dancing: The Musical Films*. New York: Wings Books, 1985.

Pike, Bob, and Martin, Dave. *The Genius of Busby Berkeley*. Reseda, Calif.: Creative Film Society, 1973.

Ringgold, Gene, and Bodeen, DeWitt. *Chevalier: The Films and Career of Maurice Chevalier.* Secaucus, N.J.: Citadel Press, 1973.

Rodgers, Richard. *Musical Stages: An Autobiography.* New York: Random House, 1975.

Thomas, Bob. *Clown Prince of Hollywood: The Antic Life and Times of Jack L. Warner.* New York: McGraw-Hill, 1990.

———. *Thalberg: Life and Legend.* New York: Doubleday, 1969.

Vidor, King. *A Tree Is a Tree.* New York: Harcourt, Brace, 1952.

Weinberg, Herman. *The Lubitsch Touch.* New York: Dover, 1977.

D. MISCELLANEOUS BOOKS

Bordman, Gerald. *American Musical Theatre: A Chronicle.* 2nd ed. New York: Oxford University Press, 1992.

Jauss, Hans Robert. *Toward an Aesthetic of Reception.* Trans. Timothy Bahti. London: Harvester Press, 1982.

Kreuger, Miles. *Show Boat: The Story of a Classic American Musical.* Rev. ed. New York: Da Capo Press, 1990.

Lissauer, Robert, *Lissauer's Encyclopedia of Popular Music in America: 1888 to the Present.* New York: Paragon House, 1991.

Mordden, Ethan. *Broadway Babies: The People Who Made the American Musical.* New York: Oxford University Press, 1983.

E. SELECTED PERIODICALS

Billboard

Close Up

Exhibitors Herald-World

Film Daily

Fortune

Harrison's Reports

Los Angeles Times

Motion Picture

Motion Picture Herald

Motion Picture News

The Nation

New York Herald-Tribune

The New Movie

The New York Times

The New Yorker

Photoplay

Time

Vanity Fair

Variety [Weekly]

Index

Page numbers in italics refer to photographs appearing on those pages.

Jolson, Al, 5, 13, 27, 27 n. 12, 30, 31–35, *36*, 37–40, 46, 49–53, *51*, 55, 59, 61, 82, 103, 132, 143–44, 152–54, 169, 169 n.9, 211, 240, 245, 264, 335, 359, 367–70, 376, 378, 378 n.6, 390, 400–401, 413–15, *414*, 432, 434, 435; emulators of, 48, 93, 143–60 passim, 214, 215

Jolson, Harry, 152

Jordan, Dorothy, 98, 98 n.13, *134*, 258 n.6, 289, 405

Joyce, Peggy Hopkins, 401 n.19

Joyner, Joyzelle, 257–58, 258 n.5

Judels, Charles, 273

June Moon, 115

Just Imagine, 112, 121, 256–58, 261, 270, 329, 383, 403, 406

Kahn, Gus, 406

Kaley, Charles, 136, 204, 206

Kalman, Emmerich, 301

Kalmar, Bert, and Ruby, Harry, 112–13, 225, 268–69, 274, 381, 382, 412

Kalmus, Herbert T., 72, 73, 122–25, 327–28. *See also* Technicolor

Kalmus, Natalie, 293. *See also* Technicolor

Kane, Helen, 132, 179, 206, 249

Kaufman, George S., 93, 93 n.8, 403

Kaye, Danny, 264, 277

Kearns, Allen, 134, 252

Keaton, Buster, 132, 163 n.1, 164, 167, 167 n.6, 168, 210, 262, 271–72, 272 n.5, 277

Keeler, Ruby, 28 n.14, 75, 153, 192 n.3, 211, 256, 335, 373, 375–76, 376 n.3, 376–78, 378 n.6, 384, 389–92, *393*, 400–401, 426–27, 434

Keene, Richard, 176

Keith-Albee Circuit, 30

Kellum, Orlando E., 15

Kelly, Gene, 3, 5, 129, 143 n.1, 168, 435

Kelly, Kitty, 352, 400

Kelly, Patsy, 399

Kelly, Paul, 401 n.19

Kelton, Pert, 233, 405

Kennedy, Joseph P., 11, 48, 86, 319–20

Kennedy, Merna, 95, 96, 98, 414

Kenyon, Doris, 56

Kern, Jerome, 82, 90, 222, 232, 234 n.8, 237, 332, 422–23

Kibbee, Guy, 192 n.3, 414, 426

Kid Boots, 222, 224

Kid Millions, 404 n.21, 427

Kid from Spain, The, 366–67, 367 n.17, 369, 377, 391

Kiepura, Jan, 381, 434

Kiki, 333 n.6

Kinetophone, 14–15

Kinetophonograph, 14

King, Carlotta, *79*, 80, 92–93, 103 n.16, 138, 280, 307, 329

King, Charles, 63, *67*, 71, 75, 75 n.17, 109, 133, 163 n.1, 164, 165, 168, 200–201, 201 n.8, 225, 270, 329, 340

King, Dennis, 134, 293–95, 329, 381

King, Jack, 112, 259

King of Jazz, 9, 11, 115, 127–28, 179, 180 n.16, 181–87, *185*, 295, 297, 324, 333, 338, 365, 381, 392, 421

King Kelly of the USA, 427

King of Kings, The (1927), 73 n.14, 170

King Kong (1933), 227, 361, 377, 385, 388

Kiss Me Again (1931), 121, 305–6, 329, 330, 338, 341, 342, 394 n.15

Kiss in a Taxi, A, 226

Klages, Raymond, and Greer, Jesse, 112

Knight, June, 400

Kober, Arthur, 383

Kohler, Fred, 207

Kolker, Henry, 414

Korda, Alexander, 255, 317

Kubrick, Stanley, 259

Kusell, Maurice, 131, 131 n.17, 219–21, 335

La Plante, Laura, 82, 90, 141, 141 n.20, 185, 297, 377

Lady in Ermine, The. See *Bride of the Regiment*

Lady's Morals, A, 127, 287, *288*, 337, 428

Laemmle, Carl, Sr., 54, 81–82, 90, 91, 95–96, 181, 182, 186, 297, 333, 381, 392

Laemmle, Carl, Jr., 95, 181, 297

Lahr, Bert, 10, 238, 263, 348

Lake, Arthur, 100, 102, 103 n.16, 252, *253*

Lake, Hariette [Ann Sothern], 173, 428 n.15

Lane, Burton, and Adamson, Harold, 397

Lane, Lola, 98, 238 n.11

Lane, Lupino, 130, 292, 302, 304

Lang, Eddie, 183

Lang, Fritz, 256, 344

Lang, June, 422 n.10

Langdon, Harry, 368 n.18, 369, 384

Lange, Arthur, 114, 168

Lauder, Harry, 28 n.14, 53, 177

Laughing Sinners, 337 n.7

Laughton, Charles, 178

Laurel, Stan, and Hardy, Oliver, 69 n.11, 163 n.1, 164, 167, 262, 270, 284–85, *285* n.5, 381, 417–19

Lauste, Eugene, 15

Lawrence, Gertrude, 31, 84, 120, 133, 135, 142, 187, 235 n.9, 251

Lawson, John Howard, 397

Laye, Evelyn, 137, 333–34, *334*

Leathernecking, 136, 240, 240 n.13, 329

LeBaron, William, 227

Lee, Davey, 50, *51*, 52, 153–54, 154 n.8, 421

Lee, Dixie, 174, *175*, 176

Lee, Dorothy, 87, 227, 228 n.3, 269, 298, 307, 352, 412

Lee, Gwen, 136, 163 n.1

Lee, Lila, 151, 157, 300 n.13

Lee, Rowland V., 179

Lee, Sammy, 70, 72, 129, 132, *139*, 164, 168, 397, 421

Legion of Decency, 361, 408, 411–12, 413

486 | *Index*